GROUPS

A COUNSELING SPECIALTY

FIFTH EDITION

Samuel T. Gladding
Wake Forest University

PEARSON

Merrill
Prentice Hall

Upper Saddle River, New Jersey
Columbus, Ohio

Library of Congress Cataloging-in-Publication Data

Gladding, Samuel T.
  Groups : a counseling specialty / Samuel T. Gladding. -- 5th ed.
    p. cm.
  Rev. ed. of: Group work. 4th ed. c2003.
  Includes bibliographical references and indexes.
  ISBN-13: 978-0-13-173595-8
  ISBN-10: 0-13-173595-0
  1. Group counselling.   I. Gladding, Samuel T. Group work.   II. Title.
  BF636.7.G76G55 2008
  158′.35--dc22   2007010033

Vice President and Executive Publisher: Jeffery W. Johnston
Editor: Meredith D. Fossel
Senior Editorial Assistant: Kathleen S. Burk
Production Editor: Mary Harlan
Production Coordinator: Kelly Ricci/Aptara, Inc.
Design Coordinator: Diane C. Lorenzo
Text Design and Illustrations: Aptara, Inc.
Cover Design: Jason Moore
Cover Image: Jupiter Images
Production Manager: Susan Hannahs
Director of Marketing: David Gesell
Marketing Manager: Autumn Purdy
Marketing Coordinator: Brian Mounts

Earlier editions of this text were published under the title *Group Work: A Counseling Specialty.*

This book was set in ITC Garamond by Aptara, Inc. It was printed and bound by Courier/ Westford. The cover was printed by Phoenix Color Corp.

Pearson Education Ltd.
Pearson Education Singapore Pte. Ltd.
Pearson Education Canada, Ltd.
Pearson Education–Japan

Pearson Education Australia Pty. Limited
Pearson Education North Asia Ltd.
Pearson Educación de Mexico, S.A. de C.V.
Pearson Education Malaysia Pte. Ltd.

10 9 8 7 6 5 4 3 2 1
ISBN 13: 978-0-13-173595-8
ISBN 10:   0-13-173595-0

To my wife
Claire
and my children
Ben, Nate, and Tim
Who have all taught me anew that
sensitivity is a strength,
listening is a skill,
love is an action, and
life is a gift to be shared.

ABOUT THE AUTHOR

Samuel T. Gladding is a professor and chair of the Department of Counseling at Wake Forest University in Winston-Salem, North Carolina. He has been a practicing counselor in both public and private agencies since 1971. His leadership in the field of counseling includes service as president of the American Counseling Association (ACA), the Association for Counselor Education and Supervision (ACES), the Association for Specialists in Group Work (ASGW), and Chi Sigma Iota (international academic and professional counseling honor society). He has also been the vice president of the Counseling Association for Humanistic Education and Development (C-AHEAD).

Dr. Gladding is the former editor of the *Journal for Specialists in Group Work* and the author of more than 100 professional publications. In 1999, he was cited as being in the top 1% of contributors to the *Journal of Counseling and Development* for the 15-year period from 1978 to 1993. Some of Dr. Gladding's most recent books are *Family Therapy: History, Theory, & Process* (4th ed., 2007), *The Counseling Dictionary* (2nd ed., 2006), *The Creative Arts in Counseling* (3rd ed., 2005), *Counseling: A Comprehensive Profession* (5th ed., 2004), *Becoming a Counselor: The Light, the Bright, and the Serious* (2002), and this edition of *Groups: A Counseling Specialty.*

Dr. Gladding's previous academic appointments have been at the University of Alabama at Birmingham, Fairfield University (Connecticut), and Rockingham Community College (North Carolina). He was also Director of Children's Services at the Rockingham County (North Carolina) Mental Health Center. Gladding received his degrees from Wake Forest (B.A., M.A.Ed.), Yale (M.A.R.), and the University of North Carolina–Greensboro (Ph.D.). He is a National Certified Counselor (NCC), a Certified Clinical Mental Health Counselor (CCMHC), and a Licensed Professional Counselor (North Carolina). Dr. Gladding is a former member of the Alabama Board of Examiners in Counseling and the Research and Assessment Corporation for Counseling (RACC).

Dr. Gladding is the recipient of numerous honors, including the Lifetime Achievement Award from the Association for Creativity in Counseling; the Chi Sigma Iota Thomas J. Sweeney Professional Leadership Award; the Counseling Association for Humanistic Education and Development Joseph W. and Lucille U. Hollis Outstanding Publication Award; the Association for Counselor Education and Supervision Professional Leadership Award and Outstanding Publication Award; the Association for Specialists in Group Work Eminent Career Award; and the North Carolina Counseling Association Ella Stephens Barrett Award for Leadership and Service to the Counseling Profession. He is also a Fellow in the Association for Specialists in Group Work and in the American Counseling Association.

Gladding is married to the former Claire Tillson and is the father of three children—Ben, Nate, and Tim. Outside of counseling, he enjoys tennis, swimming, and humor.

PREFACE

Groups are a part of everyday life. We are born into a family group, and many of the most important events of our lives transpire in the educational, recreational, and work groups of which we are a part. Almost everyone is influenced daily by some type of group, and it can be justifiably argued that we truly become human through our interactions in groups. Sometimes just the memory of a group experience or the attractions of an upcoming group event can have a powerful impact. The groups with which we directly and indirectly associate affect us all.

The helping professions have worked with people in groups since the early 1900s. Professionals realize that groups have the power not only to help heal but also to harm. Working with persons in groups has become an increasingly popular, diverse, and viable means of promoting change and the accomplishment of tasks. Because each group is different, group workers must be equipped with a variety of skills.

ORGANIZATION

This book examines essential skills required to be an effective worker with groups in multiple settings. Part One of this text concentrates on the history, trends, dynamics, leadership, development, ethics, and diversity that are a part of the lives of groups. Through the 10 chapters in this section, the evolution of groups as a specialty is chronicled and explored in four primary areas: task/work, psychoeducation, counseling, and psychotherapy. Skilled group workers are aware of and comfortable in dealing with the dynamics and leadership requirements in each of these special domains. They are also cognizant of the development of groups over time, from their forming to their adjourning. Ethical and legal aspects of working in groups are discussed, too, along with the influence of culture on groups, which has its own chapter and is integrated throughout other chapters in this text.

Part Two examines the role of groups throughout the life span. These chapters cover issues and procedures for working with groups that focus on children, adolescents, adults, and older adults. Each of these age and stage groups has special needs that can be addressed positively in a group setting. Different types of groups appropriate for various life span periods and circumstances are highlighted and discussed.

The final part of this book concentrates on theoretical approaches to leading groups, describing 10 of the most prominent approaches. Each theory is examined in regard to its premises, practices, leadership, emphases, outcomes, strengths, and limitations. The specific theories explored here are psychoanalysis, transactional analysis, person-centered, existential, Adlerian, reality therapy, Gestalt, psychodrama, rational-emotive behavior, and behaviorism.

NEW TO THIS EDITION

You will notice a number of differences in this fifth edition of *Groups: A Counseling Specialty.* Some are obvious; others are subtle. One obvious difference is that the title has dropped the word "Work" in favor of using just the word "Groups." Another change that spans both the obvious and subtle domains is that more than 165 references have been added and incorporated into the body of the text, along with more than 60 new "Case Examples" and 50 "Questions from Experience." This latter addition is meant to help you tap into your own experience and reflect on how aspects of groups discussed in the book already affect your life. Another difference is that the theories section has shrunk from five to four chapters. Each theory discussed continues to have a "Learning More" subsection, in which readers can find Web sites and original sources to consult in exploring that theory further.

Chapter 10, on diversity, now includes a brief subsection on working with Arab American clients as well as ways of doing group work with African Americans, Asian Americans, Hispanics/Latinos, Native American Indians, European Americans, and gay/lesbian/transsexual clients. Other material related to working with these populations is incorporated throughout the rest of the chapters. The text is more multicultural than ever before.

Finally, in addition to these features, the appendixes include three Association for Specialists in Group Work documents related to best practices, diversity, and standards of training in group work. These documents enhance the book's emphasis on the ethics and practice of working with various kinds of groups.

Ancillaries available for instructors are an Online Instructor's Manual with Test Bank, and PowerPoint® slides. The Companion Website at **www.prenhall.com/gladding** offers chapter-specific resources for students.

A PERSONAL NOTE

I decided to write this book after reflecting on my own history in groups. In the late 1960s and early 1970s, I was exposed to a variety of groups, including what were then known as T-groups. I participated in group marathons, psychoeducational groups, self-help groups, task groups, and counseling groups. I took formal courses in conducting groups at Yale, Wake Forest, and the University of North Carolina at Greensboro. Later, I joined such organizations as the Association for Specialists in Group Work (ASGW) and the North Carolina Group Behavior Society. In my initial employment in a mental health center, I was required to lead psychotherapy, counseling, and psychoeducational groups. In private practice and in my duties as a college professor and administrator, I have added task/work groups as a part of my experience.

Fortunately, I have had some excellent instructors and colleagues over the years. They include Wesley Hood, Larry Osborne, Peg Carroll, Diana Hulse-Killacky, Jerry Donigian, Bob Conyne, Chuck Kormanski, Rosie Morgannet, Beverly Brown, Janice DeLucia-Waack, Marianne Schubert, Johnne Armentrout, and John Anderson. I have also been enriched as a practitioner and a writer from my experience as president of the ASGW and editor of the *Journal for Specialists in Group Work*.

ACKNOWLEDGMENTS

I am grateful for the input of professional group workers who reviewed various editions of this text since its original publication in 1991. They include Adrian Blow, St. Louis University; Roberto Clemente, University of Northern Iowa; Robert Conyne, University of Cincinnati; Dana Edwards, Georgia State University; Thomas Elmore, Wake Forest University; Stephen Feit, Idaho State University; Richard Hawk, Tuskegee University; Diana Hulse-Killacky, University of New Orleans; Dennis Kivlighan, University of Missouri, Columbia; Brent Mallinckrodt, University of Oregon; Diana McDermott, University of Kansas; Bernard Nisenholz, private practice, California; Susan Orr, California State University, Sacramento; John G. Pappas, Eastern Michigan University; Sally E. Thigpen, Northeast Louisiana University; and Charles Weiner, Henderson State University.

I want to especially thank the following reviewers for their helpful comments and suggestions for the fifth edition: Fred Bemak, George Mason University; Brian J. Den, Georgia State University; Jean E. Griffin, University of Nevada–Las Vegas; Susanna A. Hayes, Western Washington University; Barbara Couden Hernandez, Indiana State University; Kathleen M. May, University of Virginia; J. J. McWhirter, Arizona State University; and Steven Pfeiffer, Florida State University.

Others who have been of great assistance to me with this project are former graduate students Jo Spradling (University of Alabama, Birmingham), Paul Myers (University of Alabama, Birmingham), Regan Reding (Wake Forest), Beverly Huffstetler (Wake Forest), and Erin Binkley (Wake Forest). All have been exemplary in helping me ferret out original sources, in proofing pages, and in making changes at times in my sentence structure to improve the clarity of this text. Then, of course, the professionals at Merrill Education/ Prentice Hall—including my former editors, Vicki Knight, Linda Sullivan, and Kevin Davis, and present editor, Meredith Fossel—gave me much to think about as well as encouragement.

My family group, especially my wife Claire, has been patient and supportive during my writing and rewritings. Claire has given me encouragement, support, and a healthy helping of humor throughout this process. My children—Ben, Nate, and Tim—have also been wonderful in inspiring me to finish my work so I could do things with them (which I have). They are now ages 20, 18, and 16, far from the tender ages of 4, 2, and just born when I began this project. Thus, it is not surprising that this text is dedicated to my family group—Claire and the boys.

CONCLUSION

In concluding the fifth edition of *Groups* I am more aware than ever of the importance of collaboration in accomplishing goals and fulfilling dreams. The poet John Donne was correct in reminding us that we are not isolated islands sufficient unto ourselves. We are connected to humanity and have the power to help or hinder one another's growth and development. It is in the mixing of personalities and processes that the heart of group work lies, through which our past gains meaning, and from which our present and future are created.

Samuel T. Gladding

DISCOVER THE COMPANION WEBSITE ACCOMPANYING THIS BOOK

THE PRENTICE HALL COMPANION WEBSITE: A VIRTUAL LEARNING ENVIRONMENT

Technology is a constantly growing and changing aspect of our field that is creating a need for content and resources. To address this emerging need, Prentice Hall has developed an online learning environment for students and professors alike—Companion Websites—to support our textbooks.

In creating a Companion Website, our goal is to build on and enhance what the textbook already offers. For this reason, the content for each user-friendly website is organized by chapter and provides the professor and student with a variety of meaningful resources.

Common Companion Website features for students include:

- **Chapter Objectives**—outline key concepts from the text.
- **Interactive Self-quizzes**—complete with hints and automatic grading that provide immediate feedback for students. After students submit their answers for the interactive self-quizzes, the Companion Website **Results Reporter** computes a percentage grade, provides a graphic representation of how many questions were answered correctly and incorrectly, and gives a question-by-question analysis of the quiz. Students are given the option to send their quiz to up to four email addresses (professor, teaching assistant, study partner, etc.).
- **Essay Questions**—these questions allow students to respond to themes and objectives of each chapter by applying what they have learned to real classroom situations.
- **Web Destinations**—links to www sites that relate to chapter content.

To take advantage of the many available resources, please visit the *Groups: A Counseling Specialty,* Fifth Edition, Companion Website at

www.prenhall.com/gladding

BRIEF CONTENTS

CONTENTS

NOTE: Every effort has been made to provide accurate and current Internet information in this book. However, the Internet and information posted on it are constantly changing, so it is inevitable that some of the Internet addresses listed in this textbook will change.

PART ONE

HISTORY AND OTHER ASPECTS OF GROUP DEVELOPMENT

CHAPTER 1

HISTORY AND TRENDS OF GROUP WORK

Laima Druskis/PH College

*Nathaniel joined a band of rebels
and from that colonial action
a nation sprang and a government grew.
I, seven generations removed,
ponder the boldness of his group
wishing for such courage
in my deepest interactions
And knowing on some level at times
his resolve is mine.**

*From *Ancestral Thoughts* by Samuel T. Gladding, © 1988.

W e live in a world of groups. Crowds, committees, congregations, delegations, commissions, team, boards, bands, squads, throngs, and mobs are just a few of the words we use to describe the groups we are aware of or interact with on an everyday basis. We even name our college and pro team mascots for groups of animals such as packs (wolves), prides (lions), herds (buffalo), and even horned frogs (i.e., Texas Christian University). There is power and potential in groups, and as people we seem to recognize that almost instinctively. Indeed, just as with our ancestors, our well-being or our demise depends on the groups we are in whether by choice or circumstance.

The history of groups is as old as the history of people. From the beginning of humankind, individuals have gathered together to create, achieve, and resolve matters not possible otherwise. The legacy of group actions carries over generations and either inspires or suppresses behaviors. Groups are a natural way for people to communicate and interrelate with one another. No written history indicates when or where the first groups were formed, but all cultures have made use of groups in their growth and development. "Since ancient times people have speculated about how certain groups such as communities and social systems shape human behavior (e.g., Plato's *Republic* or Thomas More's *Utopia*) and have experimented to see how they can devise groups . . . to change human behavior and thus the social system" (Luchins, 1964, p. 5).

Groups are defined in many ways, but the following definition adapted from Johnson and Johnson (2006) encompasses the main qualities of most forms of groups. A **group** is a collection of two or more individuals, who meet in face-to-face interaction, interdependently, with the awareness that each belongs to the group and for the purpose of achieving mutually agreed-on goals. From family councils to town meetings, groups are an important component of everyday life. Healthy groups are contextually unique, complex in regard to their multiple transactions, and open systems as well (Conyne & Bemak, 2004).

Group work encompasses all types of activities performed by organized groups—for example, the accomplishment of task or work goals, such as constructing a house or leading a campaign, and educational endeavors, such as team teaching. In human service occupations we usually think of groups as dedicated to psychotherapy and counseling. "In earlier days many similar activities performed by social workers were called 'group work'" (Lifton, 1972, p. 13). Today, the concept is more specialized, which has increased the recognition of the profession and "raised the standard to which group workers may aspire" (Wilson, Rapin, & Haley-Banez, 2004, p. 20). The Association for Specialists in Group Work (ASGW) (2000) defines **group work** as

> a broad professional practice involving the application of knowledge and skill in group facilitation to assist an interdependent collection of people to reach their mutual goals, which may be intrapersonal, interpersonal, or work related. The goals of the group may include the accomplishment of tasks related to work, education, personal development, personal and interpersonal problem solving, or remediation of mental and emotional disorders. (pp. 329–330)

This chapter examines significant events in the development of groups and group work. It also focuses on major trends in group work and the future of groups. With an understanding of the history, present status, and probable future of groups, practitioners are more likely to have a comprehensive picture of what groups have been used for and what they are capable of doing. As Claiborn (1987) contends, "The past has a nice way of getting us to think about the present" (p. 286). It guides us, as people and professionals, in assessing where we are, as well as where we want to be.

USES OF GROUPS BEFORE 1900

Before 1900, organized groups were generally formed for functional and pragmatic reasons. Most were large, and their primary emphasis was in distributing information. Instruction or correction of behaviors was accomplished mainly through educational means. Immigrants, the poor, and the mentally ill were among those populations receiving special attention in large groups. Social workers and physicians used group structure to help these individuals gain knowledge about themselves and others.

An example of how groups were used at the time can be found in the work of Jane Addams at Hull House in Chicago. Addams formed groups of new immigrants and the poor to help them understand their environments better and to assist each other in breaking down barriers that impeded them. What she did would be classified now as the beginnings of **social group work** (Pottick, 1988). She organized individuals into purposeful and enriching groups that engaged in reading, crafts, and club activities. In addition, she discussed with group participants matters such as hygiene and nutrition, which helped them make needed personal changes. The model of group work set up by Addams emphasized "the larger social community" in which group members had common origins, goals, and needs. It was a forerunner "to later therapy groups emphasizing the participants' membership in a common social system or organization (e.g., the Tavistock, T-group, and theme-centered models)" (Shaffer & Galinsky, 1989, p. 2).

Overall, the actual development of groups in the late 1800s and early 1900s was a dynamic movement that included contributions from the emerging disciplines of psychology, sociology, philosophy, and education (Bonner, 1959). The group movement developed not because of one individual or discipline but rather because of the need for social reform and education. The use of large groups for mainly instructional purposes evolved to the use of small groups for various purposes. By the beginning of the 20th century, a group movement had begun that would slowly emerge and grow in scope, size, and impact.

GROWTH OF WORK WITH GROUPS: 1900 TO THE PRESENT

1900 to 1909

Joseph Hersey Pratt is credited with having organized the first formal group experience that was not primarily educational or task/work oriented. He started a psychotherapy group for tuberculosis outpatients in 1905 at the Massachusetts General Hospital in Boston. He was one of the first to write about the dynamics that occur within group settings, and his work served as a model for other leaders exploring processes within their groups (Appley & Winder, 1973). Pratt started his group primarily for humane and economic reasons. The group served as a source of support and inspiration for tuberculosis patients whose conditions were chronic and cyclical and whose circumstances often led to personal discouragement and depression (Seligman, 1982). The group saved both Pratt and his patients time and effort in treating this disease by providing information and encouragement in a common setting; that is, messages did not have to be repeated to each patient one at a time. Furthermore, Pratt noticed that the people in the group not only became more concerned with one another over time but also had a positive influence on one another. It is to Pratt's credit that he recognized the therapeutic power of groups.

At about the same time Pratt was forming his hospital groups, efforts were being made to establish groups in the public schools. In 1907, Jesse B. Davis, principal of Grand Rapids High School in Michigan, directed that one English class per week would be devoted to "Vocational and Moral Guidance" (Glanz & Hayes, 1967). Unlike Pratt, Davis did not emphasize the dynamics of the group process. Rather, he stressed the functionality of a group as an environment in which to learn life skills, values, and the importance of citizenship.

After the death in 1908 of Frank Parsons (who is credited as being the founder of modern-day counseling), counselors in many guidance settings, such as the Vocational Bureau of Boston, began to see vocationally undecided individuals in small groups as well (Brewer, 1942). The emphasis at such agencies, as in the schools, was to use groups as a way of dispensing information and providing educational and vocational guidance.

1910 to 1919

The initial progress in group work slowed from 1910 to 1919, although educational and task/work groups were used to a considerable extent. For instance, soldiers were instructed in groups during World War I, and teamwork was emphasized during the war for both civilians and military personnel. During this conflict, psychological group tests, such as the Army Alpha and Beta intelligence tests, were developed and administered. Groups were also used in a limited way to treat combat-fatigued soldiers.

Except for the period from 1916 to 1918, the focus in the United States during this time was on the individual and individual achievement. There was, however, growth in select American schools and organizations in studying group educational approaches to learning. Also, in Europe, Jacob L. Moreno published a significant, philosophical paper on group methods, written under the name of J. M. Levy (Milman & Goldman, 1974). It stressed the psychoanalytic and social psychological perspectives of individuals working together.

1920 to 1929

Several important events in the development of groups occurred in the 1920s. First, in 1922, Alfred Adler initiated a new and systematic form of group guidance and counseling that became known as **collective counseling** (Dreikurs & Corsini, 1954). Adler employed his treatment method with both prison and child guidance populations. In the child guidance clinics, he established a team of helping specialists, such as psychiatrists, psychologists, and social workers, to interview children. Parents and children were helped by the team to realize that problems with children usually are related to problems in the family. Families, especially parents, became more motivated to find solutions to problems by employing this principle. Adler and his associates devised family group meetings, or **family councils**, as a means of getting input from everyone in the family on how to resolve difficulties and improve family relations. Adler's work was a forerunner of applying group techniques to a natural group: the family.

A second major event in the 1920s was Jacob L. Moreno's formulation in 1921 of the **Theater of Spontaneity** (*Stegreiftheatre*), a first step in his creation of psychodrama. Moreno's ideas would later influence other theorists, such as Fritz Perls "in his founding of

Gestalt technology and William Schutz in his formation of encounter techniques" (Shaffer & Galinsky, 1989, p. 9). Some of the ideas stemming from psychodrama, such as role playing, the taking of "stage center," the emphasis on here-and-now interaction, the promotion of catharsis, the focus on empathy, and the encouragement of group members helping one another, are incorporated in many forms of groups today. Moreno's innovations in the field of group psychotherapy challenged old methods of working with individuals who were experiencing mental turmoil.

Related to Moreno's work, although entirely independent from it, was Trigant Burrow's (1928) focus on the interpersonal relationships of individuals. Burrow thought that interpersonal relationships play a crucial role in the formation and enactment of psychotherapy. He believed isolation was detrimental to mental health.

A final significant occurrence during the 1920s was the investigation of small groups. Researchers began to learn which types of interactions were the norm in small-group settings and how groups influence individuals (Allport, 1924). Individual versus group performances were also evaluated (Gordon, 1924; Watson, 1928). These studies grew in number and importance during the 1930s and 1940s. Because of this scientific approach, the concept of groups gained respect, and the power of groups became more recognized.

1930 to 1939

The 1930s are noted in group work history for five major events. First, group guidance and educational publications and practices increased (e.g., Allen, 1931; McKown, 1934). Second, Jacob Moreno continued to write and make creative presentations. Third, there was an increase in the number and quality of fieldwork studies by sociologists, such as Muzafer Sherif (1936), Theodore Newcomb (1943), and W. F. Whyte (1943). A fourth event during the decade was the founding of the first major self-help group in America, **Alcoholics Anonymous (AA).** A final noteworthy phenomenon of the 1930s was the movement of psychoanalytic treatment into the group domain and the discovery of several dynamics that operate in group psychotherapy (Kline, 2003). Each of these events will now be examined.

Group guidance and education in schools centered on vocational and personal themes. Initially, these activities were the responsibility of homeroom teachers. Some schools even referred to homeroom as "the **'guidance hour'** or 'guidance room'" (McKown, 1934, p. 53). In this arrangement, the teacher's responsibilities were "to establish friendly relationships, to discover the abilities and needs, and to develop right attitudes toward school, home, and the community" (Strange, 1935, p. 116). Group guidance continued this way until the 1950s.

Jacob Moreno's most productive writings and presentations started in the 1930s and continued for several decades. He introduced the terms *group therapy* and *group psychotherapy* into the vocabulary of helping professionals in 1931 and 1932 (Corsini, 1957; Moreno, 1966). He also devised one of the earliest forms of group treatment: *psychodrama* (Moreno, 1945). **Psychodrama** is an interpersonal approach in which participants act out their feelings regarding past or present events and attempt to clarify conflicts. This type of therapy and the emergence of therapy in small groups, which became more prevalent in the 1930s, opened the way for the theoretical conceptualization of group counseling. Although Allen (1931) used the term *group counseling* at about the same time that Moreno used *group therapy,* Allen was referring basically to group guidance procedures. It was not until the 1940s that group counseling, as it is known now, appeared.

The third major event of the decade—studies of groups in natural settings—used various investigative methods to gather data. Sherif (1936), for instance, studied the influence of groups on the establishment of social norms by charting the response of individuals inside and outside a group setting to a particular stimulus called the *autokinetic movement.* He found that individuals who had been a part of a group tended to view this light phenomenon within the range established by their group. Likewise, Newcomb (1943) found that students from politically conservative homes tended to become more liberal because of the prevailing norms of their peer groups. Finally, Whyte (1943) studied larger social systems by moving into the slums of Boston in 1937 for 3½ years. He found that gangs, clubs, and political organizations had a dramatic impact on individuals' lives.

In the late 1930s AA was established by founders who came to realize "the potency of individuals meeting together and interacting in a supportive way to produce change" (Posthuma, 2002, p. 3). It evolved into an organization that continues to help alcoholics gain and maintain control of their lives by remaining sober. Many of the techniques used in AA are similar to those found in other self-help groups—for example, listening, empathizing, supporting, and teaching.

Psychoanalytic group analysis also emerged in the 1930s (Kline, 2003). One of the leaders of this movement was Trigant Burrow, who studied how social forces affect behavior and stressed the biological as well as the interactive principles of group behavior. The biological principles he described as a process called **phyloanalysis.** Other pioneers of psychoanalytic group analysis were Louis Wender (1936) and Paul Schilder (1939). Wender's work resulted in interventions for inpatient groups. He also was one of the first group workers to describe group therapeutic factors, such as intellectualization, person-to-person transference, and catharsis in the family. Schilder's efforts focused more on the interactions among individual group members (Appley & Winder, 1973).

1940 to 1949

The 1940s are often seen as the beginning of modern group work. Two major directions in the formal development of groups took place during this time: (1) the theoretical writings and practices of Kurt Lewin and Wilfred Bion and (2) the establishment of group organizations. Lifton (1972) observed that the climate in which group work developed during this time reflected the reaction of American and British societies against authoritarian dictatorships and showed a major concern with promoting democracy.

Kurt Lewin (1940, 1951) is generally recognized as the most influential founder and promoter of group dynamics during this era (Johnson & Johnson, 2006; Luft, 1963). A refugee from Nazi Germany, Lewin worked tirelessly to research and refine group dynamics and surrounded himself with energetic and brilliant people. He began writing in the 1930s, but the major impact of his work emerged in the 1940s. Lewin's approach, **field theory,** emphasizes the interaction between individuals and their environments. It is based on the ideas of Gestalt psychology. For Lewin, the group is a whole that is different from and greater than the parts that comprise it.

It was Lewin, "the practical theorist" (Marrow, 1969), who was instrumental in establishing a workshop on intergroup relations in New Britain, Connecticut, in 1946. The workshop led to the formation of the **National Training Laboratories (NTL)** in Bethel, Maine, and the growth of the **basic skills training (BST)** group, which eventually evolved into the **training group (T-group)** movement. Lewin discovered through his collaborative research that group discussions are superior to individual instruction in changing people's ideas and behaviors. His emphasis on a here-and-now orientation to the environment and his point that changes in a group's behavior depend on an "unfreezing" and "freezing" process of human behavior were major contributions to understanding groups. Lewin first applied the concept of *feedback* to group work.

Wilfred Bion (1948), a member of the **Tavistock Institute of Human Relations** in Great Britain, also stressed the importance of group dynamics. Bion was psychoanalytically trained but broke away from Freudian concepts, such as the idea that the family is the basic group model. Instead, Bion stated that group phenomena may be radically different from those within a family (Mackler & Strauss, 1981). His focus was on group cohesiveness and forces that foster the progression or regression of the group. Bion found that he could characterize the emotional pattern of a group as either a **"W" (work group)** or a **"BA" (basic assumption) activity**, which was an antiwork group. BA groups could be broken down further into three subpatterns: *BA Dependency* (where members are overdependent on the group leader), *BA Pairing* (where members are more interested in being with one another than in working on a goal), and *BA Fight–Flight* (where members become preoccupied with either engaging in or avoiding hostile conflict).

During the 1940s, two major group organizations and publications were founded. The first organization was the **American Society of Group Psychotherapy and Psychodrama (ASGPP)**, which Moreno established between 1941 and 1942. The second was the **American Group Psychotherapy Association (AGPA)**, a psychoanalytically oriented organization established by Samuel R. Slavson in 1943. Two pertinent journals started during the 1940s were *Sociatry* in 1947, which was retitled *Group Psychotherapy* in 1949, and the *International Journal of Group Psychotherapy* in 1949. Each journal reflected the philosophy of its founder, Moreno and Slavson, respectively. With the inception of these professional societies and their journals, "group work was recognized as a legitimate specialty with its own standards and research base" (Kottler & Forester-Miller, 1998, p. 340).

1950 to 1959

The 1950s were characterized by a greater refinement in group work and more emphasis on research. For example, in regard to group behavior, Bales (1950) noted that, in most groups, stereotyped roles tend to emerge over time. He listed 12 broad categories, from positive reactions (e.g., shows solidarity) to negative reactions (e.g., shows antagonism).

Group procedures also began to be applied to the practice of family counseling at this time. Among the pioneers in this area was Rudolph Dreikurs, who began working with parent groups (Dreikurs, Corsini, Lowe, & Sonstegard, 1959). Dreikurs employed Adler's theory and ideas in setting up these groups, which were primarily educational in nature. Another clinician, John Bell (1961), also started using groups in his work in family therapy. Beginning as early as 1951, he conducted family therapy sessions like group counseling sessions. Bell treated families as if they were strangers in a group. He relied on stimulating open discussions to solve family problems and, as in group counseling, he encouraged silent members to speak up and share ideas. Nathan Ackerman (1958), Gregory Bateson (Bateson & Ruesch, 1951), and Virginia Satir (1964) were significant professionals during this decade, too. Their independent but similar focus was on modifying the psychoanalytic model of group therapy for working with families. Ackerman and Satir were more clinically oriented and developed techniques for treating dysfunctions in families. Bateson concentrated more on research, especially group dynamics within families.

The last major development in groups during the 1950s was the implementation of new group concepts. A group "vocabulary" was developed to describe phenomena within group sessions. For example, Richard Blake and Jane Mouton initially used the term *developmental group* during this decade. The first textbook in group work was published in 1958: *Counseling and Learning Through Small-Group Discussion* by Helen I. Driver. Terminology for working with groups mushroomed in the 1950s.

As language and terms for groups increased, a shift occurred in the type of groups that were created. Group guidance began to wane in the late 1950s and was replaced by group counseling as a major way to bring about behavioral changes, especially in educational settings (Gazda, 1989). Group psychotherapy increased in popularity as tranquilizing drugs made working with groups in mental health settings viable. The Japanese implemented a new type of group called the **total quality group** under the direction of work group master W. Edwards Deming (Hillkirk, 1993). This type of group, which focused on problem solving related to consumer satisfaction and quality issues in business, would later influence American industry.

1960 to 1969

Group work, especially group counseling and psychotherapy, was popular in the 1960s. Part of the reason for the flourishing of groups during this time was the result of events occurring in society. "The Vietnam War, hippie movement, racial strife, and social activism increased public awareness of the power that groups can have to promote community change" (Kottler & Forester-Miller, 1998, p. 341).

Some of the most creative leaders in the history of group work came into prominence during this time. Group practice became so popular that the *New York Times* designated 1968 as "the year of the group." Many forms of group work were initiated or refined during the 1960s, including encounter groups, sensory awareness groups, growth groups, marathons, and minithons. It seemed to be a decade in which there was a group for everyone and everyone was in a group. The "increased interest in and respect for group counseling and psychotherapy marked the beginning of the reversal of the negative attitude toward the efficacy of group work that was strongly adhered to by most of the psychoanalytic community at the time" (Ward & Litchy, 2004, p. 105).

Two of the most popular groups were encounter groups and marathon groups. Carl Rogers (1970) coined the term **basic encounter group**, which was later shortened to *encounter group,* to describe his approach to group work, an extension of his theory of individual counseling (Rogers, 1967). Encounter groups are often known as *personal growth groups* because the emphasis in these groups is on personal development. Encounter groups are sometimes also referred to as **sensitivity groups**, a term that focuses on individuals' awareness of their own emotional experiences and the behaviors of others. In encounter groups, emphasis is placed on the exploration of intrapsychic and interpersonal issues (Eddy & Lubin, 1971), and a feeling of community and connectedness is promoted.

Marathon groups were devised by George Bach and Fred Stoller in 1964 as a way of helping people become more authentic with themselves and switch from "the marketing stance of role-playing and image making" (Bach, 1967, p. 995). Marathon groups are usually held for extended periods, such as 24 or 48 hours, and group members are required to stay together. Fatigue is an important factor in these groups, as members become tired and experience a breakdown in their defenses and an increase in their truthfulness result- ing in self-growth. Bach (1967), especially, devised creative ways to help people in these groups (and later marriages) resolve interpersonal conflict by learning how to fight fairly.

With the popularity of groups came abuses (Stanger & Harris, 2005). Many well- intentioned individuals and some charlatans established groups with no clear ideas about how to run them. As a result, some individuals became casualties of the group movement. They were instructed to do such things as yell at others, physically attack those they dis- liked, or simply disrobe and lay all their defenses aside. The publicity seekers and entre- preneurs who set up these groups received reams of publicity, most of which was bad. By the end of the 1960s, the group movement was under attack, and the field had been set back considerably. Many individuals made cults out of groups and impaired the function- ing of those who participated in their activities (Landreth, 1984).

However, positive and important events also occurred during this period, especially in the development of group theory and practice. Among the most popular theorists- practitioners of this decade were those who took a humanistic-existential orientation. In addition to Rogers and Bach, four were important:

- Fritz Perls (1967), who conducted numerous workshops at the Esalen Institute in California demonstrating his Gestalt theory through the use of a group setting (Frew, 1983);
- Eric Berne (1964, 1966), who highlighted his therapeutic approach, **transactional analysis (TA)**, in group settings;
- William C. Schutz (1967), who illustrated through group work that individuals can take care of their interpersonal needs for inclusion, control, and affection through groups (Schutz, 1958) and stressed the use of nonverbal communication, such as touching or hugging, in groups; and
- Jack Gibb (1961), who studied competitive versus cooperative behavior in groups and discovered, among other things, that competitive behavior in one person fos- ters competitive behavior, as well as defensiveness, in others.

1970 to 1979

In the 1970s, group work continued to grow, but not without controversy. Irving Janis (1971) created the term **groupthink** to emphasize the detrimental power that groups may exert over their members to conform. He showed that a groupthink mentality can be devastating to the growth of individuals and the problem-solving ability of the group itself.

Walter Lifton's (1972) book of this period reflects the turmoil and concern surround- ing the use of groups that had begun in the 1960s. He cites Jane Howard's (1970) book *Please Touch* as an example of an attempt to answer the critics of group work, who basi- cally characterized sensitivity groups as antidemocratic and morally degrading. Howard's description of her movement from one encounter group to another debunked some pop- ular misconceptions of these groups as "hotbeds" for junkies and addicts, but her book raised other issues, such as the importance of group leadership and the screening of group members. The controversy surrounding groups in the 1970s was due to their rapid, almost uncontrolled, growth in the late 1960s and the fact that guidelines for leading and conducting group experiences themselves were not well defined.

In partial answer to this need for more professionalism in the conducting of groups, the **Association for Specialists in Group Work (ASGW)** was formed in 1973 by George Gazda and Jack Duncan as a divisional affiliate within the American Personnel and Guidance Association (now the American Counseling Association). The association grew rapidly during the 1970s and was active throughout the decade in promoting responsible group leadership and setting up standards under which group leaders should operate (Carroll & Levo, 1985).

Group research also came into prominence during the 1970s, with the percentage of research articles on groups rising to 20% as compared to only 5% in the 1950s (Kottler & Forester-Miller, 1998). Irvin Yalom and George Gazda conducted particularly important work. Yalom (1970), in a marker event, published the first edition of his classic book, *The Theory and Practice of Group Psychotherapy.* In it he analyzed group methods and processes and described 11 **curative (therapeutic) factors within groups**, "the most central and necessary of which are group cohesiveness and interpersonal learning" (Ward & Litchy, 2004, p. 106). In addition, Yalom and Lieberman (1971) found that leadership style in groups influences how individuals fare in such settings. Aggressive, authoritarian, and confrontational leaders and those who are most distant and cool produce the most group casualties. Gazda was largely responsible for collecting primary accounts of how different group workers, especially psychotherapists and counselors, conceptualized and practiced their approaches (Elliott, 1989). He helped link group leaders together.

1980 to 1989

In the 1980s, the popularity of group work for the masses increased, as did the continued professionalism of the group movement itself. The AGPA was one of the associations that continued to refine group theory and practice. For instance, the AGPA published a collection of articles edited by James Durkin (1981) that examined how **general systems theory**, which emphasizes circular causality as opposed to linear causality, could be utilized in groups.

In addition to the expansion of theory, the number of different types of groups grew. Self-help groups, in particular, mushroomed. It was estimated in 1988 that between 2,000 and 3,000 self-help groups operated in the United States. These mutually supportive groups usually did not include professional leaders but were led by paraprofessionals or group members. Examples of such groups then and now are Alcoholics Anonymous, Narcotics Anonymous, Weight Watchers, and Compassionate Friends. Educational groups also received increased attention during this decade. Noted leaders in the group work area, such as George Gazda (1989), proposed the use of **developmental group counseling** with multiple populations for teaching basic life skills.

A code of ethics for group workers was published by the ASGW in 1980 and revised in 1989. [Ethical standards for working with groups have now been incorporated into the American Counseling Association *Code of Ethics* (2005)]. Standards for training group leaders were proposed by the ASGW during the decade and adopted in 1991. By the end of 1989, the ASGW had attracted more than 5,000 members. The AGPA and other group organizations also increased their memberships in the 1980s.

In summary, by the end of the 1980s, group work was recognized as a viable means of helping individuals in a variety of settings. More types of groups were available than ever before, with a new emphasis on self-help, social skills, development, and ethics. More care was being focused on evaluating the effects of group experiences, and the number of research articles on group work was increasing.

1990 to 1999

In the 1990s, group work continued to flourish. In 1991, the Group Psychology and Group Psychotherapy division of the American Psychological Association was established. It began publishing its own journal, *Group Dynamics,* in 1997 and attracted a number of psychologists to its ranks.

More mature group organizations continued to prosper, too. For example, the AGPA celebrated its 50th anniversary in 1992 and set up a certification for group psychotherapists, the Clinical Registry of Certified Group Psychotherapists, in 1994. A number of new books and a plethora of scholarly articles were also published in the decade. Group work was increasingly utilized in school settings, especially as a way of influencing educational endeavors and social skills (Hudson, Doyle, & Venezia, 1991). However, group work also focused on groups for special populations, such as those in the midst of divorce, adult offenders, people from different cultures, and people with disabilities. A particularly innovative specialized type of group for the treatment of Borderline Personality Disorders, **dialectic behavior therapy**, was developed in the early 1990s by Marsha Linehan (1993) and her research team. The approach, based on cognitive behavior therapy, uses a psychosocial method that teaches coping skills to group members during a weekly 2.5-hour session. Such skills as interpersonal effectiveness, distress tolerance, reality acceptance skills, emotion regulation, and mindfulness are taught. The clinical effectiveness of DBT has empirical support.

The number of individuals interested in working with groups also increased in the 1990s for almost all group associations. More emphasis was also placed on specialty groups, for example, depression, bulimia, and sexual abuse. In 1991, the ASGW approved and published professional standards for the training of group workers in four main areas: psychoeducational, task/work, counseling, and psychotherapy groups. A distinction in these standards was made between core group competencies and group work specialties, with specialists already having mastered core skills (ASGW, 1991, 2000). Furthermore, research from a variety of sources on different types of groups supported their effectiveness and cost efficiency (Kline, 2003).

In addition to these activities, more training and educational opportunities were offered in groups by almost all professional associations. For example, the ASGW and the AGPA held annual national conferences on group work and sponsored continuing education courses at various sites around the United States.

Furthermore, the 1990s were filled with a wide variety of self-help groups and support groups. Parenting groups became more popular, and the number of **cooperative learning groups** increased. In addition, **focus groups**, composed of representative samples of individuals concerned with issues, products, or outcomes, came into wider use and provided important information for businesses, politicians, and policy makers. Probably the greatest growth in the use of groups, at least in North America in the 1990s, was in work settings. In these environments, the use of task/work groups grew dramatically as organizational hierarchies began flattening out and workers became more collaborative in achieving goals (Hulse-Killacky, Killacky, & Donigian, 2001).

CURRENT TRENDS IN GROUP WORK

In the early years of the 21st century, groups continue to be popular in multiple settings. "Generally, groups work for an ever-increasing number of client complaints" and concerns (Barlow, Fuhrman, & Burlingame, 2004, p. 10). Counselors, coaches, teachers, politicians, and corporate researchers have made groups more a part of their personal and professional lives than ever before. Books on the therapeutic aspects of groups, such as Paul Solotaroff's *Group* (1999), sell well. "Small groups are now well accepted as a method of providing support, as well as promoting change, effective decision making, problem solving, team building, and social skill building" (Kottler & Forester-Miller, 1998, pp. 341–342). Specialty group practice and research into specialty areas of group work flourish. In addition, there is an emphasis on the refinement of standards needed to conduct groups. Other trends affecting group work are in training and education, technology, research, the development of brief solution-focused ways of delivering group services, and the use of dialectical behavior group therapy to treat individuals who tend to harm themselves.

Training/Educating Leaders and Members in Group Work

The training and educating of group leaders has become more sophisticated recently as the dynamics within groups have become better understood (Ward, 2004a). For instance, Riva and Korinek (2004) have found that group work instructors can "intentionally model effective group leader behaviors and use these behaviors and the students' responses to them as powerful ways to augment the didactic material being taught about group dynamics and theory" (p. 55). They suggest activities instructors can use during the initial, middle, and final stages of a group, such as providing a high degree of structure in early group meetings to increase cohesion and reduce anxiety.

In addition to modeling, group training now focuses on presenting skills in steps. No longer are novice group leaders told that they must observe the dynamics in a group and help group members understand what is going on within themselves and their interpersonal relationships. Instead, Stockton, Morran, and Nitza (2000) have developed a conceptual map for leaders to follow. Processing, according to these researchers, can be conceptualized as four interrelated steps:

- identifying critical incidents of importance to group members,
- examining the event and member reactions,
- deriving meaning and self-understanding from the event, and
- applying new understanding toward personal change. (p. 347)

By learning such a cognitive map, group leaders and members come to have a better understanding of how to initiate and facilitate processing activities. This model requires flexibility in its application because of the dynamics involved in groups. However, it gives group workers a checklist of tasks to keep in mind.

Likewise, in introducing graduate students to the dynamics within a group, Romano and Sullivan (2000) have developed the **simulated group counseling model** (Romano, 1998). For this model to be effective, students role-play different group members in an ongoing group experience lasting 8 weeks. The advantages of this model are that students are provided with a safe and realistic experience for learning how groups develop. Furthermore, dual-relationship ethical concerns are reduced because professors are not dealing with actual self-disclosures from students in personal growth groups. Thus, professors do not find themselves in the ethical bind of being an evaluator of students academically while also gaining intimate personal knowledge about those students.

A related simulation model for group work training is known as **process-play** (Brenner, 1999). In this procedure, "students participate in a here-and-now focused, process-oriented training group, but their interactions are guided by superficial characteristics specified as the mask (e.g., responding differently to persons who are tall or who are wearing green) rather than interpersonal dynamics" (p. 147). The masks stimulate group conflict resolutions in and of themselves without relying on member self-disclosures or traditional role playing. Thus, student privacy is protected while interpersonal learning takes place.

Technology and Group Work

The use of technology worldwide "ranges from a minimal encounter constituting information exchange or referral to resources, to more interactive exchanges constituting the dissemination of information, provision of support, and offerings of electronic counseling" (Bowman & Bowman, 1998, p. 432). Computers, cell phones, computer simulation, and other forms of technology have altered the ways people interact individually and in groups. Whereas electronic course tools, such as the "bulletin board" of WEB-CT, have been used to deliver group theory in rural areas (O'Halloran & McCartney, 2004), technology has been used in a number of other ways also. "As technology becomes more advanced, easier to use, and more affordable, opportunities for enhancing traditional group activities with technological approaches continue to grow" (Smokowski, 2003, p. 21). This technology has taken numerous forms, including the use of chat rooms, computer conferencing, listservs, and news groups (Bowman & Bowman, 1998; Hsiung, 2000; Page, 2004).

Collectively, the computer support for a group activity is referred to as **groupware**. For instance, groupware is used to set up "chat rooms" at various sites on the World Wide Web, allowing people who are physically separated to have in-depth discussions on subjects of common interest. Likewise, in some educational settings, computers provide a means for class discussion outside of regular meetings. Electronic mail systems, keypad voting systems, and computer support for group decision making are some of the manifestations of groupware. In these cases, the messages sent are linear, and those who participate in them do not have an opportunity to read nonverbal cues and responses, such as body posture or voice tone. Nevertheless, computers promote psychoeducational and task/work group development, at least in regard to the exchange of information.

In addition, Internet Web sites have emerged for group associations that are international in scope, such as the International Association of Group Psychotherapy (IAGP). National group organizations, such as the Latin American Federation of Group Psychoanalytic Psychotherapy and the Argentine Association for Group Psychology and Psychotherapy, have also created Web sites.

An example of how computers are being used in, and having an impact on, support groups comes from research conducted at Stanford University. In this study, the content of 300 messages from an online eating disorders support group were analyzed. Messages consisted primarily of personal disclosures, advice, emotional support, and other kinds of information. Messages were posted around the clock, including 31% of the postings that were sent from 11 p.m. to 7 a.m. The kinds of messages sent over the computer reflected the same pattern found in face-to-face groups (DeAngelis, 1997). A benefit of this group format was that messages could be and were sent at any time. A drawback was that, when inaccurate or unhealthy information was sent, it was not challenged immediately, if ever.

Group use of computers holds promise for the future, especially for helping group members stay in contact with one another and exchange information. "Computer-mediated support groups are a growing phenomenon" (Shaw, McTavish, Hawkins, Gustafson, & Pingree, 2000, p. 157). Online groups can take two forms. They may be either **asynchronous** (e.g., with an e-mail listserv, "where messages formatted as typed text can be sent at any time whether or not the receiver is on-line") or **synchronous** (e.g., "where group members must be on-line and logged into the site of a group at a designated time") (Page et al., 2000, p. 134). Both have advantages and disadvantages; synchronous discussions are more challenging because of technological limitations and scheduling problems (Romano & Cikanek, 2003). Because of the availability of new software programs, such as The Palace, visual, auditory, and spatial cues can be simulated, and the group virtual room and experience can become more personal. PalTalk also has possibilities as a convenient format for online discussion groups (Page et al., 2003). The "cutting edge of current technology appears to be synchronous video groups" using Polycoms connected with high-speed Internet (Page, 2004, p. 615).

Finally, online learning is growing in training group leaders in a content area. For instance, Krieger and Stockton (2004) describe how a course on developmental theory and structuring therapy groups for younger populations was offered online. The 5-week course made it possible for a variety of school personnel to gain access to practical information while also offering them a chance to experience a different type of learning environment that fit into their schedules.

Studies on Group Effectiveness

Research shows that group work is an effective method for providing services to others (Kivlighan, Coleman, & Anderson, 2000). Meta-analyses, which make it possible to more clearly compare outcomes of different group formats and individual versus group treatments, have been published (BarNir, 1998; McRoberts, Burlingame, & Hoag, 1998). For instance, Toseland and Siporin (1986) reviewed 32 studies comparing individual and group formats. They found that the two modalities were equally effective in 75% of cases, and groups were more effective in the other 25% of cases. In a more recent study, Burlingame, Fuhrman, and Mosier (2003) conducted a meta-analysis of 111 studies on groups published over a 20-year period. Their work provided evidence of the overall effectiveness of group psychotherapy in particular and, to a lesser extent, of other group treatments. As Ward (2004) points out, group work has come a long way from being seen as an adjunct to individual therapy to now being seen as a robust treatment that stands on its own.

Yet group research is in its infancy compared with research in many other social sciences (Christensen & Kline, 2000; Stockton & Morran, 1982). There is still much that we do not understand about the intricacies of complex interactive variables found in groups. In other words, research is yet to be conducted on "which variables in which combinations lead to . . . effectiveness in various types of groups" (Ward, 2004, p. 156). In order for this situation to be rectified, researchers will have to devise more sophisticated techniques to measure change, and clinicians and researchers will have to interact more (Hall & Hawley, 2004).

Overall, increased concern and attention are being devoted to group research including an exploration of group forms that have fallen out of favor. For instance, Stanger and Harris (2005) are analyzing how marathon groups can be conducted in university counseling centers and beyond. Their emphasis is on setting up a structure by which these groups can be conducted in a safe and therapeutic manner. They are also measuring primary domains of a client's counseling experience for persons undergoing individual counseling, weekly group counseling, or marathons.

In addition to research in these areas, professional group associations are giving awards and grants for group research and recognizing major researchers in special ways. For instance, the entire September 2005 edition of the *Journal for Specialists in Group Work* was devoted to the contributions of Rex Stockton, especially his writing and research on group counseling over a 30-year period (Toth, 2005). Furthermore, group researchers, such as DeLucia-Waack (1997a, 1999a), are identifying group outcome and process instruments and assessing them in such areas as validity and reliability. Greater emphasis is being placed on investigating the effectiveness of important concepts crucial to group work, such as feedback and group climate, through measurements, such as the Corrective Feedback Self-Efficacy Instrument (Page & Hulse-Killacky, 1999) and the Group Climate Questionnaire (Burlingame, Fuhriman, & Johnson, 2004). Resources for identifying both methods and measures of evaluating group outcome and process are being published as well.

Finally, qualitative, as well as quantitative, methods of conducting research on groups are emerging (e.g., Christensen & Kline, 2000). This more phenomenological approach holds promise for exploring dynamics within groups. Specifically focusing on the evaluation process in groups is also being emphasized. Research practitioners, such as Smead (1995), are posing questions that should be asked in evaluation, such as "How do you plan to determine whether a member has changed due to the group experience?" "How are you going to determine whether your goals and objectives have been met?" and "How do you plan to evaluate leader performance?" (p. 27).

Brief Group Work and Managed Care

Brief group work began as an alternative to long-term group therapy (Piper & Ogrodniczuk, 2004). Today it is especially valued as a response to managed care and other health management programs that have imposed the expectation of quick results on the healthcare and mental health communities and limit the number of sessions they reimburse for treatment (Cornish & Benton, 2001). In addition, brief group therapy has been found to be efficient, cost-efficient, and the treatment of choice for certain types of problems (e.g., adjustment, trauma reaction) (Piper & Ogrodniczuk, 2004).

Solution-focus theory and therapy was one of the first forms of brief group work practiced. Although this approach was originally developed as a model for working with individuals and families, deShazer (1985, 1988), LaFountain and Garner (1996), and Sklare, Sabella, & Petrosko (2003) applied it to working with young adolescent (i.e., middle school children) and to individuals with recurring problems in a group setting. Likewise, Coe and Zimpfer (1996) outlined advantages of using solution-focused theory in groups in the mental health care arena. All followed the principles of solution-focused brief counseling, which assumes that treatment will be brief, that all complaints are alike, that participants are goal oriented, and that the focus of counseling and therapy will be on finding solutions (e.g., exceptions to when difficulties occur). Using these principles, they discovered a number of advantages to applying the theory to working with a group, including being able to gather together clients with heterogeneous problems who were available at a specified time and not being dependent on role models. Best of all, solution-focused brief counseling groups produced results. Coe and Zimpfer (1996) conceptualized how the theory could be applied to different stages of group development, whereas Sklare et al. (2003) further enhanced the potency of this approach by using solution-focused guided imagery.

The importance of brief treatment in group work cannot be overstressed, as it appears to meet the requirements of managed care companies and of many clients, the vast majority of whom come for eight or fewer sessions regardless of the services offered (Cornish & Benton, 2001). In fact, an integrated group counseling approach using the principles of brief dynamics and solution-focused therapy has been pioneered in a university counseling setting, with good results reported (Cornish & Benton, 2001). A brief approach in group work adds new vitality to working with groups of all kinds and is simultaneously pragmatic. "Given the realities of managed care and the time that individuals are willing to invest in therapy, the life span of any one therapeutic group is limited. There is, therefore, a need to help members of psychoeducational, counseling, and therapy groups focus on their goals and possible interventions as quickly as possible" (Bridbord, DeLucia-Waack, Jonrd, & Gerrity, 2004, p. 301). The brief, solution-focused approach does that.

THE FUTURE OF GROUP WORK

Group work has come a long way in its brief formal history, and, undoubtedly, it will be robust and permeate almost all segments of society on a global level in the future. However, predicting where group work will go in the future is difficult. As Conyne (2003) reminds us: "The world changes at such an explosive rate that prognostication perhaps should not even be attempted" (p. 293). Nevertheless, trying to map the direction of group work is important to the health and well-being of the profession. The more accurately professionals can anticipate where groups are going, the better they can train themselves and others to meet needs. After all, "counselors of the twenty-first century will be expected to provide a variety of group work applications" (Conyne, 1996, p. 155).

One direction group work appears to be going is following some of the predictions outlined by Zimpfer (1984) in that it is becoming more concrete and structured in regard to treatments for precise diagnoses. There is an increased emphasis on group systems theory as well and how it "can provide a variety of directions for innovations in group research and practice" (Connors & Caple, 2005, p. 93). Furthermore, a greater variety of groups are being created, including approaches that are more educational and growth inducing than ameliorative or adjustment focused. In relation to the greater breadth of groups offered, participants are now conceived as collaborators in treatment rather than as passive receivers. In addition, groups are being offered for a wide variety of populations, such as male inmates (Morgan, Garland, Rozycki, Reich, & Wilson, 2005), persons with multiple sclerosis (Gordon, Winter, Feldman, & Dimick, 1996), survivors of childhood sexual abuse (Gerrity & Peterson, 2004), depressives (Rice, 2004), substance abusers (Kominars & Dorheim, 2004), and those in grief (MacNair-Semands, 2004).

Linked to the area of specialization is the challenge for group workers to use the power "of the group" more fully in the future (Glassman & Wright, 1983). Groups that are able to harness the resources within themselves are more constructive and effective in promoting change and fostering support.

SUMMARY AND CONCLUSION

Group work has developed differently throughout its historical growth. During its initial stages in the early 1900s, the emphasis on groups was mainly on functionality. For example, Joseph Hersey Pratt first used groups to teach patients ways of caring for themselves, and it was only accidentally that he discovered groups had a healing effect. Similarly, during World War I, groups were used strictly for their utilitarian benefits. In the 1920s and 1930s, natural groups were studied closely, and the first major theorist in the group movement, J. L. Moreno, emerged. Kurt Lewin, a contemporary of Moreno, was an equally powerful figure in laying the foundation for group theory, influencing the development of the National Training Laboratories and the Tavistock Small Group movement in the 1940s.

In the 1950s, the distinctions between group work and family therapy arose. The language and vocabulary used in describing group work were refined, and the total quality work group emerged. In the 1960s, amid societal unrest, group work became popular with the general population in preventive and remedial ways. It was seen as a viable alternative to individual counseling, especially in educational settings. Many different forms of groups were developed; indeed, the 1960s was the decade of the group, and a number of important theorists came into prominence during this time.

Group work research and the growth of self-help groups were refined during the 1970s and 1980s. Task/work groups became more important and influential from the 1970s until the present. Psychoeducational groups reemerged as important during the 1980s and 1990s. Professional standards and ethics for group leaders were adopted during these decades, and group organizations begun earlier continued to flourish as new ones were founded. Self-help and support groups also grew in number and importance.

Recent trends in group work include new training and educational methods that increasingly use simulation and role-play. Technology, especially computers, is also becoming more popular. Along with these shifts is a greater emphasis on research involving groups and new theories employed in conducting groups, such as solution-focused therapy. Overall, present trends and the future of group work appear to be robust, especially in regard to the increased attention being paid to more specialized types of groups for particular populations with specific concerns or problems.

By being attuned to the history and current state of group work, those who study it will understand how groups have evolved, where they are now, and how they are likely to develop. Groups have been and will continue to be popular in a variety of settings, such as educational institutions, businesses, and community organizations. Group work is moving toward another plateau of sophistication and promise, making the future exciting.

CLASSROOM EXERCISES

1. Discuss with two other classmates your experiences in various groups, focusing as much as possible on the qualities of task/work groups in which you have participated. Concentrate on the factors that make some groups better than others, and share your conclusions with the class as a whole.

2. In groups of two, research a major figure in the history of group work (e.g., Jane Addams, Jacob Moreno, Irvin Yalom). Note this individual's contributions to the development of group theory or practice. Report your findings to the class in the form of an oral report.

3. Informally survey your campus or community in regard to the types of groups that are offered. Assign two classmates to gather information on selected groups, such as charity groups or fraternities. Examine the purpose of each group and how it functions. Share your findings with your class.

4. Access the World Wide Web home pages of the Association for Specialists in Group Work (ASGW), the American Group Psychotherapy Association (AGPA), the International Association of Group Psychotherapy (IAGP), the American Society of Group Psychotherapy and Psychodrama (ASGPP), and other groups. As a class, discuss what you found most helpful on the sites and what other materials you would like to see included.

CHAPTER 2

TYPES OF GROUP WORK

George Dodson/PH College

You and I live in different worlds
spinning around each other
in a patterned orbit that draws us close
but keeps us from really meeting.
Thus, we work hard to bridge the gaps—
the distances between our lives—
and search for words that touch
the inner cores the burn within.
I grow weary in reaching out
for you are but one among many
in my ever-expanding universe
that ebbs and flows with time.
Living in space and in harmony
is exciting and dynamic
but sometimes in the quiet
*there is inner turmoil.**

*From *Earth Traveler* by Samuel T. Gladding, © 1997.

Until the early 1990s, groups within the helping professions were categorized mainly in terms of counseling or psychotherapy. In actuality, group workers led and were aware of other types of groups, such as psychoeducational and work groups. However, no standards were set for leading groups outside the counseling and psychotherapeutic arenas. For this reason, in 1991, the Association for Specialists in Group Work (ASGW) developed standards and competencies for the preparation of group workers in four distinct group work specializations: task/work, psychoeducational, counseling, and psychotherapy. These standards were revised in 2000, although much of their basic thrust remains the same. (See Appendix C for the 2000 edition of *Professional Standards for the Training of Group Workers*.)

Developing standards and competencies for group workers was a major breakthrough. By explicitly defining what group workers need to do with specific group types, the standards identify, define, and establish skills that need to be acquired and developed. Thus, the evolution of a typology is an aid in efforts to determine and use evidence-based interventions to enhance outcome treatments (Ward, 2006). Furthermore, as a result of the standards, exemplary training models have been set up in educational institutions. By having such models, programs that prepare group specialists from a variety of disciplines can point to examples of what should be done in the preparation process (Conyne, Wilson, & Ward, 1997).

This chapter explores each group work specialty (i.e., task/work, psychoeducational, counseling, and psychotherapy) in the context of its purpose, structure, and intended outcome. Other models, past and present, for classifying group work, especially the groups and process (GAP) model, are discussed as well. The ways in which group purposes and skills can be combined are illustrated through an examination of the ways in which self-help groups operate. By being aware of different types of groups and their purpose and function, group workers can conduct and participate in a variety of groups in an effective and ethical way.

MODELS OF SPECIALTY GROUPS

Before exploring the four specialty groups, let us examine, briefly, how they came into being. In truth, there is no systematic way these groups came to be recognized. Rather, the process was one that developed over time and came in spurts. In fact, the classification system for categorizing group work is still being debated, as is discussed later in this chapter.

Need was part of the reason for the development of specialty groups. Group workers needed a way to describe what they were doing and what could be expected. For example, **contact-focused group theory** was an early forerunner of the specialty group model. The focus of this theory was on the purpose of groups. Three primary contact groups described in this theory were group guidance, group counseling, and group psychotherapy. Mahler (1971) differentiated among these groups as follows: (a) the group's initially defined purpose, (b) the group's size, (c) the management of the content, (d) the length of the group's life, (e) the leader's responsibility, (f) the severity of the problem, and (g) the competency of the leader.

To further distinguish among these three groups, Gazda (1989) emphasizes that guidance, counseling, and psychotherapy groups may be viewed along a continuum.

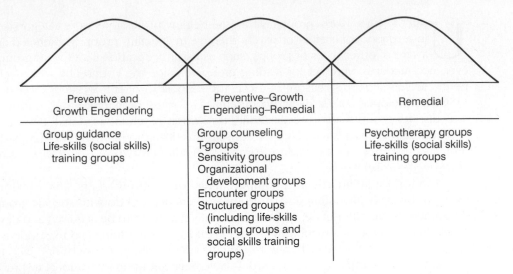

Figure 2.1
Relationships among group processes.
Source: From *Group Counseling: A Developmental Approach* (4th ed., p. 9) by George M. Gazda, 1989, Boston: Allyn & Bacon. Copyright © 1989 by Allyn & Bacon. Reprinted with permission.

Overlapping goals, professional competencies, and unique distinctions are visually high-lighted in this model (see Figure 2.1).

A model even more comprehensive and useful in conceptualizing groups was the first **specialty/standards model** pioneered by Saltmarsh, Jenkins, and Fisher (1986). This model evolved out of the realization that groups differ in their purpose and functioning. Therefore, not all groups are created equal, and to try to conduct them in similar ways is neither prudent nor possible. Thus, Saltmarsh et al. set up a model of group work known by the acronym TRAC, with each letter representing an area in the total picture of group work: tasking, relating, acquiring, and contacting (see Figure 2.2).

The main characteristic that distinguishes one type of group from another in this model is the focus. *Tasking groups* are focused on task achievement. *Relating groups* emphasize the options for movement within the life of each person. *Acquiring groups* are directed toward learning outcomes that members can apply to others. In contrast, *contacting groups* are focused on the individual growth of members (Saltmarsh et al., 1986, p. 34).

It was possible by using this model to explain how groups that start out in one major area (e.g., tasking) may move into other areas (e.g., relating). For example, a group set up for a special event, such as staging a race for a charity, may evolve into one where members simply enjoy getting together and hold frequent "reunions." The **TRAC model of groups** clearly delineates group process and management and the types of specialty groups found in each of four areas. It was the forerunner of the ASGW (1991, 2000) *Professional Standards for the Training of Group Workers,* which concentrates on task/work, psychoeducational, counseling, and psychotherapy groups and is the focus of the next sections of this chapter.

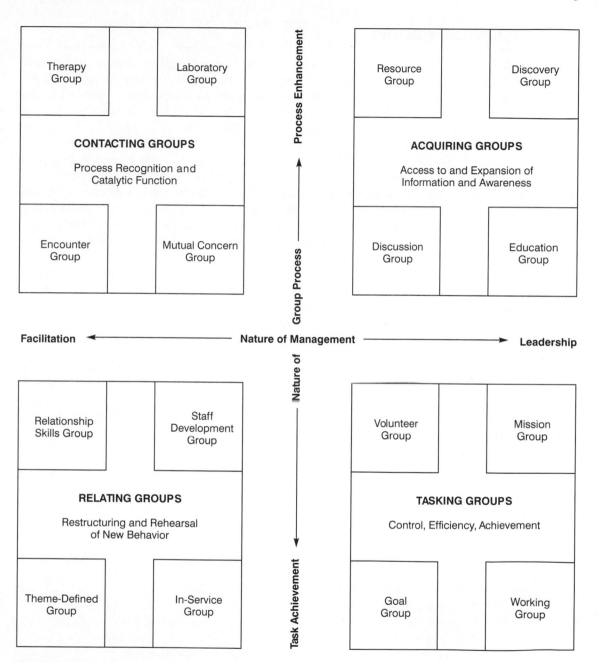

Figure 2.2

The TRAC map of group processes and management.

Source: From "The TRAC Model: A Practical Map for Group Processes and Management" by R. E. Saltmarsh, S. J. Jenkins, and G. I. Fisher, 1986, *Journal for Specialists in Group Work, 11,* p. 32. © ACA. Reprinted with permission. No further reproduction authorized without written permission of the American Counseling Association.

TASK/WORK GROUPS

Task/work groups "promote efficient and effective accomplishment of group tasks among people who are gathered to accomplish group task goals" (ASGW, 2000, p. 330). There are as many types of task/work groups as there are kinds of tasks and work. The major types of tasking groups, according to Saltmarsh et al. (1986), are volunteer groups, mission groups, goal groups, and working groups. Task/work groups also take the form of "task forces, committees, planning groups, community organizations, discussion groups, and learning groups" (ASGW, 1991, p. 14). Regardless of type or form, all task/work groups emphasize accomplishment and efficiency in successfully completing identified work goals (i.e., a performance, an assignment, or a finished product) through collaboration (Stanley, 2006). Unlike other groups examined here, task/work groups do not focus on changing individuals. Whether the group is successful depends on group dynamics—the interactions fostered through the relationships of members and leaders in connection with the complexity of the task involved.

Because task/work groups run the gamut from informal subcommittee meetings to major Hollywood productions, the number of members within a task/work group may be large, but this type of group usually works best with fewer than 12 people because unintended subgrouping does not occur. The length of a task/work group varies, but most are similar to other groups in that they have a beginning, a working period, and an ending. Total quality groups found in business settings are a good example of task/work groups. These groups apply group methods "to solve problems related to consumer satisfaction and quality" (Smaby, Peterson, & Hovland, 1994, p. 217). Juries are another good example of task/work groups. The movie *12 Angry Men* not only illustrates how some task/work groups operate but shows the many facets of group process as well (Armstrong & Berg, 2005).

Like other types of groups, task/work groups run best if the following assumptions are met:

- If the purpose of the group is clear to all participants,
- If process and content issues are balanced,
- If the systems of the group as a whole, leader, member, and subsets of members are recognized and acknowledged,
- If time is taken for culture building and learning about each other,
- If the ethic of collaboration, cooperation, and mutual respect is developed and nurtured,
- If conflict is addressed,
- If feedback is exchanged,
- If leaders pay attention to the here-and-now,
- If members are active resources,
- If members learn to be effective and influential participants,
- If leaders exhibit a range of skills for helping members address task and human relations issues,
- If members and leaders take time to reflect on what is happening (Hulse-Killacky, Killacky, & Donigian, 2001, pp. 21–22).

There are, however, at least two major differences between task/work groups and other types of groups. First, these groups may disband abruptly after accomplishing their goal. In this way they have the most similarity to psychoeducational groups that may end hurriedly because of time constraints, especially in a school setting. If members or leaders pay little attention to the termination stage in a task/work group, then members may feel incomplete when the group is finished. A second difference between task/work groups and other types of groups is that task/work group members and leaders may have considerable contact with others in an organization in which the group is housed. The reason is that task/work groups need input and feedback from persons who are not group members.

◆ *Questions from Experience* ◆

Task and work groups can either be rewarding or disappointing. You have probably been in both kinds of groups. What is the most rewarding task/work group you were ever in? What made it so? What was the worst? What factors contributed to your being disappointed in the group?

An Example of Task/Work Groups: Teams

Task/work groups "have great importance for our everyday lives, our jobs, our government, and our world" (Stanley, 2006, p. 27). A special type of a task/work group is a team. A **team** is a group of "two or more people who interact dynamically, interdependently, and adaptively and who share at least one common goal or purpose" (Azar, 1997, p. 14). In this respect, a team is more than the sum of its parts. Teams differ from other types of groups in four main ways (Kormanski, 1999; Reilly & Jones, 1974): (a) They have shared goals, as opposed to individual goals, as in most groups; (b) they stress interdependency more; (c) they require more of a commitment by members to a team effort; and (d) they are by design accountable to a higher level within the organization. "A lack of commitment to the team effort creates tension and reduces overall effectiveness" (Kormanski, 1999, p. 7).

Teams differ from task/work groups in at least a couple of ways. For one thing, more interdependence and accountability are evident in a team than in a task/work group. In addition, in a team effort, there is more sharing of information and work toward a common goal than in a task/work group. The result is usually a greater bonding of members to one another and more cooperation and unity in achieving a common objective (Katzenbach & Smith, 1993). Table 2.1 describes other differences between teams and task/work groups.

Although teams can be classified in many ways, one of the more common is by setting. From this perspective, teams are primarily found within work, sports, and learning situations (Johnson & Johnson, 2006). For example, teams are found in environments such as surgery, military exercises, and flying. In a work team, the emphasis is on interpersonal interaction in which members' proficiency and success in doing their jobs are maximized and their efforts are coordinated and integrated with the other team members.

A second way to classify a team is by how it is used. Common uses include problem solving (e.g., ways to improve quality, efficiency, and the work environment), special purpose

Table 2.1
Task/work groups versus teams.

Working Groups	Teams
A strong, clearly focused leader is appointed.	Shared leadership responsibilities exist among members.
The general organizational mission is the group's purpose.	A specific, well-defined purpose is unique to the team.
Individual work provides the only products.	Team and individual work develop products.
Effectiveness is measured indirectly by group's influence on others (e.g., financial performance of business, student scores on standardized examination).	Effectiveness is measured directly by assessing team work products.
Individual accountability only is evident.	Both team and individual accountability are evident.
Individual accomplishments are recognized and rewarded.	Team celebration. Individual efforts that contribute to the team's success are also recognized and celebrated.
Meetings are efficiently run and last for short periods of time.	Meetings with open-ended discussion and include active problem solving.
In meetings members discuss, decide, and delegate.	In meetings members discuss, decide, and do real work together.

Source: From D. W. Johnson and F. P. Johnson, *Joining Together: Group Therapy and Group Skills.* Copyright © 1994 (5th ed., p. 539). Reprinted by permission of Allyn & Bacon.

(e.g., facilitate collaboration between unions and management), and self-management (e.g., a small group of employees who produce an entire product or service).

A final way teams can be classified is in regard to what they recommend, do, or run. Teams that recommend include task forces that study and help find solutions for problems, whereas teams that do focus on performance (Katzenbach & Smith, 1993). It is rare for a team to run something, such as an organization, especially if it is large and complex.

A number of guidelines should be considered in establishing teams. First, it is important that teams be kept small. Because large numbers of people generally have difficulty interacting constructively in a group, the ideal size of a team will be 10 or fewer members. Second, team members should be selected on their already established expertise and skills as well as those they have the ability to master. Therefore, effective teams are heterogeneous, and their members possess a variety of task/work and teamwork abilities. In such groups, team members will often serve as "external memory aids" for one another and "divvy up what needs to be remembered about a task, with individual members remembering different aspects of the task and everyone knowing who knows what" (Azar, 1997, p. 14). A final necessity for forming a team is to bring together the resources necessary to function, including both tangibles and intangibles, such as materials, support personnel, space, and time.

Once a team has been established, it must be structured and nurtured (Johnson & Johnson, 2006). A crucial ingredient in this process is giving the team a mission and the independence to operationalize the goals that go with the mission. Teams function best when they have a meaningful and worthwhile purpose. A further necessity in structuring and nurturing a team is to "provide opportunities for team members to interact face-to-face and promote one another's success" (Johnson & Johnson, 2006, p. 547). Frequent and regular meetings are one way this may be done in a face-to-face way, but electronic communication, such as e-mail, fax, and phone time, can also be counted as time spent together.

Other matters that must be attended to in structuring and nurturing a team, according to Johnson and Johnson (2006), include the following:

- Paying "particular attention to first meetings," especially what those in authority do in such meetings since they are the role models for the members
- Establishing "clear rules of conduct," especially pertaining to attendance, discussion, confidentiality, productivity of members, and constructive confrontation
- Ensuring accountability of the team as a whole and its members individually
- Showing progress, especially obtaining easy goals early in the life of the group
- Exposing the team to new information and facts that "help them redefine and enrich their understanding of their mission, purpose, and goals"
- Providing "training to enhance both taskwork and teamwork skills"
- Having "frequent team celebrations and opportunities to recognize members' contributions to the team success"
- Ensuring "frequent team-processing sessions" so the team can examine how effectively it is working and discuss ways to improve (pp. 547–548)

Overall, teams that function best emphasize continuous improvement of themselves on an interpersonal, process, and product basis. They work as a group to create a culture that is supportive for members—one that gives them a sense of identity. At the same time, team members focus on specific goals and missions they wish to accomplish and make sure their energy is constantly focused on outcomes that are directly related to their purpose. Effective teams also train together, with the result being better performance over time, increased productivity, and fewer mistakes (Azar, 1997).

CASE EXAMPLE: Bradley at the Bat

Bradley has always loved baseball. He was never a great player, but he has now joined the city recreation league and is a member of his company's team. He plays second base, and his colleagues applaud him for both his effort and, at times, his efficiency.

Bradley is the lead-off batter. His job is to get a hit and get on base. He finds that whenever he comes to the plate his teammates cheer for him whether he gets a hit or not. That makes him feel good, and as a result he tries harder.

Bradley has noticed recently that he is becoming closer to his fellow workers at his company. In other words, there seems to be a spillover effect, and whether he is at the ballpark or at his computer, Bradley is trying hard to do a good job. He notices that he and others now, regardless of where they are, use phrases such as "Let's have a winning attitude here" and "Let's do this—for the team."

When have you seen a team positively affecting one of its members? What do you think this says about the power of teams and teamwork?

PSYCHOEDUCATIONAL GROUPS

Psychoeducational groups were originally developed for use in educational settings, specifically public schools. "The developmental nature of psychoeducational groups [proved] very useful when working with children's self-concepts and attitudes toward school" (Villalba, 2003, p. 264). One of the first types of groups to evolve in the development of group work, they were premised on the idea that education is treatment not only because of the knowledge acquired in the process but also because of the perceptions that may be changed as a result (Young, 1998). Basically, psychoeducational groups, with well-organized and structured activities and exercises, helped increase the self-worth of participants (Villalba, 2003). Sometimes these groups are simply referred to as **educational groups** or **guidance groups**.

Regardless of their name, "psychoeducation group work emphasizes using education methods to acquire information and develop related meaning and skills" (Brown, 1997, p. 1). Thus, psychoeducational groups are able to function on multiple levels and with a wide variety of clients. They can be preventive, growth oriented, or remedial in their purpose and focus. Because of their versatility, psychoeducational groups are increasingly being used in various settings outside of schools, including hospitals, mental health agencies, correctional institutions, social service agencies, and universities (Jones & Robinson, 2000; Morgan, 2004). They include "discussion groups, guided group interactions, recovery groups, support groups, orientation groups, educational groups, or student-centered learning groups" (Torres Rivera et al., 2004, p. 391).

"The overarching goal in psychoeducational group work is to prevent future development of debilitating dysfunctions while strengthening coping skills and self-esteem" (Conyne, 1996, p. 157). For instance, Hage and Nosanow (2000) reported that an 8-week, 90-minute psychoeducational group for young adults from divorced families helped participants "reduce isolation, establish connectedness, and build a stronger sense of their own identity and empowerment" (p. 64). In addition, Morgan (2004) states that cognitive-behavioral or behavioral approaches for offenders and mandated clients work well, especially if the psychoeducational group is structured on a topic such as stress management, problem-solving, or life skills. Because of their flexibility and efficiency, psychoeducational groups may even be preferred in counseling and psychotherapy environments "when managed care policies demand brief and less expensive treatment" (Brown, 1997, p. 1). They may also be preferred when the leader is less clinically experienced and wants the group members to realize immediately why they are in a group.

The size of psychoeducational groups will vary across settings (e.g., whether the activity is in a self-contained classroom or in a public lecture hall), but a range from 20 to 40 individuals is not unusual. In such large groups, discussion and skill practice can take place in subgroups. However, if subgroups are set up, then they must be small enough to ensure that each member of the subgroup is not seriously limited in the available **airtime** (i.e., "the amount of time available for participation in the group"; Brown, 1997, p. 4). Therefore, subgroups should be limited to 10 to 12 adult members at most, and fewer if the members are children.

The leader of psychoeducational groups is in charge of managing the group as a whole, disseminating information, and breaking groups into subgroups when necessary. A leader who is not an expert in the group's focus area must bring in someone who is. The leader's responsibilities then include managing the expert's presentation as well as the group's activities. The juggling of data, along with processes ensuring that group members benefit from the group experience, is demanding. Timing is crucial, and the group leader must be cognizant of group members' readiness to approach certain activities (Jones & Robinson, 2000). To do the job well, a psychoeducational group leader should take preventive steps before the group's first session. These include planning for session length, session frequency, number of sessions, and what will occur within sessions (i.e., the curriculum). Follow-up planning for subsequent sessions is crucial.

In the planning process, it is vital that the leader focus specifically on the design of the group. Such attention to detail is a highly involved endeavor but has a tremendous payoff in keeping the group focused and on course (Furr, 2000). In designing a group, Furr advocates a six-step process: (1) stating the purpose, (2) establishing goals, (3) setting objectives, (4) selecting content, (5) designing experiential activities, and (6) evaluating. Such a procedure leads to purposeful and meaningful outcomes.

Although the length, frequency, and number of sessions of psychoeducational groups will differ according to the ages of the people involved and the stage of the group, these groups usually last from 50 minutes to 2 hours. In general, psychoeducational groups work best when they have a regular meeting time, such as once a week. The number of sessions offered will depend on the purpose, but the range varies from 4 to 20 or more sessions. The average number of sessions is 8 to 10. However, all of these parameters are subject to change as "emerging policies on parity for insurance coverage of mental health services . . . influence the length and focus of many psychoeducation groups, as part of the mental health care system" (Brown, 1997, p. 13).

In general, psychoeducational groups stress growth through knowledge (ASGW, 1991, 2000). Summing up previous comments about such groups, Torres Rivera et al. (2004) state that the focus of psychoeducational groups is on transmitting, discussing, and integrating factual knowledge. Because of this focus, psychoeducational groups are "amenable to certain technological applications," such as computer-assisted programs, video and audio transmissions, and computerized simulations (Bowman & Bowman, 1998, p. 434). Content includes, but is not limited to, personal, social, vocational, and educational information. Activities in these groups can take many forms but usually are presented in the form of nonthreatening exercises or group discussions (Bates, Johnson, & Blaker, 1982). For instance, in working with individuals who have undergone cardiac transplantation and their families in a psychoeducational short-term group, Konstam (1995) found that framing anger in a positive way helped the group to discuss this normally "taboo" emotion for heart patients. Furthermore, the group process helped members realize they were not unique in their experiences of anger. By the end of the group, anger had significantly decreased.

One way to improve psychoeducational groups is to give members **out-of-group homework exercises** (Morgan, 2004). For instance, instead of just talking about the positive aspects of anger, group members might be assigned a photo opportunity of taking pictures of anger at work in a positive way. They might find that mild forms of anger or frustration can lead to people planting gardens, paving roads, or clipping hedges, all of which have a positive outcome.

◆ *Questions from Experience* ◆

When have you been a member of a psychoeducational group? What did you learn from the experience? How did it help you or give you fresh insight or knowledge?

An Example of Psychoeducational Group Work: Life-Skills Development Groups

A special form of the psychoeducational group is the life-skills development group. The concept of **life-skills groups** began to emerge in the 1970s when theorists such as Ivey (1973) and Hopson and Hough (1976) started using terms such as *psychoeducation* and *personal and social education.* In the 1980s, the momentum for this approach gained further impetus through the social skills and life-skills training methods advocated by Gazda (1989). The emphasis on life-skills training and its importance in society continues.

Life-skills training focuses on helping persons identify and correct deficits in their life-coping responses and learn new, appropriate behaviors. Sometimes these corrective measures are achieved in individual counseling, but often they are carried out in a group setting. One example is helping parents relate effectively to their children with disabilities (Seligman, 1993). The focus of life-skills training is on immediate remediation and future prevention. The training itself is primarily developmental. The group emphasis is on "how to." Activities within the group may include the use of films, plays, demonstrations, role-plays, and guest speakers.

A life-skills emphasis is appropriate for individuals in schools, colleges, families, work settings, clubs, and other natural group environments. Because many troubling situations arise in groups, the group setting provides an excellent place in which to work on resolutions. Because of the focus on life skills, such as increasing appropriate interpersonal communications or assertiveness abilities, "the growth process proceeds more comfortably, more observably, and with more precise attention given to the specific ingredients that induce change" (Zimpfer, 1984, p. 204).

Through life-skills training, people can be taught on an intrapersonal level how to prevent potential problems, such as depression, from occurring (Sommers-Flanagan, Barrett-Hakanson, Clarke, & Sommers-Flanagan, 2000). They can also be reinforced for taking corrective measures on behavioral and cognitive levels if difficulties arise. For example, Waldo and Harman (1999) found that the communication and interpersonal relationships between state hospital patients and staff improved and became more enjoyable when Bernard Guerney's (1977) Relationship Enhancement (RE) therapy approach was used in a group with both.

A number of steps are involved in learning life skills, many of which are the same as those that Johnson and Johnson (2006) describe in learning group skills:

1. Understand why the skill is important and how it will be of value to you.
2. Understand what the skill is, what the component behaviors are that you have to engage in to perform the skill, and when it should be used.
3. Find situations in which you can practice the skill over and over again while a "coach" watches and evaluates how you are performing the skill.

4. Assess how well the . . . skill is being implemented.
5. Keep practicing until the skill feels real and it becomes an automatic habit pattern.
6. Load your practice toward success [i.e., set up practice units that can easily be mastered].
7. Get friends to encourage you to use the skill.
8. Help others learn the . . . skill. (pp. 53–54)

Through implementing these procedures, group members enable both themselves and others. The result is a kind of snowball effect wherein skills continue to build on skills in an effective and complementary way.

Life-skills development groups ideally offer both the opportunity to learn new ways of behaving and the support necessary to continue to exercise them. Leaders and members can learn through each other's feedback and evaluations whether the strategies they employed have been useful and thereby improve their mastery or delivery of skills for future situations. Participants who profit most from these types of groups are those who have enough time and practice to integrate what they have learned in the group fully into their real-life situations.

CASE EXAMPLE: Patrick Practices His Psychoeducational Group Skills

As a group leader, Patrick wanted to experiment in finding out what methods worked best in leading a psychoeducational group for preteens. Therefore, when he made his lesson plans for his four fifth-grade classes, he used different ways of presenting the material: role-play, lecture, PowerPoint, and a combination of these methods. He gave each class a pre and post test to see what they knew and what they learned. He also measured how much they enjoyed the class.

Patrick was not surprised to find that the more active role-play format received the highest rating. He was also not shocked to find that the lecture method was least well received. Interestingly, the classes learned about the same amount of information regardless of the method used, and in a follow-up test a few weeks later, Patrick found that the class that used a combination of methods had the highest knowledge retention.

Patrick's results might be different from others because of his circumstances. Therefore, think of your own life experience and how you have learned best and with the most enjoyment when in a psychoeducational group. Was there a method used, other than those just mentioned, that helped you grasp or retain the material that was presented?

COUNSELING GROUPS

Counseling groups are preventive, growth oriented, and remedial. These groups are "generally considered to be a treatment mode that is equal in effectiveness to individual counseling" (Stockton, Morran, & Krieger, 2004, p. 65). The focus of **counseling groups**, which are also referred **to as interpersonal problem-solving groups,** is on each person's behavior and development or change within the group and through the help of the group. Thus, although goals are personal, the group as a whole may also share them. For instance, some counseling groups may concentrate on ways for each individual in the group to deal with disabling emotions, such as anger, whereas others may focus on disagreeable feelings, such as anxiety. Regardless, the interaction among persons, especially in problem solving, is highlighted (ASGW, 1991, 2000). These groups emphasize group dynamics and interpersonal relationships. Although psychoeducational groups are recommended for everyone on a continuous basis, counseling groups are more selective. These groups are ideal for individuals experiencing "usual, but often difficult, problems of living" (ASGW, 1991, p. 14) that information alone will not solve.

The size of counseling groups varies with the ages of the individuals involved, ranging from 3 or 4 in a children's group to 8 to 12 in an adult group. The number of group meetings also fluctuates but will generally be anywhere from 6 to 16 sessions. The leader is in charge of facilitating the group interaction but becomes less directly involved as the group develops.

Usually, the topics covered in counseling groups are developmental or situational, such as educational, social, career, and personal. They also tend to be of short-term duration. Counseling groups are a more direct approach to dealing with troublesome behaviors than are psychoeducational groups because they target specific behaviors and are focused on problem solving, instead of being aimed at general difficulties that may or may not be pertinent to every member's life. For instance, Finn (2003) described a nine-session counseling group to help students cope with loss in which members used artistic means, such as drawing, music, and drama, to access the underlying feelings and thoughts common to grief and process what they were going through. The focus in this counseling group was on a common experience, loss, that had taken many forms but that was disruptive in these adolescents' lives until dealt with openly.

A major advantage of counseling groups is the interpersonal interaction, feedback, and contributions group members experience from one another over time. Certainly that was true in the grief group just described.

One form a counseling group may take is **adventure counseling**. This type of group grew out of the Outward Bound movement of the 1960s, which was originated by educator Kurt Hahn in order to enhance emotional and physical abilities in clients by having them deal with safe but risk-taking events in the wilderness (Gillen & Balkin, 2006). Like other groups, these groups go through a number of stages. They focus on the promotion of long-term change and the opportunity to learn new coping skills. They may be used as adjuncts in hospital and clinical settings. Fletcher and Hinkle (2002) found that integrating an adventure component into an institutional setting produced positive results in participants such as enhanced self-confidence, self-concept, and well-being. Other findings support enhanced benefits, such as more immediate insight and quicker movement through developmental stages within the group.

◆ Questions from Experience ◆

If you started a counseling group, do you think you would incorporate physical activities, such as the arts or movement, into it, or do you think you would concentrate mainly on having members talk about their concerns? Why would you do what you do, and how would it help the group develop?

An Example of a Counseling Group: A Counseling Group for Counselors

Often counseling groups are conducted in schools or agencies with clients who want or need to focus on a developmental or situational problematic aspect of their lives, such as making a career decision or resolving negative feelings toward specific persons or experiences. The purpose of the group and its members is clear.

The counseling group chosen as an example here, a counseling group for counselors, can be enhancing for several reasons. For example, it promotes a dialogue among members of a profession who may otherwise not meet together at any other regular time. One of the most important dimensions of this type of group, however, is to help counselors deal with what Kottler (1986) describes as the "toxic effect" that comes from working with people in pain. The toxic effect includes physical and psychic isolation, repeated feelings of loss in regard to client termination, and interpersonal distancing from family and friends who may perceive counselors interpreting their words and actions. Thus, as Guy (1987) recommends, counselors need periodic, regular counseling to keep themselves well and functioning in an adequate and effective manner.

A counseling group for counselors can be conducted in a number of ways, but Emerson (1995) has set up an open-ended group model that appears to be most appropriate for practitioners in local communities. Her model is premised on Coche's (1984) suggestion that experienced group counselors reexperience participation in a counseling group. Specifically, Coche states that this reexperience can help group workers go beyond blasé and stereotypical responses, make them more aware of group participants' feelings, and resensitize them professionally to their power as group leaders.

In a counseling group for counselors, just as in other group counseling, self-disclosure and exploration of one's strengths and weaknesses are important for the development of the group members and the group as a whole. **Yearbook feedback**—that is, saying nice but insignificant things about a person, as high school students do when they write in annuals—is a tempting but nonproductive strategy. Instead, group members must deal with anxieties about their concerns as the group develops in an atmosphere of mutual trust where calculated risks are taken. When this type of behavior occurs, persons who risk making themselves known and attempt to engage in new or different behaviors gain the most from the group experience.

As in other counseling groups, counselors in counseling groups may experience some negative as well as positive outcomes. For instance, Gene may have suppressed anger and may erupt over what seems like an innocent remark directed at him. In such a case, the group needs to help Gene recognize both from where his anger is coming and toward whom or what it is really directed. Likewise, secrets may keep Bogusia from sharing significantly with the group and may inhibit the group's development if they are not acknowledged and shared. On the positive side, the awareness of personal growth that comes in problem solving and sharing may lead to members developing greater confidence in themselves as counselors, friends, family members, or parents. For example, Cassandra may discover from feedback in the group that she is perceived in a positive way congruent with her own self-concept. Thus, she may become even more open and available to those around her.

CASE EXAMPLE: Cassie Tries a Counseling Group

Cassie was in a natural disaster and was having trouble coping afterwards. A friend suggested that she sign up for a counseling group offered by the local mental health authority. Cassie was reluctant at first, but after a couple more sleepless nights, she relented and joined a group.

The group leader, Martin, made it clear that members were free to work on issues that were of most concern to them. Cassie chose her experience in the natural disaster. She was not the only person struggling with reliving such a bad memory.

In the group Cassie was able to verbalize her anger, angst, and anguish. She was able to come to terms with what she did and did not do to help others and herself. As the group ended, Cassie, who kept a journal, told the other group members: "I was wrung out when I came to the group, now I'm writ out."

When have you felt it would be helpful to be in a counseling group to deal with a life issue? Is that still an issue you could use some help with?

PSYCHOTHERAPY GROUPS

A psychotherapy group is sometimes simply called **group psychotherapy** or group therapy. It is a group that addresses "personal and interpersonal problems of living . . . among people who may be experiencing severe and/or chronic maladjustment" (ASGW, 2000, p. 331). Such a group is remedial in nature and emphasizes helping people with serious psychological problems of long duration by "confronting them with "their unconscious conflicts so that they may be resolved" (Lev-Wiesel, 2003, p. 240). As such, this type of group is found most often in mental health facilities, such as clinics and hospitals. As an entity, a psychotherapy group may be either **open ended** (i.e., admitting new members at any time) or **closed ended** (i.e., not admitting new members after the first session).

One of the primary aims of the group psychotherapy process is to reconstruct, sometimes through depth analysis, or to rectify through various treatment modalities the personalities or intrapersonal functioning of those involved in the group (Brammer, Abrego, & Shostrom, 1993; Gazda, Ginter, & Horne, 2001). The size of the group varies from 2 or 3 to 12 members. The duration of the group is measured in months, or even years. The leader of the group is always an expert in one of the mental health disciplines (i.e., psychiatry, psychology, counseling, social work, or psychiatric nursing) and has training and expertise in dealing with people who have major emotional problems. The leader's responsibility is to confront as well as to facilitate.

It should be noted that, although group psychotherapy is focused on severe problems, it is not wise or effective to include only individuals with personality disorders or diagnosable mental disorders, according to the latest edition of the American Psychiatric Association's *Diagnostic and Statistical Manual* (Yalom, 2005). Instead, a variety of individuals (i.e., a heterogeneous group) works best. To select such a group, leaders must prescreen carefully, preferably using prescreening instruments, such as the Group Therapy Questionnaire (GTQ) (MacNair-Semands, 1997). Leaders of psychotherapy groups most often operate from a theoretical position (e.g., psychoanalysis, Gestalt, existential).

◆ *Questions from Experience* ◆

How do you think group counseling and group psychotherapy differ? How are they the same? What concerns, besides those already mentioned, do you think would be appropriate for a psychotherapy group?

An Example of Group Psychotherapy: Group Work with Abusers and the Abused

Working with abusers or the abused requires a different approach from that used in other forms of group work. Individuals who are abusers, or who have been abused by others, have great difficulty in establishing healthy intrapersonal and interpersonal relationships (Vinson, 1992). They suffer from a variety of symptoms ranging from poor impulse control in the case of abusers to poor self-concept in the case of the abused. Many persons in either category have trouble working through their problems on an individual level. Abusers "usually have long histories of abuse, extremely strong defenses against change, and relatively little ability to follow through on commitments" (Fuhrmann & Washington, 1984, p. 63). The abused, especially those who have been sexually molested as children, tend to shut down, suppress, or distract themselves to the point of not dealing with what happened to them (Emerson, 1988; McBride & Emerson, 1989). In both types of cases, denial is a major means of dealing with present and past situations.

Group psychotherapy is often effective with such individuals for at least two reasons. First, many perpetrators of abuse and their victims are socially isolated and, therefore, welcome a structured experience in which they can "tell their story" and become more connected with others. Second, groups composed of members with similar backgrounds, such as abusers, are more resistant to manipulation by their members.

Almost all psychotherapy groups for abusers and the abused make use of basic group techniques, such as role playing, modeling, feedback, and confrontation (Fuhrmann & Washington, 1984; Vinson, 1992). The degree and type of change that occurs in group therapy is related to both the emphasis in the group and the group's developmental stage (Wheeler, O'Malley, Waldo, Murphey, & Blank, 1992). Psychotherapy groups that work best are composed of volunteers who are prescreened before being selected. However, because of the seriousness of abusive disorders, some groups are mandated as a part of court-ordered treatment and are filled with openly resistant clients. In such situations, group leaders must know how to work with resistance, such as not opposing it, but talking it through. Because of the volatility present in abuse groups, co-leaders are often recommended.

Probably the abusive disorder in which group psychotherapy strategies are most prevalent is with addiction, ranging from "foodaholism" (Stoltz, 1984) to chemical dependency (Clark, Blanchard, & Hawes, 1992; Kominars & Dornheim, 2004). In such groups, it is helpful but not always necessary to have leaders with experience in working through the abuse involved. A group leader does not have to have been abused or have been an abuser to be effective with group participants in this personality reconstruction process, but a thorough understanding of the individual, group, family, and community dynamics that contribute to abusive disorders is essential. For example, if Zelda undertakes conducting such a group, not only does she need to have established expertise in dealing with the dynamics underlying the abused or abusers, but she also must have established a network of community resources she can utilize in helping her group members reconstruct their lives. See Figure 2.3 for a summary of the four main types of groups.

CASE EXAMPLE: Garrett and the Psychotherapy Group

Garrett has been in and out of the state mental hospital three times. Having read the book *A Mind that Found Itself,* he realizes that he is much like the author, Clifford Beers, who had moments of clear thinking amid times of despair. In one of his clearest moments, Garrett decides to enroll in a psychotherapy group to help himself.

The group is open-ended, with new members coming in all the time and old members leaving. Yet, Garrett finds that the constant leadership of the group worker keeps him focused on not getting too upset when his day is interrupted or when he makes mistakes. He takes his medicine every day and talks about the time when he may no longer need medication. Overall, he is better adjusted than before because he is becoming more aware of himself and what he can do to help himself.

What people do you know, either from a distance or up close, who you think could benefit from a psychotherapy group? Do you think most people who need psychotherapy groups are on medications? Why or why not?

MIXED GROUPS AND A PROPOSED REGROUPING OF CATEGORIES

Some groups simply do not fit into any of the four major categories of groups just described; that is, it is hard to classify them as mainly task/work, psychoeducational, counseling, or psychotherapy groups. "Overlapping and blending of group types in the same group experience often best represents the reality of the evolving practice of group work" (Ward, 2006, p. 95). Furthermore, as Waldo and Bauman (1998) assert, the four main categories of groups are problematic "in that the goal and process dimensions of group work are combined within each category" (p. 164). Groups that defy classification are sometimes described as **mixed groups** because they encompass multiple ways of working with their members and may change their emphasis at different times in the development of the group.

Waldo and Bauman (1998) have proposed using multiple dimensions to describe groups. They point out that, although there are at least five dimensions that could be used in categorizing groups—goals, process, members, setting, and leader—"it is possible to arrive at a meaningful and practical categorization of groups through the use of the first two dimensions, goals and process" (p. 169). Their nomenclature for goal category includes the terms

- development; that is, forward motion and expansion,
- remediation; that is, overcoming or correcting manifest problems, and
- adjustment; that is, assisting members in coping with problems or circumstances that cannot be remediated.

The process dimension of their proposal retains three of the titles and process descriptions currently employed by the ASGW: psychoeducational, counseling, and psychotherapy.

Type of Group	Emphasis	Setting	Size	Duration Number of sessions
Task/Work	Promote efficiency and effective accomplishment of group goals	Almost any environment—work, school, religious settings, community organizations, civic groups	Work best with 12 or fewer members because otherwise subgroups may form	Time depends on task, but most task/work groups last from a half hour to 2 hours. Meetings may be regular or spontaneous depending on objective and whether setting is formal or informal
Psychoeducational	Acquire information and develop related meaning and skills	Hospitals, mental health and social service agencies, educational and religious settings, work environments	20 to 40 is average	50 minutes to 2 hours. Regular meetings usually weekly—average number of sessions 8 to 10, although many may be just for one session
Counseling	Prevention, growth, remediation, interpersonal and group dynamics	Schools, universities, mental health agencies, employee assistance programs, etc.	8 to 12 adults, smaller size for children, may vary depending on whether open or closed ended	20 to 90 minutes on average with longer lengths for adults. Regular meetings usually weekly
Psychotherapy	Personal and interpersonal problems of living—some severe; remedial, reconstructive	Hospitals, clinics, mental health and social services agencies	Depends on whether open or closed ended	60 to 120 minutes. Regular meetings often last over a number of months or years

Figure 2.3
Comparison of four basic types of groups.

Therefore, when goals and process are placed as two dimensions of a matrix, they form nine categories of group work, as represented in Figure 2.4.

Waldo and Bauman (1998) have validated their goals and process, or **GAP, matrix for groups** by having independent raters categorize randomly selected articles on group work under this system as well as the ASGW's four types of groups. They found much more agreement (100% vs. 33%) for raters using the GAP model and point to the utility, specificity, and research implications of their system as opposed to the four-group specialty system of the ASGW.

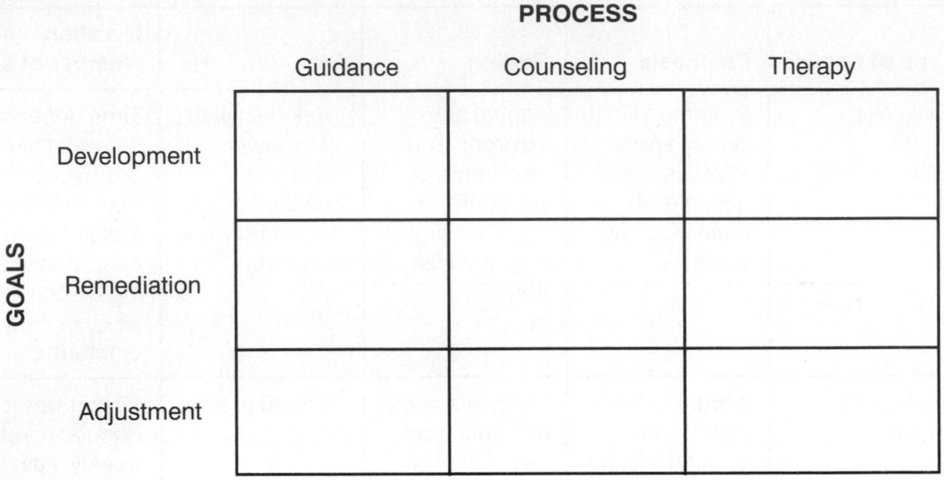

PROCESS

	Guidance	Counseling	Therapy
Development			
Remediation			
Adjustment			

GOALS

Figure 2.4

The proposed goals and process (GAP) matrix for groups.

Source: From "Use of the Proposed Goals and Process (GAP) Matrix for Groups" by M. Waldo and S. Bauman, *Journal for Specialists in Group Work*. Reprinted with permission of Sage Publications.

In response to the GAP matrix for groups, Conyne and Wilson (1998) point out that, although the system has many merits, if it were to be adopted as proposed it could undermine the ASGW training standards, which are a firm foundation for training, research, and practice and "whose positive effects are only now just beginning to emerge" (p. 183). Another drawback to the GAP model is that it does not consider task/work groups (Keel, 1998). Furthermore, the model is not as applicable as it would seem to such areas as psychoeducational groups for college students and, in fact, may complicate training for professionals entering student development and related fields (Taub, 1998b). Another drawback is that the model itself may need further refinement. For instance, the GAP model might be more useful if three dimensions (i.e., members, settings, and leaders) initially discussed by Waldo and Bauman were included as well as the dimensions of goals and process (Gerrity, 1998).

In response to the criticisms of their GAP model, Bauman and Waldo (1998) have revised their system to incorporate the four ASGW group classifications in regard to goals and process (see Figure 2.5). The discussion among group leaders about classification systems continues.

Regardless of how groups are classified, there are many examples of how groups may overlap in purpose, process, and content. For instance, a group might begin with multiple purposes (i.e., psychoeducational, psychotherapeutic, and task oriented). Such groups can be found among a number of self-help or mutual help groups.

Self-help groups and **mutual help groups** are synonymous (Klaw & Humphreys, 2004, p. 630). They take two forms: those that are organized by an established, professional helping organization or individual (**support groups**) and those that originate spontaneously and stress their autonomy and internal group resources—"self-help" groups in the truest sense (Riordan & Beggs, 1988). Although distinctions in support groups and self-help

PROCESS: the type of interaction characteristic of the working stage of the group			
Task/Work Facilitation: Discussion. Applying principles of group dynamics and employing methods such as collaborative group problem solving, team building, program development consultation, etc.	Guidance: Psychoeducation. Transmitting, discussing, and integrating factual information and building skills through the use of planned skill-building exercises	Counseling: Interpersonal Support. Using interactive feedback and support with a here-and-now focus	Therapy: Eliciting. Evoking emotional response and in-depth exploration of concerns

GOAL: purpose that guides direction of group

Task Performance: to complete a task or to improve performance on a task	TYPICAL (e.g., faculty meeting)	LIKELY (e.g., customer relations personnel training)	UNLIKELY	VERY UNLIKELY
Development: to promote growth and enhance individual life competencies	UNLIKELY	TYPICAL (e.g., career development workshop)	LIKELY (e.g., personal growth group)	UNLIKELY
Remediation: to overcome or correct existing problems	LIKELY (e.g., Boy/Girl Scout meetings)	LIKELY (e.g., spouse abusers group)	TYPICAL (e.g., interactional support group for foreign students)	TYPICAL (e.g., group for couples having severe conflicts)
Coping: to manage and contend effectively with unalterable	LIKELY (e.g., sheltered workshop)	TYPICAL (e.g., living skills—schizophrenia)	LIKELY (e.g., support group—diabetes)	UNLIKELY

Figure 2.5

The revised goals and process (GAP) matrix for groups.

Source: From "The Revised Goals and Process (GAP) Matrix for groups" by S. Bauman and M. Waldo, *Journal for Specialists in Group Work, 23*(2), p. 222. Reprinted with permission of Sage Publications.

organizations can be made regarding leadership and control (Silverman, 1986), these groups share numerous common denominators, including the fact that they are composed of individuals who have a common focus and purpose. They are psychoeducational, psychotherapeutic, and usually task driven. In addition, members of these groups frequently employ basic counseling techniques, such as reflection, active listening, and confrontation.

The civil rights movement of the 1950s and 1960s laid the foundation for the self-help and support group movements (Vander Kolk, 1985). Minorities, especially African Americans, realized during this time that they would have to band together and rely on their own resources if they were to make substantial gains and obtain major changes in American society. Other factors, such as the success of earlier self-help and support groups (e.g., Alcoholics Anonymous, Weight Watchers) and the failure of federal programs to take care of needs they were intended to address, also contributed to the momentum behind this movement.

Many support and self-help groups seem to be successful in assisting their members to take more control over their lives and function well. The narrow focus of these groups is an asset in achieving specific goals. There are more than 800 self-help organizations in the United States alone. "Indeed, mutual help organizations exist for almost every major chronic condition and leading cause of morality" (Klaw & Humphreys, 2004, p. 631). Furthermore, these groups are utilized with "approximately 7% of American adults (about 11 million people)" participating in them every year and approximately 18% having done so in their lifetime (Klaw & Humphreys, 2004, p. 632).

A national survey revealed some important facts about the characteristics of self-help group participants. First, with the exception of groups for eating problems (whose membership is composed almost entirely of Caucasian women), African Americans and Whites are equally likely to attend all types of self-help groups. Furthermore, individuals with low incomes ($0–$20,000/year) are more likely to participate than are middle-class and affluent individuals. Finally, individuals who are divorced or separated and have less social support are more likely to attend groups than are married individuals and individuals with extensive social support. Given these data, we may conclude that self-help groups have significant potential to benefit diverse racial groups and individuals with low financial and social resources (Klaw & Humphreys, 2004, pp. 632–633).

In addition to the foregoing, within a self-help group context a group member is empowered because he or she both provides as well as receives services. Thus, the positive self-identity of these individuals grows. Furthermore, "self-help groups can be successfully incorporated into professional programs in a fashion that enhances outcomes with little additional cost" (Klaw & Humphreys, 2004, p. 635). Thus, mental and physical health can be improved through the use of self-care groups, and they can lower health care cost if utilized by health care and health promotion programs (see Figure 2.6).

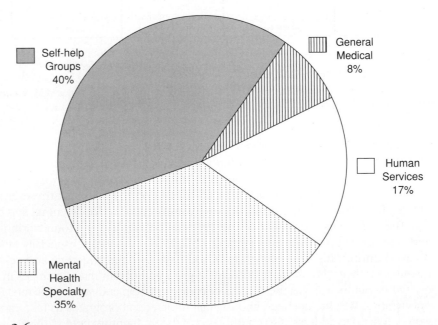

Figure 2.6
Help-seeking visits for addiction and psychiatric problems by U.S. adults.
Source: From Klaw, E. & Humphreys, K. (2004). The role of peer-led mutual help groups in promoting health and well-being. In DeLucia, J. L., Gerrity, D. A., Kalodner, C. R., & Riva, M. T. *Handbook of Group Counseling and Psychotheory* (p. 633). Thousand Oaks, CA: Sage.

Some of the most common self-help groups are those for chronic conditions such as arthritis (Young at Heart) and psychiatric disabilities (Recovery, Inc.), as well as those established to combat leading causes of mortality such as tobacco (Nicotine Anonymous) and illicit drugs (Narcotics Anonymous).

◆ *Questions from Experience* ◆

What surprises you about self-help groups? What facts about these groups did you already know or assume?

An Example of a Mixed Group: A Consumer-Oriented Group

A support group that encompasses self-help and functions from a psychoeducational and task/work perspective is a consumer-oriented group. Consumer-oriented groups are formed on the basis of need and may be either short term or long term, depending on the problem or concern. For instance, consumer-oriented groups may revolve around long-term themes, such as protection of the environment. In such cases, they tend to be ongoing, with individuals joining or dropping out of the group depending on the sociopolitical climate and the impact of specific events on their lives. Short-term consumer groups focus on immediate issues, such as highway safety in a particular locale, increased taxation, reassessment of property, or school zone districting in a community. These groups are usually spontaneously organized and less hierarchical than long-term consumer groups. After their issue is settled (e.g., new stop lights are installed, school zones are redrawn), the short-term groups usually disband. They work in such cases much like task/work groups.

Consumer groups are sometimes impaired, at least initially, because there is no immediately recognized leader. When this occurs, the group must wait for one to emerge. Often considerable chaos ensues while members jockey for positions and direction. Consumer groups that are most successful have both *rigor* (i.e., structure and a plan of action) and *vigor* (i.e., constant communication and contact with officials), whereas those that fail primarily have only one or neither of these qualities.

Consumer groups that meet in public and wish to elicit community support need to identify responsible persons who will arrange for a variety of tasks that must be carefully and efficiently carried out if the group is to be successful. Many of these tasks are rather mundane and mechanical, but they are crucial in promoting the outcome of the group—for instance, arranging for audiovisual equipment and food, if necessary.

One of the more important dimensions to planning consumer group meetings is the seating arrangement of the room. At least six arrangements will enhance or detract from the task of the group, depending on how they are used (Wilson & Hanna, 1986) (see Figure 2.7). Consumer group leaders should be aware of these designs when setting up their meetings to enhance the use of their time and the resources of the people involved. For instance, if Benjamin, the leader of a consumer group, mainly wants the group to hear new information, he may arrange the room and program as a symposium. However, if he wants group members to become active and discuss strategies for dealing with a particular matter, he may use a round-table format and arrange as many tables as needed to accommodate

Format Called	Arrangement Suggested	Reason for Using	Method
Round Table		To promote equality of feelings; maximize participation of all members; ensure as much spontaneity as possible.	Group discussion of problems and solutions for the purpose of making a good decision or sharing information.
Symposium		To present a variety of views in the form of short speeches or reports for the benefit of the audience.	Moderator introduces the panel; provides history of the issues at hand; presents each speaker in turn; monitors time; thanks the participants; ends the meeting with a brief charge to the audience or a summary of the issue.
Panel Discussion		To conduct a semistructured discussion of issues on a topic for the benefit of an audience.	Moderator introduces the panel and problem and keeps the discussion flowing; restates often; controls (somewhat) equal and fair time allocation. Members are responsible for developing points of view and have some control of agenda.
Forum		To encourage audience participation on issues surrounding a topic.	Moderator introduces the program and speaker, who presents a brief statement and interacts with the audience. Moderator participates to encourage audience involvement. A variety of discussion formats can be used.
Colloquy		To inform an audience through the use of planned questions designed to get unprepared responses from participants for the benefit of the audience.	Moderator introduces the speaker and panel of questioners, then regulates rotation and time. Sometimes summarizing, sometimes clarifying, moderator does not participate as a panelist.
Whole-House Decision Making		To debate issues as a body, then decide, using appropriate voting methods.	Moderator regulates the discussion and debate, attempting to get maximum input from both sides in order that members of the house may cast informed votes. Parliamentary procedure is commonly used to govern the event and facilitate orderly progress.

Figure 2.7

A guide for planning group meetings.

Source: From *Groups in Context* by G. L. Wilson and M. S. Hanna, 1986, New York: Random House. Copyright © 1986 by McGraw-Hill. Reprinted with permission of The McGraw-Hill Companies.

the size of the group. After discussing issues for a specified length of time, each table leader can then report back to the group as whole.

SUMMARY AND CONCLUSION

This chapter has covered past and present proposed categories for classifying groups. Past models include those that were contact-focused or specialized, yet flexible, as in the TRAC Model. In 1991 the four major types of groups (psychoeducational, counseling, psychotherapy, task/work) as proposed by the ASGW became a standard for categorizing groups. This system was revised in 2000 when it was realized that some groups, such as many self-help groups, are mixed and incorporate multiple dimensions of the four ASGW group emphases in their functioning. The GAP group model is the most recent innovation in the group classification system. Its usefulness is now being openly discussed among group experts.

Group workers who narrow their skills to working with only one type of specialty group will limit their flexibility in working with people in groups. Although specializing can increase expertise in a particular area, human service professionals, such as counselors, psychologists, social workers, and psychiatric nurses, are called on to deal with a variety of clients in multiple ways. Sometimes conducting a psychoeducational group will be more productive than running a psychotherapy group, and sometimes psychoeducational group skills are necessary to facilitate a psychotherapy group (MacNair-Semands, 1998). Working in task/work groups will be required regardless of what else the clinician does.

From case conferences to task force teams, everyone who works as a professional helper needs to know how to facilitate a group that is focused on achieving a product other than individual change. Therefore, it is essential to adhere to and master the standards and competencies that professional associations such as the ASGW (2000) have laid out. Group work involves types of groups, but it is a complex and demanding process in its actual application.

CLASSROOM EXERCISES

1. In a group of three, identify two life skills, such as applying for a job or making conversation in a social situation, that you think could be taught in a psychoeducational group. Outline the ways you would teach these skills. Confer with another threesome about the skills they have selected and the approach they have decided to use in this process. Select one skill and approach from your combined group of six, and as a group present it to the class.

2. Read recent periodicals in your library to gain a sense of how task/work groups and teams are used in business and nonbusiness environments. In a group of three, discuss the articles that each of you has selected. Share your ideas about ways to use task/work groups and teams in the helping professions.

3. In dyads, read and critique a recent research report or journal article on the effectiveness of a counseling or psychotherapy group. Report your findings to the class as a whole in a brief oral presentation.

4. You have been asked to train a group of novice group workers and teach them about the four major types of specialty groups. From what you have read in this chapter, how would you go about accomplishing this task? Would you incorporate the GAP model into your training? If so, how? Share your outline for presenting your material with your class and get their feedback.

CHAPTER 3

GROUP DYNAMICS

Ken Karp/PH College

*Emotions ricochet around the room
   fired by an act of self-disclosure
      in an atmosphere of trust.
I, struck by the process,
     watch as feelings penetrate the minds of members
        and touch off new reactions.
Change comes from many directions
    triggered by simple words.* *

*From *Group Dynamics* by Samuel T. Gladding, © 1989.

Groups are dynamic entities that have a direct and indirect impact on their members (Bion, 1959; Yalom, 2005). "In any group, it is a mistake to ever conclude that nothing is happening within or between its members" (Conyne, Wilson, & Ward, 1997, p. 32). The presence of others may improve or impair the performance and development of persons depending on their background and preparation (Zajonc, 1965). When individuals are accustomed to working with others and well prepared for a group experience, the group enhances their performances and they add to the group. In contrast, when individuals are used to working alone and are not well prepared for a group experience, their behavior may be detrimentally affected by being in the group and they may detract from the group as a whole. Thus, a **social influence** emerges in a group that manifests itself by altering actions, attitudes, and feelings (Asch, 1951; Conyne, 1983; Festinger, 1954; Sherif, 1937).

Research taken from three separate disciplines—individual psychology, social psychology, and sociology—focuses on explaining these and other interactions that occur in groups and how groups influence their members (Munich & Astrachan, 1983). Basically, people act differently in groups than they do by themselves. As a general rule, **primary affiliation groups** (i.e., those with which people most identify, such as a family or peers) exert greater pressure on individuals than **secondary affiliation groups** (i.e., those with which people least identify, such as a city or confederation).

CASE EXAMPLE: Alberto Wreaks Havoc

When he is with his family, 13-year-old Alberto is polite and well behaved. So it was a shock when Mrs. Hernando received a call from the director of the camp Alberto was attending during the summer asking that she and her husband come and get him. When the Hernandos arrived at the camp, the director informed them that Alberto had broken into the kitchen with several other boys and literally dumped flour all over the tables and chairs.

When questioned, Alberto could not give a rational explanation. He said he simply thought it was funny and that the camp staff would not care. He was simply having a good time with his new friends. His behavior at camp was far from that he displayed at home with his family and peers.

What do you think happened to Alberto? Based on what you have read, why might it have happened?

The influence of groups on members, and what has grown to be known as **group dynamics**, was first studied as a phenomenon in work environments. Indeed, "the origins of group dynamics are largely in social and industrial psychology and stem from the efforts of experts in these fields to understand group influence on individual behavior and on productivity in the workplace and in other human groups" (Friedman, 1989, p. 46). Elton Mayo and his associates at the Hawthorne Plant of the Western Electric Company conducted the initial landmark study on the influence of groups (Mayo, 1945). This research group investigated the effects of manipulating physical features in the work setting. It was discovered that physical aspects of the work environment were not as important as social factors within the work group itself. Changes in behavior as a result of observation and manipulation of conditions in an environment became known as the **Hawthorne effect**.

Although Mayo's work involved group dynamics, he did not describe it this way. Rather, the term came from Kurt Lewin (1948), who was the first to use it. For Lewin, group dynamics includes everything that goes on in a small group. He was especially interested in how the climate of a group and its processes influenced the interactions of group members and ultimately outcomes. He thought many factors contributed to the overall concept of group dynamics, including the group's purpose, communication patterns, power and control issues, and member roles. For instance, a psychotherapy group for survivors of natural disasters, such as a tsunami, hurricane, or earthquake, has a purpose and intensity quite different from those of a research group formed to study the Internet's effects on community values. Member roles and interactions are not the same, either, and the intensity or temperature of these types of groups differs dramatically. By understanding forces operating within a group and their interplay, group specialists are able to discern the nature of groups and how interactions among participants affect a group's development.

GROUP CONTENT AND GROUP PROCESS

Included in the term *group dynamics* (i.e., forces within a group) are two powerful elements that have a major bearing on a group's development and productivity: **group content** (i.e., information within and purpose of the group) and **group process** (i.e., interactions and relationships among members within the group). The amount and mixture of group content and group process ultimately determine the dynamics within a group.

Group Content

Group content involves the actual words, ideas, and information exchanged within a group as well as the purpose of the group. For example, in a psychoeducational group, participants may talk about the facts surrounding the purpose of the group, such as how to prevent the spread of AIDS. However, no group runs well on facts and information alone. After some time in most groups, members have enough basic knowledge to accomplish their goals. This point does not mean that new and pertinent information should not be added to the group over time—quite the contrary, because groups absorb and deal with information developmentally. Rather, it means that more information is not necessarily better. Large quantities of information in short periods are not generally useful because they cannot be adequately digested. For instance, in a group for victims of a disaster, information on recovery is given in pieces over time because otherwise group members become overwhelmed, confused, or discouraged.

People in groups, just like people individually, do not make most of the important decisions of their lives based on cognitive knowledge. Instead, good decision making involves interaction with others in pursuit of a purpose. It is based on members having pertinent information, an opportunity to understand their options, and a chance to assess what they are thinking and feeling with other people they trust and value. That is where group process comes in.

CASE EXAMPLE: Professor Drone Goes On and On

Despite his sincerity and sense of caring, Professor Drone gets terrible student evaluations. He complains to his colleagues and tries harder each semester without making any substantial progress. He is knowledgeable and amicable but his students do not learn a lot. The reason: He drones on with lecture notes from the minute he starts class until the bell rings. Students do not interact except to occasionally squirm and roll their eyes.

What would you advise Professor Drone to do besides "try harder"? Be specific.

Group Process

Group process is the interaction of group members with one another, often in some meaningful way. For example, Joe may feel he cannot speak up in a group because another group member criticized one of the first things he said in the group. His lack of trust and inhibition detracts from the group because he remains silent. If Joe is an especially astute observer of people or has insight that would really help the group, his nonparticipation in the group hurts that much more. Regardless, other members will eventually notice Joe's withdrawal. Then either the group will spend time attending to Joe—trying to coax him into contributing when they could be focusing on other goals—or they will criticize him even more, thus alienating him significantly from the group. Therefore, attending to process within the group is vital to the group's well-being.

As groups develop, less time generally is spent on content material, and more is focused on process functions. There is often a relational paradox. Individuals, especially those who have been in nonmutual relationships, want to become connected with others. Out of a sense of fear or hurt, however, as with Joe in the preceding illustration, they simultaneously employ strategies that restrict or limit their ability to become close to others (Comstock, Duffey, & St. George, 2002). Therefore, they disconnect. They may reconnect (when trust is built) and enhance their connection (when they feel safer yet).

Seven types of group processes that most frequently occur in groups related to this paradox and the dynamics surrounding it have been outlined by Donigian and Malnati (1997):

- **Contagion**—In this process, member behavior elicits group interaction. For instance, if Bette talks to others in a group about her emptiness and loneliness, then she may elicit an emotional and physical reaction from other group members as some cry and some lean forward to listen more intensely.
- **Conflict**—Matters involving conflict usually revolve around significant issues in people's lives, such as authority, intimacy, growth, change, autonomy, power, and loss. All group members and leaders experience conflict during the life of a group. How a group leader handles conflict makes a difference. For example, if in a group counseling session Rex, the group leader, pushes Stu to have a fight with Keith, Rex may be vicariously meeting needs he never satisfied in adolescence, but he may not be helping Stu or Keith to resolve their differences.
- **Anxiety**—The tension involved in anxiety and the uneasy feelings that go with it are universal. To cope with the discomfort of some emotions in a

group, members typically employ one of two strategies. The first is a
restrictive solution, such as changing the subject, attacking a group member, intellectualizing, detaching from the group, or ignoring a group member. Thus, if Karen feels uncomfortable discussing her personal life, she
may flippantly say, "But my situation is just like everyone else's."

A second, healthier strategy for dealing with anxiety is to employ
enabling solutions (Whitaker & Lieberman, 1964). These types of solutions revolve around open listening and discussion about the anxiety that
is present. In such a situation, Roosevelt might say to Regina, "Tell me
more about how you felt when your mother criticized you." Overall, "anxiety is a mobilizer of group process," especially if it is faced openly and honestly (Donigian & Malnati, 1997, p. 62).

- **Consensual validation**—The process of consensual validation involves
checking one's behaviors with a group of others. In this interaction, people are questioned, confronted, or affirmed either individually or within
the group. Thus, in a group for overeaters, members might question one
another about their interactions involving food to find out how unusual or
common their behaviors are.

- **Universality**—It is comforting to know that others within a group have similar
experiences and feelings. Such insight helps people feel they are in the same
ballpark as the rest of the group members. In the universality process, this discovery enables group participants to identify and unify with one another. For
instance, in a psychoeducational group involving families with adolescents,
families in the group may be relieved to know they are not the only ones having difficulties with parent–teen communications. If a group is going to be productive, it is essential for universality to occur early in its development.

- **Family reenactment**—Families of origin continue to influence people
throughout their lives (Kerr & Bowen, 1988). Because groups resemble
families in many ways, it is natural that some behaviors by group members
are connected to issues they never resolved in childhood. The group is
either helped or hindered by such actions, depending on whether group
members are assisted in focusing on the present or allowed to lapse into
the past. In the first case, the group member and the group work through
issues. Thus, Pedro may say to Veronica, "I need you to help me hear what
you are saying. Your actions are a lot like those of my mother, with whom I
was constantly arguing." In the second scenario, group interactions
become distorted or toxic. An example of this type of behavior is when
Sally repeatedly tells David, "I'm not listening to you. You sound just like
my father, and he never had anything worthwhile to say."

- **Instillation of hope**—In some groups, especially those involving counseling and therapy, many members may feel hopeless. They believe their environment controls them and thus they will never be different or change. It
is, therefore, vital that these group members be helped to come to terms
with their own issues. Through such a process, all group members can
come to realize that their issues are resolvable. In such a situation, Kathy
may begin to believe she can be different because William has gotten better
and his problems were similar to hers when the group began.

Balance Between Content and Process

Process must be balanced with content regardless of the type of group being conducted (Kraus & Hulse-Killacky, 1996). Process, along with content, is at the heart of decision making. Leaders can use two sets of questions to guide the interplay between content and process (Hulse-Killacky, Killacky, & Donigian, 2001).

Content questions include:

> *What do we have to do?*
> *What do we need to do to accomplish our goals?*

Process questions center on:

> *Who am I?*
> *Who am I with you?*
> *Who are we together?* (p. 9)

Interpersonal dimensions of a group take on increased importance as the group moves toward its objectives (Armstrong & Berg, 2005). The ideal balance between content and process can be seen in a bell-shaped curve (Figure 3.1) in which content and process look like a single thread even though they are two separate fibers (Hulse-Killacky, Schumacher, & Krause, 1999).

When process and content are out of balance, there may be too much of one, or the two may not be intertwined. For example, a group can begin with an overfocus on process (see Figure 3.2). In such a group, an experiential activity that does not tie in with the rest of the group session is used to get members emotionally involved. For example, a leader may take one of the energizer exercises from Keene and Erford (2007), such as "It's Snowing" (p. 26) where everyone represents himself or herself as a snowflake in the introduction segment of the group and highlights unique personal qualities. However, in this unbalanced scenario the activity is then never connected to the work of the group. Another such scenario may occur if Peggy, the group leader, has group members talk to one another initially about the most important event that shaped their lives and then

Figure 3.1

Balanced process and content.

Source: From "Leadership in Groups: Balancing Process and Content," presentation at the annual convention of the American Counseling Association, April 1994, Minneapolis, MN. Reprinted with permission of Diana Hulse-Killacky, Becky Schumacher, and Kurt Kraus.

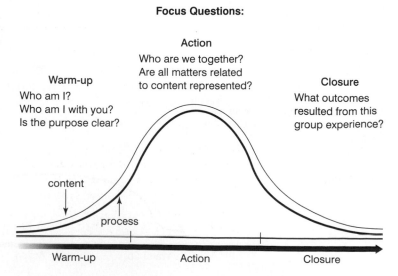

Focus Questions:

Action
Who are we together?
Are all matters related
to content represented?

Warm-up
Who am I?
Who am I with you?
Is the purpose clear?

Closure
What outcomes
resulted from this
group experience?

content

process

Warm-up   Action   Closure

Figure 3.2

Process first, content after.

Source: From "Leadership in Groups: Balancing Process and Content," presentation at the annual convention of the American Counseling Association, April 1994, Minneapolis, MN. Reprinted with permission of Diana Hulse-Killacky, Becky Schumacher, and Kurt Kraus.

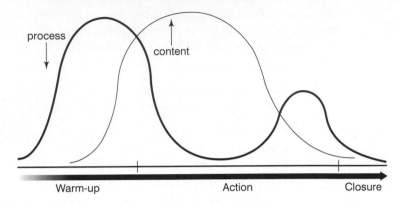

"Now for the first half hour tonight we are going to play some 'noncompetitive games' in the hope. . . ."

moves onto having the group solve a problem concerning the selling of tickets to an upcoming play, without connecting the group experience to the work activity.

The opposite of such a scenario is for a group to stay focused on content (Figure 3.3). This type of arrangement occurs frequently in task/work groups in which members may not even be introduced to one another before the group leader states what the group will do for the day. In a content-dominated group, process is inhibited and members often withdraw from the group mentally or physically because they never felt a part of it to begin with.

Therefore, groups that work well, regardless of their emphasis, are those in which group members and leaders are aware of the need to have content and process balanced. In such groups everyone works continuously to make sure neither gets out of line.

◆ *Questions from Experience* ◆

What is the best-run group that you have ever been a member of? What made it so? What was the worst? What made that a bad experience? In your evaluation of these groups, think how content and process were handled.

Figure 3.3

Content-inhibiting process.

Source: From "Leadership in Groups: Balancing Process and Content," presentation at the annual convention of the American Counseling Association, April 1994, Minneapolis, MN. Reprinted with permission of Diana Hulse-Killacky, Becky Schumacher, and Kurt Kraus.

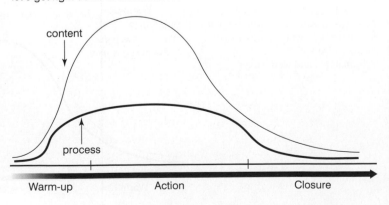

"We have lots to do today. So let's get right down to business. . . ."

THE GROUP AS A SYSTEM: A WAY OF EXPLAINING GROUP DYNAMICS

Because content and process must be balanced to have productive group dynamics, a question that arises is "How?" One answer is to think of the group as a **system**, a set of elements standing in interaction with one another (Agazarian, 1997; Connors & Caple, 2005). Each element in the system is affected by whatever happens to any other element. Thus, the system is only as strong as its weakest part. Likewise, the system is greater than the sum of its parts (Gladding, 2007). An example of a system is a living organism, such as a plant or an animal. However, a group can be conceptualized as a system, too, and as such is made up of three crucial parts: the group leader, the group members, and the group as a whole (Donigian & Malnati, 1997).

For the system to be healthy and productive, each of these parts must function in an interactive and harmonious way as a unit and with the other two parts of the system. Thus, if group members are constantly in conflict with one another, then the group will not work well as a whole regardless of how talented the leader might be. Likewise, if group members work well together but are led by a leader who is unable to use this strength, then the group as a whole will underfunction. Finally, if group members and the group leader are both healthy, but no one in the group knows anything about how a group functions over its life span or the group has no goals, then the group as a whole will suffer.

Systems theory goes a long way in explaining how groups work and group dynamics (O'Connor, 1980). In a systems context, group members are always deciding between their needs for *differentiating themselves* (i.e., taking care of their needs to do things by themselves) and *integrating with others* (i.e., doing things with others) (Matthews, 1992). From a systems perspective, group leaders must orchestrate their efforts in helping members and the group as a whole to achieve a balance of individual and collective needs as the group develops. Multiple factors—such as interpersonal relationships, the mental health of the individuals involved, and the skill of the group leader—affect the group. The dynamics within the group are complex and connected. Although some factors influence others directly (i.e., in a **linear** or cause-and-effect way), most factors influence each other **systemically** (i.e., in a circular manner) (Bertalanffy, 1968; Donigian & Malnati, 1997; Matthews, 1992).

From a systems perspective, even small or seemingly insignificant events make a difference in the group. For instance, the presence or absence of a group member affects how a group operates. Similarly, the withholding or divulging of feelings has an impact. Even inevitable events, such as the passage of time, influence both the lives of group members and the life of the group as a whole. Consider, for example, the Beatles. During the 1960s, each member of this band—Paul McCartney, John Lennon, George Harrison, and Ringo Starr—changed not only himself but also the outward appearance, musical style, and performance of the others and the group as a whole. The Beatles of 1969 were not the same group in the way they operated (or even looked) as the Beatles of 1964 (Forsyth, 2005). The point is that groups as systems with many parts are constantly in a state of flux. In a more mundane illustration, if Bill feels uncomfortable in the presence of Norm and Nancy, then their absences from the group will most likely result in Bill being more active, which in turn will lead to new information being added to the group and a new interactive group process.

The complexity of working with groups as distinct types of entities must be properly understood to promote healthy atmospheres within them (Korda & Pancrazio, 1989). Persons who are uninformed or ignore how groups function usually become frustrated and bewildered. They do not help the group grow and may even behave inappropriately by encouraging behavior that group members are not ready to handle yet.

CASE EXAMPLE: Retro Rick

Rick is 50, married, and the father of three children. He works in information technology. Because he wants to expand his circle of male friends, he joins a local "growth group" of men who are at various life stages. Instead of talking about his own situation, Rick tries to be "cool." He talks about himself in singular terms and as if he were single and still in his 20s. He seeks out the younger men in the group to "hang with." Everyone is confused as to what Rick is doing. As one of the men his age says to him: "You are not 'youthing,' you are aging. 'Time passages' is more than a song by Al Stuart."

What do you think is happening in the group? What aspects of health and dysfunction are present? How could the group be healthy as a system?

One method of assessing which types of factors most influence certain group situations is by studying the research on groups as systems in such journals as *Small Group Behavior,* the *Journal for Specialists in Group Work, Group Dynamics,* and the *International Journal of Group Psychotherapy.* Good research that is clearly and concisely written can convey a considerable amount of information. Direct group observation or participation is a second means of comprehending the evolving nature of groups and how members are influenced by one another and external forces (e.g., cultural surroundings). This method gives firsthand knowledge about how a group is operating. A third way of assessing group influences is feedback from outside objective observers or a critique of group videotapes. This last means of obtaining data, especially if outside observers use video, allows a thorough examination of the group as a system and enables one to both see and hear what is occurring within.

INFLUENCING GROUP DYNAMICS

Given that group dynamics can be explained from a systems perspective, it behooves group workers to take advantage of this knowledge. They can do so by setting up conditions and structures that will help the group potentially run better and more smoothly in both the long and the short run. Although veteran group leaders "develop skills to assess the dynamics of group members and use their skills to anticipate and react to group movement" (Gerrity, 1998, p. 202), most group workers are wise to spend time and energy attending to the preplanning part of a group, the group structure, group exercises, group interaction, and members' roles.

Preplanning

The dynamics of a group begin before the group even convenes. In the pregroup stage, the leaders plan what type of group to conduct, in what setting it should be held, how long it will last, who should be included, and how it will be evaluated. All of these considerations are an essential part of facilitating a successful group (Glaser, Webster, & Horne, 1992). If leaders are not sure of the type of experiences they wish to set up and for whom, then the group will most likely fail.

The first factor that must be considered in preplanning is **clarity of purpose**—what the group is to accomplish. For a group to be successful, it must be relevant and meaningful for all of its members. Otherwise, they are likely to withdraw or disengage. For instance, a psychoeducational group focusing on careers may have an appeal to senior high school students but not be relevant to primary school children unless it is modified to their level and presented so that they see a connection between themselves and future careers.

In addition to clarity of purpose, a **group setting** (i.e., its environment) will influence how well it runs. Settings should be rooms that are quiet, comfortable, and off the beaten track. The type of environment, one that promotes positive group dynamics, is not found by accident. It must be carefully selected because the group's functioning ultimately depends on it. Members who feel secure in an environment are more willing to take risks and use themselves and the group to the fullest.

A third factor that must be considered in preplanning a group is time. A group session should not be too long or too short. Sessions running more than 2 hours may cause members to become tired and lose interest. Likewise, with the exception of some children's groups, most groups need about 15 minutes to "warm up" before they start working. Therefore, groups that meet for less than half an hour do not have time to accomplish much. The ideal time frame for most groups is between an hour and an hour and a half. A few groups, such as marathons, use extended periods to help lower defenses through the effects of fatigue. In this way, they promote identity and change. Most groups, however, meet weekly within the period just described. Such a schedule allows group members and the group as a whole to obtain a comfortable pace or rhythm.

Even in a small group, size makes a difference in group dynamics. Research indicates that increasing the size of a group (beyond 6 to 14 members) decreases its cohesiveness and member satisfaction (Munich & Astrachan, 1983). One study indicated a significant reduction in interaction among group members when the group size reached 9, and another marked reduction when the group size reached 17 or more (Castore, 1962). In such cases, **subgrouping** (in which two or more members develop a group within the group) tends to occur. The result of subgrouping is that some members become silent while others dominate. Competition for airtime, focus, and inclusion becomes intense (Shepherd, 1964). Thus, the atmosphere of the group changes. Groups with fewer than 5 members (except those composed of elementary school children) tend not to function well, either. In such groups, too much pressure is placed on each group member to perform or contribute. There is virtually no opportunity in a group of 5 or fewer to choose not to participate.

Another component of a group that affects its dynamics is membership, in regard to both the mixture and the number of people in it. **Heterogeneous groups** (i.e., those composed of persons with dissimilar backgrounds) can broaden members' horizons and enliven interpersonal interactions. Such groups may be helpful in problem solving, such as in psychotherapy and counseling groups. Yet, **homogeneous groups** (i.e., those centered around a presenting problem or similarity in gender, ethnicity, sexual orientation, or sociocultural background) are extremely beneficial in working through specific issues. They normalize "one's experience and the sense of shared struggle in a common area"

Table 3.1
Factors involved in preplanning a group.

Clarity of purpose	What the group is to accomplish
Setting	The environment
Time	The length of the group meeting
Size	How many people will be involved
Membership	Heterogeneous or homogeneous
Goals	Expected or planned outcomes
Commitment	Voluntary or mandated attendance
Openness	Consideration of novel ideas and actions
Risk taking	Engaging in new thoughts and behaviors
Attitudes	How members and leaders perceive tasks and others

(Perrone & Sedlacek, 2000, p. 244). Task/work groups, as well as some counseling and therapy groups, are often homogeneous for this reason. A potential drawback to homogeneous groups, however, is "when group members gain the belief that only others who are similar (adult children of alcoholics, abuse survivors) can fully understand or help" them (MacNair-Semands, 1998, p. 209). That aside, it is the nature and purpose of the group that usually determines what its member composition will be.

Other factors affecting group dynamics that must be preplanned are the fit between members' goals and group goals (expected or planned outcomes), the level of membership commitment (i.e., whether members are joining the group voluntarily or because of external pressures), the openness of members to self and others, a commitment to take or support risks, members' attitudes toward leadership and authority, and the leader's attitude toward certain member characteristics. The point is that group dynamics are a result of interaction patterns that develop because of careful or careless preplanning (see Table 3.1).

Group Structure

Group structure refers both to the physical setup of a group and to the interaction of each group member in relation to the group as a whole. Both types of structure influence how successful or harmonious the group will be and whether individual or group objectives will be met. Leaders and members have the ability to structure a group for better or worse. In this section, the physical structure of a group is examined; the essence of group interaction will follow in a later section.

The **physical structure** (i.e., the arrangement of group members) is one of the first factors to consider in setting up a group. Physical structure has a strong influence on how a group operates. If members feel they are physically removed from the group or are the center of it, then they will act accordingly.

The seating arrangement in a group is, therefore, important. Many groups, regardless of purpose, use a **circle** format. In this configuration, all members have direct access to one another (Yalom, 2005). Equality in status and power is implied. The disadvantage of

Figure 3.4

Optimal group structure/
interaction.

Source: Adapted from "Some Effects
of Certain Communication Problems
on Group Performance" by H. J.
Leavitt, 1951, *Journal of Abnormal
and Social Psychology, 46,*
pp. 38–50.

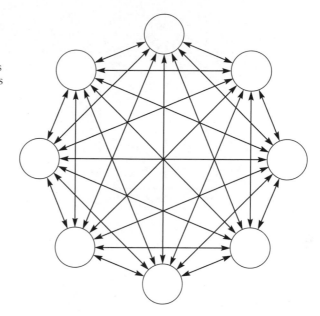

this arrangement is the lack of a perceived leader in the structure unless the identified
leader is active and direct. Overall, the circle lends itself to being a democratic structure
for conducting group work and is probably the best structure for ensuring equal airtime
for all group members (see Figure 3.4).

However, the circle is not the only way to set up a group. Other formats yield different
types of interactions. In an experiment to determine the effects of various structures on
group performance, Leavitt (1951) devised three communication networks in addition to
the circle (see Figure 3.5): the "chain," the "Y," and the "wheel."

In the **chain** arrangement, people are positioned or seated along a line, often according to their rank in the group. Communication is passed through others from a person at
one end of the configuration to a person at the other end. The chain is a popular way to
run some group organizations. For example, the military conceptualizes its command
structure as "the chain of command." However, a chain is seldom used outside a hierarchical association because of the indirectness of communication, the lack of direct contact
with others, and the frustration of relaying messages through others. In a group, for
instance, Janet will probably become exasperated if she has to communicate her wishes
and thoughts through Georgia, who in turn has to relay them to Penny, who then conveys
them to the leader.

In contrast, the **wheel** arrangement has a "center spoke," the leader, through whom
all messages go. Although members have the advantage of face-to-face interaction with the
leader in this structure, they may become frustrated by the inability to communicate with
another group member directly. In the wheel configuration, some members are not
informed about what their colleagues are doing. For example, supervisors in a factory may
work as the center spokes in a wheel formation and have different personnel report to
them. If they do not give as well as receive information, then their workers will not know
how the plant is operating or which issues need to be addressed.

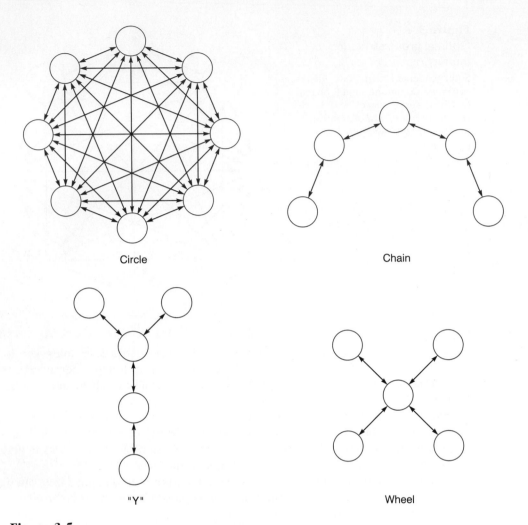

Circle

Chain

"Y"

Wheel

Figure 3.5
Effects of group structure on group performance.
Source: Adapted from "Some Effects of Certain Communication Problems on Group Performance" by H. J. Leavitt, 1951, *Journal of Abnormal and Social Psychology, 46,* pp. 38–50.

The final type of group structure Leavitt (1951) experimented with was the **Y**, which combines the structural elements of the wheel and the chain. In this arrangement, there is a perceived leader. The efficiency of the unit is second only to that of the wheel in performance. Like a chain, however, the Y may frustrate group members who wish to have direct contact and communication with one another. Information is not equally shared or distributed.

In most cases, the importance of structure will vary according to the type of group being led. For instance, in a psychoeducational group, members may be arranged in yet another structure—**theater style**—in which they are seated in lines and rows. Because of the emphasis in psychoeducational groups on obtaining cognitive information, this arrangement may be useful. However, group members are cut off from interaction with one another in a theater-style arrangement because they are all facing the same way. In contrast, if psychotherapy groups are to work well, they should be structured so that members can easily interact with one another verbally and physically, such as in a circle. Similarly, positive dynamics are crucial to the success of most task/work groups. Some of these groups will employ a more hierarchical structure, such as a "chain of command," to operate efficiently. However, many organizations are moving to flatten hierarchies by using group circle formats. This trend is prevalent in businesses and associations that operate according to a quality management style (Walton, 1991).

Group Exercises and Activities

The outcome of a group is dependent not only on the variables present at the beginning of the experience but also on the number and kind of structured exercises and activities used during the group (Carroll, Bates, & Johnson, 2004). The question of whether prepackaged activities have a place in groups is one that group leaders and members must deal with constantly. There are certain advantages and disadvantages to employing exercises in a group setting (Carroll et al., 2004; Jacobs, 1992). For example, if the leader knows a particular game or exercise is likely to result in a positive outcome, then it may be used as a catalyst, especially early in the group's life, to bring people together. In this capacity, games and exercises can play a vital part in promoting group dynamics.

An example of a purposeful activity a leader might use to begin a group is the exercise "Adverbs" (Gladding, 2004). In this activity, group members pass around a pencil to one another in a circle saying and demonstrating any word that ends in "ly" in the process. Thus, Juanita might say to Charlene who is seated on her right, "I am passing this pencil to you quickly" and in the process give the pencil to her quite fast. Charlene, in turn, would then turn to the person on her right and use another "adverb" and motion such as "slowly," "clumsily," "hesitantly," and so forth, until the pencil had gone around the group several times. At that point, the leader and members would talk about ways of doing things and behaving in the group that the exercise demonstrated.

Overall, **group exercises** can be beneficial if they promote a positive atmosphere in a group. Jacobs, Masson, and Harvill (2006), for instance, state that exercises have a number of benefits, among which are

1. They may generate discussion and participation, thus stimulating members' energy levels and interaction.
2. Exercises may help the group focus on a particular topic or issue. This is especially true in task groups.
3. Group games help shift the focus from one area to another. Although effective group leaders should be able to redirect the focus without employing games, some exercises provide a natural bridge to important group topics.
4. Games and exercises promote experiential learning, which means that members will probably go beyond their thoughts in self-exploration. Furthermore, exercises such as rounds provide the group leader with useful information about the group and what needs to be done to move forward.
5. They increase the comfort level of participants and help them to relax and have fun. Learning takes place best when it is enjoyable.

Group exercises and activities "are commonly used in groups to activate the group, encourage members to take risks, and provide a learning experience that moves the group members" (Riva, 2004, p. 63). Basically, these ways of working with a group are "either intrapersonal or interpersonal, and the type of communication is either verbal or nonverbal" (Trotzer, 2004, p. 77). Interpersonal activities involve interacting with other group members in dialogue—for example, introducing oneself to the group and answering questions. If the activity is nonverbal, words are not used, such as the exercise 'changing seats' [asking select members or an entire group to change seats]. Intrapersonal activities are those in which an exercise is done alone at first and then shared and explored with others at a later time. . . . Nonverbal activities include private, personal experiences. . . . (Carroll, Bates, & Johnson, 2004, pp. 116–117) Overall, when combined four possible categories emerge that are of low, medium, or high intensity in the four categories below.

1. **Verbal Intrapersonal.** A low-intensity verbal intrapersonal exercise would be having group members draw pictures of how they perceive the world and using these pictures to introduce themselves verbally to the group.
2. **Verbal Interpersonal.** An example of a low-intensity verbal interpersonal activity would be having group members divide into small groups and discuss their sibling positions. Then the group as a whole would reassemble and members would talk about how they view the world based on past perceptions.
3. **Nonverbal Intrapersonal.** A low-intensity nonverbal intrapersonal exercise would be what is known as "body relaxation," where the leader would talk members through relaxing parts of their body starting with the feet and ending with the head. Members' eyes would be closed the whole time.
4. **Nonverbal Interpersonal.** In a nonverbal interpersonal activity, members might line up from most to least about any concern that is relevant for the group at the moment such as anxiety. Members would then get a chance to compare where they stand in regard to others in the group.

Overall, exercises and activities can be used almost anytime in the group process, as long as they do not become gimmicks and are processed afterward so that members gain insight into themselves personally and as members of the group. Activities may consist of different forms, for example, written, verbal, art, movement, and combinations, too (Dossick & Shea, 1988, 1990). The important point to remember in using exercises and techniques in groups is that timing and instructions are everything. A poorly timed event with unclear instructions may damage the group instead of promoting cohesion, insight, and movement. If employed too frequently, group activities can negatively influence the group by taking the focus off its purpose. There are also some ethically questionable exercises that promote anxiety and do harm; Gazda (1989) thus advises that group leaders who use them do so cautiously.

Group Interaction

Group interaction can be described as the way members relate to one another. It consists of nonverbal and verbal behaviors and the attitudes that go with them. Group interaction exists on a continuum, from extremely nondirective to highly directive. For example, in some psychotherapy groups, members may be quite reserved and nondirect in their interactions with others, at least initially. In many task groups, however, members may be direct and verbal. The type of group interaction (e.g., nonverbal, verbal communication) as well as its frequency makes a difference in how or whether the group develops. Each factor is examined separately here, even though none of these components operates in isolation from the others.

Nonverbal behaviors make up "more than 50 percent of the messages communicated in social relationships" and are usually perceived as more honest and less subject to manipulation than verbal behaviors (Vander Kolk, 1985, p. 171). The four main categories of nonverbal behavior, according to Vander Kolk, are *body behaviors, interaction with the environment, speech,* and *physical appearance*. Group leaders and members have many nonverbals to watch. For example, when Sue wraps her arms around herself, does it mean that (a) she is physically cold, (b) she is imitating Heather, or (c) she is psychologically withdrawing from the group? The meaning of nonverbal behaviors cannot be assumed. In addition, the same nonverbal behavior from two different people may not convey the same message. Walters (1989) has charted behaviors frequently associated with various group members' emotions. Nonverbal behavioral expressions should always be noted (see Table 3.2).

Verbal behavior is also crucial in group dynamics. One of the most important variables in group work to track is who speaks to whom and how often each member speaks. On a formal basis, there are ways to chart such interactions, such as **sociometry**, a phenomenological methodology for investigating interpersonal relationships (Treadwell, Kumar, Stein, & Prosnick, 1997). For example, by using a **sociogram** (a tool of sociometry that plots out group interactions), a group leader might learn that Melissa addresses most of her comments in the group to one of three people. Such data might be helpful to the leader and the group in examining or modifying their interactions (see Figure 3.6).

However, most leaders operate informally and map in their minds awareness of how group members speak and to whom. They also pay attention to silence and how it is observed and respected. It is difficult for some groups to deal with silence but less likely to be bothersome in certain psychoeducation and task groups in which members are not especially attuned to it.

Group discussion is usually important to the functioning of any type of group. In task, psychoeducational, counseling, and psychotherapy groups, discussion allows members to process information relevant to making decisions (Forsyth, 2005). Alternative courses of action can be considered more thoughtfully when the group as a whole discusses them. The amount of time spent in an active discussion of issues influences the quality of the group's decision (Laughlin, 1988).

Sometimes groups will use their time unwisely and collectively engage in what is known as the **Law of Triviality** (Parkinson, 1957). According to this law, the time a group spends discussing any issue is in inverse proportion to its consequences. For example, in an hour-long task group, 50 minutes might be spent talking about whether a group celebration should be held on a Thursday or a Friday and 10 minutes might be spent in planning the activities and considering a budget for the event.

Members' Roles

A **role** is "a dynamic structure within an individual (based on needs, cognitions, and values), which usually comes to life under the influence of social stimuli or defined positions"

Table 3.2

Behaviors frequently associated with various group member states.

	Head	Face	Mouth	Eye Contact	Hands	Posture
Despair/ Depression	Down	Sad frown (eyebrows down at outer ends)	Tightness	Little or none; may cover eyes with hand	Autistic behaviors; body-focused self-stimulating movements	Approaches fetal position
Excitement/ Euphoria	Mobile movement	Mobility of expression	Smiling; laughing	Tries to capture and to hold eye contact of all other persons ("Look at me.")	Sweeping, expansive movements	Frequent change; seductive
Fear/Anxiety	Stiff movement; chin down	Flushing	Tightness; clenching teeth	Darting glances to others; wants to keep watch on others by not meeting their gazes ("I'll watch you.")	Tightness; gripping; sweaty palms ("clenched and drenched")	Frequent movement; crouching; hunching shoulders
Hostility/Rejection of another person Active/Overt	Head, and often chin, thrust forward and/or tilted upward	Angry frown (eyebrows down at center)	Lips tensed and pushed forward slightly	Defiant	Clenching; fist; thumping (symbolic hitting)	Poised on edge of chair
Passive/Covert	Down; turned away slightly	Squinting of eyes	Closed; normal	Aversion; blank staring	Body-focused movements; self-inflicting behaviors	Infrequent change
Dependency/ Attraction toward another	Head slightly down while making eye contact ("Poor me.")	Mirrors expression of other	Frequent smiling	Frequent	Reaching motions	Quasi-courtship
Resistance to Learning	Turned; rolled back	Rigidity of expression	Tightness	Avoidance	Clenched; looking at watch; body-focused movements	Held in; stiffness of limbs

Source: From Richard P. Walters, "Nonverbal Communication in Group Counseling" from *Group Counseling: A Developmental Approach*, 4th ed. Copyright © 1989. Adapted by permission by Allyn & Bacon.

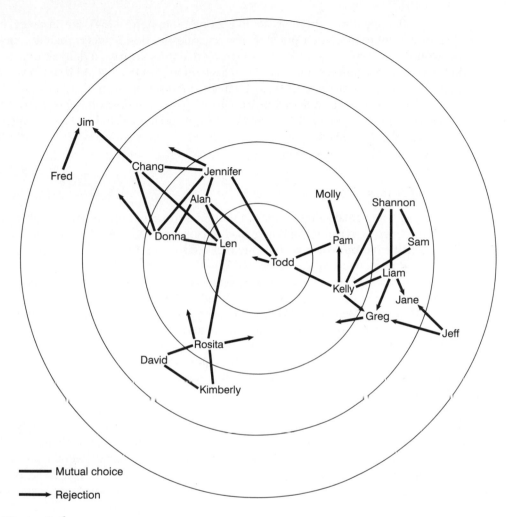

Figure 3.6
Sociogram depicting choices and rejections of classmates.

(Munich & Astrachan, 1983, p. 20). The manifestation of a role is based on the individual's expectation of self and others and the interaction one has in particular groups and situations. For example, Mabel, a reflective and introverted person, might take the role of a "group observer" in an active counseling group. By so doing, she could give feedback to the group as a whole without exposing personal feelings. Every person has multiple roles he or she can fulfill. When groups change or when people change groups, roles are frequently altered.

Roles are usually different from the overall identity of individuals. For example, persons may play certain roles in their vocational life, such as being a sales clerk or a computer operator, but not envision themselves exclusively as their occupation. Therefore, although Terri sells shoes, she does not consider herself as just a salesperson. Nevertheless, roles strongly influence how individuals act in a group (Shepherd, 1964). For instance, entrepreneurs may want to push their point of view regardless of how it affects their acceptance into the group. Sometimes roles become so strong that persons have a difficult time separating themselves from the roles they play. Such a situation may be enacted if persons mainly see themselves in terms of a role they played in childhood. For example, adult children of alcoholics (ACoAs) often play one of four roles to adapt to their environments: hero, scapegoat, lost child, or mascot (Harris & MacQuiddy, 1991; Wegscheider, 1981). Unfortunately, in such circumstances, the persons may become trapped in dysfunctional ways of relating that will detrimentally affect them in all but psychotherapeutic groups.

Types of Roles

One way to conceptualize most roles in groups is to view them as primarily functioning in one of three ways: facilitative/building, maintenance, and blocking (Capuzzi & Gross, 2006).

A **facilitative/building role** is one that adds to the functioning of a group in a positive and constructive way. Members who take on such a role may serve as initiators of actions and ideas, information seekers, opinion seekers, coordinators, orienters, evaluators, or recorders. Group facilitating and building focuses on helping everyone feel like a part of the group. Members who function in this way help the group develop while keeping conflict to a minimum. Group facilitators and builders do their best work during the initial formation of a group. For instance, in a task group, Dottie may take the role of being an opinion seeker. Before the group moves on its decisions, she makes sure all views are heard by asking more quiet members for their input.

A **maintenance role** is one that contributes to the social-emotional bonding of members and the group's overall well-being. When interpersonal communication in the group is strained, there is a need to focus on relationships (Wilson & Hanna, 1986). Persons who take on such roles are social and emotionally oriented. They express themselves by being encouragers, harmonizers, compromisers, commentators, and followers. For example, in a counseling group, Ned may help by serving in the role of a harmonizer as he assists members in seeing the differences they have and pointing out how these differences can give each group member a new perspective on the world. In group maintenance, group members are encouraged to openly express "both positive and negative feelings, supportive responses to member concerns and contributions, and acceptance of differences" (Shaffer & Galinsky, 1989, p. 25).

A **blocking role** is essentially an antigroup role. Individuals who take this role act as aggressors, blockers, dominators, recognition seekers, and self-righteous moralists. For instance, those who perceive themselves as outsiders, like Lucy who has been placed in a psychoeducational group for punishment, may actively attempt to keep the group from discussing a proposed topic. Such a member may also seek to divert attention away from the group's goal by being negative and preventing the group from accomplishing anything.

Fortunately, few members act out a pure role. Hansen et al. (1980, pp. 442–446) have compared two of the most prominent classifications of group member roles as described by Benne and Sheats (1948) and Bales (1951). Their classification differs slightly from that just described, but the basic roles and concepts they outline overlap considerably (see Figure 3.7).

Group Building and Maintenance Roles
(Positive Social-Emotional Roles)

- *Facilitator or Encourager*—In this position, individuals play the role of a counselor's helper. They make sure everyone feels comfortable. Their motive often is to keep the focus off themselves.

- *Gatekeeper or Expediter*—Individuals in this role make sure the group operates within its proposed norms. They act like a counselor assistant and may generate hostility from others if they become too active.

- *Standard or Goal Setter*—This role is similar to that of gatekeeper, and individuals who take it push for establishing group norms and lofty goals. They are often unsure of themselves.

- *Harmonizer or Conciliator*—These are group mediators who seek to keep conflict down and emotionally control the group. They are afraid of the group getting out of hand emotionally.

- *Compromiser or Neutralizer*—Persons who assume this role suggest cognitive solutions/alternatives for group member differences. The same internal dynamics are probably occurring within them as with harmonizers; that is, they are afraid of too much emotion.

- *Group Observer*—These people provide feedback to the group by summarizing content or process within the group. They rarely participate directly in the group, though, because of the risk of exposing their thoughts and feelings.

- *Follower or Neuter*—The individuals who assume this role express a lot of agreement with the group but are so unsure of themselves that they rarely offer their own opinions.

Group Task Roles (Instrumental or Task Roles)

The tasks undertaken by group members at this time help the group move toward accomplishing its goals.

- *Initiator-Energizer*—Individuals who assume this role prod the group to move and take action. They may be seen as hasslers.

- *Information or Opinion Seekers*—This role involves gathering more data, both affectively and cognitively, so the group may act. Persons who assume this role may push other group members to disclose before they are ready.

- *Information or Opinion Giver*—Persons in this role seek to give information, advice, or opinions to others in the group. They assume they have correct facts and proper attitudes. They are often annoying but can act as a catalyst to spur the group on.

Figure 3.7
A classification of group membership roles.

- *Elaborator and/or Coordinator*—Group members in this position are reality oriented, and they make sure that the group is, too. Their logic often gets in the way of creativity.
- *Orientor-Evaluator*—The individual who assumes this role acts as the group's judge in evaluating how well it is doing in achieving its tasks, both quantitatively and qualitatively.
- *Procedural Technician*—One or more followers in the group may take this role, which involves concentration on the achievement of group goals. As such, this role is similar to the gatekeeper role previously discussed in the group-building section.

Individual Roles (Negative Social-Emotional Roles)

Individuals who assume these roles are self-serving rather than group oriented. They lack solid interpersonal relationship skills and can benefit a great deal from a group. Yet, their presence within the group makes it difficult for the group to operate. Several of the most prominent of these antigroup roles as described by Vander Kolk (1985) are as follows:

- *Aggressor*—This person disagrees with most group members' ideas and behaviors. He or she may try to impose his or her ways on others.
- *Blocker*—These individuals are very rigid about what should be discussed, and often they resist the wishes of the total group and impede its progress.
- *Recognition Seeker*—The role consists of bragging and calling attention to self at the expense of others and the group in general.
- *Playboy/Playgirl*—The behavior of this person, for example, nonchalant or cynical, lets other group members know he or she is not invested in the group.
- *Help-seeker/Rescuer*—People who assume the help seeker role elicit sympathy from the group and are dependent. Rescuers meet their own needs but do not really help members function better.
- *Monopolist*—These individuals talk incessantly (because of their anxiety) about issues only tangentially related to the group. They alienate other group members and must be controlled.
- *Do-gooder/Informer*—The do-gooder wants to do what is right for others, whereas the informer wants to share information about someone in the group outside the group session. Both seek to enhance their image.
- *Withdrawn/Hostile Members*—These individuals seek to avoid group interaction and participation by being silent or intimidating. Both behaviors result in greater self-protection.

Figure 3.7, *continued*

Source: Adapted from *Group Counseling: Theory and Practice* (2nd ed., pp. 442–446) by James C. Hansen, Richard W. Warner, and Elsie J. Smith. Copyright © 1980 by Houghton-Mifflin Company. Used with permission.

Problems in Carrying Out Roles

Sometimes problems arise in the fulfillment of roles (Hare, 1962). Both internal and external factors contribute to these problems, and there is seldom a simple cause. Four major forms of role difficulties are role collision, role incompatibility, role confusion, and role transition. In **role collision**, a conflict exists between the role an individual plays in the outside world (e.g., being a passive observer) and the role expected within the group (e.g., being an active participant). In **role incompatibility**, a person is given a role within the group (e.g., being the leader) that he or she neither wants nor is comfortable exercising. **Role confusion**, sometimes known as **role ambiguity**, occurs when a group member simply does not know what role to perform. This often happens at the beginning of groups or in leaderless groups where members do not know whether they are to be assertive in helping establish an agenda or passive and just let the leadership emerge. Finally, in **role transition**, a person is expected to assume a different role as the group progresses but does not feel comfortable doing so. For example, in self-help groups, experienced members are expected to take on leadership, rather than "follower," roles. Yet, some group members do not feel comfortable doing so.

In most groups, maintenance and task roles need to be balanced. "Too much attention to socioemotional functioning can cause the group to wander and lose sight of its goals; in similar fashion, overemphasis on task can result in disruption and dissatisfaction if members have no outlet for their grievances and no way to resolve their conflicts" (Shaffer & Galinsky, 1989, pp. 25–26).

THE EFFECT OF POSITIVE AND NEGATIVE VARIABLES ON GROUP DYNAMICS

Many group specialists (e.g., Corey, 2004; Jacobs et al., 2006) have listed a number of variables within groups essential to group life and functioning. Psychotherapeutic and counseling groups seem to have been especially targeted by experts in this regard. Yet, the factors generally noted are applicable to most psychoeducational and task/work groups, too. These variables include member commitment; readiness of members for the group experience; the attractiveness of the group for its members; a feeling of belonging, acceptance, and security; and clear communication. These factors are often collectively conceptualized as **positive group variables**. For example, if group members speak from an "I" position, everyone in the group becomes clear about what they are saying and can respond appropriately. Positive forces within the group, when expressed to the fullest extent possible, can lead to a group that is both cooperative and altruistic (McClure, 1990).

Yalom (2005) was among the first to delineate positive primary group variables based on research he conducted with others on therapy groups. He has called these positive forces **curative (therapeutic) factors within groups**. These variables are expressed in successful groups through a variety of means. They often affect the interactions of members and the group as a whole in complex ways. For counseling and psychotherapy groups, these therapeutic factors are as follows:

- **Instillation of hope**—assurance that treatment will work. For example, the leader might say at the beginning of a group: "I think we will be able to accomplish most of your goals through our work in this group."

- **Universality**—what seems unique is often a similar or identical experience of another group member. For example, the leader might say: "Isaiah, it seems that you and Austin share a similar concern about how you can find balance in your lives."
- **Imparting of information**—instruction about mental health, mental illness, and how to deal with life problems usually through group discussion. For example, a member might share that she has read that to stay mentally healthy, a person needs 8 hours of sleep at night.
- **Altruism**—sharing experiences and thoughts with others, helping them by giving of one's self, working for the common good. For example, Jessica might inform the group that she is going to work a night at the homeless shelter and invite them to work there too.
- **Corrective recapitulation of the primary family group**—reliving early familial conflicts correctly and resolving them. For example, Louise may find that through her interactions with Roscoe she is able to find ways of disagreeing with a male slightly older than her, like her brother Taylor, without becoming emotionally upset if he does not accept her argument.
- **Development of socializing techniques**—learning basic social skills. For example, Aiden may come to realize through the group experience that people like to be invited to do activities rather than carped at to do them.
- **Imitative behavior**—modeling positive actions of other group members. For example, Jayden may learn ways of requesting what he wants by imitating the behavior of Colin.
- **Interpersonal learning**—gaining insight and correctively working through past experiences. For example, Virginia may see through talking with members of the group that her bossy behavior in the past has gotten her nowhere.
- **Cohesiveness**—the proper therapeutic relationship among group members, group members and the group leader, and the group as a whole. For example, after everyone in the group shares their thoughts about racism, they may feel closer together.
- **Catharsis**—experiencing and expressing feelings. For example, Julia may cry softly when she realizes how much hurt she has been carrying around for so long.
- **Existential factors**—accepting responsibility for one's life in basic isolation from others, recognizing one's own mortality and the capriciousness of existence. For example, Sebastian may come to the realization through talking with older members of the group that his life is half over and that he needs to work hard on improving himself if he is ever going to live his dreams.

Yalom (2005) contends that these variables constitute both the "actual mechanisms of change" and "conditions for change" (p. 4). The interplay of the factors varies widely from group to group.

To Yalom's (2005) list, Bemak and Epp (1996) have added what they consider to be a 12th factor—love. They believe that although love may contain aspects of some of Yalom's other factors, it stands alone as a contributor to the healing process in group psychotherapy. "Love's nature and dynamics in groups . . . can have many variations"—for instance, transference as well as genuineness (p. 119). According to Bemak and Epp, "the unmasking of transference and the fostering of open expressions of giving and receiving love are essential healing factors in the group therapy process and in the development of healthier human beings" (p. 125).

Yalom's (2005) conceptualization of group dynamics, with the addition of Bemak and Epps's (1996) contribution, is extremely useful for conducting group counseling and psychotherapeutic sessions. It gives group leaders and members ideas and experience-based realities on which they need to focus. Such variables are like a map that can guide the group process. For instance, if a group member, Sarah, refuses to work through past family impasses and treats another group member, Charles, as if he were a rejecting parent, then the leader and other members can take steps to correct this behavior. In this case, the group might confront Sarah with how she is acting and role-play situations to help her recognize and resolve previous dysfunctional patterns that are interfering with her present functioning.

In addition to positive variables and therapeutic forces, **negative group variables** operate. These variables include, but are not limited to, avoiding conflict, abdicating group responsibilities, anesthetizing to contradictions within the group, and becoming narcissistic. If most or all of these variables are present, then a group will become regressive and possibly destructive (McClure, 1990, 1994). In such cases, the whole group and the individuals within it lose.

Avoiding conflict involves the silencing of members who expose the group's shortcomings or disagree with the majority's opinions. Silencing is often done through coercion or acts of domination. For example, whenever Debbie tries to tell the group she does not feel understood by the other members, she is belittled through comments such as "That's touchy/feely stuff, Debbie—get real" or "You are being oversensitive." As time passes, Debbie learns not to speak. A destructive dynamic is set in motion by avoiding conflict and silencing dissent. If it remains unchallenged and unchanged, then the group becomes unhealthy.

One of the most destructive behaviors for groups to take is to become narcissistic. "**Narcissistic groups** develop cohesiveness by encouraging hatred of an out-group or by creating an enemy. . . . As a result, regressive group members are able to overlook their own deficiencies by focusing on the deficiencies of the out-group" (McClure, 1994, p. 81). In the process of projecting their feelings onto others, group members create an illusion of harmony that binds them together. For example, a student newspaper is launched with the intent of attacking the president of a university. Within the group, members focus on "digging up dirt" and disregard any positives they find. A bunker mentality develops in which the president becomes the enemy and the student newspaper, the source of all truth. Member disagreement is handled by dismissing anyone from the paper who does not agree with the party line. Cohesiveness is developed through rewarding member writers who can find the most damaging material to print.

Occurring in regressive groups, along with the avoidance of conflict and the development of group narcissism, is **psychic numbing**, in which members anesthetize themselves to contradictions in the group. In the student newspaper example, writers may break into an office to get information they want and not feel guilty about breaking an ethical or legal code. Overall, a regressive group expresses an abdication of responsibility for the group and a dependency on its leader. Members do not take on the role of being leaders or facilitators of the group but rather become obedient followers. They do not take risks and, in effect, give their power away to influence the group. In such cases, the group is left without means to correct itself and will continue to be destructive unless a crisis occurs that influences its members to behave differently (Peck, 1983).

LEARNING GROUP DYNAMICS

Knowledge of group dynamics that is both experiential and cognitive can help a group worker either lead or be in a group. Such learning may take place in multiple ways. One model is based on interdisciplinary education and involves five activities that help participants gain greater insight into the ways their group is functioning (Marotta, Peters, & Paliokas, 2000).

1. *Videotaping*—Through observing their personal and collective interactions in a group, participants may note verbal and nonverbal behaviors of members and how these actions affected the group and its development. They may also note group roles, if any, that stand out.

2. *Journaling*—A journal is a weekly log of the content and process that occurred in a group and one's reactions to particular activities, exchanges, or the group as a whole. By writing immediately after a group is completed, participants capture present thoughts and feelings related to what happened in the group. By reading their logs later, they may gain insight into patterns occurring within the group.

3. *Outdoor Experiences*—Participating in an outdoor exercise can help individuals explore their cooperative and competitive styles and how these mesh with the group as a whole. The group can be seen more fully as a dynamic entity in events such as rope courses, where if the group is to be successful, everyone must participate and negotiate in regard to overcoming an obstacle or completing a task.

4. *Simulation games for team building*—"Problem-based learning situations in the classroom are isomorphic to issues that professionals will encounter in the workplace" (Marrotta et al., 2000, p. 21). A task such as having a group, along with the teacher, design a logo for a class can bring out or highlight behaviors that either help or hurt the group reach a goal. By having the group analyze what happened in the process, members can see more clearly the dynamics involved in what happened and how they contributed.

5. *Sociometrics and learning integration*—A final way to help facilitate the learning of group dynamics is through the employment of sociometric techniques. These activities can provide perspective on each member's learning style and on various aspects of group dynamics, such as leadership, boundaries, and subgroups. All of these can be depicted through visual models. For example, individual students might be given Tinkertoys to create a visual model of their understanding of the development of cohesion. The crucial component in this activity, as with the others, is debriefing, discussion, reflection, and the fostering of insight.

GROUP, INDIVIDUAL, AND FAMILY DYNAMICS

Working with groups is both similar to and different from working with individuals or families. Individual, group, and family approaches to helping have some parallels in history, theory, technique, and process. However, because of the unique composition of each, the dynamics of these ways of working are distinct (Gladding, 2005). The number of variables and interactions differ as does the focus. A skilled group worker who has knowledge of individual and family helping dynamics is able to compare and contrast what is occurring in the group with what might be happening in another setting and, more important, to assess what may be needed. **Awareness** of individual and family helping dynamics assists a group worker in realizing whether referral of a member is in order. The complexity of working with others is a process that involves knowing what to do, when to do it, and what the probable outcomes may be. In this section, the dynamics of individual, group, and family work are discussed in regard to persons, processing, and consequences.

Persons

In examining the entities of groups, individuals, and families, one immediate common denominator is apparent. All are bodies, singularly or collectively, with defined boundaries and interrelated parts. An intervention cannot be made at any level without affecting other aspects of the body. For example, even on the individual counseling level, a counselor cannot work from a strictly behavioral perspective without influencing the cognitive and affective aspects of the client. However, in working with individuals, only one person is the focus of attention. The influence of others may be discussed, but they are not a part of any direct form of helping. In addition, single individuals may or may not be behaviorally or emotionally connected with others. Therefore, attention is almost always centered on intrapersonal issues.

With groups and families, the focus is on more than one person. It is often simultaneously intrapersonal and interpersonal. Trotzer (1988) and Vinson (1995) point out that groups share many similarities with families. For instance, both have hierarchies (i.e., power structures), roles, rules, and norms. In addition, both groups and families move through phases and stages during the counseling process, with group leaders being more active in the initial sessions of any therapeutic interventions. In groups and families, a tension also is manifest overtly and covertly that must be resolved or managed if members are going to work well together. A final similarity between groups and families is that all members in their units affect both. Thus, if a member of a group or family is dysfunctional, then the entire group or family will work in a dysfunctional way.

Groups are distinct from families in that the members come together initially as strangers for a common purpose (Becvar, 1982; Hines, 1988). They have no experience of working together. Families, in contrast, have members with a shared history of interactions. This history may hinder or facilitate any actions taken in trying to offer assistance, but interventions made in family work usually occur faster and with more impact because of the family's common background. Another difference in working with groups and families is the purpose for the treatment. In groups, intrapersonal change may be just as important as interpersonal change, whereas in families the focus is usually on changing the family system. Although groups may resemble families at times in how they work, groups dissolve after a set time, whereas families continue. Overall, as Becvar (1982) states, the group is not a family and the family is not a group.

Processing

In group work, "**processing** refers to helping group members identify and examine what happened in the group and their individual experiences of the event, as well as how the event occurred and how different members responded to it. Processing activities and events in the group helps group members better understand their experiences in the group and relate these to their personal lives" (Glass & Benshoff, 1999, p. 16).

Processing with individuals, groups, and families is similar in several ways. One important similarity involves an examination of what is involved. In essence, all effective processing can be thought of as following the **PARS model (Processing: Activity, Relationship, Self)**, even though this model was originated for group work (Glass & Benshoff, 1999). As shown in Figure 3.8, processing following this model includes three stages: reflecting, understanding, and applying. In *reflecting*, individuals retrace the steps of a particular activity and essentially ask, "What did we do?" An individual may reflect with a counselor, group members may reflect with one another and the leader, and family members may reflect with one another and the therapist. "Reflection allows participants the opportunity to recreate the experience by describing actions the group [or the individual] went through to complete the exercise" (Glass & Benshoff, 1999, p. 18). In the *understanding* stage, the focus is on participants discussing specific interactions as well as offering explanations and interpretations of what occurred, especially in relationship to others. On the group and family level, this stage is more complete because of the others immediately involved. Finally, in the third stage of PARS, the emphasis is on *applying* what has been learned through experience and interaction in the session to one's own life. Without this last stage, which involves a transfer of insight and learning, processing is not complete.

In addition to the PARS processing model, some common counseling and psychotherapy theories are used as guides in individual, group, and family work (Horne, 2001; Patterson, 1986). For instance, Bowen and Adlerian theory may be employed in helping adolescents differentiate themselves from their families in a counseling group format and thus become less anxious personally and within their family context (Nims, 1998). Likewise, person-centered and behavioral theories have been translated to working with people in individual, group, and family environments. However, an individual theory of helping may not be appropriate for use in some group and family situations, just as some approaches created by group workers and family therapists are not geared for individually oriented helpers.

	Activity	Relationships	Self
Reflecting	*Reflecting-Activity*	*Reflecting-Relationships*	*Reflecting-Self*
Understanding	*Understanding-Activity*	*Understanding-Relationships*	*Understanding-Self*
Applying	*Applying-Activity*	*Applying-Relationships*	*Applying-Self*

Figure 3.8
The PARS Model.

Source: From "PARS: A processing model for beginning group leaders" by J. S. Glass and J. M. Benshoff, 1999, *Journal for Specialists in Group Work, 24*(1), p. 18. Reprinted with permission of Sage Publications.

Consequences

In addition to both subtle and obvious differences in processing and employing theories, a major difference in working with individuals, groups, and families is what happens after helping ends. Success and failure have different consequences. If the individual or the group work does not go well, then those involved may be disappointed. However, with few exceptions, they leave the experience and those involved with it behind them. Families, however, live together through any attempts at helping, and change may promote tension both during and after the process.

Overall, individual, group, and family approaches overlap and yet are distinct from one another. The participants, how they are involved, and how they relate to the professional clinician and the others outside of treatment sessions must be taken into consideration in any comparison. Likewise, a crucial aspect of the process of working with these populations in different phases and stages of their development is which theories of helping are used and how. The leader's role in each differs in regard to what is highlighted in inducing change.

SUMMARY AND CONCLUSION

This chapter has focused on group dynamics. In most groups, it is crucial that group leaders and members be aware of these dynamics because such forces help influence group development for better or worse. Several key areas of group dynamics have been discussed. For instance, the content and process in a group must be recognized for what they are and what they contribute. It is also crucial that content and process be balanced. Furthermore, in fostering change, it helps to perceive the group as a living system with interacting parts that affect one another.

In influencing the dynamics of groups, leaders must preplan and clarify the purpose of their groups. This type of action before the group begins can be instrumental in positively affecting the way the group functions. In addition to a clear purpose, leaders should plan for a quiet, conducive environment for their groups. Planning groups with regard to time, size, mixture of people, and goals is also crucial. Group structure in terms of member positioning and group interactions, especially verbal and nonverbal behaviors, must be taken into account. If groups are to prosper, they must spend their time wisely and be as inclusive of all their members as possible.

Members' roles must also be considered. In healthy groups, members may switch roles and be facilitative or supportive. Antigroup roles, such as being aggressive, must be dealt with to prevent groups from being regressive and destructive. At the same time, positive group variables, such as clear communication and acceptance, must be promoted. Ways of helping groups include the limited use of group exercises and employing basic helping skills. Learning activities that promote insight into how groups operate is helpful, as are teaching devices that highlight group dynamics. In working with groups, leaders are best able to understand and make appropriate interventions if they are aware of the differences and similarities in group dynamics compared with those of individuals and families in helping situations.

In summary, groups are a unique way to work with individuals in resolving past problems, accomplishing present tasks, and undertaking future goals. Those who wish to participate or specialize in them are wise to realize that groups are dynamic entities with lives of their own that differ from those of their members. Those who are knowledgeable about how groups operate know what to expect and can help facilitate positive action in themselves and others.

CLASSROOM EXERCISES

1. In groups of three or four, discuss what you consider to be the most important positive group variables mentioned in this chapter. Are some variables more important for some types of groups than for others? Which ones does your group think would be most crucial in the following types of groups: (a) a group for troubled adolescents, (b) a social skills learning group for mentally challenged adults, (c) a grief group for those who have lost loved ones, and (d) a task/work group planning for a lecture series? Compare your discussion with those generated by other class members.

2. Pick a role mentioned in this chapter with which you feel comfortable. Why do you find this role attractive? Think about whether you have played this role in groups before. Also describe what role in the group you consider least desirable and why. Discuss your findings with another class member.

3. This chapter mentioned ways of influencing a group. Discuss in subgroups of three ways you might pragmatically exert a positive presence in a group. Especially concentrate on the importance of factors that affect group dynamics, and identify whether these factors are primarily those related to content or process.

4. Observe or recall a group that you are or have been involved in, and note which factors mentioned in this chapter are or were prevalent in the life of the group. How do you think the group could be improved? What is your feeling after this observation about the influence of groups on people and people on groups? Discuss your impressions with the class as a whole.

CHAPTER 4

EFFECTIVE GROUP LEADERSHIP

Ken Karp/PH College

Before me is an opening in time
  behind lies a lifetime of training,
At both sides, and strategically located around a circle,
  are those who depend on my skills
    as they wait in anticipation.
Within me there is measured anxiety
  outside I show a calm facade;
The group begins
  with the soft sound of words,
    quiet nervous laughter, and a few faint smiles,
      all deft attempts to join with others
        and create simple trust
          in a smoke-free environment
            filled with hope and uncertainty. *

*From "In Anticipation" by Samuel T. Gladding, © 1989.

Leadership and groups are eminently connected. "Leadership is necessarily concerned with group activity" (Gardner, 1990, p. 80). Hundreds of research studies have been conducted to identify personal or professional attributes of leaders (Johnson & Johnson, 2006; Napier & Gershenfeld, 2004). Although some characteristics associated with group leadership (e.g., caring, openness, strength, awareness, warmth, flexibility, sensitivity) have been pinpointed, many unknown dimensions persist. In fact, leadership is probably "one of the most observed and least understood phenomena on earth" (Burns, 1978, p. 2). Nevertheless, the role of the leader is crucial to the overall functioning of groups. "The leader plays a vital role in both the dynamics of the group and the outcome of its members" (Riva, Wachtel, & Lasky, 2004, p. 37). In addition, "a group is a mirror of its leader. A group draws definition from its leader. It will be only as good as the leader, as good as his or her skills, and as good as the leader's own being" (Bates, Johnson, & Blaker, 1982, p. 73).

Many issues surround group leaders and leadership. Some of them deal with substance, such as the mastery of skills; others, with style and personality. There are different types of leaders, just as there are distinct types of groups, and the appropriateness of an individual for a particular group depends on many complex and interrelated factors. The way a leader functions in one group may be totally inappropriate in another (Forsyth, 2005; Kottler, 2001). For example, a **transformational leader** (i.e., a person who empowers group members and shares power with them in working toward the renewal of a group) may be needed when a group is floundering. However, a **traditional leader** (i.e., a person who is controlling and exercises power from the top down as an expert) may be appropriate in running a hierarchical group that is diverse and whose members are physically separated.

In this chapter, multiple aspects of leadership are examined—for example, styles, personalities, and core and specific skills. Which behaviors and competencies work best in particular circumstances is also considered, along with other group leadership functions, co-leadership, training, and supervision. However, first we turn our attention to defining *leadership*.

LEADERSHIP: A CONCEPT IN SEARCH OF A DEFINITION

The word *leader* first appeared in the English language in the early 1300s, and the word *leadership* in the early 1800s (Johnson & Johnson, 2006). Yet, despite the long history associated with defining leaders and leadership, much disagreement persists among social and political scientists about exactly what a leader is. There is no one definition of either word. Indeed, the concepts "leader" and "leadership" have been defined in more different ways than almost any other concept associated with group structure (Johnson & Johnson, 2006). For example, Bass (1995) states that

> leadership has been conceived as the focus of group processes, as a matter of personality, as a matter of inducing compliance, as the exercise of influence, as particular behaviors, as a form of persuasion, as a power relation, as an instrument to achieve goals, as an effect of interaction, as a differentiated role, as initiation of structure, and as many combinations of these definitions. (p. 38)

Clearly, disagreement prevails about what a leader and leadership are in both the theory and the practice of group work (Barker, 1997; Stockton, Morran, & Velkoff, 1987).

Despite definition disagreements, some common factors in leadership can be distinguished. Forsyth (2005), for instance, defines leadership as "a special form of social interaction: a reciprocal, transactional, and transformational process in which individuals are permitted to influence and motivate others to promote the attaining of group and individual goals" (p. 343). This definition encompasses many of the most important factors of leadership (i.e., social, reciprocity, legitimate influence, motivation, and cooperation for the achievement of common goals) and distinguishes leadership from control (Parsons & Shils, 1951) and power (French & Raven, 1960). Forsyth's definition is the basis on which leadership is conceptualized in this chapter. It is assumed that a leader is one who implements a number of facilitative qualities in a group, such as envisioning goals, motivating people, and achieving a workable unity in an appropriate and timely way (Carroll, Bates, & Johnson, 2004; Gardner, 1990).

GROUP LEADERSHIP STYLES

Leaders help groups get organized and develop. Therefore, the style that a group leader displays has a direct effect on the behavior of group members and group dynamics (Sampson & Marthas, 1981). Leaders who operate exclusively from one point of view are more likely than others to influence members' behaviors in a specific way, for better or worse. For example, leaders who are always telling their group members what to do may get immediate tasks accomplished but at the price of membership flexibility and innovation. Most effective group leaders show versatility (Kottler, 1994). They modify their leadership pattern to coincide with the purpose of the group and its membership.

Choosing a style of leadership depends on a multitude of factors, such as the leader's personality and the purpose of the group. Lewin (1944) identified three basic styles of group leadership: authoritarian, democratic, and laissez-faire. Lieberman, Yalom, and Miles (1973) describe six basic styles: energizers, providers, social engineers, impersonals, laissez-faires, and managers. Hansen, Warner, and Smith (1980) contend that most models are either refinements or elaborations of Lewin's concepts; therefore, the focus of this section is on Lewin's three styles, what the choice of each yields, and so-called leaderless groups.

Authoritarian group leaders envision themselves as experts and tend to be rigid and conventional in their beliefs (Cheng, Chae, & Gunn, 1998). They believe they understand group dynamics and, therefore, are best able to explain group and individual behavior. These leaders interpret, give advice, and generally direct the movement of the group much as parents control the actions of a child. They demand obedience and expect conformity from their followers. Authoritarian leaders are often charismatic and manipulative (McClure, 1994). Frequently, they structure their groups using the wheel model (explained in Chapter 3), which results in an autocratic **leader-centered group**. All information is filtered through them, and they decide which information to share with the group (see Figure 4.1). Such leaders may also coerce group members under their charge because they basically believe people are not ambitious and are somewhat lazy. This style of leadership is also sometimes referred to as *guru oriented* (Starak, 1988). McGregor (1960) characterizes this type of leader as a so-called **Theory X leader**. Adolf Hitler, Fidel Castro, and Mao Tsetung exemplified this type of leadership, although some charismatic political and corporate leaders may display characteristics of this style in a more healthy way. Most leader-centered groups place

Figure 4.1
Authoritarian leadership.
Source: From *Group Counseling: Theory and Practice* (2nd ed., p. 391) by James C. Hansen, Richard W. Warner, and Elsie J. Smith. Copyright © 1980 by Houghton Mifflin Company. Used with permission.

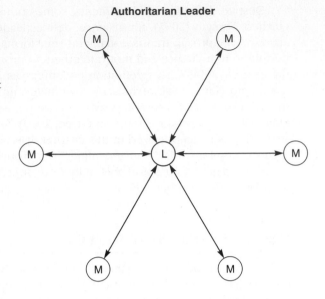

a strong emphasis on the personality of one individual, giving that person a great deal of power and trust. In these groups, chaos erupts when the recognized leader is absent.

Some group workers prefer an authoritarian leadership style. They often equate group leadership with instructing or controlling. Authoritarian leaders may achieve much during periods of crisis because of their commanding style and the needs of followers. Authoritarian leaders are powerful and usually safe from exposure of any personal vulnerability. They direct action and yet are protected by structure and function from self-disclosing.

Democratic group leaders are more group centered and less directive than authoritarian leaders. Leaders operating from this perspective, such as Carl Rogers (1970), trust group participants to develop their own potential and that of other group members. These leaders serve as facilitators of the group process and not as directors of it. They cooperate, collaborate, and share responsibilities with the group. Those who embrace this perspective are more humanistically and phenomenologically oriented (see Figure 4.2). McGregor (1960) refers to group centered leaders as **Theory Y leaders**. They think that people are self-starters and will work hard if given freedom. Leaders who have exemplified this approach to a group facilitate conditions to "promote self-awareness and options to develop the guru within" (Starak, 1988, p. 104). Mohandas Gandhi and Martin Luther King, Jr., led using this style.

Leaders who are inwardly comfortable and trust group members to take care of themselves and others often use this approach. The advantage is a sharing of power and responsibility. Group members can interact openly. Trust, once established, is fostered under this type of leadership, as is calculated risk taking.

Laissez-faire leaders are leaders in name only. They do not provide any structure or direction for their groups, so members are left with the responsibility of leading. As a result, the group operates from a **group-centered perspective**, focusing on members and interpersonal processes. The disadvantage of this type of leadership is that the group as a whole may be slow to establish agendas and achieve goals. Some inexperienced group

Figure 4.2

Democratic leader.

Source: From *Group Counseling: Theory and Practice* (2nd ed., p. 391), by James C. Hansen, Richard W. Warner, and Elsie J. Smith. Copyright © 1980 by Houghton Mifflin Company. Used with permission.

Democratic Leader

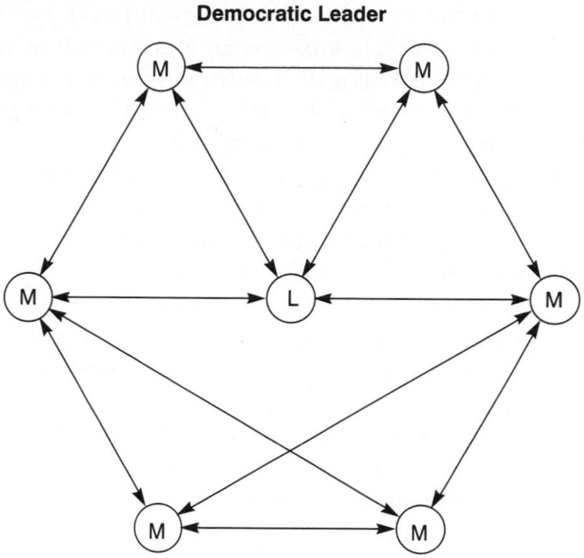

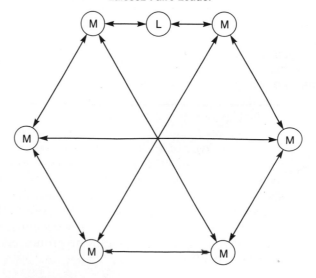

leaders choose this style in an attempt to be nonthreatening; others pick this style to avoid making any hard decisions, thereby increasing their popularity. (Being liked or popular is not a key characteristic of being an effective leader, by the way.) Still others believe that this group style works best and that the group must take care of itself from the beginning. Unfortunately, many laissez-faire group leaders and their groups do not accomplish anything because no clear purpose and goals emerge. Interactions within a laissez-faire group are represented in Figure 4.3.

Figure 4.3

Laissez-faire leader.

Source: From *Group Counseling: Theory and Practice* (2nd ed., p. 391), by James C. Hansen, Richard W. Warner, and Elsie J. Smith. Copyright © 1980 by Houghton Mifflin Company. Used with permission.

Laissez-Faire Leader

At the extreme of a group-centered approach is what Ouchi (1981) describes as Theory Z, which stresses that a group will manage itself through the participation of its members. A **Theory Z leader** is, therefore, a facilitator who helps encourage group members to participate in the group and to trust that individual and collective goals will be accomplished through interaction.

Whether a group is leader or group centered depends on who set it up, under what circumstances, and for what purpose (Gardner, 1990).

So-called **leaderless groups** rotate the leadership role among their members. In these groups, leaders emerge as the group develops. One type of leaderless group is the self-help group (e.g., Alcoholics Anonymous, Parents Anonymous), briefly described in Chapter 2. Another form is the mutual support group exemplified by some women's groups that form around such concrete and specific purposes as the accomplishment of goals, babysitting cooperatives, or a hobby or interest such as hiking or quilting (Kees, 1999). In many forms of these groups, this style of peer leadership works well. In such cases, nonprofessional leaders develop as their group progresses. They usually end up creating a leadership style that feels comfortable for them, such as being confrontational or collaborative. Occasionally, they undergo brief leadership training by reading manuals or taking courses. Although some leaders of leaderless groups are effective, this approach is basically developed through trial and error. It has the potential to be destructive as well as constructive.

CASE EXAMPLE: Omar's Emergence

When Jared joined the Gamblers' Anonymous group, two aspects of the group struck him. First, he was one of the younger members. Second, the group was led by a rather old, grizzly man by the name of Omar. Jared was not sure if he could relate to anyone in the group that well, but Omar immediately made him feel welcomed and a part of the group by relating part of his life story. It seems that Omar had come into this group several decades ago at about the same age as Jared. An older member, who was then the leader of the group, had helped him understand both the nature of his problem and himself. Omar had been grateful and had vowed that he would do the same if given the chance. Now he was the leader and he was fulfilling his pledge.

When have you received the guidance and attention of someone who was older and wiser than you? How do you think it helped you?

Another type of leaderless group meets alternatively with and without a leader (Mullan & Rosenbaum, 1978; Wolf, 1963; Yalom, 2005). Such groups may increase the creativity and participation of individuals and the group as a whole. However, notable group specialists (Gazda, 1989; Yalom, 2005) warn about the dangers of these groups, especially when they are composed of moderately or severely disturbed individuals. In such cases, if a leader is not present, the group may get entirely out of hand and do considerable damage to its members. As a result, the group regresses, and everyone ultimately suffers (McClure, 1990).

LEADERSHIP STYLES FOR DIFFERENT GROUPS

Different types of groups demand specific styles of leadership (Association for Specialists in Group Work, 2000). For example, in psychoeducation and task/work groups, leaders do best when they are direct and keep the group focused on the topic or job at hand. Psychotherapy and counseling groups, however, require that leaders provide support, caring, and sometimes confrontation and structure. They are more intrapersonal in nature. Regardless, the ASGW *Professional Standards for the Training of Group Workers* (2000) "specifies a minimum level of 1 hour a week of planning time for group leaders (either individually or with a co-leader). According to these standards, leading effective groups demands constant assessment of leader skills and interventions, group development, and individual progress of group members" (DeLucia-Waack & Fauth, 2004, p. 137).

Shapiro (1978) states that group leadership is often focused on either the interpersonal or the intrapersonal aspects of a group. The **interpersonal style of group leadership** focuses on transactions among individuals in the group, whereas the **intrapersonal style of group leadership** stresses the inward reactions of individual group members. Both styles of leadership have their place in a group, and effective group leaders use both styles at times. For instance, as a group leader of a counseling group, Don may ask Phyllis to reflect on her last outburst directed toward Mary Ann. Later, Don may solicit opinions from the group about how Phyllis could relate more positively with Mary Ann. Ideally, counseling group leaders begin by concentrating on the group's interpersonal dimension. Later, when members are more comfortable with one another, the leaders integrate intrapersonal material into the group. Other types of group leaders, such as those who lead psychoeducational groups, may engage in the process in an entirely different way.

Leadership may also focus on the accomplishment of tasks versus the development of personal relationships. Whether a leader exercises task or relationship leadership depends on who he or she is, what is happening, and when (or whether) goals must be accomplished. For example, if the group leader is heading a work group whose members know one another well, then he or she may focus on the task to be accomplished because members already have a sense of "we-ness." If, however, a leader is conducting a psychotherapeutic group, then he or she is most likely to focus on the cohesiveness of personal relationships before attempting to work on individual or group goals. Hersey and Blanchard (1969) have elaborated on different styles of leadership dealing with people and tasks over a group's life cycle. In their model, leaders choose an emphasis depending on whether they are people or task oriented. In reality, most group leaders will consider both aspects of a group.

Regardless of emphasis, leaders need to be attuned to and use "core mechanisms of group process and change" (Polcin, 1991, p. 10). These **core mechanisms of group leadership** are emotional stimulation, caring, meaning attribution, and executive function. Lieberman et al. (1973) first described these universal central factors and distinguished them from a group leader's orientation (i.e., theoretical approach).

In all types of groups, leaders must promote sharing on an affective as well as an intellectual level (i.e., **emotional stimulation**). Feelings, as well as thoughts, need to be expressed. For example, instead of asking Stephanie what she thought about Wanda's remarks, the group leader could ask her how she felt about them. Furthermore, group leaders must show **caring** (i.e., a genuine concern for others), through their openness and honesty with group members. Thus, Logan needs to let Dominic know that he honestly wants to know what he is thinking and that he values their relationship whether they have the same ideas or not. **Meaning attribution** refers to the leader's ability to explain to group members in a cognitive way what is occurring in the group. For instance, the leader might say, "Members of the group seem reticent to talk today about themselves. It appears we are having a hard time trusting one another." To function optimally, group leaders need "to learn how to attribute meaning to the events and experiences occurring during the life of a group" both for others and for themselves (Conyne, 1998, p. 255). Finally, in the **executive function** role, leaders manage the group as a social system that allows the group and its members to achieve specific goals (Polcin, 1991). In this role, leaders may remind the group periodically what it has done and what it is doing in regard to agreed-on goals formulated earlier. For instance, the leader may say: "We have formulated a plan. Our challenge now is to implement it."

◆ *Questions from Experience* ◆

Which of the core mechanisms of group leadership do you see yourself best at implementing? What experience(s) in your life give you insight into that strength(s)?

PERSONAL QUALITIES OF EFFECTIVE GROUP LEADERS

Every group leader brings his or her personal qualities to a group, including preferred ways of perceiving the world and experiences in relating to oneself and others. Group leaders must ask themselves such questions as "Who am I?" "Who am I with you?" and "Who are we together?" (Hulse-Killacky, Schumacher, & Kraus, 1994).

The way the questions are asked, as well as the answers that are derived, plays a strong part in determining how one's personal qualities translate into leadership. For example, if a person does not have a strong sense of self, then it is doubtful he or she will be effective as a group leader. Similarly, if an individual cannot keep his or her identity while appreciating others, then it is unlikely that this leader will exert a strong influence in the group. Personal qualities of effective leaders have traditionally been explained through examining their personality traits or learned skills. Effective group leaders probably use the strongest aspects of their personalities and knowledge and combine these with experiences in their leading of groups (Johnson & Johnson, 2006).

The Trait Approach

A traditional school of thought in human history is that some persons emerge as leaders because of their personal qualities. This point of view was advocated by Aristotle, Thomas Carlyle, and Henry Ford (Forsyth, 2005) and remains popular today in some circles. Some group work specialists have compiled long lists of ideal qualities they believe are essential to the personality of an effective group leader, a so-called **trait approach** to group leadership (Johnson & Johnson, 2006). Proponents of this viewpoint believe that specific personality characteristics are essential for successful leadership (Latham, 1987).

Table 4.1
Some personality correlates of leadership behavior.

Personality Characteristic	Type of Relationship	Personality Characteristic	Type of Relationship
Achievement drive	Positive	Energetic	Positive
Adaptability	Positive	Extroversion	Unclear
Alertness	Positive	Nurturance	Unclear
Ascendance	Positive	Responsible	Positive
Attractiveness	Unclear	Self-confidence	Positive
Dominance (bossy)	Negative	Sociability	Positive
Emotional balance	Unclear		

Source: Adapted with permission of The Free Press, a Division of Simon & Schuster, Inc., from *Bass & Stodgill's Handbook of Leadership* Third Edition by Bernard M. Bass. Copyright © 1974, 1981, 1990 by The Free Press.

Two examples of this approach are those given by Slavson (1962) and Corey and Corey (2006). Slavson posits that the personal qualities of group leaders include poise, judgment, empathy, ego strength, freedom from excessive anxiety, a desire to help people, tolerance of frustration, imagination, intuition, perceptiveness, and an ability to avoid self-preoccupation. Corey and Corey include such qualities as courage, willingness to model, presence, goodwill and caring, belief in group process, openness, nondefensiveness in coping with attacks, personal power, stamina, willingness to seek new experiences, self-awareness, humor, and inventiveness. The number of ideal qualities appears to be almost infinite, and it is unlikely that many potential group leaders will possess them all.

The trait view of leadership, although popular and appealing, has little support in research. No single personality type is best suited to be a group leader. Rather, effective group leaders possess a combination of certain personal qualities—a "personality profile" (Stogdill, 1974) that facilitates their communication with group members. These qualities promote the successful integration of the leader and the group and help the group work more efficiently toward common goals (Stogdill, 1969, 1974). Although research indicates that some personality qualities correlate with leadership, it is the combination of factors (e.g., emotional stability and independence) working in interaction that makes a difference (Brandstatter & Farthofer, 1997; Stogdill, 1974) (see Table 4.1).

PERSONALITY AND SPECIFIC GROUPS

As indicated previously, studies point out that people who are effective in some groups, such as those that are relationship oriented, may not be skilled in other groups, such as those that are task oriented (Forsyth, 2005). For example, Stockton and Morran (1982) and Yalom (2005) found that those who conduct counseling and therapy groups are most effective when they are (a) moderate in the amount of **emotional stimulation** they give the group (e.g., challenging, confronting, emphasizing the disclosing of feelings), (b) moderate in the expression of **executive functions** (e.g., setting rules, limits, norms), (c) high in **caring** (e.g., offering support, encouragement, and protection), and (d) high in the use of **meaning-attribution** skills (e.g., clarifying, interpreting).

The research also indicates that ineffective group leaders are characterized as aggressive, authoritarian, pressure oriented, disrespectful of members, confrontational, egocentric, inappropriately self-disclosing, and poorly timed interveners (Lieberman et al., 1973). Experienced leaders act more like one another than inexperienced leaders do (Kottler, 1994).

Leaders who have been well trained in personal counseling are often assumed able to transfer their relationship skills to conducting groups. However, such is not the case. The dynamics associated with working with individuals, as opposed to groups, differ considerably. Just wanting to be a good group leader is not enough; one must have experience. Indeed, "group leaders must experience the power of group dynamics both as a member and a leader to truly understand them" (DeLucia-Waack, 2000c, p. 325).

Consequently, would-be group leaders need to explore through both experience and reflection whether they are suited by temperament and skills to operate as the leader of a group. Bates et al. (1982) recommend that potential group leaders examine their own personalities by using Jungian-based instruments, such as the Myers-Briggs Type Indicator (Myers, 1962), to understand how they might function in a group. Other group experts recommend different ways of assessing oneself (Kottler, 1994).

THEORY AND EFFECTIVE GROUP LEADERS

The principles that guide group leaders are known as **theory**. The word *theory* receives mixed reactions in the field of group work because it is overused and often misunderstood. Basically, a theory is "a way of organizing what is known about some phenomenon in order to generate a set of inter-related, plausible, and, above all, refutable propositions about what is unknown" (Blocher, 1987, p. 67). A theory guides empirical inquiry and is useful in testing hypotheses. It is different from a *philosophical assumption* (which is largely untestable and focused on values) and a *process model* (which is a "cognitive map" that provides a "direct and immediate guide for counselor action" [Blocher, 1987, p. 68]).

On one hand, some individuals believe that theory is of minor importance and has little effect on practice. This position was especially prevalent in the 1960s, when many new types of groups sprang up without solid theoretical foundations (Ruitenbeek, 1970). On the other hand, some think knowledge of well-developed theory is essential to becoming a competent practitioner (Lewin, 1951). The place of theory in group work depends on the type of group being conducted.

Most major theoretical positions "consider the use of groups as a preferred mode of treatment" (Peterson & Nisenholz, 1987, p. 210). Operating from a theoretical base has definite advantages. However, choosing a theory or theories can be problematic, especially in group work. Among the advantages of theories is that they are practical. A good theory helps a practitioner understand and find meaning in experiences by providing a conceptual framework. "Like the scientist, a counselor [or a group worker] uses scientific theory to organize his or her knowledge of behavior" (Claiborn, 1987, p. 288). The lack of a theoretical framework can result in confusion.

A second advantage of theory is that it serves as a guide to expected behavior. In group counseling, for instance, a **settling-down period** usually occurs in which members test one another and the group before the group unifies. Group leaders guided by such theoretical knowledge are better prepared to respond appropriately to settling-down times than those who are unaware.

A third advantage of a theory is its **heuristic** (i.e., research) dimension. Theory is the foundation on which research is built. Research, in turn, strengthens the quality of theory. It is difficult, if not impossible, to have a theory without a research component. Another advantage of knowing and operating from a theoretical perspective is that the practitioner and group may make more progress than they would otherwise. Group leaders without any theory behind their interventions will probably find that their groups never reach a productive stage.

A further argument for the employment of theory in groups is that it helps practitioners formulate their own personalized approach to the groups in which they work. Patterson (1985, 1986) has made the point that some practitioners continue to repeat mistakes of the past or rediscover events of past decades because they are ignorant about how theories developed. Leaders who are most aware of what has been will most likely be skilled innovators of new methods and more highly developed in their ability to integrate and personalize information and process.

CASE EXAMPLE: Manuel Makes a Change

Manuel never had formal training in conducting groups. Instead he was asked one day to lead an inpatient group at the hospital where he worked and for several years he had done so. He was therefore surprised when a new employee, Mattie, was assigned to conduct the group with him. He was even more taken aback when Mattie asked him what theory he employed in leading the group.

After realizing he lacked theoretical skills, Manuel decided to attain training. He became a reality therapist and in the process cringed as he remembered how he used to be obsessed with getting his group members to delve into their pasts. He now realized that focusing on the present was much more practical.

What orientation do you have in your group work? What have you seen others do that works?

Finally, knowledge of theory generally helps group leaders formulate a specific approach for each group member. It is the leader-as-scientist's task to enhance the fit between the hypothetical group member and the actual one. Theory allows for the making and testing of predictions about how the group member will behave in response to particular environmental conditions, including selected interventions (Claiborn, 1987).

Group leaders may have difficulty choosing a theory because some theories tend to be "either too specific or too general to account for all the elements involved in the complexity of human behavior" (Ohlsen, Horne, & Lawe, 1988, pp. 48–49). Theories are also incomplete, and practitioners who stick with only one theory may be hard-pressed to explain certain actions in their groups.

A second problem in selecting a theory is that theories may become political. Practitioners of specific approaches tend to reinforce one another and exclude others. Although this practice may produce theoretical enrichment, it often sets up a **we/they mentality** in which practitioners of other points of view are seen as "uninformed," "naive," or "heretical."

In such cases, potential contributions to a theory from outside sources are never made, and questionable assumptions are not examined thoroughly.

A third drawback of theories is that they have many overlapping dimensions. For example, terms originated by Alfred Adler and Carl Rogers, such as *empathy, acceptance,* and *inferiority complex,* have essentially been incorporated into major leadership theories. As a result, the meaning of these concepts can be quite different from their origins. Such imprecise usage can be confusing to novice practitioners and the general public.

Another troublesome aspect about theories involves research. Some research (e.g., Korchin, 1976) supports the premise that theoretical orientation and outcome are unrelated. Basically, this research states that experienced therapists tend to be more effective and similar in what they do than inexperienced therapists. If research continues to uphold this finding, then group leaders, especially those with a counseling background, may pay less attention to theoretical orientations.

A further limitation of theories, and a potentially dangerous one, is that group leaders who use theory may notice only select details about their group members (Kottler, 1994). In such cases, both members and leaders are placed in potential jeopardy. For example, if Kathy ignores the more angry side of Bree and other group members because her theory is based on emphasizing positives, then she may find that she is unable to deal with the group's collective anger.

Related to this limitation are group leaders who become locked into a theory so tightly that they become rigid, inflexible, and mechanical in practice. These leaders have poor interpersonal relationship skills because they are focused on what the theory directs rather than what their group members need. For instance, if a theory directs leaders to simply reinforce and not confront, then group members will find select behaviors influenced positively and other actions and considerations stunted.

SKILLS OF EFFECTIVE GROUP LEADERS

Group leader skills are displayed in different ways and at various stages during the life of a group. Therefore, to make appropriate leadership decisions, group leaders must be well educated and know which skills are at the core of leading an effective group. In addition, the skills employed by the leader must be timely and appropriate. A variety of group techniques are possible, but effective group leaders also use themselves, other group members, and the group process itself in helping facilitate change. No "cookbook" is available detailing exactly when to use specific interventions. Responsibility ultimately falls on group leaders to determine what to do, when to do it, and how.

Core Group Skills

Regardless of the type of group, some critical core skills must be exercised if the group is to be successful. The Association for Specialists in Group Work's (1991) *Professional Standards for the Training of Group Workers* lists 16 such skills:

1. Encourage participation of group members.
2. Observe and identify group process events.
3. Attend to and acknowledge group member behavior.

4. Clarify and summarize group member statements.
5. Open and close group sessions.
6. Impart information in the group when necessary.
7. Model effective group leader behavior.
8. Engage in appropriate self-disclosure in the group.
9. Give and receive feedback in the group.
10. Ask open-ended questions in the group.
11. Empathize with group members.
12. Confront group members' behavior.
13. Help group members attribute meaning to the experience.
14. Help group members to integrate and apply learning.
15. Demonstrate ethical and professional standards of group practice.
16. Keep the group on task in accomplishing its goals. (p. 14)

Some of the core group skills are solely the responsibility of the leader, such as modeling effective group leadership behavior and engaging in appropriate self-disclosure in the group. A leader who does not model or self-disclose will have a negative impact on the group as whole. Thus, when the group leader, Ralph, is asked by a member if he has ever been put down by his boss, he needs to answer truthfully and briefly (if appropriate) rather than ask why he is being questioned. Other core group skills depend more on the cooperative efforts of a group leader and members—for instance, giving and receiving feedback in the group (Morran, Stockton, Cline, & Teed, 1998).

Overall, group leaders need to realize that they must work with group members if core skills are to be carried out appropriately. For example, if Patricia, the leader, gives feedback to her group about their behaviors but claims feedback she receives from group members is merely the result of projection, then the group will stop working well. In this situation, Patricia becomes disconnected from the group as a whole.

Specific Group Skills

In considering which competencies to use, group leaders should recognize that a number of group skills are the same as those displayed in working with individuals. For example, group leaders must be empathetic, caring, and reflective. At the same time, a number of special skills are unique to group leaders and to the groups they are leading. Group work is an interactive system in which attention to one group member or topic will have an impact on all group members and the group process. Thus, group leaders must also be engaged in

- drawing out and cutting off members,
- opening and closing group meetings in ways that keep the group on task and respectful of individual members,
- ensuring that all members have the opportunity to express themselves,
- assigning tasks based on members' strengths, and
- sharing leadership toward specifically defined goals. (Stanley, 2006, p. 26)

Corey (2004) has formulated a chart based on Nolan's (1978) ideas about group leadership that points out some of the essential skills that group leaders must have at their command (see Table 4.2).

Table 4.2
Overview of group leadership skills.

Skills	Description	Aims and Desired Outcomes
Active Listening	Attending to verbal and nonverbal aspects of communication without judging or evaluating.	To encourage trust and client self-disclosure and exploration.
Restating	Saying in slightly different words what a participant has said to clarify its meaning.	To determine whether the leader has understood correctly the client's statement; to provide support and clarification.
Clarifying	Grasping the essence of a message at both the feeling and the thinking levels; simplifying client statements by focusing on the core of the message.	To help clients sort out conflicting and confused feelings and thoughts; to arrive at a meaningful understanding of what is being communicated.
Summarizing	Pulling together the important elements of an interaction or session.	To avoid fragmentation and give direction to a session; to provide for continuity and meaning.
Questioning	Asking open-ended questions that lead to self-exploration of the "what" and "how" of behavior.	To elicit further discussion; to get information; to stimulate thinking; to increase clarity and focus; to provide for further self-exploration.
Interpreting	Offering possible explanations for certain behaviors, feelings, and thoughts.	To encourage deeper self-exploration; to provide a new perspective for considering and understanding one's behavior.
Confronting	Challenging participants to look at discrepancies between their words and actions or body messages and verbal communication; pointing to conflicting information or messages.	To encourage honest self-investigation; to promote full use of potentials; to bring about awareness of self-contradictions.
Reflecting Feelings	Communicating understanding of the content of feelings.	To let members know that they are heard and understood beyond the level of words.
Supporting	Providing encouragement and reinforcement.	To create an atmosphere that encourages members to continue desired behaviors; to provide help when clients are facing difficult struggles; to create trust.
Empathizing	Identifying with clients by assuming their frames of references.	To foster trust in the therapeutic relationship; to communicate understanding; to encourage deeper levels of self-exploration.

Note: The format of this chart is based on Edwin J. Nolan's article "Leadership Interventions for Promoting Personal Mastery," *Journal for Specialists in Group Work,* 1978, *3*(3), 132–138.

Skills	Description	Aims and Desired Outcomes
Facilitating	Opening up clear and direct communication within the group; helping members assume increasing responsibility for the group's direction.	To promote effective communication among members; to help members reach their own goals in the group.
Initiating	Taking action to bring about group participation and to introduce new directions in the group.	To prevent needless group floundering; to increase the pace of group process.
Goal Setting	Planning specific goals for the group process and helping participants define concrete and meaningful goals.	To give direction to the group's activities; to help members select and clarify their goals.
Evaluating	Appraising the ongoing group process and the individual and group dynamics.	To promote deeper self-awareness and better understanding of group movement and direction.
Giving Feedback	Expressing concrete and honest reactions based on observation of members' behaviors.	To offer an external view of how the person appears to others; to increase the client's self-awareness.
Suggesting	Offering advice and information, direction, and ideas for new behavior.	To help members develop alternative courses of thinking and action.
Protecting	Safeguarding members from unnecessary psychological risks in the group.	To warn members of possible risks in group participation, to reduce these risks.
Disclosing Oneself	Revealing one's reactions to here-and-now events in the group.	To facilitate deeper levels of interaction in the group; to create trust; to model ways of making oneself known to others.
Modeling	Demonstrating desired behavior through actions.	To provide examples of desirable behavior; to inspire members to fully develop their potential.
Dealing with Silence	Refraining from verbal and nonverbal communication.	To allow for reflection and assimilation; to sharpen focus; to integrate emotionally intense material; to help the group use its own resources.
Blocking	Intervening to stop counterproductive behavior in the group.	To protect members; to enhance the flow of group process.
Terminating	Preparing the group to end a session or finalize its history.	To prepare members to assimilate, integrate, and apply in-group learning to everyday life.

Among the specific skills that differ significantly between group and individual work are the following:

- **Facilitating**—In groups, the leader facilitates by helping open up communication among group members (e.g., "Ryan, how do you want to respond to Kyle?"). In individual counseling, facilitation involves a more personal focus (i.e., opening people up to themselves, such as "Melissa, how did that feel to you?").

- **Protecting**—The skill of protecting is two dimensional in group settings. On one hand, it involves the leader safeguarding members from unnecessary attacks by others in the group. On the other hand, protecting "refers to a broad category of leader interventions aimed at preventing members from taking unnecessary psychological risks in the group" (Morran, Stockton, & Whittingham, 2004, p. 93). It is not a skill usually used in individual counseling. For example, as Emma struggles in controlling her anger, the leader wants to make sure she does not receive hostile and unsympathetic responses from others and that she does not go too far, too soon, in disclosing reasons for her anger.

- **Blocking**—Blocking is related to protecting. In blocking, the leader intervenes in the group activity to stop counterproductive behavior. This intervention can be done on a verbal or nonverbal level. In individual and counseling sessions, the leader will block a person from counterproductive behavior, such as rambling or storytelling, by confronting, intervening, or cutting off (Morran et al., 2004). Therefore, if Darlene dominates the group for 10 minutes with a story that seems to have no point, the leader may give her both a hand signal and a verbal message that she needs to conclude what she is conveying within a couple of minutes.

Six other skills not included in Corey's chart are also vital in some group work settings: linking, diagnosing, reality testing, modification, delegating, and creativity.

- **Linking**—Linking is "an intervention often used to connect what one group member is saying or doing with the concerns of one or more other members" (Morran et al., 2004, p. 96). For instance, in a psychoeducational group, the leader might link Matthew and Cheri together by stating, "I hear that both of you are concerned about what to say to other people after you have said 'hello.'" Through linking, interaction among members is encouraged within the group. Linking also promotes the development of facilitative relationships that have been found to be essential for effective group functioning (Morran et al., 2004, p. 96).

- **Diagnosing**—In this activity, the leader identifies certain behaviors and categories into which a person or group fits. Diagnosing in groups does not usually include psychological instruments but is based more on leader observations. For instance, in a task/work group, a leader may notice that the group has a tendency to blame rather than to develop constructive ideas for different ways to do things. To help the group grow, the leader must be a good observer who knows how to overcome distractive or disruptive behavior.

- **Reality testing**—This skill is used when a group member makes an important decision, such as changing jobs or taking a risk. At such moments, the leader will have other group members give feedback to the one who is contemplating a change on how realistic they consider the decision to be. For instance, members might tell Jack that they think he has the skills to be successful in sales as well as in public relations. Through this process, the person is able to evaluate more thoroughly his or her decision.

- **Modification**—Modification is a skill "designed to elicit potentially productive feedback from a group member" (Clark, 1995, p. 14). It is primarily employed when one group member gives another group member negative feedback that the second group member either cannot accept or becomes defensive about. Its purpose is to safeguard members and create a constructive atmosphere in the group. For instance, if Jayne tells Dylan, "You are selfish and never share your thoughts with the group," she could be asked to restate her thoughts and end up saying, "I think you have something to offer the group, and I'd like to hear more from you." In modification, the group leader must use a logical sequence by first "acknowledging the emotional reaction of a member" receiving negative feedback and then affirming the "potentially constructive intent" of the sender (Clark, 1995, p. 16). Finally, by using a convincing tone of voice, the leader needs to persuade the sender to restate the feedback message so it can be properly heard and received.
- **Delegating**—In delegating, the group leader assigns a task to the group or one or more of its members. The task can be as simple as observing and sharing impressions of what is happening in the group. For example, "Yvonne, I would like for you to let the group know when you think there is a lot of energy in it." Delegating can be complex, too, such as asking a member or members to lead the group. The idea behind delegating is to share the responsibility for the development of the group with the group.
- **Creativity**—The act of creativity is one where a person takes elements within the environment and arranges or rearranges them in such a way that something new and useful is formed. Often insight, meaning, and synergy occur in the process. By its very nature, group work is creative; therefore, group leaders need to be skilled in divergent ways of thinking and behaving (Bowman & Boone, 1998). Group leaders with a heightened capacity for creativity can help themselves and the group be more productive in times of crisis and form a sense of community. When creativity is employed, problems can also be viewed differently, and lives and interaction patterns transformed.

Overall, more than 2 dozen leadership skills can be used in various types of groups. Initial research by Toth and Stockton (1996) suggests that general group skills, such as here-and-now interventions (i.e., immediacy) as well as specific skills (e.g., blocking), can be taught using a systematic, microskills format as first devised by Ivey (1971). The implementation of this research is yet to come, but the identification and mastery of leadership skills are important. By being familiar with the skills and how they are employed, group leaders increase the range of alternative actions (Ivey & Ivey, 2007) that they can use at appropriate times in the life of the group.

GROUP LEADERSHIP ROLES AND FUNCTIONS

In addition to displaying a wide variety of skills, group leadership requires that leaders function in specific roles, at various times during the life of a group (DeLucia-Waack, 1999c). A group leader must be versatile and focused in various ways at different times.

Experience, coupled with training, permits leaders to operate in such a manner. There are six essential roles and functions that leaders must carry out over the life of the group: "(a) group member selection, (b) pregroup preparation, (c) positive leader-member relationship, (d) leader's use of structure, (e) group cohesion, and (f) leader communication and feedback" (Riva et al., 2004, p. 38). The specifics of these roles will be discussed in later chapters. However, it is crucial to remember that there are skills and behaviors associated with each distinct role and function. For instance, at the beginning of the group, a leader is much more likely to function in an active and direct way than during the middle phase of the group process, when group members are busy with their own activities.

It is also important to realize that group leaders operate in certain ways whether the groups are counseling, therapy, psychoeducational, or task/work oriented. Leaders must recognize which strategies will work best and when. Bates et al. (1982) characterize four main roles and functions that group leaders need to display at various times: traffic director, modeler of appropriate behavior, interactional catalyst, and communication facilitator.

Each of these roles takes specific skills. In the **traffic director** role, for instance, leaders "help members become aware of behaviors that open communication channels and those that inhibit communication" (Bates et al., 1982, p. 96). The role is both proactive and reactive in the prevention of certain behaviors (e.g., blocking "why" questions, focusing on the past, gossiping) and the promotion of others (e.g., actively listening, responding in a nonjudgmental way). In a similar manner, in the role of **modeler of appropriate behavior**, leaders must consciously pick actions they think group members need to learn through passive and active demonstrations. These ways of modeling can include deliberate use of self-disclosure, role-plays, speech patterns, and acts of creativity (Kottler, 1994). For example, when group leaders employ voice tones that signify happiness or sadness, they are directly and indirectly helping their group members learn ways to express their feelings.

The **interactional catalyst** role requires that leaders promote interaction between group members without calling attention to themselves. One way to do this is to look at various members when it might be appropriate for them to respond. Being an interactional catalyst is a functional process that continues throughout the group and can take various forms, such as questioning whether two or more group members have something to say to each other and then being silent to see what happens.

CASE EXAMPLE: Nolan Gets a Nod

Nolan characterized himself as a "shy guy" who was "willing to try almost anything once." So when he joined a singles group, he thought he would have plenty of opportunities to try many things. Instead, the group was dominated by a few individuals and Nolan had a hard time getting a word in edgewise, until one day when the group leader looked around the group during a moment of silence and gave a nod to him as if saying: "Please feel free to speak and share your opinions." That is what Nolan did, and almost immediately afterwards, he became more involved.

Have you ever been brought out by someone through either verbal or nonverbal means? Do you recommend that others do it? Why?

Finally, in the **communication facilitator** role, group leaders reflect the content and feeling of members and teach them how to do likewise. For instance, leaders may note that when someone is conveying that they are depressed they do not smile or have a lilt in their words. Therefore, this process focuses on both the expression of words and the emotion behind the communications. In addition, the importance of speaking congruently is stressed—that is, using "I" messages to state what one wants or what one thinks.

Leaders and Group Conflict

In addition to the four tasks just described, a primary function of group leaders is dealing constructively with conflict. The display of conflict is normal within a group and is especially prevalent in certain group stages, such as "storming" (Tuckman, 1965). Conflict and challenges in groups, if managed properly, offer opportunities for growth within the group. However, "one of the most difficult aspects of group leadership is the ability of the group leader to respond to conflict or challenging incidents in the group" (Kraus, DeEsch, & Geroski, 2001, p. 31).

Five specific techniques for managing conflict in groups have been proposed by Simpson (1977) and elaborated on by Kormanski (1982): withdrawal from the conflict, suppressing the conflict, integrating conflicting ideas to form new solutions, working out a compromise, and using power to resolve the conflict.

- **Withdrawal from the conflict**—This strategy involves leaders distancing themselves from conflict and postponing interventions. It has the advantage of letting leaders gather more data and observe longer without becoming excessively involved. It also allows leaders to consult and use resolution strategies later if issues are not settled. The disadvantages of this approach are that conflict may escalate, and withdrawal is completely ineffective in dealing with a crisis.
- **Suppressing conflict**—As a strategy, suppression consists of playing down conflict. It is often used when issues are minor. It keeps emotions under control and helps group leaders build a supportive climate. Suppression is most effective when conflict issues are unimportant or when focusing on a relationship is more important than concentrating on an issue. The disadvantages of suppression are that it fails to resolve conflict and allows feelings to smolder and possibly erupt later. In addition, leaders may be perceived as weak or insensitive when they use this strategy.
- **Integrating conflicting ideas to form new solutions**—Consensus is the idea behind integration. In using this strategy, group leaders try to get all parties to reexamine a situation and identify points of agreement. The goals are to develop new alternatives, learn how to open up lines of communication better, and build cohesive unity and commitment. One example of integration is **mediation**: having a third party hear arguments about a situation and then render a decision. The disadvantages of the integrative approach include the large amount of time it takes to implement and the unwillingness of some individuals to set aside their own goals and work for the good of the group.
- **Working out a compromise**—In this method, each party involved gives up a little to obtain a part of what they wanted and avoid conflict. The result is a win–win situation in which cooperative behavior and collaborative efforts are encouraged. This approach is extremely effective when resources are limited and

group members are flexible—for example, in a work group in which little money is available to spend on research and salaries. Compromising is a good strategy to use in avoiding win–lose situations. Negotiation is a good example of compromise. The disadvantages of compromise are that some parties may inflate their wants to get more, and the eventual action taken may be ineffective or less than desirable.

- **Using power to resolve the conflict**—The power strategy involves "the imposition of someone's will on someone else" (Kormanski, 1982, p. 116). The source of power may be derived from either a person's status or personality. **Position power** is most often used when immature relationships between individuals exist (Hersey, Blanchard, & Natemeyer, 1979). It is derived from the status of people's titles, such as "group leader" or "group facilitator." **Personal power** is employed more frequently in mature relationship situations. The source of power in such a situation is from the individual and his or her ability to persuade others to follow a selected course of action.

By using power, a leader is able to resolve a crisis quickly. However, the use of power creates a win–lose atmosphere in which the losers may harbor feelings of resentment or powerlessness and may seek subtle or blatant revenge on those who have won. Arbitration is an example of a typical use of power. Table 4.3 shows which techniques are most preferred under certain group circumstances.

◆ *Questions from Experience* ◆

Which of the leadership strategies for managing conflict do you most prefer? When have you used this strategy? Which of the strategies do you least prefer? What makes it unattractive for you?

Table 4.3
Contingency assessment guidelines.

Preferred Technique	Contingency Factor
Withdrawal	Important information is lacking. Choosing sides is to be avoided.
Suppression	An important relationship is involved. The issue is unimportant.
Integration	Group commitment is needed. The group will put group goals first.
Compromise	Resources are limited. A win–win set is desired.
Power	Time is limited (crisis situations). A continued deadlock persists.

Source: From "Leadership Strategies for Managing Conflict" by C. Kormanski, 1982, *Journal for Specialists in Group Work, 7,* p. 117. © ACA. Reprinted with permission. No further reproduction authorized without written permission of the American Counseling Association.

Overall, a prerequisite to becoming an effective leader is learning which strategies and roles to employ in conflict situations and when. Kraus et al. (2001) encourage leaders to approach such situations first by attending to and valuing them. Leaders must "internally process challenges in part by asking themselves supervision-like questions before effective interventions can follow" (p. 32). They suggest a "menu" of six nonexhaustive and nonexclusive questions that cover such important topics as member selection, systems theory, group dynamics and stages, individual members' group issues, emerging themes, and leader introspection (see Table 4.4). "By leaders carefully considering which perspective—which cuisine—may offer the best opportunity to harness the positive energy present in the group at that moment, an appropriate approach will follow"

Table 4.4
The Menu.

1. Were group members appropriately selected?
   - Does each member of the group present a concern that is related to the purpose of the group?
   - Is the member safe in the group and the group safe with the member?
   - Is each member at an appropriate level of functioning for this group (cognitive and psychological)?
2. Is the challenging incident related to the group system?
   - How are all members contributing to this moment?
   - What does this incident tell me about the functioning of the group?
   - How is this incident affecting the group? Its members? The whole group? The subgroups?
3. Is the incident a function of the stage or of the dynamics of this group?
   - How much of this is a function of normal group development?
   - How can I facilitate a process with the group so those members can try new behaviors?
   - To which therapeutic forces do I need to attend to help the group in this stage of group development?
4. Is this incident a symptom of an individual member's style of functioning?
   - How does this exemplify this individual member's presenting problem?
   - How can I intervene to promote insight?
   - How can I respond in a way that keeps all members invested in the group?
   - How can I include other group members?
5. Is this incident related to issues raised in the group?
   - How does this incident exemplify underlying core issues?
   - How can I intervene to facilitate insight related to the content and themes of this group?
   - How can I help members make intra- and interpersonal meaning of this incident?
6. Is this incident an artifact of my own responses to the group or to individual members?
   - How am I responding personally to this incident?
   - How is my response related to my own personal style?
   - What does my intuition tell me about what is happening in the group?

Source: From "Stop Avoiding Challenging Situations in Group Counseling" by K. L. Kraus, J. B. DeEsch, & A. M. Geroski, 2001, *Journal for Specialists in Group Work, 26*(1), p. 33. Copyright 2001 by Sage Publications, Inc. Reprinted by permission of Sage Publications, Inc.

(p. 44). Other experiences, such as observing or co-leading actual groups, can also be enlightening in learning how to handle conflict and not become defensive when challenges occur.

CO-LEADERS IN GROUPS

A **co-leader** is a professional or a professional-in-training who undertakes the responsibility of sharing the leadership of a group with another leader in a mutually determined manner in order to facilitate counseling, therapy, or group member interaction. The use of co-leaders in groups occurs often, especially in groups with a membership of 12 or more. The efficacy of using co-leaders depends on many factors, including economic considerations, advantages to the group, and the compatibility of the leaders. "Group co-leaders' concerns about their competence . . . [are] among the most significant factors influencing the development and enactment of their co-leader relationship" (Okech & Kline, 2006, p. 166).

Advantages

The advantages associated with co-leading a group, according to experts such as Carroll et al. (2004), Corey and Corey (2006), and Jacobs, Masson, and Harvill (2006), include the following:

- **Ease of handling the group in difficult situations**—When two leaders are present, they may help each other facilitate the movement of the group. For example, one leader can shift the topic or the focus of the group if the other leader gets bogged down. Before and after group sessions, co-leaders can plan strategies and discuss problems that they, members, or the group as a whole are experiencing.
- **Uses of modeling**—With co-leaders, group members are exposed to two models of human interaction. They see how individuals can relate to each other in positive ways and how they can disagree and still cooperate. When co-leaders are of the opposite gender, members may grow by more fully realizing and reliving earlier family dynamics and working on any unresolved issues that are brought up (Alfred, 1992; DeLucia-Waack & Gerrity, 2001).
- **Feedback**—Regardless of the issues members discuss, they usually receive twice the leader feedback when the group is co-led. This input helps members realize more fully how others perceive them and gives them a different perspective than they would receive otherwise. For example, one co-leader may comment on intrapersonal aspects of a group member's behavior, whereas the other focuses on interpersonal relationships. In such situations, leaders may also stimulate each other more and take corrective measures to avoid **burnout** (i.e., becoming physically and emotionally exhausted). Leaders, like members of the group, may grow more than they would if they were leading the group alone.

- **Shared specialized knowledge**—In groups with co-leaders, there is a primary advantage for all concerned when the leaders share specialized training with each other and the group. This type of sharing can come in response to a situation in the group, such as dealing with anger, and can be done privately or publicly. In these cases, everyone benefits because information is presented and discussed in a more dynamic and expanded manner than is possible in a one-leader group.
- **Pragmatic considerations**—In a co-led group, it is possible for one leader to cover for the other if a group session must be missed because of illness or professional considerations. Coverage allows the group to continue and evolve.

Limitations

The limitations of co-leading a group are also important to consider. The disadvantages this effort entails have the potential to be very destructive. "Unless partners can work as a complementary team, much group time can be wasted in power plays, bickering, and mutual sabotage" (Kottler, 1983, p. 178). Among the potential liabilities of co-leading are the following:

- **Lack of coordinated efforts** (Okech & Kline, 2006; Posthuma, 2002; Stockton & Morran, 1982)—The degree to which a group grows depends on the coordination of its leaders. When leaders do not meet to process what has occurred in the group or to agree on where they want to lead the group, destructive conflict within the group may occur, and the outcome of the group may be less than desirable. In such situations, the leaders may work, knowingly or not, at cross-purposes.
- **Too leader focused**—The old saying that "too many cooks spoil the broth" may apply to some groups with two leaders. In these cases, the presence of two leaders, especially if both are strong personalities and leader centered, will work against the good of group members because too much attention is concentrated on the leaders. One leader may also dominate another and call attention to the leadership role instead of the goals of members. In such cases, the impact of both group leaders is eventually diminished (Alfred, 1992).
- **Competition** (Posthuma, 2002; Trotzer, 2007)—Competition may be manifest in several ways—for example, through trying to gain the attention of the group or through using opposing theories. The point is that competition between group leaders will cost the group part of its efficiency and productivity. Leaders may also lose respect for each other in such an atmosphere.
- **Collusion**—In the collusion process, a co-leader establishes an informal alliance with a group member to address disliked qualities of the other co-leader. The result is an unloading of unexpected emotion onto the nonaligned leader and a splitting of the group into factions.

Overall, when leaders decide to lead a group jointly, they must work as a team. Such an approach takes considerable preparation. The process develops over time and goes through stages (Fall & Wejnert, 2005; Okech & Kline, 2006). For example, in the initial forming stage of a group, co-leaders "are uncertain about the expectations of the group and of one another" (Fall & Wejnert, 2005, p. 315). Likewise, co-leader relationships develop over time and co-leaders experience storming, norming, performing, and adjourning in a parallel manner to that of group members. Okech and Kline (2005) found that co-leaders believe that their effectiveness as co-leaders depends on the quality of their relationships. Thus, co-leading is a double-edged sword in that it can both relieve and promote stress depending on how well the leaders relate to one another. Gazda (1989) states that "supportive feedback, mutual trust and respect, and a liking for each other appear to be at least minimal requirements" for co-leaders to work well together and be of benefit to the group (p. 64).

In addition to developing a strong relationship, co-leading requires that both leaders be competent to begin with and that they be able to express a wide range of facilitative skills (e.g., self-disclosure, timing) in an appropriate manner. It also demands that co-leaders be consistent and noncompetitive (Stockton & Morran, 1982). The three main models of co-led groups are those in which the lead is (a) **alternated** (i.e., one leader takes responsibility for a specific period or a session, and the other leader provides support); (b) **shared** (i.e., each leader takes charge momentarily as he or she sees fit); or (c) **apprenticed** (i.e., a more experienced leader takes charge of the group to show a novice how to work with groups).

Overall, co-leading can be either a bonus or a bust to group members and to group leaders. When co-leaders develop a positive relationship in their group approach, they have a greater capacity for helping individuals and the group than does a single leader (Trotzer, 2007). It is the development of the right conditions that either makes or breaks co-led groups.

◆ *Questions from Experience* ◆

When have you co-led a group or been in a group that was co-led? How was it, and why do you think it functioned in the way it did?

GROUP LEADERSHIP TRAINING

"Training in group counseling typically includes four essential components: academic, observation, experiential, and supervision" (Riva & Korinek, 2004, p. 55). Yet, one of "the weakest areas of the group work movement throughout the decades has been the lack of attention paid to the training of group leaders" (Shapiro & Bernadett-Shapiro, 1985, p. 86). Until recently, little was published about training group leaders (Dye, 1997). Indeed, in the early days of group work (the 1950s and 1960s) before training standards were established, almost anyone could claim to be a group leader and start a group. Many such individuals were well intentioned but used predominantly individual counseling techniques to work with groups. The results were less than desirable and many times harmful. The self-anointed approach is no longer recognized or considered ethical by major group associations. Such an approach does not ensure quality or uniformity in treatment.

Most people are not natural leaders of groups (Gardner, 1990). It takes time and training to perfect group leadership skills. Yalom (2005) strongly advocates that potential group psychotherapy leaders participate in groups as a part of their training. This is a group process model of training (Stockton, Morran, & Krieger, 2004). Yalom notes that the accreditation committee of the American Group Psychotherapy Association has recommended a minimum requirement of 60 hours of participation in group for those in training to become leaders. Yalom also believes leadership training should provide an opportunity for a beginner to serve an apprenticeship with a more experienced clinician. Jacobs et al. (2006) also point out the importance of being in groups to fine-tune skills. The idea behind this approach when used as a model for training group leaders is that people must experience the power of the group as followers before they can become group leaders. Indeed, many self-help group leaders hone their skills in this way. However, being in a group is inadequate instruction for becoming a group leader. Likewise, a sole emphasis on simple didactic instruction or mere observation of a group at work is deficient as the major way to train group leaders.

In addition to an experiential base, group leaders must have specialized knowledge in the theories, dynamics, and interpersonal, ethical, research, and stage components of group work (Association for Specialists in Group Work, 2000). Leadership skills for conducting groups require input and cultivation of many sources. Effective group leaders must be able to perceive what is occurring in the group, select appropriate interventions, and risk implementing the interventions they have chosen (Stockton, McDonnell, & Aldarondo, 1997). Only the well-trained professional can make therapeutic moves in a group on a consistent basis (Vriend, 1985). Among the methods that have been established to train group leaders are (a) group-based training (Pearson, 1985), (b) the group generalist model (Anderson, 1982), (c) the educational and developmental procedure (Tollerud, Holling, & Dustin, 1992), (d) systematic group leadership training (Harvill, Masson, & Jacobs, 1983; Harvill, West, Jacobs, & Masson, 1985), (e) the critical-incident model and intervention cube concept (Childers, 1986), and (f) skills-based training models (e.g., DeLucia-Waack, 2001a).

The first way of obtaining the specialized training necessary for working with groups that is examined here is **group-based training** (Pearson, 1985). In this model, trainers first identify and define specific skills used in groups, providing examples in which each skill might be used. The flexibility of using various skills is stressed. Next, both videotapes and role-plays are used to show trainees how a particular skill is employed. The third step in this procedure is structured practice, in which each trainee demonstrates how he or she would use the skill that has been demonstrated. This enactment is then critiqued. Finally, group leader trainees, after learning all the group skills, are asked to demonstrate their group facilitation skills in 20-minute, unstructured practice sessions. They are observed leading a group and are given feedback on the use of skills they implemented during this time as well as those that they did not use. The way this training model works is represented in Figure 4.4.

A second way of preparing group facilitators is the **group generalist model**, which includes a five-step process outlined by Anderson (1982) as follows:

1.   The trainer models leader behavior for the total group.
2.   The group is broken down into subgroups of five or six, and each subgroup member practices leading a small group discussion.

3. After each discussion, some aspect of the subgroup's behavior is processed (e.g., anxiety).
4. The subgroup critiques the leader's behavior.
5. Following practice by each trainee, the total group shares observations and conclusions about the activity. (p. 119)

A third model for training group leaders is the **educational and developmental procedure**. It consists of four components: (a) content, (b) decision making, (c) eventual leadership style, and (d) dual process (Tollerud et al., 1992). All of these components are connected to a supervisor, "whose role is to make timely decisions as to how and when these components are implemented into the training" (p. 97). The focus of content is on factual information. Decision making involves choosing what to do and how to do it based on an understanding of group dynamics and self-knowledge. Leadership style deals with the complex set of expectations and tasks that face new group leaders. Finally, dual process is the idea that the group leader-in-training is a member of two groups at once. The first group is composed of those the trainee is leading; the second is composed of peers. The experiences from each group can be used in the other (see Figure 4.5).

Systematic group leadership training is a fourth way of teaching basic skills to beginning group leaders. It is a six-step method that includes the videotaping of trainees as they lead a group before they are introduced to the skill to be learned (steps 1 and 2). Then the trainees read about and see a new skill demonstrated (steps 3 and 4). Finally, trainees critique their original videos and then make new videotapes demonstrating the

Figure 4.4

Major components of the group-based skills training format.

Source: From "A Group-Based Training Format for Basic Skills of Small-Group Leadership" by R. E. Pearson, 1985, *Journal for Specialists in Group Work, 10,* p. 152. © ACA. Reprinted with permission. No further reproduction authorized without written permission of the American Counseling Association.

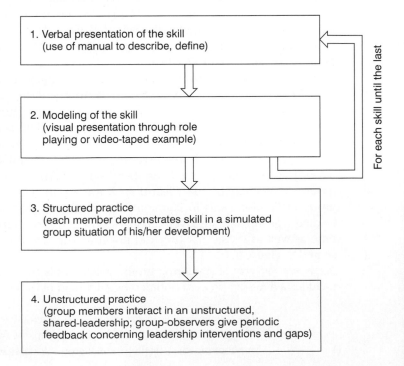

Figure 4.5
An educational model for teaching in group leadership.

Source: From "A Model for Teaching in Group Leadership: The Pre-Group Interview Application" by T. R. Tollerud, D. W. Holling, and D. Dustin, 1992, *Journal for Specialists in Group Work, 17*(2), p. 97. © ACA. Reprinted with permission. No further reproduction authorized without written permission of the American Counseling Association.

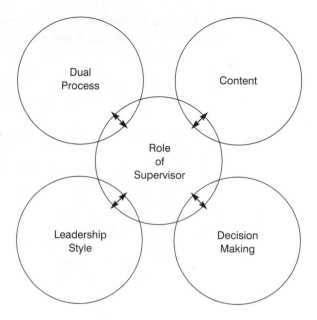

skill they have just been taught (steps 5 and 6) (Harvill et al., 1983). As first proposed, systematic group leadership training focused on six group leadership skills:

- **Cutting off**—This skill is used to stop group members who continue to speak in an unfocused way and help them concentrate on a point. For example, the leader might say, "Sharon, you seem to be repeating yourself. See if you can make your point in a sentence. Then let's hear from someone else."
- **Drawing out**—Drawing out occurs when the leader "directly invites comments or involvement from one of more group members. It is often used to encourage participation from members who find it hard to share with others or with those who share on a surface level but avoid deeper issues" (Morran et al., 2004, p. 95). For example, as the leader, Rudy might ask Fred and Alma if they have thoughts about the matter before the group because they have been quiet during the group's discussion.
- **Holding the focus**—This skill helps members concentrate on a specific topic or person for a set length of time. For example, if the group has been talking about risk taking and Wanda changes the subject, then the leader may simply say, "Wanda, let's conclude our discussion on risk taking before we deal with anything else."
- **Shifting the focus**—Sometimes leaders need to move group members to a different topic or person. For instance, the group leader may say to the group as a whole, "It appears we have exhausted our ideas about how to take risks. I would like to see us talk about the drawbacks, as well as the advantages, of risk taking."
- **Using eyes**—Scanning the group and noticing nonverbal reactions is a helpful skill for group leaders. For instance, the leader may notice that Kathryn's eyes are focused on the floor instead of on Jean, to whom she is talking.
- **Tying things together**—When leaders tie things together, they connect members with one another in regard to their similarities just as in linking. Therefore, Inez

and Pablo are connected or "tied together" by a leader who realizes they both have a passion for computers and software programs and who points this commonality out in the group.

Research findings support that four of these skills—cutting off, drawing out, holding the focus, and shifting the focus—are significantly improved following systematic group leadership training.

The **critical-incident model** and **intervention cube** concept make up a fifth way of training group leaders. This approach, as first set forth by Cohen and Smith (1976) and later expanded on by Donigian and Hulse-Killacky (1999), focuses on a number of critical incidents in the life of a group. The trainee, after studying group dynamics, watches a videotape of his or her instructor handling a number of different situations in a group. Then the trainee co-leads a group under the instructor's supervision, during which he or she makes strategic interventions geared to the incidents in the particular group (Childers, 1986). Trainees are taught self-management skills and ways to deal with specific group situations. They learn on both a personal and a professional level. This type of training, when combined in an integrative way with the type of nonperfectionistic thinking pattern proposed by Miller (1986), can help beginning group leaders be less rigid and more sensitive, caring, and helpful to others.

Skills-based training models for group workers have also become more prevalent and popular, and a number of instruments have been developed to assess group leadership skills (DeLucia-Waack, 2001). A particularly strong model, the **Skilled Group Counseling Training Model**, has been proven to be effective through research (Smaby, Maddux, Torres-Rivera, & Zimmick, 1999). It is especially helpful in assisting beginning group workers to "learn and transfer group counseling skills to actual group counseling sessions" (Downing, Smaby, & Maddux, 2001, p. 158). This model, which can be tested through use of the **Skilled Group Counseling Scale**, "includes 18 skills organized into three stages of counseling: exploration, understanding, and acting" (p. 158). An equally important instrument for measuring skills is the **Group Leader Self-Efficacy Instrument (GLSI)**, a 36-item scale that measures group leader self-efficacy (Page, Pietrzak, & Lewis, 2001). **Self-efficacy**, according to Bandura (1986), is a person's judgment of his or her capability to organize and execute a course of action required to attain a designated type of performance. The GLSI appears to have sufficient validity and reliability to measure the self-efficacy of individuals learning to perform group leader skills and, therefore, can be employed to ensure that new leaders are competent in their purported abilities.

Overall, the concepts and methods used in most of these approaches to training include the basic prerequisites for an effective group leader as articulated by Trotzer (2007). They also incorporate, for the most part, the literature on the training needs of preservice group leaders as summarized by Stockton and Toth (1996), which states that group leaders need the following components in their educational programs:

(a) grounding in theory through the accumulation of didactic material,
(b) opportunities to observe groups in action and to learn and practice group skills before they actually lead a group,
(c) participation in a personal growth group experience to observe group development from a member's perspective and develop as a person, and
(d) practice in leading or co-leading a group under careful supervision. (p. 275)

Yalom (2005) concurs with this holistic, research-based, balanced, and multidimensional emphasis in training. He stresses that group leadership training goes beyond techniques in emphasizing the importance of helping students to evaluate their own work in a critical fashion and to maintain sufficient flexibility (both technically and attitudinally). According to Yalom, becoming a mature clinician requires evolving. Every group is a learning experience. An open attitude toward learning is especially true for effective and mature group leaders, regardless of their specialty area in working with groups.

GROUP SUPERVISION

"Supervised experiential training is a key component of group leader instruction" (Stockton & Toth, 1996, p. 280). Supervision increases supervisees' independence and self-confidence (Linton, 2003). Therefore, group supervision is an essential and complementary activity for becoming competent at group leadership (DeLucia-Waack, 2002). It may be done in conjunction with the other three components of group leadership training.

Supervision for group workers is also essential after formal training. Without ongoing supervision and evaluation, original errors made by a group leader may be reinforced by simple repetition (Yalom, 2005). For example, Isabel may continue to gloss over feelings in group members unless she is confronted about both what she is doing and why. Furthermore, supervision enables group leaders to address repeatedly problematic thoughts and issues they may have, such as those involved in eating disorders (e.g., perfection, independence), so that they do not become troublesome and intrusive (DeLucia-Waack, 1999b). Group workers who do not have supervision "got stuck in patterns of dysfunctional behavior and do not know how to get out" (DeLucia-Waack, 1999c, p. 132).

One way to minimize problems and processes in group supervision is to make it developmental and comprehensive. "At any particular moment, the supervisor must consider the level of cognitive complexity of the supervisee, the developmental level of the group, the level of training of group members, and the interactive effects of these variables with one another" (Hayes, 1990, p. 235). The anxiety of the group leader must also be assessed and dealt with in supervision because "anxiety may impact cognitive development" and the functioning of the leader in the group (Duncan & Brown, 1996, p. 252).

The American Group Psychotherapy Association recommends a minimum of 180 hours of supervision for group leaders-in-training. According to Trotzer (2007), one good way of being supervised is to have two potential group leaders co-lead a group under the supervision of a more experienced leader. This type of supervision is less threatening to a novice group leader than trying to co-lead with an experienced group leader. It also requires less time on the supervisor's part and allows him or her to be more objective in critiquing the new group leaders. This technique may also include videotaping and observations by a group team behind a one-way-mirror that in turn can result in further supervision by a supervisor working with the observation group.

Peer group supervision is another way of providing group leaders with supervision. "The support for peer group supervision is based on the belief that it offers opportunities for vicarious learning in a supportive group environment. It is argued that once established, this environment contributes to decreased supervisee anxiety, increased self-efficacy and confidence, and enhanced learning opportunities" (Christensen & Kline,

2001, pp. 81–82). This type of supervision also may reduce hierarchy and dependency needs found within individual supervision. Furthermore, it may make the most of supervisory time and expertise, although in the beginning it requires an investment in structuring the group. Research by Christensen and Kline (2001) using a process-sensitive peer group found peer group supervision to be an effective way of helping supervisees learn essential skills "that enable them to supervise each other in a peer supervision environment" (p. 97).

A less effective way of supervising is through listening to an audiotape of a group. In this type of supervision, voice tones and member input are readily picked up, but other nonverbal dimensions of the group are missed. The least effective way of conducting group supervision is having a supervisee report either orally or in writing what occurred in the group. Such self-reports are usually selective in what they report and miss the subtleties of sessions (Freeman & McHenry, 1996).

A final way supervision may occur is to have group leaders in a group that is supervised. This type of group supervision saves time and resources (Gillam, Hayes, & Paisley, 1997). It is usually reserved for novice counselors who are learning generic counseling skills, but it can also be employed with group leaders either during formal education classes or as continuing education (Werstlein & Borders, 1997). In such a process, group leaders bring in videotapes or role-play problematic situations in the group and receive supervision from the supervisor in charge of running the group and from their peers. In academic and practice settings, a group of this kind may function primarily as a task group, and "highly task-oriented behaviors may predominate across all stages" of its development (Werstlein & Borders, 1997, p. 132).

If supervision is successful, then group leader trainees will grow in four areas (Bernard, 1979; Freeman & McHenry, 1996; Lanning, 1986). First, they will improve their **process skills**—that is, observable behaviors used to run groups, such as summarization, immediacy, and confrontation. DeLucia-Waack (2002) recommends that a Group Processing Sheet be utilized in the process skills area. This sheet is made up of two parts: Group Process Notes to record "the events of the group session as part of the official notes for the group and/or individual client files" and a Processing of the Group Session section to help group leaders analyze what happened in the group in terms of therapeutic factors, critical incidents, effective interventions, and counter-transference" (p. 346). By improving process skills, group leaders become more versatile in their interactions with group members and the group as a whole.

A second area in which group leader supervisees will become better through supervision is in using **conceptual skills**—that is, thinking skills that enable them to delineate dominant themes and the concerns of clients while simultaneously choosing a particular helpful response. Conceptual skills deal with the whole picture of what is occurring within the group and are crucial to the development of a group. Conceptualizing is helped through filling out the Group Processing Sheet, as is the third area in the domain of **personalization skills**. These skills are associated with using one's own personal attributes, such as openness or humor, to full advantage in a group setting. Finally, in supervision, supervisees are assisted in improving their **professional skills**, such as behaving appropriately in a crisis, safeguarding confidentiality, and turning in reports connected with the group on time. Overall, supervision contributes to both specific and general learning experiences of group leaders in training.

Group Processing Sheet

Group Process Notes

Date: Session#:   Group Leaders:

Members present: Members excused: Members not excused:

Themes for the session
   Content:
   Process:

Notes for the group
   Opening:
   Working:
   Ending:

Notes about each group member
   Member A:
   Member B:
   Member C:
   Member D:
   Member E:
   Member F:
   Member G:
   Member H:

Processing of the Group Session

Comments about the group
   Content:
   Process:
   Specific members:
   To be discussed in supervision:

Evaluation of intervention strategies
   Executive functions:
     What worked?
     What didn't (and what could you do differently next time):
   Meaning attribution
     What worked?
     What didn't (and what could you do differently next time):
   Caring
     What worked?
     What didn't (and what could you do differently next time):
   Emotional stimulation
     What worked?
     What didn't (and what could you do differently next time):

(continues)

Critical incidents related to therapeutic factors: (instillation of hope, universality, imparting of information, altruism, the corrective recapitulation of the primary family group, interpersonal learning—input, interpersonal learning—output, cohesiveness, catharsis, existential factors, identification, self-understanding). Briefly discribe the three most critical incidents that happened this week in group and how each illustrates a therapeutic factor.

1.
2.
3.

Countertransference

Toward specific members: Briefly discribe the feeling toward the member, who the person reminds you of (if any), and how you behave based on this toward the member. Is your reaction based on something that a person is doing in group or based on assumptions you are making about the person based on relationships with others? What could you do in the future to respond to this person as they are in the group and not as if they were someone else?

1.
2.

Toward specific incidents or group topics: Briefly describe the event, the feeling(s) elicited from you as a result of the event, what other situation this reminds you of, what behavior it is based on, what your personal reactions and issues are related to this event, and what you can do differently in future interactions:

1.
2.

Tape transcription

Choose a 20-minute segment of the tape and transcribe it using the following format:

Leader statement
Type of statement
Member statement
Consequence
Other possible response(s)

Source: From J. L. Delucia-Waack, *Journal for Specialists in Group Work,* 2002, *27*(4), 355–356. Copyright 2002 by Sage Publications, Inc. Reprinted by permission of Sage Publications, Inc.

SUMMARY AND CONCLUSION

This chapter has focused on the complex nature of group leadership. The concept of leadership is often misunderstood, but some of its common factors include multiple relationships in which there are reciprocity, legitimate influence, motivation, and cooperation for the achievement of beneficial goals. To be an effective group leader, a person must show some versatility and realize that different styles of leadership are appropriate in certain situations. Leaders who are too rigid and use one style (e.g., authoritarian, democratic, laissez-faire) may be less helpful than those who are flexible and developmental.

The personal qualities of group leaders are also important. No one trait is essential for leaders to possess. However, the display of some personal qualities (e.g., support, warmth) in certain quantities will facilitate the movement of the group and the growth of members. Which qualities and quantities are vital depends on the dynamics of a particular group. The way theories and theoretical skills are employed is also linked to the nature of the group being led. Some theories are helpful and advantageous to the leader and members; others are not.

Some skills are unique to certain groups, whereas others are universal to all areas of human relations. As group work has grown, it has become increasingly important for group workers to become skilled in core competencies appropriate for running any type of group as well as for them to master specific group competencies targeted for specialty groups. General core group skills come first. From these skills group workers can hone and refine their abilities when working in specialty areas. No one skill is crucial for a group leader to possess, but knowing what to do and when to do it is essential. Leadership in skill deployment is developed through experience, course work, and supervision. Skills, if properly applied, can help members and groups achieve individual and overall goals. Knowing when and how to use a particular skill separates successful and unsuccessful group leaders.

Group leaders function in a variety of ways—for example, as traffic directors, catalysts, and managers of conflict. Therefore, leaders must be sensitive to themselves and their constituents. Sometimes working with a co-leader can be helpful in learning how to integrate personal and professional skills, especially if the experience is under supervision. Group leadership training is a must for those who expect to work on more than a one-to-one basis. Such training will often be composed of three elements: telling, doing, and showing. It is important that group leaders get a feel for what working with a group is like before they actually direct one. The process of updating leadership skills is continuous, and models for learning these skills have proliferated and improved in recent years.

In summary, groups are a unique way to work with individuals in resolving problems or accomplishing tasks. Group leadership involves being not only knowledgeable about group operations but also skilled through an integrative experience on how to help members and the group as a whole move in productive directions.

CLASSROOM EXERCISES

1. Why do you think the terms *leader* and *leadership* are so misunderstood? What qualities do you consider essential for a group leader? If possible, tell about a leader who has personally influenced you and how you were affected. What did that person do with the group you were in that you admired most?

2. List personal and professional qualities and skills you possess that would help you lead a group of your choosing. Which qualities and skills do you think you need to cultivate more? Discuss your self-assessment with two other class members. Notice how your ideas and theirs change or remain the same in this process.

3. Find an article on the supervision or training of group leaders (consult the *Journal for Specialists in Group Work, Small Group Behavior,* or *Counselor Education and Supervision*). Share the content with the class and your instructor; other class members will do the same. From the ideas presented, discuss what the process of supervision entails in group work.

4. Discuss how you feel about conflict in a group with another class member. After you have identified your feelings, look at the five ways of managing conflict suggested in this chapter. Which ones are you most uncomfortable with? Why? Describe a specific way you can work to improve your management of group conflict.

CHAPTER 5

BEGINNING A GROUP

Prentice Hall School Division

Knowing that most beginnings are awkward
we wait anxiously for words or actions
to break the silence of this gathering
and give our group its genesis.
Strangers to each other,
and to ourselves at times,
we slowly move into awareness
of our own uniqueness
Coupled with impressions
of the specialness of others.*

*From Beginnings by Samuel T. Gladding, © 1993.

G roups develop in a healthy way, dissolve because of lack of care, or end up in disarray. Understanding how to begin and nurture a group significantly improves the chances that the goals of the group and its members will be achieved and chaos will be avoided.

Almost all functional groups go through developmental stages. The generally agreed-on number of stages in their evolution is between four and five. For example, Tuckman and Jensen (1977) identify the stages as *forming, storming, norming, performing,* and *adjourning.* Similarly, Kormanski and Mozenter (1987) state that groups develop out of **awareness** and then move on to *conflict, cooperation, productivity,* and finally *separation,* whereas Trotzer (2007) conceptualizes groups as moving through the stages of *security, acceptance, responsibility, work,* and *closing.* Ward (1982) characterizes group stages in a four-part sequence as *power, cohesiveness, working,* and *termination,* and Gazda (1989) does the same in including the stages of *exploration, transition, action,* and *termination.* I describe a four-stage process as well—*formation/orientation, transitioning* (i.e., storming and norming), *performing/working,* and *mourning/termination.* On the outskirts of this stage norm is Yalom (2005) with three stages—*orientation, conflict,* and *cohesiveness*—and Corey (2004) with six stages: *formation, orientation, transition, working, consolidation,* and *follow-up/evaluation.* Not all theorists agree that stages do or must exist in groups, at least in a progressive fashion (Yalom, 2005). However, developmental stages have been identified in learning groups (e.g., Lacoursiere, 1974, 1980), therapy groups (e.g., Brabender, 1985), and training groups (e.g., Dunphy, 1968).

Regardless of how many stages there are in group development, the beginning stage is an important and usually a multidimensional event. The most obvious beginning of a group is when group members and leaders assemble for the first session. However, before the initial meeting, many processes have already been completed—for example, formulating the idea for the group, screening members, and selecting preliminary individual and group goals. Even after the group meets initially, it continues to evolve and can be conceptualized as forever forming, with certain issues returning from time to time to be explored in greater depth—the so-called **cyclotherapy process** (Yalom, 2005). Some of the issues

Stages/transitions of group development.

STAGES/ TRANSITIONS AUTHOR	1	2	3	4	5	6
Tuckman (1965), Tuckman and Jensen (1977)	Forming	Storming	Norming	Performing	Adjoining	
Gazda (1989)	Exploratory	Transition	Action	Termination		
Yalom (2005)	Orientation	Conflict		Cohesiveness		
Trotzer (1999)	Security	Acceptance	Responsibility	Work	Closing	
Gladding (2008)	Forming/ Orientation	Transition Storming/Norming		Performing/ Working	Mourning/ Termination	
Corey (2007)	Formation	Orientation/ Exploration	Transition	Working	Consolidation/ Termination	Follow-up/ Evaluation

Source: From Capuzzi, D., Gross, D., & Stauffer, M. (2006). *Introduction to Group Work,* 4th ed. Denver: Love Publishing Co., with permission.

with which groups continually struggle are anxiety, power, norms, interpersonal relationships, and personal growth (Cohen & Smith, 1976; Kormanski, 1999).

The focus of this chapter is on what is considered to be the **forming, or orientation, stage of the group**, which is a time of initial caution associated with any new experience. Personal relations are characterized by dependence, and group members attempt to be accepted and safe by trying to keep things simple and free of controversy so they can avoid being rejected by others, the leader, or even themselves. This feature of the group is particularly strong in counseling or psychotherapy groups in which individuals do not know each other well, but it can also be part of task/work and even psychoeducational groups where members have a common shared history. Regardless, discussions are usually superficial during forming, centering around historic or future events that do not have a direct impact on the group or its members (Tuckman & Jensen, 1977).

STEPS IN THE FORMING STAGE

Forming is a process that involves several steps. Although some of these steps may be completed concurrently, none may be skipped if the group is going to form properly and prosper. Group workers are wise to consult such documents as the Association for Specialists in Group Work's (ASGW) *Best Practice Guidelines* (1998) if they want to have successful groups and work within appropriate ethical and professional standards.

Step 1: Developing a Rationale for the Group

A group begins conceptually with the generation of ideas. Behind every successful group is a *rationale* for its existence. The more carefully the reasons for conducting a group are considered, the more likely it is that there will be positive responses and outcomes. Therefore, a clear rationale and focus are of uppermost importance in planning. Group leaders who are unclear about their purpose will end up being nonproductive at best and possibly harmful.

For example, school counselors may wish to make sure that all members of a sixth-grade class learn appropriate ways of interacting with the opposite gender. One counselor decides to run a series of psychoeducational groups with the sixth-grade students based on the rationale that students first need knowledge before they can act properly. This counselor plans a sequential series of interactive presentations. Another counselor at the same school does not think through the process and impulsively decides to conduct counseling groups with the sixth graders to deal with this same topic. There is no rationale for such groups—they are not well suited for children who have not expressed a concern about this subject, and they take considerable time to conduct. The outcome of the two groups run by these counselors would vary greatly because of the initial thought processes of each.

Step 2: Deciding on a Theoretical Format

In addition to developing a rationale for which type of group to conduct, group workers must consider the theoretical format from which they will work. Some group leaders

Table 5.1

Characteristics of counseling groups according to focus.

Characteristics Variables	Group Focus		
	Extrapersonal	**Interpersonal**	**Intrapersonal**
Type	Task	Process	Therapy
Expectation	Action	Development	Remediation
Time Focus	Future	Present	Past
Leader Role	Directive	Facilitative	Responsive
Structure	High	Variable	Low
Stigma	Very low	Low	Moderate
Confidentiality	Not necessary	Desirable	Necessary
Size	3–30+ members	6–20 members	5–10 members
Member Consistency	Frequent changes	Occasional changes	Few changes
Duration	1–30+ sessions	5–20 sessions	12–30+ sessions

Source: From "A Curative Factor Framework for Conceptualizing Group Counseling" by M. Waldo, 1985, *Journal of Counseling and Development, 64,* p. 53. © ACA. Reprinted with permission. No further reproduction authorized without written permission of the American Counseling Association.

pretend not to work from a theoretical basis, claiming they will let their groups decide how to develop. Yet, even this type of purported atheoretical stance is really a theoretical statement about how the leader thinks and conducts a group.

Ward (1982, 1985) notes that each major theory of group work has limitations and strengths. Leaders who are most aware of these areas before groups begin can choose a format appropriate to their group even if it is **eclectic** (i.e., a composite of theoretical approaches). In choosing a theoretical format, the limitations and strengths of each approach must be considered. All types of groups deal with individual, interpersonal, and group focus levels. A theoretical format should function on intrapersonal, interpersonal, and extrapersonal matters, but in varying degrees. The theoretical base of the group should match the needs of participants and the group as a whole (see Table 5.1).

Waldo (1985) has conceptually described levels of functioning in a group as **I/We/It**. His thoughts parallel Hulse-Killacky's ideas concerning process and content. "I" is the individual, intrapersonal focus on beliefs, attitudes, and feelings; "We" is the interpersonal dimension, or the relationship among group members; and "It" is the extrapersonal emphasis on issues, tasks, or group concerns. Leaders who wish to facilitate interpersonal ("We") development of members might choose a theoretical format that promotes this process, such as a person-centered counseling group, whereas those emphasizing individual ("I") development might plan to employ an active psychoeducational group. Regardless of the approach chosen, planning for a group must consider that groups contain many variables, among them people, processes, and products. "Group work is challenging and complex because groups are complex" (Ward, 1985, p. 59).

CASE EXAMPLE: Joan and the Sound of Silence

Joan has seen a need in her school to address bullying. She wants to run an interpersonal group based on person-centered theory. She also wants to have the group focus on prevention and be developmental. Joan thinks it would be best to start her group with the younger children first. She assembles first graders, whom she screened to select those who are most passive and the least likely to complain about being picked on. However, during the first session of the group she is frustrated because no one talks about themselves or their feelings. Although Joan has had good intentions, she has overlooked the fact that a homogeneous group of shy kids is not one that is likely to be verbal, especially using a person-centered approach.

What would you suggest she do? When? How? And why?

Step 3: Weighing Practical Considerations

After a clear, convincing rationale and theoretical format have been determined, group proposals should stress specific, concrete, and practical objectives and procedures. Considerations such as meeting time, place, and frequency cannot be overlooked if the group is to be successful (Jacobs, Masson, & Harvill, 2006). Group leaders must be sensitive to political and practical realities as well. Some good group ideas never get implemented because colleagues fear, misunderstand, or disapprove of the group leader's plans. For example, a high school guidance group focusing on understanding opposite-sex relationships might be prohibited or canceled if the principal of the school thinks sex is to be the main agenda item of the group. In a case like this, the group leader should first thoroughly brief the principal and then the parents of the teens to prevent a negative reaction.

CASE EXAMPLE: Careful Candace

At the beginning of the school year, Candace sent out a needs survey to her 10th-grade students. She found that one area a majority of them wanted more information on was on the impact of over-the-counter drugs on health. Rather than start a group on "Drugs 101," Candace talked to her principal about the survey results and then sent an e-mail to her students and their parents. She followed this communication up by gaining permission from her administration to conduct a psychoeducational group on over-the-counter drugs and then explaining to the PTA what she had in mind. Before recruiting group members, she sent out another e-mail to the 10th-grade class and their parents informing them about what she planned to do and how and inviting their questions and comments. When she did recruit and conduct the group, no one seemed upset and the group went well.

What else do you think Candace could or should have done?

Overall, the setting in which the leader works will influence the formulation of a group proposal. For instance, an employee assistant professional might propose an adjustment group for recent retirees in a community center, whereas a college counselor might focus on offering a series of guidance presentations on careers in the student university center. Counselors and therapists in private practice will generally have more flexibility and fewer administrative procedures than those who work in the public domain. However, institutions do not protect private practitioners who conduct groups. Therefore, private practitioners must be as careful and meticulous as other group practitioners in their proposals. A partial secret of success in all cases is detailed preparation. A good model that reflects adequate preparation is a proposal that includes the broad range of information presented in Figure 5.1. This model can be adapted to meet the needs of group leaders interested in serving other populations.

Step 4: Publicizing the Group

Corey and Corey (2006) note that how a group is announced influences both the ways it will be received by potential members and the kind of people who will join. Some of the best ways of announcing the formation of a group are through word of mouth with professional colleagues, personal contact with potential members, and written announcements to a targeted audience. There are advantages and disadvantages to each of these ways of **publicizing a group**. For example, announcing the formation of a group through word of mouth to professional colleagues may personalize the information but fail to reach a large number of individuals who might wish to participate. The same is true if a group leader simply contacts those he or she thinks might benefit from the experience. Written announcements to selected audiences are likely to reach the most people, but they may not be clear enough to specify who should be a member of the group. Therefore, some persons who are not suited for the group may apply, or too many persons may apply, requiring the group leader to spend a large amount of time screening them.

The *Best Practice Guidelines* published by the ASGW (1998) is a definitive and comprehensive document that provides guidance on the proper conduct expected of those who lead groups, including preparation procedures. Professional group workers have also focused on specific issues regarding content that should be addressed. Among the best of these checklists is one by Tollerud, Holling, and Dustin (1992). Another checklist on specific issues regarding content is found in Figure 5.1.

Step 5: Screening and Pretraining

The maturity, readiness, and composition of membership play a major role in determining the success of a group (Riva, Lippert, & Tackett, 2000). Therefore, potential group members should be **screened** (i.e., interviewed either individually or in a group before the group's first meeting in regard to their suitability for the group) and carefully chosen whenever possible. (Exceptions to selecting members are likely to occur in psychoeducational and some task/work groups.) In the pregroup screening process, the leader must address potential group members' readiness to be in a group and their goals (MacNair-Semands, 1998).

Most experts in the group field endorse either an **individually conducted pregroup screening procedure** or a **group-conducted pregroup screening process** (Couch, 1995; Riva et al., 2000). Both formats are essentially intake interviews—ways of determining who should join a particular group and who should not. In pregroup screening sessions, the

Proposal for a group

I. Type of Group

This will be a (task/work, psychoeducational, counseling, psychotherapy) group for people between the ages of (____ and _____) or with the following interests or aspirations: (_____). The group will specifically focus on _____. It will not concentrate on _____. The group will meet for a (limited, unlimited) time starting with a meeting on (fill in specific date, length of meeting, and place).

During the initial session, the leader will give specific suggestions to participants in getting the most from their group experience.

The fee (if any) for this group will be _____.

II. Rationale, Goals, and Objectives

The rationale for conducting this type of group is as follows:

1.

2.

3.

Goals and objectives for the group are as follows:

1.

2.

3.

III. Rights and Expectations of Group Members

Group members have rights as well as responsibilities. It is expected that group members will be active participants. However, members will decide at what level they participate, how much they reveal about themselves, and when they wish to share information. Ethical guidelines of _____ will be followed.

IV. Group Leader

Name(s) of the group leader(s), degrees, professional and personal backgrounds and experiences, qualifications for leading groups, and other pertinent information.

V. Basic Ground Rules

To obtain the most from the group, members will be asked to suggest ways of conducting it. However, these generic rules will be followed:

1.

2.

3.

VI. Topics for the Group

Certain topics will be given emphasis, but group members will have the opportunity to discuss the aspects of those topics that are most meaningful to them. Following is a sample of some possible topics for the group to explore. Other topics of concern to group participants can be developed.

1.

2.

3.

Figure 5.1

Checklist of specific issues on content.

group leader and potential members can interview each other about different aspects of the group process and themselves. The group leader may ask a number of questions to potential group members during the screening, but queries that are open ended and elicit personal responses and interpersonal styles seem to work best (Gladding, 1994; Riva et al., 2000). For example, a prospective member of a group might be asked: (a) "What has been your past experience with groups?" (b) "What has led you to want to be a part of this group?" (c) "What can you contribute to this group?" and (d) "How do you express your emotions, especially your negative ones?"

In the pregroup screening process, the group leader must also determine the level of interpersonal behavior or comfort with others that potential group members have. Such a determination is "essential to groups that focus primarily on group interaction and group process" (Riva et al., 2000, p. 167). The goal is to determine whether a particular group is right for a particular person at a specific time. Through screening members, premature termination is avoided, goals and processes involved with the group are clarified, and members are empowered to take an active part in the group.

According to Couch (1995), there are a number of interdependent steps necessary for conducting an effective pregroup screening interview:

1. *Identify needs, expectations, and commitment.* Of these factors, commitment is considered the most crucial. Thus, the group leader might ask: "Since there are a number of group experiences from which you could chose, why do you particularly want to be in this group? What do you want to get out of it?"

2. *Challenge myths and misconceptions.* It is crucial that potential members have accurate information and not misinformation like that sometimes given on television or in the movies (Childers & Couch, 1989). Some of the common misunderstandings about groups, especially counseling and psychotherapy groups, include "groups are for sick people," "groups are artificial," and "groups force people to lose their identity." The group leader might help in clarifying this matter by asking a potential member: "How do you perceive this group developing? What are your concerns in being a member of it?"

3. *Convey information.* The nature and limits of confidentiality are particularly helpful to communicate, but group stages, roles, and the importance of balancing content and process may be quite useful to explain as well. To address this matter, the group leader might simply talk about the length of the group, what might occur, and the importance of a member paying attention to nonverbal as well as verbal interactions.

The uniqueness of school environments may make the pregroup screening process distinct for school counselors who lead groups. These group workers may concentrate on developmental issues when interviewing potential menbers. They may also form groups based on program goals and student standards (Hines & Fields, 2002). Written parental consent for children under 18 to participate in a group is needed as well.

One way, other than screening, to ensure that members are ready for the group is through **pretraining** (i.e., orienting group members on what to expect of the group before it ever meets). "Such an investment should enhance the functioning of the group, speed its work, reduce dropouts, and increase the positive outcomes" (Zimpfer, 1991, p. 264). Pretraining has been positively associated with cohesion, member satisfaction, and comfort with the group (Burlingame, Fuhriman, & Johnson, 2004). It can be done on an individual or a group basis. When conducted individually, the possibility always exists that a leader will accidentally leave out some vital details about the group. The advantage of such a process, however, is that the rapport between the member and the leader may increase. A group session, in contrast, is a more uniform, although less personalized, way of pretraining. Such a session focuses on topics that might be explored in the group and gives members an opportunity to assess whether they wish to invest themselves in this particular group. It also gives the leader an opportunity to see how potential members of the group interact in a group setting. Group pretraining is not required; however, the more thoroughly prepared potential members and the group leader are, the more likely it is that the dropout rate will be low, the communication clear, and the cohesion of the group as a whole great (DeRoma, Root, & Battle, 2003; Yalom, 2005).

An example of pretraining illustrates its essence. In a group that is voluntary and therapeutic, potential members should be informed of which techniques and procedures will be used, the qualifications of the leader, fees (if any), types of records kept, member responsibility, personal risks involved, and the types of services that can realistically be provided (ASGW, 1998). They may even be shown clips of selected group videotapes, such as those created by Irvin Yalom, Rex Stockton, Gerald Corey, or Peg Carroll. Their questions about the group should be answered as well.

When the group leader is unsure about how specific to be, it is better to err on the side of caution and give group members a thorough explanation of group and administrative procedures. In no case should the leader make promises or guarantees. Facts concerning the formation and procedure of a group are preferably put in writing.

Step 6: Selecting Group Members

The selection of group members is usually a two-way process. Exceptions occur in some psychoeducational groups, in which material is presented to a captive audience, such as in schools or the armed forces, and in task/work groups, such as in businesses, where individuals are grouped with one another because they work in the same office. When potential group members and the leader are mutually involved in the selection process, both have input into deciding who will be included or excluded.

People who are invited to join the group should be individuals likely to benefit from the experience. Essentially, they should be those who have specific goals in mind, who have allayed their fears of what a group might do, and who feel comfortable in their roles and sensitive to their surroundings.

Individuals who do not appear likely to contribute to the growth of the group or who lack personal maturity are prime candidates for exclusion from it. Such persons include those who are extremely hostile, self-centered, unmotivated, crisis oriented, or mentally unbalanced as well as those who are unable or unwilling to self-disclose, express feelings, or tolerate anxiety (Corey, 2004; Riva et al., 2000). Other individuals who may be excluded from a particular group are those who are either too different or too similar to other potential group members. Many of these individuals may benefit from personal one-to-one counseling.

Members of extremely heterogeneous groups may not relate well to each other and may experience a good deal of interpersonal conflict (Melnick & Wood, 1976); members of extremely homogeneous groups, in contrast, may relate too well, may not work hard on individual or group tasks, and may stay on a superficial level. Over time, heterogeneous groups may be most effective for intensive group therapy procedures in which the emphasis is on personality change (Kellerman, 1979), whereas homogeneous groups may be most appropriate for individuals who need support or have more focused problems, such as solving a dilemma on a job-related task. Clearly, both advantages and disadvantages are inherent in heterogeneous and homogeneous groups (Furst, 1953).

A potential group member should never be coerced to join a group. Likewise, if a potential group member and the group leader determine that group work "does not show promise as a source of help," then the group leader should work with the interviewee in looking for other sources of assistance (Ohlsen, Horne, & Lawe, 1988, p. 37).

CASE EXAMPLE: Savage Sue

Henry had one spot open in a counseling group he was forming at his agency for adults in mid-life. The group was heterogeneous and Henry thought that Sue, a mid-40s Caucasian woman, would be a good fit for the group. When he broached the subject of the group with her, Sue declined. Undeterred, Henry persisted and finally got Sue to join by telling her that if she did not, the group would fail and that the other group members really needed the experience.

The group turned out to be a bad experience for everyone involved. Sue did not show up half the time and when she did come, she was passive-aggressive. Henry really got mad toward the end of the group and blasted Sue for her behavior. Her response was: "Well, I told you I did not want to be a part of the group in the first place."

Put yourself in Henry's shoes. What would you do now? What would you do the next time you start to form a group?

Step 7. Selecting a Group Leader

Certain qualities distinguish an effective group leader. Some of these have been discussed previously and will not be reiterated here. The selection of a leader by a potential group member is emphasized because the selection process hinges partly on professional qualities and partly on personal qualities. It is easier to deal with professional issues because, in the pregroup screening procedure, the potential group member can and should ask about the group leader's qualifications. The group leader can voluntarily offer information about his or her educational preparation and experience in conducting groups. Such professional disclosure is considered a must at this point in group formation (ASGW, 1998).

Personal information about the group leader's style in sessions is also important (Trotzer, 2007). The leader's style may incorporate humor, self-disclosure, confrontation, or other helping modalities. The leader's style and personality are important aspects of the group for the potential member to consider. If the potential group member does not think that the group leader is one with whom he or she can comfortably work, then it is best to find another group to join.

TASKS OF THE BEGINNING GROUP

Group leaders and members have varied tasks to accomplish during the first sessions of a group, including these: (a) dealing with apprehension, (b) reviewing members' goals and contracts, (c) specifying more clearly or reiterating group rules, (d) setting limits, and (e) promoting a positive interchange among members so they will want to continue (Weiner, 1984). Failure to accomplish any of these tasks may result in the group not functioning properly. Each of these tasks is examined individually.

Dealing with Apprehension

Apprehension is synonymous with anxiety. Too much or too little anxiety inhibits the performance of the group and its members (Yalom, 2005). Therefore, it is appropriate that group members and leaders have a moderate amount of apprehension when they begin a group. It helps them key in on what they are experiencing and what they want to do. Apprehension differs in psychotherapeutic and psychoeducational groups, in which there is an individual focus to the apprehension, and task/work groups, in which there is a group focus to the apprehension. For example, in a therapy group, Ellen may be anxious about whether others will see her as capable, whereas in a task group she may be anxious about whether the group can perform its assignment.

It is helpful, and sometimes necessary, after each group session for group leaders to deal with any misunderstandings that may have arisen because of anxiety. For example, if James is berating himself in front of his counseling group for being defensive when asked a question about his attitudes toward race, then the leader may say, "James, I hear you are concerned about two aspects related to the question Jan asked you about race. One is your verbal answer; the other, your failure to live up to your own expectations. I wonder what feelings got in the way of your handling of Jan's question." Such an observation and invitation give James a chance to deal with his emotions, especially his apprehension about saying the right words and being perfect. By clarifying what has happened, James and the group as a whole are able to move on.

Reviewing Goals and Contracts

Goals are specific objectives that an individual or the group wishes to accomplish. Group goals are announced at the time a group proposal is formulated and again during the pregroup interview. Group members should keep these objectives in mind throughout the group process. Likewise, individual goals are worked out in the pregroup screening session and are consistent with the group's overall goals. In counseling, psychoeducation, and task/work groups, such goals may have a universal quality about them, for example, understanding careers. In psychotherapy groups, especially with individuals in severe distress, the goals and contracts may vary widely. For example, such groups may contain members who are trying to resolve grief as well as those who are attempting to overcome depression.

A thorough way of clarifying group and individual goals is to have the group leader restate the purpose of the group during the first session and have each member elaborate on his or her goals. In some cases and with some theories (e.g., Gestalt, behaviorism,

As a member of this group, I, John Smith, make this contract to achieve the following goals.

What (i.e., goal)	How	When	Where
(1) share my thoughts	verbal	each session	in group
	verbal	each day	home
	verbal	each class	school
(2) eat healthy	choice	each meal	everywhere
(3) exercise	discipline	each day	home
(4) control anger	choice	each time	home
	choice	each time	in group

_____John Smith_____   _____January 31, 2007_____
signature   date

Figure 5.2

Sample contract on goals for an individual group member.

transactional analysis), members are asked to formulate a **contract** (i.e., an agreement of what will be done and when) (Corey, 2004; Donigian & Hulse-Killacky, 1999). A written contract helps members specify what, how, when, and where they will work to make changes related to their goals (see Figure 5.2).

However, as important as it is to formulate and verbalize goals, "simply asking members to write about their group or asking members to write specific goals prior to the beginning group are not sufficient to influence group process, perceptions of involvement, or ability to give feedback significantly" (Bridbord, DeLucia-Waack, Jones, & Gerrity, 2004, p. 301). It is in the verbalization and feedback interaction that goals tend to be clarified and strengthened.

Specifying Group Rules

Rules are the guidelines by which groups are run. They are established both before and during the group process. In pregroup screening sessions, leaders take the initiative in setting up rules. For example, most groups have rules set by the leader, such as no physical violence, no drugs, and attendance at all meetings. Rules should be stated in a positive rather than a negative way; thus, "No physical violence" is better expressed as "Members will respect the physical and psychological space of others at all times."

During the first session of the group and afterward, members make contributions to rules by which the group will abide, for example, "Smoking will be permitted outside the group room but not during the group session." It is important to formulate a rationale behind every group rule rather than to set rules in an arbitrary and "thou shall not" manner that invites violations and game playing (Yalom, 2005).

One rule that is usually agreed to, but difficult to enforce, is **confidentiality**—the explicit agreement that what is said in the group will stay in the group. It should be noted here that confidentiality is the "ethical cornerstone" of group counseling and psychotherapy (Plotkin, 1978). It is also a valued component of many task/work and psychoeducational groups, for it is "a prerequisite for the development of group trust, cohesion, and productive work" (Gazda, 1989, p. 303). However, confidentiality is sometimes violated, either intentionally or unintentionally. At the beginning of the group, members and leaders should review possible ways that confidentiality might be violated, including revealing identification information about group members or talking about group interactions outside of the group.

Leaders also need to be sure of their responsibilities regarding confidentiality, for example, protecting group members' files or computer records and erasing or destroying audiotapes and videotapes after they have been used to critique group progress. Leaders often take responsibility for keeping confidences by reviewing group codes of ethics and legal precedents. They usually do so outside the presence of the group. However, the extent to which leaders go to maintain confidence may be productively discussed in the group itself, especially if members raise issues pertaining to it.

When breaches of confidentiality occur, they disrupt the functioning of the group and promote distrust among group members. Therefore, it is crucial that group rules or procedures be in place to deal with such possibilities. The group that can agree in the initial session on the nature of rules and the consequences for breaking them is far ahead of the group that bypasses this procedure.

Setting Limits

Limits are the outer boundaries of a group in regard to behaviors that will be accepted within the group. They are set both explicitly and implicitly in group settings. Explicitly, these limits take the form of rules regarding acceptable behaviors and procedures related to time (Napier & Gershenfeld, 2004). When members violate an explicit limit, the group corrects them. For example, if Kathy tells Connie what Louise said in confidence in a group counseling session, then Kathy may be dismissed from the group, asked to apologize to Louise, or taken to task by members about the seriousness of what she did.

Implicit limits are more subtle and involve such actions as the attention of the leader to a particular member or the verbal reinforcement or discouragement of certain content topics (Jacobs et al., 2006). For example, the leader may instruct group members who ramble on about their families: "Keep your comments about past family matters brief and to the point so the group can help you." The leader may also use eye contact to encourage or suppress dialogue. Skilled group leaders use their power of facilitating and setting limits in both direct and indirect ways.

Promoting a Positive Interchange Among Members

Promoting a positive interchange among members of a group is initially the task of the group leader. If positive interchanges among group members can be facilitated, then group members will begin to share openly with one another, and the group atmosphere will be enhanced.

The leader can establish a positive tone by (a) being enthusiastic, (b) drawing out members, (c) holding the focus on interesting topics, (d) shifting the focus when the topics are irrelevant or interesting to only a couple of members, and (e) cutting off any hostile or negative interactions (Jacobs et al., 2002). If such a productive tone is not created, then group members may drop out, close up, or attack each other.

Another way to promote a positive interchange within the group is to use **interactive journal writing**. In this process, members keep logs of their thoughts, feelings, impressions, and behaviors within a group and exchange them in all directions—members to leaders, members to members, and leader to members (Parr, Haberstroh, & Kottler, 2000). When conducted so that members are well prepared for it, this type of process may promote group cohesiveness, trust, altruism, catharsis, hope, and self-understanding. It can be used in all stages of a group.

RESOLVING POTENTIAL GROUP PROBLEMS IN FORMING

A number of problems can occur during the formation of a group and afterward. Some of these difficulties involve people; others are related to procedures. One of the best ways to handle potential group problems is to prevent them. Prevention involves following the steps for forming the group already mentioned in this chapter. When prevention is not possible, the leader and group can work to bring about resolution. Member interaction patterns that are particularly troublesome are addressed first in this section, then initial group procedures.

People Problems

Despite careful screening, some group members display difficult behaviors early in the group process. Those who cause the most concern, especially in counseling groups, are individuals in the group who monopolize, withdraw, intimidate, verbally ventilate, focus on others, seduce, or show intolerance (Edelwich & Brodsky, 1992). **Subgroups** (i.e., cliques of members who band together) may also be troublesome. Sometimes, group leaders will become too involved in the content of what is being expressed in the group and not notice interactional patterns. By concentrating on the styles of different group members, however, leaders are better able to plan and lead future sessions. Seven common membership roles often displayed during the first session are covered here, along with the problem of subgroups. In dealing with people problems, group leaders are advised to avoid labeling individuals. The tendency that goes with labels is to stereotype individuals and to perceive situations as always falling within a certain behavioral range (Kline, 1990).

Manipulators

Members who are **manipulators** are characterized by their subtle and not-so-subtle use of feelings and behaviors to get what they want. Often they are angry and bring into the group unresolved life problems centering on control. For example, Jose, in his manipulator role, may say to the group, "If you're not going to give me what I want, then I'm leaving this group."

Reframing, conceptualizing potentially destructive acts in a positive way, may help manipulative individuals. For example, the leader may say to Leonardo after he has falsely and vigorously accused the group of breaking confidentiality, "Sounds like what you want from this group is specific help in learning how to trust them." The group leader or members may also intervene by blocking manipulating actions, such as threatening or pleading. At the beginning of a group, manipulators will often struggle with group leaders for control. They should not be allowed to usurp the leader's function, or the group will fail.

Resisters

Resisters are also often angry or frustrated and bring these feelings with them to the group. They do not participate in group exercises or tasks and act as barriers to helping the group form. For example, Brandy may say to the group, "I don't see any sense in telling you how I feel. That won't really help me."

Leaders can help resistant group members build trust in the group by inviting them to participate but not insisting that they do. This is an affirmation approach and allows resisters and leaders a chance to explore this behavior later (Larrabee, 1982). A second way of working with these individuals is to confront and interpret in a reflective manner what is happening with them (Vriend & Dyer, 1973). For instance, in the previous example, a group leader may say to Brandy, "I hear you have been disappointed with the groups in which you have previously participated. They have not been very productive for you." Often the feelings of resistant members are dealt with best in the working stage of the group.

Monopolizers

People who are **monopolizers** dominate the conversation in a group and do not allow other members a chance to verbally participate. Monopolizers initially offer group members relief because they focus attention on themselves and away from everyone else. These individuals are dealing with underlying anxiety but often become sources of irritation for other group members. One soliloquy does not a monopolizer make, so anxious members should not be characterized as exhibitors of this behavior too early. At the same time, members who display this pattern from the beginning need the help of the leader and other members to realize how certain behaviors hurt their interpersonal relationships and which other actions they could take to improve them. The sooner the nonproductive talk of the monopolist is addressed, the more productive an outcome can be reached (Ohlsen et al., 1988). The technique of cutting off, highlighted later in this chapter, is an excellent way to deal with monopolists.

Silent Members

Silent members may or may not become involved with the group. Sometimes, silence is used to cover hostility (Ormont, 1984). Members who are silent are often nonassertive, reflective, shy, or just slow in assessing their thoughts and feelings. The best way to determine the meaning of silence is to give a person a chance to respond, such as answering a question, and to notice what happens. A simple question such as "What do you think about what other group members have been saying?" is often enough to draw a silent member into the group.

Acceptance of silence by the group leader and the creation of opportunities by the leader for silent members to become more involved usually rectify any negative impact that may be associated with these individuals or this behavior. If a group member remains silent throughout the group experience, then he or she will probably not get as much from the process as more active members (Conyne & Silver, 1980).

Users of Sarcasm

Persons who express themselves through **sarcasm** differ from those who are outwardly angry. **Users of sarcasm** mask their feelings through the use of clever language that has a biting humor. For instance, the sarcastic member may say, "Oh, joy, now I get to tell you about how I feel. Isn't that just thrilling!"

The group leader can help the sarcastic member work on expressing anger more directly. This skill is accomplished by identifying what is happening in the group member's life and by having the group member explore what the behavior means for him or her both now and where it was learned. The leader may also invite other group members to give the sarcastic member feedback on how they respond to sarcastic ways of relating.

CASE EXAMPLE: Irksome Erika

Erika entered the psychotherapy group because she was unhappy with her life. She thought it would be easy to change, but after four weeks she became skeptical. She expressed her feelings through belittling other members. For example, she would say: "Oh my, has Cora gotten cold feet?" or "Oscar, aren't you filled with confidence today! I can just see it oozing out of your skin.'

When Erika did not stop these kinds of remarks, the group jumped in to confront her. For instance,

Blanche told Erika: "I don't think your comments are helpful to you, the group, or the person you are addressing them to. They just have a bitter flavor about them."

Although Erika did not change herself quickly, she did begin to soften her tone after a couple of weeks.

What might you have said to her? What else might have been helpful to her?

Diagnostic Analyzers

Individuals who have a passing knowledge of psychology or mental illness may attempt to diagnose or explain other group members' problems in clinical terms. These people get caught up in thinking that everyone in the group has a deep-seated problem that can and should be explained by using the *Diagnostic and Statistical Manual (DSM)*. Their belief is that once an explanation of a behavior is given, group members will act differently. Thus diagnostic analyzers are quick to provide cures and an abundance of answers and explanations to others. They focus on solving other people's problems.

The group leader can help counter this tendency and assist the diagnostic analyzer by pointing out that everyone has difficulties and that only those with extreme troubles are diagnosed by DSM standards. More importantly, the leader can assist the analyzer by having this group member focus on what he or she would like to get out of or take away from the group. This type of personal gain and centering can aid the analyzer in realizing that he or she has more to get from the group than is possible by concentrating on others.

Focusers on Others

This final category of behavior involves **focusers on others**—those who become self-appointed group "assistant leaders" by questioning others, offering advice, and acting as if they did not have any problems. These individuals are often challenged by group members and can be helped to overcome this other-focused behavior by being taught that self-disclosure is more helpful to most people than a style devoid of personal involvement. They may also be given permission during this stage of the group to make wishes for themselves. For instance, the leader may ask, "Latoya, if you could have some new traits for yourself, what would they be?" In essence, other-focused group members must be helped to realize the value of becoming personally committed to the group.

Overall, it is important that group members be given time to express themselves and not be labeled or stereotyped early in the group process. Leaders must also trust their feelings and reactions in regard to difficult group members. In some instances, a difficult group member may have to be removed from the group, but this measure is a last-resort strategy (Kline, 1990). Such a process creates anxiety in other members about whether they might also be removed. Before ever taking such a step, the leader needs to try to help the group help itself by working through thoughts and feelings about certain behaviors. Allowing group members to give and receive feedback enables them to obtain insight and change the troublesome and disruptive behavior. In short, "the presence of 'problem members' is a golden opportunity to facilitate group development and move the group to greater levels of intimacy and heightened functioning" (Kline, 1997, p. 95).

Subgroups

Group leaders may help prevent the formation of subgroups by focusing on the uniqueness of each individual and his or her connectedness with the group as a whole. Leaders may also discourage the formation of subgroups by making their expectations known in regard to such groups in the screening interview, pregroup training, and the initial group session. When subgroups do develop, however, they must be dealt with directly, or they may have a deleterious effect on the group member interaction. Trotzer (2007) describes three ways of handling subgroup behavior (outside of prevention):

1. "Bring all coalescing, colluding, and subgrouping behavior that occurs in the group to the group's attention." For example, point out that John, Jim, and Mary seem to be acting as a team on their own and not with the other members of the group.
2. "Establish a guideline and expectation that the group be informed about extra group activities among members." In such a case, one of the group rules can be that all meetings of group members outside the regular schedule of the group be reported to the group at large before sessions begin.
3. "As a group leader, do not collude with subgroups overtly or covertly by not disclosing what you perceive and/or know about the subgroup." If a group leader remains silent on realizing that a subgroup has formed, he or she is hurting the group as a whole. Speaking out may risk alienating members of the subgroup for a while, but not doing so poses an even greater risk of losing the group as a whole.

Group Procedural Problems

Both the group leader and members often feel anxiety, awkwardness, and anticipation at the beginning of an initial group session. Because every group is different, even veterans of group experiences may feel some apprehension. Most group members will try to put on their best behavior and be friendly and positive, but potential problems may arise at certain points. The best way to deal with these areas is to prevent them from developing. At other times, however, corrective measures may need to be taken.

Opening the Group

Beginning the first group session is often a difficult experience, especially for the novice leader. It is what Donigian and Hulse-Killacky (1999) describe as a **critical incident in the life of the group** (i.e., an event that has the power to shape or influence the group positively or negatively). How it is handled can make a major difference in what happens later in the group. Some practitioners, such as Coulson (1972, 1974), choose to begin a group in silence, but most group leaders are more structured. They have general openings, or leads, at their command, such as "Let's get started" or "It is time to begin" (Carroll, Bates, & Johnson, 2004).

Along with these general leads, several other options are available for beginning the first group session. Jacobs et al. (2006, pp. 86–90) suggest eight different ways. Each is dependent on the style of the leader and the purpose of the group.

1. "Start with an opening statement about the group; then conduct an introduction exercise." This type of procedure is usually employed with psychoeducational or task/work groups, although it may be used in therapeutic groups. It involves the leader taking about 5 minutes to describe the format and purpose of the group and introduce him- or herself. This process is followed by a brief exercise, such as members introducing themselves.
2. "Start with a long opening statement; then get right into the content of the group." In this style, which is often used in educational and task groups, the leader begins by giving members an explanation of the group's content or purpose. He or she then quickly gets group members involved in the group without introducing them to one other because either the group is too large or members already know one another.
3. "Start with a long opening statement about the group and its purpose; then conduct an introduction exercise." This procedure is used when the group's focus is educational or task based. In the long opening statement, the leader reminds group members of their purpose and then helps the group get down to business by describing what the group is going to do. This option works best when the information given is interesting and informative. A mistake that may be made is for the leader to talk too long—for example, over 15 minutes.
4. "Start with a brief statement about the group; then get into the content." This opening is ideal for task/work groups in which members know one another and the group's purpose is clear. In this opening, members freely exchange ideas and suggestions at the initial group meeting.
5. "Start with a brief statement about the group; then have the members form dyads." In this type of opening, the purpose of coming to the group is clear, and

members have some comfort in being in the group. Breaking into dyads helps group members focus more on content or the purpose of the group experience.

6. "Start with a brief statement about the group; then have members complete a short sentence-completion form." The sentence-completion format is useful in helping members focus on the purpose of the group. It is employed in task/work, psychoeducational, and therapy/counseling groups when no introductions are needed.

7. "Start with an introduction exercise." This type of introduction is employed when group members have a strong idea of the group's purpose. This process helps members introduce themselves and immediately focus on the content of the group. A number of creative exercises can be used. For example, Lessner (1974) suggests that group leaders use nondidactic poetry, such as that written by Lawrence Ferlinghetti or A. R. Ammons, when they begin a new group. The selection is read aloud, and then all group members describe how they are like an image in the poem, such as a leaf, a rock, or a tree. They then introduce themselves to the group by stating not only their name but also an image with which they identify. Texts such as Jacobs' (1992) *Creative Counseling Techniques* are excellent resources for picking or modifying a procedure with which to begin. For example, Jacobs points out that props, such as cups and chairs, can often illustrate to group members what words alone cannot convey.

8. "Start with an unusual opening—one that grabs the members." The idea behind this type of beginning is to get group members' attention in ways that would otherwise not be possible. For example, a leader might stage a verbal argument with a co-leader on ways to effectively communicate. Group members would then be asked to offer feedback on what they saw. A discussion would ensue about communication and ways to do it effectively.

Overall, there is no single type of introduction that will work consistently for every group or every group leader. The style of introduction is largely determined by the interpersonal skill of the leader and the nature of the group.

◆ *Questions from Experience* ◆

Think of the groups you have been in during your lifetime. How did the groups that were most productive start? How did those you least enjoyed and profited from begin?

Other aspects of the group at its beginning that will be problematic if not addressed are structure, involvement, cohesion, hope and risk taking, and the termination of the session. Therefore, these processes are examined more thoroughly here.

Structure

Group leaders in the initial stage of a group must make decisions on **structuring the group** (i.e., running the group according to a prescribed plan or agenda). Those conducting task/work and psychoeducational groups will be much more direct than leaders of counseling and psychotherapy groups. The advantages of structuring a group are that it promotes group cooperation, lessens anxiety, highlights individual performance, and facilitates the inclusion of everyone in the group (Bach, 1954). Structuring may also give leaders confidence and help them concentrate on group goals. The disadvantages of structuring are that it may discourage personal responsibility and restrict freedom of expression. Unstructured groups, though promoting more initial anxiety and discontent, also ultimately create high group cohesiveness and morale (Trotzer, 2007).

Regardless of who promotes involvement, the structuring of a group is inevitable. As Corey and Corey (2006) remind group workers, the proper question is not whether a group leader should provide structure but rather what degree of structure should be provided. A major guideline for the amount of structure will be the leader's theoretical stance. Overtly and covertly, members look to the leader for structure and answers, as well as for approval and acceptance (Yalom, 2005). It is important that the leader not over- or understructure the group experience during the beginning sessions.

Dies (1983) has given some guidelines for proper structuring in the initial stage of group development. These ideas include an awareness by leaders that directly structuring the group in its early stages facilitates the group's development and may promote the establishment of trust and the accomplishment of goals. However, structuring depends on the type of group. It can include indirect modeling of behaviors by the leader as well as confrontation of actions. Once the group begins to work well, leaders who use a lot of structure ease up on this process.

Involvement

Involvement of group members, in which they actively participate with one another and invest themselves in the group, is necessary for first sessions to work best. Structured exercises, such as those proposed by Johnson and Johnson (2006), are excellent in bringing people together in a creative and enjoyable way. However, there is no instant intimacy or involvement of group members with one another.

During the first sessions, group leaders must facilitate member interaction. The use of structured activities is one way to accomplish this goal. By discussing specific concerns related to the exercises, group members are able to stop concentrating on group acceptance issues and start focusing on individual goals. Therefore, there is a place in some groups for these activities on a limited basis. In deciding how to get members involved, leaders should focus on the primary purpose of the group before they decide on a strategy for achieving this goal. The most productive groups are composed of members who realistically deal with themselves, others, and issues.

Group Cohesion

"The effective development of any group requires that members share an image of the group" (Hansen, Warner, & Smith, 1980, p. 492). Unfortunately, in the initial stage of group work, "members bring individual images of the group" (p. 492). Not only is a common identity lacking, but often group members are unsure of themselves, resist any directions from the group leader, or "play it safe" by showing a reluctance to join with others.

One way to break down this difficulty and build **group cohesion**—that is, a sense of "We-ness"—is to allow individuals to voice their concerns freely and fully. By participating in this way, members gain a sense of ownership in the group because they have invested in it. Another way to enhance group cohesiveness is through the use of the arts (e.g., drawing, photography, literature) in helping group members express their feelings and thoughts more clearly (Gladding, 2004; Shechtman & Perl-Dekel, 2000). Art techniques in groups are usually fun, nonthreatening, and involve self-disclosure. The participatory process also promotes a sense of openness, trust, and security in the group as a whole as well as in its members. These perceptions lead to positive group member interactions, such as cooperation on tasks, resolution of differences, and agreement on group goals.

Although group cohesion usually does not manifest fully until the norming (or identity) stage of the group, the seeds for its development are planted early. They are rooted in attachment, as members learn to trust and interpersonally relate (Pistole, 1997).

CASE EXAMPLE: Colleen's Cohesive Experience

Colleen was skeptical about being involved in a women's group. She was drawn to it because of her social isolation, but she was wary of it because she thought it would be too "touchy feely" and that all she would get from it would be an emotional purge. When she expressed her skepticism about the group during its initial session, she was surprised to hear other women voice the same concern. That made her feel closer to these strangers.

Colleen was drawn into the group even more when the leader asked members to draw a line with markers showing the emotions they were experiencing as they began the experience. Colleen used a bright orange marker. Her line was jagged up and down the page. When processing it, she was not sure if it represented anger, frustration, or nervousness. She laughed as she told the group, and in a good-natured way they laughed, too.

What do you think Colleen thought about the group after these two experiences? What else might you have done as the leader to have helped Colleen find her place in the group?

Hope and Risk Taking

Promoting hope is one of the basic "therapeutic" factors described by Yalom (2005). If members are hopeful that their situations can be different and better, then they are likely to work hard within the group. Leaders can instill hope during the initial sessions of the group in several ways. For instance, they can convey information to members about group process, validate commonalties among members, and accentuate the positive (Couch & Childers, 1987). They can also use humor or give general examples of how hope has been conveyed in other groups (Gladding, 1994).

If members are able to experience a sense of **universality** (i.e., commonness with others) within the group, then the group will feel more cohesive (MacKenzie & Livesley, 1983). They are then more likely to take risks that, when successfully completed, will add to their sense of accomplishment and attractiveness to the group. "The degree of risk should not be excessive at this point, or the disclosure too threatening to other members" (MacDevitt, 1987, p. 79). Therefore, leaders must strive for balance in the area of self-disclosure. Leaders who can facilitate the disclosure by members of limited and nonthreatening information in the early stages of the group are appropriate in what they are doing and on their way to conducting a successful group.

Termination of the Session

The termination of a group session is filled with many feelings—anxiety, relief, sadness, and joy. It is just as important to end a group session appropriately as it is to begin it correctly. Too often, not enough attention is focused on closing a session; a group leader may simply announce, "Time is up." Corey and Corey (2006) recommend that at least 10 minutes be set aside at the end of a group for reflection and summarization. Otherwise, group members may become frustrated and fail to gain insight into themselves and others. They also suggest that, at the end of regular sessions, group members leave with some unanswered questions, some reflection about their involvement in the group, some self-report about what they are learning, some concentration on what they would like to explore during the next session, and some feedback from others about positive changes in their behaviors.

The initial sessions of a group are crucial in establishing such a pattern. Even if a group does not make it through more than a few sessions, many group members may experience "considerable relief" because they are able to release repressed feelings (i.e., catharsis), see themselves as possessing commonalties with others (i.e., universality), find themselves caring about the fate of others (i.e., altruism), and experience hope about their personal futures (Zimpfer, personal communication, December 1989).

USEFUL PROCEDURES FOR THE BEGINNING STAGE OF A GROUP

No one way or technique is appropriate for all aspects of a group as it begins. The reason is simple: each group is unique. Yet, there are some universal group procedures that seem to work well in most groups, especially at the beginning of the group. Following are a few of these.

Joining

Joining is the process by which members connect with one another psychologically and physically. Joining requires that leaders and members exert some effort to meet and find out more about each other. Joining can occur in several ways. Probably the most common is for members to introduce themselves, stating their names and some brief background information. A more exciting way of joining is through an **icebreaker**—that is, an activity designed to promote communication between two or more people. Such an activity can take many forms. For instance, members can simply take turns stating their name and a favorite food or activity. Such a superficial icebreaker is appropriate in most task/work and psychoeducation groups. Counseling and psychotherapy groups, however, are better served when members go into more depth about themselves and explain their reasons for becoming a part of the group. They can do this in a straightforward verbal way. They can also do it more creatively by engaging in activities, such as "making bags" that are decorated on the outside with symbols of their life, for example pictures, and that contain within more symbolic information about concerns they have and that they will disclose when ready (Gladding, 2004).

Linking

Linking is the process of connecting persons with one another by pointing out to them what they share in common. It strengthens the bonds between individuals and the group as a whole. For example, the leader may point out how two participants are dealing with issues involving loss or transition. The leader may also help the group realize through linking sentences that one of the issues during the session has been the establishment of trust. In such a case, the leader might say, "I have observed today that some of you are struggling with a common problem. Henry, Alice, Alicia, and Ernie, you all have talked about being unsure of whether you can say what you really feel in the group. The issue of trust seems important and one that is shared."

Linking is employed throughout the life of a group, but it is especially powerful at the beginning stage. Through linking, group cohesion is developed. Some group workers consider linking to be development because, as the group progresses, more themes, interpersonal relationships, and issues tie the group together and facilitate a sense of interrelatedness (Trotzer, 2007). This developmental quality of linking is more likely to occur if the process is used from the start of the group.

◆ *Questions from Experience* ◆

Think of when someone helped you become aware of an interest or hobby that you shared with another person. What was it like for you to gain this awareness? What did you want to do with this knowledge?

Cutting Off

Cutting off is defined two ways. First, it is making sure that new material is not introduced into the group too late in the session for the group to deal with it adequately. For instance, if Janice, a group member, relates that she would like to share an important secret with the group and only 5 minutes remain in the session, then the leader may cut her off. The cutoff will most likely focus on the limited amount of time left in the session. In such a procedure, the member is invited to bring up the secret information next time, and the group can begin the session with it.

The leader might phrase a cutoff statement this way: "Janice, I think the group is receptive to hearing from you but is unable to because of the time. I regret that what you wished to share has surfaced so late in the session. I need you to save this material until next session so we can deal with it properly and give it, and you, the consideration you are due."

Cutting off is also preventing group members from rambling. For instance, if Mark begins to relate his life history to the group, when all he has been asked to do is briefly introduce himself, then the group leader may cut him off by saying something such as, "Mark, we will go into more depth about our backgrounds as the group goes on. Now we need to move on to the next person to make sure everyone has an opportunity to be introduced." By cutting Mark off, the leader keeps the group on task and teaches proper conduct to Mark and others in the group.

Drawing Out

The opposite of cutting off is **drawing out**, in which the leader purposefully asks more silent members to speak to anyone in the group, or to the group as a whole, about anything. For example, the leader might say, "Andy, we haven't heard from you about this matter." By using the drawing-out technique, the leader helps members feel more connected with one another. Drawing out also helps members invest more in the group as well as recognize their thoughts. At the same time, other group members receive valuable information about the person who is being drawn out. This technique is particularly appropriate for group members who tend to be introverted or reflective.

Clarifying the Purpose

Sometimes members unintentionally bring up material that is not appropriate for a beginning session or the overall purpose of the group. In such situations, the leader should **clarify the purpose** of the group with the individuals and the group as a whole, the stage the session has reached, or which behavioral interactions are appropriate. For example, the group leader may say, "Frank, your comments are quite interesting, but I am not sure where you are going with them in regard to the topic we have been dealing with. Remember, in this group we are focusing on improving our interpersonal communication skills."

SUMMARY AND CONCLUSION

Beginning a group is a major undertaking filled with complex tasks. Group leaders can be overwhelmed by all the demands associated with this responsibility if they are not prepared properly. Therefore, carefully prepared proposals and selection of group members are musts if the group is to be successful. These processes take time and effort but are likely to pay off for the leader in such ways as receiving approval from colleagues, obtaining appropriate group members, gaining clarity on group and individual goals, and ensuring as much as possible confidentiality and proper procedure. Groups that begin well are more likely ultimately to do well.

Group leaders need to be prepared for developmental and unexpected events within the group, such as members who play certain roles and processes that contribute positively or negatively to group and individual growth. Structuring the group and confronting problems when they occur are important for an overall successful outcome. There is no way to know exactly what will happen when, but group leaders who have a knowledge about how to open and close first group sessions, as well as how to help group members get what they both want and need, are valuable resources whose importance cannot be underestimated.

CLASSROOM EXERCISES

1   Draw up a proposal for a group you would like to lead following the model presented in this chapter. Present it to three other people in a small group of four and elicit their feedback about ways to improve your ideas. Take turns listening to others in the group and making positive suggestions to them on ways to refine what they are proposing.

2   Using seven volunteer class members, assign one to play the role of the group leader who will screen the others as potential group members for a personal growth group. Have the leader interview members individually and in subgroups of two or three. Notice which questions are asked and how the interview process differs on an individual and small-group basis. Then have the leader screen members for a task-oriented group. How do the questions differ? Discuss as a class what you observed.

3   Invite a group leader to speak to your class about how he or she conducts the initial sessions of groups and gets them off to good beginnings. Specifically focus on how the leader deals with the matter of confidentiality and troublesome group procedures such as those discussed in this chapter.

4   What ground rules do you consider essential for conducting an initial group session? How would these rules differ if the group were therapy oriented as opposed to task oriented?

CHAPTER 6

THE TRANSITION PERIOD IN A GROUP: NORMING AND STORMING

Ken Karp/PH College

In the midst of struggles, stagnation, and stress
  we gather as pilgrims on a journey
    to explore the territories of our minds
      and the spaces that separate us from others.
The air is tense with anxiety
  as we venture into the unknown.
Like the settlers of yesterday's time
  we strive to take in all we encounter.
Enlivened by a new awareness
  *we are moved to consider change.**

*From "A Restless Presence: Group Process as a Pilgrimage," by S. T. Gladding, 1979, in *School Counselor, 27,* pp. 126–127. © ACA. Reprinted with permission. No further reproduction authorized without written permission of the American Counseling Association.

Groups and their members seldom stay the same. The enthusiasm that is prevalent in the initial group meeting, for instance, usually wanes by the second or third meeting, and participants may experience a letdown. This type of behavior is to be expected. Another predictable development is the movement of members from talking about past history to concentrating on the here and now. The shift to an emphasis on the present may not occur without the leader's guidance, but in most groups it takes place on two levels—the personal and the group as a whole (Sklare, Keener, & Mas, 1990; Yalom, 2005). This event, in which members are willing to risk more and move past the superficial, signals the end of the forming stage and the beginning of transition.

The **transition period** in the group is the time after the forming process and before the working stage. In groups that last 12 to 15 sessions, this period begins in the second or third group session and usually extends for one to three meetings. In other words, the transition period in a group takes an average of 5% to 20% of the group's time. This period, which is a two-part process, is characterized by the expression of a number of member emotions and interactions.

Transition begins with a **storming** stage in which members start to compete with others to find their place in the group. This unsettling aspect of the group involves struggles over power and control that may be both overt and covert (Carroll, 1986). Anxiety, resistance, defensiveness, conflict, confrontation, and transference are frequent feelings that surface at this time (Corey & Corey, 2006; Gladding, 1994a). If the group successfully weathers this turbulence, then it moves on to a norming stage in which there are resolutions, the building of cohesiveness, and the opportunity to move forward in growth (Ward, 1982). The purpose of the group and the skill of its leader influence the general ebb and flow of these processes, but the personalities and needs of members and their levels of trust, interest, and commitment also play a major part (Jacobs, Masson, & Harvill, 2006; Zimpfer, 1986). Because every group is unique, leaders and members have to pay special attention to group dynamics and personal feelings to maximize the benefits from these two experiences.

In this chapter, attention is concentrated on how the qualities displayed in the storming and norming stages of a group (i.e., the transition period) are influenced (Tuckman, 1965; Tuckman & Jensen, 1977). Each group and group experience is different, but the development of the group involves the interdependence of task goals and interpersonal relationships (Napier & Gershenfeld, 2004). Characteristics associated with transitions in the group follow some general universal patterns, whether they are stage (development) or theme (issue) oriented. The overall patterns must be considered if the group is to effectively negotiate through this period and eventually be productive. The two predictable processes in the group's transition—storming and norming—have characteristics uniquely their own.

STORMING

Storming is a time of conflict and anxiety, when the group moves from **primary tension** (i.e., awkwardness about being in a strange situation) to **secondary tension** (i.e., intragroup conflict) (Bormann, 1975). During this period, if the group is functioning well, it works out its "threshold for tension" and reaches a balance between too little and too much tension. Group members and leaders struggle with issues related to structure, direction, control, catharsis, and interpersonal relationships (Hershenson & Power, 1987; Maples, 1988). Although frustration and noise sometimes increase during this stage, *quiet storming* in the form of avoidance may also take place. It is important that "the group and its members express and explore differences between and among members" if the group is to be productive (Donigian & Malnati, 1997, p. 64). Members need to work through past nonproductive ways of relating, create new repertoires, and establish their place in the group.

CASE EXAMPLE: Olivia Gets Stuck in Storming

Olivia is a new group leader. She has never read a book on leading groups or received supervision. Yet she thought it would be fun to form a group within her service club. For the first few sessions all went well as members bantered about as they did at their weekly meetings. Then when the discussions got more serious in regard to what the group would do to better the club, tension arose. Put quite simply, there are three competing ideas out on the floor and there is a lot of competition to see which one emerges as the strongest. The group now has three subgroups and a few independent thinkers. Tempers are beginning to flare just a bit, and Olivia is worried that someone may get either mentally or physically hurt.

What would you recommend she do? When? How?

Each group experiences the storming process differently (Rybak & Brown, 1997). Some may encounter all the problems associated with this period, whereas others may have few difficulties. A group's development may be arrested here by either dwelling on conflict or ignoring it and never move on to the working stage (Forsyth, 2006). When this happens, conflict becomes destructive, and disagreements spiral upward, "characterized by power, manipulation, coercion, threats, and deception" (McRoy & Brown, 1996, p. 12). Therefore, it is essential that the group leader help members recognize and deal with their conflict and any anxiety and resistance associated with it (Gladding, 1994a; Mahler, 1969). They may do so through either conflict resolution or conflict management.

Conflict resolution "is based on the underlying notion that conflict is essentially negative and destructive" (Rybak & Brown, 1997, p. 31). Therefore, the primary focus is on ending a specific conflict. For instance, the leader may ask Kevin and Opal to stop calling each other names or making absolute, general statements about each other. **Conflict management** is premised on the "basis that conflict can be positive" (Rybak & Brown, 1997, p. 31); thus, the focus is on directing conflict toward a constructive dialogue (McRoy & Brown, 1996). For instance, if Petro and Heather accuse each other of being insensitive, then they may be asked to show each other which actions they would like to see in the other.

When group leaders employ either a conflict resolution or a conflict management approach, the potential benefits of conflict in a group are numerous. For instance, conflict can open up relationship development in the group by highlighting interpersonal boundaries between members (Durkin, 1975). It can also help the group as a whole overcome resistance to change from receiving more information. Other positive functions of conflict that come from resolving or managing it include releasing tension, strengthening relationships, and reevaluating and clarifying goals (McRoy & Brown, 1996; Schmidt & Kochan, 1972). Satisfactorily dealing with conflict results eventually in a "degree of interdependence versus independence that is acceptable in the relationship between members and within the group as a whole" (Rybak & Brown, 1997, p. 31).

Storming has some central characteristics that determine which way conflict will be handled and how the group will progress: peer relationships, resistance, and task processing.

Peer Relationships in Storming

During the storming stage, group members are initially more anxious in their interactions with one another because they are afraid of losing control, being misunderstood, looking foolish, or being rejected (Corey & Corey, 2006). Some avoid taking a risk by remaining silent at this time; others who want to establish their place in the group deal with their anxiety by being more open and assertive (Bach, 1954; Yalom, 2005). For instance, Cheryl may remain quiet during storming and simply observe the group members' interactions. However, Tony may be verbally aggressive and express his thoughts about every idea raised in the group.

The concern for power is also prevalent during storming. **Power** is "the capacity to bring about certain intended consequences in the behavior of others" (Gardner, 1990, p. 55). The struggle for power occurs soon after group members have oriented themselves to the group formation (Yalom, 2005). Attitudes toward power become important because the ways in which group members deal with this issue influence how conflictual or cooperative a group will become (Johnson & Johnson, 2006).

Power within a group can take many forms. **Informational power** is premised on the idea that people who know more are able to exert control over situations, including those involving people. **Influential power** is based on the idea of persuasion and manipulation of others through convincing them that a certain course of action is correct. **Authoritative power** is predicated on social position or responsibility in an organization. Authoritative means, such as "pulling rank," may be employed to try to influence members of groups that include individuals of unequal status, such as those in task/work groups.

◆ *Questions from Experience* ◆

When have you seen any of the three types of power explained above displayed? When have you exercised power of any type, especially in a group? How do you feel about exerting power of any type? How do you feel when power is exerted on you?

The principles that operate in dealing with power are similar regardless of the type of power being expressed. At first, members will attempt to resolve power concerns in ways that resemble those they have used outside the group—for example, by fighting or fleeing. If these strategies work, then members will continue to employ them. If not, members will formulate new ways of handling potentially conflictual situations. For example, when Tracy finds that yelling at other group members does not influence them and make them respect her, she may try having one-to-one conversations or persuading the group that she should be respected by telling members stories about what she has done in the past.

Members' attitudes about trusting the group and its leader are also an issue during storming. There is usually a good deal of mistrust in others during the storming stage, based partly on lacking experience in dealing with the group and partly on resolving anxiety and power issues while moving from a superficial group toward becoming a unified one. Too much mistrust will hinder people in the group from becoming cohesive. However, blind trust uninformed by experience (e.g., telling group members your intimate thoughts before getting to know them fully) is also inappropriate.

Connected to the issues of anxiety, power, and trust among peers is the question of the quality of verbal interaction. Negative comments, judgments, and criticisms are frequent during storming as members deal with issues of control, conflict, and dominance in the establishment of a hierarchy (Maples, 1988; Schutz, 1971; Yalom, 2005). For instance, members may focus on the content of the message. In such situations, their responses would most likely be statements such as "I cannot understand why you allowed that to happen to you," "I don't think you were very smart in letting that occur," or "If I were you, I would have. . . ."

CASE EXAMPLE: Critical Carl

He swore he was only being truthful, but every time a group member brought up a situation in which he or she had been wronged, Carl pounced on the event like a lion on a gazelle. He was relentless in his criticism and judgment. Members either fought with him or stopped talking to him. Finally, several members of the group pointed out to Carl what he was doing. He protested but to no avail. It took considerable time, but finally Carl realized what he was doing and modified his behavior.

Why do you think Carl was resistant to changing his critical demeanor? What strategies outside of verbal confrontation do you think would help an overly critical person modify a behavior?

If all goes well during the storming stage, then group members come to understand themselves and one another better. They begin to develop empathy for one another, too. However, to make progress, the group must work collectively through its resistance to change.

Resistance During Storming

Resistance is best defined as any behavior that moves the group away from areas of discomfort, conflict, or potential growth. It appears to increase especially during the early part of the storming stage (Higgs, 1992). Forms of resistance are multidirected and aimed at discussion material (e.g., "I don't want to talk about that"), the leader (e.g., "You're the leader; you show me how to change"), other members (e.g., "I think Jenny doesn't like me. I'm leaving"), questions of control (e.g., "I don't feel safe in here and I'm not going to say anything until I do"), or the group in general (e.g., "You guys are a bunch of losers. I don't have anything in common with you").

Group leaders who are unprepared for such experiences may become defensive when this kind of behavior happens. In such situations, the group is thrown into chaos, and the leader may feel personally attacked or insulted. When this behavior occurs, responses by members and the leader are usually angry and unproductive. For example, Helen may say, "June, if you don't like this group and what is being discussed here, you can quit and find another group." June may reply by yelling, "You aren't in charge and have no right to tell me what to do!"

Some forms of resistance are more subtle than others. For example, group member behaviors may appear to be accepting on the surface but are really resisting underneath. The most prevalent forms of subtle *indirect resistance* are described in the following subsections.

Intellectualization

Intellectualization is a behavior characterized by an emphasis on abstraction with a minimal amount of affect or emotion (Clark, 1992). The person uses thoughts and a sophisticated vocabulary to avoid dealing with personal feelings. Such a process helps the member become detached from the group. For example, a psychotherapy group member might say to the group, "Many people think they are being threatened when others disagree with them." Unless this comment contains some personal feelings, such as "I feel that this group is rejecting me when members disagree with me," it is difficult to make a meaningful response.

Questioning

In interpersonal relationships, a question is often a disguise for a statement (Benjamin, 1981). If members are constantly **questioning** one another, then they are safe from exposing their true selves. Questions also keep the group focused on why something occurred in the past and thereby prevent members from concentrating on what is happening now. In a resistant counseling group, members may use questions such as, "Do we really have to talk about how we feel?" or "How come John is not saying as much as Susan about his past group experience?"

To counter questions, group leaders need to take corrective actions. One of the best strategies is for leaders to ask members to use the word "I" before beginning a sentence, such as "I feel nervous." A complementary strategy is for leaders to simply say, "Since most questions are really statements, I want each of you to rephrase your query as such" (Sklare et al., 1990). Thus, in the examples just given, statements would be "I do not want to talk about my feelings" and "I wish John would say as much as Susan about his past group experience." Through such approaches, members and the group as a whole are invited to examine their thoughts and feelings in a productive way.

Advice Giving

Advice giving involves instructing someone on what to do in a particular situation. Advice is seldom appropriate or needed in most groups (Sack, 1985). It prevents members from struggling with their own feelings and keeps the advice giver from having to recognize shortcomings in his or her life. In a resistant group member, advice may be general or specific, but it is usually not helpful. For example, Jan may say to Wanda, "I think what you need to do is to exercise more. Until you feel better about your body, you will never feel good about yourself." This advice may have merit but, because the members do not know one another well at this time, it will probably be seen as criticism and separate Jan and Wanda even more.

Band-Aiding

The cleverly named concept known as **band-aiding** involves the misuse of support. It is the process of preventing others from fully expressing their emotional pain through ventilating their feelings (i.e., catharsis). Band-aiders soothe wounds and alleviate feelings when just the opposite would be more appropriate. For example, in a psychotherapy group, Ralph may try to calm Jason physically and psychologically when Jason is shouting about the way he was treated by his parents. If Ralph succeeds in his effort, then he prevents Jason from releasing his feelings and thereby dealing with them. Jason may then continue to be angry and, at times, project his emotions onto others. This may result in extending the storming stage of the group.

CASE EXAMPLE: Band-Aid Bob

He had been hurt badly in the breakup of an intimate relationship, and Bob still carried the wounds. He thought he had joined a grief support group, but he soon found out he had become a member of a denial troupe. The members simply did not want to listen to or hear about pain. Therefore, Bob became more and more frustrated.

He wanted to get his feelings out. Instead, he was being blocked from moving on in his life.

What are some ways Bob could have handled this situation besides becoming frustrated and mad about it? When have you seen people or groups band-aid someone? What was the result?

Dependency

Group members who display **dependency** behavior encourage advice givers and band-aiders. They present themselves as helpless and incapable but refuse to listen to feedback. They are "help-rejecting complainers" (Yalom, 2005). For example, Joyce may say to Tom, "What would you do in my situation? You are more experienced than I am. I need your help." If Tom responds by taking charge of Joyce's life, then neither he nor Joyce is helped because Joyce becomes more dependent on Tom, and the two begin to relate as unequals in a one-up/one-down position.

Other forms of resistance, discussed next, are more direct and potentially more destructive.

Monopolizing

Monopolizing occurs when a person or persons in the group dominate the group's time through excessive talking or activity that is often irrelevant to the group's task. At other times, their points are pertinent but so full of unimportant details or movement that the group is unable to process what they have heard. In either case, this form of resistance keeps the group from working on either individual or group projects.

Monopolizers may be helped by (a) confronting them, (b) teaching them new skills to deal with anxiety (e.g., progressive relaxation), or (c) giving them feedback on how their old or new behaviors affect interpersonal communications (Krieg, 1988; Yalom, 2005). In some cases, the group leader may display a hand signal to remind the monopolizer that he or she needs to change behaviors.

Attack on the Group Leader

An **attack on the group leader** is probably the most direct form of resistance that causes groups difficulty. Many theories view an attack on the leader as an opportunity to shape new norms and enhance group movement (Donigian & Hulse-Killacky, 1999). It is, however, vital that the group leader not ignore an attack. Sometimes attacks are justified, especially if the group leader has been insensitive to members' needs. However, such is not always the case.

Processes that contribute to leader attacks in almost all groups are subgrouping, fear of intimacy, and extragroup socializing. For example, if subgroups develop in the group, then isolated thoughts and ideas may germinate in regard to the leader's competence. It does not take long for such negative thoughts to surface and be expressed. These difficulties and attacks can be prevented if members are screened, pregroup training takes place, and rules for the group are clearly defined in the beginning. For example, in a psychotherapy group, Zack may be asked to wait to participate in the next group being offered because he appears unable to think through situations by himself. When the leader has doubts about whether someone is ready for a group, it is probably better to err on the side of caution and deny the person a particular group experience.

When an attack on the leader comes, however, it must be addressed and dealt with immediately. Otherwise, the group will become unsafe for any risk-taking behavior and will disintegrate into a series of attack sessions in which members feel threatened and drop out (Yalom, 2005). In other words, *perpetual storming* will prevail. One of the best strategies for group leaders to use in dealing with attacks is to face them directly and attempt to determine the underlying variables that have led to them, such as unresolved feelings. It is best that the leader do this in a nondefensive and open manner. For example, if Ben, as the leader, is being attacked for not creating a safe and trusting atmosphere, then he may state, "As I listen to what you are saying, I'm aware that you would like me to do more. I'd like to know what you have specifically in mind. I'd also like to know how you would like others in the group to act so that you would feel safer and more trusting."

Task Processing in Storming

Task processing (i.e., ways of accomplishing specific goals) appears to regress during storming. No longer do members or leaders concentrate as directly on objectives as they did at the beginning of the group. Rather, there is a great deal of attention on personal matters, such as group safety, leader competence, trust, and ways of interacting. It is healthy that this "pause" in the group takes place, for it allows everyone the opportunity of reevaluating goals and directions. More important, it provides a chance for group participants to "look" before they "leap" toward the process of change.

A potential problem in this suspension of effort to accomplish a task is that someone in the group may be blamed, or scapegoated, for the group's lack of achievement (Rugel, 1991). To **scapegoat** is to project the group's problems onto a single individual instead of the group taking responsibility for creating and resolving its difficulties. If such an event occurs, then the group spends additional time and energy working on interpersonal issues that must be resolved before the group as a whole can get back on task. It is crucial that members and leaders take responsibility for their own actions at this point in the life of the group. For example, in response to Marc being blamed by several group members for present problems, Jean may say, "I think the situation we are currently in is the result of more than one person's actions. We have all contributed in our own unique ways to this situation. If we are going to help one another, then we need to explore what we have done up to this point and try to do some things differently."

If members can be helped by the leader and one another to express their feelings in relation to individual or collective goals, then scapegoating is less likely to happen, and greater awareness will most likely evolve (Saidla, 1990). This process is helpful in the eventual achievement of selective tasks and the healthy growth of the group and its members.

Working Through Storming

Several methods have already been mentioned for working through particular forms of problematic intra- and interpersonal group issues during storming. However, there are global and uniform means of helping the group as a body during this time as well. One way to help group members work through their feelings in storming is to use a **process observer** (i.e., a neutral third-party professional who observes the group and gives it feedback on its interpersonal and interactive processes). As Trotzer (1997) states, "The foundation for effective problem-solving and conflict resolution is effective group process . . . . Impasse and polarization arise with conflict when group process is defective or ignored" (p. 6).

By giving the group feedback as to what he or she sees occurring, a process observer can help the group become more open in acknowledging and constructively responding to tensions and anxieties that may be present in group member relationships. For example, the process observer may say to the group, "I have noticed that Rick and Darla seem to be struggling with each other regarding what the group will focus on today while the rest of the group is silent. This pattern has been going on about 10 minutes now. I wonder what is happening with the group?" Framing an observation in such a factual way allows all members of a group to hear it and allows members besides Rick and Darla to deal with what appears to be a covert conflict. By starting early to observe what is going on among group members, the members and the group as a whole can attempt to change behaviors or modify ways of interacting.

A second way to work through the storming stage is to use the process of **leveling**, in which members are encouraged to interact freely and evenly (Kline, 1990; Kottler, 1994).

In leveling, the leader draws out group members who are underparticipating, and those who are excessively active are helped to understand the impact of their actions through group feedback. For instance, if Tonya is always making a comment after each group member voices a concern or makes a statement, then the leader may intervene by saying, "Tonya, do you realize how your active participation in the group affects other members' abilities to get involved?" If Tonya does not acknowledge any awareness, then the leader may ask the group to help Tonya become more sensitive to how her actions are preventing others from becoming involved in the group. A slightly different strategy would work for Al, who is not speaking up in the group. An open invitation by the group leader might be, "Al, we haven't heard from you today. What's on your mind?" If leveling works well, then the verbal behavior within the group is modified so that members participate evenly. When everyone in the group interacts, issues that have the potential to cause conflict may surface and be resolved sooner.

Another method for working through storming is for group members to acknowledge what is occurring in the group independent of a process observer. If group leaders or members deny that the group is in unrest or even conflict, then confusion will arise. In addition, members will not trust themselves, take risks, or believe the leader. In most groups, members can handle honesty better than denial or deception (Gladding, 1994a). They may agree with Walter, who says to Michelle and Megan, "I wish you guys would resolve your personal disagreement so we can move on toward working on our goals." By facing the fact that storming is happening, members and leaders know what they are up against and can thereby give themselves permission to be less frustrated and display greater tolerance of what is happening. Acknowledgment also enables members to make plans and develop a greater sensitivity to the situation so that it can be improved.

A final global way of dealing with the storming part of transition is to get **feedback** from members about how they are doing and what they think needs to be done (Ponzo, 1991). The feedback process can take place in a formal or an informal way. Using **informal feedback**, the leader may ask members to give their reactions to a group session in an unstructured way at any time they wish. Such an invitation is likely to increase spontaneity and sensitivity. For instance, Bettie may say, "Oh, I just realized something I'm doing. Every time Patricia talks, I tune her out. She reminds me of my mother with whom I had real trouble. Yet, just now, Patricia, I heard your comments about your own pain, and I suddenly became aware that you are your own person."

◆ *Questions from Experience* ◆

Which of the strategies just described do you think you would employ in a group that was storming? Which would you not employ? Why?

Formal feedback is structured. It may be set up, for example, through the use of what is known as **rounds** (i.e., having each person in the group make a comment). In rounds, each individual has the same amount of time, usually 1 or 2 minutes, to say whatever he or she wishes. Through using rounds, especially those that are time specific, everyone gets equal "airtime," to give input and make suggestions. In formal feedback rounds, the views of the group as a whole are heard. Formal feedback may also include the use of **logs** or **journals** (i.e., members' written comments made after a group). Ideally, logs are written and read between group sessions by the group leader, who gives feedback to group members and even the group as a whole regarding specific and general comments. "Collected logs can be a robust diary of the entire group experience, documenting ups and downs, the progress or lack of it, and can sometimes serve as a map showing members' growth" (Riordan & White, 1996, p. 98).

Results of Working Through Storming

When the group works through storming, especially in regard to resistance, the group will take on a new dimension characterized by members making emotional space for one another and being accommodating. Additional changes will include "more plain talk, open risk taking, overt agendas, increased intimacy, greater appreciation for one another, more intense emotions, and an emphasis on the present" (Ormont, 1988, p. 44). Members may also decide to revise their goals or alter their style of interpersonal relationships as a result of working through storming.

Altering interpersonal relationship style is especially important to the group's future development. Often members enter a group with a limited response range. For example, in the area of conflict management, members may only know or feel comfortable using one or two of five dominant **conflict management orientations**: competing, accommodating, avoiding, collaborating, or compromising (Thomas & Kilmann, 1974). These conflict management styles can be characterized as follows:

- **Competing** occurs when individuals pursue their own concerns at other people's expense—for example, Heather insists that she be picked up from school at 5 p.m. even if it means others have to rearrange their schedules to do so.
- **Accommodating** happens when individuals neglect their own concerns to satisfy the concerns of others—for example, Anna gives up an hour of sleep each night so that she can fix breakfast for her suite mates.
- **Collaborating** occurs when individuals work with others to find solutions that fully satisfy the concerns of both—for example, the Brown family searches until they can find a movie that they all want to see.
- **Avoiding** is seen when individuals do not immediately pursue their concerns or those of other persons—for example, Sam lets his wish to be a pilot take a backseat while he checks out the reactions of others to his tentative choice of a job.
- **Compromising** is in effect when individuals attempt to find an expedient, mutually acceptable solution that partially satisfies both parties—for example, in peace negotiations, representatives from countries may have to give up some of the things they want in order to get a final agreement.

Although each of these responses has advantages (e.g., in regard to time limits, competing may work best), group members who are limited in their responses may restrict their ability to relate to all members of the group. Such a case would occur if Kenneth constantly challenged other members of his work group to "put up or shut up." By altering

Figure 6.1

Five conflict-handling modes.

Source: From "Constructive Management of Conflict in Groups" by R. C. Mitchell and R. R. Mitchell, 1984, *Journal for Specialists in Group Work, 9,* p. 141. © ACA. Reprinted with permission. No further reproduction authorized without written permission of the American Counseling Association.

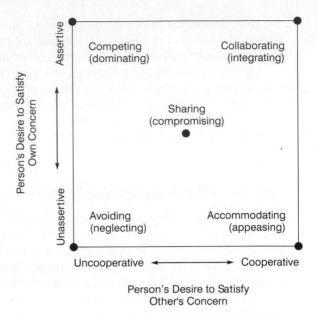

their style of conflict management, members increase their flexibility and the probability that the conflicts they have with other members will have a more positive than negative outcome (e.g., provide vivid feedback, motivate individuals to search for creative alternatives) (Mitchell & Mitchell, 1984) (see Figure 6.1).

Different types of groups will vary in the length and depth of their experience in storming and amount of conflict (Jacobs et al., 2006). For psychotherapy groups, the impact of the storming period on the group itself will be greater and last longer than for psychoeducational groups. In fact, psychoeducational groups are usually low in interpersonal conflict, and the duration of such conflict is relatively brief if it occurs at all. Psychotherapy groups, in contrast, are generally intense, and the storming period can be quite long. Regardless of the time and intensity, storming provides a time for group members to become realistic and active in examining their goals and working out relationships in their interactions with others. For most groups, the interdependency among group members and the stability of the group as a whole cannot deepen until intragroup hostility has surfaced, been acknowledged, and been dealt with (Bennis & Shepard, 1956). Therefore, the work done during storming is the foundation on which most groups will be built (Mahler, 1969).

NORMS AND NORMING

There is both a distinction and a relationship between the concept of norms and the group experience of norming. **Norms** are expectations about group members' behaviors that should or should not take place (Forsyth, 2006). "Group norms regulate the performance of the group as an organized unit" (Napier & Gershenfeld, 2004, pp. 101). Words commonly associated with norms are "ought, should, must, or better" (Shepherd, 1964,

p. 123). In some groups, especially those that are open ended, group norms may be unclear, confusing, ambiguous, arbitrary, and restrictive. In most groups, however, norms are clear and are constructed both from expectations of the members for their group and from the explicit and implicit directions of the leader and more influential members (Yalom, 2005). Therefore, most norms are based on input from everyone involved in the group and ensure group predictability and survival.

At the beginning of a group, norms may not be as clear or as well defined as they will be later. As the group develops, group members and leaders become more aware of the verbal and nonverbal rules they wish to follow to achieve their goals. They also become better acquainted with one another.

Group norming is the feeling of "We-ness," identity, groupness, or cohesiveness that comes when individuals feel they belong to an association or organization larger than themselves. The process of norming is often characterized as one of the major aspects of groups (Tuckman, 1965; Tuckman & Jensen, 1977). Like storming, norming is a crucial part of the group process because it sets the pattern for the next stage: performing (i.e., working). In the norming stage, enthusiasm and cooperation are often expressed (Hershenson & Power, 1987). In many ways, it parallels the forming stage in its emphasis on positive emotions. However, because group members are more informed and experienced with one another, they can concentrate on themselves and one another better in the group. Although some groups experience norming as a distinct stage in their development, others find the process to be continuously evolving. Two main aspects of norming are peer relations and task processing.

Peer Relationships During Norming

During the norming stage, several important changes occur in peer relationships. Among these are outlook and attitude. Group members usually have a positive attitude toward others in the group and the experience itself during norming. They feel a newfound sense of "belongingness" and "groupness" (Saidla, 1990). This positive mindset is likely to result in learning, insight, and feelings of support and acceptance. Members are willing to give of themselves and committed to taking needed actions. They expect to be successful. Peer interactions are manifest through identification, here-and-now experiences, hope, cooperation, collaboration, and cohesion.

Identification

A sense of **identification** is a "normal" developmental process in which individuals see themselves as being similar to one another (Freud, 1949). For example, in a counseling group, Allison and Lynn may come to realize they have many similar tastes, from food to clothes to reading materials. Identification explains why group members often become emotionally attached to their leaders and give them power. It also explains why some strong friendships begin in groups. Identification must be taken into account when considering the behavior of groups of all sizes. Those groups in which there is more identification with the leader or other members will be more cohesive and less resistant to change than those that are not. In norming, identification with others grows.

CASE EXAMPLE: Becoming Mobile, Agile, and Hostile

When I was in my 20s, I became a member of the United States Army. The training they put me through during the 6 weeks of basic training molded me into a person who thought of himself as a part of a greater whole. Although individually I was "mobile, agile, and hostile," I also identified myself as part of a larger group that was the same. My identity went beyond my dog tags. I was a part of the armed forces.

My experience is not that different from what you may have experienced in being a member of a club, art group, or athletic team. What words, slogans, logos, and mascots do you identify with and why? Gauge the strength of your relationship with entities with which you identify.

Here-and-Now Experiences

Although group progress can be charted on a session-by-session basis, the best way to help individuals and the group make progress is to deal with immediate feelings and interactions (i.e., **existential variables**). Conflict, withdrawal, support, dominance, and change all need to be acknowledged as they occur. Feelings from ecstasy to depression also must be addressed as they surface. Group leaders and members can link the present with past trends, but it is crucial that behaviors and emotions be recognized and worked on when they arise (Kelman, 1963). Some individual and group experiences will focus on what Yalom (2005) describes as personal issues about one's own life and death. Others will be directed toward obtaining specific goals, such as learning to accept others who differ or finding new, appropriate ways to interact with members of the opposite sex (Carkhuff, 1971; Rose, 1982; Watson & Tharp, 1981).

Hope

The experience of **hope** occurs on both a cognitive and an emotional level in groups. Cognitively, hope is the belief that what is desired is also possible and that events will turn out for the best. Emotionally, hope is the feeling that what one wishes for will occur. The importance of hope is that it energizes group members and the group as a whole. Furthermore, hope helps groups envision meaningful, but not yet realized, possibilities (Gladding, 1994b).

In norming, groups and their members need to hope and usually do so. Psychotherapeutic group members may hope, for instance, that they have the courage to overcome past tragedies, whereas counseling group members may hope they can purposefully plan a future different from their past. Task/work group members may also express hope in combining their talents so that new products can be marketed. Likewise, psychoeducational group members may hope they can learn to integrate new life skills into their daily lives.

Cooperation

Cooperation occurs when group members work together for a common purpose or good. During norming, group participants become relaxed and work better together.

Vying for position, which is so prevalent in storming, diminishes. In some task/work groups, cooperation increases because there is increased awareness of a group goal and members realize more fully what each can do for the other (Johnson & Johnson, 2006). In psychotherapeutic groups, cooperation is often the result of better understanding and communication worked out in the storming stage. In such cases, it is based on a hope for change (Weiner, 1984).

Collaboration

Collaboration goes hand in glove with cooperation. Members who think they can work in a harmonious, cooperative manner are likely to share facts and feelings about themselves and other matters with the group; that is, they collaborate. Furthermore, they are prone to work with other group members in sharing a vision and making that goal a reality.

Collaboration is probably seen most clearly in task/work groups in which members work on a tangible product. However, in counseling groups, collaboration is also expressed when members assist one member in obtaining a personal goal even when there is no observable reward for the rest of the group.

◆ *Questions from Experience* ◆

When have you seen a group work hard for the benefit of one of its members? Even when it appears only the member benefits, what else might be happening?

Cohesion

The last factor in the interpersonal process of norming, **cohesion**, has received a great deal of attention. It is "widely recognized as central to the success of groups" (Nitza, 2005, p. 274). Cohesion can be thought of as a sense of "Groupness" or "We-ness." Groups that establish such a spirit (and keep it) run harmoniously as a unit. Morale, trust, and solidarity increase, as do actions involving self-disclosure. The chief concern of the group during this time is intimacy and closeness (Yalom, 2005). In a cohesive atmosphere, emotional closeness becomes acceptable.

There is a difference between "total group cohesiveness and individual member cohesiveness (or, more strictly, the individual's attraction to the group)" (Yalom, 1985, p. 49). Yet, a positive correlation often exists between the two, with members of groups attracted to a particular group contributing to it. Group and individual cohesion can be measured by behaviors, such as attendance, punctuality, risk taking, self-disclosure, and dropout rates. Cohesive groups are more effective in their communication patterns, and members communicate with one another frequently. Cohesive groups also appear to have considerable fun together and yet are achievement oriented, especially on difficult tasks (Johnson & Johnson, 2006). They are able to express their hostilities and conflicts openly and come to some resolutions. Well-functioning athletic teams are cohesive.

The advantages and limitations of group cohesion are notable. On the positive side, it has generally been demonstrated that members of cohesive groups "(1) are more productive; (2) are more open to influence by other group members; (3) experience more security; (4) are more able to express hostility and adhere more closely to group norms; (5) attempt to influence others more frequently; and (6) continue membership in the group longer" (Bednar & Lawlis, 1971, pp. 822–823).

However, cohesion can be problematic. Among the potential difficulties with cohesion is that group participants may decide they like the positive atmosphere so much that they are unwilling to talk about anything that might be upsetting. In such groups, harmony is stressed over everything, and a type of **pseudo-acceptance** (i.e., false acceptance) prevails. This type of atmosphere prevents anxiety (Miles, 1957), but it keeps the group from progressing. Groups that finally settle down into the performing or working stage are those that can discuss negative, as well as positive, material.

Task Processing During Norming

One main task objective in the norming stage is for members to reach an agreement on the establishment of *norms,* or rules and standards from which to operate the group. Some norming is done on a nonverbal, mostly unconscious, level, but other aspects of norming are conducted verbally. Through norms, group members learn to regulate, evaluate, and coordinate their actions (Gibbs, 1965). Groups typically accept both *prescriptive norms,* which describe the kinds of behaviors that should be performed, and *proscriptive norms,* which describe the kinds of behaviors that are to be avoided (Forsyth, 2006).

Norms are value laden and give a degree of predictability to the group that would not be there otherwise (Luft, 1984). Often, they evolve so gradually that they are never questioned until they are violated. Basically, norms allow the group to begin to work, although not all norms are productive (Wilson & Hanna, 1986).

Another main, task-related goal of the norming stage is **commitment** (Maples, 1988). The commitment is to the group as a whole and its rules as well as to individual goals. The group and its members begin to operate on a higher level when commitment is a central part of the group. Eventually, participants come to "evaluate their performances and the performances of others in terms of accomplishment of the group's goals" (Napier & Gershenfeld, 2004, p. 194). This sense of commitment carries over and intertwines with the group at work (Schutz, 1958). It is at this point that the group and its members can begin to see the tangible results from their dreams and efforts. Groups in which members are most committed to one another are more likely than not to be productive in achieving tasks as well as successful in feeling good about the group experience.

Examining Aspects of Norming

Norming is generally characterized in terms of behaviors and feelings expressed by group members toward one another. Although it is difficult to measure the impact of emotion on the group, there are ways of examining behaviors during this stage that are both concrete and scientific. One way involves peer relationships. This method uses a research-based theory of personality and group dynamics that is referred to by the acronym **SYMLOG** (System for the Multiple Level Observation of Groups) (Bales, 1980; Bales, Cohen, & Williamson, 1979).

The SYMLOG model yields a field diagram that pictures how members of a group are rated on three dimensions: dominance versus submissiveness, friendliness versus unfriendliness, and instrumentally versus emotionally expressive. In addition, it yields a total of 26 roles found in groups. One way to use this instrument is to rate each group member's tendency to engage in any of the 26 roles on the instrument and then to summarize the scores along the three dimensions. For instance, an industrialist such as Dr. Z might be classified as UF (assertive and businesslike), whereas a talk-show host such as David Letterman might be UPB (entertaining, sociable, smiling, and warm). By using SYM-LOG, the interactional dynamics and personality of the group can be better understood because the homogeneous or heterogeneous nature of the group is clearer.

Promoting Norming

Norming can be promoted through actions by either the group leader or group members. Several human relations and specific group skills can be used in this process. Chief among these skills are supporting, empathizing, facilitating, and self-disclosure.

Supporting

Supporting is the act of encouraging and reinforcing others. Its aim is to convey to persons that they are perceived as adequate, capable, and trustworthy. Through the act of supporting, group members feel affirmed and are able to risk new behaviors because they sense a backing from the group. The result is often creative, surprising actions that are novel and positive. For example, in a counseling group, Trip (speaking for the group) may say to Burgess, "I, and we as a group, really think you can be more assertive in letting your spouse know what you want." The results are that Burgess comes into the group the following week and presents a one-person play called "How to Be Assertive" in which she humorously, yet sensitively, shows how she used the group's support to ask her husband for what she wanted.

Empathizing

Empathizing means putting oneself in another's place in regard to subjective perception and emotion while keeping one's objectivity (Brammer & MacDonald, 2003). It demands a suspension of judgment and a response to another person that conveys sensitivity and understanding. Again, during the norming stage, expressing empathy takes on special significance. Members need to listen to both the verbal and nonverbal messages of others in the group and be responsive. For instance, in a psychotherapy group, Nancy may say to Fred, "It seems to me you are sad. Your voice is low, and your eyes are focused on the floor." Such a message reflects an understanding of another person's voice and body signals and opens up potential dialogue and problem-solving avenues.

Facilitating

The act of **facilitating** involves using clear and direct communication channels among individuals. It is an activity usually assumed by a group leader, although members of the group may engage in this process at times. Part of facilitation is to make sure messages are sent and received accurately. The leader may say, "Tammy, when Mark said he was glad you had resolved your differences, you looked a bit perplexed. I wonder what you were thinking?" In this case, Tammy may shrug off the suggestion that anything was bothering her, or she may confess that it feels unusual for her not to be at odds with Mark. In either case, Mark, Tammy, and the group as a whole get the benefit of making sure these two group members are feeling connected so that underlying problems do not arise later to the detriment of the group as a whole.

Self-Disclosure

One of the strongest signs of trust in a group is **self-disclosure** (i.e., revealing to group members information about oneself of which they were previously unaware) (Jourard, 1971). Self-disclosure is enhanced when members feel safe. Through self-disclosure, barriers that inhibit communication among individuals are torn down. A sense of community and camaraderie is established. Leaders may model disclosure behaviors to show which materials should be revealed and how. It is best to first disclose materials related to individuals and experiences in the group. Through such a process, members' bonds become stronger.

Results of Norming

If the process of norming goes well, then the group will be ready for the next step in its developmental process—working. Members will feel connected with the group and will be able to concentrate on being productive, rather than protecting themselves. Just as Maslow's (1962) hierarchy of personal needs builds from the basics up, such is also the case in groups. When members feel secure and linked with others, they are free to begin cooperating and coordinating their efforts to achieve specific goals.

Norming gives group members guidelines under which to operate. They are, therefore, able to gauge how well they are doing individually and as a group. If discomfort is evident in the group, then members may realize that they or the group as a whole is regressing instead of progressing. It is from the baseline of norming that the group is measured or referenced.

Overall, norming has the effect of helping members in the group feel good about themselves and the group as a whole. Norming is like a breath of fresh air after the turmoil of successfully resolving the difficulties of the storming stage. Norming allows members to clear their minds, reassess their goals from a realistic perspective, feel good about themselves and the group's progress, and make new plans for the working stage of the group. Such processes help group members and groups as a whole renew their efforts toward achievement.

SUMMARY AND CONCLUSION

The transition period of groups is multifaceted and complex. If it is successful, then this time will be a takeoff point for the group's work. Ideally, transition is a two-part process. Group members resolve conflict in the storming stage of the transition period, and then they are able to set up and follow rules (i.e., norms) as well as form a cohesive bond with one another (i.e., norming). In such cases, the group ends the transition period ready to get down to work collectively and personally and to be productive.

In practice, groups are unique and differ in the way they develop because of their members, leaders, climates, and goals. A number of procedures can be enacted to facilitate the group's development and that of its members during this time. Some of these activities are as simple as recognizing what is happening (i.e., promoting awareness). Others are more complicated and require that the leader learn appropriate skills or enlist members' help and participation (e.g., empathy, support).

In this chapter, common aspects and problems of the transition period of group work have been discussed, particularly in regard to personal and task-related consequences. In the processes of storming and norming, group leaders and members must be cognizant of and emotionally attuned at all times to each other's intrapersonal and interactional patterns. If the overall outcome of groups is to be productive, then individuals and the group as a whole must make a transition from the more superficial stage of forming to the more demanding stage of working. To do so, they must learn to relate to one another as well as to plans and purposes.

CLASSROOM EXERCISES

1. Under your instructor's direction, have group members enact resistant roles: withdrawing, monopolizing, attacking the group leader, and so on. After about 15 minutes of role-playing, ask group members what they think would be helpful to them in overcoming resistance to specific situations. Discuss their ideas and the class's ideas in regard to dealing with resistance.

2. Discuss with a classmate and then the class how you, as a group leader, would promote cohesion. Refer to different techniques mentioned in this chapter as well as to other ideas or procedures you think would be beneficial.

3. Which types of self-disclosure have you seen in groups to which you have belonged? What impact did these revelations have on you? Discuss your experiences in a group of four. Then talk about how the act of self-disclosure differs for individuals in task/work groups as opposed to counseling, psychotherapy, and psychoeducational groups.

4. What part do you think hope and commitment play in the storming stage of group work? What other factors have you seen successfully employed in helping individuals reach a settlement of conflict or differences? Discuss your ideas and experiences with two classmates and then the class as a whole.

CHAPTER 7

THE WORKING STAGE IN A GROUP: PERFORMING

Scott Cunningham/Merrill

In the calmness of reflection
we examine the depths of our lives
and the purposes for which we have come together.
I am amazed that out of silence
and through a sharing of support
a whole new group has evolved.
In the process of working
we have welded an identity
from where we shall stand
and likewise be moved. *

*From *In Reflection* by Samuel T. Gladding, © 1993.

Members of successful, ongoing groups usually experience a number of adjustments and changes before they begin to work. However, after a group makes the transition from forming to resolving conflicts and norming, the **working stage** begins. This stage focuses on the achievement of individual and group goals and the movement of the group itself into a more unified and productive system (Maples, 1988).

The working stage is also described as the group's "performing stage" (Tuckman & Jensen, 1977) and its "action stage" (George & Dustin, 1988). It is a time of problem solving that usually lasts longer than any of the other group stages. In groups of all types, somewhere between 40% and 60% of the total group time will be spent in this stage. Task/work groups will generally spend a higher percentage of their time here than will counseling, psychotherapy, or psychoeducational groups because of their purposes and the ways they are run. The working stage is often regarded as the most productive stage in group development and is characterized by its constructive nature and the achievement of results.

During the working stage—as compared to the other stages—group leaders and members feel more freedom and comfort in trying out new behaviors and strategies because the group is settled and issues, such as power and control, have been worked through enough for members to trust one another. At this stage in the group's development, "therapeutic forces," such as openness to self, others, and new ideas, "are well-established" (Ohlsen, Horne, & Lawe, 1988, p. 88). A healthy group, regardless of its purpose, displays a great amount of intimacy, self-disclosure, feedback, teamwork, confrontation, and humor. These positive behaviors are expressed in interpersonal relationships among members (i.e., in peer relations). Other behaviors of the group during this stage are primarily focused on task-related endeavors, such as achieving specific goals. Both peer- and task-related dimensions of a group in the working stage are considered in this chapter along with generic core skills.

PEER RELATIONSHIPS

In the working stage of most groups, there appears to be genuine concern on a deep, personal level by members for one another. Participants are more *intimate* after control problems have been resolved (Schutz, 1973). Feelings of empathy, compassion, and care abound, and groups gradually grow closer emotionally. This interpersonal bonding, or **cohesiveness**, usually increases, even in task/work groups, as group members interact and understand one another better. This process has positive repercussions in terms of member satisfaction as well as individuals' feelings about themselves and the group as a whole (Perrone & Sedlacek, 2000).

Emotional closeness is especially likely to grow if group members can identify socially with one another and if they have been successful in working through their struggles together. An appreciation of cultural differences is helpful in this process. Whereas the previous stages of the group were characterized by concerns of being *"in and out"* (i.e., becoming a member of the group, as opposed to being an outsider) and *"top to bottom"* (i.e., establishing one's place in the group structure), the working stage of the group focuses on *"near and far"* (Schutz, 1966). Participants establish how physically and psychologically close they wish to be to others and behave accordingly.

Along with positive feelings about the group and the constructive behaviors of its members comes a greater willingness to self-disclose (i.e., reveal information about oneself to the group). Society generally discourages **self-disclosure** (Jourard, 1971), and in some groups, such as task/work groups or psychoeducational groups, it may be inappropriate for members to be too open. For example, if members talk extensively about family secrets in psychoeducational groups, they most likely have overstepped appropriate limits. However, self-disclosure has a place in most groups.

Self-disclosure involves more than simply talking about oneself. It is a multidimensional activity. It involves listening and receiving feedback as well as speaking. It is related to many other factors, such as the type of group that one is in, the level of others' disclosures, group norms, and timing (Morran, 1982; Stockton & Morran, 1980; Wilson & Hanna, 1986).

CASE EXAMPLE: Self-Disclosing Sally

The group Sally has been in for the past 5 weeks is a counseling group composed of women who have all been abused. Sally has had little to say, although she has been very involved mentally. However, in the middle of the session after LaToya has shared, Sally speaks up. She discloses to the group not only the abuse of the past but the reasons why she did not leave her situation earlier. It is something that is hard for her to do and yet something she feels "comfortable" in doing. At the end of her self-disclosure, Sally admits she was scared to bring up her situation. Yet, she says that the disclosures of others and the fact that she is feeling comfortable with others made her want to let them know about her situation.

What do you think is healthy about Sally's actions? What are some potential dangers or drawbacks?

The **Johari Awareness Model**, sometimes called the *Johari Window,* is a good representation of what happens in the arena of self-disclosure when a group is in the working stage (Luft, 1984). This model also illustrates how appropriate disclosure develops during the life of the group (see Figure 7.1).

The first quadrant (the **open quadrant**) contains information that is generally known to self and others. For example, Flo knows that the group is aware that she chews her nails. In the working stage, this quadrant expands. Members learn one another's names, stories, and likes and dislikes. With an expansion of knowledge, participants are able to interact more fully and freely with one another. Exchanges of thoughts and feelings move to a deeper and more personal level. What was previously hidden to others and even to oneself is now exposed and dealt with openly.

The second quadrant (the **hidden quadrant**) contains undisclosed information known only to oneself. This quadrant shrinks during the working stage, through self-disclosure. For example, group members become aware of the experiences others have had, such as the fact that Larry has traveled extensively or that Jackson studied abroad. This information would not be apparent unless it was willingly revealed. Members become increasingly comfortable with one another as a result of finding out more about one another. This comfort leads them to take further risks in revealing hidden secrets to the group as a whole, as Sally did in the example given earlier. When this process happens, members who

Figure 7.1

Johari Window.

Source: From *Group Processes: An Introduction to Group Dynamics,* Third Edition, by Joseph Luft. Copyright © 1963 by Joseph Luft. Reprinted by permission of Mayfield Publishing Company.

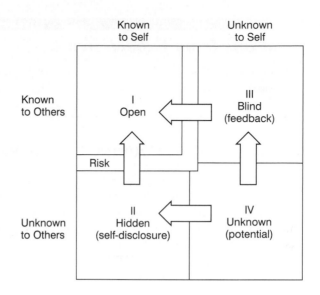

have opened up, and the group as a whole, are freer to explore other personal and interpersonal dimensions of relationships that were previously limited to them.

The third quadrant (the **blind quadrant**) is originally unknown to oneself but known to others when the group began. For instance, Tom may be unaware that his face twitches slightly before he speaks in the group, but everyone else sees it. In the working stage, the personal unknown area diminishes. Feedback is a key ingredient in this process, as members share their impressions of one another. There is a risk in giving and receiving feedback of this nature, for all comments may not be positive. Therefore, group leaders need to monitor and, if necessary, intervene to be sure effective feedback takes place at this time and throughout the group. Through sharing on a number of levels, members come to know about how they are seen and are able to interact on a deeper and more authentic level in the group.

The fourth quadrant (the **unknown quadrant**) is full of potential. It contains material hidden from self and others because of a lack of opportunity. As the group progresses, this quadrant shrinks. It may be developed in the group because of crises or opportunities. Basically, the possibilities and potentials that individuals possess lie dormant until opportunities arise to express them. In the working stage of the group, some situations develop in which, unknown to the group or the person, an untapped talent emerges. For example, Brenda, a shy group member, may suddenly take the lead when the group is in the midst of a dilemma, such as searching for ways to deal with a rival group in a positive way. Although unexpected, this type of emergent behavior is usually welcomed by all within the group because it represents growth.

Overall, in the working stage of the group, members become increasingly aware of individual participants and the world of each person. More sharing of past and present experiences and perceptions ensues. In addition, risk taking increases. The group and its members achieve growth and freedom. New discoveries open the group and its members to other insights and actions as well. A long-term, closed group membership is especially prone to display the behaviors just described.

◆ *Questions from Experience* ◆

When have you seen someone and the group they were in surprised by that person's actions? What do you think happened to trigger this behavior? How was it similar or different to the process that has been described in Quadrant 4?

TASK PROCESSES DURING THE WORKING STAGE

The major emphasis in the working stage is productivity, whether the results are tangibly visible or not. Group members focus on improving themselves or achieving specific individual and group goals. One way productivity may be increased is by encouraging equal member airtime through making the **rounds** (Yalom, 2005). This procedure has been elaborated on previously, but its importance as a process in a group that is working cannot be overestimated. Members who are given time during the group to discuss issues of concern to them will invest more deeply in the group with each session and will do the type of work that can benefit themselves and the group as a whole. For example, if in a counseling group Timothy realizes the group will help him in finding new ways to overcome his shyness with women, then he is likely to attend all group meetings faithfully and participate actively. The only problem with the technique of rounds is having enough time for all members to articulate and work on situations to the extent they wish.

A second way tasks are accomplished at the working stage is through **role playing**. In role-plays, members are given a chance to assume an identity that differs widely from their present behavior. Role playing is a tool for bringing patterns of behavior and their consequences into focus "by allowing participants to experience the situations concretely . . . gain insight into their behavior, and practice the skills required to manage the situation constructively" (p. 55) (Johnson & Johnson, 2006). This psychodramatic technique can be powerful in helping group members see and feel how certain actions will be experienced before they actually occur outside the group (Shaffer, 1997).

Trust and caring are vital in the role-playing process, and specific ideas about what the group member wants to accomplish are helpful. In a role-play, the participants set up an imaginary life situation and ask others in the group to play certain parts while they respond in a prescribed way, such as remaining calm. After the action is completed, the member and the group discuss benefits, consequences, and alternative ways of behaving in the given situation.

CASE EXAMPLE: Name-Calling Nanette

Nanette is an overweight, unkempt, and lethargic 6th grader. She is teased a lot in school. The counseling group she is in is working with her on controlling her temper. She is asked to play the role of being nonchalant when others poke fun at her. She pretends the words are like raindrops bouncing off a finely waxed car. She is in the driver's seat and can remain cool instead of revving up. Nanette finds her role refreshing and she is surprised that she can control her temper.

What other roles might Nanette play that would help her? How might she transfer what she does in a role-play to real life?

A group member can have a frustrating experience in a role-play and still benefit from it. For instance, Helen asked her psychoeducational group members to role-play a situation with her in which she confronted her boss about his rude and demeaning behavior to her. Although group members tried to assist Helen in their enactment of roles, Helen was not sure after the role-play ended whether she had found a way to address her boss or not. However, as she continued talking, Helen began to realize that, although she had not achieved all that she wished, she did feel some relief and confidence about the situation and had a base from which to continue.

Another task process that is prevalent in the working stage is **homework**, or working outside the group itself. Group members often find that they need to carry behaviors they practice within the group to situations outside the group. Although the group or its leader may not give members a specific assignment, they will often try out new skills and bring their experiences back to the group to process. In this way, participants receive twice the benefits they would otherwise; that is, they get to practice skills in a real-life situation, and they get to interact with the group about the experience.

An example of homework is a member practicing being calm when his colleagues in a work setting make demands on him. In returning to the group, he can not only relate how his homework went but also receive support and suggestions from other group members on future homework assignments. Homework generally varies in its intensity and importance. Sometimes, simple and less noticeable acts, such as calling friends, going to a meeting, or inviting someone over for refreshments, are vital homework tasks.

◆ *Questions from Experience* ◆

Outside of an educational setting, when have you had homework or given yourself homework? How did that work for you? How have you seen homework benefit others?

A final dimension that must be considered in the working stage of the group is **incorporation** (i.e., a personal awareness and appreciation of what the group has accomplished on both an individual and a collective level). When the working stage of a group ends, members should have a feeling and knowledge of what was achieved and how. Through incorporation, members realize the value of the group in their lives and remember critical times in the group regarding what they or other members of the group said or did. Incorporation prepares members to move on to the termination stage. For example, in thinking about the group as it progressed, Eileen was able to realize that she took risks in the group by disclosing information she had never revealed before. Instead of being devastating, this experience gave her a sense of relief and direction. She was able to take satisfaction in what she had done and began to see that she could accomplish goals outside the group. Her gratitude for the group and for what she learned as a result of being in the group increased.

TEAMWORK AND TEAM BUILDING DURING THE WORKING STAGE

Teamwork and team building are vital in the working stage of groups (Kline, 2001; Ward, 1997). A **team** is "a number of persons associated together in work or activity" (*Merriam-Webster's Collegiate Dictionary,* 2003). The outcome of a team effort is seen most graphically in athletic or artistic competition in which members of a group act and perform in a coordinated way to achieve a goal, such as scoring points or dancing in a unified and coordinated manner.

Groups sometimes function as teams, whether planned or not. However, selecting members of a group who will function best in a team environment ensures the best possible results. One way of selecting members is by using the **Team Player Inventory (TPI)**, a 10-item assessment instrument that denotes the degree to which individuals are predisposed toward organizational team-working environments (Kline, 1999). The TPI is the "only measure that is specifically designed to assess predisposition of individuals working in teams" (p. 110). Furthermore, the TPI is practical in determining whether "there are team members who view team work environments as primarily negative" as well as identifying individuals who "are positively predisposed to working in a team environment" (p. 110).

After team members are selected, the next major step is promoting a team spirit. This process increases the likelihood that a group will work together constructively. It is done through encouraging **teamwork** (i.e., all members of a group working together cooperatively) through team building. The process of **team building** takes time and may assume different patterns over time (Kormanski, 1990, 1999). For example, some teams may build through completing tasks together, whereas others may do so through extended group discussions. Groups that work to achieve consensus, promote interpersonal relationships, and minimize conflict perform best.

In psychoeducational groups, teamwork and learning are promoted by emphasizing how groups can achieve tasks that cannot be accomplished by an individual alone (Gough, 1987). For instance, if an academic class is given a long reading assignment that could not be covered by one class member in the time allotted, a study group team could come together and distribute the readings. Then each member could become an expert on an area that he or she would later teach the group when they reassembled (Light, 1994).

Teamwork is considered so important to many organizations that teachers from graduate business schools to elementary schools often break their classes into teams at the beginning of a term to help them to master material and to learn how to work cooperatively with others. A team can be a socializing as well as a productive experience. The founder of reality therapy, William Glasser (1986a), considers teams to be an essential part of his theory, especially as it relates to control within self and others. Teamwork and the team building that goes with it can also be applied to counseling and psychotherapy groups in stressing the importance of the interpersonal dimension in one's own growth and development.

Effective development of a team (i.e., team building) can take other forms as well. Maples (1992) has proposed one model of developing a group into a team. She premises her model on the assumption that group members trust one another and are motivated for success. Basic components of this model involve choice and ownership. Groups that make positive choices that lead to success do so from a stance of openness, honesty, compassion, enthusiasm, integrity, and a commitment to communication. The ownership of the group is achieved in such cases through patience, objectivity, personal responsibility, and investing energy in the group. Keeping focused in the present, being sincere, and at times being introspective or humorous are other factors that help the group achieve a sense of unity as a team. Maples suggests that groups also need **ice-breaking exercises** (i.e., introductory activities that link people together). Such exercises increase the group's awareness of one another or remind members of what they did in previous sessions.

CASE EXAMPLE: Bulldozing Barney

Barney believes that it is always best to get down to business as soon as possible. Therefore, when his task group comes into a room, he gives them an agenda and tells them what they are going to do. He then begins the meeting by going item by item through the handout. Barney's group appears to be unmotivated, and they are behind other groups at the same company who have had a similar assignment.

What do you think is going on inside the group? How do you think Barney is feeling? Thinking?

Ward (1997, pp. 115–116) has listed six other factors that either contribute to or distract from the development of teams:

1. *"Leadership style"*—A democratic style works best in building teams because of its cooperative emphasis.
2. *"Member maturity and motivation"*—The more of each, the better.
3. *"Group task or purpose characteristics"*—Some tasks lend themselves to cooperative work more than others.
4. *"Membership stability and group size"*—Irregular attendance is distracting, and having either too many or too few members prohibits the development of a team effort.
5. *"Time availability"*—It is crucial that group goals match time availability.
6. *"Organizational, institutional, cultural, and societal expectations"*—The setting in which a group is conducted will influence whether teamwork is valued, as will the backgrounds of those involved.

PROBLEMS IN THE WORKING STAGE OF GROUPS

Despite good intentions, some groups are more productive than others for a variety of reasons, including pregroup preparation, the composition of group members, the group's focus, and group leadership/followership interactions. Among specific problems that arise during the working stage are fear and resistance, challenges to leaders, and a lack of focus on achieving individual and group goals. These problems are expressed in numerous ways, such as intense emotionality in members, projection or scapegoating of a member, and lack of constructive participation. Focusing on issues outside the group, such as gender or race, or turning inward as a group to be protective (i.e., collusion) are also problematic and are considered here.

Racial and Gender Issues

Matters pertaining to race and gender are manifest in some groups more than others, but they occur in most types of groups in both subtle and blatant ways. The thoughts and feelings surrounding these descriptors of persons reflect societal attitudes in general. In regard to race, Rokeach, Smith, and Evans (1960) propose that racial prejudice is based on assumptions about the beliefs and attitudes of persons of a given race. Some groups may struggle or engage in high conflict because of racial prejudices among members. Other groups deal with racial issues through denial (Lanier & Robertiello, 1977). Individuals who hold stereotyped views and act accordingly are **culturally encapsulated** (Wrenn, 1985) and behave in a rigid and stereotyped manner (Ivey, Pedersen, & Ivey, 2001). Contact with others from different cultures in a group context often helps members become more aware of their racial feelings. It can have "the healthy effect" of making them realize their ethnocentric assumptions and limiting beliefs, "thus leading to a broader view of human nature" (Walsh, 1989, p. 547).

The same dysfunctional/functional and nonproductive/productive dynamic of prejudice and stereotypes may occur in regard to gender, too (Sullivan, 1983b). In such cases, the words *male* and *female* are highlighted at the expense of the concept *person.* The result is that males and females must learn new roles within the group that give them greater freedom to be flexible and competent. Sometimes others hamper this new learning, but it has a good chance of success if it is begun early in the group's development. Leaders must work with the group to prevent or limit negative outcomes among members by increasing sensitivity and decreasing the escalation of conflict (Korda & Pancrazio, 1989). Generally, the issue of gender is highly visible and dealt with constructively by group leaders and members as part of larger issues in the working stage.

Group Collusion

Group collusion involves cooperating with others unconsciously or consciously "to reinforce prevailing attitudes, values, behaviors, or norms" (Butler, 1987, p. 1). The purpose of such behavior is self-protection. Its effect is to maintain the status quo in the group. For example, in work groups, when subordinates agree with their boss to keep from being fired, they are engaging in a collusion process. The same is true in psychoeducational groups when students concur with their professors to receive a good grade.

Most groups experience some degree of collusion but, in extremes, group collusion prevents open discussion, critical thinking, and problem solving. Such closeness, and the conformity promoted by it, may lead to a destructive process that is regressive in nature. Janis (1972, 1982) has called this phenomenon **groupthink**. In a groupthink situation, there is a "deterioration of mental efficiency, reality testing, and moral judgment that results from in-group pressures" (Janis, 1972, p. 9). Forms of groupthink may become destructive and even deadly. Evidence of the lethal nature of groupthink can be found in the Bay of Pigs invasion of the Kennedy administration; the mass suicide that occurred in Jonestown, Guyana, under the leadership of the Reverend Jim Jones; and the Branch Davidian tragedy in Waco, Texas. In less severe cases, groupthink inhibits growth and represses individual and group development. For example, in some work groups, criticism of a new or existing product may be suppressed because of groupthink. Ignoring the groupthink attitude and expressing criticism may cause talented individuals to lose their jobs and influence in a company. The cartoon "Dilbert" regularly illustrates examples of groupthink.

To prevent group collusion from occurring to any great extent, group membership should be diversified. In addition, open discussion should be promoted, and goals and purposes should be continuously clarified. As a precautionary measure, some type of

devil's advocate procedure should be actively implemented. This procedure entails asking one or more members in the group to question group decisions with a firm skepticism before the group reaches a conclusion (Forsyth, 2005; Tjosvold, 1986). Such an approach is especially helpful "when the decision scenario involves high uncertainty (little predictability) but plenty of available information" (Chen, Lawson, Gordon, & McIntosh, 1996, p. 589). Interpersonal relationship skills should be strengthened as well. "Groups who wish to structure themselves to avoid faulty decision making are well advised to have impartial leadership and methodical procedures where they avoid overestimation of the group, closed-mindedness, and pressures toward conformity" (Schafer & Crichlow, 1996, p. 429).

CASE EXAMPLE: Danielle as the Devil's Advocate

Danielle is not very popular in her work group. She is always questioning. She wants to know what the expected outcome of an action might be, and if she does not get a specific answer, she will not cooperate with the group. Everyone in the group is tired of her "attitude" and they are now signing a petition to get her transferred.

Why do you think the group's action is a good or bad idea? What else might they do? What else might Danielle do to help make the group more productive?

THE WORKING STAGE OF THE GROUP AND GROUPS THAT WORK

Just as there is a difference in the dynamics that underlie the working stage of a group's development, there is also a difference in working and nonworking groups. For instance, members of working groups have a sense of cohesion and trust with one another. They work in the present and are willing to take risks in self-disclosing or sharing ideas. When disagreement exists in the group, members acknowledge it and deal with it in an open manner. Communication is clear and direct, and members use one another as resources. In addition, working groups are aware of the group progress and process. They accept responsibility for doing their part within the group in relation to either their own or group goals. They give honest feedback to one another without fear of reprisal. They are hopeful and secure within the group and are, therefore, able to maximize their thinking, feeling, and behaving capabilities. Corey and Corey (2006) have identified about 20 characteristics that compare working and nonworking groups (see Figure 7.2).

It is evident from examining their list that Corey and Corey believe leaders and members both play a vital, interactive part in the success or failure of the group. Research confirms such a view. Leaders who have prepared themselves and their members adequately beforehand are more likely than not to be successful. However, despite preparation, incidents may happen within a group in the working stage that cause problems. For example, the death of a loved one may influence a group member to focus on his or her internal agendas rather than the group's task. Likewise, an unresolved conflict between group members may break down the harmony and constructive nature of the group.

The following lists represent some basic differences between productive and nonproductive groups. As you study the lists, think of any other factors you could add. If you are or have been in a group, think about how these characteristics apply to your group experience.

Working Group	Nonworking Group
Members trust other members and the leaders, or at least they openly express any lack of trust. There is a willingness to take risks by sharing meaningful here-and-now reactions.	Mistrust is evidenced by an undercurrent of unexpressed hostility. Members withhold themselves, refusing to express feelings and thoughts.
Goals are clear and specific and are determined jointly by the members and the leader. There is a willingness to direct in-group behavior toward realizing these goals.	Goals are fuzzy, abstract, and general. Members have unclear personal goals or no goals at all.
Most members feel a sense of inclusion, and excluded members are invited to become more active. Communication among most members is open and involves accurate expression of what is being experienced.	Many members feel excluded or cannot identify with other members. Cliques are formed that tend to lead to fragmentation. There is fear of expressing feelings of being left out.
There is a focus on the here and now, and participants talk directly to one another about what they're experiencing.	There is a "there-and-then" focus; people tend to focus on others and not on themselves, and storytelling is typical. There is a resistance to dealing with reactions to one another.
The leadership functions are shared by the group; people feel free to initiate activities or to suggest exploring particular areas.	Members lean on the leader for all direction. There are power conflicts among members as well as between members and the leader.
There is a willingness to risk disclosing threatening material; people become known.	Participants hold back, and disclosure is at a minimum.
Cohesion is high; there is a close emotional bond among people, based on sharing of universal human experiences. Members identify with one another. People are willing to risk experimental behavior because of the closeness and support for new ways of being.	Fragmentation exists; people feel distant from one another. There is a lack of caring or empathy. Members don't encourage one another to engage in new and risky behavior, so familiar ways of being are rigidly maintained.
Conflict among members or with the leader is recognized, discussed, and often resolved.	Conflicts or negative feelings are ignored, denied, or avoided.

Figure 7.2

Contrasts between a working group and a nonworking group.

Working Group	**Nonworking Group**
Members accept the responsibility for deciding what action they will take to solve their problems.	Members blame others for their personal difficulties and aren't willing to take action to change.
Feedback is given freely and accepted without defensiveness. There is a willingness to seriously reflect on the accuracy of the feedback.	What little feedback is given is rejected defensively. Feedback is given without care or compassion.
Members feel hopeful; they feel that constructive change is possible—that people can become what they want to become.	Members feel despairing, helpless and trapped, victimized.
Confrontation occurs in such a way that the confronter shares his or her reactions to the person being confronted. Confrontation is accepted as a challenge to examine one's behavior and not as an uncaring attack.	Confrontation is done in a hostile, attacking way; the confronted one feels judged and rejected. At times the members gang up on a member, using this person as a scapegoat.
Communication is clear and direct.	Communication is unclear and indirect.
Group members use one another as a resource and show interest in one another.	Members are interested only in themselves.
Members feel powerful and share this power *with* one another.	Members or leaders use power and control over others.
There is an awareness of group process, and members know what makes the group productive or nonproductive.	There is an indifference or lack of awareness of what is going on within the group, and group dynamics are rarely discussed.
Diversity is encouraged, and there is a respect for individual and cultural differences.	Conformity is prized, and individual and cultural differences are devalued.
Group norms are developed cooperatively by the members and the leader. Norms are clear and are designed to help the members attain their goals.	Norms are merely imposed by the leader. They may not be clear.
There is an emphasis on combining the feeling and thinking functions. Catharsis and expression of feeling occur, but so does thinking about the meaning of various emotional experiences.	The group relies heavily on cathartic experiences but makes little or no effort to understand them.
Group members use out-of-group time to work on problems raised in the group.	Group members think about group activity very little when they're outside the group.

Figure 7.2 (*continued*)

Source: From *Groups: Processes and Practice, 4th edition*, by G. Corey and M. S. Corey © 1992. Reprinted with permission of Wadsworth, an imprint of the Wadsworth Group, a division of Thomson Learning. Fax 800 730-2215.

STRATEGIES FOR ASSISTING GROUPS IN THE WORKING STAGE

When groups are not doing well in the working stage, several approaches can rectify the situation: modeling by the leader (Borgers & Koenig, 1983), exercises (Corey, Corey, Callanan, & Russell, 1992), group observing group (Cohen & Smith, 1976), brainstorming (Osborn, 1957), nominal-group technique (NGT) (Delbecq & Van de Ven, 1971), synectics (Gordon, 1961), written projections (Hoskins, 1984), group processing (J. Donigian, personal communication, July 8, 1994), and teaching of skills (Toth & Erwin, 1998).

Modeling by the Leader

The **modeling** method is used to teach group members complex behaviors in a relatively short time by copying or imitating. Modeling depends on timing, reinforcement, the amount of positive feedback received, the view of the group leader, the degree of trust, and the amount of motivation for imitation. Borgers and Koenig (1983) stress that group members borrow from leaders and other members what they need to function better and become more their own persons. Leaders can promote working in the group by displaying behaviors congruent with this stage, such as self-disclosure, or by having a core of group members with whom others can readily identify display such actions. The latter strategy of having peers help peers is especially effective if the members who are modeling behaviors are similar to those they are helping in regard to age, gender, and background (Cox, 1999).

Exercises

Exercises involve less direct showing and more an experiential integration. "The term *exercise* is used among group leaders to refer to activities that the group does for a specific purpose" (Jacobs, Masson, & Harvill, 2006, p. 207). There are different views about whether preplanned exercises should be used in groups and when. On one end of the spectrum is a view represented by Rogers (1970), who advocates the avoidance of "any procedure that is planned" (p. 56). On the other end of this continuum are leaders who simply employ a series of exercises in their groups from group exercise books (e.g., Pfeiffer & Jones, 1972–1980).

A more moderate approach is using exercises in groups at specific times for specific reasons (Carroll, Bates, & Johnson, 2004). As Jacobs et al. (2006) point out, a leader may employ group exercises for at least seven reasons:

1. To increase the comfort level
2. To provide the leader with useful information
3. To generate discussion and focus the group
4. To shift the focus
5. To deepen the focus
6. To provide the opportunity for experiential learning
7. To provide fun and relaxation (p. 205)

All of these reasons make it likely that sometimes group leaders will employ a prestructured exercise during the working stage of the group. Preplanned exercise experiences should not be used indiscriminately or even frequently in the working stage of most groups. However, interventions such as these, when well planned and tailored to a particular situation, can increase member awareness and responsiveness to self and others. Whether exercises are used in group work depends on the need for these devices, the comfort of the group and its leader with them, and the potential benefits and liabilities of using such procedures (Wenz & McWhirter, 1990).

As previously discussed, an icebreaker at the beginning of a group can be a potent stimulant, as can a well-timed intervention at a critical moment in the group's development. For instance, if a counseling group appears to be anxious and overly concerned about one of its members, Michelle, and is talking *about* her instead of *with* her, then the leader might simply ask the group to gather in a tight circle with arms interlocked. Michelle would then be invited to try to break through the circle, which, even if successful, would be frustrating and aggravating. From this brief exercise, the leader could help the group focus on its dynamics and the group processes that keep the group from discussing their anxiety about Michelle with her.

Regardless of the types of exercises used, "it is the processing of those activities that translates what happens in group into interpersonal and intrapersonal learning for group members" (DeLucia-Waack, 1997b, p. 82). Through processing of an experiential exercise, group members may "develop a plan of action for transferring . . . learning to their lives outside of the group" (Kees & Jacobs, 1990, p. 23). This benefit may be especially powerful because it offers group members new possibilities for influencing the course of their lives positively.

Despite benefits, group exercises have disadvantages, too (Gladding, 2004). If they are used too often, group members may become overly dependent on the leader. They may make some group members angry or resentful because members may feel a lack of control over what will happen next. Finally, if employed too frequently, exercises can disrupt the natural development of a group. Therefore, prudence is called for when exercises are used in groups.

◆ *Questions from Experience* ◆

When have you been in a group where the leader used exercises? How did you like the experiential nature of what you did? What drawbacks or doubts did you have in following the leader's directions? If you were running a group, when might you use exercises? Why?

Group Observing Group

Group observing group requires that the group break up into two smaller groups in any way the leader directs and that each observe the other function (as outsiders). This process is sometimes called a **fishbowl procedure** (see Figure 7.3).

After the group observations are completed, the group reunites, and members give one another and the group as a whole feedback on what was observed. The intent of this activity is to help members focus on common concerns that outweigh differences and to begin working harder (Cohen & Smith, 1976).

For example, Carolyn might notice that the group she is observing struggles with the problem of making sure everyone who wants to contribute gets heard. This awareness helps her realize that her own group is not unique in its quest to be fair to all members

Figure 7.3
Group observing group.

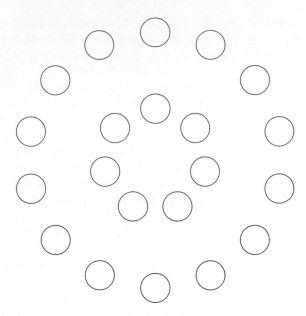

and make sure they have a say. She also realizes some things she could do differently in her own group, such as being an encourager of those who are most reflective and less likely to participate overtly.

A variation on the fishbowl is the two-way fishbowl, that is, the 2-FB model (Hensley, 2002). This model is primarily a group training approach that can be used in academic classes. Participants learn about group theory, process, and leadership by taking on and integrating four different roles: class participant, group member, observation team member, and group leader. Each role provides students with a different lens through which to view and then reflect on the evolution of working groups as they move in and out of these various roles.

Brainstorming

Brainstorming, a way to stimulate divergent thinking, requires an initial generating of ideas in a nonjudgmental manner (Osborn, 1957). The premise of this approach is that critical evaluation of ideas and actions often holds back creativity and member participation. Therefore, in this procedure, the ideas of every person are recorded first before any comments are made. Quantity is emphasized in this process—the more ideas, the better. Only after a large number of ideas have been written down do members go back and evaluate the feasibility of what they have contributed. This results in an increase in group activity and responsibility as well as an emphasis on reality. However, by the time ideas are judged along qualitative lines, many thoughts have been contributed that would not have been voiced otherwise.

Nominal-Group Technique

Another helpful procedure for getting the group to work is the **nominal-group technique (NGT)**. This process has up to six steps (Delbecq, Van de Ven, & Gustafson, 1975).

In the first step, the group leader introduces the problem or issue briefly and then asks members to silently, and individually, generate a number of ideas or solutions connected with the statement. Members are given 10 to 15 minutes to complete this exercise and are asked to do it in writing. The second step involves members' sharing of ideas, with each person stating an idea in a round-robin fashion and the group leader writing that idea and an identification code on a blackboard or flip chart before the next person speaks.

The third step requires a discussion of ideas for clarification, with "What did you mean when you said...?" dialogue. The fourth step has members write their top five ideas or solutions on an index card. The leader then collects the cards, a vote is tallied, and the information is fed back to the group as a whole. In the fifth step, a short discussion of the vote follows. At this time, members can again raise points, seek clarification, or solicit comments. The final step is a possible revote, which usually takes place if the discussion on the original vote has brought out new information that members want to consider in light of their earlier decision.

NGT does not require the open exposure of members as much as brainstorming. However, it is quite useful in getting group members to think and to work on problematic situations, especially in task/work groups. Overall, NGT places more objectivity in the group decision-making process than almost any other method.

Synectics

A novel way of helping groups in the working stage become more productive is **synectics**. The word *synectics*, from the Greek, means the joining together of different and apparently irrelevant elements. Synectics theory applies to the integration of diverse individuals into "a problem-stating, problem-solving group" (Gordon, 1961, p. 1). Synectics follows the general pattern of group discussions—problem statement, discussion, solution generation, and decision (Forsyth, 2006). There are several important differences, however.

First, throughout the discussion, members are asked to analyze all sides of an issue by adopting a spectrum policy. This policy is the recognition that few ideas are totally good or bad. Next, members are encouraged to express their wishes and hopes throughout this process. Although they may not receive what they wish for, members are able to clarify what they want more clearly through this process and to relieve some pent-up frustrations.

A very refreshing and stimulating part of synectics is called **excursions**. In these activities, members actually take a break—a vacation—from problem solving and engage in exercises involving fantasy, metaphor, and analogy. For example, members might play with how many career paths they could take to get elected president of their country. The idea is that the material generated in these processes can be reintegrated into the group later, specifically to issues that are of individual and group importance.

Written Projections

Written projections are yet another means to help a group during the working stages. Members are asked to see themselves or their groups in the future having been successful and to describe what the experience was like. Group members are able to play with their fantasies at times as well as be realistic. An example of projection that captures the spirit of this approach is the writing of a **therapeutic fairy tale** (Hoskins, 1984). Within 6 to 10 minutes, members are to write their story beginning with "Once upon a time" and including (a) a problem or predicament; (b) a solution, even if it appears outlandish; and (c) a positive, pleasing ending. The time limit helps members focus on the task and prevents resistance.

A group member in a therapeutic group once wrote this fairy tale:

> *Once upon a time, there was an old woman who had managed, like the woman in the shoe, to raise a number of children. The only problem was that the children now knew what they wanted to do with their lives and the old woman did not. At first, she got depressed and thought if she got sad enough the children would come back to her. They did, but they were angry and put her in a mental health facility. She tried getting even more down, but her strategy just didn't seem to help. The children abandoned her.*
>
> *One day the old woman woke up and said to herself, 'Today, I'll wear purple, a healing color, and I will go out in the wards and say hello to everyone I meet.' She did and, to her amazement, most of those she encountered responded back in a positive way. She felt better, they felt better, and as a result she realized all the world could now be her surrogate children. So, she left the hospital with a good feeling and a great plan and lived happily both with her children and her neighbors.*

Group Processing

Another strategy for helping groups maximize their resources in the working stage is through group processing. "**Processing** can be defined as capitalizing on significant happenings in the here-and-now interactions of the group to help members reflect on the meaning of their experience; better understand their own thoughts, feelings, and actions; and generalize what is learned to their life outside the group" (Stockton, Morran, & Nitza, 2000, p. 345). **Group processing** "refers to the dynamics that naturally occur in the group" (p. 345) or, as Yalom (2005) has characterized it, "the nature of the relationship between interacting individuals" (p. 143). To enhance processing for group workers and group members, the strategy of note-taking is recommended (Falco & Bauman, 2004; Hall & Hawley, 2004). Such a procedure prevents "**memory decay**" (where more frequent life events of members overshadow previous group experiences). In addition, making process notes provides group members with an opportunity for self-reflection and growth by motivating group leaders and members to "recall each session in detail in order to provide meaningful insights" (Falco & Bauman, 2004, p. 186).

◆ *Questions from Experience* ◆

When have you made notes about an event in your life, that is, a journal, log, or diary? Were you surprised when you reread this material and remembered events you had forgotten? How do you think making notes in a group would help you in the group? What might be some drawbacks?

As discussed in Chapter 6, another way to make the most of processing is to bring a **process observer** into the group. This person is a professional human services worker (e.g., counselor, psychologist, social worker) who is neutral in regard to the group agenda and personalities in the group but who helps the group understand the dynamics within their setting by observing and feeding back to them what is occurring between members and in the group itself. The job of the process observer is not to judge but to inform the group objectively about what is occurring (Trotzer, 2007). For instance, in a task group, the observer might say something like the following: "I noticed during this portion of the group that Beverly was trying to make sure the group was aware of the ramifications of investing money in the foundation. She did this through providing the group with a lot of facts. Bree, you were most supportive of Beverly and encouraged her. Chuck, you were also suppor- tive but you seemed to grow impatient as Beverly's presentation continued. Michael, on the other hand, I observed you wanted to end the discussion and kept asking the group if there were other agenda items to cover. I'm not sure exactly what that was about."

Hearing such feedback, group members are then free to discuss and process what the observer has presented. They may do so through talking with one another, owning their feelings, or asking the observer for more detailed or clearer information. In any case, through process observation, the work of the group is enhanced because members begin to see patterns in themselves and others and to address issues related to who they are with one another as well as the content on which they are focusing (Kormanski & Eschbach, 1997). It is prudent for most groups, regardless of their emphases, to have the process observer "report" either right before or after they take a break or when they seem to be getting bogged down. Process observing energizes the group as well as gives it use- ful information.

Teaching of Skills

A final strategy for improving performance in the working stage of a group is teaching skills. Sometimes group members are not successful because they do not know how to relate well to others, such as giving and receiving interpersonal feedback (Toth & Erwin, 1998). Novice group participants may be especially lacking in feedback skills.

Through teaching members skills, group functioning improves. The reason is that members feel more confident in their abilities and indeed improve them. Basic counseling responses in groups can be learned in a systematic and interesting way (Haney & Leib- sohn, 2001).

OUTCOMES OF THE WORKING STAGE

The end result of the working stage of a group is usually tangible. Goals have been worked on and achieved. Some of these goals take the form of personal objectives. For example, in counseling and psychotherapy groups, members are usually involved in improving par- ticular areas in their lives. Other goals evolve as the result of a combined group vision and effort. Group members often gain a clearer idea of what they have accomplished in the working stage when they put their group session goals down on paper before each session (see Figure 7.4).

One of the most productive aspects of the group in the working stage is the learning and sharing of ideas and information among members. As a result, the entire group membership

Group Session Goal Chart

Your Name:_____   Date:_____   Group Session:_____

What I want to accomplish today	What I need to do to accomplish it	The resources in the group that can help me	How I will know if I accomplished my goal for today

Figure 7.4

Group session goals chart.

Source: Adapted from *The Theory and Practice of Group Psychotherapy* (4th ed.) by Irving D. Yalom, 1995, New York: Basic Books. Copyright © 1970, 1975, 1985, and 1995 by Basic Books, Inc. Reprinted by permission of Basic Books, a member of Perseus Books, L.L.C.

is enriched. Some groups achieve the ability to generate new thoughts spontaneously. "Group stuckness" cannot remain if the group is really working.

An important aspect to realize about any group is its cyclical nature between task and social/emotional vectors (Bales, 1951). Certain roles are primarily task oriented, such as presenting material in a psychoeducational group. Others are either positive or negative in regard to the creating of social/emotional atmospheres, such as welcoming people to the group or ignoring them. Leaders and members must be vitally aware of roles, because by being so, they can best promote strategies and resolutions.

Other procedures used in the working stage of a group overlap with techniques previously described in prior group stages. For instance, in counseling and psychotherapy groups, as participants make discoveries about themselves, they experience an emotional *catharsis*—a release of pent-up feelings. In such cases, they may cry, laugh, become angry, or tap into any other feeling state that has been released. For example, in a psychotherapy group, Irene found herself still mad at her childhood siblings for teasing her about matters over which she had no control, such as where she lived and what her parents did for a living. Her awareness and release of bottled-up feelings were therapeutic, as was the discussion she had later with her group members.

Sometimes, group members will add actions to the emotions they are experiencing during the working stage. It is hoped participants can gain insight and become more cognitively aware of themselves and their options during this stage through such means. If this developmental process occurs, members **cognitively restructure** their lives (i.e., they begin to think of and perceive themselves differently). They see that, although change is difficult, they are not helpless and the situation is not necessarily hopeless (Ellis, 1977, 1986; Watzlawick, 1983). Expressing negative emotions without cognitive restructuring only reinforces such feelings.

With this heightened awareness come increased intermember exchanges and a giving and receiving of honest, direct, and useful information. Group members seem to genuinely care how others perceive their behaviors in the working stage. The impact of their actions in promoting or inhibiting relationships becomes valued. The focus is on the present, and it may include **confrontation**. The idea behind confrontation is for members to challenge one another to examine the discrepancies between their words and actions. For example, in a counseling group, Paul may say to Allison, "I hear that you really want to make your own decisions, but I see that you are constantly asking your mother for advice. Help me understand how these two behaviors relate." Confrontation does not usually lead to conflict or withdrawal. Instead, members become more thoughtful about what they are doing and why.

Feedback, which is known as "immediacy," "here-and-now interventions," and "impact disclosure," is the pantheoretical intervention in group work (Claiborn, Goodyear, & Horner, 2001). It refers to the response of one individual to the words and actions of another (Yalom, 2005) and is used in the working stage of a group and indeed throughout the group. Feedback usually involves sharing relevant information with other people, such as how they are perceived or how they behave, so they can decide whether to change. Information should be given in a clear, concrete, succinct, and appropriate manner. Feedback is not usually unidimensional (i.e., about one thing) (Bednar & Kaul, 1985; Morran, Robison, & Stockton, 1985) but rather often encompasses a variety of information both conscious and unconscious. Timing and the type of feedback given are important variables on its impact. Positive feedback is generally received more willingly and has a greater impact than negative feedback (Dies, 1983; Morran et al., 1985). However, research shows that the positive–negative sequencing of feedback increases the acceptance of negative feedback (Kivlighan & Luiza, 2005). Likewise, group members rate specific feedback about behaviors as being more effective than general or nonspecific feedback (Rothke, 1986; Stockton & Morran, 1980).

In giving feedback, it is important to "carefully assess" a person's readiness to receive a corrective message (Stockton, Morran, & Harris, 1991, p. 253). It is also essential to allow enough time for processing feedback messages. If adequate time is not allowed, then group members may rationalize or forget the messages they receive. Overall, the quality of feedback is higher during the latter stages of the group at work and is likely to be more accepted by members then. This may be due to a number of factors including less projection or transference (Lev-Wiesel, 2003). Regardless, it is important that feedback be given within the group throughout the entire group experience (Morran et al., 1985). The group leader can do much to facilitate feedback exchanges in a group. Activities that may be employed include

- structured feedback exchange exercises (where the leader sets up ways for members to give exchanges to one another, such as in writing),

- modeling (where the leader regularly gives feedback to members in a direct and caring manner),
- connecting (where the leader helps a group member relate feedback to a goal or behavior),
- consensual validation (where the leader uses other group members to give their reactions to feedback directed at a particular group member), and
- feedback paraphrasing (where the leader has the recipient of feedback repeat what he or she heard in his or her own words) (Morran, Stockton, Cline, & Teed, 1998).

Using a variety of feedback methods may be most helpful in getting messages across.

CASE EXAMPLE: Unaware Olga

Olga joined the psychotherapy group because she felt that she had a way of alienating people from her. Sure enough, she did. When QuiQue stated he was thinking of taking a social skills class, Olga said: "That's stupid!! Be a man!" Zack, the leader, and the rest of the group wrote Olga notes of concern about her action, but Olga did not slow down in her blatant criticism of others. She thought Julie was "a tramp" for flirting with men and told her so.

At this juncture, Zack asked if someone in the group might model other ways for Olga to express her disdain for what Julie was doing. Katie did using milder language. Others followed. Still, Olga was outspoken and usually hurtful when she responded to others. The next time Olga exploded it was at Zack, who this time responded by paraphrasing, saying: "Olga, it sounds like you hate me."

Olga finally got it. "Oh," was all she could add. "I didn't realize my words were so powerful."

After that, Olga watched her words and actually asked others to help her frame her thoughts in a gentler style.

What do you think about the way Olga received feedback? Would other ways of giving feedback been more effective? For instance?

The **corrective emotional experience** is another benefit that can come in the working stage of the group. Yalom (2005) describes this experience as the hallmark of the working phase of therapy groups. A group supportive enough to permit the risk taking that goes with this experience must have been developed beforehand. If it has, then the corrective emotional experience has several components. The first is that the group member must risk making "a strong expression of emotion, which is interpersonally directed." "Reality testing," which allows the group member "to examine the incident with the aid of consensual validation from the other members," is also necessary. Then the group member must recognize "the inappropriateness of certain interpersonal feelings and behavior or the inappropriateness of certain avoided interpersonal behavior." Finally, the group and its leader must help the member going through this experience in every way possible "to interact with others more deeply and honestly" (p. 26).

In addition to increased intimacy, openness, and feedback, another quality that is useful, important, and likely to be helpful during the working stage is **humor**—the ability to laugh at oneself or a situation in a therapeutic and nondefensive manner (Watzlawick, 1983). Groups that last make more frequent and longer use of humor than those that are short lived (Scogin & Pollio, 1980). In a successful working stage, seriousness may be interspersed with laughter as members gain better insight into themselves, others, and the dynamics of life inside and outside the group. Humor may have a potential benefit for a group by easing tension, distilling hostility, promoting positive communication bonds, and fostering creativity (Baron, 1974; Fine, 1977; La Gaipa, 1977; Murstein & Brust, 1985).

The exact role humor plays in a group is not always easy to determine. Certainly, it may distract members from their work or be used to make put-downs. Therefore, it is important for groups to notice when and how humor is used to determine its impact. There are always opportunities to cultivate humor by taking advantage of paradoxes within the group, discrepancies, the unpredictable, the unanticipated, universal truths, the absurd, and the familiar (Napier & Gershenfeld, 2004). For example, in a round, the group leader asks members to remember a funny experience in their lives that made them more aware of their humanness. Sam relates that because of his cultural background, he had not understood that a "Danish" was a sweet pastry as well as a person from Denmark. When he was invited by his group to "go get a Danish," he just looked at them in amazement and questioned why they would want to do something like that. It was only when his peers escorted him to a bakery that he fully understood what they were talking about and laughed with them at the misinterpretation (Gladding, 2002).

Well-conducted counseling, psychotherapeutic, task/work, and psychoeducational groups often make use of humor. Sharing a lighter moment from one's personal experience or enjoying an illustration that makes a point while being amusing helps people remember and enjoy a laugh together at no one's expense. Humor also helps individuals and group members as a whole bond and gain insight (Fry & Salameh, 1993). It influences them positively about working together.

SUMMARY AND CONCLUSION

The working stage is when the group should be most productive in resolving or solving personal, task, or educational issues. If for some reason this stage of the group does not go well, then group members may leave the group frustrated and disheartened. In addition, attempts at termination will be impeded. Members who have had a bad experience in the group during this stage are less likely to want to participate in collective efforts again. In contrast, when the group functions well in the working stage, members are positively influenced.

Some of the factors of which group leaders and members must be aware and execute to help groups help themselves have been highlighted. Among these important elements in assisting the group to be productive are modeling, structured exercises, groups observing groups, brainstorming, the nominal-group technique, synectics, written projects, group processing, and teaching skills. When groups are successful in the working stage, they achieve goals and move toward termination. Members of such groups increase their insight and use of basic therapeutic devices through such devices as feedback, confrontation, corrective emotional experience, and humor. Overall, in successful groups, the working stage is one that is remembered fondly and proudly by its members.

CLASSROOM EXERCISES

1. Divide into groups of four. Discuss the use of humor in groups for facilitating the group process. What are the advantages and limitations of using humor in task, guidance, and therapy groups?

2. Write a "therapeutic fairy tale" about some aspect of your life. In groups of two, discuss how you reacted to this exercise and for which populations you think it would be appropriate. Share your story and ideas with others in the class, if you wish.

3. How does a representation such as the Johari Window help you understand the similarities and differences between working and non-working groups? Talk with another classmate and then the group as a whole.

4. Discuss in a group of five the nominal-group technique. Use the technique, as explained in this chapter, to generate ideas about how, when, and with whom NGT would be most effective.

CHAPTER 8

TERMINATION OF A GROUP

Susan Oristaglio/PH College

I travel back to the land of my genesis
as a different man in a changing world,
like Joseph, after his stay in Egypt.
At the end of night, I will begin,
by exploring the light and hope of dawn,
recalling the length of just past days,
and feeling the warmth of lasting friendships.
Amid the abundance of still fresh memories
I will journey on a path of transition
into the unknown and ever evolving
as I experience the fullness of time
that leads to closure and permanent growth.*

*From Transitions by Samuel T. Gladding, © 1994.

The termination of a group member, a group session, or an entire group experience received relatively little attention in professional group publications until the 1970s. For example, it was not until 1977 that Tuckman and Jensen added the stage "adjourning" to the developmental model of groups devised by Tuckman in 1965. Part of the reason for the neglect of termination in group work was the assumption that ending a group experience on any level is a natural phenomenon that most leaders and participants know how to do.

Yet, termination is never simple. Group leaders, members, and the group as whole may handle it awkwardly or ineptly. Through design or neglect, proper preparations are often not made for termination (Shapiro, 1978). However, termination is filled with thoughts and feelings that tend to influence individuals long after the group experience is just a memory (Stein, 1993). According to Corey (2004), the termination stage is equally as important as the beginning stage of a group. During the forming stage of a group, members get to know one another better; during the termination stage, they come to know themselves on a deeper level. If termination is properly understood and managed, it can be an important force in promoting change in individuals (Yalom, 2005).

Primary activities of group members in termination are to (a) reflect on their past experiences, (b) process memories, (c) evaluate what was learned, (d) acknowledge ambivalent feelings, and (e) engage in cognitive decision making (Wagenheim & Gemmill, 1994). Through members' participation in these activities, they are helped to integrate and use information gleaned from the group experience in outside situations (Lieberman, Yalom, & Miles, 1973; Woody, Hansen, & Rossberg, 1989). They are able to generalize learning from one situation to another (Carroll, Bates, & Johnson, 2004; Shulman, 1999). For instance, if Maria realizes in the group that she has the ability to confront individuals and does not have to just placate them, then she can use this skill in her work situation when individuals constantly make demands on her.

Overall, **termination** is a transition event that ends one set of conditions so that another experience can begin (Cormier & Hackney, 2005). It is considered the last stage of the group process, but in reality it marks a new beginning. Termination provides group members an opportunity to clarify the meaning of their experiences, consolidate the gains they have made, and make decisions about the new behaviors they want to carry away from the group and apply to their everyday lives. It is influenced in a positive or negative way by the leader's action and direction. It differs for members in closed-ended versus open-ended groups because members of closed-ended groups prepare for and experience termination collectively, whereas members of open-ended groups prepare for and experience termination individually.

Within termination are many issues and processes. One concern is **emotional ambivalence**. Often there are feelings of loss, sadness, and separation (Gladding, 1994a; Hulse-Killacky, 1993; MacKenzie & Livesley, 1984). Frequently, these feelings are mixed with those of hope, joy, and accomplishment (Schutz, 1967). Almost always, there are issues involving "unfinished business," transference, and countertransference (Kauff, 1977; Tudor, 1995). How to solidify and translate learning accomplished within the group to outside experiences is still another aspect of termination. Therefore, it is crucial to the health and well-being of everyone in a group that termination be handled correctly. If the change, loss, and grief that are a part of termination are not acknowledged and overtly handled, then gains made within the group by its members will be minimal (Stein, 1993).

In this chapter, several different aspects of group termination are covered. First, proper preparation for termination is examined. Second, the effect of termination on the individual is explored. Next, ways of handling premature termination are discussed, especially when the ending is involuntary. Fourth, proper methods of ending single group sessions are noted, along with appropriate ways of ending the group as a whole. Finally, the issues of problems in termination and of group member follow-up are addressed. In each of these situations, the responsibilities of leaders and members are highlighted.

PREPARING FOR TERMINATION

Proper preparation for ending a group begins in the planning stage. Leaders should have in mind not only what type of group they wish to conduct but also how long it will meet and how it will end. They are guided in these decisions by theoretical and pragmatic considerations, such as which approach has shown positive results with certain populations and problems as well as which facilities are available and when (Cormier & Hackney, 2005).

To ensure proper group procedures from start to termination, leaders must establish appropriate boundaries. **Boundaries** are physical and psychological parameters under which a group operates, such as beginning and ending on time or sitting in a certain configuration, such as a circle (Carroll et al., 2004). Leaders who do not keep these dimensions of a group in mind basically "are abdicating their responsibility and reinforcing a perception many group members may already have—that people often don't mean what they say, that they cannot be trusted" (Bates, Johnson, & Blaker, 1982, p. 88). Therefore, planning for termination should go hand in glove with other theoretically based group procedures and be a coordinated process. The impact of termination is both direct and subtle on the growth of individuals and the group as a whole.

CASE EXAMPLE: Ernie Tries to End a Group

The last thing Ernie thought he needed was instruction on how to end a group. He had been in groups before that just seemed to end and he thought he would know both the time and the way to finish the counseling group he was leading. Trouble was, he did not have the foggiest idea how he would know what to do and when. Therefore, week after week group members attended, and Ernie pretended that that was what was supposed to happen.

However, after about 6 months into the group, members began to attend irregularly. There was a lack of energy in those who did attend, and everyone looked to him to make the situation better.

Finally, Ernie announced to the 7 of 12 members still coming that after today's meeting, the group would not meet again. Many of the members were upset or mad. All but one member shared their anger with Ernie. He was visibly shaken by the time everyone left. It was not as he had hoped.

What could Ernie have done to have made the transition smooth? Do you think group members were justified in being angry at him? How would you have felt had you been one of the members?

Termination occurs on two levels in groups: at the end of each session, and at the end of a certain number of group sessions. Both types of termination have step processes within them that are predictable. In considering termination, group leaders should make plans accordingly. One of the best guidelines for making plans to terminate is based on a model for ending family therapy sessions, whose main idea is that, regardless of theory, termination entails four steps: (a) orientation, (b) summarization, (c) discussion of goals, and (d) follow-up (Epstein & Bishop, 1981).

During orientation, the subject of termination is raised. At times during the process, group members are reminded when a session or a group will end. During summarization, material and processes that have occurred in the group are reviewed. Ideally, both the group leader and group members participate in this summary. During the discussion of goals, the group focuses on what members will do after the session or the group ends. In the final step, follow-up, group members inform one another of the progress they have made in obtaining their objectives. Through reminding themselves of these steps and procedures, group leaders help themselves, group members, and the group as a whole end successfully.

In open-ended therapy groups, such as those for psychiatric patients, termination is highly individualized, but even these situations contain some predictability. For example, Yalom (2005) states that most psychiatric patients in outpatient groups require approximately 12 to 24 months to undergo substantial and durable change. Working though issues in these types of groups takes time. Therefore, trying to end a group before its members are ready for closure is ill advised and can be detrimental.

In closing a group session, a leader should inform members that the group is ending about 5 to 30 minutes before its conclusion. Such an announcement (i.e., orientation) does not have to be elaborate. Rather, the leader can simply say during a pause or a brief interruption, "I see we have about 15 minutes left. What do we need to do collectively or individually to end on time?" In a therapy group, the amount of time needed to bring about closure is almost always greater than in a task/work or psychoeducational group. Regardless, this orientation to the end makes it possible for the group members to summarize, set goals, and plan for follow-up if they wish.

In ending a total group experience, the orientation to termination involves a planned number of sessions that are devoted to the topic of closure. In closed-ended counseling and psychotherapy groups, at least two to four sessions should be focused on the ending (Gazda, 1989; Maples, 1988). Task/work groups may decide to disband more rapidly, but they also need time to get used to the idea of no longer being a group. The time is needed because, in some task/work groups, members hinge part of their identity to the group (Stein, 1993). Ideally, group members review what was completed, assess output versus objectives, assess the group's ability to meet the evaluation of those who use or view group output, and prepare group output for final disposition (Keyton, 1993). In psychoeducational groups, members are usually aware in advance that the group will be time limited. However, a reminder is often appreciated and keeps the group on task and mentally prepared for the final ending. A straightforward orientation to termination followed by the other steps in the termination process helps members accomplish their pregroup goals and clarify any questions they have of themselves or others. As in other environments, members who gain the most from a group experience are informed in advance what will happen during the time they are together and what is expected of them. The process of termination is no exception to this rule.

◆ *Questions from Experience* ◆

With what groups have you identified in your life? How did it feel to leave these groups? What was the best experience you had when the group ended? What was the worst? How can this information inform you about terminating a group?

EFFECTS OF TERMINATION ON INDIVIDUALS

Termination's impact on individuals depends on many factors. These include whether the group was opened-ended or closed-ended; whether members were, in fact, prepared in advance for its ending; and whether the speed and intensity of work within sessions was at an appropriate level to allow participants to properly identify and resolve concerns or problems (Tudor, 1995). If handled inappropriately, termination may adversely affect persons and inhibit their growth. "If handled adequately, the process of termination in itself can be an important role in helping individuals develop new behaviors" (Hansen, Warner, & Smith, 1980, p. 539). Often from the death of relationships, whether physical or psychological, comes a new understanding of who one was with others and who one is now as a result (Hulse-Killacky, 1993). However, for such benefits to occur, group members must work through their feelings just as people who experience death and grief do (Kübler-Ross, 1973).

The behavior of group members at the end of the group indicates how they think and feel as well as what they have experienced (Luft, 1984; Shulman, 1999). Members who are anxious at or during termination may feel they cannot function without the group's support. Participants who are sad may be afraid they will not see others in the group again. Those who are angry may think they have not accomplished what they should have done (Ellis, 1988). For example, if Jane says to the group that she is "upset" about its ending and wishes to continue longer, she may be indirectly stating that she wants reassurance from group members that she is competent to deal with situations by herself.

Usually the range of feelings among individual group members is wide. In some cases, group members emphasize only the positive aspects of what has occurred in the group instead of what they have learned. This type of focus is known as **farewell-party syndrome** and tends to avoid the pain of closure (Shulman, 1999). However, the most likely overriding emotion at the end of a group is one that can best be described as mixed or bittersweet (Goodyear, 1981).

The best way for individuals to end a group is to reflect on what they have experienced and make way for new beginnings outside the group. However, the achievement of this ideal is not always possible. Therefore, group leaders may have to focus special attention on the issue of separation with some people more than others (Corey, Corey, Callanan, & Russell, 2003). For example, the leader may have to spend more time with Jason at the end of a psychotherapy or counseling group because of his unstable background. In contrast, the leader may spend less time with Jacob because of his emotionally secure past. For Jason, the fear that he will be unable to find supportive relationships in other settings can be countered by a leader who helps him remember the risks he took in the present group and ways he achieved his group goal in a personal and satisfactory way.

Regardless of how careful and thorough the leader is during the termination stage, a few group members may occasionally need more help. For these people, three options are productive:

1. individual counseling, in which unique concerns can be given greater attention;
2. referral to another group or organization, in which more specific or specialized assistance can be rendered; or
3. **recycling**, in which the individual can go through a similar group experience again and learn lessons missed the first time.

In all of these cases, the focus is on helping group members maximize their capabilities and obtain their goals. Through these procedures, group members discover more about themselves, try to better understand others, and take steps toward creating the types of communities or organizations they need.

PREMATURE TERMINATION

Sometimes, individuals quit a group abruptly or the group experience ends suddenly because of actions by the leader. Both cases are examples of **premature termination** and may result in difficulties for the participants (Donigian & Hulse-Killacky, 1999). Various theoretical perspectives and practitioners handle such situations differently. For example, a person-centered group and leader may trust a group member's judgment that leaving before the group is scheduled to end is the best action, whereas a reality-therapy orientation may concentrate on trying to persuade a member not to leave. A psychodynamic perspective may explore intrapersonal reactions associated with premature termination.

There are guidelines (e.g., Association for Specialists in Group Work, 1998) to follow in premature termination cases regardless of the reason for the action or the group leader's theoretical persuasion. Most of these guidelines apply to psychoeducational, counseling, and psychotherapy groups because the impact of premature endings is greatest on these types of groups. Task/work group members and leaders, however, may also make use of these guidelines.

Generally, three types of premature termination must be dealt with: the termination of the group as a whole, the termination of a successful group member, and the termination of an unsuccessful group member (Yalom, 2005).

Premature Termination of the Group as a Whole

Premature termination of the whole group may occur because of a group leader or group member action. Group leaders may appropriately terminate the group prematurely if they become sick, move, or are reassigned to other duties. In all of these situations, group members may feel incomplete and try to reestablish contact with the leader (Pistole, 1991).

To handle these types of premature termination properly, leaders need to have at least one group session to say good-bye to the group as a whole, or they need to be able to contact group members directly. The logistics of making such arrangements is sometimes difficult. Inappropriate premature group termination, however, is even more stressful.

Group leaders who prematurely terminate groups because they feel personal discomfort, fail to recognize and conceptualize problems, or feel overwhelmed by member problems do themselves and the group a disservice by leaving the group and its members with unresolved issues.

Premature Termination Initiated by Group Members

For individuals, premature termination may be due to appropriate or inappropriate reasons, and the experience may be successful or unsuccessful. Yalom (2005, p. 233) lists a number of reasons that are often given by individuals who leave psychotherapy and counseling groups prematurely: (a) "external factors" (e.g., scheduling conflicts, external stress), (b) "group deviancy" (i.e., members who do not "fit in" with others), (c) "problems of intimacy," (d) "fear of emotional contagion" (i.e., a negative personal reaction to hearing the problems of other group members), (e) "inability to share the doctor" (i.e., wanting individual attention from the group leader), (f) "complications of concurrent individual and group therapy," (g) "early provocateurs" (i.e., overt, strong rebellion against the group), (h) "inadequate orientation to therapy," and (i) "complications arising from subgrouping." Of these reasons, those involving external factors, not fitting in, and complications of concurrent individual and group therapy are most likely to be appropriate factors in deciding to end a group experience early. It should be cautioned, however, that group members may rationalize reasons for premature endings.

The other reasons given by Yalom (2005), with the exception of inadequate orientation, are associated most often with the immaturity of group participants. Immature individuals, who are usually unsuccessful in the group process, avoid dealing with loss by physically removing themselves from the group. They deny their need for self-exploration and understanding. They often prevent themselves from experiencing deep personal growth by making a few changes in behavior and then leaving. At other times, if such group members do not remove themselves but consistently and disruptively act out, then the leader may have to ask them to leave. This type of behavior is in marked contrast to successful group members who terminate prematurely for legitimate reasons and take the time to say good-bye to others in the group before they go.

CASE EXAMPLE: Eileen's Exit

Eileen felt more uncomfortable with her counseling group every week. She thought others were talking more, gaining greater insights, and growing healthier than she was. That bothered her a great deal. She thought of leaving but decided her parents would not approve. Therefore, she struggled in the group. One day she simply arrived early, left a note on the leader's chair, and went home.

When she received phone calls later that night after the group, she did not answer. Instead, she binged on ice cream in her freezer and turned up the volume of the television.

What do you think she could have done that would have been more constructive and productive? How? When?

Preventing Premature Termination

If a group appears to have a high potential for premature termination, steps can be taken to prevent it. For instance

- groups should start and end on time,
- members should commit to attend a number of sessions,
- members should be treated in a personal and professional way,
- clarity and conciseness should be used in talking about individual and group issues, and
- reminders should be sent to members if there are long intervals between group sessions (Young, 1992).

Other steps can be taken to soften or alleviate premature termination and its potential negative impact. The first action is for the leader or members to inform the group as soon as possible about their departure from the group. Individuals need time to prepare for transitions and loss. The more time available, the better, especially if the departure is unexpected. For example, a leader who must move because his or her spouse is relocating may telephone group members to prepare them for this event before the next session, especially if the move is unforeseen or sudden.

A second procedure group leaders can follow when faced with a member wanting to leave prematurely is to discuss thoroughly the ramifications of such a move with the member and the group in a safe, protected atmosphere (Corey & Corey, 2006). Often, members will not leave a group prematurely if they are given a chance to talk things out and explore their feelings more thoroughly. For instance, Peter may think he has been slighted but may feel differently once he has had a chance to face the issue in the group. Through this type of contact, he may recognize his tendency to flee situations when he is uncomfortable and acknowledge that he may have to change his lifestyle if he stays in the group.

Finally, in the case of premature termination, members should be helped to realize what they have gained from the group and what positive steps they can take in the future to build on these achievements. Giving members feedback is one valuable way to help them adjust to an abrupt ending (Wagenheim & Gemmill, 1994). If Penny, for instance, decides she wants to work on a project on her own without input from the group, then members can tell her before she leaves what she has meant to them or the group as a whole. In such a situation, Dick might say, "Penny, I have really benefited from the energy you have generated in this group," whereas Robin might respond, "Penny, I find what you want to do to be refreshing and inspiring." When this feedback procedure is used, all members leave on a positive note and are more likely to benefit from the group.

Occasionally, a member will drop out of the group with no warning and without saying good-bye. In such cases, the group leader should follow up and ask the absent member why he or she left the group prematurely. The member should be invited back to discuss his or her thoughts and feelings with the group as a whole and to say good-bye and achieve closure when appropriate. Best practices guidelines (Association for Specialists in Group Work, 1998) and ethical codes (e.g., American Counseling Association, 2005) state that no undue pressure should be used to force a person to remain in or to return to a group or a counseling situation. However, the benefits and liabilities of staying in the group can and should be explored openly.

◆ *Questions from Experience* ◆

When has someone you had a relationship with suddenly disengaged from activities you did together? How did you feel about the disconnection? What would you have liked to have had happen? Relate that emotion and the positive action you would like to have seen from your friend or acquaintance to the act of premature termination.

TERMINATION OF GROUP SESSIONS

There are numerous ways to end group sessions when the group has come to its planned conclusion. For each group session, the appropriate format for closing will depend on the type of group that was conducted, the purpose of the particular session, and the content of the session. The leader should vary the ending of the group whenever possible so members do not get bored with the same routine. Among the most effective formats for closing a session are having the members summarize, having the leader summarize, using a round, using dyads, and getting written reactions (Jacobs, Masson, & Harvill, 2006). Rating sheets and homework are also recommended (Wagenheim & Gemmill, 1994).

Member Summarization

In member summarization, one or more members of the group summarize what has transpired during the session, describing what has happened to them individually and how they have gained from the particular session. If done regularly, it challenges members each week to think about what they are both giving and getting from the group (Corey et al., 2003). At least 10 minutes should be allotted to this exercise, but it is important that group members not become bored. Thus, each member who speaks must keep his or her summary brief. For example, member comments at the end of a session might go as follows:

Samuel: I've learned a lot just by listening today. I've found out I share many of the same feelings about taking risks that Russell does.

Mary Grace: I was surprised that the focus of the group today centered on risks. I expected we would talk about past events, not present challenges. This session has got me thinking about what I will do in regard to my work situation.

Russell: It was a risk for me to speak up today and talk about my feelings in regard to taking risks, such as moving to a new city. Although I still have mixed emotions about what I am going to do in the future, I'm glad I spoke up.

Chip: I'm glad you initiated our focus on risk taking, Russell. There are some situations in my own life that involve risks that I want to talk about next time.

Leader Summarization

When leaders summarize, they give a personal reaction to what they perceive to have occurred in the group. Leaders may comment on "the cohesion of the group, the degree to which members freely brought up topics for work, the willingness of members to take risks and talk about unsafe topics, the degree to which members interacted with one another, and the willingness of members to discuss negative concerns or feelings" (Corey et al., 2003, p. 168). For example, the leader may say on such occasions, "I like the way Julie confronted Joe on the issue of anger. I don't know that you resolved how anger should be handled, but at least you started a dialogue. I was also pleased to see Sheree assert herself. Sheree, I have wondered about your silence, so it was good to see you come out. Markus, I was impressed with your comments, too, about trying new behaviors when in a different environment. I'll be interested in what you do this week in that regard. Thom, it seemed to me that you were avoiding confrontation with Diana today. It might be productive for you and Diana to talk about that next session."

The leaders' advantage in summary situations is the emphasis they can place on certain points and comments. The disadvantage is that leaders may neglect some important developments during the session or fail to mention the contributions of one or two members. Also, leaders may misinterpret behaviors or interchanges.

Rounds

The exercise of **rounds** (sometimes called **go-rounds**) is a variation on member summarization, except in this procedure every group member comments briefly (usually in a sentence or two) about highlights of the group session. Rounds are a way of completing loose thoughts, ending on a positive note, and ensuring that each member feels involved in the group (Trotzer, 2007). Every group member gets equal airtime and leaves with a feeling of having participated in the group.

CASE EXAMPLE: Robin Makes the Rounds

At the ending of a group, Robin wanted to make sure everyone had a say about the way the psychoeducational group had gone. Although it was unusual, she decided to let each person present say a sentence or two about what they had learned in the group. To her surprise, the process went well, and as one member put it toward the end of the round, "Everyone has reminded me of important points I do not want to forget."

When have you ever been reminded of ideas from someone? How often has it been in a group setting? How frequently has it been at the close of a unit of study or an interpersonal experience? How might you use what you know from these experiences in your work at the end of a group?

Dyads

By having members form into groups of two, or **dyads**, at the end of a session, group leaders make sure all members are involved in termination, and at the same time, the group is energized. Often, group leaders may decide to pair participants up at the end of a session if they are working on similar concerns or problems. For example, if Tom and Jeanne are both striving to be better listeners and more empathetic, then they may be put together to talk and practice skills connected with their concerns. If there are no obvious pairings, then members are free to choose their partners or work with those assigned to them.

Written Reactions

Writing is frequently used at the termination of group sessions. It is an aid to promoting reflection because of the time and structure group members have to devote to it. Furthermore, writing can demystify the group process, encourage deeper participation, validate members' feelings about group experiences, and increase cohesiveness among members of the group (Cummings, 2001).

Several forms of written reactions can be used at the end of group sessions. One is an exercise in which members are asked to take a few minutes during the closing of a session and write their reactions to what has happened. This procedure is conducted infrequently, and members may or may not share their writing, depending on the time left in the session and the leader's instructions.

A second form of this procedure is for group members to write regularly at the end of each session in **journals**, or **logs** (Gladding, 2004; Riordan & White, 1996). In this process, group members are required to write their reactions to the events of each session. This process enables them to spot inconsistencies in their reactions more quickly than if they simply talked about them. A paper trail is established that group members and the group leader may later consult in charting the personal effect of the group. "Indeed, the collected logs can be a robust diary of the entire group experience, documenting the ups and downs, the progress or lack of it, and can sometimes serve as a map showing members' growth" (Riordan & White, 1996, p. 98). There is no one agreed-on time at which logs should be written after the end of a session. "Logs written immediately following the session will tend to reflect more accurately the emotions experienced within the session, while those written following a reasonable time lapse will present observations digested and organized in a fashion compatible with the self-concept" (Riordan & Matheny, 1972, p. 381). Either way, some information and insight will usually surface.

Writing and exchanging **journal letters** is a third way of ending group sessions (Cummings, 2001). In this practice, group members and the leader write about their experiences in an ongoing group and give their letters (usually one or two pages) to each other (i.e., members to leader and leader to members). In the case of students learning about groups, such an exchange helps "correct misperceptions, encourage risk taking in self-disclosure and in challenging of other group members, reinforce helpful leadership behaviors that members had used in the sessions, and answer questions posed by group members" (p. 11).

A fourth form of writing is to combine the written word with either music or drawings (Wenz & McWhirter, 1990). For example, in summing up a session or a group, members may be invited to draw logos that represent their lives or to bring in music that symbolizes through lyrics or a melody what they are. In the case of Elaine, she drew a tree that was green and full as her logo, with words underneath it:

I have grown to be me,
All that I hoped in the group I could be.
Now I am moving on.

Logos can be created by first asking members of groups to doodle. After a few minutes, they are invited to find part of the doodle to expand in making their logo. They are also encouraged to think of words and phrases that come to mind as they embellish their drawings and to jot these descriptors down for when they write about what they have drawn.

Finally, the group leader can make written notes about or to members at the end of each session, which may or may not be shared with the group or individuals (Yalom, 2005). When the leader chooses to write notes about members, this usually takes the form of a private, clinical record. When the leader writes notes to group members on their logs, the response is aimed at promoting insight and communication with individuals. In some group exercises, the leader or other members give written responses to the group as a whole.

Rating Sheets

Another way of closing a group and obtaining an accurate picture of how the group assessed the session is by having the leader distribute a **rating sheet** to members that they fill out and return before they leave. Members can rate themselves, other members, and the leader on a number of dimensions, including involvement, risk taking, goals, emotional involvement, feedback, and productivity (Corey et al., 2003). They can give their opinions on how satisfactory the group was for them and how they think it could be improved. To be effective, a group session rating sheet should be brief. Sometimes it can be set up in the form of incomplete sentences, as follows:

1. The thing I liked most about today's group was _____ .
2. My best and most productive time in today's group was _____ .
3. The thing I will remember most about today's group is _____ .
4. I think that today's group could have been improved if _____ .
5. My suggestions for making the group even better are _____ .

Homework

The closing of a group may often occur with the assignment of **homework** (i.e., work done after the group session is over). Such "real-world," nongroup experiences can include thinking, feeling, or behavior experiences. Homework may be especially important in task/work groups in which members need to complete assignments so the group can finish a project. Homework is also important in counseling and psychotherapy groups because it helps members find ways of transferring learning in the group to events in their everyday life. Getting homework assignments at the close of the session allows group members to be more concrete in determining their between-group goals.

◆ *Questions from Experience* ◆

When have you found homework assignments helpful to you? What made them that way?

TERMINATION OF A GROUP

The termination of a group is filled with a mixture of emotions and tasks. It is a time when members' behavior undergoes noticeable changes (Davies & Kuypers, 1985). In successful groups, there is an increase in positive feedback and a certain amount of distancing as members anticipate change. In unsuccessful groups, anger and frustration may emerge along with distancing as members realize they will not attain individual or group goals. "Embedded in the process of termination are issues of the individual's separateness, autonomy, and independence from the group" (Ohlsen, Horne, & Lawe, 1988, p. 93). Leaders and members who successfully complete this stage of the group have and employ certain interpersonal and process skills. These interpersonal and process skills are concentrated on here because they serve as a model to emulate.

Movement into the stage of termination rests squarely on the shoulders of group leaders. Although members of all groups realize the group will end, it is the leader who provides the type of guidance that will make the process positive and productive. One way leaders do this, as previously noted, is through setting a **time limit for the group** (i.e., a number of meeting times that are announced in advance). A second way they help the group terminate is through **capping**—easing out of emotional interaction and into cognitive reflection (Bates et al., 1982). Skilled group leaders realize that if members leave groups too stirred up emotionally, then they may not remember much, if any, of what they learned within the group. Therefore, leaders make a purposeful attempt to promote more cognitive interpersonal and intrapersonal interactions as the group moves into disbanding.

A third way group leaders can ease termination is to model appropriate termination skills and call the group's attention to what needs to be done in bringing about closure. For example, to establish closure as the group terminates, members may be asked to reflect on the group experience:

> *What was most helpful?*
> *What did they learn from the group?*

Even more specific than reflections may be when members are asked to identify aspects of the group and of individual members that were most helpful (DeLucia-Waack, 1998). In this process, group leaders approach the group in a matter-of-fact and reflective manner and help focus group members memories and thoughts.

A number of capping (i.e., closure) skills enable the group to close appropriately. In their interactions with the group as a whole, leaders must use these skills to the maximum. Because time and modeling processes have been covered previously, capping skills, especially as they relate to affective aspects of the group, are focused on here.

Capping Skills in Terminations

Some groups need less time to close than others do. For instance, task and psychoeducational groups usually end when they have completed their mission. The group members may make **summarizing** reflections that recall significant events or learning experiences in the group at its end. However, other procedures are not always used. In contrast, psychotherapy and counseling groups may struggle with multiple issues during closure because of the more personal and intense nature of material covered. In actuality, all types of groups can benefit from capping skills in closure. When these skills are employed properly, group members gain a sense of completeness that the group has ended and a new time in their lives has begun. Some of the most important capping skills for groups to employ at the termination of the group as a whole are as follows:

1. Reviewing and summarizing the group experience
2. Assessing members' growth, change (or achievement)
3. Finishing business
4. Applying change to everyday life (implementing decisions)
5. Providing feedback
6. Handling good-byes
7. Planning for continued problem resolution (Jacobs et al., 2006, p. 362)

Reviewing and summarizing the group experience is the first way to ask members to cap the group. This procedure involves having members recall and share special moments they remember from the group. One way to implement this review is by asking members to recollect their most salient memories from each of the group sessions. Giving the members copies of their feedback sheets on individual sessions may enhance this experience, but it is not absolutely necessary. At review and summary times, group leaders or other group members may guide participants through the process in ferreting out important points they wish to remember or contribute to the group.

For example, in her review of the group, Carolyn became stuck in remembering exactly when she made her first major contribution to the group.

Carolyn:	I think it was during the fifth session that I noticed how we all shared a common concern about not being recognized for the work we do and pointed it out to the group as a whole. I was pleased that I did that, and I think you, as members of the group, were, too. I just wish I could remember when I did that.
Group Leader:	Carolyn, although you cannot remember the exact session, what would you like for us as a group to remember?
Carolyn:	Two things. First, I made a contribution, and second, I helped us all realize more clearly a common bond—concern over not being recognized. I think the second contribution was important to the group as a whole in what eventually happened here.

Assessing is a technique similar to reviewing, but in **assessing members' growth and change**, the emphasis is on individuals' memories of themselves at the beginning of the group and now. The idea of such a capping exercise is to have members see and share significant gains with themselves and others. If group logs have been used, then members may consult them before sharing with one another. The important point of this exercise is for members to recognize their own growth. For instance

Marge:	When I came here, I was scared. I felt I was the only one who was self-conscious about how she looked physically. Through this group, I have grown to understand that everyone, including really attractive people like you, Betsy, worry about how you present yourself. I am more confident than I was when we began this group that I can overcome my feelings. I have also learned, through my conversations with you, some things that I can do to enhance my appearance.

Finishing business is a crucial task at the end of a group. **Unfinished business** is basically "when someone hurts another, or is hurt by someone, and fails to resolve [the] problems with the relevant person" (Ohlsen et al., 1988, p. 128). Unfinished business may develop in groups because of their fast pace and lack of time to process all of the material that arose. Unresolved, unfinished business festers like an untreated wound and can hamper personal functioning. The "hurt" may distract a person from concentrating on what he or she needs to do and has a negative impact on the group itself. In either case, clear communication, congruence, and direct confrontation of the event with the significant person are needed for resolution and to start the healing process. During termination, group members are encouraged to complete this process, feel relief, and start mending and growing. Different theoretical approaches will direct exactly how this may be done, but sometimes the learning of a new behavior is required. In completing this task, it is crucial not to bring up new business.

For example, if Tamara thinks Wendy has put her down in the group, she needs to voice her concern during the termination stage, if not before. Then, if she is shy, she may need to assert herself and ask for what she wants or thinks she needs, such as an apology or an explanation. From that point, there is clarification, negotiation, and, if successful, resolution. When the process is over, Tamara and Wendy should be able to move on with their lives, each other, and the group.

The process of *applying change to everyday life* involves rehearsal, role-play, and homework. **Rehearsal** can be done in the group setting with members showing others how they plan to act in particular situations. This type of demonstration can be made more concrete and meaningful when others in the group play the roles of significant people in such environments. Some common mistakes that members make in rehearsals and role-plays are focusing on the change in others instead of self, becoming impatient with the slowness of others' change, and relying too much on the group's jargon (Corey et al., 2003; Shulman, 1999). Usually, rehearsals and role-plays will occur in the working part of the group and only be reviewed at termination.

Sharing homework is a transitional exercise that often follows rehearsal and role play-ing in which group members actually practice in public what they have done experientially in the group. Homework is usually specific and allows group members to report their results to the group, decide more clearly what they wish to change, and make a transition from group to personal norms. Homework has been covered before, but the important points to remember are that it (a) is a continuous technique that may be employed in many different types of group sessions and (b) should always be processed.

Providing feedback is crucial to the closure of a group and is an integrating experience. It provides an opportunity for leaders and members to reinforce each other for the progress they have made as well as to deal with their thoughts and feelings about making meaningful changes. Feedback should be honest, specific, sincere, and as positive as possible, although leaders and members occasionally can use it "to confront members who are still denying problems or who have not taken responsibility for their behavior" (Jacobs et al., 2006, p. 365). It is helpful for members to write down specific feedback. Otherwise, they tend to forget what was said (Wagenheim & Gemmill, 1994). After the group has ended, members can use written records of feedback to see whether they are continuing to make progress toward being the type of person they were becoming when the group ended.

Expressing farewells allows the group to wrap up, at least on an affective/cognitive level. By **saying good-bye**, members are encouraged to own their feelings and express their thoughts at this time, especially in regard to what others in the group have meant to them. Members may reminisce about significant group events at this time, "remind each other of the way they were, and give personal testimonials about how much they have been helped" (Hansen et al., 1980, p. 546). The group leader may also deal with feelings about separation if they come up.

Sometimes there is a resistance to saying good-bye, for this is the final capping experience. In such cases, group leaders can set the tone for the closing moments by sharing their feelings of satisfaction with the work the group has done and by inviting members to express themselves in a farewell. For some members, there is a need for touching, shaking hands, or hugging. Depending on the type of group, one or more of these demonstrative ways of saying good-bye may be appropriate, but it is best for leaders and members to err on the side of caution if they are ever in doubt as to how to say good-bye. This means using a verbal approach. The important thing in good-byes is that thoughts and feelings be expressed in a constructive manner.

Often, especially in closed-ended groups, structured exercises can be used in this farewell process (Cohen & Smith, 1976; Pfeiffer & Jones, 1969–1975; Schutz, 1967; Trotzer, 2007). These exercises can help bring a ceremonial close to the group and reach a climactic and conclusive ending. One such structured exercise is the awarding of certificates for attending the group. Another is a **pat on the back**, in which members draw the outline of their hand on a piece of white paper that is then taped on their back. Other group members then write closing comments on the hand outline or the paper itself that are positive and constructive about the person (see Figure 8.1).

The final step in closing a group is *developing a specific plan for continuing each member's progress* after the group ends. This *planning for continued problem resolution* may be completed before or after individual good-byes are said. It should include when and how certain activities will be carried out, but "others' expectations should not be part of the plan" (Vander Kolk, 1985, p. 204). In essence, this activity is a variation on what Corey et al. (1992) describe as **projecting the future**, in which group members are asked to imagine the changes they would like to make in the short and long term. However, this planning process is more concrete and may involve the use of a written contract between

Figure 8.1
A pat on the back.

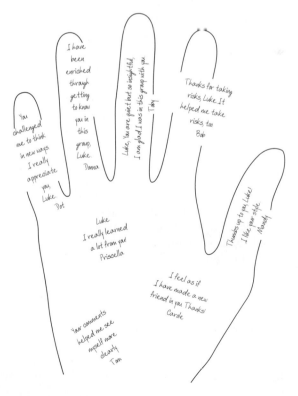

the group member and the group that spells out in a realistic way how the member will implement the plan. Such a procedure can be quite productive in a task/work group as well as a therapeutic group. For example, Bob may state to the group and to himself that within the next 3 months he will complete his survey to find out how customers in his department like the services they are being offered. He will then send group members the data he collects.

PROBLEMS IN TERMINATIONS

Sometimes group members (and occasionally group leaders) have difficulty with the stage of termination. In such cases, they will attempt to deny that they are close to ending and will not do work connected with closure and transition. At other times, they will encounter difficulties in transference issues with the leader or other members. Another scenario may be the group leader's countertransference in relationship to one or more members. Finally, the issues of closure and transition may or may not be handled correctly. Each of these four possible problem areas is examined here.

Denial

Denial is acting as if an experience, such as a group, will never end. It can be expressed in a group on a limited or mass level (Donigian & Hulse-Killacky, 1999; Yalom, 2005). Usually the denial of termination is an individual matter, although some groups at times act as if the group experience will continue indefinitely. In cases of denial, the group leader must remind participants, especially in closed-ended groups, when the last session will be and encourage them to prepare accordingly (Carroll et al., 2004). In cases in which the group or individuals refuse to deal with termination issues, the leader needs to focus specifically on these areas. This focus may involve consultation with another professional, as well as individual sessions with denying members, or a special session or two with the group as a whole.

For example, when John led a six-part psychoeducational group on home repairs, members of the group told him after the fourth session that they would not let him end the group. Collectively, they insisted they wanted more and would not stop learning. To John's credit, he thanked the group for its confidence in him and compliments to him, but at the beginning of the fifth session, he also stated firmly and matter-of-fact way that the group would end in one more session. He gave group members additional information about other courses they might find of interest and referred them to the community college's director of continuing education for information on other available classes.

Transference

Transference is the displacement of affect from one person to another (Gladding, 2006). It has many sources but basically operates on an unconscious level and is manifest most directly when individuals attempt to relate to other persons in ways inappropriate for the situation.

Within a group, a variety of transference processes may emerge. For instance, "transference may occur among the group members themselves, between each member and leader, and between each member and the group as a whole" (Lev-Wiesel, 2003, p. 227). Group leaders and members in counseling and psychotherapy groups are often the objects of multiple transferences—that is, distorted perceptions. However, transference can occur in task/work and psychoeducational groups, too. For example, at various times in the group, leaders and members may be perceived by other participants as experts, authority figures, superheroes, friends, or lovers. There is a natural tendency for many group participants, especially adult children of alcoholics (ACoAs), to interact in the group as they did in their family of origin (Brown & Beletsis, 1986).

One way of dealing with transference perceptions is to become aware of them, that is, recognize them for what they are initially in the group and encourage participants to give both positive and negative feedback to others throughout the group process. This is a tricky process to keep in balance, and group leaders may be wise to seek consultation or supervision in such situations. The curative factor for multiple transference characteristics in groups, according to Yalom (2005), is the primary recapitulation of the primary family group, and it represents a second way to deal with transference. Yet a third way of dealing with this difficulty is called the group stories fabric technique (GSFT) (Lev-Wiesel, 2003). In this last method, group members recount personal stories and give as well as receive feedback to these stories by other group members. The stories within the stories told by members, that is, the **metastories**, reflect individuals' transference issues. Implementing the GSFT is complex and takes time. It involves the group work leader weaving the stories of group members into a "single, unified story that reflects the issues and concerns of all the group members" (p. 233).

Regardless of which method may be utilized, at the end of the group, if transference is still present, the group itself may be used as a whole even more to help individuals deal with their unresolved issues, including the revealing of feelings and the realistic exploration of them. Individual counseling for persons with transference problems, after the group terminates, may also be appropriate.

CASE EXAMPLE: The Group That Would Not Die

Shelby had done all he could to inform the counseling group he was leading that it would end. However, he agreed to extend it for four more sessions. Yet when the time came, members insisted that the group be extended again. Shelby did not think that was wise and tried to wrap the group up in the last of the sessions.

Nevertheless, the group kept going even without its leader and members kept calling Shelby and asking him to return. Since he feared that the group members would eventually become tired of one another and that the group might deteriorate, Shelby came to the third meeting of what he called "the group that wouldn't die." At that meeting he explained once again the benefits of a time-limited group and the fact that once an experience ended, participants could begin a new group and learn even more. His words finally had an impact and the members of the group, after doing rounds, decided to quit.

What do you think you might have done had you been in Shelby's shoes?

Countertransference

Countertransference is usually thought of as the leader's emotional responses to members that are a result of the leader's own needs or unresolved issues with significant others. However, in addition to leader–member interactions, countertransference can occur between members of unequal status. "Countertransference origins likely to be evoked in group therapy include reactions to authority, conflict, and anger; narcissistic needs; cultural values; excessive need for control; family issues, and separation-individuation issues. . . . Countertransference *triggers* are the therapy events and/or client characteristics that evoke therapists' unresolved conflicts" (DeLucia-Waack & Fauth, 2004, p. 139). Group leadership may also trigger a group worker's unresolved conflict because of its complex and interactive nature.

The first step in dealing with countertransference is to recognize how it is being manifest. Watkins (1985) states that countertransference is being exhibited when leaders are overly solicitous, distant, protective, nonconfrontational, competitive, resistant, overly identified with, or romantically or socially attracted to group members. There are a number of ways to manage countertransference, including denial and repression. However, the best way to combat these feelings and actions is direct supervision and individual therapy. It is crucial in ending a group that countertransference issues be resolved.

Handling Termination Correctly

As evidenced in the literature on termination, there is no one way to handle it correctly. However, some specific signs indicate that termination is being conducted incorrectly. For example, if a group is closed abruptly and issues about ending are not processed, then the group is being closed improperly. "More often than not, this problem is observed when the group is of the short-term, weekend encounter variety where there is no follow-up period built into the process" or when the group leader is "from out-of-town and conducts a combination training-therapy workshop" (Gazda, 1989, p. 307).

Another sign that the group is being terminated incorrectly is when members are left with a number of unresolved issues. In open-ended groups, this problem may be handled by extending the number of sessions in the group (Yalom, 2005). In closed-ended and time-limited groups, leaders must try to resolve as many of these issues in the time left in the group and make appropriate referrals or offer individual counseling to those who still have difficulties when the group ends.

Overall, termination is a gradual process, and group leaders who handle it properly let it evolve over time. "Embedded in the process of termination are issues of the individual's separateness, autonomy, and independence from the group" (Ohlsen et al., 1988, p. 93). The pain and anxiety of separating from the group (if they occur) are best dealt with at this time by using capping techniques. As stated previously, capping involves a cognitive sharing of events that are removed from immediate here-and-now situations. Examples of capping include reflecting on past experiences, remembering meaningful group events, reminiscing about the way one entered the group, and talking about present and future plans (Gladding, 1994a; Yalom, 2005). The sharing of this information can be done on an individual basis through a brief leader–member exit interview before the group's final session or within the confines of the last few sessions of the group itself.

FOLLOW-UP SESSIONS

Follow-up is the procedure of reconnecting with group members after they have had enough time to process what they experienced in the group and work on their goals or objectives. Usually follow-up is planned for 3 to 6 months after a group ends, either with the group as a whole or with the leader and a group member. There are several ways to follow up with group members once a group has ended. The first is to arrange for a private interview with each group member a few weeks to a few months after the group terminates (Corey et al., 2003). These interviews focus on the achievement of individual goals of group members. They give leaders and members a way of assessing what has happened to members since the group terminated. At these times, the impact of the group on members can be examined more closely, and any unresolved business can be discussed. Leaders also have an opportunity at such sessions to suggest other resources or opportunities for group members.

A second variation on the follow-up of group members is to hold a reunion about 3 to 6 months after its termination (Cormier & Hackney, 2005). These sessions may take the form of parties or may be conducted in a business-style manner. Regardless, it is important that leaders and members be given the opportunity to reconnect with one another and share their unique experiences. The best way to plan for reunions is to announce them before the group officially ends. In this way, group members are more motivated to follow through on changes to which they have committed during the group.

Another way to conduct a follow-up is with an **evaluation questionnaire**. This serves the purpose of helping group members be concrete in assessing the group in which they have participated. These questionnaires can take many forms but are best if kept brief. An evaluation questionnaire should cover at least (a) the leadership of the group, (b) the facilities in which the group was held, and (c) the group's effectiveness in achieving its objectives.

Leadership can be assessed through asking such questions as whether the leaders (or co-leaders) were personally and professionally responsible and whether they were effective in helping the group and its members. Questions related to whether the group began and ended on time are also appropriate.

Queries related to facilities should focus on the location, comfort, and usefulness of the room in conducting a group. If a room is too noisy or cold, or even if it is the wrong shape, the group will be affected.

Final inquiries on a follow-up questionnaire should deal with the effectiveness of the group. If the individuals involved had their personal and collective needs met through the group, then the group was successful. It may take months before such an assessment can accurately be made.

A final, frequently used method to evaluate a group is through writing a journal. A journal, or log, may be a valuable document for later examining what actually happened and when within the group (Adams, 1993). Individuals who keep journals may discover through reading their writings how they progressed during the group. Leaders may especially benefit by sharing their journals with other professionals as a means of supervision and feedback. In such a process, they may gain insight into their own strengths and weaknesses in handling particular group stages, difficult group members, and forms of group behavior. For example, Tyro may note his initial concern about Alicia in his journal. Later, he may look back to his writing and recognize how she has grown, regressed, or stayed the same. The key to this insight would become clear because of his writing.

Among the benefits of keeping a journal are its immediacy and availability for the group member or the leader. A journal is a paper trail that can be kept in a special place so that it is always accessible. Journals also allow group members to release their emotions and check the reality around them. By recognizing themes within one's journal, a person can examine predominant ways of reacting toward a person or a situation. If such expression is irrational or irresponsible, then the group member can work within or after the group to become more skilled in making another response. Finally, journals help group members clarify their thoughts. For example, by journal writing, Jill may discover she is mad at herself for not taking risks rather than angry at Amy for talking too much.

SUMMARY AND CONCLUSION

Termination is an important stage in groups, both on an individual session basis and as an overall process. The impact of termination on group participants and the group as a whole can be either positive or negative. Thus, it is crucial that group leaders and members have an awareness of termination and its importance even before the group starts.

Until the late 1970s, termination was not given much attention because it was assumed that group leaders would know how to close off groups. Since that time, however, termination has increasingly been recognized as a distinct process in group work and has been the subject of numerous research studies. On an individual level, group members may either resist or gradually move toward termination. Some members, who have not been properly screened or who are immature, may leave the group early. Leaders and members must deal with these situations as well as with unavoidable premature exits due to circumstances beyond a leader's or a member's control. Ways of handling these situations vary, but general guidelines exist. One of these guidelines is to recognize that major theoretical positions

deal with premature termination differently. Another guideline is to be aware that termination is a gradual and stepwise process.

Appropriate ways of ending individual sessions and the group as a whole also exist. Group leaders must take precautions and necessary steps to see that groups run on time and that members realize the importance of participating in the group while there is time. Ways of encouraging members to do so include offering structured exercises, such as making the rounds, as well as setting up parameters and focus. It is the leader's responsibility to make sure the group stays on track in closing and to help members who have unfinished business or other problems at the time of termination. Follow-up on either an individual or group basis is a way of helping members concentrate on what they have achieved within the group as well as what they wish to accomplish. Structured exercises used throughout the termination process, such as journal keeping or feedback questionnaires, will help leaders and group members to end a group positively and productively.

Table 8.1 summarizes the stages of groups including termination.

Table 8.1

Characteristics of the five group stages.

Forming	Storming	Norming	Performing/Working	Mourning/Termination
Characterized by initial caution associated with any new experience; attempt to avoid being rejected by others.	**Characterized** by a time of conflict and anxiety; group moves from primary to secondary tension; attempt to balance between too much and too little tension.	**Characterized** by a feeling of "We-ness" that comes when individuals feel that they belong to the group; often enthusiasm and cooperation at this time.	**Characterized** by a focus on the achievement of individual and group goals and the movement of the group into a more unified and productive system.	**Characterized** by participants coming to know themselves on a deeper level; primary activities in termination—reflect on past experiences, process memories, evaluate what was learned, acknowledge ambivalent feelings, engage in cognitive decision making.
Peer relationships: group members tend to be superficial and center conversation around historical or future events that do not have a direct impact on the group.	**Peer relationships:** group members tend to be more anxious in their interactions with one another; concern for power is prevalent.	**Peer relationships:** identification with others in the group; hope, cooperation, collaboration, cohesion.	**Peer relationships:** genuine concern on a deep, personal level by members for one another; greater willingness to self-disclose on the part of members; increased awareness in the group about individual participants and the world of each person.	**Peer relationships:** feelings of empathy, compassion, and care abound; participants relate to one another on a deep and sometimes emotional level; feelings of warmth and sorrow often occur simultaneously.
Task processing: dealing with apprehension; reviewing members' goals and contracts; specifying more clearly or reiterating group rules; setting limits; promoting positive interchange among members so they will want to continue.	**Task processing:** concentration on direct objectives diminishes; a healthy "pause" takes place; scapegoating might take place.	**Task processing:** members must agree on the establishment of norms from which to operate the group; groups accept both prescriptive and proscriptive norms; importance of commitment is stressed during this time.	**Task processing:** major emphasis on productivity whether the results are tangibly visible or not; maintenance of interpersonal relationships must be attended to and balanced with productivity.	**Task processing:** major emphasis on promoting a successful end to the group and relationships in the group; consolidation of gains, finding of meaning in group, making decisions for new ways of behaving; prepare for a new beginning after group ends.
Useful procedures: joining, linking, cutting off, drawing out and clarifying purpose.	**Useful procedures:** leveling, feedback, informal and formal feedback.	**Useful procedures:** supporting, empathizing, facilitating, self-disclosure.	**Useful procedures:** modeling, exercises, group observing group, brainstorming, nominal-group technique, synectics, written projections, group processing, teaching skills.	**Useful procedures:** summarization, rounds, dyads, written reactions, rating sheets, homework, time limits, capping skills, and modeling.

CLASSROOM EXERCISES

1. As a class studying groups, bring in song lyrics, poems, or short stories that deal with the theme of termination. Examine how writers treat the subject, and discuss those whom the class feels personify these themes.

2. In a group of three, think of an exercise you could use to help a group terminate—for example, the making of a group collage. As a triad, formulate directions to do your exercise and conduct it before the class as a whole. Try to make your exercise as concrete and creative as possible.

3. Discuss in a group of three what you would do as a group leader in the following situations:
    a. A group member at the last session angrily attacks you as the leader and says his experience in the group has been worthless.
    b. Five of eight group members ask you during the last session to extend the group for at least four more sessions.
    c. After the close of an individual group session, a member lingers and tells you she must talk about something she did not reveal in the group today.

    Share your strategies for dealing with these situations with the class as a whole.

4. Role-play a group session in which one member gets up and leaves the group (during the fourth session). Have group members and the leader react in ways they feel at the moment. Then have other class members who have been on the outside of this demonstration give the inside group feedback about what they observed and what they might do.

CHAPTER 9

ETHICAL AND LEGAL ASPECTS OF GROUP WORK

Michal Heron/PH College

I am taken back by your words—
To your history and the mystery of being human
    in an all-too-often robotic world.
I hear your pain
    and see the pictures you paint
        so cautiously and vividly.
The world you draw is a kaleidoscope
    ever changing, ever new, encircling, and fragile.
Moving past the time and through the shadows
    you look for hope beyond the groups you knew
        as a child.
I want to say: "I'm here. Trust the process."
But the artwork is your own
    so I withdraw and watch you work
        while occasionally offering you colors
            and images of the possible.**

*From "Journey" by Samuel T. Gladding, © 1990, *Journal of Humanistic Education and Development, 28,* p. 142. Copyright ACA. Reprinted with permission. No further reproduction authorized without written permission of the American Counseling Association.

Group leaders are constantly making decisions. Much of what they decide is guided by the ethical guidelines of the professional organizations to which they belong and the legal codes of local, state, and federal governments (Remley & Herlihy, 2005). At times, practitioners are confused about whether their decision making is based on ethical guidelines, legal standards, or both. *Ethics* and the *law* are not one and the same. Rather, "they can probably be best conceptualized as two over-lapping circles which share a common intersection" (Kitchener, 1984a, p. 16). Ethical and legal opinions complement and contradict each other. Group leaders who make the best and wisest decisions are those who are informed by as many sources as possible.

Information alone, however, is not enough. Knowledge in and of itself does not guarantee proper ethical behavior (Welfel, 2006). Group leaders and members must also practice what they learn. "Conduct and character are correlated" (Hayes, 1991, p. 24). It is only with practice that those who work in groups become skilled at discerning the rationale for their behaviors and the consequences of them (Foltz, Kirby, & Paradise, 1989). Therefore, ethical and legal decision making is a dynamic activity that needs careful attention if group leaders are to stay current and act in the best interest of their group members. "It becomes every group leader's responsibility to attempt to think ethically and behave professionally" (Gumaer & Scott, 1986, p. 149). "Ethical decision making is an ongoing process with no easy answers" (Moleski & Kiselica, 2005, p. 3).

In this chapter, the nature of professional and personal ethics is examined, along with some specific ethical guidelines for group leaders. Potential problems related to ethics in group work are examined, as are issues involving the training of group leaders in ethics. In addition, the nature of law and legal codes is explored because they affect the field of group work. Potential legal problems in groups are also discussed. Although many ethical and legal matters are fairly straightforward and clear-cut, some are not. Group work is a complex process, and those who are most involved in it must be multifaceted.

THE NATURE OF ETHICS AND ETHICAL CODES

Ethics may best be defined as suggested standards of conduct based on a set of professional values (Gladding, 2006). To behave in an ethical way is to act in a professionally acceptable manner based on these values. Ethics address what is right and correct and are deduced from values (Welfel, 2006). All ethical issues involve values as grounds for decision making. Some of the dominant values underlying the practice of ethics are based on the virtues of autonomy, beneficence, nonmaleficence, justice (i.e., fairness), fidelity, and veracity (i.e., truthfulness) (Kitchener, 1984b; Meara, Schmidt, & Day, 1996).

Autonomy is the promotion of self-determination or the power to choose one's own direction in life. In groups, it is important that members feel they have a right to make their own decisions. For example, if Kathy is struggling in a counseling group about whether to marry, then she needs to feel she is not being pressured by the group to decide one way or the other.

Beneficence is promoting the good of others. It is assumed in groups that leaders and members will work hard for the betterment of the group as a whole. For example, in a career support group, members who find out information concerning employment opportunities will share those tips with others in the group.

Nonmaleficence means avoiding doing harm. To act ethically, members of groups must be sure the changes they make in themselves and the help they offer others are not going to be damaging. For instance, Yoko, a Japanese American, may not be helped if she takes a group leader's advice and becomes more assertive with her family of origin.

Justice (i.e., fairness) refers to the equal treatment of all people. This virtue implies that everyone's welfare is promoted and that visible differences in people, such as gender or race, do not interfere with the way they are treated. Thus, Mohammed is not made to feel apart from the group because he is the only Arab American in it.

Fidelity refers to loyalty and duty. It is keeping one's promise and honoring one's commitment. In group work, fidelity involves stating up front what the group will focus on and then keeping that pledge. In such situations, trust is established, and group members are able to accomplish what they set out to do. For example, a psychoeducational group basically deals with information. Therefore, if Mark joins such a group, he expects that the group leader will not ask him to disclose personal information about himself that might be embarrassing.

Veracity is truthfulness. In group work, veracity is important in almost all phases of the group's development. Group members and leaders who are not truthful with themselves or others set up situations in which a good working relationship is impossible to achieve. For instance, in a therapy group, if Tosha tells the group she is not offended by a remark by another member when she really is, then her behavior in the group may change and the group as a whole may deteriorate because of this untruthfulness. Generally, veracity in groups has to do with both inter- and intrapersonal honesty.

At first glance, the practice of ethics does not appear to be difficult. Indeed, individuals who are sheltered from complex interpersonal relationships may find it relatively easy to behave ethically. However, when behavior is considered in the multifaceted world of a group of diverse people, the matter of ethics and acting ethically may become complicated. A uniform code of ethics is needed as a guide in such situations.

A **code of ethics** is a set of standards and principles that organizations create to provide guidelines for their members to follow in working with the public and with one another. Codes of ethics are constantly evolving. "Parts of ethical documents are aspirational in nature . . . and not enforceable, while other sections require strict professional adherence" (Rapin, 2004, p. 152). In short, ethical codes do not address all possible situations.

In a field such as group work, in which practitioners come from varied backgrounds, often some question arises as to which code of ethics to follow and when (Page, Mitchell, Olson, & Vernon, 2000). The reason is that within each specialty (e.g., counseling, medicine, nursing, psychology, social work), codes of ethics have been developed. Some do not deal with aspects of group conduct, and some contradict one another (Corey, Corey, & Callanan, 2007). In addressing the field of counseling specifically, Herlihy and Remley (1995) point out that "the existence of multiple codes of ethics creates a confusing situation both for professionals and for consumers" (p. 130). Their observation is pertinent to the field of group work.

One document that specifically addresses ethical issues in group work is the *Best Practice Guidelines* of the Association for Specialists in Group Work (ASGW) (1998; see Appendix A). This document provides "structure to the planning, performing, and processing tasks required for effective and ethical practice in counseling and psychotherapy groups" (Rapin, 2004, p. 159). It should be used along with the more general Codes of

Ethics from one's professional association, because together these documents give guidance for ethical interaction in groups. They are based on years of group experience and were developed in response to the need to outline proper behaviors and correct questionable practices within the group field. Two other documents, the ASGW's *Principles for Diversity-Competent Group Workers* (1999; see Appendix B) and its *Professional Standards for the Training of Group Workers* (2000; see Appendix C), are also important sources of ethical information, as they outline the qualifications of group leaders in different types of groups and ways of working with diverse groups.

It is important that group leaders be aware of these codes, standards, and guidelines as well as others like them from similar helping professions, such as social work and psychology. Although codes of ethics, best practice guidelines, and professional training standards are not entirely satisfactory because in many situations no one behavior seems entirely ethical, ethical codes, guidelines, and standards such as those just mentioned give group workers a starting place to find answers and resolutions. Therefore, these documents should be studied and discussed throughout a professional's career. An advanced group leader is expected to operate much more ethically than one with less experience (Kottler, 1994).

CASE EXAMPLE: Sunny's Sad Situation

The principal of her school asked Sunny, a classroom teacher, to lead a counseling group for elementary children. Sunny had no background in group work, but she did not want to disappoint her principal. Therefore, she consented.

Matters went from bad to worse quickly. Sunny invited acting-out kids to be in her group without getting their parents' permission or even notifying them. By the second session, Sunny found that she faced both a disorganized situation in her group and a bunch of angry parents. Being clueless, she moved quickly to seek advice from the school system's attorney.

How could Sunny have avoided this situation? What would you have advised her to do had she come to you before consenting to lead the group? Afterwards? What positive role could ethics have playing in this scenario?

MAJOR ETHICAL ISSUES IN GROUP WORK

A number of major ethical issues are involved in most kinds of group work. For some types of groups, such as task/work groups, a few of these issues will not be as prevalent as for other types of groups, such as psychotherapy or counseling groups. Among the most important issues are those involving training of group leaders, screening of potential group members, the rights of group members, confidentiality, personal relationships between group members and leaders, dual relationships, personal relationships among group members, uses of group techniques, leaders' values, referrals, records, and termination and follow-up. All of these issues are discussed here.

Training of Group Leaders

Certain personal characteristics are vital for group leaders: self-awareness; genuineness; the ability to form warm, caring relationships; sensitivity and understanding; self-confidence; a sense of humor; flexibility of behavior; and a willingness to self-evaluate. Without these personal qualities, potential group leaders would have difficulty in their interpersonal relationships and would not be effective. Usually, individuals wishing to become group leaders will obtain specialized training in one of the four areas of group work specialization: psychoeducation, counseling, psychotherapy, or task/work. However, it is the responsibility of professional education programs, such as those accredited by the Council for the Accreditation of Counseling and Related Educational Programs (CACREP), to be sure that persons whom they graduate are personally integrated and have received the experiences and possibly therapy they need to work out biases and use strengths (Yalom, 2005).

In addition to personal qualities, the training of group leaders involves selected course work and experience in core group skills, such as being able to identify the basic principles of group dynamics (ASGW, 2000). It is also important for them to be involved in different types of group experiences, both as participants and as leaders or co-leaders (Corey et al., 2007; Yalom, 2005). Just as the ASGW (2000) has published its professional standards (see Appendix B), so has the American Group Psychotherapy Association (AGPA) (2002) and other professional group associations. Personal-growth experiences are seen by group associations as part of the total program for aspiring group leaders.

Regardless of the standards followed, group leaders must recognize their limitations (Welfel, 2006). Those who do not possess professional credentials in an area in which they wish to practice either must not practice or must be supervised by a professionally qualified person (ASGW, 1998). It is essential that leaders and members have a clear conception of the type of group to which they belong and the kind of goals they wish to achieve (Gumaer & Martin, 1990). One way for beginning group leaders to gain clarity and experience, in addition to those ideas mentioned previously, is to join a **training group** (Corey & Corey, 2006). In such a group, beginning leaders can learn to recognize and work out major personal and professional issues that affect their ability to conduct groups—for example, criticism, anxiety, jealousy, or the need for control.

Screening of Potential Group Members

A second major issue in group work is screening potential members, which is more difficult than it seems. It becomes even more complicated when the group is composed of nonvolunteers.

Screening is actually a three-part process. It begins when group leaders formulate the type of group they would like, and are qualified, to lead. Next is the process of recruitment, in which the leader must make sure not to misrepresent the type of group that is to be conducted. In the recruiting process, potential members have a right to know the goals of the group, the basic procedures to be used, what will be expected of them as participants, what they can expect from the leader, and any major risks as well as potential values of participating in the group. Recruiting is often conducted in a number of ways, including the distribution of flyers as well as direct, personal contact with potential group members and helping professionals who may know individuals appropriate for such an experience.

Finally, the leader screens applicants on a one-to-one or small-group basis to be sure they are able to benefit from and contribute to the group (Riva, Lippert, & Tackett, 2000). This type of screening is valuable because it provides an opportunity for the group leader

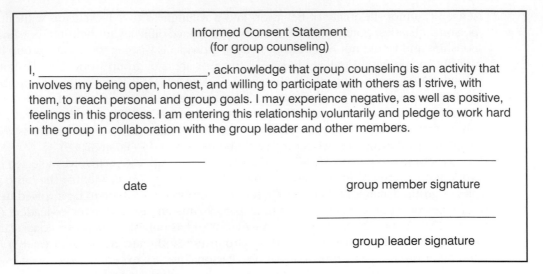

Figure 9.1
An informed consent statement.

to establish rapport, clarify norms and expectations of group behavior, and answer any questions the individual may have about the group.

An important aspect of screening, besides the personal contact it provides, is finding out whether a potential group member is currently in any other kind of mental health treatment, such as individual counseling. If a person is, then it is essential for the group leader to contact the other mental health services provider and inform him or her about the potential member's desire to participate in the group. The potential group member ultimately must decide in collaboration with this professional whether to join the group. The potential member needs as much information as possible about the benefits and liabilities of such action. It is advisable at the end of the screening process, and before accepting a member into the group, that the leader obtain a member's signature on an **informed consent statement** (Welfel, 2006) (see Figure 9.1). Such a process acknowledges that the individual is aware of the group activity in which he or she is about to participate and is doing so voluntarily.

Rights of Group Members

Group members have rights that must be respected and protected if the group is going to work well. These rights are similar to the rights of others who are consumers of professional services. "Group members need to understand what choices they have in participating and what consequences will occur if they refuse" (Rapin, 2004, p. 159). Overt ways of conveying this understanding is important in both voluntary and involuntary groups (such as those that are court ordered or conducted in an inpatient facility). In some types of groups, such as counseling groups, recipients of services can be alerted to their rights through the distribution of prepackaged materials, such as those produced by Chi Sigma Iota (International Academic and Professional Counseling Honor Society) and the National Board of Certified Counselors (see Figure 9.2). These materials along with a verbal explanation of them are crucial to fully informing individuals of their rights.

Counseling Services:
Consumer Rights and Responsibilities
Consumer Rights

- Be informed of the qualifications of your counselor: education, experience, and professional counseling certification(s) and state license(s).
- Receive an explanation of services offered, your time commitments, and fee scales and billing policies prior to receipt of services.
- Be informed of limitations of the counselor's practice to special areas of expertise (e.g., career development, ethnic groups, etc.) or age group (e.g., adolescents, older adults, etc.).
- Have all that you say treated confidentially and be informed of any state laws placing limitations on confidentiality in the counseling relationship.
- Ask questions about the counseling techniques and strategies and be informed of your progress.
- Participate in setting goals and evaluating progress toward meeting them.
- Be informed of how to contact the counselor in an emergency situation.
- Request referral for a second opinion at any time.
- Request copies of records and reports to be used by other counseling professionals.
- Receive a copy of the code of ethics to which your counselor adheres.
- Contact the appropriate professional organization if you have doubts or complaints relative to the counselor's conduct.
- Terminate the counseling relationship at any time.

Consumer Responsibilities

- Set and keep appointments with your counselor. Let him/her know as soon as possible if you cannot keep an appointment.
- Pay your fees in accordance with the schedule you pre-established with the counselor.
- Help plan your goals.
- Follow through with agreed-upon goals.
- Keep your counselor informed of your progress toward meeting your goals.
- Terminate your counseling relationship before entering into arrangements with another counselor.

This statement was prepared jointly by the National Board for Certified Counselors and Chi Sigma Iota to help you understand and exercise your rights as a consumer of counseling services. NBCC and CSI believe that clients who are informed consumers are able to best use counseling services to meet their individual needs.

Figure 9.2

Counseling services: consumer rights and responsibilities.

Source: National Board for Certified Counselors, Greensboro, NC, and Chi Sigma Iota (International Academic and Professional Counseling Honor Society), Greensboro, NC. Reprinted with permission of the National Board for Certified Counselors.

In addition, specific guidelines pertaining to rights and risks in particular group situations should be covered (Remley & Herlihy, 2005). Group members should be told before the group begins that their participation in the group is voluntary or involuntary accordingly and what will be the consequences if they choose not to participate, if they are disruptive, or if they leave the group. Furthermore, group members should be informed of their rights to resist following instructions or suggestions of leaders and other members. They should expect to be treated individually and respectfully and to be protected from physical and psychological threats and intimidation. They should also be informed as clearly as possible about what the group leader can and cannot do. Basically, group members have the right to know as realistically as possible what type of group procedures will be used, what they can and cannot do, and what the risks are in their participation.

Confidentiality

Confidentiality is the right of group members to reveal personal thoughts, feelings, and information to the leader and other members of the group and expect that information to not be disclosed to others outside the group. Not keeping confidences is like gossiping and is destructive to the group process. Underlying the keeping of confidence is the matter of trust. If groups of any kind are going to be productive, then members must trust one another.

Group leaders should deal with the importance and reality of confidentiality during the pregroup screening process. It should be stressed to potential group members that everyone in the group is expected to maintain confidentiality as a means of creating trust, cohesiveness, and growth (Corey et al., 2007; Cottone & Tarvydas, 2007). At the same time, the leader must acknowledge that he or she cannot guarantee confidentiality and that there may be certain cases in which ethical or legal considerations may force the leader to break confidentiality (Welfel, 2006). For example, Section B of the American Counseling Association's *Code of Ethics* (2005) deals with confidentiality, privileged communication, and privacy and spells out as clearly as possible when confidentiality must be broken, such as when clients are being dangerous to themselves or others or when legal requirements demand disclosure.

When group leaders find or suspect that members have broken confidentiality, they need to address the matter quickly and directly with the group as a whole. For instance, if Paul, as group leader, learns in a counseling group that Bonita has told her closest friends about Jill's reactions to her failed marriage, then Paul needs to raise the issue before the group for discussion and suggestions. The atmosphere surrounding such an experience will be tense and should be serious.

In efforts to prevent breaks in confidentiality, leaders need to reaffirm periodically to group members the importance of not discussing with others what occurs in the group (Corey et al., 2007). This approach keeps the matter of confidentiality constantly before the group and may serve a preventive function by increasing members' awareness so that they do not unintentionally discuss material outside the group. Unfortunately, leaders and members cannot prevent breaks of confidentiality after a group ends, and this reality must also be addressed.

◆ *Questions from Experience* ◆

When have you had your own or a friend's confidentiality broken? What were the results of this breach? How did you feel? What did you do? What do you think you should do if this happens in a group now?

Personal Relationships Between Group Members and Leaders

The degree and kind of relationship between group members and leaders will vary from group to group. In task/work groups, for instance, casual contact between group members and leaders is usually unavoidable and may even be productive. However, in therapeutic groups, such contact is likely to be inappropriate and could be destructive to the persons involved as well as to the group as a whole. It is more likely that relationships between group members and leaders will be detrimental to the group as a whole if they are not carefully handled. Such relationships can lead to favoritism or to a failure to focus on important personal topics within the context of the group itself. Usually, outside personal contact between group leaders and members in therapeutic or counseling groups is discouraged or prohibited because this behavior may foster dependency or may lead to unhealthy dual relationships.

Dual/Multiple Relationships

Dual/multiple relationships occur when group leaders find themselves in two or more potentially conflicting roles with their group members, such as "professional (e.g., professor, supervisor, employer) or personal (e.g., friend, close relative, sexual partner)" (Herlihy & Remley, 2001, p. 80). "Although certain dual/multiple relationships may seem unavoidable and may even seem harmless, they carry the potential for harm because of the inherent vulnerability of the client and the imbalance of power between counselor and client" (Neukrug, Milliken, & Walden, 2001). In a counseling training program, for instance, a group leader might also be a member's teacher and have the responsibility of assigning grades. The fact that the group leader might come to know something about the member's background could potentially have a detrimental effect on the member's grade (Davenport, 2004). For example, Patricia, the group leader, might find out that Jenny, a group member, is a lesbian. If Patricia has unresolved issues or biases involving homosexuals, she will treat Jenny differently than before. Regardless of the exact setting, dual relationships can negatively affect the people involved in subtle and obvious ways. Therefore, they are best avoided.

In academic settings, Remley and Reeves (1989) advise counselor educators to avoid dual and multiple relationships such as requiring or allowing students to participate in a group experience led by the educators as a part of a course. Most of these situations usually involve a conflict of interest. Ways of resolving these circumstances include (a) using faculty-supervised post-master's students to lead groups for entry-level students; (b) using a blind-grading system; (c) requiring students to participate in externally supervised groups; (d) employing role-play techniques; (e) having students co-lead their own groups while the instructor observes; and (f) using a "fishbowl training" technique in which students co-lead their own groups alternating between an inner and outer circle, again with the instructor observing and helping the group process what occurs (Forester-Miller & Duncan, 1990; Kane, 1995).

However, how to handle potentially dual or multiple relationships is not as easy or as prescriptive as it may seem on the surface. In a nonacademic setting, especially where people are unaccustomed to receiving help from an outsider, cultural respect must be balanced with ethical considerations (Moleski & Kiselica, 2005). For example, to refuse to receive a gift from a group member of Japanese descent might do more harm than good because it might be seen as an insult to the gift giver.

This last issue on balance and perspective brings up an important point about the difference between a dual relationship and a relationship with dual qualities (Aponte, 1994). For instance, a group leader may know about a member's personal issues and yet be able to treat the member fairly and appropriately. However, most relationships with dual or multiple qualities, such as conducting a group and grading participants or offering group counseling to a friend, are fraught with the potential to become contaminated. Therefore, if there is the slightest doubt about whether a group worker is about to enter into such a relationship, then the leader should err on the side of caution.

If a potential dual or multiple relationship cannot be avoided, such as in a rural setting where there are limited services, then all parties concerned should carefully explore the potential benefits and pitfalls in the affiliation before entering it. If possible, it is wise to have an outside neutral party strictly monitor the relationship on a regular basis. This type of an arrangement is preventive and follows the ethical principle that "the professional should, at all cost, do no harm to the client" (Sklare, Thomas, Williams, & Powers, 1996, p. 265).

Personal Relationships Among Group Members

The matter of personal relationships among group members is another ethically gray area. Context is one of the major deciding factors. In some settings, for example, work environments, schools, or mental hospitals, group members will inevitably interact with one another outside the group. In other settings, such as outpatient treatment groups or special task forces, this type of interaction is unlikely to occur naturally. Most group leaders do not make hard and fast rules about personal relationships among group members because this type of rule is impossible to enforce (Jacobs, Masson, & Harvill, 2006). There are some cases, such as in self-help groups, in which contact with members outside the structured group may be therapeutic. However, in most counseling and psychotherapy groups member-to-member contact outside the group results in the formation of subgroups or hidden agendas, which can be detrimental. Therefore, discouraging socialization in these types of groups is a prudent policy (Remley & Herlihy, 2005).

Overall, for most groups, the focus should be on open relationships within the group setting. There is a rich and subtle interplay between the group member and the group environment, and each member at once shapes and responds to his or her social microcosm. The more spontaneous the interaction is, the more varied will be the environment and the greater the likelihood that problematic issues will be touched on for all the members (Yalom, 2005).

Uses of Group Techniques

Group techniques or exercises are structured ways of getting members to interact with one another. They can have a powerful impact on group members and positively affect how people work together or change. However, when leaders misuse group techniques they can also inhibit the natural ebb and flow of a group (Carroll & Wiggins, 1997). For instance, Meg may start each group counseling session with a structured exercise to avoid having to grapple with the hard job of focusing on group process and the difficult issues that have arisen in the group. In such a situation, Meg may accelerate the pace of the group, but at a cost. As Yalom (2005) states, "The group pays a price for its speed; it circumvents many group development tasks and does not develop a sense of autonomy and potency" (p. 472). Therefore, the use of group techniques as in Meg's case is ethically questionable.

Corey (2004) believes that structured exercises are best used when they are focused on group goals or group members' achievements. Group leaders face ethical problems when they lack the skill or sensitivity to use exercises properly or when they "deskill" group members by making them overly dependent on the leader and less likely to help one another (Jacobs et al., 2006; Yalom, 2005). In such cases, leaders may generate more feelings or nonverbal expressions than they or the group can handle and ultimately may lead the group to a dead end (Carroll & Wiggins, 1997; Corey & Corey, 2006). In choosing an exercise for a group, the leader should always have a rationale and tailor the exercise to fit the particular needs of the group. Using techniques isolated from relationships and theories amounts to the employment of "gimmicks," which is an unprofessional and unethical way to work (Patterson, 1985a).

CASE EXAMPLE: Jerry Puts Gimmicks into Gear

Jerry was leading a group for the first time. Not knowing exactly what to do to get the group moving, he used a warm-up exercise initially. It worked like a charm. Group members quickly started talking to one another and Jerry noted that the group went well.

Since he was leading a psychotherapy group, Jerry believed it would be good to start each group with an exercise. He quickly learned the meaning of the term "diminishing returns," as each week the activities he brought in seemed to be less powerful than the week before. Group members did not seem particularly interested in beginning the group that way, especially if they had unfinished business from the week before.

What would you tell Jerry to do at this point? What are other positive and negative aspects of beginning a group with an activity or gimmick?

Group leaders can employ at least 14 different kinds of exercises in the groups they conduct: written, movement, dyads and triads, rounds, creative props, arts and crafts, fantasy, common reading, feedback, trust, experiential, moral dilemma, touching, and group decision (Jacobs et al., 2006). Whenever an exercise is used in a group, it should be processed so that it allows group members to become better informed about themselves and the group. Therefore, at least twice as much time should be allowed for the processing of exercises as for completing them. Ways of processing include sharing in small groups, sharing in the group as a whole, sharing through writing, using rounds, or employing some combination of these methods (Jacobs et al., 2006).

Leaders' Values

Group leaders have values and, for better or worse, values influence the goals, methods, and ultimately the success of group work and counseling (Corey et al., 2007; Mitchell, 1993; Patterson, 1958; Williamson, 1958). Leaders who try to hide their values may actually do more harm than good in certain situations. For instance, if Jana dislikes the patronizing way Carolyn responds to other group members but does not voice her value about members leveling with one another, then the group may either avoid interactions with Jana or scapegoat her. However, leaders must be careful not to impose their values on group members. Such action short-circuits members' exploration, especially in counseling and psychotherapy groups, and results in confusion and chaos.

Group members have the ultimate responsibility to make their own decisions. However, leaders help members explore their values more thoroughly while maintaining their own. If group leaders and members have conflicts about values, then leaders are responsible for making referrals (Corey et al., 2007). Leaders must stay attuned and be aware of the impact of values in a group of any kind.

Referrals

Referrals (i.e., transfers of members to another group) are made when group leaders realize they cannot help certain members achieve designated goals or when a conflict between leaders and members has proven unresolvable. The group leader is responsible for making appropriate referrals when necessary because he or she cannot be all things to all people. The process of making a referral involves assessing one's own values and limitations as a group leader and listening to individual group members concerning their particular needs.

Group leaders should maintain an extensive and current list of referral sources. The referral process itself involves four steps: "(1) identifying the need to refer; (2) evaluating potential referral sources; (3) preparing the client for the referral; and (4) coordinating the transfer" (Cormier & Hackney, 2005, p. 294). For instance, if Dot realizes in her psychotherapy group that she cannot help Mahalah, then she may first arrange to meet with Mahalah after a group session and discuss the situation with her. Before the meeting, Dot should prepare a list of potential referral sources and have these ready for Mahalah to see during their session together. If Mahalah is not ready for a referral, then Dot may have to meet with her again. After Mahalah has been persuaded of the wisdom of the referral, Dot should work with her on the arrangements.

Records

When conducting groups for counseling or therapeutic purposes, it is important that group workers keep records. Such documentation helps the group worker concretely review what happened in the group, when it occurred, and who was involved. By reviewing past events, issues and agendas that develop in the group can be better addressed, and the group worker can document for third parties, such as courts or managed care agencies, information that may be relevant to any ethical or legal issues that arise.

Written records should be kept in locked files in a secured area. The area also should be locked and have limited access. One way to keep records is to write them in a problem-oriented format. However, such a procedure "tends to transcribe clients' experiences into the official language of diagnostic labels" and can be dehumanizing (Chen, Noosbond, & Bruce, 1998, p. 405). Another possibility is to document the experiences of group members and the group as a whole in what Yalom (2005) describes as a *process summary*. Using this method, the group worker highlights group process, "reinforcing clients' understanding of the highly charged here-and-now experiences" of the group (Chen et al., 1998, p. 405). A third alternative is for the group worker to write a therapeutic document to the group using key phrases, responses, and descriptions of vivid nonverbal behaviors, thereby capturing the dynamics of a session (Chen et al., 1998). Group members can then discuss the document and their reactions to it at the beginning of the next session. They can also use the document as a reflective tool outside of group sessions to evaluate themselves or the group and to make appropriate changes.

Termination and Follow-Up

"Termination and follow-up become ethical issues more because of errors of omission rather than errors of commission" (Gazda, 1989, p. 307). Groups need to reach some form of closure before ending. By doing so, they help promote and maintain changes members have made while in the group (Yalom, 2005). For long-term groups, the termination process may mean several sessions devoted to winding down and tying up loose ends, whereas for short-term groups, a few hours devoted to this activity will be all that is necessary. Issues related to attachment, loss, and meaning are primarily dealt with in termination (Corey et al., 2007; Cormier & Hackney, 2005; Patterson & Eisenberg, 2000). The important point is that these issues involving separation and consolidation be addressed. For instance, in a psychotherapy group, Lars, who lost his parents early in life, may be particularly upset or angry that the group is ending. He may have unresolved issues in dealing with loss. Although he modified his behavior and thinking in the group, he may revert back to his former style if he is not helped by the group and the leader to come to an acceptable resolution about the group ending.

The ethical issue in follow-up usually centers on its neglect rather than its inclusion. Group leaders should make themselves available to group members for consultation as well as follow-up meetings after the termination of a group. If group leaders are negligent about this important procedure, then group members may not adequately assess the impact the group has had on them and are unlikely to continue working on their goals as specifically as they would otherwise. Besides providing for the welfare of group members, follow-up after termination also has the added benefit of helping group leaders evaluate the effectiveness of what they did in the group and improve their group leadership styles. "Perhaps the most meaningful evaluation material can be gained by a group leader 30 days or more after a group ends. At that time the members are more independent of the leader and perhaps can be more honest" (George & Dustin, 1988, p. 115).

Again, consider the case of Lars. If he receives follow-up, then he will most likely feel that he has not been abandoned. Furthermore, he can focus during follow-up on the improvements he has made since the group ended and be reinforced for this new behavior.

◆ *Questions from Experience* ◆

Think of when you received follow-up from a professional (or even a nonprofessional) about a service or product you purchased. How did you feel when you received the contact? What were your impressions of the person and the service or product? Do you think members of counseling groups might have similar thoughts and emotions?

MAKING ETHICAL DECISIONS

Because group leaders face such a wide variety of issues, it is crucial that they know beforehand how they will make ethical decisions. Although such decisions can be made in many ways, some approaches to ethical decision making can make the process operate more smoothly. Two are discussed here.

The first is making ethical decisions according to both principle ethics and virtue ethics (Corey et al., 2007). **Principle ethics** are ethics based on obligations. They focus on finding "socially and historically acceptable answers to the question, 'What shall I do?'" (p. 10). Codes of ethics are based on principle ethics (i.e., actions stemming from obligations). **Virtue ethics** focus on "the character traits of the counselor [or group worker] and nonobligatory ideals to which professionals aspire rather than on solving specific ethical dilemmas. Simply stated, principle ethics asks 'Is this situation unethical?' whereas virtue ethics asks 'Am I doing what is best for my client?'" (p. 10). In a group, the client is the group as a whole as well as the individuals found therein. Therefore, integrating principle ethics and virtue ethics becomes complex.

A second way of making ethical decisions is to use specific steps as a guideline. For example, in the case of promoting beneficence and enhancing ethical decision making, a mnemonic device that reminds group leaders and members of what they should do can be helpful. One device created for these situations is the **A-B-C-D-E Worksheet** (Sileo & Kopala, 1993) (see Figure 9.3). The letters stand for assessment, benefit, consequences and consultation, duty, and education. Some of the points are more applicable in certain situations than in others, but the device gives practitioners an idea of what they can use to enhance the group's good.

In addition to using this type of worksheet on a particular aspect of group ethical decision making, members can take general steps in the overall process. For example, in ethical decision making, Hill, Glaser, and Harden (1995) suggest a seven-step model to follow in a sequential fashion. This model begins with the recognition that a problem exists and ends with continuing reflection. It is one that involves client collaboration in the process, which Walden (1997) states empowers the client—in this case, the group. Thomas (1992) recommends a less elaborate model. First, she attempts to define a situation. Then she consults ethical codes for information and guidance. A continuum of alternative actions is

A = Assessment
1. What is the client's mental state?
   a. What are his/her strengths, support systems, weaknesses?
   b. Is a psychiatric/medical consult necessary?
2. How serious is the client's disclosure? Is someone at risk for physical harm?
3. What are my values, feelings, and reactions to the client's disclosure?

B = Benefit
1. How will the client benefit by my action?
2. How will the therapeutic relationship benefit?
3. How will others benefit?
4. Which action will benefit the most individuals?

C = Consequences and Consultation
1. What will the ethical, legal, emotional, and therapeutic consequences be for:
   a. The client?
   b. The counselor?
   c. Potential clients?
2. Have I consulted with colleagues, supervisors, agency administrators, legal counsel, professional ethics boards, or professional organizations?

D = Duty
1. To whom do I have a duty?
   a. My client?
   b. The client's family?
   c. A significant other?
   d. The counseling profession?
   e. My place of employment?
   f. The legal system?
   g. Society?

E = Education
1. Do I know and understand what the ethical principles and codes say regarding this issue?
2. Have I consulted the ethical case books?
3. Have I recently reviewed the laws that govern counseling practice?
4. Have I been continuing my education through journals, seminars, workshops, conferences, or coursework?

Figure 9.3

An A-B-C-D-E Worksheet for ethical decision making.

Source: From "An A-B-C-D-E Worksheet for Promoting Beneficence When Considering Ethical Issues," by F. J. Sileo and M. Kopala, 1993, *Counseling and Values, 37*, 89–95. Copyright ACA. Reprinted with permission. No further reproduction authorized without written permission of the American Counseling Association.

generated next. At either end of the spectrum will be choices ranging from "take radical action" to "take no action," with more moderate suggestions in the middle part of the choice curve. The next part of the process is to evaluate all suggested actions in regard to other persons' welfare and professional responsibilities. After the consequence of each action is examined, some tentative decision is made and finally implemented. Records are kept, at least of the final outcome.

One unique psychoeducational group experience for ethics-based decision making is conducted through the Arizona courts with the adult criminal diversion programs. These programs offer alternatives to prosecution for persons formally charged with criminal offenses—usually first-time offenders with misdemeanors (Alexander, 1999). In this program (four sessions of 2 hours each), group members work to solve their own and other members' real problems. They do so through tapping into universal values that they already hold, such as goodness, thoughtfulness, tolerance, responsibility, and honesty, as well as learning how to make better decisions. In this program, ethics-based decision making "entails the following steps: (a) identify the problem, (b) research the facts, (c) identify all of the people who will be affected by this decision, and (d) list all of the solutions you can think of and evaluate each alternative" (Alexander, 1999, pp. 210–211). Homework is given, case studies are featured, and members are encouraged to think creatively, such as using brainstorming, metaphorical thinking, and generating unconventional ideas. In this way, opportunities for making choices (and making better decisions) are expanded.

PROMOTING ETHICAL PRINCIPLES IN GROUP WORK

The promotion and implementation of ethical conduct in groups occur on two levels: training and practice. There is an opportunity in educational settings to instill in prospective group leaders a knowledge of and a feel for ethics (ASGW, 1998; Hayes, 1991; Paradise & Siegelwaks, 1982). Indeed, such a procedure is crucial to the welfare of group leaders and other helping professionals in general. For individuals already in practice, training in the ethics of working with groups can best be achieved through continuing educational opportunities and peer supervision.

Training Group Leaders

Training group leaders to address ethical issues is a multidimensional process. On one level, group leaders must become familiar with ethical codes and standards. On another level, they must get to know their own ethics and values. On a third level, prospective group leaders must practice recognizing ethical dilemmas and making ethical decisions. Finally, individuals must become aware of the development of ethical decision making over time so they can assess their own development as practitioners.

All of these different aspects require integrating if individuals are to be properly educated. Indeed, as Kitchener (1986) points out, the training of potential group leaders requires sensitizing them to ethical standards and issues, helping them learn to reason about ethical situations, developing within them a sense of being morally responsible in their actions, and teaching them tolerance of ambiguity in ethical decision making.

To become familiar with ethical codes, best practices, and standards in group work is initially as simple as reading pertinent documents and articles. This type of approach has often been used. Although it may expose persons to the basics of what are commonly accepted guidelines in the practice of group work at a particular time, it does not teach them that ethics are normative rather than factual (Wilcoxon, Remley, Gladding, & Huber, 2007). Ethics "inevitably change both as new scientific evidence dictates new approaches and as our culture changes" (Gazda, 1989, pp. 297–298). A prime example of the rapid change in ethics is the revision of the ASGW's *Ethical Guidelines for Group Counselors* (1989) and the decision by the ASGW not to use these guidelines after the mid-1990s and instead to use the ACA's code of ethics (2005) and the ASGW's own best practices (1998) document as standards for ethical conduct. Training group leaders in ethical decision making today thus involves examining particular codes of ethics, guidelines, and standards while simultaneously exposing prospective group leaders to vignettes related directly to ethical cases (Gumaer & Scott, 1985). Casebooks and videotapes on ethics are very helpful in this procedure (e.g., Corey & Herlihy, 2006; Corey, Corey, & Haynes, 1998).

On a second level, ethical training requires individuals to examine and understand their own personal codes of ethics (Van Hoose & Kottler, 1977; Van Hoose & Paradise, 1979). Group discussion related to general dilemmas can increase ethical awareness and help individuals gain more self-understanding (Paradise & Siegelwaks, 1982). For example, in a classroom situation, a teacher may use a values scale, like those generated by Milton Rokeach (2001), to help class members assess the values they hold most closely. The teacher may also present controversial group case histories to the class and ask members to focus on ways they would handle these situations.

A third way to emphasize ethics is on an integrated level. Prospective group leaders can gain a greater exposure to dealing with ethical dilemmas from a practical viewpoint through role-plays in simulated groups and direct participation in practitioner training groups (Conyne, Wilson, & Ward, 1997). Using these methods, leaders-to-be get a feel for decision making and group dynamics. This type of knowledge is crucial for potential group leaders who do not have a good understanding of making decisions within the dynamics of a group. It can help them learn to reason and risk as well as prevent them from becoming ineffective, harmful, and unethical.

Finally, as a last part of training, individuals who aspire to be group leaders should be exposed to developmental theories of ethical reasoning so they can gauge their own professional growth (Welfel, 2006). Models such as those developed by Van Hoose and Paradise (1979) hold promise for helping persons in training to gain a clearer understanding of their own level of functioning (see Figure 9.4).

Continuing Education and Peer Supervision

For practitioners already in the field of group work, the matter of keeping up with ethical codes and growing as an ethically based professional can be met by taking continuing education courses and by undergoing peer supervision. Almost all professional associations offer programs on ethics at their national, regional, and state conventions. **Continuing education units (CEUs)** for participating in professional programs help group workers stay attuned to the latest developments in areas related to group work. For example, programs

Stage I. **Punishment Orientation**

Counselor decisions, suggestions, and courses of action are based on a strict adherence to prevailing rules and standards, i.e., one must be punished for bad behavior and rewarded for good behavior. The primary concern is the strict attention to the physical consequences of the decision.

Stage II. **Institutional Orientation**

Counselor decisions, suggestions, and courses of action are based on a strict adherence to the rules and policies of the institution or agency. The correct posture is based upon the expectations of higher authorities.

Stage III. **Societal Orientation**

The maintenance of standards, approval of others, and the laws of society and the general public characterize this stage of ethical behavior. Concern is for duty and societal welfare.

Stage IV. **Individual Orientation**

The primary concern of the counselor is for the needs of the individual while avoiding the violation of laws and the rights of others. Concern for law and societal welfare is recognized, but is secondary to the needs of the individual.

Stage V. **Principle or Conscience Orientation**

Concern is for the legal, professional, or societal consequences. What is right, in accord with self-chosen principles of conscience and internal ethical formulations, determines counselor behavior.

Figure 9.4

Stages of ethical behavior.

Source: From *Ethics in Counseling and Psychotherapy* (p. 117) by W. H. Van Hoose and L. V. Paradise, 1979, Cranston, RI: Carroll Press. Reprinted by permission of Sulzburger & Graham Publishing.

on group dynamics, group leadership, and group standards are frequently offered at helping relationship conventions. Many professional associations require that their members participate in such activities (Corey et al., 2007).

Continuing education can be supplemented with **peer supervision**, in which practitioners meet regularly to consult with one another about particularly difficult group situations (Ohlsen et al., 1988). Through this type of experience, practitioners, especially those in private practice, become more informed, establish support, avoid burnout, and stay more aware of the ethical dimension of working with clients in particular cases. It is interesting to note that peer supervision is conducted in a group environment, which can also provide information on dealing with, among other topics, issues in running groups (Greenburg, Lewis, & Johnson, 1985).

Both continuing education and peer supervision can be helpful in subtle and blatant ways to professionals who practice group work. In addition to giving them more knowledge and procedures to use in groups, these educational methods can create new awareness of even minor misconduct in the group leader or in the group. Through this awareness, such behavior can be eliminated. For example, in some groups, a promise is made that no pressure will be put on a participant, but then nonactive members are encouraged in subtle ways to be involved in the group (Kottler, 1994). In helping themselves and their groups make ethical decisions about incidents like this one, group workers increase the safety and efficiency of their groups as well as their own self-knowledge.

RESPONDING TO ALLEGED UNETHICAL COMPLAINTS

It is unusual for a group member to file an unethical complaint against a group leader. However, such incidents occasionally happen, especially in counseling and psychotherapy groups. When they do, the group leader, as a helping professional, needs to take appropriate actions. Two essential actions are to notify his or her professional liability insurance carrier and "ensure that an attorney is promptly retained" (Chauvin & Remley, 1996, p. 564). The reason is that allegations in an ethical complaint can be used as the basis for a lawsuit. Therefore, ethical complaints must be treated seriously.

If an ethics complaint is lodged against a group worker, it will usually be made with a group with which the worker has an affiliation, such as a professional association's ethics committee or a state licensing board. The group worker will have an opportunity to respond to the charges, and the committee or board will then act as a jury. Charges may be dismissed or upheld. If they are upheld, then the group worker may be disciplined through a reprimand, suspension, probation, or revocation of membership or licensure. Regardless, it is in the group worker's best interest to be discreet. If an emotional outlet is needed to handle the stress associated with such a process, then the group worker should seek professional counseling services (Chauvin & Remley, 1996). As with all matters pertaining to adversity, prevention is the first and best practice when dealing with ethical matters.

Overall, "ethical conduct results from a combination of didactic knowledge, an understanding of problem-solving approaches, a clear conception of philosophical principles . . . that underlie a formal code of ethics, and a basically sound character that leads one to respond with maturity, judgment, discretion, wisdom, and prudence" (Bersoff, 1996, p. 90).

CASE EXAMPLE: Hostile Henry Strikes Again

Although they were both in the same profession, Henry hated Fielding. He thought Fielding was a little too good and was too kind. Therefore, when Henry heard rumors that Fielding had said something outrageous as the leader of a psychotherapy group, he immediately filed an ethics charge against him with his national professional group and the state licensure board.

The information Henry received was wrong, and he later retracted his charge. Fielding had been hurt professionally and personally by then. What would you advise Fielding to do? What would you do in regard to Henry if you were the national group or the state licensure board?

LEGAL ISSUES IN GROUP WORK

Ethics and the law are separate but sometimes overlap (Remley, 1996). By their very nature, ethical codes and laws tend to be reactive, emerging from what has occurred rather than anticipating what may occur (Corey et al., 2007). **Law** refers to a body of "agreed-upon rules of a society that set forth the basic principles for living together as a group. Laws can be general or specific regarding both what is required and what is allowed of individuals who form a governmental entity" (Remley & Herlihy, 2005, p. 3). Some ethical issues, such as telling the truth, have legal ramifications when violated. There are also situations regarding issues such as confidentiality and advertising in which conflicts may emerge between legal and ethical systems. Therefore, group leaders are well advised to have knowledge of both ethical codes and legal precedents.

Often, when persons feel wronged by professional helpers, the helpers' actions will be judged according to the standards of the group with which their services are most identified (Woody, Hansen, & Rossberg, 1989). The conduct of group leaders, for example, would likely be compared with the type of behavior considered appropriate in the ASGW's *Best Practices Guidelines* (1998) or a similar definitive document. Thus, group workers must keep up with professional and legal developments on a regular basis. This means staying abreast primarily of community, state, and national standards and knowing what to do in the case of legal action (Bernstein & Hartsell, 2005).

Community, State, and National Standards

Group leaders who function successfully are aware of "community standards, legal limitations to work, and state laws" governing the practice of groups, especially those that directly affect counseling or psychotherapy (Ohlsen et al., 1988, p. 391). This type of information may be best obtained from these sources:

1. Civic, religious, and business leaders of the community in which the group worker resides;
2. Professional state counseling boards;
3. State departments of education;
4. Persons involved in the state or national divisions of major professional counseling associations;
5. Liaison personnel in national professional associations;
6. Local attorneys; and
7. Members of the state attorney general's office.

It is not unusual for helping professionals, such as group workers, to fail in their practices because they have not paid enough attention to community, state, and national standards (Woody, 1988). Knowing theories and techniques of group work is not enough to make practitioners successful, especially those who operate in diversified settings or who wish to operate as private practitioners (Paradise & Kirby, 1990).

The best procedure to employ in preventing legal difficulties is to do one's professional "homework" beforehand. This means reading and studying major references on legal decisions that have an impact on conducting groups. For example, major sources explaining the relationship between the law and mental health practices include those by Anderson and Hopkins (1996); Bernstein & Hartsell (2005); Cohen and Mariano (1982);

Hummel, Talbutt, and Alexander (1985); Sidley (1985); Swenson (1997); Van Hoose and Kottler (1985); and Woody & Associates (1984). The ACA's legal series, edited by Theodore P. Remley Jr. (1996), is excellent in this regard, too. Primary sources for researching legal opinions include the *United States Supreme Court Report* (for Supreme Court decisions), the *Federal Reporter* (for U.S. Courts of Appeals decisions), and the *Federal Supplement* and *Federal Rules* (for U.S. District Court decisions). An official state reporter, such as *Connecticut Reports* or *Alabama Reports,* usually disseminates state court decisions. A frequently used legal research source is *Shepard's Case Citations,* which follows "the judicial history of a targeted case" (Woody & Mitchell, 1984, p. 32).

Bibliographies on group work are a rich source of obtaining information on all professional aspects of groups. With the use of the Internet and computer technology, specialized bibliographies can be put together quickly and cost-efficiently. Reading journal articles, books, and monographs and attending workshops on trends and issues in human services all should be included in group workers' schedules. Consultation with professional peers on landmark legal decisions, such as *Tarasoff v. Board of Regents of the University of California* (1969), is also vital.

Legal Action

Legal action is most likely to be taken against a group worker, especially in a psychotherapy or counseling group, if members think they have suffered physical harm, emotional trauma, or psychological or financial damage as a result of participating in a group experience (Shaffer & Galinsky, 1989; Swenson, 1997). Such legal action usually is in the form of a **malpractice** suit that implies the group leader has failed to render proper service because of either negligence or ignorance. "The word 'malpractice' means bad practice," and "the claim against the professional is made by a 'plaintiff' who seeks a monetary award based on a specific amount of damages physical, financial, and/or emotional" (Gazda, 1989, p. 299). Practitioners can best avoid these suits by maintaining reasonable, ordinary, and prudent practices (Crawford, 1994). For example, keeping written records of groups under lock and key and securing electronically stored records are musts (Swenson, 1997).

Specific practices that are most likely to prevent lawsuits include these:

1. Screening to reject inappropriate potential group members
2. Spending extra time at the beginning of the first group session to discuss group rules and group members' responsibilities
3. Following the ethical codes of professional organizations to which one belongs
4. Practicing only those theories and techniques in which one has actual expertise
5. Obtaining consent or contracts in writing from members (or in the case of minors, their parents)
6. Warning members about the importance of confidentiality and the exceptions in which member confidentiality will have to be broken
7. Staying abreast of recent research, theory, and practice techniques within one's specialty
8. Empowering members to evaluate their own progress and be in charge of their own progress

9. Obtaining regular peer supervision of one's work
10. Following billing regulations and record-keeping practices to the letter of the law (Anderson & Hopkins, 1996; Corey et al., 2007; Hummel et al., 1985; Paradise & Kirby, 1990; Van Hoose & Kottler, 1985)

If a malpractice suit is filed, especially as a result of a counseling or psychotherapeutic experience, then plaintiffs must show that

1. a therapist–client relationship was established,
2. the therapist's conduct fell below the minimal acceptable standard for the case,
3. the conduct of the therapist was the cause of injury to the client, and
4. an actual injury was sustained by the client (Schultz, 1982).

Although the therapist–client relationship may be established easily (e.g., through producing a bill or receipt for services), other criteria in malpractice suits are more difficult to prove. In suits charging that the group leader's conduct fell below minimum standards, the measure usually used in such cases is what other practitioners in the same geographical area would do under similar circumstances (Wilcoxon et al., 2007). Group workers who are in contact with and in line with other practitioners in their area are less likely to be affected by this criterion, although local standards are increasingly being replaced with those on the national level.

The question of whether the group leader's conduct caused injury to a person is easiest to prove if the acts and injury are closely related in time (Wilcoxon et al., 2007). Finally, in deciding whether a group member sustained an actual injury, one or more of the following effects must be shown:

- Exacerbation of a previous symptom
- Appearance of a new symptom
- Client misuse or abuse of therapy (e.g., increased intellectualization or dependency)
- Client overextension of self (e.g., taking on inappropriate tasks)
- Disillusionment with therapy (e.g., feelings of hopelessness and depression) (Strupp, Hadley, & Gomes-Schwartz, 1977).

CASE EXAMPLE: Phyllis Becomes a Plaintiff

Phyllis joined her therapist's psychotherapy group because she had issues revolving around unresolved grief from her childhood. About halfway through the group, the leader became demanding. He insisted that if group members were going to get better, they needed to "spill their guts" and "get on with life." Feeling pressured, Phyllis complied with the leader's demands. She later came to regret her actions, especially when she found out that information she had disclosed in the group was out in the public domain.

In response, Phyllis quit the group and sued the leader. She was visibly upset. The case was settled out of court, with the leader apologizing to Phyllis and returning the money he had charged her. Phyllis wanted to press the case further, but she could not prove she had been harmed in an irreparable way. Furthermore, the leader had kept careful records, which documented that Phyllis had asked him to "push her" to talk before the group.

Even though Phyllis was limited in what she could do legally, do you think she had some ethical recourses? If so, what would they have been?

Most malpractice suits in group work will center on **unintentional civil liability** (i.e., a lack of intent to cause injury). For example, Lilly may claim that a group leader caused her harm by not letting her fully express herself when he blocked her from verbally attacking another group member with whom she disagreed. However, in some cases, "intentional" harm becomes the issue in question. **Intentional civil liability** cases include situations in which there are issues regarding

> *battery* (the unconsented touching of a person),
> *defamation* (injury to a person's character or reputation either through verbal *[slander]* or written *[libel]* means),
> *invasion of privacy* (violation of the right to be left alone), or
> *infliction of mental distress* (outrageous behavior on the part of the therapist) (Wilcoxon et al., 2007).

These types of cases are usually more clear-cut than those involving unintentional actions. In all cases, group specialists, especially those who work in psychotherapeutic or counseling groups, are advised to study their professional standards and codes of ethics carefully before, during, and after group sessions. In all cases, professionals who work with groups should carry **professional liability insurance** (i.e., insurance designed specifically to protect a group worker from financial loss in case of a civil suit). Any court litigation can be costly, and even the most careful group leader may be the subject of legal action. Thus, purchasing liability insurance (usually available through professional associations) and carefully keeping up to date on ethical and legal matters may be two of the best practices that group leaders can employ in helping themselves operate on the highest possible level.

◆ *Questions from Experience* ◆

Who have you known who has been in a civil court case? What did they have to pay their attorney? How much do you think malpractice insurance would cost? Check.

SUMMARY AND CONCLUSION

This chapter has covered various aspects of ethical and legal issues regarding group work. Many of the topics focus on group leaders' responsibilities to their members and themselves. However, some material in this chapter is specifically targeted toward the rights and responsibilities of group members. It is assumed by most individuals who join a group that their leaders will be ethical and professional. However, that is not always the case, and some group members become casualties of their experience. To insure against this, most professional associations, particularly the Asso- ciation for Specialists in Group Work and the American Group Psychotherapy Association, have constructed best practice guidelines, ethical codes, and professional standards by which group leaders and groups should abide. These documents are probably more relevant to leaders of psychotherapy and counseling groups, but they also apply to those who work in psychoeducational settings and with task/work groups. By adhering to such guidelines, codes, and standards, group leaders tend to maximize the benefits and minimize the harm that a group can do to individuals (Lakin, 1985).

Nevertheless, group leaders must pay attention to specific ethical issues, including their training and competence; screening potential members; informing members about the group and the rights they have; ensuring confidentiality to the greatest extent possible; establishing appropriate relationships among group members and between the leader and members; owning but not imposing their own values; using group exercises properly; making appropriate referrals; transcribing and keeping appropriate records; and employing termination and follow-up procedures correctly. Group leaders and members must also scrutinize how they make ethical decisions.

None of these are simple tasks that are easily accomplished on a one-time basis. Therefore, group leaders must constantly monitor their behavior and keep current on ethical matters. "A combination of good personal character and virtue with sound thinking and good decision-making skill . . . ensures the best solution to an ethical dilemma" (Sileo & Kopala, 1993,

p. 90). Prospective group leaders may receive cognitive and experiential training in ethics while they are still in training, whereas more experienced leaders (who are supposed to be more knowledgeable about ethics) must rely more on continuing education experiences and peer supervision.

Legal aspects of group work are similar to those involving ethics in some ways, although there may be overlap. It is important for group specialists to do their homework in researching legal cases that affect human services professionals and consult with others about ways to behave within the limits and spirit of the law. Getting to know community, state, and national standards for the practice of their profession is a major way to do this. If practitioners encounter legal difficulties, then they need to know the difference between unintentional and intentional malpractice suits and what they need to do in such cases. It is also crucial that all group leaders carry professional liability insurance.

CLASSROOM EXERCISES

1. Compare the ethical codes of as many professional associations as you can in regard to the practice of group work. Once the codes are collected, have half of the class note the similarities within them and the other half of the class highlight their differences. Discuss your findings and their implications for working with groups.

2. Pretending you are a group leader, think of what you would do in the following two situations and then role-play these scenes with fellow classmates:
   a. A group member of the opposite sex, whom you find attractive, asks to meet with you outside the confines of the group. The member states the purpose of such a meeting in vague terms, but he or she assures you that it is important.
   b. You discover that several of the group members are talking about group activities and individuals to their friends. This

   is the fourth meeting of the group, and everyone is present.
   How did your thinking change or stay the same after these role-playing situations?

3. Have each member of the class write a potential ethical dilemma within a group context in which they are currently involved. Collect the situations and, as a class, discuss with your instructor some strategies that might be employed to deal with these situations.

4. As a class, visit the reference librarian of your library. Ask him or her to show you the resources most readily available for tracking down legal information on counseling cases. If possible, have the librarian follow a case through its introduction and appeals. Discuss with a classmate how you could make use of the resources you have at your disposal for keeping up with the legal aspects of group work.

CHAPTER 10

GROUP WORK WITH CULTURALLY DIVERSE POPULATIONS

Michael Littlejohn/PH College

With age she has learned
to forgive the groups
that mistreated her
because of her color.
Each Saturday she now bakes bread
and takes it to the local mission
where she stays to cut and serve it
with love and a main dish.
Her grace has overcome years of hatred
angry words and hours of sadness
her brightness exudes a subtle warmth
everyone calls her "Rainbow."*

*From *Rainbow* by Samuel T. Gladding, © 1997.

Diversity exists in a variety of ways: "race, ethnicity, language, culture, gender, socioeconomic class, sexual orientation, religion, ablism and disability, and more" (Diller, 2007, p. xii). It is a fact of life, especially in complex, pluralistic societies like those in North America, Europe, and Australia, which are composed of people who differ widely in regard to their lifestyles and worldviews. Diversity is also prevalent in other cultures and countries, such as China and Israel, where differences in communication styles, messages, and behaviors affect the ways in which groups are set up and conducted (Conyne, Wilson, & Tang, 2000; Shechtman & Peri-Dekel, 2000). Therefore, it is essential that group workers acknowledge and appreciate differences and "take them into consideration when attending to groups in different countries and cultures" (DeLucia-Waack, 2000b, p. 228).

When individuals in groups feel threatened by differences, they become defensive and withdraw from interactions with those with whom they are uncomfortable. They may also manifest their discomfort through stereotyping and showing prejudice and discrimination toward others. "Racism, sexism, religious intolerance, and homophobia poison the quality of life for victims and perpetrators of intolerant acts alike" (Lee, Armstrong, & Brydges, 1996, p. 8). In a segregated and encapsulated environment (Wrenn, 1962), it is difficult for these individuals to free themselves of negative feelings, thoughts, and behaviors.

However, groups of all types provide one way to help resolve misunderstandings and projections. By working collaboratively with persons who differ from themselves, group members can not only achieve common goals but in the process can also (a) bridge the gap of differences, (b) become more creative in their problem solving, (c) grow in their cognitive and moral reasoning, and (d) learn to view matters from a new perspective (Johnson, 2000).

A HISTORICAL OVERVIEW OF CULTURAL DIVERSITY IN GROUPS

Surprisingly, the emphasis on cultural diversity in group work is a relatively new frontier that few group professionals or associations have dealt with in depth (Bemak & Chung, 2004; Chau, 1992; Conyne et al., 2000). For instance, it was not until 1996 that the Association for Specialists in Group Work (ASGW) set up a task force to incorporate multicultural competencies into its standards. Still later, in 1997, the ASGW endorsed the Multicultural Counseling Competencies and Standards of the Association for Multicultural Counseling and Development (Sue, Arredondo, & McDavis, 1992). In 1999, the ASGW adopted its own Principles for Diversity-Competent Group Workers but did not operationalize this document with articles (see Appendix B).

Three reasons account for this delay in dealing with culture and diversity in groups. First, despite early work in the late 1940s by Kurt Lewin and his associates "to train community leaders to work more effectively in reducing tensions among interracial groups and to facilitate changes in racial/ethnic attitudes," this emphasis of the group movement was forgotten and discarded soon after Lewin's death in 1947 (Merta, 1995, p. 567). Second, during the development of the group movement of the 1960s and 1970s, culturally diverse group members were not considered to be significantly different from dominant group members in regard to concerns and issues. Finally, cultural minority members were not thought to have a great deal more influence on group dynamics than those from the dominant cultural group (Brinson & Lee, 1997).

However, recent thinking has returned to Lewin's emphasis on the use of groups both to promote racial and ethnic harmony and to help people from different backgrounds understand themselves and others better. For instance, Molina, Brigman, and Rhone (2003) have found that elementary school children can be taught learning skills to help them increase their understanding and appreciation of diverse cultures.

In addition, reports from group leaders, working with older populations, indicate that the cultural backgrounds of group members often have a powerful impact on interpersonal relationships and the work that the group does (Conyne et al., 2000; Rose, 2001). In such groups, "culture becomes the foreground rather than the background for the group process" (Baca & Koss-Chioino, 1997, p. 130). Therefore, an effective group worker must consider the cultural background and influences of group members in all types of groups. "Culturally sensitive practice plays a critical role in the delivery of group counseling services" and in group work in general (Johnson, Torres, Coleman, & Smith, 1995, p. 144).

CASE EXAMPLE: Deidra Diverges from Diversity

In setting up an advertising task group at work, Deidra decided to form a homogeneous group of her peers. She was single, young, attractive, well educated, and had a quick wit. She thought having a group with characteristics similar to her would be fun and productive. At first it was. The group came up with a number of new ideas for promoting the company's product.

Then, the group began to falter. They were good at targeting a population like themselves, but as Lawrence, a member of the group, said: "We really don't know what's it's like to be Hispanic or disabled." Thus, after a heady start the group disbanded in disgrace. They simply ran out of ideas.

What do you think might have happened had Deidra formed a heterogeneous group? Why?

CHALLENGES OF CULTURALLY DIVERSE GROUPS

Culturally diverse groups are found in a number of settings. However, the contexts in which they are most likely to be conducted are

  (a) racial-cultural sensitivity groups, increasingly being held on college and university campuses,
  (b) alcohol and other drug abuse recovery programs,
  (c) groups conducted inside correctional facilities, and
  (d) career development and job training programs. (Johnson et al., 1995)

To work effectively with culturally diverse populations in a group context, group leaders must make three modifications in regard to traditional ways of working in a group. First, they must understand what a culture is. A number of definitions of culture exist, but Sternberg (2004) gives one of the best in stating that culture is "the set of attitudes, values, beliefs, and behaviors shared by a group of people, communicated from one generation to the next via language or some other means of communication" (p. 325). Because many different groups of people live in the United States, Canada, the United Kingdom, and other pluralistic nations, *most group work is multicultural in nature.* Indeed, the term *multicultural,* which stresses this diversity among people, has become quite common in the professional helping literature as well as society at large.

Second, group theory and technique must be modified and applied to different cultures in ways that are congruent with the beliefs and behaviors of those cultures (DeLucia-Waack, 1996b, p. 218). This type of behavior is beginning to occur. A notable example is the application of cognitive appraisal theory to psychoeducational multicultural groups (McCarthy, Mejia, & Liu, 2000). In this model, based on the work of Roseman, Antonion, and Jose (1996), group members are taught to identify linkages between appraisals of events and people and their emotions. They learn, for instance, that there are various interpretations individuals can make about events and people, including negative, positive, and surprise. A four-stage model is useful in presenting this information and includes a didactic introduction, discovery, deeper insight, and a final integration and appraisal flexibility phase. In the process, participants might learn that changing their appraisal of an event by attributing the cause to themselves, instead of to other persons, leads to a different emotion and may consequently result in a greater understanding of cultures outside of their own.

◆ *Questions from Experience* ◆

When have you been in a group, or even just with another person, where your interpretation of an event was different? What do you think was behind this difference in perception? How did it make you feel? How did you see similar events from then on?

Finally, for group work to be multicultural, group theory and techniques must be developed that "acknowledge, explore, and use group member differences to facilitate change and growth" (DeLucia-Waack, 1996b, p. 218). This last change, which stresses the use of differences to enhance group effectiveness, has been slow to emerge. Works by Greeley, Garcia, Kessler, and Gilchrest (1992) and Johnson et al. (1995) have led the way in this particular area. Still, almost all formalized group approaches, especially in the Western World, are based on European-American models (Bemak & Chung, 2004).

Further complicating the issue of conducting multicultural groups are the various definitions of multiculturalism that have been advocated. Multiculturalism as a movement has been defined traditionally in terms of cultural, ethnic, and racial differences. In this somewhat narrow definition, an emphasis is placed specifically on the collective history of a people as an identified group as well as individual differences among members (Atkinson, Morten, & Sue, 1993; Harper, 1984; Vacc & Wittmer, 1980). However, culture may be defined broadly, too, and may include such factors as demographic variables (e.g., age, gender, residence), status variables (e.g., social, educational, economic), and affiliations (both formal and informal) (Pedersen, 2000). Thus, there is a fine line between too narrow and too broad of a definition of culture.

A broader definition of culture is probably preferred because of its inclusive rather than exclusive focus. Under such a definition, the almost 20% of Americans who have some type of disability as defined by the Americans with Disabilities Act of 1990 are included. So are persons with varied sexual lifestyles, such as gays, lesbians, and bisexuals

(Brown, 1996). Unquestionably, most groups are multicultural in this broadest sense of the word in that they are heterogeneous and incorporate within them people with a number of differences (Yalom, 2005). For purposes here, the word *multicultural* is used in the broadest way. However, because of page limitations, the focus in this chapter is on a limited number of distinctly recognizable cultural groups, African Americans, Hispanics/Latinos, Asian Americans, Native Americans, Arab Americans, European Americans, and gays/lesbians.

MYTHS ABOUT MULTICULTURAL GROUPS

A number of myths surround multicultural groups, some perpetuated by professionals with the best of intentions. Yet, the fact is that myths are only partially true and, therefore, must be resolved if people from different cultures are to work well together. DeLucia-Waack (1996b, pp. 219–221) has articulated four myths that need to be dispelled if diverse groups are going to be productive.

Myth 1: "Discussion of racial or cultural differences will offend group members."   The reason some group workers do not address cultural issues is that they fear a discussion of these matters will be offensive to group members or make them uncomfortable. Yet, as DeLucia-Waack (1996b) points out, "in reality, the acknowledgement of cultural differences may increase group cohesion" (p. 219). The reason is that, once acknowledged, the subject area is no longer taboo and what was in effect known by everyone on a covert level is now overt. This knowledge can be especially useful if it is addressed in a sensitive manner. Thus, within a group, the leader might say to Lilly, "As an African American house-wife, how does what Jane, as a European American housewife, is advocating resonate with you?" In such a situation, Jane and Lilly may find both similarities and differences in what they think based on culture and status. By discussing cultural differences openly, they will not misunderstand or misperceive each other based on silence or presumptions.

Myth 2: "Groups can be truly homogeneous."   Even when groups seem homogeneous, they are not. People are unique in many ways (e.g., gender, age, marital status, family of origin, occupation, beliefs/values). Therefore, what may appear alike on the surface may be exactly that—veneer. Once group workers can break through the myth of homogeneity, then true progress can be made in highlighting both differences and similarities among people. The group is then freed to use the unique as well as the universal potential within the group as a whole (Pedersen, 1997b). Thus, after the leader acknowledges that Raphael and Jorge differ in their thoughts and objectives, even though they are brothers, the two group members and the group as a whole will begin to make progress in achieving individual goals.

Myth 3: "Group member differences do not affect the process and outcome of task and psychoeducational groups."   The basis of this myth is that task and psychoeducational groups are not affected by process as much as counseling and psychotherapy groups are. These groups are believed to be primarily content oriented. Yet, in getting to content, task and psychoeducational group members are influenced by the beliefs, experiences, and cultural interactions that are a part of their background. Therefore, culture plays a major part in how and when members in task and psychoeducational groups interact. For instance, DeLucia-Waack (1996a) relates the story of trying to lead a stress management workshop for a group of eight Italian male students who were new to the United States. Although well intentioned and well prepared, she found that these men did not think a woman should be teaching a class of men and that their cultural norms did not permit the disclosure of weaknesses to other men, let alone a woman!

Myth 4: "Group work theory is appropriate for all clients."   Theories on groups and how they work, at least in most of North America, are, as pointed out previously, "based on Eurocentric notions of mental health and functional relationships" (DeLucia-Waack, 1996b, p. 221). These tenets of health include a focus on the individual, verbalization as the primary means of communication, unstructured interactions among group members, an emphasis on risk taking, and the importance of the group leader or facilitator. In reality, these emphases are not shared worldwide. Group members are unique, and what may be the norm for one may not be the norm for another. Thus, if groups are going to work, then members must discuss norms and work out a framework that will be helpful to all.

If group leaders and members notice and address myths before the group begins, such as in the screening stage of the process, then greater understanding and a better outcome will most likely result. Along with a focus on myths, group workers must help the group to formulate and reach appropriate goals.

CASE EXAMPLE: Myra's Myths and Mindsets

Myra had been told all of her life that Whites were all pretty much alike. Her family had told her not to trust them, for they would take advantage of her whenever they could. Thus, when a White woman befriended Myra in her counseling group, Myra was suspicious. She knew the woman must want something and that she would pay a price for friendship. Therefore, Myra avoided the woman and seldom spoke to her.

Later when the group had a reunion, Myra was surprised to find out that the woman she had avoided was good friends with many of her friends. She was shocked. She could not believe it. Not only that, the woman had some situations similar to Myra's. By avoiding her White group member, Myra had missed a number of opportunities for companionship, support, and insight.

How do you think myths and mindsets can be overcome? What historical examples can you think of where the thinking of one or more persons was changed? What insights can you glean from such examples?

GOALS OF MULTICULTURAL GROUPS

Like all successful forms of group work, multicultural groups are goal directed. Although goals will differ from group to group, these goals may be described as falling into categories that are primarily remedial, preventive, or task oriented. Goals also focus on intra- and interpersonal processes. In addition, goals are geared toward both general and specific topics that are of concern to those within their ranks (Corey, 2004). Thus, a primary challenge of conducting multicultural groups relates to the different views, values, and interpersonal styles that members display as well as how these forces are both managed and highlighted in productive ways. If the group is conducted properly, then members who differ from one another will begin to trust and help one another in learning new, different, and productive ways of acting and interrelating (Pedersen, 1997b). Through such a process, individuals, subgroups, and the group as a whole will benefit. For instance, if Maria assists Jen in verbalizing her frustrations with school policies, then the two may become emotionally closer to each other and work more closely with their fellow group members in proposing new and better school policies.

According to DeLucia-Waack (1996a), multicultural groups, regardless of their emphasis, have three common goals: (a) to understand the situation that brought the person to the group from a cultural perspective; (b) "to approach all events and behavior in the group from a functional perspective" (p. 171); and (c) to help members make sense of "new behaviors, beliefs, and skills within a cultural context" (p. 171). These goals hold up across group types. If participants do not comprehend why they are in a group, what they can learn from the group, and what implications their new behaviors, beliefs, or skills have for them within the context of where they live, then the group experience will be of minimal use to them.

◆ *Questions from Experience* ◆

When have you ever been in a group where it was obvious that one or more members did not want to be a part of the group? How did their actions affect the group? How do you think their actions could have been muted or modified?

ASSESSING CULTURAL DIVERSITY IN A GROUP

It is imperative that group workers understand the cultural backgrounds of their clients before attempting to work with them and that they have a broad and culture-centered perspective. As previously noted, groups composed of people from culturally different backgrounds will have diverse values and worldviews (DeLucia, Coleman, & Jensen-Scott, 1992). By recognizing these differences and the cultures from which they sprang, group leaders can design appropriate interventions (Pedersen, 1997a). However, the extent of diversity is dependent on a number of factors, including time, acculturation processes, the socioeconomic environment of persons, and even the number of group members from a particular background. (By the way, including just one member of a culturally distinct group in a group is usually not very productive. That person may have difficulty identifying with others in the group and may be stereotyped by the group.)

Therefore, group workers need to assess multiple factors that will either benefit or hinder the group's development. This type of assessment is complex. For instance, some people may be deeply affected by their collective history, whereas the influence is minimal for others. In making an assessment, the pregroup screening stage of forming the group is the place to begin. In screening, group leaders may keep in mind that some cultural groups do better in certain types of group environments. For instance, many Asian Americans do not respond well to traditional group psychotherapy processes because their culture teaches them not to share personal problems or confront others in public. In contrast, other cultural groups, such as African Americans and Hispanic/Latino Americans, do extremely well in a variety of group settings (McWhirter, McWhirter, & McWhirter, 1988).

For most cultural groups, core group skills and principles will work on some level. However, for other groups, depending on their specific composition, there is a need to develop culture-specific strategies (Sue, 1992). Thus, in planning and implementing a culturally diverse group, the leader must conceptualize and work both broadly, in terms of what is generally known, and specifically, in terms of the persons who actually comprise the group. Outcomes in groups "are dependent, in part, on the match between the group leader's and the client's respective stages of racial consciousness" (Johnson et al., 1995, p. 145). Therefore, before Dwight, a European American, decides to lead a multicultural counseling group, he must ask himself questions about his own awareness of his heritage and the heritage of others in the group and how it will affect the final results.

LEADERSHIP IN CULTURALLY DIVERSE GROUPS

As implied previously, before beginning a group, it is important for leaders to examine their own thoughts and feelings about people who are culturally or otherwise distinct from themselves. Self-awareness regarding cross-cultural interactions is a "must" for those who would lead (Bieschke, Gehlert, Wilson, Matthews, & Wade, 2003). Such an examination allows leaders to deal constructively with prejudices, biases, and racist elements in their lives that have either been passed on from a previous generation or learned through isolated incidents and generalized. For example, a group leader of Asian American descent who grew up in an affluent but isolated neighborhood might have negative feelings about working with Mexican Americans if he or she has never encountered persons from such a background before and has heard disparaging remarks about them as a group. The point is that when thoughts and emotions about culturally different groups of people are not dealt with before a group begins, they may well play themselves out detrimentally within the group itself (Allport, 1954; Donigian & Malnati, 1997). For example, the leader in the illustration just given might hold stereotypes of Mexican Americans, such as that they are all illegal immigrants and not well educated. Such stereotypes might psychologically impede the leader's ability to hear and communicate accurately with members of this group.

In conducting groups that include members who are culturally distinct, leaders must sensitize themselves continually to cultural variables and individual differences so that they become more conscious of the issues of culture that influence their own backgrounds and those of group members (DeLucia-Waack, 2004). "A culturally responsive group leader is aware of his or her own cultural values, assumptions, and biases and how these might impact upon the group process" (Brinson & Lee, 1997, p. 47). He or she also is "autonomous"; that is, the group leader is comfortable with his or her identity and able to empathize with culturally different group members' feelings.

Skilled multicultural group counselors realize that among group members, multicultural differences tend to occur early in the life of a group "and discomfort associated with multicultural issues tends to occur towards the end of groups" (Bieschke, Gehlert, Wilson,

Matthews, & Wade, 2003, p. 325). This process of examination and "becoming" inevitably lasts a lifetime. However, parts of it are achieved in stages, with the group leader becoming more skilled with each culturally diverse group conducted (Marbley, 2004). Such groups give life and possibility to those involved with them because differences in group members become assets in the group's development. In addition, there is an understanding of how values and beliefs are shaped and influenced by social environments.

Increasing the awareness and abilities of group leaders in culturally diverse groups may be done in multiple ways. Strategies most often employed are

(a) consultation or group co-leadership with minority counselors already serving specific cultural groups;

(b) participation in cultural immersion experiences (e.g., significant holidays and events);

(c) actively taking inventory of the needs and issues of minority groups in their communities; and

(d) language training when possible (or at least becoming familiar with the correct pronunciation of ethnic names, values, and traditions) (Johnson et al., 1995, p. 149).

A fifth strategy is for group leaders to examine their family as the place where they learned about their culture and relationships with others (Ivey & Ivey, 2007). Constructing a genogram and interviewing family members about their cultural experiences and expectations can often give insight into the sources of particular beliefs and outlooks.

A final strategy is the employment of both didactic and experiential education. On the didactic side, there is the study of cultures and the heritages of people. This type of knowledge can be obtained through reading books and articles that relate to global and specific traditions and customs in the lives of various people (Chiu, 1997). On the experiential side, course work can be set up to sensitize group workers to themselves and group members who differ from them (Greeley et al., 1992). Integrating this cultural knowledge into real groups is the challenge.

Counselors-in-training may need to work through the strong emotional reactions and paralyzing feelings they experience when dealing with multicultural counseling training on any level. One way to handle the intense emotions, such as guilt or shame, that come with such training is through the use of small, supportive, and accepting groups (Parker, Freytes, Kaufman, Woodruff, & Hord, 2004). This type of a group, which is nonjudgmental in nature, may help neophyte counselors share thoughts, feelings, and actions that they would not do otherwise. Through such a process multicultural counseling competencies are enhanced.

In summary, to be a leader of a multicultural group with skills and competencies, a leader must

• have "an awareness of different cultural worldviews and the subsequent impact on group work interventions"

• have a self-awareness, in particular of racial identity and personal and cultural worldviews, and

• have a focus "on the development of a repertoire of culturally relevant group work interventions" (DeLucia-Waack, 2004, p. 167).

CASE EXAMPLE: Edward Enters a Multicultural Group as a Leader

Edward is a native of Africa and the son of immigrant parents. He is bilingual. Until age 4 he lived in Kenya. Since then, he has lived in Canada. As a mental health worker, he has decided to start a group for recent immigrants from Africa. He is aware of his heritage as well as his values, but he is not as familiar with the lives of recent immigrants.

Because he is married and the father of young children, Edward does not have time to participate in a lot of new cultural experiences. However, he approaches his group with new knowledge he has attained through attending a recent course on the lives of African immigrants. He has also conducted personal interviews with some recent immigrants. Therefore, he is prepared to address situations affecting his group members when the group begins.

What else might Edward do to make himself more competent? What do you consider to be your greatest strength in addressing multicultural issues?

WORKING WITH DIFFERENT CULTURAL POPULATIONS IN GROUPS

The 2005 census indicated increasing diversity in the population of the United States. The following percentages reveal how many of the 296 million respondents reported themselves to be of a particular race: African American, 12%; Native American, 1%; Asian American, 4%; Hispanic, 14%; European American (i.e., White Non-Hispanic), 67%, two or more races, 2% (U.S. Bureau of the Census, 2005).

Accompanying this growing diversity is the increasing need for professional and personal sensitivity to others in groups, especially multicultural groups (DeLucia et al., 1992). "Implicit in multicultural group work is the fostering of acceptance, respect, and tolerance for diversity within and between members" (Bemak & Chung, 2004, p. 36). Therefore, group workers from all cultures in the United States will need to expand their knowledge about cultural variables. People from various cultures do not think or act alike, nor do they come to groups for the same reasons. Among the most important pieces of knowledge group workers need regarding diversity in groups is information about group process in naturally occurring groups—for example, the African American church, Latino clubs, Native American tribal councils, and Asian American family groups. "In many cases, group process in these kinship units often significantly predates what we know as group work" (Lee, 1995, p. 4). One dynamic that occurs in multicultural group counseling is the use of defense mechanisms, particularly splitting and projection identification, which are used "in groups to protect against feelings of inadequacy and vulnerability, which underlie racial and cultural prejudice" (Cheng, Chae, & Gunn, 1998, p. 373). Excessive splitting and projection identification lead to scapegoating that in turn leads to fragmentation and a failure to build a sense of community within the group.

While acquiring process knowledge, group workers should attune themselves to the nonverbal behaviors of group members. Nonverbal behavior can have various meanings among different cultures. For instance, cultural differences in eye contact abound (Ivey & Ivey, 2007). European Americans usually value direct eye contact when listening and less while talking, whereas African Americans often have the reverse pattern. Likewise, direct eye contact may be avoided entirely by some groups of Native Americans when talking about something serious. Distance is another nonverbal behavior that should be understood. Conversational distance of an arm's length is comfortable for many North Americans, but many Hispanics/Latinos prefer half that distance. The point is that, in conducting any group, cultural heritage will influence levels of comfort and patterns of interaction for better or for worse depending on the knowledge of group leaders and other group members.

Some of the qualities that affect particular minority and majority cultural groups follow. It should be noted that although these characteristics may generally apply, they "warrant ongoing scrutiny because they are based more on anecdotal reports than on systematic research and because they often fail to consider within group differences (e.g., socioeconomic status, acculturation level) and between group differences (e.g., between Japanese Americans and Vietnamese Americans)" (Merta, 1995, pp. 573–574). Individuals within a group and even groups in different regions of a country will vary in their customs and traditions. Therefore, group workers can never assume that persons from certain backgrounds will behave in a set way. In fact, to make such an assumption is to stereotype and act with prejudice.

African Americans

African Americans are quite diverse, and within-group differences are great. Yet, collectively, most African Americans share a common bond that is the result of the legacy of slavery and bondage that prevailed in the United States from 1619 to 1865. During those almost 250 years, African Americans were bought and sold as chattel. The history of discrimination that followed their freedom from slavery has influenced most members of this group in significant ways. For example, skepticism or suspicion of European Americans is pervasive among African Americans (Gossett, 1998). However, commonly shared positive values among African Americans include the importance of family, creative expression, and spirituality (Gainor, 1992; Rollock, Westman, & Johnson, 1992; Williams, Frame, & Green, 1999).

Although "African Americans generally minimize the use of professional counseling services," group work is appropriate for counseling African Americans (Pack-Brown & Fleming, 2004, p. 183). Group work is especially relevant if it is "grounded in the African American worldview" (Williams et al., 1999, p. 260). The reason is that "African American culture has typically provided a network of support systems through community resources" which the group may parallel (Pack-Brown & Fleming, 2004, p. 183). African American culture is communalism (i.e., a collective identity) that is manifest in strong kinship ties and an emphasis on social responsibility for others, even those outside of one's immediate family (Perrone & Sedlacek, 2000). A "'safety in numbers' principle makes it easier" for some African Americans to disclose before a group than before an individual professional helper (Merta, 1995, p. 574).

In groups, African Americans may share, cooperate, and have their personal experiences validated. "In addition, group counseling experiences may help African Americans increase their sense of hope and optimism, decrease their feelings of alienation, develop more effective coping techniques, and acquire more effective socialization skills" (Ford, 1997, p. 103).

"The African American community often presents a challenge to group leaders who are unfamiliar with the African American worldview and life experiences" (Pack-Brown & Fleming, 2004, p. 189). For instance, in group work, African Americans express themselves in various ways, such as displaying "their emotions in culturally specific language patterns or by displaying nonverbal behavior in a demonstrative manner" (Brinson & Lee, 1997, p. 48). Therefore, when leading a group composed of African Americans, a group leader who is not African American must be aware of both the verbal and the nonverbal traditions of members and not ascribe negative connotations to normal means of expression. Likewise, in leading groups whose membership contains only some African Americans, a non–African American not only needs to realize regular cultural ways of expression but also must help educate and sensitize other non–African Americans to these patterns.

In working with African Americans in counseling and therapeutic settings, group leaders have found the creative arts, "especially music, poetry, literature, folklore and graphic expression," to be useful aids in promoting group interaction (Brinson & Lee, 1997, p. 52). Gender issues are often unique and because of discrimination, oppression, racism, historical hostility, and cultural stereotypes, getting African American men to participate in counseling or group work is a challenge (Muller, 2002). African American women are, as a group, more receptive, but they "must contend with long-standing negative, stereotypical image [too] of being Black and female" (Pack-Brown & Fleming, 2004, p. 188). Therefore, group workers must be sensitive and appropriate in involving this segment of the African American population in groups.

In work with African Americans, especially if the group workers are European Americans, care must be taken in setting up the group so that members will be able to share freely and benefit from the group. The process of setting up may therefore involve not only the topics of sessions but self-examination and input from professionals in the African American community as well (Muller, 2002). For African American women on predominantly White college campuses, an Afrocentric group counseling approach has been found to be beneficial (Brown, Lipford-Sanders, & Shaw, 1995). Such an approach centers on positive African values within a cultural context. Also, an African American Women's Spirituality Group has been found to be an effective intervention for African American women because it connects them with others around shared cultural experiences (Williams et al., 1999). Two resources that introduce models for group work with African Americans are the videos *I Am Because We Are! Afrocentric Approaches to Group Work* (Pack-Brown & Whittington-Clark, 2002) and *Images of Me: A Guide to Group Work with African American Females* (Pack-Brown, Whittington-Clark, & Parker, 1998).

◆ *Questions from Experience* ◆

What other general characteristics are prevalent in African American men and women? In African Americans as a group? If you are not African American, how do you think you could build trust within a group that was composed of a number of African Americans? What would you do differently than you usually do? What would be the same?

Hispanic/Latino Americans

Like other ethnic and cultural groups, there is considerable variety in populations that are characterized as Hispanic/Latino. There are four major Hispanic/Latino subgroups in the United States: Mexican Americans (65%), Central and South Americans (21%), Puerto

Ricans (10%), and Cuban Americans (4%) (Diller, 2007; Rivera, 2004). Shared values among these groups include the importance of family, interdependence and cooperation, the worth and dignity of the individual, and an acceptance of life as it exists (Diller, 2007). Differences include the use of language, religious rituals, and celebrations. Therefore, if group workers are going to be effective leaders, they should be aware of different Hispanic groups and the cultural gulfs, as well as bridges, that unite and separate them (Altarriba & Bauer, 1998).

The professional literature notes that group work with Hispanic/Latino Americans can be beneficial and take a number of forms. For instance, Gonzalez-Lopez and Taylor (1997) have found that group therapy with Latinos and Latinas can transform their thinking.

In groups for Hispanics/Latinos, group counselors should generally be active, validating, and supportive (Baca & Koss-Chioino, 1997). In addition, recommendations have been made regarding language, especially in groups in which members' first language is Spanish. For instance, Espin (1987) recommends that leaders of such groups be bilingual: For many members of Hispanic/Latino groups, Spanish is the language of emotions because it was in Spanish that affective meanings were originally encoded. Salgado de Synder (1987) also recommends that Spanish be used in Hispanic/Latino groups, along with English, to facilitate the emergence and discussion of taboo topics, such as sexuality, that may have been lost in the process of acculturation.

In working with Hispanic/Latino groups, sex-role socialization issues and cultural identity may affect the process, too. "Hispanic women tend to be more reserved than Hispanic men" (Brinson & Lee, 1997, p. 48). Therefore, the group leader may need to use a skill such as drawing out to help Hispanic women—who have been most socialized in their cultural tradition—to voice their opinions and actively contribute to the group. One way to accomplish this goal is through the use of a "comadre or compadre" group approach where group members offer social support and a sense of community like extended family members (Rayle, Sand, Brucato, & Ortega, 2006). In such a group setting, stress may be reduced and depression modified while a sense of belonging, respect, and affirmation is enhanced. This effect may be especially notable in recently immigrated, monolingual Mexican women.

On college campuses, groups that support **Chicanas** (i.e., women of Mexican descent) may also be valuable and effective in helping them succeed. One such group, built around Yalom's (2005) 11 therapeutic factors, was found to help Chicanas "build personal and professional support systems, feel validated with respect to common experiences and educational concerns, develop skills and strategies to negotiate personal and educational difficulties, and discuss cultural values within a group context" (Gloria, 1999, p. 256). Likewise, Hispanic/Latino males may be reluctant to disclose information that they perceive as threatening their masculinity or machismo (Baruth & Manning, 2007). For this reason, group workers need to be encouraging and patient in conducting groups with Hispanic/Latino males.

Considerable anecdotal information is available about the effectiveness of group work with Hispanics/Latinos in such areas as academic skills, value clarification, problem solving, self-esteem, and pride in one's cultural identity (Merta, 1995). For instance, Baca and Koss-Chioino (1997) have presented a model for group counseling with Mexican-American adolescents specifically targeted toward teens in this population who have behavior problems, including substance abuse. Overall, groups for Hispanic/Latinos have proven quite productive, especially for Mexican Americans.

CASE EXAMPLE: Tanya Is Tempted to Betray Her Heritage

Tanya is the only person of Hispanic/Latina heritage in her psychoeducational group. Her parents immigrated to North America from Mexico when she was a child. Most of her life she has lived in a "White neighborhood" and played with children whose native language is English. As she learns in her group, there are many cultures within the United States, and her Hispanic/Latina one is strong and filled with many traditions.

At first Tanya is proud of her heritage, but she is teased outside the group for that. Therefore, she begins to speak up less in the group and her comments become more limited. It is obvious to the group leader, Michael, that Tanya wants to say more than she is saying. He wants to help her own her feelings and yet he does not want her to create such a stir that there is a backlash.

What do you think he could do to help Tanya and the group be more accepting and open? What do you think he should avoid doing?

Asian and Asian Pacific Americans

"The demographic profile of Asian and Pacific Islander Americans includes an array of more than 40 disparate cultural groups" (Sandhu, 1997, p. 7). "Each group has its own distinct historical and sociopolitical backgrounds, languages, identity, issues, cultures, and challenges" (Chung, 2004, pp. 200–201). Thus while Asian Americans and Pacific Islander Americans are often lumped into one main category, there are wide inter- and intragroup differences that may make it difficult for group workers to deal effectively with unique issues of particular individuals (Chen & Han, 2001). Furthermore, the myth that members of this population are the "model minority" and have no serious problems is exactly that—a myth. "In actuality, Asians in the U.S. not only face many of the same problems as other minorities, such as racism and stereotyping, but the very press coverage which extols their virtues often complicates and exacerbates those problems, especially for those Asians who for many reasons, cannot meet the expectations raised" (Cheng, 1995, p. 8). Therefore, for group workers, Asian Americans are a challenge. Members of this population must be understood and worked with beyond the myths that surround them.

One issue that must be addressed in working with Asian and Asian-Pacific American culture groups is the disparity "between group work values (e.g., openness, expression of feelings, directness) and the cultural values of Asian Americans (e.g., verbal nonassertiveness, reluctance to display strong emotions in front of strangers, and unwillingness to disclose personal problems to strangers)" (Merta, 1995, p. 574). The importance of "saving face" and not embarrassing oneself or disgracing one's family is also highly prized by many Asian Americans (Fukuyama & Coleman, 1992; Kim, Atkinson, & Umemoto, 2001; Leong, 1992). The means for preventing a clash in values and the loss of face may be demanding and require an adjustment in the ways leaders conduct groups, especially counseling and therapy groups. Many Asian Americans and Asian-Pacific Americans have been taught to respect authority and see a group leader as a person of authority (Chung, 2004; DeLucia-Waack, 1996b). Because of this cultural introjection, they will not challenge the group leader even when such a challenge might be beneficial to everyone in the group.

One way to work with groups of Asian Americans, especially college students, is to offer "groups which focus on practical concerns to them rather than on forums which focus on more personal concerns" (Cheng, 1996, p. 10). For work with college students, groups that feature topics such as career choices, immigration, academic topics, and communication skills seem to be successful and well attended. Cheng (1996) also recommends that groups for Asian American students be short term (one to five sessions) in addition to theme centered.

Another successful way of conducting groups with Asian Americans and Asian Pacific Americans is a stage-specific interactive approach (Chen & Han, 2001). In this model, group workers "carefully respond to specific tasks and challenges that arise in each stage" of the group (p. 113). For example, in the forming stage, group leaders need to realize that nonverbal messages from Asian American members, such as silence, may convey respect rather than resistance, and they must treat these behaviors accordingly. Similarly, in the working stage of the group, leaders need to realize that emphasizing Asian Americans' strengths, rather than their pathologies, helps them to move more toward a sense of choice and control.

An approach for Native Hawaiian adolescents in particular is culturally consonant group counseling using values, concepts, processes, and techniques of Ho'oponopono (i.e., an indigenous interpsychic and intrapsychic healing method) (Kim, Omizo, & D'Andrea, 1998). In this problem-solving approach, the emphasis is placed on values such as *aloha* (i.e., love and caring), *lokahi* (i.e., unity and harmony), and *ohana* (i.e., extended family). Although more research needs to be conducted using what the authors set up as a 10-week group, indications are that Hawaiian adolescents with low self-esteem may benefit from such an experience.

Overall, most kinds of groups that are well designed seem to work in a therapeutic way for Asian Americans and Asian Pacific Americans. A particular population that may find group work beneficial is Southeast Asia refugees. "Several studies have pointed toward its effectiveness with this population" (Chung, Bemak, & Okazaki, 1997, p. 207). Highly traumatized refugees may especially find solace in group therapy (Chung, 2004).

◆ *Questions from Experience* ◆

What other general characteristics than those mentioned here are prevalent in Asian American men and women? In Asian Americans as a group? If you are not Asian American, how do you think you could build rapport within a group that was composed of a number of Asian Americans? What would you do differently than you usually do? What would be the same?

Native Americans

"Long before the notion of group counseling was a glimmer in the eyes of the early pioneers of the counseling profession, Native peoples throughout North and South America were using group approaches for therapeutic benefits of creating and maintaining harmony and balance in the personal, social, environmental, and spiritual realms of people's lives" (Garrett, Garrett, & Brotherton, 2001, p. 17). Native Americans generally share some common values, such as an emphasis on cooperation, health, holism, sharing, spirituality, healing, and an extended-family orientation (Colmani & Merta, 1999; Dufrene & Coleman, 1992; Garrett, 2004). Thus, in work with Native Americans, groups have been found to be more appropriate than individual counseling (Appleton & Dykeman, 1996). "Native Americans are a group-oriented people who consider the whole greater than the sum of its parts" (Garrett & Osborne, 1995, p. 34). In fact, healers in Native American society rarely treat individuals in isolation from their family, friends, and neighbors (Thomason, 1991).

"Approximately 50% of the Native American population resides in urban areas," so it is important to consider the degree of traditionalism versus the degree of acculturation to mainstream American values and cultural standards before treating Native people (Garrett, 2004, p. 170). In general, Native Americans cultural values revolve around harmony, noninterference, and the balancing of dualities.

Yet because of the strong tradition of groups in Native American cultures, several group approaches to working with Native Americans seem to work well. One such approach, for young men in particular, is the **sweat lodge ceremony**, in which about 10 participants undergo a ritualized cleansing of the mind, body, and spirit through structured processes in a small turtle-shaped dwelling known as a *sweat lodge* (Colmani & Merta, 1999; Garrett & Osborne, 1995). The sweat lodge, where blasts of hot steam are created by pouring a special mixture of water and herbs over heated rocks, becomes "a type of counseling center and place for group therapy" (Lake, 1987, p. 8). The four-phase process of the sweat lodge ceremony is similar to other group process models in that it includes an entrance (i.e., exploration), a threshold (i.e., transition), purification (i.e., working), and an emergence (i.e., consolidation/closure) (Garrett & Osborne, 1995). Within this process and in other gatherings is the "**talking circle**" tradition (Garrett, 2004). The group leader uses a go-round procedure, and everyone assembled uses "I" statements to express their thoughts and feelings, in both prayer and conversation, about themselves, their families, their connections with others, and their future. The process itself includes the 11 therapeutic factors identified by Yalom (2005), but it also contains strong moral-cognitive development and cultural identity components for Native Americans (Colmani & Merta, 1999).

Research also supports the use of art therapy in groups for Native Americans. "Art media provide clients culturally sensitive avenues for expression through nonverbal forms" (Appleton & Dykeman, 1996, p. 225). In a group consisting of Native Americans and people of other cultures, the arts can be an especially powerful form of communication because "American Indian group members may be reserved in their level of self-disclosure when they are among non-Indians" (Brinson & Lee, 1997, p. 48). Art therapies in groups overcome barriers of culture, socioeconomic status, and other surface differences while inspiring, directing, and healing intrapersonal and interpersonal rifts (Gladding, 2004).

The **inner circle/outer circle approach** is another way of working with Native Americans in groups. Group members divide up and sit in two concentric circles. Inner circle members then describe what is painful or frustrating in their lives with their fists clenched so that they can feel the tension physically as well as emotionally (Garrett et al., 2001). They then turn around to the outer circle members, who sit with open palms. When the outer circle group has granted permission, the tensions of the inner circle are slowly released into their open hands. Each outer circle member in turn takes the opportunity to share with his or her inner circle member specific themes, key words, or underlying feelings. The outer circle member may also request guidance or support from a community circle outside of the outer group and use the insight or action from the community circle with the inner circle group member. Much of the therapeutic value of this approach comes from the interaction of the circles and the bringing together of people physically, mentally, and spiritually through an interrelationship process.

Overall, Native Americans tend "to value a group orientation and may find group work the preferred modality of treatment . . . [especially if the group leader is] perceived by the Native American group members as genuine, considerate, and nonmanipulative" (Merta, 1995, p. 576).

Arab Americans

Arab Americans are a fast-growing and mosaic group coming from 22 countries as diverse as Egypt, Lebanon, Morocco, Yemen, Tunisia, and Palestine. There are more than 3.5 million Arab Americans in the United States, most of whom are Christian, with a sizable portion being Muslims (http://www.aaiusa.org/arab-americans/22/demographics, August 19, 2006; Negy, 2004). However, "Arabic and Muslim cultures often overlap. Thus, although the majority of Arab Americans are Christian, Muslim traditions and values are often upheld by Muslim and Christian Arab Americans alike" (Nasser-McMillan & Hakim-Larson, 2003, p. 151).

Arab Americans vary among themselves. Potential differences include social class, level of education, language (Arabic has distinct dialects), relative conservatism of the country of origin, time of immigration, and level of acculturation (Abudabbeh & Aseel, 1999). Despite such cultural variations, sufficient commonalities exist that special attention from service providers is warranted.

Arab cultures tend to be of a high context rather than of a low context such as in North American society. Therefore, Arab Americans as a group usually differ significantly from traditional Americans in that they emphasize social stability and the collective over the individual.

The family is the most significant element in most Arab American subcultures, with the individual's life dominated by family and family relations. Education is valued in Arab American households with approximately 4 in 10 Americans of Arab decent having earned a bachelor's degree or higher (http://www.aaiusa.org/arab-americans/22/demographics, accessed August 19, 2006).

When working with Arab Americans, especially immigrants, it is crucial for group workers to remember that there is a sharp delineation of gender roles in such families. Furthermore, patriarchal patterns of authority, conservative sexual standards, and the importance of self-sacrifice prevail. There is also an emphasis on the importance of honor and shame because people in Arab cultures only seek outside help from helpers, such as group workers, as a last resort (Abudabbeth & Aseel, 1999). Complicating matters even more is the fallout, tension, and distrust from September 11, 2001 (Beitin & Allen, 2005).

Therefore, clinical recommendations for working with groups in this population include

- being aware of their cultural context,
- being mindful of the issue of leadership and the importance that authority figures play in their lives,

- being attentive to the part that the extended family plays in decision making,
- being sensitive to the large part culture plays as an active and tangible co-participant in treatment,
- being conscious of the fact that a strength-based approach to treatment is both desirable and works better,
- being active as a group worker and balancing the role so as not to be seen as a rescuer or a threat.

Group workers can help Arab Americans by helping them access groups where they can find support and become members of a larger community that is dealing with issues as they are. Group counseling or therapy poses "some potentially problematic issues for particular clients. This is especially true for the war refugees from Iraq, due to the paranoid symptoms that often accompany the diagnosis of PTSD in clients who have experienced wartime trauma. On the other hand, parenting groups and 12-step programs seem to be effective with some non-refugee Arab immigrant groups, perhaps due to the collectivist nature of the Arab culture in the countries of origin" (Nasser-McMillan & Hakim-Larson, 2003, p. 154).

◆ *Questions from Experience* ◆

What other general characteristics are prevalent in Arab American men and women that you know? In Arab Americans as a group? If you are not Arab American, how do you think you could conduct a group that was primarily composed of Arab Americans? What would you do differently than you usually do? What would be the same?

European Americans

People descended from European ancestors comprise the largest number of people in the United States and make up what is known as the *majority culture*. Descendants of Germans, Irish, English, French, Italians, Poles, and Russians are among the most numerous of the European Americans. They all share some similarities, with the most obvious being their white skin color. This similarity has both positive and negative attributes. On the plus side, it provides an outer link of similarity and some assumptions of alikeness that bring people together. On the minus side, skin color may lead to some insensitivity about self or others. "White Americans often have difficulty perceiving themselves as members of a cultural group and often refer to themselves and others as 'American' or 'a person' without regard to race" (Brown, Parham, & Yonker, 1996, p. 510). Indeed, White racial identity theory argues not only that within-group differences exist among Whites but that these differences are based on the degree and type of identity people of white skin color have with White culture (Carter & Akinsulure-Smith, 1996).

Regardless of skin color or identity, European Americans differ dramatically among themselves, just as in other cultural groups. Their values, religious traditions, and customs vary. For instance, historically, persons who came from northern European countries and arrived in the territory that would become the United States in the 1600s and 1700s discriminated against the ancestors of southern Europeans arriving in the late 1800s to the early 1900s. Thus, many second- and third-generation European Americans may share much more in common with minority culture populations, especially in regard to struggles against prejudice, than would seem likely or obvious. Recognizing these within-group differences can help group workers to avoid stereotyping, generalizing, and treating all European Americans the same. It can also help facilitate their linking of European Americans to other members of groups from outwardly different backgrounds.

Nevertheless, as a group, people of European origin in North America "have been in a position of social and cultural dominance with respect to other groups" (Lee, 1997, p. 19). European Americans have generally defined the lifestyles, attitudes, and values of society. As a group, European Americans are time conscious and view nature as something to be conquered. Furthermore, collectively (but with notable exceptions), they are future-time oriented, competitive, individualistic, rational thinkers, democratic, driven by a strong work ethic, and generally live in nuclear families (Carter, 1991; Katz, 1985). European Americans who understand their own world view, cultural values, and racial identity are more likely than not to have a positive influence on others in groups who both differ from and are similar to them.

There is no professional literature on working with European Americans in groups. Until recently, it has been assumed that, unless otherwise stated, groups either include a majority of European American participants or they are conducted by a European American. That assumption is probably still more correct than not, as authors of groups that focus on cultural minorities identify their groups as such (e.g., African American, Hispanic). Therefore, it is difficult, if not impossible, to tease out guidelines for working with European Americans in groups. Nevertheless, there are two factors that are helpful. The first is to realize that, as with other cultural groups, there are more within-group differences than between-group differences among European Americans. Therefore, just as with other groups, it is important to focus on differences as well as similarities among participants.

Second, in working with European Americans in groups, it is crucial to address matters that affect members socially, such as the fact that American culture is becoming increasingly diverse. These social factors are probably of greatest concern to the group as a whole and cause them the most anxiety and difficulty.

GROUPS FOR GAYS, LESBIANS, AND BISEXUALS

In recent years, gays, lesbians, and bisexuals (GLBs) have become increasingly visible in American society. As a group, they comprise approximately 10% to 15% of the overall population (Dorland & Fischer, 2001). However, regardless of their visibility or their number, GLBs are still discriminated against in many ways both in the public domain (Khng, 2001) and in other settings. Thus, as individuals, GLBs have distinct concerns related to their lifestyles in particular and life problems in general. Some of these concerns, such as sexism and homophobia, are of special significance, but other matters include career and life development issues.

The lifestyles of GLBs vary from being hidden or invisible, to coming out, to openly acknowledging their sexual orientation. Groups devoted specifically to working with members of each group, who often have more in common than not, have proven useful and productive, at least according to anecdotal reports. Mixed groups, whose members have heterosexual, homosexual, and bisexual identities, have also been successful

(Firestein, 1999). In working with GLBs in groups, it is important to remember that they are a diverse population. There are large within-group differences as well as between-group differences among members.

Groups have been used to work with GLBs in adolescence as well as with more mature populations. For instance, support groups for sexual minority youth have been found to be a means for members of this population to talk about their concerns with a counselor in school (Muller & Hartman, 1998). Groups have also been employed to work with bisexual men (Wolf, 1987). Such groups allow bisexual men to share their experiences and gain support from one another. Regardless of members' age, the matter of confidentiality is of uppermost importance in groups for GLBs. It is also critical that group workers who lead GLB groups explore their own sexuality (Hitchings, 1994) and understand how social influences affect the personal and interpersonal lives of group members (Cowie & Rivers, 2000).

CASE EXAMPLE: Gloria Joins a Group

Gloria has wrestled with her homosexual tendencies for years. Now at 19 she has decided that she is a lesbian and she wants to "come out" to others. She joins a counseling group in order to work on this issue. The group comprises a number of individuals from various backgrounds and with diverse issues.

When Gloria brings up her wish to the group, some members are accepting and encouraging. Others seem horrified and intolerant. Fred, as the leader, tries to bring the group together to be supportive of Gloria. He encourages members to ask Gloria questions and to help her explore herself to the fullest. Most members do so. However, there are two members who condemn Gloria and threaten to leave the group. Fred stops the group for the day and asks all members to explore their own sexuality and be ready to talk about it next session.

What do you think of Fred's plan? What are some other ways Fred could handle this situation?

SUMMARY AND CONCLUSION

In this chapter, group work has been examined from a multicultural perspective. As Horne (1996) has stated in reviewing the literature on group work, "There is much greater diversity in the populations we now serve" (p. 2). Groups are composed of individuals with all types of cultural backgrounds, and to ignore the cultural differences among members and treat everyone the same in a group is to negate the richness inherent in the group membership. Yet, theoretically and pragmatically, multicultural group work, especially that focused on working with groups composed of members

from different cultures, has been slow in its evolution. Even more discouraging has been the dearth of literature and practice on working positively in groups with differences.

The reasons for the lack of progress in multicultural group work can be attributed to myths and fears as well as the sheer complexity of developing an applicable multicultural group work theory. Yet, goals, assessments, and ways of working with specific minority and majority populations are coming to the forefront in ever increasing numbers. Attention is now being paid to group leaders' awareness of cultural distinctions and appropriate actions they need to take in regard to these differences. Similarities between groups are also being noted. Pedersen (1997b) suggests that a culture-centered perspective promotes understanding, freedom, health, and justice.

With information on different cultural groups being published more frequently in professional journals, there is hope that practical as well as theoretical work in this area will increase. It is from this literature and study of general and specific information, as well as practice, that group leaders must mature in understanding the groups they assist. Along with this understanding must come direct contact with members of other cultures and experiences in cultures other than one's own. Finally, group workers must simultaneously explore their own cultural heritage and become aware of both the positive and negative aspects of their learned values. Through a lifelong commitment to learning about different cultures, group workers can become effective in leading and participating in groups that are culturally heterogeneous.

CLASSROOM EXERCISES

1. Make at least three visits to a naturally occurring culture group (e.g., club, church group). Observe how members of the group interact in similar and different ways. Describe for the rest of the class what this experience tells you about the group. What is your reaction to what you saw?

2. What general steps would you take in leading a task/work group composed of individuals from different cultural backgrounds? How would your steps be different if this group were a counseling/therapy group? Would leading a diverse psychoeducational group require that you do anything different from what you have already proposed?

3. Because literature on working with culturally diverse groups is still relatively new, go to your library and find an article on the subject. Critique it. What new information not covered in this chapter did you find?

4. What myths do you think are prevalent about members of your cultural group? What reality (or kernel of truth) underlies these myths? How do you think a group leader would work with a group composed of members of your culture based on the truth as opposed to the myth?

PART TWO

GROUPS THROUGHOUT THE LIFE SPAN

GROUPS FOR CHILDREN

I watch the children line up like ducks
all in a row, except one.
Noisily they ramble past concrete walls
follow-the-leader style
behind a blond-haired woman
in a light yellow dress
who quietly talks to them through her motions.
Today is picture day in the school
with a jolly old man who says: "Cheese"
tossing tidbit compliments before boys and girls
as they fix their smiles at him.
In just a flash roles are caught,
a moment recorded, and lines form again.
Straight and precise the children walk
all except one, who in dimly-lit halls,
rapidly steps in a zigzag manner
defying a rule and defining himself.*

*From "Still Life" by Samuel T. Gladding, 1975, *North Carolina Personnel & Guidance Journal, 4,* p. 28. Copyright by Samuel T. Gladding. No further reproduction authorized without written permission from the author.

C hildren are not miniature adults. They have specific needs, wants, wishes, frustrations, joys, and fears, some of which are best shared in a group. In growing up, developmental, emotional, and behavioral problems affect more than 20% of all children (Shechtman, 2004). Unless these situations are addressed, they will fester and will often plague the lives of these individuals. Therefore, it is best to work with children during times of development, pain, or crises. Groups are an ideal place for such work to occur.

However, group work with children, defined here as groups for children under age 14, requires a special knowledge of child development and group theory. "Children have shorter attention spans, are more likely to project their feelings onto others, tend to need more structure and direction, and have much less control over their situation and environment" (DeLucia-Waack, 2000a, p. 132). Thus, to be helpful to children, group workers must be attuned to children's issues and needs in a distinct way. For instance, as opposed to adults, children usually respond better to nonverbal techniques than they do to verbal exercises because of their limited vocabularies and their dispositions to display feelings through play instead of words (Thompson & Henderson, 2007). Group specialists must adapt their approaches to the social, emotional, physical, and intellectual levels of this population (Johnson & Kottman, 1992).

When children face natural age and stage developmental tasks together (e.g., learning how to work cooperatively, learning how to express emotions appropriately), they frequently master more than the specifically targeted skills. Social interactions with other children and adults often promote within them a sense of well-being and lead to the prevention of future problems as the children develop human resources and models to go with their already formed cognitive and behavioral skills (Boutwell & Myrick, 1992; Cobia & Henderson, 2007). Through being exposed to new people and ways of handling situations, their growth is enhanced on all levels. In children's groups, timing as well as content is crucial, and learning occurs best at what Havighurst (1972) describes as a **teachable moment**, a time when children are ready and able to learn.

Since the late 1960s, small-group work, especially in school settings, has proven its efficacy and has become a major model by which children are helped (Bowman, 1987; Shechtman, 2004). This type of work concentrates on promoting life skills and correcting faulty assumptions. In elementary and middle schools (where most children under 14 are educated), psychoeducational and counseling groups are used to help children not only learn new skills but also become aware of their values, priorities, and communities. Indeed, the research shows that approximately 70% of children's groups take place in schools (Shechtman, 2004). Small groups give students the opportunity to "explore and work through their social and emotional challenges with others who are experiencing similar feelings" (Campbell & Bowman, 1993, p. 173). For example, group counseling is often employed with children who have special life event concerns, such as separation from a parent through divorce (Cappetta, 1996; DeLucia-Waack & Gerrity, 2001; Yauman, 1991) or failing grades (Boutwell & Myrick, 1992). Group counseling is also appropriate for children who have disruptive or acting-out behavior problems, such as violent outbursts, excessive fighting, defiance, maladjustment, and an inability to get along with peers and teachers (Brantley, Brantley, & Baer-Barkley, 1996; Nelson, Dykeman, Powell, & Petty, 1996). For some children with severe problems, family therapy outside or inside the school environment is necessary (Hinkle, 1993; Whiteside, 1993).

In almost all their daily environments, children spend a great deal of time interacting in groups, so these settings are ideal places to conduct both preventive guidance work as well as remedial counseling (Campbell, 1993; Gumaer, 1984; Kulic, Horne, & Dagley, 2004). The most basic underlying principle of dealing with children in groups stresses that groups are natural childhood environments and, therefore, have the power to hurt or to heal (March, 1935). Care must be exercised in working with children in group settings to prevent harm and promote health. Readiness for group guidance and psychoeducational experiences "is determined by the developmental level of individuals and their corresponding need system" (Gazda, 1989, p. 33). Readiness for group guidance and counseling is determined by the amount of dissonance children feel between how they are acting and what they see others their age doing. Overall, the key to working with children in groups is readiness on the part of both the leader and the children.

CASE EXAMPLE: Sabrina's Exhaustive Experience

As the new counselor at her school, Sabrina wanted to prove her worth to others. Thus, during her first month, she set up six groups ranging from a friendship group to a grief group. She was enthused at first and poured herself into working with the children in her groups. However, conducting six groups a week began to get old soon, and Sabrina found she was tired of the meetings she had set up.

When she tried to terminate some of the groups, both the children and their parents complained. They liked meeting, and everyone seemed to be getting something from the groups. Finally, over the protest of everyone, Sabrina ended the groups. She was simply too exhausted to continue. Clearly, she was not as ready for the experience as the children.

If you had been Sabrina, how would you have handled your newness to the school and the setting up of groups? When she became overextended, what do you think Sabrina could have done besides shutting down the groups? What part do you think readiness had to do with this situation?

TYPES OF GROUPS FOR CHILDREN

Developmental and nondevelopmental factors determine what types of groups are set up for children. **Developmental factors** include variables such as the age, gender, and maturity level of those involved. **Nondevelopmental factors**, in contrast, encompass less predictable qualities, such as the nature of the problem, the suddenness of its appearance, the intensity of its severity, and the present coping skills of children and their families.

As mentioned previously, groups for children generally take the form of guidance and psychoeducation (i.e., learning a new skill or experience) or counseling and psychotherapy (i.e., rectifying or resolving problematic behaviors, assumptions, or situations). The emphasis, regardless of the type of intervention, is on children's healthy development (Baker, 1996). Interventions vary depending on the children (or parents and teachers) with whom the group worker is interacting. However, some generalizations can be made. First, group guidance and psychoeducation usually involve the group worker in the role of an information giver with a large group of children. In such situations, the group worker functions as an instructor or a guide and may work directly with teachers. For example, a group worker and teacher may jointly present information on ways of dealing with grief and sorrow effectively.

In this case, the teacher may read a short book, such as Judith Viorst (1971), *The Tenth Good Things About Barney*. Then the group worker may use discussions and role-plays to help the class apply the lesson to their lives—for example, when a pet dies, it is okay to be sad and appropriate to talk about what the pet meant to you and how you loved it.

It is not easy to give individual attention to all members of a psychoeducational group (Myrick, 2003). Consequently, the experience is usually less personal and more limited in scope than a counseling or psychotherapy group. However, psychoeducational groups, like group counseling and psychotherapy, can be an effective way to help children unlearn inappropriate behaviors and master new ways of relating more easily through interaction and feedback in a safe practice situation with their peers (Thompson & Henderson, 2007). For example, in a psychoeducational group, Chad may learn ways to be assertive in verbally asking for what he wants from June instead of being inappropriately aggressive by bullying or hitting. He may also learn constructive ways to deal with situations when he does not get what he wants.

Second, guidance and psychoeducational groups primarily focus on improving skills and awareness in personal and interpersonal areas, such as values, attitudes, beliefs, social maturity, and career development, but they are not limited to these general growth topics. Group counseling and psychotherapy, however, are more remediation based and deal with such personal and interpersonal concerns as "self-concept, social skills, interpersonal relationships, problem solving, academic skills, communication skills, and values" (Franks, 1983, p. 201). Therefore, when the fifth-grade class participates in a group psychoeducational experience, it is assumed they are generally healthy but uninformed about a subject area, such as boy–girl relationships.

Third, although there is often an overlap in the subject areas covered in the activities of the groups just mentioned, the number of children involved in psychoeducational groups and counseling and psychotherapy groups usually differs. The latter types of groups focus on more specific concerns and in greater depth. Not as many individuals can be included.

Finally, the amount of risk taking and the overall process of these ways of working with groups tend to be distinct. Greater personal risks are taken in group counseling and psychotherapy, and these groups are held in a less structured environment than is found in group guidance and psychoeducation (Myrick, 2003). In addition, learning is usually more cognitively based in guidance and psychoeducational groups, whereas it is more emotionally based in counseling and psychotherapeutic groups.

◆ *Questions from Experience* ◆

Think of skills you learned in groups growing up from those in schools to those in religious or civic settings. What skills have stayed with you from those times? How did the presence of peers help or hinder your mastering of information or behavior?

Group Guidance for Elementary/Middle School Children

Group guidance for children of elementary and middle school age may be conducted in school, community agencies, or both (Corey & Corey, 2006). **Preschool and early school-aged children** include ages 5 through 9, and **preadolescents** are defined as children in the latency period ranging in age from 9 to 13 years. Children below the age of 5 are usually not included in groups because of the egocentric nature of their development. However, exceptions can be made for more mature 3- and 4-year-olds, and children below age 5 may successfully be included in prosocial learning groups (Golden, 1987).

Because group guidance in the schools is a preventive approach, counselors usually act as group leaders. Traditionally, they have presented their lessons to groups of children within a regular classroom environment. These offerings are varied and can range from a puppet show on friendship for preschoolers to realistic portrayals of preteen situations, such as those shown in the award-winning Public Broadcasting System's *DeGrassi Junior High,* for older children. Other lessons center on a variety of subject areas, such as personal or mental health, boy–girl relationships, getting along with parents, and cooperation with peers. Career development and self-exploration are two particularly proactive topics often explored (DeLucia-Waack, 2000). Making the transition from elementary to middle school is another (Akos & Martin, 2003). This last type of group may be especially potent in reducing student anxiety, preventing negative outcomes associated with transition, establishing supportive networks among peers, and positively influencing the developmental paths and school success for preadolescents.

Two excellent resources for conducting group counseling activities with elementary students are:

Rosemarie Smead's 's (1994) *Skills for Living: Group Activities for Elementary School Students*, where Smead not only describes how to conduct specialized groups for children but also provides readers with ways of working with parents, teachers, and principals; *and*

Ann Vernon's (1990) *Thinking, Feeling, Behaving: An Emotional Educational Curriculum for Children Grades 1–6,* where Vernon provides a bevy of activities for this age population based on Rational Emotive Behavior Therapy (REBT).

School guidance and counseling journals, such as *Professional School Counseling,* also contain a wealth of ideas. For instance, one interesting and classic group psychoeducational activity found in the predecessor of this publication is the "Get Along Gang" (Bond, 1993), an activity aimed at helping third-graders contain their anger. In this experience, the counselor presents name calling as a game. Name-callers win if another person gets angry at being called a name. To win the game, students who are called names must not get angry or show their anger.

Group guidance works best when counselors know what they want the group to achieve. One classic model for reaching this goal is known as SIPA (structure, involvement, process, and awareness) (Tyra, 1979). In *structuring,* counselors ask children to listen or do new activities according to certain guidelines. *Involvement* consists of getting the group to be active participants. (Even children who do not wish to participate may report back to the group as observers after an activity is over.) *Processing* is composed of sharing ideas, and *awareness* is consolidating what was learned in the guidance time. An example of a SIPA group is one Kizner (1999) offered in an elementary school setting to adopted children. The 12-session group consisted of presenting information about adoption, preparing an autobiography, fostering student's self-esteem, expressing feelings, and having discussions around adoption-related issues.

Many psychoeducational groups revolve around activities and are subsequently called **activity group guidance (AGG)** (Hillman & Reunion, 1978). These activities are developmental in nature and typically include coordinated guidance topics. For example, in promoting self-understanding and understanding of others, puppets, drawings, and music are often used (DeLucia-Waack, 2001b; Egge, Marks, & McEvers, 1987; Gladding, 2004; Harper, 1985). These artistic activities are nonthreatening and enhance interaction and motivation in ways that language alone cannot do. For some children who are not in contact with their emotions, songs that they have written and sung to different tunes can give them an awareness of themselves not possible otherwise (Miles, 1993). Because of the inherent power of active developmental media, they are often packaged in commercial classroom guidance programs, such as **Developing Understanding of Self and Others—Revised (DUSO–R)** (Dinkmeyer & Dinkmeyer, 1982). A typical AGG session has three stages:

1. A 10-minute warm-up in which the group and leader discuss an appropriate guidance principle
2. A planned activity that attempts to implement the guidance principle for the day
3. A follow-up discussion, lasting about 5 to 10 minutes, in which the group reviews the impact of the guidance principle activity on themselves (Hillman & Reunion, 1978)

At other times, group workers implement group activities on their own, sometimes in various formats. For example, they may decide to have the group express a variety of feelings through making rhythmic sounds on their knees to represent the emotions at different times of the day or in different situations. Such an activity can help build empathy and foster prosocial behavior (Akos, 2000). In cases such as these, children may sound out in a group a variety of feelings, such as sad, mad, unsure, happy, and satisfied. Then, as in the more structured methods, group discussions take place (Gladding, 2004).

In guidance and psychoeducational groups, a variety of techniques work well, and group workers should move developmentally from more simple activities to those that are more complex. For example, learning or becoming aware of one's emotions should be followed by activities that promote the recognition of feelings in others. Such a process could be achieved by having children participate in a game that Akos (2000) calls "Referential Communication." This activity requires children to sit in a circle with paper and crayons. They are asked to draw a green triangle in the middle of their paper. Then each child takes turns giving a command as to what to draw next. When the activity is over, the children show their drawings and talk about the differences in them as well as how easy or hard it is to understand the perspective of other group members.

Campbell (1991) gives four techniques for working with undermotivated children in psychosocial groups: (a) using guided fantasy, (b) focusing on specific behaviors to be improved, (c) creating positive affirmations (i.e., positive statements about oneself), and (d) employing visualizations. One or more of these techniques may not work with some children, but probably some will. The point is that variety is the essence of group guidance and psychoeducational lessons.

A relatively new model for offering group guidance and psychoeducational material in middle schools is for counselors to train teachers to provide this service. Through such an arrangement, the productivity of school counseling personnel can be increased while reducing the need for more staff (Rolland & Neitzschman, 1996). The basic material taught to teachers by counselors who use this model is the core group counseling skills as defined by the Association for Specialists in Group Work. After mastering these skills, teachers and counselors work even closer together than they might otherwise, and students are better served.

Group Counseling Within the Schools

Group counseling within schools is essential to the healthy growth of elementary and middle school students. Psychoeducational and counseling groups, "where a counselor works with a group of 6 to 8 students, greatly increases the number of students who can benefit from working with a school counselor" (DeLucia-Waack, 2000, p. 131). Such groups are becoming the preferred method of counselor intervention because they enable "a counselor to see more students and to use counselor time to its maximum" (Boutwell & Myrick, 1992, pp. 65–66). In small group settings, the affective as well as the cognitive and behavioral domains of students are explored.

Sometimes group counseling is focused, such as in the *Fresh Start Club* for elementary school children who have been retained at grade level (Campbell & Bowman, 1993). In situations in which the group is structured, the emphasis is placed on positive aspects of an experience in addition to group support. In group counseling, opportunities are also provided for learning about self and others through less structured interactions.

Group counseling usually takes one of three approaches in dealing with persons and problems: (a) crisis centered, (b) problem centered, and (c) growth centered (Myrick, 2003). **Crisis-centered groups** are formed because of some emergency, such as conflict between student groups. These groups usually meet until the situation that caused them to form has been resolved. Group counseling provides individuals with a means to examine their situation and to think together about some possible solutions (Myrick, 2003). Sometimes, groups formed because of a crisis continue meeting after the crisis has passed and develop into either problem-centered or growth groups. For example, after a fight between some fourth- and fifth-graders, children in one school formed a "peace group." The purpose of the group was originally to promote ways to resolve problems among the children who had been in open conflict. As the group continued to develop, however, its purpose was enlarged to finding ways to spot problematic situations in the school and correct them in a productive way.

Problem-centered groups are small groups set up to focus on one particular concern—for example, coping with stress. They are useful to students who have one major difficulty, such as being under too much pressure—for instance, children who have demanding parents who insist they excel in school and extracurricular activities, such as athletics or dance. Like the members of crisis-centered groups, those involved with problem-centered groups are usually highly motivated and committed to working on their situations and themselves.

To illustrate a problem-centered group, Clark and Seals (1984) describe a three-phase open group counseling approach for ridiculed children that provides support "to children who long for acceptance" (p. 161) and who have a problem getting it. In the initial phase of the group, the focus is on establishing a relationship based on trust and encouragement. Children who get involved in the group feel a sense of **universalization**, realizing they are not the only ones who face being ridiculed. In the second phase, erroneous thoughts and distorted cognitions are challenged (see Table 11.1). The final phase of the group serves to promote positive behaviors, including the working out of strategies to deal with peers who ridicule. Role-plays are often used in this phase, and interpersonal interaction and cooperation are encouraged.

Table 11.1
Basic mistakes of ridiculed children.

Erroneous Statement	Type	Corrected Statement
"Everyone hates me."	Overgeneralizations	"I do have one friend."
"They're all out to get me."	False or impossible goals of security	"Six children make fun of me."
"There's nothing I can do about it."	Misperceptions of life and life's demands	"I can avoid some of the teasing."
"I can't do anything right."	Minimization or denial of one's worth	"I am very good with computers."
"I'll get them all back someday."	Faulty values	"Why waste my time on getting revenge?"

Source: From "Groups Counseling for Ridiculed Children" by A. J. Clark and J. M. Seals, 1984, *Journal for Specialists in Group Work, 9,* p. 160. Copyright ACA. Reprinted with permission. No further reproduction authorized without written permission of the American Counseling Association.

Another problem-centered group is the *friendship group* (Coppock, 1993). This group is for students who have been referred to a school counselor for specific problems, such as misbehavior, lack of social skills, or poor academic performance. It is closed ended, lasting from 6 to 8 weeks. In it, students are invited to "develop and practice friendship skills" (p. 152). These skills revolve around nonthreatening activities, such as introducing oneself to another, playing games (e.g., receiving compliments), making up adventures (e.g., imagining oneself in a new place and time), and solving problems, especially those that are of a personal nature. This last part of the group is done only if students are developmentally ready to work with the group on a problem and only after problem-solving skills have been discussed and demonstrated in the group.

Growth-centered groups focus on the personal and social development of students (Myrick, 2003). Their purpose is to enable children to explore their feelings, concerns, and behaviors about a number of everyday subjects. For instance, Rose (1987) describes a time-limited group for children ages 6 to 12 that promotes social competence. Although the group is behaviorally based and uses a number of behavioral principles, such as rehearsal, instruction, modeling, feedback, coaching, assignments, and social rewards, the basic format of the group could be modified to work with children who are not in distress but who wish to improve their social functioning. Although personal skills may be taught to children in group guidance classes, growth-centered groups allow a more personal touch to be added to the learning process and give the group worker an opportunity to get to know children more deeply and help them in specific ways.

Group Guidance and Counseling in Community Settings

The basic dynamics of group guidance and counseling for children in settings outside school environments do not differ substantially from those conducted within schools. Community settings with groups for children, such as churches, clubs, and mental health centers, basically structure and run their groups in a manner similar to that used in educational institutions. A major difference, however, between schools and community agencies is the populations of children served. Community organizations will usually have more homogeneous groups than will schools. This difference occurs because children group themselves in organizations according to their interests and because mental health professionals in agencies often start groups for certain "types" of children—for example, the shy low achievers, abused children, or those with severe conduct disorders.

Nevertheless, this lack of diversity can be overcome through group exercises. For example, a structured technique, such as the *Human Rainbow,* makes it possible for children to recognize unique as well as universal qualities in themselves and others. In this structured activity, children first create masks and then form a circle—a human rainbow—around the room. Afterward, they discuss similarities and differences among people and address areas in human relations in which they have a major concern (Buban, McConnell, & Duncan, 1988).

It is important in community settings, as well as educational institutions, that group guidance or counseling activities be presented in an appealing way. One means to do so is to advertise groups as "clubs." By forming clubs instead of guidance or counseling groups, children avoid any stigmas attached to mental health activities. In the process, they can become more involved in the group and, thereby, get more from the experience.

CASE EXAMPLE: Sadie's Seasonal Affective Disorder Group

Sadie identified three girls in her school who were affected by seasonal affective disorder (SAD). She thought if she formed a group for them that focused on good things in their lives, she might suppress their sadness. Therefore, she formed a theme group that she called a club named "GLAD" (Great Lassies and Dames). The idea behind the club was to study the lives of girls and women who had overcome obstacles and achieved fame.

The club got off to a great start. Everyone read inspirational stories and talked about the remarkable girls and women that could serve as role models for them. The third week, Kari asked if she could invite a friend. Since the group had not been advertised as closed, Sadie was unsure what to do.

Would another person without the characteristics of the first three be detrimental to what she was trying to accomplish? What do you think? What would you do in this case?

SETTING UP GROUPS FOR CHILDREN

In designing group experiences, group workers must consider the maturity of the children with whom they are working and the purpose of the group. Assessing children's maturity is most frequently accomplished by establishing regular contacts with them. Determining topics for the group to explore can be accomplished through the use of "sociograms, self-concept inventories, incomplete sentence activities, and children's drawings" (Gerler, 1982, p. 87). Decisions can also be made when counselors conduct needs assessments with students, teachers, parents, and other related school personnel or when counselors hear several students voicing similar concerns over a short period. Regardless of how the decision is made, many questions must be answered before the group begins, including these:

1. What medium will be most used in group communication?
2. What structure will be employed?

3. What materials will be used in the group?
4. How will group members be recruited and screened?
5. How long will group sessions meet?
6. How many children will be in the group?
7. What will the gender mix be?

Nonverbal Versus Verbal Communication

Gazda (1989), in concurrence with other authorities in the field of children's group counseling, such as Dinkmeyer and Muro (1979), Keat (1974), and Slavson (1945, 1948), states that children under 12 years of age should participate primarily in groups that involve play and action, using techniques such as sociodrama, child drama, and psychodrama. Ginott (1968) also recommends the use of active play therapy for young children (under age 9) in groups, specifically, water colors, finger paints, clay, and sand, and Jones (2002) advocates group play therapy with sexually abused preschool children. As Campbell (1993, p. 10) states, "Toys have been referred to as the words children use to express emotions." Opposed to this **action-centered view of groups** are professionals such as Ohlsen, Horne, and Lawe (1988), who believe that children can be taught the proper ways to express themselves verbally and that verbally oriented groups are viable with even very young children.

In practice most counselors combine a mixture of verbalization and activity in their group sessions in a manner that is most helpful to their participants. In doing so, those who most favor verbal interaction hold onto the belief that the interplay of words and roles will "change the cognitive map and action patterns of a group member," whereas those who are activity oriented "believe that personality modifications occur through activity" (Kaczkowski, 1979, p. 45). There is some truth in both points of view.

Group Structure and Materials

In addition to deciding on the primary way of obtaining information from children, professionals who conduct such groups must also formulate how groups will be structured. **Highly structured groups** have a "predetermined goal and a plan designed to enable each group member to reach this identified goal with minimum frustration" (Drum & Knott, 1977, p. 14). Such groups are usually used for teaching skills that may be transferred to a wide range of life events. Often, groups are highly structured at their beginning and become less structured as group members get to know one another better. Unstructured groups, in contrast, are used in more experientially based situations in which process is emphasized rather than product. It is rare for a children's group of any kind to be totally unstructured.

Group workers must also decide how materials used in the groups will be employed. If the emphasis of the group is on completing a project (e.g., drawing a figure) as opposed to experiencing a feeling (e.g., free-hand drawing), then the materials that are distributed and instructions given should reflect this. There are basically four approaches to this process: (a) unstructured material, unstructured approach; (b) unstructured material, structured approach; (c) structured material, unstructured approach; and (d) structured material, structured approach (Kaczkowski, 1979). Each approach has its advantages and limitations (see Table 11.2).

Table 11.2

Relationships among key elements in group work.

Group	Goal	Leader	Child	Materials
Unstructured material, unstructured approach	Recognition of self Understanding that impulse can be controlled Living within social boundaries Self-responsibility	Cognitive stimulant Rewards Intrudes (approves, disapproves, etc.) Provides materials but not goals	Forced to think Free to use material	Conducive to creation, control, and change No end product Freedom of action
Unstructured material, structured approach	Improved self-concept Improved impulse control Improved social interaction	Preselects activity Acts as participant Helps child manipulate things and people in acceptable manner	Forced to think about something Tests reality Learns basic interaction with others	Designed to place limits on action Develops some skill Process rather than product emphasis
Structured material, unstructured approach	Reduce egocentric behavior Build relationship between things and people Deal effectively with social realities Evaluation of personal goals	Selects materials with child Facilitates interpersonal relations Active in skill presentation (minimal emphasis) Identification figure Rewards behavior	Learns practical working relationships Externalizes hostility Respects properly	May facilitate skill development Used to develop relations and cooperation No end product Has an acceptable standard of performance
Structured material, structured approach	Improved social reality Development of acceptance Reality relationships	Selects materials with child Provides for success Formal Teaches skill Facilitator	Completes project Tries to exhibit selective behavior Independent	Conducive to generating a product Cognitive or creative skill development Enhances reality relations

Source: From "Group Work with Children" by H. Kaczkowski, 1979, *Elementary School Guidance & Counseling, 14*, p. 47. Copyright ACA. Reprinted with permission. No further reproduction authorized without written permission of the American Counseling Association.

The key to making the group a productive vehicle for helping children is for the group worker to use a leadership style that will enable him or her to blend meaningful materials with an appropriate degree of verbalization and activity. For instance, in group counseling, a leader may employ a democratic style that encourages sharing and openness. By creating such an atmosphere and modeling appropriate behaviors, group leaders establish trust within the group and set concrete examples of how change can be accomplished.

◆ *Questions Based on Experience* ◆

When have you seen a leader relate well to a group of children? What did the leader do that made him or her attractive to the children? Which of those same traits or techniques could you employ if working with a group of children?

Recruiting Members and Screening

Once preliminary decisions about form, structure, and materials are made, the group worker begins the task of recruiting members. One of the best ways to accomplish this task is to provide parents, teachers, and students with an **information statement** that describes what the group is about and what is expected of its members (Ritchie & Huss, 2000). Flyers, bulletin boards, newsletters, and word of mouth may be used in various ways in this effort. Children who are potential group members, especially for topic-focused group counseling, will often ask to join a group.

Not all children who volunteer or who are referred are appropriate for a group. Therefore, a pregroup screening process must be used. Prescreening has special importance with children's groups because of the ethical and legal responsibilities involved in conducting groups for minors (Ritchie & Huss, 2000). "Issues such as the client's right to privacy, informed consent, and parental involvement take on special significance when treating minors in groups" (p. 147). For instance, in regard to privacy, "counselors in schools or community agencies should be careful that their recruitment process does not label potential group members and violate their right, and the right of their parents to privacy" (p. 148). For instance, it would be unwise to form a group for "antisocial boys." Although a label of this nature may seem absurd, it has happened, and group workers need to be careful in describing and advertising their groups. In an extreme case, parents might sue the counselor for slander or damages caused by associating their child with a negative label.

Assuming that counselors have taken appropriate precautions, the next step after recruitment is screening. One way to screen potential participants is through pregroup assessment methods. These methods may be informal or formal. An informal method is having a child write out what he or she wishes to get from a group. A more formal method is using instruments specifically designed for this purpose, such as the *Group Psychotherapy Evaluation Scale* or the *Group Assessment Form* (DeLucia-Waack, 1997a). Individual or small-group intake interviews can also be employed by group workers to talk with children about the group and its purpose (Corey & Corey, 2006).

If, based on relevant inclusion criteria, the counselor thinks certain children can bene-fit from the group and these children display an interest, then the children are invited to join (Kochendofer & Culp, 1979; Silverman, 1976). Selection is crucial to the group's suc-cess because group member satisfaction and identity with the group will influence group cohesion and ultimately affect personal outcomes.

When group workers and children decide that the group is appropriate, letters requesting permission for participation must be sent to parents. Children must sign con-sent forms, too, so that everyone is in agreement before the group begins about the pur-pose of the group and the procedures involved. Thus, group work with children is more difficult to set up than group work with adults because of the many considerations involved in protecting children's rights (Corey, Corey, & Callanan, 2007).

Group Session Length and Number in Group

Opinions vary on how long group sessions should last and how many children should be included in a group. One general guideline is the younger the children, the shorter the session and the smaller the group (Myrick, 2003; Vinson, 1992). When groups become too large (e.g., nine or over), members do not get an opportunity to participate as much with one another, and the dynamics of the group change. In such situations, subgroups may form, or "in groups" and "out groups" may develop.

The number who can be included in large group guidance activities is virtually unlim-ited. However, most counselors think in terms of 25 to 30 students. This enables the group to be conveniently subdivided into five or six small working teams with about five or six students each (Myrick, 2003). Small groups within the group can be further subdivided, if necessary, into triads and dyads.

In group counseling, numbers are of concern. Group size should always be deter-mined after examining the purpose of the counseling group, the developmental needs of the students, and the time available (Gumaer, 1986; Posthuma, 2002). When working with children ages 5 to 6, sessions may be held for only 20 minutes each two or three times a week and the number of children allowed to participate may be limited to 3 or 4 (Thomp-son & Henderson, 2007). As children mature, the time allotted for each session and the numbers included go up. For example, preadolescent children (ages 9 to 13) may meet in groups of 5 to 7 for as long as a regular classroom period (45 to 50 minutes), although the time allotted usually is around 30 minutes (Jacobs, Masson, & Harvill, 2006).

Gender and Age Issues

A final consideration in setting up a group is a decision regarding the sex and age range of the participants. On the issue of gender, there is considerable disagreement. For example, Ginott (1968) believes that children of different sexes should be mixed in preschool group settings but that school-age children should be separated. Gazda (1989) also believes that school-age children should be segregated by sex, but not until the ages of 9 or 10. He con-tends that around the time of puberty, girls begin to mature more rapidly than boys, and the two genders do not mix well in groups. By contrast, Ohlsen (1977) advocates that groups include both girls and boys because he feels that group counseling is the safest place for girls and boys to learn to cope with each other regardless of social or sexual development. This same point of view is held by Thompson and Henderson (2007), who stress a balance of both sexes in a group unless the problem to be discussed is such that the presence of the opposite sex would hinder discussion—sex education topics, for example.

In regard to age, a general rule of thumb is to group children with those who are within about one chronological year of one another (Gazda, 1989). Exceptions are made when more aggressive children are grouped with older children and less mature children are grouped with younger children. Some children with severe problems may be better candidates for individual counseling.

ROLE OF THE LEADER IN CHILDREN'S GROUPS

The leader's role in children's groups varies. In group guidance, the leader is a teaching facilitator who encourages self-exploration. Guidance lessons are planned in cooperation, and often participation, with classroom teachers. Sometimes a counselor and a teacher will co-lead a group and map out their developmental curriculum far in advance. At other times, they will make use of **timely teaching**, when a particular event stimulates thinking and discussion among students (Faust, 1968). Many group guidance leaders operate from an atheoretical base in regard to the process of change. They stress developmental learning. Others are more integrative or holistic. Yet a third group of leaders concentrate solely on a single area of change, such as in the affective, behavioral, or cognitive domain.

In relation to the approach taken, leaders of children's guidance and psychoeducational groups also influence what happens in the groups by the way they arrange chairs. Myrick (2003) states that students can be seated in five basic arrangements (see Figure 11.1). When the classroom is arranged in a **row formation**, attention is focused toward the front. This arrangement is good for making a presentation, but it limits, and even inhibits, group interaction. In the second formation, a **circle**, student eye contact is increased and equality is promoted, but if the class group is too large (e.g., more than 20), students may lose a sense of connectedness with others. In the **semicircle arrangement**, students can see one another, and discussion is likely to involve almost everyone. However, if the group is too large (e.g., more than 20), students may not feel that they are a group.

The fourth arrangement, **in and out circles**, is often referred to as the **fishbowl**. The inner circle promotes a sense of closeness, but those in the outer circle may feel left out and become bored. To help promote participation by everyone, group leaders can assign tasks for the outside group members to do (e.g., taking notes on group interactions) while they observe the inside group. They can also rotate groups in and out of the inner circle on a regular, timely basis. Another way to encourage participation by everyone is for leaders to leave an empty chair in the inner circle where those in the outer circle can sit and observe directly on a one-by-one basis what is happening in the inner circle.

Finally, the group guidance leader can use another structured arrangement known as **discussion teams** to promote involvement in guidance and psychoeducational activities. In this arrangement, students are divided into teams that are then seated in semicircles

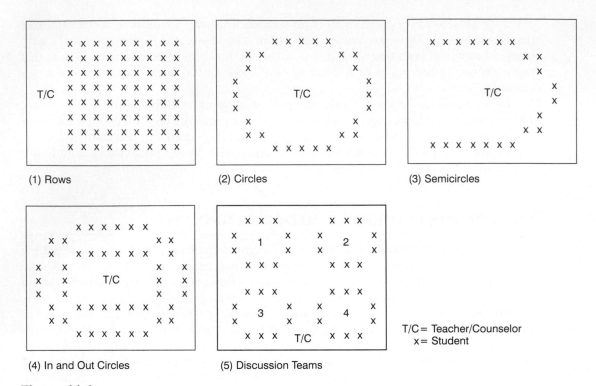

Figure 11.1

Managing large groups: Seating arrangements.

Source: From *Developmental Guidance and Counseling: A Practical Approach* by R. D. Myrick, 1997 (3rd ed., p. 240), Minneapolis: Educational Media Corporation. Copyright © 1997 Educational Media Corporation. Reprinted with permission.

around the room. This formation has the advantage of getting students involved with one another and raising the level of excitement among the children. The disadvantage is that interaction is mainly limited to a small number of individuals, and other group members get to participate in only one group.

In group counseling, leaders have more of a tendency than in group guidance to have a theoretical orientation and act accordingly (Long, 1988). For example, the Adlerian group leader functions as an open, democratic individual who is based in the here and now. These leaders vary in their techniques, but in working with children's groups, they are prone to emphasize encouragement and the law of natural consequences (Dinkmeyer & Sperry, 2000). Leaders who are psychoanalytically based (and work more in group psychotherapy than in group counseling) focus on the release of feeling through catharsis and the analysis of transference and interpretation (Corey, 2004). In contrast, group counselors who take a Rogerian approach in their group work with children "put far greater emphasis on the facilitative quality of the counselor as a person. . . . The counselor's personhood [is] the basic catalyst that prompts group participants to make progress or not" (Boy & Pine, 1982, p. 179).

Leaders in rational-emotive behavior therapy groups with children stress the teaching of rational thinking (Ellis, 1974a; Weinrach, 1995). However, leaders in transactional analysis (TA) prefer to work with children in groups to promote the confrontation of games and help children learn basic TA concepts by seeing them demonstrated in themselves and others (Harris, 1967; Thompson & Henderson, 2007). In a similar way, leaders who adhere to Gestalt theory work in groups to promote awareness and support personality change from within (Corey, 2004). Leaders in solution-focused groups help group members concentrate on a solution rather than a problem. This emphasis may be especially helpful in increasing success because of its positive and specific nature (Murphy, 1997). Finally, leaders of behavioral and cognitive-behavioral groups, which are the most popular for the treatment of children (Shechtman, 2004), focus on teaching children appropriate prosocial skills and helping them eliminate dysfunctional behavior (Rose, 1987). A critical component in bringing about behavioral change is promoting behavioral awareness—that is, "increasing students' ability to identify socially inappropriate behaviors, antecedents, and consequences and to use self-selected contingencies positively" (Safran & Safran, 1985, p. 91).

Basically, the "principles of group counseling apply to all ages. However, the group counselor [leader] must adapt his or her techniques to the clients' social, emotional, and intellectual development, as well as their ability to communicate verbally" (George & Dustin, 1988, p. 136).

CASE EXAMPLE: Claire Chooses an Approach

Claire wants to help her fourth-graders become more team oriented. She thinks that will help them become more academically accomplished as a group. She thinks an Adlerian approach would work best because of its social emphasis. She finds that the class becomes closer as a result of her theory selection and implementation. Yet, she is not sure what another theory might produce.

What would you advise? What would be the advantages and limitations of your choice?

STUDIES ON THE OUTCOME OF CHILDREN'S GROUPS

Because psychoeducational and counseling groups have been conducted with elementary and middle school children for years, numerous studies have been made on them. Unfortunately, only a few of those studies have been research based (Shechtman, 2004). Nevertheless, as Bowman (1987) discovered in a national survey, counselors, especially school counselors, consider groups to be vital in reaching some students whom they would otherwise miss. Furthermore, DeLucia-Waack and Gerrity (2001) point out that "groups provide elements of support, altruism, universality, and cooperation that individual counseling cannot provide" (p. 281). The following are some examples of outcomes from group counseling with children over the years.

In regard to fourth- and fifth-graders who were children of alcoholics, Riddle, Bergin, and Douzenis (1997) found that they benefited in a number of ways from group counseling. In particular, the self-concepts of these children, as measured by the *Piers-Harris Children's Self-Concept Scale,* improved. In addition, these children increased their social skills and lowered their anxiety over the 14-week period of the groups. They also acquired information about the disease of alcoholism and learned strategies to employ to cope with parental alcoholism. Without the use of a group, these benefits, which applied to 40 students in the public elementary schools in southeast Georgia, would not have been realized on such a scale.

In another elementary school research project, Allan and Bardsley (1983) found group counseling to be helpful for **transient children** (i.e., those children who have moved to a new community and a new school) as they adapt to their environments. They describe a six-session group counseling format that positively affected students, teachers, parents, and a principal.

In working with fourth- and fifth-graders whose parents divorced, an 11-session support group for elementary school children was found to be beneficial (Tedder, Scherman, & Wantz, 1987). In this group, a developmentally appropriate introductory activity, the *caterpillar,* was used. Students filled in the eight sections of their caterpillar by drawing an expressive face in the first segment, writing three words that described themselves in segment 2, listing two of their hobbies in segment 3, writing three present feelings in segment 4, identifying where they were born in segment 5, describing where they would like to be at the present time in segment 6, listing an activity they would like to do in segment 7, and writing about a unique special personal quality in segment 8 (see Figure 11.2). The most important outcome of this research was its use of objective instruments to verify positive outcomes. Parents especially noted the impact of the group on their children's behavior.

In regard to groups for elementary school–age children whose parents are divorcing, DeLucia-Waack and Gerrity (2001) have elaborated on other research showing the effectiveness of such groups in schools and community agencies. In addition, they suggest a framework for leading counseling and psychoeducational groups for children of divorce in school, agency, and court-based programs. They stress the use of the creative arts, such as music, bibliotherapy, puppets, and drama, in such groups to help children express their feelings and practice new behaviors and skills in a safe and supportive environment.

A *Disruptive Child's Play Group (DCPG)* for third-grade children in an elementary school also produced positive results (Bleck & Bleck, 1982). After children participated in this 10-session program, their self-concept scores improved significantly compared with those for a control group. In another study on self-concept in the same year, Durbin

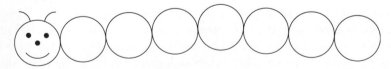

Figure 11.2

Caterpillar introductory activity.

Source: From "Effectiveness of a Support Group for Children of Divorce" by S. L. Tedder, A. Scherman, and R. A. Wantz, 1987, *Elementary School Guidance & Counseling, 22,* p. 105. Copyright ACA. Reprinted by permission. No further reproduction authorized without written permission of the American Counseling Association.

Happy	Afraid	Worried	Free Space
Sad	Timid	Mad	Lonely
Joyful	Excited	Scared	Smart
Angry	Tired	Good	Overwhelmed

Figure 11.3

Feelings bingo game.

Source: From "Multimodal Counseling: Motivating Children to Attend School Through Friendship Groups" by D. B. Keat, K. L. Metzgar, D. Raykovitz, and J. McDonald, 1985. *Journal of Humanistic Education and Development, 23,* p. 170. Copyright ACA. Reprinted by permission. No further reproduction authorized without written permission of the American Counseling Association.

(1982) found that self-concept for a sixth-grade girls' group improved significantly at the end of nine 35-minute sessions. Durbin's group followed a multimodal format based on Keat's (1979) **HELPING** framework—health, emotions, learning, personal interactions, imagery, need to know, and guidance. HELPING is an alternative model to Lazarus's (1976, 1989) **BASIC ID** approach—behavior, affect, sensation, imagery, cognition, interpersonal relations, drugs/diet. The HELPING model has been found to be a motivator for increasing daily attendance at school of third-grade boys, too (Keat, Metzgar, Raykovitz, & McDonald, 1985). It includes developmentally stimulating activities within it, such as *"Feelings Bingo,"* in which participants use "I" messages after a feeling is called and "win" by filling out their feeling card horizontally, diagonally, or any way the caller decides beforehand (see Figure 11.3).

In two studies involving *children with learning disabilities,* a population that comprises 2% to 10% of the school-age population, group counseling was found to improve self-concept, social behavior, and locus of control (Omizo, Cubberly, & Longano, 1984; Omizo & Omizo, 1988a). One of the studies (Omizo & Omizo, 1988) included participants from varied ethnic backgrounds in grades 4 to 6 and compared the 10-session treatment group with a control group. The other study, which also included a control group, was conducted with predominantly White middle-class children from ages 8 to 11 years and lasted for eight sessions. Both studies have significant implications for educators in helping children with learning disabilities to learn.

One of the most promising research studies on groups with children is a replication study conducted by Lee (1993) of classroom guidance on student achievement. In her work, Lee followed the **Succeeding in School lessons** created by Gerler and Anderson (1986). This series of 10 lessons deals with modeling after successful people in school while learning to feel comfortable and responsible. It focused on promoting cooperative efforts; enhancing student self-concept; and learning appropriate school skills, such as listening and asking for help. Although Lee's research had some flaws, she found that fifth- and sixth-graders who took part in this experience significantly improved their academic achievement in mathematics over a control group. The group also made gains in language and conduct.

In addition to the studies cited here, many others either statistically or anecdotally report positive results on the use of groups with elementary and middle school children (e.g., Daniels, D'Andrea, Omizo, & Pier [1999], on counseling groups with homeless children and their mothers; and Huss & Ritchie [1999], on support groups for parentally bereaved children). Research by Shechtman and her colleagues in Israel has been particularly strong in reporting the effectiveness of counseling groups on friendships of latency-age children lacking in social efficacy. These researchers have found such groups to lead to significant gains in intimacy, particularly in boys (Shechtman, Vurembrand, & Hertz-Lazarowitz, 1994). Some studies are now investigating the strengths and weaknesses of specific packaged types of groups. The most recent and promising of these is the Student Success Skills (SSS) model (Campbell & Brigman, 2005), a group intervention for elementary and middle school students related to school success in academic and social performance. Twenty-five school counselors who trained in this structured small group counseling approach worked with mid-range to low-performing students and saw them improve in both academic performance and behavior compared to a control group. Overall, research is making strides in informing potential group workers with children about which types of groups and experiences are effective with certain populations and when.

STRENGTHS AND LIMITATIONS OF USING GROUPS WITH CHILDREN

Using guidance, psychoeducational, counseling, and psychotherapy groups with children poses a number of advantages and limitations. How successful a particular group will be depends on many variables, such as how well prepared the leader and members are, the composition of membership, the amount of time allotted, and the group's focus.

Children who profit most from group counseling and psychotherapy share the following characteristics: They volunteer, are committed to discussing what genuinely concerns them, are committed to learning new behaviors, are interested in helping other group members learn new behaviors, and believe that their counselor or group leader and parents (and even teachers) have confidence in their ability to learn and implement new behaviors (Ohlsen et al., 1988). The opposite may be said for children who do not benefit.

Myrick (2003) lists a number of advantages and limitations for both group guidance and group counseling with children. Among the advantages of group guidance and psychoeducational activities are the following:

1. It allows the counselor/group leader to see a large number of students in a brief amount of time and work in a preventive fashion.
2. It allows the counselor/group leader to use inside (i.e., teachers) and outside (i.e., community personnel) resources to help children learn to help themselves.
3. It promotes security and comfort in children, promotes peer interaction, and enhances learning of practical ways to handle problem situations.

Among the limitations of group guidance and psychoeducational activities are the following:

1. It may be too impersonal at times and fail to help children in a practical way.
2. It may include too many individuals and prohibit general discussion or the exploration of certain subjects.
3. It may stereotype the counselor as a presenter of knowledge and inhibit the counselor from being more spontaneous.

Group counseling with children has advantages and limitations, also. Among the advantages listed by Myrick (2003) are the following:

1. It is more efficient than individual counseling because more children can be seen at any one time.
2. It is more realistic than individual counseling. Because of its social interaction base, it allows group members to share with one another frequently and learn through peer modeling and feedback.
3. It promotes support, acceptance, relaxation, risk taking, and resources for involved members.
4. It may free the counselor/group leader to make strategic intervention with members of the group.

Limitations of group counseling with children are the following:

1. It takes more time to develop trust and closeness because of the increased number of individuals involved in the counseling process.
2. It is more difficult to safeguard confidentiality and to include all members actively in group discussions and activities.
3. It is more difficult to organize group counseling activities than it is to see select children on a one-to-one basis—that is, group counseling formats require school system and/or parental permission/approval.
4. It requires leaders and members to be sensitive to topics that are inappropriate for the group and to be aware of, and counteract, nonproductive behavior of select group members.

Gumaer (1986) states that experienced middle school counselors can implement group work by recognizing its value; improving their involvement with teachers; discussing the rationale for more group work with their principals; obtaining additional training if necessary; and becoming self-motivating through initiating groups in cooperation with principals, faculty, and students. Ways in which new counselors can begin group work include selling the principal on the value of it and explaining that it is an integral part of counseling. They should also offer in-service training to teachers, set up a time to conduct a group, implement one group at a time, publicize groups, lead growth-centered groups initially, and evaluate all group experiences.

SUMMARY AND CONCLUSION

This chapter has examined the use of guidance/psychoeducation, counseling, and psychotherapy groups with elementary and middle school children. Group workers, both inside and outside schools, frequently conduct groups for children in this age range (under 14 years). To be effective, leaders must have knowledge of group dynamics, group process, and human development. They must target their activities either toward guidance and psychoeducational groups, in which learning and prevention are the chief targets, or toward group counseling and psychotherapy, in which resolution and growth are the primary concerns. Developmental and nondevelopmental situations are dealt with in these groups.

Setting up groups for children is contingent on many factors. Certainly the matter of structure is of central concern. Structure involves how much control the group leader allows members to have and how materials are used. Another important aspect is related to how long the group will meet and with whom. A general rule of thumb seems to be that the younger the children, the shorter the time of the meeting, although frequency of meetings may be increased. The debate about including both genders in groups is fairly evenly split. On the one hand, conducting groups for just one gender poses some advantages and disadvantages.

On the other hand, clinicians and researchers agree that children should be developmentally within a chronological year of one another in most cases.

The leader's role will vary in children's groups depending on the purpose of the group and the theoretical model advocated. Generally, leaders will be more active at first. Leaders use both nonverbal and verbal ways of learning, depending on the maturity of the children involved. Research supports the employment of groups in many settings with children, including those who have suffered loss, need support, or lack social skills. Multimodal group counseling and guidance seem especially appropriate because children respond to a number of stimuli at different times in their lives. Although group guidance, counseling, and psychotherapy are not without limits, counselors or group leaders often limit the effectiveness of group work by failing to use their resources sufficiently. Thus, various ways of advocating for and implementing groups have been discussed.

CLASSROOM EXERCISES

1. One way to begin a group on an elementary/middle school level is to have children engage in activities that focus on their strengths. For example, children may be asked to draw something they do well and wear it after they have shared it in the group. In groups of five, pretend you are under age 14, and try this activity. Discuss with your group, and then the class as a whole, your reaction to this exercise. As a class, devise five other activities to use in group guidance and counseling with children. List the pros and cons of each.

2. In a group of four, create an activity for a group guidance class in each of the areas listed by Keat et al. (1985) in the HELPING model. Discuss the advantages and limitations

of multimodal guidance and counseling as developed by Keat and Lazarus.

3. Compare problem-centered group counseling with growth-centered group counseling. Discuss with another student in class how problem-centered group counseling might become more growth oriented. Continue the discussion by listing strategies that a group leader could use in keeping a growth-oriented group from becoming problem centered. Share your ideas with the class as a whole.

4. Find a current research article on using groups with children. Share the results with the class as a whole in a reaction report giving the strengths and limitations of the study as you see them and how you might use this information later in working with a children's group.

CHAPTER 12

GROUPS FOR ADOLESCENTS

Shirley Zeiber_/PH College

Out of the depth of your mind come the secrets
rough diamond-shaped forms
slowly pressured in pain and cut with hope.
With inner strength
you mine repressed memories
and change your expression
as feelings are released.
Privately, I wish for more of your story
but the struggle is deep
and the thoughts are too heavy
to be quickly lightened with insight.
So with the group I patiently listen
and silently applaud your emergence. *

*From "Secrets—Revised" by Samuel T. Gladding, 1990, *Journal of Humanistic Education and Development, 28,* p. 141. Reprinted with permission.

Adolescence (defined here as the age span from 13 to 19 but extended to include some individuals up to age 25) is a difficult period in the life of many young people. It is a time of both continuity and discontinuity marked by extensive personal changes (Graber & Brooks-Gunn, 1996; Hamburg & Takanishi, 1989; Thompson & Henderson, 2007). Young adults during this time grow up physically and mature mentally, but they struggle with psychological and social issues related to their growth and development. Approximately 30% of 14- to 17-year-olds, for example, "engage in multiple-problem high-risk behaviors" (Shechtman, 2004, p. 429). Among other challenges they face, adolescents must learn to cope with crises in identity, sexual concerns, peer and friendship pressures, dramatic physical changes, career and college decisions, and movement into greater independence. They do so in an environment that, despite all outward appearance, is often filled with loneliness, anger, turmoil, frustration, and self-doubt. Life events, both positive and negative, affect their lives (Wasielewski, Scruggs, & Scott, 1997).

Adolescents are expected to behave as adults in their relationships with their peers and adults. They are given some adult privileges, such as obtaining a driver's license and registering to vote. However, most adolescents experience frustration and stress in being independent, on one hand, and yet dependent on their parents and school or community authorities, on the other. Some of their turmoil may also be exacerbated because teens are officially denied some of the most tempting status symbols of adulthood, such as sanctioned sex and the legal consumption of alcohol. Often, adolescents "seem to have to wait for circumstances to make their decisions for them, because they are not really free to decide for themselves" (Harris, 1967, p. 176). At other times, adolescents are pressured into adult roles too soon, such as facing combat in the military. Little wonder that the world, for many adolescents, is uneven and often confusing.

Yet, despite frustrations, adolescents reach out for growth and change and become the "cultural pioneers" of each generation (Dinkmeyer & Sperry, 2000). In their search for identity, they frequently create new fashions and trends. Many adolescent identities are relatively short lived and discarded with maturity—for example, wearing one's hair long or not trusting adults. Yet, the fads in clothing, music, language, and dance, while isolating some adolescents from general society, unite them with peers and in many cases help them constructively break away from their families of origin and establish a sense of individuation from others (Santrock, 2006).

Overall, *adolescence* (a term originated by G. Stanley Hall) is a time of rapid changes. It is characterized by some or all of the following: "storm and stress" (Hall, 1904), heightened emotionality, experimentation, and a desire for independence. Some of the "normal expectations" of late childhood and middle-grader adolescence have been summarized by Gumaer (1984) (see Table 12.1). These expectations differ widely but increase with each age group. The rapidity of transition associated with adolescence helps explain why many individuals in this category have difficulties in adjustment. Girls as a group appear to experience more stress than boys do, especially after age 14 (Yeaworth, McNamee, & Pozehl, 1992).

Groups of all kinds can be helpful to adolescents in making a successful transition from childhood to adulthood. They are valuable because they allow members to experience a sense of belonging, to share common problems, to find and provide support, to facilitate new learning, to help ease internal and external pressures, and to offer hope and models for change (Malekoff, 1997; Nims, 2002). A group context allows open questioning

Table 12.1
Normal expectations for children's social and emotional development.

Developmental Stage	Social Development	Emotional Development
Late childhood (8–11 years)	Peer group extremely influential. Bias and prejudice developed. Independence from family and adults developed. Team games and competition enjoyed. Opposite sex may be excluded in play. Interest in sex education and sexual differences developed.	Need to receive reinforcement and approval from peers. Strong bond, attachment to same sex. May antagonize and be hostile toward opposite sex. More willing to accept constructive criticism. Accepts responsibility for behaviors and consequences of actions.
Middle-grader adolescence (11–14 years)	Status among peers predominates behavior. Dating begins. Personal appearance becomes important. Very interested in sex and body development. Sexual experimentation begins.	Anxiety present related to acceptance by peers, status in group, personal appearance, dating, and body development. Growing need to express independence from parents. Antagonism in home may develop over "control."

Source: Adapted with the permission of The Free Press, a Division of Simon & Schuster, Inc. from *Counseling and Therapy for Children* by Jim Gumaer. Copyright © 1984 by The Free Press.

or modification of values and an opportunity to practice communication skills with peers and adults. Often adolescents find out through groups more about their "vertical attachments (parents) and horizontal attachments (peers)" (O'Malley & Allen, 1993, p. 266). In a group setting, adolescents can safely experiment with reality, test their limits, express themselves, and be heard. By participating in groups, they may develop a greater sense of identity and intimacy (Erikson, 1963, 1968). Using the processes of increased self-awareness and self-disclosure to others in the group (Jourard, 1971), along with having the opportunity to prove that they can translate their ideas into actions in the context of a community (Erikson, 1968), enables adolescents to achieve new or refined personal and interpersonal skills. Within groups, adolescents often find "genuine acceptance and encouragement" from peers and "a trustworthy adult who seems to trust and respect" them (George & Dustin, 1988, p. 142).

TYPES OF GROUPS FOR ADOLESCENTS

On a typical day, adolescents spend a great deal of their time in groups. There is the family group at home; the learning group at school; possibly a work group; and, of course, a social group. Peers are especially important to adolescents (Santrock, 2006), influencing the developing young person for better or worse. Society labels such groups as the "right" or the "wrong" crowd, and adolescents strongly identify with the values generated by their primary peer groups. In addition to these natural groups are at least two other main types of groups to which adolescents may belong and to which adults may have input. One is the developmental psychoeducational group, which is primarily voluntary and self-focused; the other is the nondevelopmental counseling or psychotherapy group, which can be voluntary or nonvoluntary and focuses on either oneself or oneself with others. Both can have a powerful impact on adolescents who participate in them.

Developmental Psychoeducational Groups

Developmental psychoeducational groups usually focus on common concerns of young people, such as identity, sexuality, self-management, parents, peer relationships, career goals, and educational or institutional problems. Individuals join these groups out of a sense of need and a desire to gain knowledge and experience that will help them better handle their concerns (Carty, 1983). Such groups are conducted in community agencies, school settings, or both (Berube & Berube, 1997). Traditionally, they have an adult leader.

Within the schools, Bowman (1987) found that the top five group topics for adolescents described by a national sample of high school counselors were career, communication skills and peer helping, decision making, study skills, and self-concept. Following up on Bowman's survey almost a decade later and using the same instrument, Dansby (1996) found in a group of Tennessee counselors that the most frequent high school group topics were somewhat similar: college plans, career choices, decision making, self-concept/self-esteem, and study skills.

Most of the counselors surveyed by Bowman (1987) believed that small-group psychoeducational and counseling services are "vital and practical to implement in their programs" (p. 261). However, both Bowman and Dansby (1996) found that high school counselors believe setting up groups with adolescents is unrealistic because of a lack of time and scheduling problems. Consequently, counselors in schools do not lead groups that often, and only about 8% to 12% of their time is spent in this activity (Akos, 2004).

When developmental psychoeducational groups are offered to adolescents, however, they seem to have positive results. For example, Milsom, Akos, and Thompson (2004) found in a pilot study that adolescents with learning disabilities who participated in a psychoeducational group increased their disability self-awareness as well as their postsecondary education knowledge while becoming better self-advocates for themselves. Psychoeducational group discussions can also facilitate the process of examining careers that adolescents may not have considered previously (Glaize & Myrick, 1984). In addition, structured groups for high school seniors can help them make the transition from school to college, the military, or a career (Goodnough & Ripley, 1996). Such groups may be especially pertinent at the end of the senior year (i.e., April and May), when peer groups are beginning to break down and adjustments in regard to the future must be made.

Related types of psychoeducational groups—for example, cognitive restructuring groups—can help students learn skills related to resolving problematic situations before they arise and thereby avert major crises (Baker, Thomas, & Munson, 1983). For example, Chong (2005) found that socio-cognitive groups for adolescents in Singapore facilitated attitudinal change and helped students become "responsible learners." Likewise, communication skills groups have been found to effectively help high school students improve their interpersonal relationships with peers in terms of sending and receiving verbal and nonverbal messages. This improvement is especially likely if role-playing exercises are included as a part of the small-group experience (Hudson, Doyle, & Venezia, 1991). Additionally, small-group work in adolescent sexuality education has proven effective both in and out of school settings. "Some adolescents' lives will be immediately and dramatically improved by sexuality education" in a group setting, whereas for others the impact will be more subtle (McMurray, 1992, p. 389). The actual and potential results for employing developmental psychoeducational groups with adolescents are great. These groups are not only efficient, effective, and important as school counseling interventions "but they also provide opportunities for students to support and learn from each other" (Milsom et al., 2004, p. 395).

Phillips and Phillips (1992) have summarized an exemplary school district's model of offering structured developmental groups. The groups set up in this model focused on the personal concerns of students. Groups of 8 to 16 met for 50 minutes (i.e., one class period) a week. They were conducted for 10 weeks during school hours, with the periods being rotated each week. All groups were co-led, with some teachers serving as co-leaders with counselors and other mental health staff. During the sessions, the group leaders used basic group counseling skills, such as reflecting content and feeling, clarifying messages, helping members recognize their own strengths and outside resources, and encouraging members to take actions that could help them resolve situations by themselves. During each session, students were reminded of group rules, such as confidentiality, but otherwise were allowed to talk freely and openly about their concerns. The outcome was both personal growth and prevention.

CASE EXAMPLE: Oscar's Career Exploration Group

As a community volunteer, Oscar gives 2 hours of his time each week to work with Hugh, the high school counselor. Instead of focusing on individual students, Oscar and Hugh decide to lead an after-school group for students who are interested in exploring careers. The group will be psychoeducational. Seventeen students show up for the group, and Oscar and Hugh structure it so that topics include careers that vary in their educational requirements. They bring in outside speakers to talk about their careers and how they decided to follow their chosen paths. The 10-week course is a huge success.

Were you Oscar or Hugh, how might you follow up this group? What careers would you include in a group like the one just described? Why?

Nondevelopmental Counseling/Psychotherapy Groups

In contrast to developmental psychoeducational groups, which focus on life skill issues for adolescents in particular, **nondevelopmental counseling and psychotherapy groups** tend to concentrate more on concerns adolescents have with adults and society, such as drug or alcohol use, school problems (e.g., poor grades, truancy), or deviant behavior. Usually, schools, agencies, or courts establish these groups, and troubled adolescents may either volunteer or be forced to attend (Jacobs, Masson, & Harvill, 2006). An excellent resource for finding experiential exercises to use with young adolescents in groups is Smead's (1996) *Skills and Techniques for Group Work with Youth,* which covers topics pertinent to the needs of this age population, such as developing self-esteem, managing stress, making friends, and coping with grief and loss.

An exemplary program for helping volunteer adolescents who experience high levels of stress and lack support is "Teachers as Counselors" (TAC), which was designed and implemented by the Spring Independent School District (Houston, Texas) (Wasielewski et al., 1997). In the TAC program, teachers who interact with students in mature, effective, and nurturing ways are selected and trained to work with adolescents. The concerns of these adolescents may be situational or developmental, such as having trouble making new friends, failing courses, having problems with physical size, or hassling with parents. The groups are composed of 6 to 10 members and meet for 50 minutes a day, 1 day a week for 10 weeks. The teachers are supervised each week when they lead student groups (usually once or twice a year) for 2 hours at a time in a group of fellow teachers. Thus, students, teachers, counselors, and the school as a whole benefit from this experience. All students who participate are free to discuss any topic that causes them stress.

◆ *Questions from Experience* ◆

The TAC model just described is one that depends on delegation and supervision to ensure that it works well. What has been your experience in delegating or supervising someone else? How do you think that experience would affect you should you decide to start a group program similar to that of TAC?

Not all counseling and therapy groups for adolescents are voluntary, of course. When potential members are not given a choice whether to participate, the result is usually resistance and reluctance. Although some of the hostility of these members may be overcome before the beginning of the group by talking to the participants and inviting them to share their thoughts and feelings, leaders of such groups face an uphill battle to create cohesion. They must be creative and innovative to turn around the negative energy. Starting with a formal presentation of the rules is not the way to begin a nonvoluntary group of adolescents. Just listening to the adolescents' complaints about having been referred to the group is a good place to start. After such feelings have been ventilated, members and leaders can begin to talk about common concerns and goals (O'Hanlon & Weiner-Davis, 1989). Several constructive ways of handling participants' negative feelings and resistance are suggested by Corey and Corey (2006):

1. *Meet with these adolescents individually before the group starts*—This pregroup meeting gives the counselor/group leader and the adolescents a chance to explore feelings connected with participation in a required group and alternatives connected with the choice of nonparticipation. Such a meeting also provides the counselor/group leader with an opportunity to explain the nature of the group

and how it will be conducted and to find out whether the adolescents have had any previous therapy experiences. Rapport may be established at this time, too. In summarizing such a pregroup meeting, an adolescent group leader may find him- or herself saying, "A lot of emotions are coming into this group, many of them associated with anger. However, the way the group is set up should give everyone a chance to express themselves and explore areas in their lives that may be problematic. I look forward to working with you as we begin our group next week."

2. *Work with the resistance that uncooperative adolescents bring rather than fighting it*—Working with resistance includes listening in an understanding, nondefensive way to adolescents' stories about the reasons they have been forced to come to a group. For example, SueAnn may say that she feels like a "victim" of a teacher conspiracy, whereas Ray may describe his situation as one in which Mr. Cardwell "really has it in for him." In these cases and others like them, the experience of being heard is helpful in breaking down hostility and building up trust. The group leader may also work with resistance by inviting certain adolescents to try the group for a few sessions and then decide whether they will continue. This type of option gets adolescents into the group and yet gives them a choice.

   If this technique does not work, then an adolescent may be invited to the group as an observer for a session. Thus, Jack, as the group leader, may say to Kate, a rebellious 15-year-old, "Although I would like for you to be a member of this group, I would first like to invite you to see how it works. You can come for three sessions as an observer. Then we can talk about what you have seen and your thoughts about the group, at which time you can join or withdraw from observing." After seeing the group in action, the adolescent can then decide whether to participate or choose another consequence imposed by others.

3. *Respond to adolescents' sarcasm or silence with honest, firm, and caring statements*—By being simultaneously firm and caring, group leaders can help non-voluntary adolescents become less emotionally upset in regard to the group, the leader, and the process. For example, leaders may tell adolescents who call them names, "I really care about you as a person, but I care about myself, too, and name calling will not be permitted in this group. I would like for you to be able to talk about your anger and other feelings, but in a direct and clear manner. That will mean using 'I' when you make a statement." Responding in this manner shows concern and care. It also establishes rules that are clear and firm. It helps the group leader and the group take care of themselves and function in a direct and nondefensive way.

Overall, developmental psychoeducational and nondevelopmental counseling/psychotherapy groups are two of the primary ways adolescents receive constructive help from adults and one another. Although such groups are found in both schools and agencies, the ways in which they are conducted may differ because schools have more internal control than most agencies. Developmental psychoeducational groups are almost always choice oriented, whereas developmental counseling/psychotherapy groups are usually geared toward both choice and change. As a rule, leaders of nondevelopmental counseling/psychotherapy groups face more of a challenge in helping participants get involved if the groups are nonvoluntary.

CASE EXAMPLE: Peter's Pregroup Preparation

Peter knows that the kids he is working with in juvenile detention do not want to be a part of a group. They have been mandated to come. Rather than start out looking at a group of angry young teenagers, he decides to visit them a day or two before the group actually starts. When he sits down with each person, he explains to them what

is going to happen and what their options are. He has them read and sign a statement to that effect, too. Thus, when the group begins everyone has had the same pregroup preparation.

What do you think of Peter's strategy? What else might he do?

SETTING UP GROUPS FOR ADOLESCENTS

Determining how a group will be set up is based on the type of group. In some groups, the material to be presented may have general applicability to a wide range of individuals. In other groups, the focus of the group is narrow and deals with specific and sometimes troublesome aspects of life, such as sexuality (McMurray, 1992) or grief (Moore & Herlihy, 1993). Cultural, situational, and developmental aspects of group content and context must always be kept in mind.

Regardless of the topic and the level at which it is aimed, group leaders still need to be careful in selecting group members. They must make sure that adolescents who are chosen are mature and motivated enough to benefit from the group and be of benefit to the group. Various factors that must be considered in working with adolescents in groups include the use of verbal versus nonverbal behavior, group structure and materials, recruiting members and screening, group session length, number of members, and gender and age issues.

Nonverbal Versus Verbal Communication

Whereas groups for elementary and middle school children are activity focused, groups for adolescents are more verbally oriented. The reason is that the majority of individuals ages 13 and older are developmentally ready and prefer to interact through speech (Santrock, 2006). Sometimes adolescents, out of fear of being rejected or ridiculed, will withdraw or hold back on topics they wish to discuss. In such cases, **nonverbal cues**, such as body posture or facial expression, will take on added significance. For instance, if Paula begins to frown when the subject of group rules comes up but does not say anything, then the group leader may say, "Paula, you are frowning. I wonder if it is in connection to what we are now discussing?" Structured exercises may be introduced into adolescent groups, especially at the beginning, to facilitate trust, cohesion, and eventually more open and honest verbal communication (Carroll, Bates, & Johnson, 2004). For example, in the introductory session of a counseling group, members might be asked to begin by comparing themselves to an animal, body of water, or machine (Paisley, Swanson, Borders, Cassidy, & Danforth, 1994). Participants could first make a drawing and then talk about their ideas, or they could just discuss their comparisons in a go-round warm-up experience. For example, if group members are asked to compare themselves to bodies of water, then statements might be made as follows:

Julie:	I am like a babbling brook. I flow in an even way most times.
Derrick:	I am a raging stream. I have a lot of anger that spills over into my life and interactions with others.
Ross:	I am a lake. Placid on the outside with a lot that waits to be discovered underneath.
Allison:	I am a mountain river, flowing hard but as yet undiscovered.

In groups for adolescents, just as in groups for adults, members should be free to decide whether to talk, but the leader should work at setting up conditions that promote positive exchanges. Sometimes these conditions involve teaching basic communication skills in a structured manner (Goldstein, Sprafkin, Gershaw, & Klein, 1980; Leaman, 1983).

Certain theories, such as Gestalt and psychodrama, focus on the congruence between verbal and nonverbal messages. Yet even leaders from primarily talk-oriented traditions, such as psychoanalysis, will be more efficient when they concentrate on noticing how congruent members' words and behaviors are. Nonverbal behavior, such as inattentiveness, conveys a great deal and may be as important as verbal messages for all adolescent groups, even task/work groups.

Another way to help adolescent group members unify their thoughts and actions is to use **action-oriented group techniques**, such as role playing and "I" statements (Corey & Corey, 2006). For example, a leader may say to Joey, "I want you to show the group what happens when you are being rejected by Pat. By role playing this situation, I think both you and the group can get a better handle on it. Would you pick someone in the group to help us all see what is happening in the situation you just described?" Appropriate behaviors that are modeled by the counselor and prestigious peers may also be useful in showing members other options that are available to them.

◆ *Questions from Experience* ◆

When have you learned a skill best from observing how someone else did it? When have verbal instructions been the best way for you to master a subject? What do you think the nonverbal to verbal ratio is in most psychoeducational groups? In most psychotherapy groups?

Group Structure and Materials

Many adolescent groups work best when they are structured around themes. **Themes** center around the genuine interests of participants. They hold group members' interest and invite their participation. Themes can vary from those that are serious, such as dealing with loss, to those that are pragmatic, such as explaining how to lead a class discussion. Flexibility can be built into theme structures, too. In a flexible theme format, the group decides week by week on the topic to be addressed. Too much choice can result in the group becoming bogged down and members losing interest. Therefore, limited flexibility

Directions: Rate each of the following problems as they apply to you at this time and indicate the degree to which you'd like help from the group with them.

1. This is a major problem of mine, one I hope will be a topic for exploration in the group.

2. This is a problem for me at times, and I could profit from an open discussion of the matter in this group.

3. This is not a concern of mine, and I don't feel a need to explore the topic in the group.

- Feeling accepted by my peer group
- Learning how to trust others
- Getting along with my parents (or brothers, sisters, etc.)
- Getting a clear sense of what I value
- Worrying about whether I'm "normal"
- Being fearful of relating to the opposite sex
- Dealing with sexual feelings, actions, and standards of behavior
- Being too concerned about doing what is expected of me to the extent that I don't live by my own standards
- Worrying about my future
- Wondering whether I will be accepted into a college
- Trying to decide on a career

Additional problems I'd like to pursue:

Figure 12.1

Problem checklist for an adolescent group.

Source: From *Group Techniques, 1st edition,* by G. Corey, M. S. Corey, P. Callanan, and J. J. Russell © 1992. Reprinted with permission of Wadsworth, an imprint of the Wadsworth Group, a division of Thomson Learning. Fax 800 730-2215.

is recommended. One way to achieve this goal is to have adolescents check off a list of the interests/problems on which they would like to concentrate. Corey, Corey, Callanan, and Russell (2003) have devised such an instrument, although any checklist of this type should be modified to reflect local concerns (see Figure 12.1).

The materials needed in a group for adolescents vary according to the type of group to be led and the personalities of the members and leaders. For some highly verbal groups, few, if any, materials will be needed. For other, less motivated and primarily nonverbal groups, many materials, in the form of activities or stimuli, will be crucial (Carroll et al., 2004). **Structured activities** (i.e., planned group exercises and activities) and associated materials will generate discussion and participation, help the group to focus, promote experiential learning, provide the group leader with useful information, increase group comfort, and facilitate fun and relaxation (Jacobs et al., 2006). Some materials in these activities are used passively, for example, having members imagine themselves as certain objects or animals. Other materials are employed in a more active fashion, such as having group members cut out pictures or paste decorations on lunch bags that symbolically represent themselves and then using the bags in introductions to the group.

One particular type of adolescent activity group that requires considerable planning and materials is sand tray group counseling with adolescents (Draper, Ritter, & Willingham, 2003). In this type of group "members build small worlds with minature figures in individual trays of sand and share their worlds as they are willing" (p. 244). With adolescents, the typical miniature collection of realistic and fantasy people, animals, plants, structures, and transportation items must almost always be supplemented with "leisure, sport, and hobby items, such as miniature basketballs, skateboards, radios, and items that symbolize academic endeavors" (p. 247).

The creative arts are a natural means also for helping to attract and retain adolescents in a variety of structured groups in insightful ways (Gladding, 2004; Rambo, 1997). Music may be especially powerful because of adolescents' general love for and familiarity with it. In addition, the power of the lyrics in certain music can help adolescents to convey thoughts that they would not be able to do otherwise (Saroyan, 1990).

Regardless of how materials are used, it is crucial that groups for adolescents do not focus on the materials to the exclusion of the meaningful process. For example, if a group uses video feedback, then the emphasis should be on how viewing certain segments of the video is helpful to members in planning alternative behaviors, not on how everyone looked or how the equipment worked.

Recruiting Members and Screening

As has been previously mentioned, not all members of groups for adolescents are recruited. For example, the members of mandatory groups may be assigned to, or drafted into, a group whether or not they wish to be involved (Leaman, 1983; Taylor, Adelman, & Kaser-Boyd, 1986). However, in voluntary groups for adolescents, recruitment is of major importance. Leaders wishing to reach as many potential members as possible should publicize the group by posting announcements on bulletin boards and making contact with students, organizations, and teachers. Members for groups can also be recruited through using questionnaires and making informal contacts.

Public relations is a crucial part of the recruitment process (Huey, 1983). Potential members and referral sources must be courted and sold on the idea that what the group is designed to do can be effective, if properly supported. Thus, the group leader must include as much information as possible on material sent to key individuals, such as administrators. However, it is also important that the group not be oversold (Deck & Saddler, 1983).

Once a pool of potential members is recruited, screening takes place as it would with any other age group. Leaders look for members who will fit together well in regard to maturity, purpose, and background. A key component of the screening interview is to keep it from becoming too formal (Jacobs et al., 2006). Leaders must develop systems that help them screen potential candidates in a minimum amount of time and yet promote two-way interaction so that the potential group members become more informed about the leader and the structure of the group. One way to establish such an interaction process is to discuss a potential situation in a group with a group member candidate. The situation could be about any subject related to the type of group for which he or she is being screened: task, psychoeducational, counseling, or psychotherapy. For example, for a task/work group, a member might be questioned about a situation in which the group strayed from its task and did not seem willing or able to get back to it. The potential member could then be asked what he or she would do to help get the group back on track.

Ohlsen, Horne, and Lawe (1988) state that attraction is a key component to the final selection of adolescents for a group. **Attractiveness** is a multidimensional concept, but basically it refers to members positively identifying with others in the group. Leaders must be careful in selecting members who can relate well to one another, not just to the leader. For example, Steve may have interests that are similar to the group leader's, but in his peer group, he is unpopular and considered to be abrasive. Unless the group is to focus on improving peer relationships, Steve would probably not be a good choice as a group member.

Group Session Length and Number in Group

Sessions with adolescents usually last between 1 and 2 hours (Gazda, 1989; Jacobs et al., 2006). They may be extended, however, and even include minimarathons lasting all day (Corey & Corey, 2006). Task/work groups that are charged with completing an assignment, such as decorating for a social event or coordinating a teen walkathon for funding cancer research, may especially benefit from longer group meetings. However, longer is not necessarily better, and a group for adolescents that lasts more than 90 minutes probably will not be productive.

In educational settings, the number of group sessions is usually dictated by divisional times in the school year, such as quarters or semesters. For instance, if a semester lasts 16 weeks, then a psychoeducational group might be geared toward a similar timetable, such as 14 weeks. Yet "the frequency of the group sessions and also the duration of the . . . sessions are directly related to the intensity of group involvement and growth" (Gazda, 1989, p. 153). If group members have major problems or deficits, then the sessions may last longer and be more frequent. Psychotherapeutic groups may especially benefit from these enlarged parameters.

The number in a group ultimately affects its outcome and rate of progress. With increased size, member interaction and relationships decrease, and the group becomes more leader centered (Gladding, 1994; Goldstein, Heller, & Sechrest, 1966). Therefore, small groups of 5 to 10 members may be ideal in working with adolescents. Gazda (1989) states that the number of adolescents he includes in a group is based on duration and frequency. When both are brief (e.g., 3 months), he prefers to work with a group of from 5 to 7. If both are longer (e.g., 6 months), then the group may include from 7 to 10 members. He notes that "as a rule, the smaller the group, the more frequently it meets, and the longer it meets, the greater the opportunity for intensity of group involvement and growth" (p. 152).

Gender and Age Issues

Whether to include both males and females in a group for adolescents depends on its purpose. Sometimes one-gender groups will be more appropriate. For instance, in a counseling or psychotherapy group dealing with the trauma and recovery from rape, it may be in the best interest of the group that only girls be included. Likewise, in a structured psychoeducational group for aggressive girls, a one-gender group with a female leader works best (Cummings, Hoffman, & Leschied, 2004). In one-gender groups, a key to the success of the group is the identity associated with gender and the topic. This type of identity comes through early socialization patterns. In summing up the research on the socialization of boys and girls in groups, Gigliotti (1988, p. 277) states that the most reliable differences show that boys play in large groups, whereas girls play in small ones. In addition, boys' friendship groups are more extensive or broadly accepting; girls' friendship groups are more stable and exclusive. Furthermore, boys in a group show more outwardly competitive behavior than girls do.

Although not dismissing gender socialization differences, Jacobs et al. (2006) believe the value of a coed group "is that there is a lot to learn about the opposite sex during the adolescent years and a coed group can be a good place to do so" (p. 401). Myrick (2003) also does not think gender makes a difference in how groups run unless a boy and a girl who are "going together" are in the same group or unless a topic related to physical growth or other sensitive sex-related issues are to be discussed.

In running **mixed-gender groups** (i.e., those that include boys and girls), especially if the focus is on social relationships and dating, it may be necessary for group leaders to develop methods to get young adolescent males involved so they will get the maximum benefit from the experience (LeCroy, 1986). Adolescent boys, as compared with adolescent girls, are usually less comfortable, less involved, and less likely to achieve as positive an outcome in groups that emphasize interpersonal relationships. Adolescent girls as a group are more interested in social relationships and are more at ease in sharing. "Adolescent females also perceive counselors and counseling 'as significantly more attractive and trustworthy,' than do adolescent males" (LeCroy, 1986, p. 505).

In regard to age, Kymissis (1993) recommends that certain adolescent ages not be mixed. For example, high school freshmen and sophomores do not mix well with juniors and seniors. However, he reports that there is little difficulty in mixing college undergraduates, although undergraduates and graduate students are not easily combined. Age in the adolescent years may not be quite as sensitive a variable as during childhood. Nevertheless, it appears that older adolescents are less affected by age differences than are younger adolescents.

CASE EXAMPLE: Agnes's Adolescent Group

Agnes is an experienced group counselor. She knows boys are more reluctant as a group to speak up once a group begins. Therefore, in selecting kids for her latest group, one of the screening devices Agnes used was a basketball. She threw each potential member a basketball and noticed how comfortable he felt with it. Based on this crite-rion and a few others, Agnes began the group by having her group go outside and shoot baskets. They all seemed to enjoy it and they loosened up with one another rather quickly.

What do you think of Agnes's screening method? What else might she have used? What should she have avoided?

ROLE OF THE LEADER IN ADOLESCENTS' GROUPS

The role of leaders in groups for adolescents is multidimensional. In addition to keeping up with the interpersonal and intrapersonal dynamics of group members, leaders must be extremely self-aware. They must be willing and courageous enough to explore, and perhaps relive, much of their own adolescent experience so that it will not interfere with their work and result in countertransference. Adolescents respond well to leaders who are open with them, enthusiastic, and caring. These types of leaders are true to themselves first and are good role models for those whom they lead. They personify congruence and are able to laugh at themselves and joke with others in a productive way—for example, noting how the palms of their hands sweated when, as a teen, they danced with a member of the opposite sex.

The roles of leaders are determined by the types of groups they lead, too. In evaluating the literature on child, preadolescent, and adolescent groups, Denholm and Uhlemann (1986) have devised a three-dimensional model with several components under each dimension. The first dimension, *developmental level,* includes three age groupings: children, preadolescents, and adolescents. The second dimension is *approach,* which is composed of four approaches to group work: activity, discussion, counseling, and therapy. The third dimension, *inquiry theme,* includes three components: theory, research, and practice (see Figure 12.2).

The classification scheme that Denholm and Uhlemann (1986) have devised has a utilitarian as well as a conceptual function. From it, the authors have classified select journals so that leaders can consult these periodicals to learn more about the types of groups they are conducting. For example, by using the Denholm and Uhlemann model, a leader looking for ideas for a counseling group for adolescents would find that issues of *Professional School Counseling* and the *Journal of Counseling and Development* provide some of the

Figure 12.2

A three-dimensional model of child, preadolescent, and adolescent groups.

Source: From "Organizing the Child, Preadolescent, and Adolescent Group Literature: A Pragmatic Teaching Tool" by C. J. Denholm and M. R. Uhlemann, 1986, *Journal for Specialists in Group Work, 11,* p. 165. Copyright ACA. Reprinted with permission. No further reproduction authorized without written permission of the American Counseling Association.

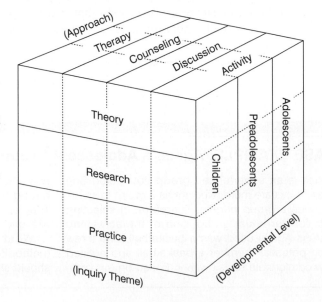

best information. This classification system saves the leader time and energy in finding practical ideas. A complete list of periodicals related to this model is shown in Table 12.2.

In general, group leaders for adolescents in high school are active. Both activity level and structure are related to the group's maturity. The theoretical persuasion of leaders also plays a vital part, as does whether the group is voluntary.

One way in which leaders can promote group cohesiveness and the acquisition of skills in adolescent groups is through modeling the types of behaviors they wish to encourage. "Good models have a tremendous impact on adolescents and can teach them how to relate openly and to help others" (Ohlsen et al., 1988, p. 279). By matching the gender between leaders and adolescents, the acquisition of modeled social skills may be enhanced (LeCroy, 1986). Leaders can also use influential peers in modeling. Thus, in an assertiveness group for girls, a female leader who is assertive can be extremely helpful in showing the girls how they can adopt and adapt an assertive approach to their unique situations. Peer leaders in adolescent groups are usually more persuasive than adult leaders in bringing about change. Therefore, adult group leaders may work well by training mature adolescents to lead groups and then supervising the adolescent leaders.

As in groups for other special populations, it is the leader's responsibility to stress the importance of confidentiality. Adolescents may use personal information gathered in a group for gossip or simply to be vindictive (Jacobs et al., 2006). In either case, the information is harmful, and such action must be prevented. One preventive measure is for leaders to state rules about confidentiality during the first session and every session thereafter. Leaders must also deal immediately with any potential breach in confidentiality and determine what has occurred. Finally, if confidentiality is broken, then leaders must either enforce rules or have the group itself deal with the problem. In any case, leader responsibility must be exercised.

Overall, leaders of groups for adolescents face a number of challenges. Some of these include being understanding, yet firm; facilitative, yet controlling; and active, yet trusting of the group process. How the group leader acts will depend on the composition, focus, and maturity of the group as well as the background of the leader. Myrick (2003) states that six basic responses make leaders more effective facilitators:

1. Using feeling-focused responses (e.g., "You seem to have some real feelings about what happened in this situation.")
2. Clarifying or summarizing responses (e.g., "So instead of responding to Laura's words, you found yourself getting depressed and withdrawing from the group.")
3. Employing **open-ended questions** (e.g., questions that invite more than one- or two-word responses, such as questions that begin with "What" or "How")
4. Giving **facilitative feedback** (i.e., telling another person the effect they have on you as a compliment or a confrontation [e.g., "Julius, I find you easy to talk with."])
5. Providing a simple acknowledgment (e.g., "Thanks" or "All right")
6. Presenting **linking** (i.e., when the leader identifies similarities and sometimes differences that are occurring among group members to help them join together, for example, "I notice that Willie and Buffy are the only ones who have taken a risk tonight.")

Table 12.2

Selected journals for each developmental area.

Inquiry Theme	Approach			
	Therapy	Counseling	Discussion	Activity
Practice	(C) American Journal of Orthopsychiatry. Child Welfare.	(C) Professional School Counseling. Journal of Counseling and Development.	(C) Professional School Counseling. Young Children.	(C) Child Care, Health and Development. Childhood Education.
	(P) Journal of Child Psychiatry. Child Care Quarterly.	(P) Professional School Counseling. International Journal of Group Psychotherapy.	(P) Professional School Counseling. Child Welfare.	(P) Child Care Quarterly. Childhood Education.
	(A) Child Welfare. Adolescence.	(A) Professional School Counseling. Journal of Counseling and Development.	(A) Adolescence. Social Work.	(A) Adolescence.
Research	(C) Group Psychotherapy, Psychodrama and Sociometry. International Journal of Group Psychotherapy.	(C) Professional School Counseling. Journal of School Psychology.	(C) Education and Treatment of Children. Professional School Counseling.	(C) Child Care, Health and Development. Child Development.
	(P) International Journal of Group Psychotherapy. Child Care Quarterly.	(P) Professional School Counseling.	(P) Professional School Counseling. Psychology in the Schools.	(P) Child Development. Runner.
	(A) American Journal of Orthopsychiatry. International Journal of Group Psychotherapy.	(A) Adolescence. Professional School Counseling.	(A) Journal of Counseling Psychology. Journal for Specialists in Group Work.	(A) Adolescence. Youth and Society.
Theory	(C) International Journal of Group Psychotherapy. Child Welfare.	(C) Professional School Counseling.	(C) The Journal: Canadian Association for Young Children. Journal for Specialists in Group Work.	(C) Child Care Quarterly: Young Children.
	(P) Social Work. Adolescence.	(P) Child Welfare. Journal of Counseling and Development.	(P) Professional School Counseling. Journal for Specialists in Group Work.	(P) Runner. The Physical Educator.
	(A) Adolescence. International Journal of Group Psychotherapy.	(A) Adolescence. Journal of Counseling and Development.	(A) Professional School Counseling. The School Guidance Worker.	(A) The School Guidance Worker.

Note: C = Children, P = Preadolescents, A = Adolescents.

Source: From "Organizing the Child, Preadolescent, and Adolescent Group Literature: A Pragmatic Teaching Tool" by C. J. Denholm and M. R. Uhlemann, 1986, *Journal for Specialists in Group Work, 11*, p. 165. Copyright ACA. Reprinted with permission. No further reproduction authorized without permission of the American Counseling Association.

Leaders of adolescent groups must be skilled and flexible in the use of these responses to avoid what Myrick (2003) describes as **low facilitative responses**:

1. *Advice/evaluation*—(i.e., telling people how to behave or judging them, for example: "Jody, you should sit up straight when you are in this group.")
2. *Analyzing/interpreting*—(i.e., explaining the reasons behind behavior without giving the person an opportunity for self-discovery, for example: "Ginger, I am sure you are tired and worn out but I am not excusing you from participating in this exercise.")
3. *Reassuring/supportive*—(i.e., trying to encourage someone, yet dismissing the person's real feelings; for example: "You can do it, Matthew. I know you feel like you can, too.")

Leaders of groups for adolescents may help themselves and their groups even more if they also make use of peer counselors or parents as consultants, when appropriate. In either case, leaders receive information and feedback they might not get otherwise.

PROBLEMS IN ADOLESCENTS' GROUPS

As with other types of groups, problematic areas that leaders must address can arise in groups of adolescents. McMurray (1992) discusses these difficulties in regard to an educational group, but these problem behaviors are not limited to just one type of group. Among the possible problems are outright disruptiveness, a hesitancy or reluctance to engage with others, polarization, attempting to monopolize, inappropriate risk taking, and overactivity or giddiness. Each of these behaviors is briefly discussed here along with a corrective response for it.

Outright Disruptiveness

Cases of outright disruptiveness in adolescent groups are more common than in adult groups because of the level of group member maturity. Disruptiveness can range from verbally yelling at other group members to attempting to pick a fight. For example, Juan may challenge another sensitive Hispanic boy in a group to be "macho" and call him names when he does not act so.

Ways of combating disruptive behavior include going over the rules of the group so that the inappropriate behavior does not occur because members are informed or warned of consequences. Having the group leader talk with a disruptive member directly before, during, or after a group meeting can be beneficial. Likewise, allowing members of the group to discuss the situation and decide what to do with the disruptive member can also be helpful. Finally, as a last resort, the disruptive person can be dropped from the group. However, taking this radical step will affect the group's dynamics and its ability to work because members will feel less secure and trusting (Donigian & Malnati, 1997). Dropping or removing a member from a group of any kind is an extreme measure that is used only if nothing else can be done.

Hesitancy to Engage with Others

A reluctance or hesitancy to engage with others can be a result of underdeveloped verbal or social skills. Sometimes, members want to act productively but simply do not know how. In such cases, engaging the problematic member either within the group context or in a leader–member conference can help to correct the situation. During these encounters, the motivation of the member can be determined. For members who wish to become more appropriate and productive, modeling and encouragement are recommended.

Polarization

Polarization occurs when a group becomes divided into different and opposing subgroups or camps. Such divisiveness may be caused by accidental circumstances, such as chance encounters of members outside the group setting, or by premeditated plans. Polarization is more easily corrected in the first case because the group and its leader can help members understand how their behavior outside the group affects the functioning of the group. However, if polarization is a result of planned actions, then a member or members may have to be dismissed for the group as a whole to work well again. This is why extra caution and time should be spent in setting up a group.

Monopolizing

Monopolizing is not unique to adolescent groups. Reasons for it, which have been discussed previously, are related to anxiety of a group member or members. Monopolizing may also be used as an attention-getter or a way of avoiding people or situations. In task/work groups, monopolizing may be handled by delegating tasks or asking for limited responses. In other types of groups, timed methods may help cut down or eliminate monopolizing behaviors. For example, the leader may ask members to respond to something occurring in the group in 25 words or less. If the monopolizer tends to exceed the word limit, then the leader or the group as a whole can use the technique of a cutoff to keep the group on task and on time.

Inappropriate Risk Taking

Sometimes group members share information too soon or reveal inappropriate information. This type of behavior is not unusual with adolescents, especially those who have limited awareness of themselves and others. For example, an adolescent boy might brag of taking drugs before fellow group members to impress them. In such cases, structured group exercises that help individuals understand themselves better in relation to others may be helpful. Reviewing group rules, talking privately with the person involved, cutting off the person's behavior, or redirecting the group as whole may be appropriate strategies for handling such a situation.

Overactivity or Giddiness

When adolescents are overactive or giddy in a group, it is attributable to several factors: the natural energy of individuals in this age group, embarrassment, the leader's or the group's failure to set limits, or boredom with the group or the topic being discussed. For example, Marsha and Suzanne may giggle and pass notes to each other constantly because of their inability to identify with the matters being raised in the group.

To respond to this type of behavior, leaders can simply acknowledge it and continue with group activities. Leaders can also discuss their feelings about the behavior with the group, or they can talk privately and individually with the member(s) most responsible for it. Another corrective action that can be taken in such a situation is to process with the group what is happening and how they as a group would like to handle the matter.

Overall, groups of adolescents have unique problem behaviors that those who work with such groups need to know about to be effective. Such information is helpful, if not vital, for leaders who plan to enter group work with adolescents. A good leader of adolescents' groups will use the power of the group as well as his or her skills.

◆ *Questions from Experience* ◆

What adolescent behaviors do you think are most disruptive in a group? When have you seen a group correct disruptive behavior in its midst?

STUDIES ON THE OUTCOME OF GROUPS FOR ADOLESCENTS

Even though groups are not as widely used with adolescents as with younger children, numerous studies have been done on their impact. Some of these reports are in the form of case studies, but many have used well-controlled research designs. Groups have been found to be effective with adolescents in promoting exploration of participants' lifestyle patterns and relationships with parents (Dinkmeyer & Sperry, 2000). Group work has also been used in helping adolescents deal with major changes in their lives, such as moving to a new school as freshmen or transfer students (Deck & Saddler, 1983; Strother & Harvill, 1986), and in reducing conflict among students in racially tense situations.

Groups are important ways to help adolescent refugees from other cultures to learn about customs and to prevent adjustment difficulties or psychological disturbances related to the resettlement experience (Tsui & Sammons, 1988). In addition, groups have a long tradition of being helpful experiences for students trying to make career decisions (Anderson, 1995; Barkhaus, Adair, Hoover, & Bolyard, 1985; Glaize & Myrick, 1984). Groups may also be used in school settings to attract and hold students in school through graduation (Blum & Jones, 1993). For instance, Sonnenblick (1997) reports forming a group as a club for high-risk middle-school girls that helped them mature and take more responsibility for themselves by participating in community service and recreational activities. In five schools cited by the American School Counselor Association as being exemplary in practice, counselors made deliberate attempts to achieve specific goals through group work (Carroll, 1981).

Figure 12.3

Conceptual model of divorce.

Source: From "Likely Candidates for Group Counseling: Adolescents With Divorced Parents" by S. G. Coffman and A. E. Roark, 1988, *School Counselor, 35,* p. 250. Copyright ACA. Reprinted with permission. No further reproduction authorized without written permission of the American Counseling Association.

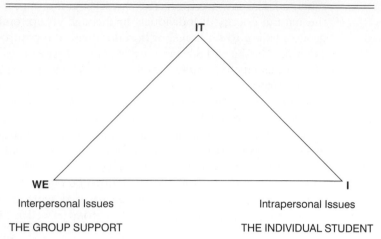

THE DIVORCE
Extrapersonal Issues the Group Has Formed to Address

IT

WE   I

Interpersonal Issues   Intrapersonal Issues

THE GROUP SUPPORT   THE INDIVIDUAL STUDENT

Likely candidates for group counseling among adolescents are potential high school dropouts (Krivatsy-O'Hara, Reed, & Davenport, 1978), high-risk adolescents with divorced parents (Coffman & Roark, 1988), adolescents who are substance abusers or delinquents (Dryfoos, 1990, 1993; Nims, 2002), and adolescents with unhealthy lifestyles and poor peer relationships (Zinck & Littrell, 2000). The group approach for all of these populations can take a systems perspective and consider the problematic behavior in its environmental context. For adolescents with divorced parents, taking a systems perspective involves focusing on helping these adolescents to realize they are not alone in their experience and that a change in the family structure, such as a divorce, has an impact on many facets of their lives. A triangle represents the three dimensions in the divorce system: the person ("I"), others ("We"), and the divorce ("It") (see Figure 12.3).

In a group for adolescents with divorced parents, information about the effects of divorce ("It") are highlighted first. For instance, the legal, adversarial, and prolonged nature of divorce might be discussed along with the stages most people go through in coming to terms with a divorce. After the group leader provides enough information, "I" and "We" interaction is focused on. Discussion of these areas may include such topics as dealing with friends, extended family members, and the separating parents as well as strategies for coping with depression, anger, and grief. In general, Omizo and Omizo (1988) have found that young adolescents who participate in divorce groups have higher self-esteem and possess a more internally based locus of control than those who do not.

In addition to a systems perspective, groups for adolescents in danger of experiencing major crises can take a skills approach. Such an approach can be seen in regard to groups for adolescents who have low motivation for learning. Thompson (1987) formulated the "Yagottawanna" (i.e., "you have to want to") group. The group relied heavily on the following concepts: "positive thinking, positive reinforcement, modeling, shaping, skill development, self-responsibility, self-discipline, and cognitive restructuring" (pp. 134–135). It consisted of nine 45-minute sessions spread over 9 weeks. The sessions were both didactic and experiential, and students were followed up on individually 2 months after the group ended. When pre- and posttest results were compared for the group, participants were found to view the group favorably and their abilities more positively.

In the area of juvenile delinquency, Zimpfer (1992) found group treatment for this population to be international in scope. "By far the most frequently reported treatment approach involves the delinquents' peers for therapeutic leverage" (p. 117). Treatment groups for juvenile delinquents seem to fall most often into the category of long-term psychotherapy. However, cognitive, behavioral, psychoeducational, psychodrama, family, and even music therapy have been employed in working with this population.

Bringing about change in the treatment of juvenile delinquents in groups seems to be most productive with youth who are first-time offenders, those who were less abused as children, and those who are from better social and economic backgrounds. The use of moral discussion groups has also been found to be helpful in rehabilitating juvenile offenders (Claypoole, Moody, & Peace, 2000). Such groups consist "of dilemma discussions, anger control, and social skills training as well as implementation of a positive peer culture into the institution" in which the juveniles live (p. 396).

Overall, it appears that groups have powerful potential for helping many adolescents to change and develop new social and academic skills. Studies with these groups need to use control groups more and refine their research methods. Nevertheless, the use of groups with adolescents in preventive and remedial ways is promising, especially in the schools.

STRENGTHS AND LIMITATIONS OF USING GROUPS WITH ADOLESCENTS

Many of the strengths and limitations of using groups with children are also found in using groups with adolescents.

Strengths

Groups are a "natural" environment in which adolescents can learn because adolescents spend a great deal of their time in groups (Carroll et al., 2004; Nims, 2002; Trotzer, 1980, 2007). Therefore, groups feel familiar to many adolescents who look forward to participating in them.

In addition, life skills may be taught to adolescents in groups through modeling, role playing, group discussions, and brief lectures (Dennis-Small, 1986; Gazda, 1989; Zinck & Littrell, 2000). Many adolescents have behavioral deficits. Through groups, they can learn important ways of coping and dealing with life stressors.

A sense of belonging is also created in groups, and adolescents are given opportunities to learn through direct interaction with or observation of other group members and the leader (Trotzer, 2007). Often this learning is carried over **(generalization)** from the group experience to the adolescent's daily life.

Groups provide for multiple feedback that can help adolescents in their personal growth and development. In addition to having the advantage of the leader's input, adolescents in groups also receive peer feedback (Myrick, 2003). Many times, the power of the peer group can be used constructively to promote needed change.

A final strength of groups for adolescents is the opportunity they provide for members to help one another (Trotzer, 1980; Yalom, 2005). It is often through helping others that an individual's own self-esteem and self-confidence are increased.

Limitations

Unless potential members are carefully screened, the group may not have enough appeal to motivate the participants. Many adolescents deny they have any type of problem and believe there is a stigma associated with discussing problems with others. Adolescent boys, especially, may feel this way (LeCroy, 1986).

Another limitation is the pressure that some adolescents may feel to conform to behaviors in which they do not believe. Peer group pressure is extremely strong in the adolescent years and may be misused in a group of adolescents unless it is carefully monitored (Corey & Corey, 2006; Ohlsen et al., 1988).

Individuals in groups may not be given enough attention. Because of their backgrounds or maturity levels, some adolescents need individual counseling or programmed learning. The group is not a suitable environment initially for some troubled young adults (e.g., those who are suicidal).

Another limitation that can develop if a group is not screened carefully is poor group communication and interaction. Often adolescents tend to "scapegoat" (i.e., blame) others for their problems. At other times, they will disrupt, criticize, or ignore others because they are so engrossed in themselves. Properly run adolescent groups screen out adolescents who are not ready to work on themselves or who are too self-centered, immature, or unhelpful (Yalom, 2005).

A final limitation of doing group work with adolescents concerns legal and ethical issues (Corey, Corey, & Callanan, 2007). To work with minors, group leaders almost always have to obtain parental consent. In addition, if leaders want their groups to succeed, then they must get the consent of the adolescent as well. Leaders may need to consult professional colleagues and associations more when working with adolescents than when working with adults. This process is time consuming and may slow down progress.

SUMMARY AND CONCLUSION

In conducting groups for adolescents, group workers must consider a number of variables. For instance, the age and developmental stage of the adolescents must be appreciated and understood before they are gathered into groups. Adolescence is a period of life filled with rapid changes and many paradoxes. It is a time of transition in which the developing young person's focus is on achieving a solid sense of identity. There is much experimentation and periods of progression and regression during this time. Adolescents often look more mature than they are and get themselves into situations for which they are not developmentally ready. In screening adolescents for groups, each potential member must be considered individually.

However, because adolescents spend a great deal of their lives in groups, working with them in a group setting is usually beneficial. Voluntary, developmental psychoeducational groups include adolescents who are concerned about particular situations. Individuals in these groups are generally quite motivated. Adolescents in nonvoluntary counseling/psychotherapy groups, which often focus on issues that are of lower priority to them, are usually less motivated and involved. In setting up either type of group, leaders must remember to pay attention to the verbal and nonverbal behavior of participants, to focus the group structure around themes, and to make sure that participants, regardless of how they are recruited, find the group to be attractive. When working with adolescents who are forced into a group situation, leaders are wise to spend time talking with them about their feelings on an individual level before the group begins. Regardless of which type of group is led, the number of sessions, length of sessions, and other ground rules for the group experience should be spelled out before the group begins. Potential problematic behaviors should also be kept in mind.

The leader of a group for adolescents, although a facilitator, is also an authority figure because of his or her adult status. Therefore, effective group workers make the most of peers within the group and model behaviors frequently. They also make themselves sensitive to age and gender issues that may affect the group's development. They even train adolescents to be peer group leaders.

When conducted properly, groups for adolescents can help them become more aware of their values and lifestyles. Groups can also help these young people overcome or cope with situational concerns, such as moving, dealing with

divorce, choosing a career, handling unplanned pregnancies, overcoming substance abuse, and becoming motivated to learn. More long-term problems involving adolescents, such as juvenile delinquency, can also be handled through group work, although with limited success.

Among the strengths of groups for adolescents is that groups are a natural way for adolescents to relate to one another. Furthermore, groups emphasize the learning of life skills, focus on generalizing behaviors practiced in the group to real-life situations, and provide multiple feedback and an increase in self-esteem that comes about through helping others. The drawbacks to working with adolescents in groups include legal and ethical considerations (e.g., obtaining parental consent), the stigma of talking to others about one's problems (especially for boys), the lack of attraction a group may have for some, and the pressure of the group to force some of its members to conform to behaviors that are against their beliefs.

CLASSROOM EXERCISES

1. Reflect on your own life as an adolescent. What were your major concerns? List the top five. In a group of three, compare your list with those of the other members. Which items are similar, and which are different? To what do you attribute the commonalties and differences? Discuss how working in a group was (or would have been) helpful to you at this stage of life. Be specific and note cultural influences in using or not using a group. Share your results with the class as a whole.

2. Discuss with another class member how you would go about setting up a nonvoluntary group for adolescents in a school or an agency in which you work or hope to work. How would this procedure differ from setting up a voluntary group for adolescents? Focus particular attention in your assessment on screening

processes, motivational issues, verbal/nonverbal exchanges, and results. Share your ideas with the class as a whole.

3. Critique a recent journal article on group work with adolescents. How did the group leader set up the experience? What made it successful or unsuccessful? Discuss your results in a group of four. As a group, make a list of factors that you obtained from reading these articles that promote or inhibit the success of groups for adolescents.

4. Pair up with another class member and talk about the different types of groups you participated in as an adolescent (e.g., Scouts, clubs, athletic teams). Discuss how you think each group affected your development as a person and what carryovers from these experiences still have an impact on you.

CHAPTER 13

GROUPS FOR ADULTS

Now matured to adulthood
embers from our past times glow
waiting to burst forth in the presence of others
like kindling and feelings
when heated and flamed.
As we grow, so does our light,
a spark that spreads like friendship in a circle,
a blaze that brightens but does not consume.
So in the warmth and reality of a group we become
stronger in reflection,
people who are openly aware of the gift
that is life
and the bittersweet insight that cycles,
like fires, have endings. . . .*

*From "Circles" by Samuel T. Gladding, 1986, in ASGW Newsletter, 14, p. 3, with permission.

Adulthood is a somewhat nebulous term. It implies that a person has reached physical, mental, social, and emotional maturity. Yet, as numerous researchers note, adulthood is a multidimensional stage of growth often characterized by a certain unevenness and unpredictability (Neugarten, 1979; Santrock, 2006). There is little uniformity to adulthood. Indeed, as Allport (1955) states, human beings are "always becoming."

For the purposes of this chapter, adulthood is conceptualized as the age period between 20 and 65 years. It includes individuals in **young adulthood** (20 to 40 years), in which identity and intimacy are two intense primary issues, as well as adults in **midlife** (40 to 65 years), in which needs related to **generativity** become the main focus (Erikson, 1963). Men and women experience this stage of life differently (Bata, 2006; Santrock, 2006), as do individuals with special needs and developmental concerns.

Wrenn (1979) advises counselors to "learn to work more effectively with adults" (p. 88). Understanding life stages and transitional experiences is a must. As Nichols (1986) points out, the **aging process** is as much a mental process of considering oneself older as it is a biological phenomenon composed of physiological changes. Responses to being an adult and grappling with issues related to it may be facilitated in groups. In such settings, people may talk with, understand, identify with, and learn from others in similar situations.

TYPES OF GROUPS FOR ADULTS

There are probably more types of groups available and run for adults than for any other age or stage of the population. Work and task groups are a primary type of group conducted for adults because many adults work outside of the home and many more are involved in volunteer civic and community activities (Hulse-Killacky, Killacky, & Donigian, 2001). Often groups at workplaces are focused on team building and the production of services, whereas volunteers attend groups whose purposes and activities are psychoeducational in nature and are devoted to accomplishing a goal for a special cause.

Counseling groups are also used for exploring the personal issues of adulthood and for helping adults deal with transitions relevant to their life-cycle changes. For instance, adjusting to marriage, parenthood, or single life are three areas on which counseling groups for adults might focus.

Likewise, group psychotherapy is employed in mental health facilities for adults whether on an inpatient or an outpatient basis (Yalom, 2005). Group therapy on this level is quite important because of its implications for society. Eliminating mental disorders and excessive stress, which impairs the functioning of adults, is crucial to well-being. Support and self-help groups for adults are also quite popular and encompass almost any specific problematic area, especially coping with addiction, abuse, and grief.

In short, adults have greater opportunities than other age groups to participate in groups on all levels. Specific examples of groups for adults are covered in this chapter.

SETTING UP GROUPS FOR ADULTS

Many of the factors that go into setting up a group for adults were covered in Chapter 5 and are not repeated here. It should be noted, however, that although it is artificial to divide adult groups based simply on the obvious characteristics of the populations involved, such as age, gender, status, and concerns, it is sometimes helpful or necessary to form adult groups on the basis of such dominant factors. For instance, the primary concerns of young adults (e.g., intimacy, beginning careers) are quite different from those of adults in midlife (e.g., generativity, advancement in careers). If there are specific developmental or situational matters that dominate a group, then these two different age populations may not mix well. Two universal issues to consider in setting up adult groups are themes and needs.

A theme is an important device used in establishing a group. Many groups for adults revolve around issues related to particular interests or concerns in life (i.e., themes). For example, psychoeducational, theme-oriented groups for college and university young adults may focus on anything from choosing a career to dealing with loneliness or disabilities (McWhirter, 1995). To be successful, the topic for a theme-based group must reflect a real-life situation that is of interest to participants, include some personalization of information, and teach some behavioral life skills connected with the subject area. In a business or a family group, cohesiveness and the value of teamwork may be important to everyone. It can be taught through adventure-based activities where participants cooperate in order to win games and experience some real or perceived risks in an outdoor setting (Gillis & Gass, 2004). Theme groups can also be psychotherapeutic and deal with such matters as chemical dependency or grief (Andrews, 1995).

A second guideline for establishing groups for adults focuses on needs, that is, necessities or obligations. For instance, many adults, such as women who work outside the home, need assistance in overcoming circumstances that limit them. A group that concentrates on overcoming barriers to advancement, such as sexism or gender discrimination, may be particularly useful for such women (Giordano, 1995; Sullivan, 1983b). Likewise, for women who work primarily as homemakers, a support group centering on common concerns such as taking care of necessary tasks, raising children, and finding meaning in life may be useful (Olson & Brown, 1986). Groups for other populations with special needs and concerns, such as those with autism, may also prove beneficial to members (Howlin & Yates, 1999).

Overall, in setting up groups for adults, the purpose of the group should be made clear, potential participants should be screened, rules governing the life of the group should be explained, members' rights and expectations should be noted, and the leader's qualifications should be communicated. Furthermore, groups for adults should be sensitive to the diversity within this population, and techniques used in such groups should be appropriate for the life experiences of the members without being forced on them.

CASE EXAMPLE: Lee Lets the Rules Slide By

When he was in the process of setting up an anger management group for men, Lee became busy with other projects as well. Although he screened each potential participant, he did not inform everyone of the rules. Ernesto was one of those. Therefore, when Ernesto lashed out at Greg in a threatening way, he was surprised to be called on the carpet for his actions. He protested to Lee that he had not been told that such behavior would not be tolerated in the group. Lee thought for a moment and realized he had not conveyed the group rules to Ernesto, so he met with him immediately after the group ended to go over this information.

Given these circumstances, what would you have done differently, if anything, with Ernesto? What are some ways to be sure that vital information is given to all members of a group before the group begins?

ROLE OF THE LEADER IN GROUPS FOR ADULTS

As with other age-span groups, the role of the leader in groups for adults varies according to type, membership, and format (open ended or closed ended) of the group.

Leaders of psychoeducational and prevention groups, such as **marriage enrichment** groups (Waring, 1988), must plan carefully what they are going to do and have a solid rationale behind their actions. Their goal is to instruct and help members learn new skills. In counseling and psychotherapy groups, theory must be the driving force behind the behavior of leaders. What leaders do and how they do it come from both a philosophical and a research base connected with the theory they embrace. Task/work groups usually do not have clear expectations of the leader except that he or she will focus on both the process and the outcome of the group (Hulse-Killacky et al., 2001).

In any type of group, the activities used by the leader may be either sequential or non-sequential. Most leaders prefer to work following a sequential pattern because this approach is both developmental and logical. However, when there is a crisis in a group or the group regresses, the leader may appropriately employ nonsequential activities to move the group forward (Donigian & Hulse-Killacky, 1999).

The skills leaders will use with adults are highlighted in Chapter 4. Before beginning a group for adults, group workers should make sure that they are familiar with such skills and have mastered them.

STUDIES ON THE OUTCOMES OF GROUPS FOR ADULTS

Just as there are more groups for adults than for any other age or stage, there have been more studies conducted on groups for adults than on any other type of group. In fact, the research on groups for adults is so extensive that it is impossible to generalize the findings. Therefore, for the purposes of this chapter, select groups in the adult age range are singled out as representative of some of the groups in which adults participate. Specific groups covered here are those for college students, for people in midlife, for specific concerns of men and women, for couples and families (both preventive and therapeutic groups), for adult offenders and abusers, and for persons with life-threatening illnesses.

Groups for College Students

Group work is important and effective in college populations. "Groups continue to be used to reach a large number of students seeking psychological services" (Kincade & Kalodner, 2004, p. 366). The reason is that many issues that college students struggle with, such as a fear of failure, mild depression, anxiety, weight control, and relationship concerns, are well suited for the types of help groups can be offered. Yet, as crucial as they are to the health and well-being of college students, only about 20% of college counseling center clients are involved in groups (Parcover, Dunton, Gehlert, & Mitchell, 2006). The explanations for underutilizing group services are numerous and include "clients' hesitancy, staff resistance to group as a preferred treatment modality, ineffective formatting (e.g., scheduling group offerings at times that conflict with class schedules), and inadequate marketing of counseling groups on campus" (p. 39). However, despite these drawbacks, groups are used in a number of ways from promoting better mental health and adjustment in students who have been quarantined (Pan, Chang, & Yu, 2005) to building a stronger sense of community on campus (Taub, 1998a).

One specific way in which groups are used in higher-education environments that is both preventive and remedial is to assist young people in separating from their families and in becoming independent adults. Studies show that group counseling based on Virginia Satir's model of treatment has proven effective in enhancing "college students' positive and definite family roles" and improving their relationships with family members (Pan, 2000, p. 316). In addition, family-of-origin groups have been found to help students "leave home" and become more self-sufficient (Mathis & Tanner, 2000; Valdes & McPherson, 1987). The tasks for college students in leaving home for membership in larger communities include "accepting new responsibilities for decision making and caring for physical needs; and mourning the losses in leaving home, for example, parents, friends, and support networks" (Vinson, 1995, p. 240). In family-of-origin groups, students explore the family context from which they came by drawing a type of family tree (i.e., a **genogram**) (see Figure 13.1).

Ideally, a genogram will represent three generations in the student's life, such as the one illustrated in Figure 13.1 by "Karen." By examining the vocational, intergenerational, marital, and relationship patterns of men and women in their families, students like Karen can gain insight into the actions of others as well as their own behaviors. In Karen's situation, her mother was frequently calling her for advice and support regarding the family and business concerns. "She felt guilt and anxiety, pulled between concern for her mother and the family business and irritation with always being brought into interpersonal conflicts having little to do with her" (Vinson, 1995, p. 248). Through construction of her genogram, Karen was able to see how she was being triangled between her mother and stepbrother and how her overfunctioning was related to the underfunctioning of various family members. Through role playing, rehearsal, feedback, and self-disclosure in a group of other college students who had also constructed genograms, Karen was able to make positive changes based on her present needs rather than inherited patterns.

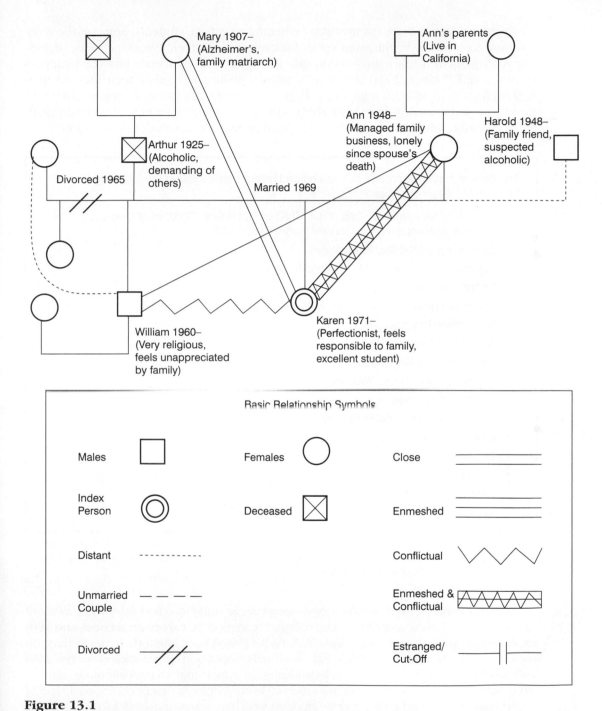

Figure 13.1

Genogram of Karen's family and basic relationship symbols.

Source: From "Employing Family Therapy in Group Counseling with College Students: Similarities and a Technique Employed by Both" by M. L. Vinson, 1995, *Journal for Specialists in Group Work, 20,* pp. 240–252. Copyright ACA. Reprinted with permission. No further reproduction authorized without written permission of the American Counseling Association.

Psychoeducational groups may also be helpful to college students. Some of the most common topics include enhancement or building of self-esteem, speech anxiety, depression management, stress management, eating disorders, and academic probation support (Kincade & Kalodner, 2004). Psychoeducational groups have also been used to help freshmen student athletes adjust to college life (Harris, Altekruse, & Engels, 2003). In these groups participants have been able to discuss relevant topics in a safe environment. Some common psychoeducational groups listed by Kincade & Kalodner (2004) are:

An informal survey of college counseling and health centers found the following topics to be common psychoeducational groups:

- Dysfunctional Family Groups (Adult Child of Alcoholics, Children of Divorce, Children of Mental Illness, General Family Dysfunction)
- Enhancing or Building Self-Esteem
- Exploring Diversity and Multicultural Issues
- Speech Anxiety
- Self-Awareness Skills for Students in the Helping Professions
- Depression Management
- Stress Management/Relaxation Groups
- The Meditative Experience
- Meditation and Stress Reduction
- Facilitating Change
- When Anger Hurts Relationships
- Eating Disorder Support
- Obsessive-Compulsive Disorder
- Academic Probation Support
- Living a Healthy Lifestyle
- Counseling and Therapy Groups

Source: From "The Uses of Groups in College and University Centers" by E. A. Kincade & C. R. Kalodner in J. L. Delucia-Waack, D. A. Gerrity, C. A. Kalodner, & M. T. Riva (eds.), (2004). *Handbook of Group Counseling and Psychotherapy*, Thousand Oaks, CA: Sage, p. 370.

Another important and popular topic among college students is becoming more aware of careers and more decisive about an after-college occupation. In **career awareness and self-exploration groups**, McWhirter, Nichols, & Banks (1984) have found that brief lectures on particular subjects, such as self-disclosure, trust, self-esteem, and communications, combined with small-group interaction, give undergraduates an opportunity to evaluate more carefully what they wish to do vocationally. Transition-to-work groups, a psychoeducational type of group, may also be used with university students who have learning disabilities (McWhirter & McWhirter, 1996). In this five-session group, resources available to group members are emphasized, including ways to communicate about disability issues, marketing oneself, legal issues regarding employment, and practical ways of compensating for one's disabilities.

For nontraditional adult college students (i.e., those outside the 18- to 21-year-old range), psychoeducational groups may be used to help them find information and resources about academic life, obtain emotional support from peers, interact socially, and meet developmental and remedial needs. Such groups are longitudinal in nature and provide both an emphasis on topics of particular concern to these students and emotional support and growth. More limited groups for adult college students can focus on other concerns, such as reentry problems, dealing with spouses or family, and competing successfully in the classroom. At the end of the college experience, a job support group can help these individuals become more easily launched into the job market and find a proper fit between their skills and employers' needs (Arp, Holmberg, & Littrell, 1986). These types of groups meet for a limited time, for example, six sessions, but provide older students a wealth of information about how to set goals, evaluate their assets, use placement centers, write résumés, and conduct themselves in interviews.

Phelps and Luke (1995) have reported that a structured counseling group for excessively self-critical university and college students works well. This type of group is set up to meet for 2 hours each week for 6 weeks and to include between 8 and 12 participants. Each session builds on the one before it and is interactive in nature, combining a mini-lecture with a group activity. Co-leaders are recommended for such groups. Group workers who wish to use such a format should be familiar with both cognitive strategies and Gestalt therapy because many of the activities for helping in this group are based on these two approaches.

Another group that has been found to be effective is for college students who are shy. This group was advertised as a "clinic" to minimize any implication of psychopathology. The 14-week, behavioral/cognitive-oriented group emphasized learning to be more relaxed in social situations; developing new behaviors (i.e., social skills) in a safe, supportive setting; identifying and changing self-defeating habits of thinking; understanding the dynamics of shyness; and realizing that a person can be both shy and happy (Martin & Thomas, 2000).

For students with test anxiety, groups may be used to help them manage their fears (Stevens, Pfost, & Bruyere, 1983). These psychotherapeutic groups concentrate on assisting students to reduce somatic tension and modify disruptive cognitions. The groups use some of the rational-emotive behavior therapy methods of Ellis (1962) and some of the cognitive-behavioral modifications of Meichenbaum (1977). This combination seems to work well, and student responses at Illinois State University, where these types of groups were first tried, have been highly favorable.

Another psychotherapeutic type of group for college students that is useful is for adult children of alcoholics, who may suffer anxiety, depression, substance abuse, and psychosomatic disorders as a result of growing up in a home in which one or both parents were alcoholics (Harman & Withers, 1992). These types of groups are usually structured so that potential group members will feel safe and be able to address issues readily.

Other types of groups commonly found in college environments include those for students who are survivors of sexual abuse, homesick, suffering grief or loss, or concerned about their sexual orientation, or for those who wish to explore health issues more deeply. Common counseling and therapy groups found in college environments (Kincade & Kalodner, 2004) appear on the following page.

A number of counseling and therapy groups are commonly found in the college environment. The list below is representative of these groups.

- Groups for Students of Various Cultural/Ethnic Heritage
- Sexual Assault Recovery
- Survivors of Sexual Abuse
- Groups for Sexual Orientation Concerns
- Women Loving Women
- Gay, Lesbian, Bisexual, Transsexual Support
- General Personal Growth Groups/General Group Therapy
- Personal Growth for Specific Populations (Adult Learners, Graduate Students, Student Athletes, Spouses/Partners/Friends of Alcohol and Drug Users, Men, Women)
- Groups for Developmental/Life Issues
- Homesickness
- Grief/Loss
- AIDS/HIV
- Health Issues/Long-Term Illness
- Current Events Support Group
- Clinical and Practical Issues in Running College Counseling Groups

Source: From "The Uses of Groups in College and University Centers" by E. A. Kincade & C. R. Kalodner in J. L. Delucia-Waack, D. A. Gerrity, C. A. Kalodner, & M. T. Riva (eds.), (2004). *Handbook of Group Counseling and Psychotherapy*, Thousand Oaks, CA: Sage, p. 371.

To assess the needs of all persons in campus communities, college officials may use a *nominal-group process* (a structured small-group technique). In such a procedure, five to nine people from different campus settings identify specific issues related to the mental health and personal needs of students, faculty members, and staff (Skibbe, 1986). Ideas are written down and discussed in a round-robin format with minimal attention devoted to relationships among group members. Ideas are then prioritized and sometimes discussed and reranked. The session takes 45 to 90 minutes, after which the group is disbanded and the members are thanked for their participation. Although this group procedure does not lend itself to statistical analysis and may not yield a representative sample of opinion, it is an enjoyable process for those involved and a fairly quick and efficient way for counselors to obtain a good idea of major issues within the campus community.

◆ Questions from Experience ◆

How did you adjust to college as either a traditional or nontraditional student? What groups, on a formal or informal basis, helped you, such as resident life hall meetings or friends with similar interests? Were you to go through the experience again, what types of groups would you recommend to the administration of your university?

Groups for Adults in Midlife

Many types of groups are available for adults in midlife (ages 40 to 65). Most, outside of task/work groups, are psychoeducational and preventive (i.e., geared toward learning and wellness) or counseling and psychotherapeutic (i.e., focused toward making choices or changes). Some of the groups mentioned in this section may be used by individuals of almost any age, but they especially tend to attract midlife adults.

In the area of psychoeducation and prevention, Parker (1975) reports on the use of systematic desensitization within a leadership group for the purpose of helping adult members become less anxious about public speaking. The results of the five-session group were that participants noticed improvements in their relaxation about public speaking and a more relaxed attitude in their personal lives in general. Bisio and Crisan (1984) used a 1-day group workshop with adults to focus on nuclear anxiety and hidden stress in life. They emphasized principles of Frankl's (1962) logotherapy and helped participants create a renewed sense of hope and purpose in life. Members of neither group desired counseling, yet both groups were therapeutic in addressing areas of immediate concern.

An interesting, interdisciplinary, positive-wellness model of group work for self-selected adults that is long term (16 weeks) is the **jogging group** (Childers & Burcky, 1984). This approach is based on the premise that physical exercise is an important element that contributes to people's abilities to perform better in all areas of life. For example, historically all types of experiential activity groups that today are represented in large-scale operations, such as Outward Bound, have reported a wide range of specific gains for participants in such areas as increased self-esteem, self-efficacy, and social competence (Hatch & McCarthy, 2003). In the jogging group an hour of exercise in the form of walking, jogging, or running is combined with another hour of group process. The group is co-led by a counselor and a health facilitator (i.e., a physician or an exercise physiologist) and follows Lazarus's (1976, 1981) multimodal *BASIC ID* concept, which focuses on behavior, affect, sensation, imagery, cognition, interpersonal relationships, and drugs/biological factors. Jogging seems to speed up the group's developmental growth just as other active outdoor experiences often do. The result is a greater awareness of self, a lowering of defenses, and a transfer and investment of physical and psychological energy into the group.

CASE EXAMPLE: Janelle Takes Her Group on a Hike

Janelle was charged by her supervisor to set up a group for depressive adults. She knew something about the effects of depression and how people who suffer with it are often lethargic. Janelle was aware, too, that a traditional group format might not be ideal for such a group.

Therefore, Janelle decided to alter the format of her group from one that was predominantly talk oriented to one that was a combination of walk and talk focused. Since all of her members were mobile, she greeted them each week in tennis shoes (and they were instructed to wear the same).

They then took a half-hour walk in a nearby park. Janelle altered the pace and route of the walk each time so that it was different. Her members at first groused a bit, but as the group progressed they seemed to not only grow accustomed to the format but look forward to it. Best of all, most reported progress in coping with their depression and some put themselves on a regular exercise routine.

When have you seen exercise be helpful and how? What other activities might be incorporated into groups for depressives? In groups for the overly anxious?

A common developmental and situational reality for adults in all walks of life is loss and grief. In working through loss, adults must accomplish four tasks related to the mourning process. Initially, they must accept the reality of the loss and then experience the pain that comes with loss. Next, they must adjust to their new environment while withdrawing emotionally from the lost relationship and reinvesting their emotional energy elsewhere (Worden, 1991). In facilitating a grieving and loss group, a closed-ended group counseling or group psychotherapy model that lasts for 2-hour sessions over 16 weeks is recommended by Price, Dinas, Dunn, and Winterowd (1995). In such a group, participants have enough time to work through their sorrow and display what Yalom (2005) describes as a therapeutic factor—"altruism" (i.e., support, reassurance, suggestions, and insight)—to other group members. In their grief work, members, who kept a journal of their experiences related to the group and role-played, worked through their situations best.

For adults who have grown up in families in which at least one parent abused alcohol, heterogeneous groups based on Yalom's (2005) therapeutic factors, especially altruism, imitative behavior, and corrective recapitulation of the family dynamic, can be empowering (Corazzini, Williams, & Harris, 1987; Harris, 1996). Such psychotherapeutic groups allow **adult children of alcoholics (ACoAs)** to question and change any of the four common behavioral roles (i.e., hero, scapegoat, lost child, and mascot) that they tended to play out to survive the instability, confusion, and fear they experienced growing up (Wegscheider, 1981). These roles are based on general systems theory and served as protection and defense against perceived and emotional or physical threat when the ACoA was young. Harris (1996) has developed a model based on interpersonal theory that depicts ACoA role behavior along two dimensions: control and affiliation (see Figure 13.2). In this model, which can be most informative for group leaders, two levels of behavior are depicted through the use of adjectives and descriptors. Level 1 behavior is the most healthy and flexible, being essentially nonpathological. Level 2 behavior is extreme and rigid. It is the type of behavior most written about in the ACoA literature and is diagnosable. By understanding this model, group leaders are less likely to stereotype and more likely to play to the strengths of ACoA members.

Because alcoholic families tend to be rather isolated (Steinglass, 1982; Steinglass, Bennett, Wolin, & Reiss, 1993), an extended system of group support is invaluable for ACoAs who wish to continue their growth toward more functional behavior. These individuals need help in learning to break the three rules that Black (1981) has identified as being universal for them: (a) do not trust, (b) do not talk, and (c) do not feel. Corazzini et al. (1987) recommend that groups of this nature work best when they are conducted in an open-ended versus a closed-ended format. Whitfield (1987) further notes that "many clinicians who work with ACoAs or other troubled or dysfunctional families believe that group psychotherapy is the major choice for recovery work" (p. 142). Such work should be combined with a psychoeducational approach to the dynamics related to addiction, dysfunction, and recovery as well as individual and family counseling.

Groups may also be used to help grown-ups who were abused as children (Courtois & Leehan, 1982). *Victims of abuse* (whether physical, psychological, sexual, or neglect) have a number of common characteristics, such as low self-esteem, self-blame, unresolved anger, and an inability to trust. Groups help them share their stories with others and feel emotional relief. In addition, group members can help one another focus on resolving present, problematic behaviors that would be difficult to do individually. "The sharing and

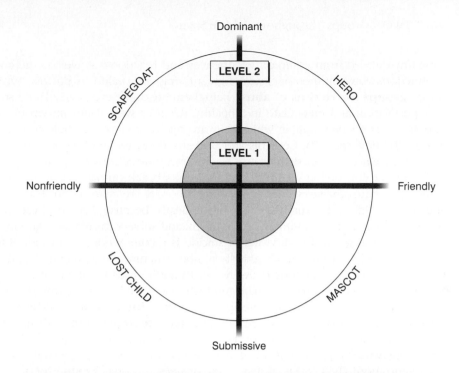

Dominant

LEVEL 2

SCAPEGOAT · HERO

LEVEL 1

Nonfriendly — Friendly

LOST CHILD · MASCOT

Submissive

	HERO	SCAPEGOAT	LOST CHILD	MASCOT
Level 1 Behaviors	controlling leading responsible taking charge being capable achieving being good hard-working taking care of helping/advising	competitive mistrusting critical ambitious antagonistic self-assured assertive proud manipulative noncooperative	quiet/shy private undemonstrative passive self-doubting insecure yielding/obedient easy to handle timid/uncertain following	cooperative receptive trusting center of attention unguarded naive/innocent overprotective reaching out distracting
Level 2 Behaviors	commanding being important rigidly autonomous egotistical structured overworking overprotecting overbearing overly parental overextended	dictatorial egotistical belligerent rebellious punishing hostile exploitative defiant irresponsible argumentative blaming	detached/isolated withdrawn inhibited/lonely docile escapist helpless subservient disengaged distrusting brooding/bitter unresponsive	childish immature hyperactive compulsive erratic acquiescing ambitionless obeying/gullible overly trusting overly distracting

Figure 13.2

Childhood roles in relation to interpersonal dimensions of behavior.

Source: From "Childhood Roles and the Interpersonal Circle: A Model for ACOA Groups" by S. A. Harris, 1996, in *Journal for Specialists in Group Work, 21*, p. 42. Copyright ACA. Reprinted with permission. No further reproduction authorized without written permission of the American Counseling Association.

empathy derived from common experiences and reactions, as well as the analysis of the interactions between members, are of great therapeutic value" (Courtois, 1988, p. 244). In short, **groups for victims of abuse** help them break the cycle of isolation so common to this population and interrelate in a healthy, dynamic way. "Many survivors come to view the group as a new family in which they are reparented as they help to reparent others" (Courtois, 1988, p. 247). Courtois and Leehan (1982) recommend that no more than six members be included in such groups to give everyone adequate "airtime" (p. 566).

Another counseling group that helps adults break out of isolation and resolve grief issues is a **group for survivors of suicide** (Moore & Freeman, 1995). The process of grieving is more difficult for survivors of a suicide death "because death in these cases is usually sudden, unanticipated, untimely, often violent, and subject to stigmatization by the community" (p. 40). A group for survivors of suicide is recommended to include 8 to 10 participants, selected after prescreening. It should be structured, closed-ended, and time limited. Eight 2-hour weekly sessions is the norm. In addition to this type of counseling group, groups for survivors of suicide can be conducted on a self-help and support group basis.

Two other types of trauma groups are **critical incident stress debriefing (CISD) groups** (Mitchell & Everly, 1993) and **solution-focused debriefing (SFD) groups** (Juhnke & Osborne, 1997). The purpose of both of these groups is to help victims of violence deal with its repercussions, such as feelings of helplessness, anxiety, depression, and disorganization. The CISD is "a structured, one-session small group experience comprising seven stages: introduction, fact, thought, reaction, symptom, teaching and reentry" (p. 67). It usually lasts 1 to 3 hours and is led by a minimum of three trained group members. Psychoeducational information is given to group participants about posttraumatic stress disorder (PTSD) symptoms so that they can recognize and get treatment for this disorder if necessary. Before and after the CISD, group members and facilitators mingle together informally for light refreshment so that they can get to know one another better and assess any areas that might need more attention.

The SFD group is similar to the CISD in its emphasis on a specific distressing incident, focus on the here-and-now, seven-stage format, inclusion of only persons who have witnessed the same violent episode, and the expertise of its leaders in postcrisis symptoms. However, the SFD is conducted over 3 weeks and enhances recovery through an extended group process. Also, following solution-focused theory, the SFD asks its participants to identify times when they are not encountering symptoms or reacting to the violence they witnessed. In addition, group members are encouraged to continue seeing themselves improving and identify what they need to do to keep improving.

Three final types of groups for adults in midlife that are psychoeducational and psychotherapeutic in nature are the career change group (Zimpfer & Carr, 1989), the career support group (Giordano, 1995), and the job support group (Riordan & Kahnweiler, 1996). There are pressures within and outside of middle-aged adults to advance in their life's work. Some midlife adults, especially those at the middle-management level, think the best way to advance is to change careers. Persons who usually consider such a strategy have a number of personal characteristics as a group. Among these characteristics are high achievement motivation, a steady and successful work record, high need for advancement, career challenge and individual satisfaction, positive self-image, high energy level, and a sense of limited chances for advancement in their present position (Campbell & Cellini, 1980). They may also face increased pressure for different behavior from their spouses

(McCullough & Rutenberg, 1988). **Career change groups** help participants sort out the reasons for pursuing a new career and whether some alternative course of action may be healthier for them. An effective career change group is holistic in nature, exploring personal and professional aspects of individuals' lives.

Likewise, **career support groups** are geared toward life-span issues of work, particularly women's work issues. "In general, women often find themselves in work situations in which they believe that their skills and abilities are underused, their pay and status are low, and few opportunities for advancement seem to exist" (Giordano, 1995, p. 5). In these situations, a support group that helps women develop successful coping mechanisms for the difficulties they encounter in their work environments is appropriate. Such a group is aimed at increasing women's feelings of self-efficacy by offering them "information to develop more effective self-care skills, offering them opportunities to perceive their qualities and strengths, and offering them validation of their current experiences" (p. 6).

Finally, there are a variety of **job support groups** (Riordan & Kahnweiler, 1996). These groups are set up for people who have lost their jobs and need emotional support, who want to learn how to achieve career goals and are willing to spend a good deal of time in doing so, or who are unemployed and are emotionally struggling with the stigma, shame, and isolation of their situations.

In all of these types of groups, clients' experiences are likely to be positive because the specific kind of support offered is geared toward their needs.

Groups for Men and Women

Men and women share many common concerns and objectives as adults. For example, "autonomy and attachment are functional adult goals, in love and work, for both men and women" (Aylmer, 1988, p. 192). Both genders also share some general experiences such as learning how to balance life demands. Thus, in some cases mixed-gender groups are not only appropriate but productive. For instance, a psychoeducational group for male and female survivors of childhood abuse and neglect, during the later stages of their recovery, may benefit both men and women as they learn different perspectives and insights from opposite-gender members (Choate & Henson, 2003).

Yet, socialization patterns dramatically influence the ways men and women perceive themselves and how they function in society (Bata, 2006; Schwartz & Waldo, 2003). Therefore, in many cases gender-specific groups may be more appropriate and give men and women a "safe place to explore new frontiers of their personal, economic, and social development" (Gonzalez-Lopez & Taylor, 1997, p. 20).

Groups for Men

"Working with men in groups has been identified as one of the most powerful and effective means of addressing the issues being faced by men today" (Andronico & Horne, 2004, p. 456). Groups can help men in identifying personal and general concerns of being male and ways of constructively dealing with issues and problems they face. For example, through groups, men can learn to resolve gender role conflicts and manage **polarities** (i.e., two interrelated, interdependent, opposite poles, such as career and family) instead of inappropriately trying to solve them through either–or choices or partner abuse (Hurst & Vanderveen, 1994; Schwartz & Waldo, 2003). Groups can also help men become more attuned to the realities of their worlds such as problems ranging from stress to self-denial (DeAngelis, 1992). Furthermore, groups can help men integrate and appreciate both their masculine and feminine sides and realize more fully the transformational aspect of their lives. As O'Neil and Egan (1992) have shown, at least 30 gender role transitions arise for some men over their life span (see Table 13.1). These "role transitions are interactive and not mutually exclusive. This means that changes in one may affect the other" (p. 312).

◆ *Questions from Experience* ◆

Not all men go through the same stages in life. What stages do you think O'Neil and Egan either need to add or delete from their chart? What stages are predominant in other men's lives? Do men, as a group, have common stages regardless of life style?

Getting men to participate in groups, although usually beneficial, is often difficult. One hindrance involves myths and misconceptions about men, groups, and men in groups. For instance, some men and some group workers believe that "men don't emote," "all men's groups are really anger groups," "men are too competitive to be supportive or each other in a group," "men aren't interested in meeting with other men," and "only male liberals have a need to express their feelings with other men." Another drawback is the belief that traditional sex-role stereotypes keep men from even thinking about being in a group. For instance, "most men still feel the pressure of fulfilling the three P's: Provider, Protector, and Procreator" (Andronico & Horne, 2004, p. 457) and fall back on their traditional roles as being independent, self-reliant, competitive, and achievement oriented. Therefore, they do not think of joining a group outside of one that they may already be in such as a team or a service group.

However, men are likely to participate in groups if the myths and sex role limitations can be addressed productively and if they are sure the group will be a safe experience. It also helps if groups for men are set up in certain ways, such as being theme oriented and psychoeducational at least initially. For example, Smiley (2004) describes a group for gay men newly diagnosed with HIV/AIDS. Such a specialized group negates the social isolation of those afflicted and offers them support, a sense of family, and a source for healing. Groups centered around themes such as work, marriage, aging, and retirement are attractive to men as a group because they do not expose them to expressing their feelings before other groups of men, they are usually time limited, and they may involve rituals (Andronico & Horne, 2004).

One of the first types of groups specifically for men was set up in the early 1970s. It was the all-male **consciousness-raising (C-R) group** (Farrell, 1974). It is interesting to note that C-R groups became popular at a time of turmoil and rapid change and paralleled one of the peaks of the women's movement. These groups did not maintain their popularity during the more conservative 1980s, yet variations of them that remain today are a viable way of helping men begin to see how they have been affected by culturally prescribed roles and how they have inhibited their own growth by following these roles.

Table 13.1
Men's gender-role transitions over the life span.

Approximate Life Stage	Gender Role Transition	Definition
Toddlerhood and Early School Age	1. Oedipal conflicts	Separation from mother and identification with father
	2. Early childhood gender role identification, learning in family	Internalization of masculine norms from father, mother; and other models
	3. Development of masculine gender role standards	Internalization of masculine expectancies and roles that govern behavior
	4. Rejection of mother and all that is feminine	Devaluation of and distancing from mother and the feminine
	5. Entering school	Formal learning where boys experience evaluation from others and self-evaluation
Middle School Age	6. Same-sex gender role preferences	Strong desire to have male companions and play activities reinforcing internalized masculine norms and standards
	7. Peer group identification—early male bonding	Internalization of male peer group gender role values and standards
	8. Heterosexual antagonism	Rejection and devaluation of girls and femininity to establish superiority of masculinity
	9. Physical maturation	Biological growth that produces changes in body and mind
	10. Interaction with female peer group norms	Contact with girls' different views of masculinity and femininity
Adolescence	11. Puberty	Physical development where the reproductive system matures and secondary sex characteristics appear, causing changes in gender role identity.
	12. Teenage gender role identification and learning	Internalization of adult expectations and norms for masculinity and manhood
	13. Tentative career choice	Early expressed interests and aspirations about chosen area of work as it relates to masculine gender role norms
	14. Dating	Social interaction with females where gender role norms and standards are expressed
	15. Initiating heterosexual or homosexual relations	Sexual activity that validates one's masculinity and value as a man

(continued)

Table 13.1 (*continued*)

Approximate Life Stage	Gender Role Transition	Definition
Early Adulthood	16. Leaving home—going to school	Departure from primary family where the man is independent and on his own
	17. Developing capacity for initimacy	Process of being personal, disclosive, and vulnerable in a relationship
	18. First job or work experience	Initial work commitment where the man's success, power, and competence are tested
	19. Marriage	Personal and legal relationship where gender role norms and standards are expressed
	20. Procreation	Sexual act where the man produces children with a woman
	21. Parenting	Becoming a father, protector, and nurturer of children
Middle Adulthood	22. Managing career and family life	The man's ability to coordinate work and home life
	23. Maintaining intimacy	The man's ability to continue being personal, disclosive, and vulnerable in a relationship
	24. Divorce	Legal and emotional processes of dissolving a marriage contract, relationship, and union
	25. Career change/transition	Events and nonevents that cause changes in the man's work status, self-assumptions, and meaning of a career
	26. Unemployment	Losing one's primary employment and sense of masculinity
	27. Aging	Becoming older, affecting a man's physical appearance and self-concept
Later Adulthood and Old Age	28. Retirement	A man's decision to withdraw from his primary occupation, work, or career
	29. Loss of stamina	A man's decreasing energy to work and live life
	30. Facing death	A man's capacity to deal with the end of his life and give up ultimate control

Source: From "Men's Gender Role Transitions Over the Life Span: Transformations and Fears of Femininity" by J. M. O'Neil and J. Egan, 1992, *Journal of Mental Counseling, 14*, pp. 313–315. Copyright ACA. Reprinted with permission. No further reproduction authorized without written permission of the American Counseling Association.

In addition, a diverse set of group formats "are applicable for helping men with their specific needs" (Heppner, 1981, p. 250). For instance, support and psychoeducational groups for single, custodial fathers have been implemented and found to be effective. One study (Tedder, Scherman, & Sheridan, 1984) revealed that men who participate in *custodial father support group* meetings make more changes in the desirable direction of learning how to take better care of their children and themselves than those who do not. A commonality of experience and purpose unites these individuals and leads to greater cohesion more quickly than is usually the case in groups for men.

Other approaches to working with men in groups include using mixed-sex groups to help men receive more varied input on who they are and what they are experiencing as males (DeAngelis, 1992). This information is compared with other group members, especially females. Groups contribute to the interpersonal growth of men, too, and help sanction the employment of unused skills, such as emotions. Furthermore, groups for men help participants observe new role models and practice what they learn within a safe environment. When leaders use social learning principles, men in groups increase their levels of affective expressiveness and ultimately their flexibility and overall functioning. Many men do best in groups when they have a chance to participate in a physical or mental exercise before the group's work actually begins. Therefore, specific exercises for this population have been developed.

Men often particpate in groups through telling stories. Therefore, group leaders may need to encourage some men to tell their stories to help them to interact with others (A. Horne, 1999). The men's movement, exemplified in the mythopoetic approach of Bly (1990), can be a power adjunct to traditional therapeutic groups for men because it encompasses the telling of stories. As a movement, "**mythopoetic** refers to a process of ceremony, drumming, storytelling/poetry reading, physical movement, and imagery exercises designed to create a 'ritual process.' Through this process, the participants explore individually and in groups their intuitive sense of masculinity, which differs from socially mediated male gender roles" (Williams & Myer, 1992, p. 395). They strive first to be personally authentic and to nurture society with their integrity. One way of conceptualizing these groups is as support groups that emphasize both the psychological and the spiritual aspects of growth (Guarnaschelli, 1994).

Groups for Women

"The evolution of women's groups in the United States can be traced to the consciousness-raising groups of the 1960s and 1970s" (S. Horne, 1999, p. 232). At first, all-women groups were controversial (Halas, 1973). However, women's groups have become "an increasingly popular therapeutic avenue to help women with issues that confront them. The formats vary from support and general therapy groups to groups that focus on specific concerns" (McManus, Redford, & Hughes, 1997, p. 22). Nevertheless, "there is not a 'typical' women's group, nor are there 'typical' women's issues" (Leech & Kees, 2005, p. 367). When working with diverse groups of women, "counselors must understand their own and their clients' unique characteristics, experiences and beliefs, the beliefs and influences of the groups of which they are members, and the universal aspects of being human" (Kees & Leech, 2004, p. 446).

There are some issues, such as dealing with chemical dependency, in which women do better in women-only treatment groups (Kauffman, Dore, & Nelson-Zlupko, 1995). Evidence also supports that group psychotherapy is effective in improving the quality of life of women with physical conditions most commonly found in women, such as breast cancer (Gore-Felton & Spiegel, 1999). Support groups for women who have particular concerns, such as those facing working mothers, may also be beneficial (Morgan & Hensley, 1998).

Although women's groups have addressed topics as diverse as spirituality and community change, some of the most focused issues in groups for women center around sexual abuse, relationships, healthy self-concept, anger, and work. Each is briefly explored here with two considerations in mind: (1) "there is considerable room for improvement in the research process for women's groups" (Leech & Kees, 2005, p. 371), and (2) groups can provide "a special environment in which women may resocialize themselves" (Sullivan, 1983a, p. 4).

In regard to sexual abuse, women who are victims of sexual assaults can form or join **rape survivors' groups** to help them recover from sexual trauma. These groups take several forms but often are conducted as group therapy (Rittenhouse, 1997). The results of such groups have been encouraging. For example, Sprei and Goodwin (1983) found that women from ages 18 to 60 who had been raped were able to decrease their sense of isolation and stigma while learning to model effective coping strategies. The group they set up was open ended and addressed issues related to information, anger, feelings of helplessness, and rape trauma. The group offered support to these women in the midst of crisis and helped them "explore behaviors, attitudes, and life choices" (p. 45). A variation of this type of group, combining rape and incest victims, has also worked well over an 8-week, 2-hour session format (Sharma & Cheatham, 1986). In both cases, consciousness raising and learning new coping behaviors were stressed. Likewise, a closed, highly structured, adventure-based group for women who self-identify as having been abused in any way has also proven effective (Kelly, 2006). Although the group purports to be psychoeducational, it has a healing and growth component that comes through processes connected with wilderness survival.

Another survivor's group based on feminist principles was found to be effective as well. In this group, each woman was treated as an expert regarding her own life, and egalitarian relationships between members and the group leader were fostered (Rittenhouse, 1997). In comparing group therapy for incest survivors, Randall (1995) found that "incest group members consistently value cohesiveness and self-understanding" (p. 237). The reason is probably that cohesiveness is associated with trust, belonging, and connectedness, whereas self-understanding has to do with historical and situational relationships with one's family of origin. In line with these two top factors, incest groups consistently ranked Yalom's (2005) therapeutic factors of identification, guidance, altruism, and interpersonal learning as low. The reason may be the self-absorbed perspective that most incest survivors take in a group.

Regardless, the success of abuse, and particularly sexual abuse, therapy groups has had a positive spillover effect in society at large. For example, from these groups have sprung psychoeducational groups for young women to prevent date violence (Rosen & Bezold, 1996). To bring the subject of incest and rape before the general public's attention, both women and men have also formed task groups. In these groups, programs have been developed on local community levels to combat demeaning and dehumanizing sexual behaviors. The impact has been pervasive, and such public figures as cartoonist Mort Walker, the creator of the comic strip "Beetle Bailey," have done something positive in regard to sexual abuse and harassment. Walker, for example, no longer draws General Halftrack chasing Miss Buxley. He has concluded that such behavior is inappropriate and should not be condoned, even in jest.

Relationship groups for women have also been found to be useful (Kees, 1999; McManus et al., 1997; Pearson, 1988). In relationship groups, the focus is on breaking out of the dependency and care-taking roles in which women often find themselves and connecting with oneself and others in a healthy and growth-producing way. Emphasis is placed on being in relationships where one's own needs as well as others' needs are met. The groups are often short term and goal oriented but can be long term and continued for the purpose of support and friendship. They sometimes revolve around themes, such as creating a better self-concept, boundary setting, and enhancing communication and relationship skills. The benefits of participation include forming new friends, expressing emotions, and changing destructive patterns.

People with eating disorders present a unique challenge to group workers. Participants must be prepared properly before their group experience, or they will drop out because of "their feelings of shame, their poor communication skills, and their avoidance of intimacy or commitment" (Cummins, 1996, p. 8). Attention to the composition and the establishment of healthy norms are important to group success and client growth as well, for "eating disorder groups often gravitate toward the needs of the 'sickest' member" (Wanlass, Moreno, & Thomson, 2005, pp. 64–65).

Eating disorders groups for women who have obsessive and distorted ideas in regard to thinness and body image may take several forms (Cummins, 1996; Gerstein & Hotelling, 1987; Kalodner & Coughlin, 2004; Zimpfer, 1990). They may be geared toward self-help or support, or they may be professionally led. Each form of eating disorders group has strengths and limitations in regard to dynamics and recovery. Self-help groups by themselves do not seem to be adequate to deal with the complex nature of eating disorders (Enright, Butterfield, & Berkowitz, 1985).

Yet participation in any of these groups can help individuals make initial contact with organized help and demystify the nature of the eating disorder. Often, relatively short-term treatment (4 months) can alter participants' behaviors and help them develop more effective coping mechanisms. "A group therapy program combining therapeutic orientations (psychodynamic, group process, and feminist)" can increase "the independence, ego strength, degree of personal control, and ability of bulimic women to form healthy interpersonal relationships" (Gerstein & Hotelling, 1987, p. 172). Cognitive-behavioral therapy, psychoeducational relational therapy, and interpersonal therapy also are useful in groups in the treatment of eating disorders, especially bulimia nervosa (Wanlass et al., 2005).

Groups dealing with anger have taken a number of forms through the years. Many have explored the nature of anger and focused on controlling it. In a women and anger group, Juntunen, Cohen, and Wolszon (1997) used a short-term (eight-session), structured, **theme group** (i.e., a psychoeducational, counseling, or psychotherapy group that focuses on a particular problem or theme) to help women understand and acknowledge the role anger has played in their lives and "to develop broader choices" in how they express anger (p. 98). The researchers found that the format for the group and its length were not satisfactory for women who wanted quick help for explosive or acting-out types of anger. However, women who had difficulty acknowledging or identifying anger seemed to benefit from the group experience, especially in hearing other women talk about anger in ways to which they could relate and in going through structured role-play activities that assisted them in recognizing, understanding, and working with their anger.

CASE EXAMPLE: Amy Confronts Her Anger

Having been abused throughout her life and into her marriage, Amy decided to join a counseling group. She was not sure what to do, though. She had always stuffed her feelings inside, and letting them out she found to be easier said than done. Gloria, the leader of her all-women's group, encouraged her to not sit passively by but to model after some of the other women in the group whom she saw getting better.

Amy did just that. She saw that Jeanette seemed to getting better and that Jeanette was vocal in expressing her emotions without going overboard. Jeanette was not afraid to cry either. Thus, through modeling Amy became more comfortable in expressing her feelings about the abuse she had received from a number of sources. After the group ended, she joined another similarly focused group because she felt she still had issues to deal with.

What does Amy's behavior tell you about the developmental nature of people and groups? What else might you have done to help Amy had you been her leader, Gloria?

Groups for Couples, Families, the Divorced, the Widowed, and the Remarried

Couples, families, and those who are divorced, widowed, or recently remarried face many stresses. Psychoeducational, counseling, and psychotherapy groups are especially popular for persons in these circumstances.

Parent Education Groups

One of the major concerns of many adults is parenting. Most adults who become parents do not receive any training in how to parent and have to learn how to work with children on a trial-and-error basis. In addition, "today's parents are raising children under social conditions decidedly different from those that the parents experienced as children" (White & Mullis, 1997, p. 47). To help parents acquire knowledge and evaluate their beliefs and attitudes, **parent education groups** were organized beginning in the late 1800s by the Child Study Association of America (Resnick, 1981). These groups initially focused on a discussion-oriented format about the needs of parents (usually mothers) and children. However, parent education groups are now considered "a form of consultation in which the consultant (leader) is assisting the consultee (parent) by teaching effective child-rearing techniques" (White & Riordan, 1990, p. 201).

Literally dozens of parenting programs operate across the United States. In these groups, single parents or couples work to develop healthy strategies for dealing with each other and their children as the family develops. Some of these parenting programs include those for abusive and neglectful parents, adoptive parents, foster parents, minority group parents, single parents, and parents of children with special needs (LeMasters & DeFrain, 1989). Most take an eclectic approach and train their leaders to understand and promote positive group dynamics to bring about constructive changes in parent–child and family interactions.

Regardless of the approach followed, White and Riordan (1990) state that there are common aspects to all parent education groups. For instance, parents are "usually sensitive to almost any issue that relates to their relationship with their child" (p. 205). They are also initially resistant to change. When directing a parent education group, a leader is wise to anticipate issues that parents might raise and be prepared to address these concerns in a productive manner. For example, parents will frequently inquire about the use of physical punishment (i.e., spanking), the importance of heredity in determining behavior, gender role appropriateness, religious beliefs as a basis for parenting, peer influences, guilt over parental decisions, and feelings about school. Effective parent education group leaders use nontechnical language in working with parents. They also thoroughly explain and demonstrate suggested interventions and accept differences in participants' backgrounds and values (Miller & Hudson, 1994). Overall, parents are best served in parenting groups when they are listened to, helped to sort through their options, and newly empowered to make decisions regarding their children. Innovative methods, such as the use of sand trays, may be used with parents who have major therapeutic concerns such as coping with adolescence substance abuse or depression (James & Martin, 2002).

◆ *Questions from Experience* ◆

What do children and parents have to learn to cope with today that was not true 20 years ago? What groups either help or hinder the development of relationships in parent–child interactions? If you were going to start a group for parents today, what would be its emphasis? Explain.

Couple and Family Group Therapy

Couple group therapy began in the 1970s and has had an uneven history (Gladding, 2007; Piercy, Sprenkle, & Wetchler, 1996). Proponents of couples group therapy list its many advantages, including (a) identification by group members of appropriate and inappropriate behaviors and expectations by others, (b) development of insight and skills through observing other couples, (c) group feedback and support for the ventilation of feelings and changed behavior, and (d) reduced cost.

Framo (1981) recommends that couple group therapy be used when preparing couples to do family-of-origin work, in which they meet with their families and work through difficulties not resolved in childhood. Couple groups are limited to three couples in this approach, all of whom have some similarity in background. Ohlsen (1979) includes five couples in his groups. He believes that having this number of couples makes the group easier to handle and provides an enriched learning environment for members.

Hendrix (1988) also uses five or more couples in his workshops, which are known as **imago (i.e., image) relationship therapy**, an eclectic approach that includes elements of psychoanalysis, transactional analysis, Gestalt psychology, cognitive therapy, and systems theory. Hendrix's approach, popularized in his book *Getting the Love You Want,* is the most structured of the couple group therapies and has revived interest in psychotherapy workshops for couples. Hendrix suggests couples go through specific exercises in a uniform manner and encourages observation of others and participation by the individual couple.

Multiple-family group therapy (MFGT) involves treating several families together at the same time with an explicit focus on problems or concerns shared by all of the families in attendance (Baltimore, 1997; Homrich & Horne, 1997). MFGT is probably the most demanding form of group work and requires its leaders to have a solid working knowledge of both group and family theories. MFGT approaches usually use co-leaders to handle the complex dynamics associated with working with so many individuals at once. This approach has many of the same advantages that couples group therapy has, including the fact that families can often serve as co-therapists for each other (Piercy et al., 1996). "Multi-family group counseling models are becoming more popular because they enable counselors to address the concerns of many people of various developmental levels in a time-efficient process" (Sayger, 1996, p. 81). **High-risk families** (e.g., those prone to violence) and **families in high-risk environments** (e.g., neighborhoods prone to violence) may especially benefit from such groups. The reason is that these groups provide "an opportunity to build a sense of community and social support, to create conditions that aid in the development of resilient children, and to empower families to use more functional strategies in their lives" (Sayger, 1996, p. 81). Another benefit of multiple-family group models is they may function in many ways (e.g., psychoeducational, task-oriented, counseling/psychotherapeutically focused).

Groups for the Divorced and the Widowed

The divorced and the widowed can best make use of groups in the process of working through their pain. In groups specifically designed to deal with their situations, the divorced and the widowed can share experiences with one another as well as obtain emotional support, receive feedback on their perceptions and behaviors, gain advice and information on dealing with problems, and get tangible assistance (Addington, 1992; DiGiulio, 1992). One model of a specific group for those who have separated has been devised by Addington (1992), who focuses the group on both the emotional impact and the emotional response of such an experience. The **emotional impact of separation** includes dealing with loss, putting the separation in perspective, becoming aware of the limited value of searching for causes of the separation, becoming more cognizant of systems interactions (e.g., family, work, social network), using the past as a guide to the future, and moving from a dyadic to a monadic identity. The **emotional response of separation** focuses on continuing relationships with an ex-spouse; recognizing the influence of the separation on family, friends, and children; working and dating; and sexual adjustment. Addington's model also includes a diagram of the grief process to help participants assess where they are in the process and to chart their progress in recovery (see Figure 13.3).

Outside of structured groups offered by professionals, most *groups for the divorced and the widowed* tend to be of a psychoeducational or self-help nature. **Parents Without Partners (PWP)** is probably the best known and most organized of such groups on a national level. PWP offers a variety of activities to its members, including interest groups, educational presentations and discussions, and recreational and social activities. Members and their children become linked to one another through these formal and informal group activities.

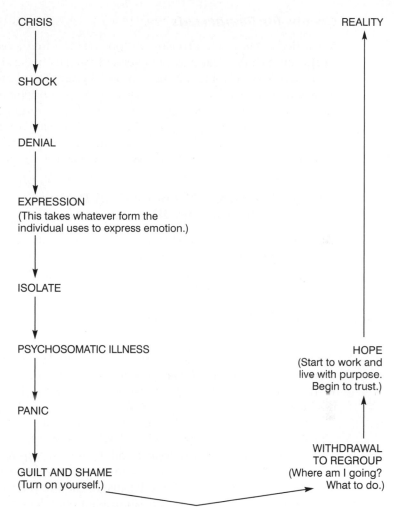

Figure 13.3
Grief process.
Source: From "Separation Group"
by J. Addington, 1992, *Journal for
Specialists in Group Work, 17,* p. 25.
Copyright ACA. Reprinted with permission. Further reproduction unau-
thorized without written permission
of the American Counseling Association.

Case Example: David Deals with His Divorce

David was seeing Walter for the pain he was continuing to incur even though he had been divorced for
2 years. Walter suggested he join a divorce group
that Walter led, in the hope that the group would be
of more help to him than Walter could be alone.

David was skeptical, but he agreed to try the
group for four sessions. What happened amazed
him. He found out that others were having similar
struggles even though they had been divorced

longer. He also found out that there were informal
support groups he could join if he wanted. In
short, David found out he was not alone and that
the more he talked in the group, the better he felt.

Why do you think David was skeptical of the
group at first? What do you think happened that
helped David begin to move on in his life? What
other things not mentioned in this brief case do
you think might be helpful for David?

Groups for Remarrieds

Remarrieds, that is, stepfamilies, are one of the three most common types of families in North America (nuclear and single-parent families being the other two). Yet, stepfamilies are especially vulnerable during their first 3 years. Therefore, a psychoeducational, closed, multicouple group intervention that focuses on enrichment is an excellent way to help such families stabilize, grow, and constructively face future challenges. Michaels (2006) has proposed a six-session group for these families using a format that emphasizes developmental, nurturing, and strengthening bonds in these families through didactic and experiential methods. Group problem-solving is utilized as well as couple-focused activities.

Groups for Adult Offenders and Persons with Life-Threatening Illnesses

Adult offenders and persons with life-threatening illnesses may seem quite different, but they share at least a few characteristics. Both categories of people are often isolated from others and struggle internally. Groups can help individuals in these circumstances, although in different ways.

Groups for Adult Offenders

The term *offender* refers to "people convicted of a crime and includes both incarcerated (i.e., housed in a secure correctional environment) and nonincarcerated (on parole, probation, etc.)" (Morgan, 2004, p. 388). In examining the literature on adult offenders, Zimpfer (1992) found that group work in prisons for those who have committed a crime has been around since the late 1950s.

Regardless, working with offenders is a challenge. Potential problematic areas include offenders' low level of trust and high levels of anger, frustration, and sense of deprivation. Therefore, a number of approaches and types of groups have been reported in the professional literature (Morgan, 2004). Some have focused on helping inmates adjust to prison life, and others on helping them readjust to the outside world. Zimpfer and Morgan point out that research in the area of treating adult offenders is growing and that group work in this area appears to be effective in producing positive outcomes. The importance of improved self-images of offenders who participate in various groups is a variable in treatment that is increasingly being noted.

Among the specific types of adult offenders targeted for treatment in groups have been those found guilty of sex offenses, people driving while intoxicated, shoplifters, domestic violence perpetrators, and crack cocaine users. Success for specific populations in this mix varies, but there is some consensus that group psychotherapy and group counseling for sex offenders is much more effective than individual treatment for this population (DeAngelis, 1992). The reasons have to do with the manipulative nature of such offenders and the power of the group to prohibit seductive or illusive behavior. Likewise, abusive men may benefit from groups, even those that are psychoeducational and open ended (Schwartz & Waldo, 1999). In such groups, they may not only find out information concerning the nature of abusive relationships but also develop healthy socializing techniques. Likewise, psychoeducational groups are helpful to other offenders in such areas as "anger or stress management, problem-solving skills, life skills, cognitive restructuring or criminal thinking errors" (Morgan, 2004, p. 389). Out-of-group homework exercises, regardless of the type of group employed, can help, too.

Grief counseling groups may be appropriate for a variety of male prison inmates who are **"disenfranchised grievers,"** that is, persons removed from their natural support systems (Olson & McEwen, 2004). Through grief counseling groups these inmates are able to give voice to their feelings, especially the loss of family, friends, freedom, privacy, and even past pain. In the process they are able to express their emotions, find connections with others who have had similar circumstances, and experience relief as well.

A cognitive, psychotherapeutic group technique for assessing offenders' (and involuntary clients') "private logic" (i.e., way of thinking) and helping them change is **sophistry** (Evans & Kane, 1996). This method enables group workers to get beyond offenders' resistance. It employs paradox (i.e., telling resistant clients not to change), hidden reasons in a group debate, and a reorientation phase to get offenders to examine defects in their thinking and to learn to practice appropriate thought processes. Sophistry basically cuts through offenders' excuses and makes covert logic overt so that it can be challenged and corrected.

Groups for Persons with Life-Threatening Illnesses

The concept of group work for persons with life-threatening illnesses originated from Joseph Hersey Pratt's idea of treating tuberculosis outpatients in a group context (see Chapter 1). More recently, psychotherapeutic groups have also been employed as a way of treating persons with other life-threatening diseases. In a review of the literature on groups for cancer patients, Harman (1991) notes the results of outcome studies with this population.

One of the most interesting of Harman's findings is that groups are still a preferred method of working with cancer patients and their families. Such groups offer education, support, and release from stress and emotion that has built up. Furthermore, groups help all involved in experiencing the therapeutic factors described by Yalom (2005) as essential to good psychotherapeutic groups: universality, cohesiveness, and the instillation of hope. Groups for those with terminal illnesses are a way to impart information in a quick and efficient manner. Finally, some forms of group work, specifically existential groups for cancer patients and those with other life-threatening illnesses, can assist such individuals in better coping with their diagnosis and living more fully in the time they have left (Spira, 1997).

STRENGTHS AND LIMITATIONS OF USING GROUPS WITH ADULTS

Strengths

One strength of using groups with adults is cost savings. Many adults have similar concerns, and it is more effective to address these common matters in a group setting than individually. Both time and money are saved in using a group to convey information or treat individuals with similar problems.

Effectiveness is another strength connected with groups for adults. For example, groups have been used to help undergraduate and graduate students master course material (Ender, 1985). These **study groups**, a type of task group, typically involve three to four students who meet at least on a weekly basis to "share information, knowledge, and expertise about a course in which they are all enrolled" (p. 469). The idea is that each group member will support and encourage the others and will obtain insight and knowledge through the group effort.

Nonproductive behavior (e.g., perfectionism) may be altered or eliminated through group work with adults. Furthermore, groups often play a key role in helping individuals in adulthood maximize their efforts and focus their energy on appropriate developmental tasks. In the process, members may form a stronger identity.

A final strength of working with adults in groups is that adults may be highly motivated to work on concerns with others and may also have an idea of outcomes they would like to achieve. Therefore, the group process may be enhanced in some cases, and results may be quite positive.

Limitations

A limitation of doing group work with adults is scheduling. Offering appropriate groups at a time and a place where potential members can attend may be a time-consuming and challenging endeavor. Adults are busy people, and setting up a group for them takes organizational skills and patience.

A second limitation of conducting groups with adults is some members' resistance to participating. For instance, many men are hesitant to enter groups because of past socialization patterns. Likewise, college students may resist group counseling because they believe it is "unpredictable, less effective than individual counseling, and detrimental to participants" (Carter, Mitchell, & Krautheim, 2001, p. 67).

Yet a third drawback to offering groups for adults is screening and assembling group members who have a common focus. Practitioners in both public and private settings often find they have a variety of individuals with whom they are working on individual concerns but that the overlap is not sufficient to justify beginning a group.

Finally, group work with adults may be difficult because of past beliefs and behavioral patterns. Adults have had longer to practice certain interactions and may take longer to change them or learn new ways of behaving.

SUMMARY AND CONCLUSION

The period of adulthood ranges from the early 20s to the mid-60s. Such a wide span in life is filled with many problems and possibilities. In young adulthood (ages 20 to 40), major concerns center on identity and intimacy, whereas in midlife (ages 40 to 65), attention is focused on generativity and fulfillment. Group work can help individuals in all stages of adulthood to clarify their focus and maximize their potential. In this chapter, groups for different ages and stages of adulthood and the gender problems that go with them have been considered.

College students and young adults, for example, are faced with major decisions involving learning, relationships, and career choices. Groups for them, especially on college campuses, are relatively short term and focus on specific agenda items. Groups can help college students and young adults become better oriented toward their environments and tasks in life, may facilitate growth, and prevent problems. However, when members of this population become stuck, they may also use groups for psychotherapy purposes.

Adults in midlife struggle to come to grips with the reality of their aging. Groups are especially helpful to midlifers in evaluating themselves in regard to family and career. Many individuals do not fully realize how their childhood influences their adulthood until midlife. For people who have grown up in families with alcohol addiction or other forms of abuse, groups can be supportive, educational, and therapeutic. Many self-help groups, such as those sponsored by Adult Children of Alcoholics, can help them break out of isolation and learn how to change dysfunctional behavioral patterns. Groups for midlifers may also focus on positive wellness, such as jogging groups, or potential change, such as those that emphasize careers.

Because men and women are socialized differently, and because biological differences often result in unique concerns, groups for one gender or the other are sometimes helpful. A process of mutual identification can be facilitated when the leader of the group and group members are all of the same sex. Role modeling is also enhanced in such groups (Gonzalez-Lopez & Taylor, 1997). Through group work, men may realize the strict limitations of traditional roles for males and make changes that allow them greater flexibility and growth. Particular problems related to work and stress may be dealt with from a psychotherapeutic and psychoeducational perspective. The mythopoetic movement is an appropriate adjunct to working in groups with men. Likewise, women may use groups to deal with career and workplace issues (Giordano, 1995). Women may also use groups to help free themselves from socialized roles that are not productive for them as adults, such as always being dependent or passive. Furthermore, they may work in groups to overcome traumatic events in their lives, such as rape, or to concentrate on self-concept issues, such as those involved in eating disorders or careers inside or outside the home.

Groups are also helpful for adults in midlife who are married or unmarried. Couple and family groups are another type of group work for midlife married adults in need of a psychotherapeutic rather than a psychoeducational approach. Groups for the divorced and the widowed, especially self-help groups such as Parents Without Partners, can offer much for this population. Parent education groups, which focus on skill development, support, and discussion, are useful for parents of all types. In these groups, parents learn to concentrate on their own behaviors as well as those of their offspring.

CLASSROOM EXERCISES

1. In groups of three, investigate the number of groups that operate on your college campus. These groups may vary from those that emphasize learning to those that are psychotherapeutically oriented. Each group in the class should concentrate on either a particular type of group or a particular organization that offers groups. Have each class group report back to the class as a whole and discuss what they have found out about the campus community and group work.

2. The transition to midlife is sometimes filled with apprehension. Have each member of the class draw a picture depicting him- or herself at young adulthood and midlife. In dyads, talk with another class member about the differences you anticipate or have experienced. What are the advantages and drawbacks of aging as you perceive them, and how might a group be helpful in this process?

3. Divide the class into two groups based on gender. Each group will review articles from professional periodicals published within the past 3 years on the use of groups with men and women. The males will review only articles on females in groups; the females in the class will do the opposite. Each group will then tabulate the results of its findings and

present this information to the whole class. After the presentation, discuss what has been found and how it might be used.

4. Interview a panel of parents (of other class members, if possible) about parenthood. List top concerns and explore how a parent edu-cation group leader might address these diffi-culties. Consult your parent panel about which interventions seem most constructive for them and why. Then discuss as a class the merits and limitations of parent education groups.

CHAPTER 14

GROUPS FOR OLDER ADULTS

When you wake up one morning
  and feel you've grown old
Take this poem down from your shelf
  And slowly read its well-wrought lines
  which fade like memories of our youth.
Those were the days on the knolls of Reynolda
  when times were measured in looks not words,
Those were the moments we wrote in our memories
  and now, like fine parchment,
    though faded they remain
clear impressions in the calmness of age
  of excitement, frivolity, and love,
  bringing warmth and smiles
    to the chill of the season:
      and brightness to a world full of grey.*

*From "A Poem in Parting" by Samuel T. Gladding, © 1968/1989/2006.

Aging is an inevitable process. Despite mythical and historical searches for the fountain of youth, everyone who lives grows older. Late adulthood begins in the 60s and extends up to approximately 120 years of age, thus making it the longest span of any period of human development—50 to 60 years (Santrock, 2006). Many people begin to acknowledge the inevitable decline in their physical powers somewhere between ages 35 and 50. Others continue to deny or even do not display many changes until quite late in life. Aging is individualized.

In previous generations, working in groups with older adults, was not a priority. The reason was that the number of individuals over the age of 65 years (a traditional time of retirement in the past) was relatively small (2% of the population in 1776; 4% in 1900) (American Association of Retired Persons, 2006). However, the percentage of those over age 65 continues to rise and is now about 12%, with 1 of every 14 people in the United States being a woman over the age of 65 (Burnside, 1993; Myers, 1990; Williams & Lair, 1988). In 2000, the number of Americans over the age of 65 was about 35 million; by 2050, the number is projected to be around 64 million. "The Census Bureau projects that one in nine baby boomers (9 million of the 80 million people born between 1946 and 1964) will survive into their late 90s, and that 1 in 26 (or 3 million) will reach 100" (Cowley, 1997, p. 59).

Although older adults (age 65 and up) are of interest to mental health professionals, existing services for this population have not kept up with demand (Knight, 1996). Many reasons account for this deficiency. One is that the number of people in this category has grown dramatically, whereas the supply of mental health workers has not risen as rapidly. For instance, since 1900, persons above age 85 have increased eightfold, whereas the population in general has increased only threefold (Hern & Weis, 1991). Another reason older adults are underserved is that mental health services have traditionally been geared toward those in middle age and younger. Further complicating the situation are the limitations some helpers place on themselves and older adults by accepting many of the myths, misconceptions, and stereotypes about the aged. For example, some may believe that older people cannot change or be creative (Corey & Corey, 2006; Greene, 1986). Acceptance of these myths leads to an "attitude bias" against working with older adults. This bias is known as **ageism** (i.e., discrimination against older people) (Butler, 1975). In actuality, many characteristics of those who are older make them excellent candidates for numerous helping services, especially group work.

Benefits and liabilities come with any age, and growing older is no exception. On the positive side, most people past the traditional retirement age of 65 (used as a marker event to separate midlife from old age) still enjoy a high quality of life and have many years to live (about a quarter of their lives) (Cowley, 1997). Often they exemplify what Erikson (1963) describes as **"wisdom"**—the ability to make effective choices among alternatives—and **"integrity"**—the total integration of life experiences into a meaningful whole. If married, older people frequently experience increased marital satisfaction and intimacy (Walsh, 1988). There is also an increase in the religious and spiritual life of many older people and with it an associated sense of well-being and meaningfulness (Levin, Taylor, & Chatters, 1994).

Because approximately 70% of persons over age 65 are grandparents, they often find enrichment and pleasure through interacting with their grandchildren (Mead, 1972; Streib & Beck, 1981). Others find significance in their lives through becoming foster grandparents or doing volunteer work. Most keep in contact with their children and are able to resolve some issues of earlier family life. A significant percentage of older adults (95%) maintain their own households and seem to value their independence. Until age 75, the majority of individuals in this age group are, as a rule, relatively free from disabling physical impairments, view themselves as basically middle-aged, and generally enjoy a variety of physical exercises and activities, including sex (Masters & Johnson, 1970; Okun, 1984). Persons in this age range are known as the **young-old**.

On the negative side, older adults as a group share many common psychological and physiological concerns. For instance, loneliness, loss, fear, or hopelessness are often prevalent among members of this group (Corey & Corey, 2006; France, 1984). "Feelings of worthlessness may develop as older individuals internalize their devalued social position and lose control over their lives" (Thomas & Martin, 1997, p. 43). Individuals over the age of 75 are considered the **old**, and those over 85 years are viewed as the **old-old**. Collectively, these groups are more likely than others to experience declines in health and overall functioning and eventually to have chronic health problems that require increased attention (Myers, 1989; Walsh, 1988). In addition, numerous individuals, especially older men, have difficulty adapting to retirement and mourn the loss of meaningful roles outside of the household. Sometimes this adjustment can lead to conflict and dysfunctioning. The poor and those who are cultural minorities usually have more trouble in old age, too, a continuation of discrimination and need they have suffered through their lives for the most part (Himes, Hogan, & Eggebeen, 1996).

Widowhood is another downside to aging. Because women have traditionally married older men and live longer than men, this possibility is of special concern to them (Neugarten, 1970). Ageism may be a painful societal force that tarnishes one's sense of pride in age. Finally, there is the prospect of facing one's own mortality. The inevitable end of life is an event some individuals in old age have difficulty accepting.

Changes required of most individuals at the older stages of life include making adjustments for declining physical strength, retirement, death of friends or spouse, and declines in income and health (Cox, 2006; Santrock, 2006; Schlossberg, Waters, & Goodman, 1995). New social roles, such as being a grandparent, must be learned; different relationships must be established with peers and children. The requirements of older adults, although not as numerous as those in adolescence, are still demanding. Not everything happens at once, however, and older individuals have time to make the transition gradually. The **"'density of time'**—its fullness and eventfulness—seems to lessen with age" (Schlossberg, 1981, p. 13).

Many of the problems associated with living over 65 years are the result of limited socialization and interpersonal activities. Others involve damaged self-image and self-esteem. Almost all of these difficulties can be constructively addressed through some form of group work. In fact, just the interpersonal nature of groups can be therapeutic for older adults, especially those who are isolated and lonely (Brandler, 1985; Henderson & Gladding, 2004; Zimpfer, 1987).

◆ *Questions from Experience* ◆

What has been your relationship with people above the age of 65? How do you feel about being that age one day? What do you think could be done to counter ageism?

TYPES OF GROUPS FOR OLDER ADULTS

Groups for those ages 65 and over are geared toward the needs of the persons involved and the expertise of the group leader(s) (Corey & Corey, 2006). On the psychoeducational and task/work side of groups are two advocacy groups for older adults: the **Gray Panthers** and **AARP**. Counseling and psychotherapy groups for this population include seven types of groups: (a) reality oriented, (b) remotivation therapy, (c) reminiscing and life review, (d) psychotherapy and counseling, (e) topic- and theme-focused, (f) member specific, and (g) eGroups.

Psychoeducational and Task/Work Groups

The two main advocacy groups for older adults have both unique and overlapping functions. As a group, the Gray Panthers addresses issues dealing with universal health care, jobs with a living wage, preservation of Social Security, affordable housing, access to quality education, economic justice, the environment, peace, challenging ageism, sexism, and racism (http://www.graypanthers.org/). Gray Panthers groups are organized nationally and at local levels.

The AARP is the country's largest nonprofit organization dedicated to the interests of mature Americans. Headquartered in Washington, DC, the AARP works in groups on the local level through education, advocacy, and community service activities (http://www.aarp.org/).

Because of the power of these two groups, many older adults join them and find both meaning and services in them. Other older adults join local religious or civic groups and benefit in a similar manner.

Counseling and Psychotherapy Groups

Of the seven counseling and psychotherapy groups, four differ significantly in both purpose and scope from the psychoeducation and task/work groups just described. They are aimed at helping mentally impaired older adults through psychotherapeutic means. The groups in this cluster are reality oriented, remotivation therapy, reminiscing and life review, and therapy. The last three groups in the counseling and psychotherapy category, topic- and theme-focused, member specific, and eGroups, are more preventive and educational in nature. Each is examined here.

Reality-oriented groups are set up for older individuals who have become disoriented to their surroundings. (Reality-oriented theory is unrelated to the theory of reality therapy developed by William Glasser.) These groups, although educationally focused, are therapeutically based in that they emphasize helping group members become more aware of their present surroundings in terms of time, place, and people (Burnside, 1986; Thomas & Martin, 2006). Group membership is limited to three or four participants when the circumstances are severe, but groups for less disoriented individuals may involve seven or eight people. Groups meet daily and, if basic information is mastered, then members progress to more creative and practical activities (Capuzzi & Gross, 1980). Because reality-oriented groups are conducted at such a low level, helping professionals with minimal training in human relationship skills are able to lead them.

Initially, these types of groups were established in institutional settings but now they are found in outpatient and day-care groups (Thomas & Martin, 2006). Regardless, they meet every day and follow a set schedule. Group sessions include sensory training, group exercises, and practical skills on a 24-hour-a-day basis (Taulbee, 1978; Thomas & Martin, 2006).

Remotivation therapy groups, in contrast to reality-oriented groups, are aimed at helping older clients become more invested in the present and future. Their membership is composed of individuals who have "lost interest" in any time frame of life except the past. The groups were originally set up in mental hospitals and nursing homes in the early 1950s by Dorothy Smith, a hospital volunteer. Participation in such groups is usually limited to 15 members who are selected for their ability to relate to others, willingness to join the group, and lack of distorted memories (Dennis, 1978). Sessions focus on nonpathological topics, such as gardening, art, or the holidays. Participants are encouraged to respond to others and to materials presented in an appropriate verbal or nonverbal manner. The goal of this process is for participants to become more cognitively organized and to increase their socialization skills through interacting with others.

According to Beaver (1983, p. 240), remotivation therapy groups follow five basic steps:

1. "The climate of acceptance"—establishing a warm, friendly relationship in the group
2. "A bridge to reality"—reading literature, keeping up with current events, investigating ideas
3. "Sharing the world"—developing a specific topic through leading questions, use of props, planned activities
4. "An appreciation of the work of the world"—stimulating the participants to think about themselves in relation to work or avocational interests
5. "The climate of appreciation"—finding joy through getting together

Often remotivation groups are preliminary to other types of group experiences, such as those involving family problems or individual concerns. Studies show positive empirical results for remotivation therapy groups (Burnside, 1986; Zimpfer, 1987), although they have been criticized too for being too rigid and disallowing feelings (Burnside, 1986).

Reminiscing and Life Review groups "are generally considered to be synonymous, defined as a naturally occurring, universal process whereby experiences and unresolved conflicts are revived, surveyed, and reintegrated into people's views of their lives" (Thomas & Martin, 2006, p. 489). These groups help individuals retrieve memories from the past, work through unresolved conflicts, reintegrate remembered experiences, and find a deeper "sense of identity and connectedness with the world" (Thomas & Martin, 2006, p. 489). Overall, these groups are aimed at increasing life satisfaction rather than improving social skills (Kennedy & Tanenbaum, 2000).

There are a number of ways reminiscing and life review groups can be structured, but DeVries, Birren, and Deutchman (1995) suggest nine guiding themes:

• History of the major branching points in life
• Family history
• Career or major life work

- The role of money in life
- Health and body image
- Loves and hates
- Sexual identity, sex roles, and sexual experience
- Experiences with ideas about death and dying and other losses
- Influences, beliefs and values that provide meaning in my life

Persons in these groups share memories, increase personal integration, and become more cognizant of their lives and the lives of those their age. Insight gained from this process helps these older adults realize more deeply their finiteness and prepare for death (Lewis & Butler, 1984).

A major therapeutic value of the reminiscing and life review group process lies in the sense of affiliation it creates among its members. These groups provide both a chance to be introspective and "an opportunity for social intimacy with others" (Singer, Tracz, & Dworkin, 1991, p. 167). Further beneficial aspects include a more positive mood among members, increased self-esteem, and enhanced life satisfaction (Thomas & Martin, 1997, 2006). In addition, members feel more competent and in greater control of their lives. Their memories give them a vehicle for communicating with others who are at their same age and stage. Isolation and loneliness are eliminated in group interactions. Through sharing, the processes of creativity and pleasure are enhanced as the individual, the group, and the group leader gain insight into a person's psychological history (Christensen, Hulse-Killacky, Salgado, Thornton, & Miller, 2006). In short, the reminiscing and life review group can be the springboard for conducting other groups or be an end in itself.

Reminiscing and life review groups are usually conducted once or twice a week for about an hour and consist of six to eight members. They may be relatively long term (more than a year) or short term (10 weeks or fewer) (Beaver, 1983; Christensen et al., 2006). The content of the group sessions is often chosen by group members but may be selected at times by the group leader(s). Popular, but not always pleasant, topics in one all-female reminiscing group of women 65 years of age and older were favorite holidays, first pet, first job, first day of school, first date, first toy, first playmate, and first memory (Burnside, 1993). Topics and themes for women and men in such groups vary. Whatever the case, content is often highlighted through the use of poetry, music, visual aids, and other memorabilia. Leaders for such groups must be skilled in group dynamics and interpersonal communication responses. They should be inquiring but not intrusive. Other helpful qualities include "delving into the daily existence of . . . group members, getting to know them as people, and overcoming pre-set notions about who elderly people are and how they experience the world" (Christensen et al., 2006, p. 86). Patience and flexibility are key ingredients that leaders need to master as well (Capuzzi & Gross, 1980).

Singer et al. (1991) provide a model of a reminiscing and life review group in an adult day-care center. In establishing their group, leaders decided on a closed-ended, voluntary group format. They screened their prospective members beforehand to ensure they were mentally alert as well as motivated for the experience. Goals for the group included decreasing social and emotional isolation, depression, and loneliness; increasing social skills and self-esteem; and enabling members to develop a social network by the end of the group. After 10 weekly 1-hour sessions, the staff of the center and members themselves noticed significant advancements in the achievement of the group's goals. Life for participants became more meaningful and enjoyable because of the respect and under-standing they found in the group. The main drawback to this particular group was that 10 sessions did not provide enough time for the members to process fully all of the material they wanted to discuss.

Therapy groups for older adults are geared toward the remediation of specific problems this population faces, such as role changes, ageism, social isolation, loss, physi-cal decline, and fear of the future (Altholz, 1978; Henderson & Gladding, 2004; Weisman & Schwartz, 1989). Sometimes persons "who are referred to group psychotherapy are . . . depressed, highly agitated and disruptive, or unable to do reality testing" (Maynard, 1980, p. 232). Others have fewer ongoing unresolved, serious personal problems, but they are still in need of help.

Generally, therapy groups for older adults are composed of between 6 and 12 mem-bers. They are usually long term (a year or more), although some groups tend to be briefer. These groups may be highly structured or relatively unstructured, but leaders need a background in gerontology as well as experience in group work with older per-sons. It is advisable for group leaders to screen potential members carefully, "assessing their competencies to process conflict and emotional issues" (Thomas & Martin, 2006, p. 489). That way, as in other groups, they do not get themselves into situations where they find a group member who is disruptive or unable to function well. Leaders of therapy groups for older adults must be knowledgeable about and skilled in the treatment of major mental disorders. It is likewise vital that they recognize and be able to deal with developmental and transitional factors connected with aging. In addition, leaders must also be encouraging of group members and willing to self-disclose when appropriate. Overall, therapy groups help their members gain a greater appreciation of themselves and where they are developmentally.

CASE EXAMPLE: Thelma Sets Up a Group for Therapy

Thelma has worked with older adults all her life. She has usually done so on a one-to-one basis. However, her facility now has a number of older adults who are socially isolated and facing physical decline. Therefore, Thelma decides to run a therapy group.

To her credit Thelma screens members, chooses eight, finds a room that is appropriate and sets up a time for the group to begin. Then, she is in a bit of a bind. She is not sure exactly how to start the group, although she has explained the purpose of the group to its members.

How would you advise Thelma to get the group going? Be as specific as you can.

Topic- and theme-focused groups are centered around a particular topic or theme, such as widowhood, bibliotherapy, sexuality, health, parenting grandchildren, spirituality, or the arts. They are psychoeducational in nature and "are designed ultimately to improve the quality of daily living for older people" (Beaver, 1983, p. 241). These groups also assist the aging to find more meaning in their lives and to establish a support group of like-minded people. Their leaders must have topic-specific knowledge of the issues being cov-ered (Myers, 1989). For instance, in groups for bereaved spouses, leaders must assist the members to cope with the pain of grief and mourning (including the "holding on" and "letting go" processes), help combat the social isolation that is so pervasive for this population, provide "consensual validation" for spouses regarding their bereavement experiences, and support members as they begin to understand the changes facing them as they begin to fashion a new future for themselves (Walter, 2005). Membership in such groups is voluntary, and the groups may be conducted in a variety of settings. "The size, composition, duration, and frequency of the group depend upon the group goals and member competencies" (Thomas & Martin, 2006, p. 490). Significant social interaction often result from such experiences.

Member-specific groups are related to topic- and theme-focused groups, but they focus more on particular transitional concerns of individual members, such as grief, hospitalization, or institutionalized day care. Basically, member-specific groups may be conducted for older adults or members of their families (Capuzzi & Gross, 1980). When these types of groups are conducted for the aging, they are aimed at helping all participants recognize and face particular concerns that are common to people who grow older, such as loss of physical strength or the effects of physical illnesses. In a similar way, member-specific groups that concentrate on families assist them in dealing with common themes related to how a group member's well-being and adjustment will affect each person in the family (Sullivan, Coffey, & Greenstein, 1987).

The same leadership skills required to lead a topic- and theme-focused group are necessary in conducting a member-specific group, but leaders must focus more on individual concerns than those of the group as a whole. For example, members of a family group with a relative who has Alzheimer's disease all may have different areas on which they wish to concentrate (Glosser & Wexler, 1985; Hinkle, 1991). There is no simple way to personalize a member-specific group.

eGroups are what their name implies. They are technology-based groups for older persons who are homebound (Thomas, Martin, Alexander, Cooley, & Loague, 2003). They may be used in multiple ways, from a life review group using eMemories and eStories to various types of support groups. Nearly half of North Americans above age 58 have access to computers and the Internet. Thus, this type of group has great potential. In addition, with ethical standards in place for online counseling both from the American Counseling Association and from the National Board for Certified Counselors, the potential use of eGroups in a professional and effective way is quite possible.

Thomas et al. (2003) recommend that potential members of such groups be referred by a professional counselor and not recruited through advertisements. In addition, they recommend that members of the group be screened. Furthermore, security and confidentiality should be maintained, and potential members who cannot guarantee security of their Internet site should be allowed only to participate in limited types of groups. Finally, each eGroup should have a counselor and a backup counselor accessible to each group member in case of a concern or emergency.

Overall, if technological skills and ethical concerns can be overcome, eGroups can help older people be connected with cohorts in other geographical areas and "build a supportive and healing community for older people who otherwise would be more isolated," therefore producing "the feeling of personal control that is so important for the empowerment and psychological and physical well-being of older people" (Thomas & Martin, 2006, p. 494).

CASE EXAMPLE: Inez Goes on the Internet

Inez self-describes herself as "a little older than a baby-boomer." She is a widow and a computer wiz. "I buy everything on line," she tells you. Because she is located in a rural area and cannot drive, she asks you about joining an eGroup. You investigate and find one that would fit her.

Inez is enthused. She signs on but does not give her real name. Then she starts describing

herself and her situation in unrealistic ways. You are monitoring the group, and finally you confront Inez with what she is doing. Her response: "I'm just having a little fun."

What might you say next? Is Inez really hurting anyone? What might you recommend that she do?

SETTING UP GROUPS FOR OLDER ADULTS

Just as with other groups, those involving older adults must be carefully and thoughtfully proposed. This means that goals should be clearly established before the group begins. Older adults generally need a clear, organized explanation of the specific purpose of a group and why they can benefit from it. The establishment of any group for older adults involves pregroup screening, especially if the group is counseling or therapeutically oriented.

Most groups for older adults are conducted on an outpatient or outreach basis, but in some cases, they are carried out in institutional settings. In outreach environments, task-oriented psychotherapy groups are beneficial because of a sense of accomplishment that these groups foster among their members through the achievement of tangible products (Zimpfer, 1987). Regardless of the setting or the focus, certain procedures should be followed when preparing to work with a group of individuals age 65 and older.

The first consideration is the physical environment in which the group will be conducted. The meeting room should be functional, geared for comfort, and in a quiet area. The ideal location is a ground-floor room with upholstered chairs, good lighting, and space for wheelchairs; it should be near a bathroom, away from steps, and with a constant temperature of about 75 degrees with no drafts. Unfortunately, this kind of environment is usually hard to find (Capuzzi & Gross, 1980; Henderson & Gladding, 2004; Hendrix & Sedgwick, 1989). Once a good setting is found, a tight circle works best for accommodating the hearing impaired and creating a sense of cohesiveness (Stone & Waters, 1991).

A second matter of importance is scheduling. Certain times of the day do not work well for meetings; for example, early evening is not good for many older group members who may have difficulty with night driving or like to go to bed early. Therefore, the group should be set up to maximize participation. This usually means finding out the schedules of potential participants and building time for group meetings around them. Once a good time is established, most groups for older adults are set up to be closed ended to build trust and develop empathy (Capuzzi & Gross, 1980; Hendrix & Sedgwick, 1989). The major exceptions to this procedure are psychotherapy groups in institutional settings or support groups such as those for the widowed that may benefit from an open-ended format (Folken, 1991; Yalom, 2005).

A third matter that must be considered is the physical ability of group members. Physical disabilities and sensory impairment can contribute to a feeling of social isolation in older adults and also inhibit their participation in a group (Myers, 1990). Some members who have lost sensory and mobility functions may require special treatment. One way to take care of their needs is to employ a **multimodal method** (i.e., using verbal and nonverbal means) for conveying information (Erwin, 1997). A warm-up activity or brief informational presentation before the group actually gets to work can help members understand the group's focus for the day.

Burnside (1978) lists a number of other factors that make groups for the aged distinct from other types of groups. These factors must be considered when setting up such groups:

- As a rule, groups for older adults tend to be smaller in size (e.g., four to eight members) than groups with other age populations, except for elementary school children. Remotivation therapy groups, which may be as large as 15 members, are a notable exception to the rule of having small groups for older adults.
- The physical environment is more important to the well-being of the group and its members than is true with other age groups. Older adults have greater difficulties with physical body systems than do other age groups because of lifestyle factors such as **hypokinesis** (i.e., physical inactivity) (Burlew, Jones, & Emerson, 1991). For some groups, physical exercise along with group activities is an excellent combination.
- Unlike the norms for some other groups, older group members are encouraged to socialize with one another outside the group setting. This type of socializing helps break down barriers that isolate older adults and is, therefore, therapeutic.
- Growth and enhancement are meaningful themes for groups for older adults. Encouragement is more appropriate than confrontation in working with this population.
- Older adults take longer to build trust than do those in other age groups (Waters, McCarroll, & Penman, 1987). The reasons for this gap vary, but they often reflect socialization patterns, such as believing that negative secrets should be kept private or feeling that no one will really understand them.

◆ *Questions from Experience* ◆

What are some characteristics of older adults not mentioned here? How might they have an impact on a group?

ROLE OF THE LEADER IN GROUPS FOR OLDER ADULTS

Almost all major theoretical approaches can be used to work with older adults (Henderson & Gladding, 2004; Storandt, 1983). Therefore, the role of the leader in groups for older adults depends on his or her knowledge of theory, the type of group to be led, the leader's previous experience and abilities, and participants' level of readiness. Hawkins

(1983) suggests the following steps for prospective leaders, especially those with little experience:

1. *Read*—It is critical to separate fact from fiction when working with members of an older population. Reading books and articles specifically geared toward the developmental and nondevelopmental issues of the aged will help leaders be more objective. Excellent reviews of the literature on groups for older adults are often published in scholarly journals (e.g., Myers, Poidevant, & Dean, 1991). A humorous yet insightful book on a wide range of topics related to aging is *It's Better to Be Over the Hill Than Under It: Thoughts on Life Over Sixty* (LeShan, 1990).

2. *Examine*—Along with reading, leaders need to examine their own prejudices and stereotypes of the old. Some leaders who grew up in a culture or subculture that stressed youth or staying young, such as the "baby boom generation," may have particular difficulty in dealing with older adults and their concerns (Folken, 1991). Leaders with negative ideas about older adults will probably be detrimental to the group and should be replaced.

3. *Meet*—It is crucial to the group's success that leaders become aware of their own perspectives on the lives of older individuals. One place such an encounter can occur is through remembering major exchanges with older adults within the leaders' families of origin. Other opportunities for such meetings are found in present settings, such as retirement homes, where leaders visit older individuals and learn more about them as persons.

4. *Fantasize*—Leaders should imagine their own lives in the future and become more aware of what their wishes, hopes, and fears might be then. For instance, leaders may envision themselves as lonely or economically destitute after retirement. Then they can empathize more with actual group members they may meet in these circumstances. By fantasizing, leaders can face their future and avoid projecting any undesirable characteristics onto those with whom they work.

5. *Learn*—Those who lead groups for older adults need to learn what social, educational, and political organizations, such as the AARP and the Gray Panthers, are available on the national, state, and local levels. These groups are often rich resources for group members.

6. *Care*—It is important, and indeed critical, that older adults realize that others, such as group leaders, sincerely care about them. Such caring adds to the self-esteem of everyone. It promotes rapport and enriches the process of being in a group (Myers et al., 1991).

In addition, leaders need to realize that the pace of a group for older adults is usually slower and the goals are more limited than for most other groups. To compensate for this slower pace and to reduce frustration, group leaders need to be accepting, remind members of positive changes, and encourage continued participation (Myers et al., 1991).

Likewise, leaders need to be cognizant that common themes in groups for older adults are loss and loneliness, death and dying, concern about physical changes, increased dependency, relationships with adult children, grandparenting, and finding meaningful and enjoyable activities in which to participate (Myers, 1989). With these themes in mind, it is understandable that the use of certain words and processes that are normally discussed in groups for other populations are not usually appropriate in groups for older adults. *Long-term goal* and *termination,* for instance, are two that should be avoided (Ekloff, 1984; Waters et al., 1987). These words have a tendency to arouse anxiety in some older persons, especially those who are frail or sick. Members may become fearful that they will not be able to attain goals or that they may suffer yet another loss. In general, a less stringent criterion for success is appropriate when working with groups for older adults. A relaxed atmosphere is also important.

Leaders also need to share impressions and experiences in their lives within the groups they conduct to keep them focused and moving. One of the most significant mistakes new group leaders make when working with older adults is not self-disclosing.

Overall, group leaders for older adults must be verbally and nonverbally active and personally and professionally concerned, as well as clear and direct. By performing in such a fashion, leaders can help move their groups away from self-centeredness to a healthy group-centeredness (Henderson & Gladding, 2004; Hendrix & Sedgwick, 1989). Group leadership skills in such cases do not differ significantly from those used with other populations, but the emphases of leaders vary. Their alertness to certain key issues—such as religion, economics, intergenerational conflict, or loss—is usually greater than would be the case in other age groups.

In summary, leaders working with older persons in groups must be sensitive to relevant issues, such as concerns with aging and death, as well as to real constraints, such as waning physical health and vitality and fewer social outlets (Jacobs, Masson, & Harvill, 2006). A major issue that most group workers face in dealing with older adults is their inexperience in knowing what their members' stage of life is like. Therefore, group workers must accept this reality and be open to being a learner, as well as a facilitator, within these groups. They must come to terms with their own aging and eventual death as well in a way that enables them to face life energetically and realistically. Personal integration of one's own life, professional knowledge of aging, and familiarity with psychoeducational and psychotherapeutic processes that will best help them relate to the aged are the key factors in becoming an effective group leader for older adults.

CASE EXAMPLE: Dora Confronts Death

Dora has a master's degree and 5 years of experience at her agency. She is from a close-knit family that is healthy and often engages in games of touch football during the holidays. In her late 20s, Dora is dedicated to the mental health of all of her clients. She always acts professionally.

As the co-leader of a group for older adults at a retirement center, Dora notices that Mr. Smoak has missed the last two sessions of the group. When she inquires about this, she is told that Mr. Smoak became ill about 10 days ago and died yesterday.

Dora is shocked. She lets her co-leader, Brian, know and they discuss the matter. Dora really liked Mr. Smoak and she feels guilty that she did not visit with him during his recent illness. She is not sure she can continue as the co-leader of the group.

How would you approach Dora if you were Brian? How could you involve other members of the group in handling this situation, or would you? Do you think Dora should continue as a co-leader of the group? Why or why not?.

STUDIES ON THE OUTCOMES OF GROUPS FOR OLDER ADULTS

Studying groups for older adults is complicated at times because, along with the inclusion of a group experience, some individuals, especially in counseling and psychotherapy groups, receive individual and medical treatments that affect how they function. Nevertheless, there are some clear-cut studies that indicate the effectiveness of groups for older adults.

In regard to reality-oriented groups, the empirical evidence for their success is not strong. The reason is possibly because of the limited nature of the clients who compose the groups or the low level of leadership skill required of facilitators (Zimpfer, 1987).

Counseling groups for dealing with the problems of the aged have been studied also. Two such examples were given in this chapter—one focused on expressing anger and alleviating depression (Johnson & Wilborn, 1991) and the other concentrated on ways of handling stress and promoting the mental health of older adults (Stone & Waters, 1991).

In the group dealing with anger, Johnson and Wilborn (1991) found that a 6-week group counseling experience did not significantly decrease anger in a group of older women. However, they found that the women seemed to value the opportunity to talk about the expression of anger and its importance in their lives. They suggested a longer period be allocated for anger-management groups for older adults in replication studies.

In the group set up to help older adults manage stress, Stone and Waters (1991) used peer facilitators in a format of four sessions, each lasting 2 hours. They emphasized the importance of personal sharing, participant control, and enhancement of self-esteem. The peer counselors who worked with this small group of 8 to 10 individuals had instant credibility because of their age, and they were perceived as strong role models and reinforcers of group members' actions. Although no formal measures of change were taken in this group, members and the peer counselors reported the group to be helpful in increasing members' abilities to handle stress, change perceptions, and realize that others shared their concerns.

Anecdotal results have also been reported from an open-ended, topic-specific support group for widowed persons in Orange County, Florida, called "The Talk Group." The idea behind this group, which started in 1983, is that a *"therapeutic alliance"* is formed between individuals in grief and those who are helping them. The result is that "bereaved individuals who enjoy a high level of social support suffer fewer depressive symptoms and somatic complaints than those who are not so well supported" (Folken, 1991, p. 173). Thus, The Talk Group appears to benefit both the newly widowed as well as the group volunteers who work in it.

Another topic-specific group that is primarily psychoeducational in nature is for grandparents who are raising grandchildren (Vacha-Haase, Ness, Dannison, & Smith, 2000). The group, based on the curriculum *Second Time Around—Grandparents Raising Grandchildren* (Dannison & Nieuwenhuis, 1996), has initially been found to help custodial grandparents establish "contact with others who face similar life challenges" and as a result to "decrease feelings of isolation" and to "increase the use of positive coping strategies" (Vacha-Haase et al., 2000, p. 76).

Therapeutic writing groups for older adults have also yielded promising results. For instance, Schuster (1998) found that, in nursing homes, residents who worked with her in a writing group took on a more positive identity and changed their familial and social relationships for the better. In this group, members wrote and then shared their writings as a way to reveal information about their thoughts and feelings.

In a nationwide study of group work in nursing homes, Mazza and Vinton (1999) found that most of the 304 respondents offered three types of groups for elderly residents—educational, support, and therapy/counseling. Most also provided educational and support groups for family members, but only 40% of the nursing homes offered therapy/counseling groups for family members. "The results of this study offer evidence that group work is generally an established part of the services offered in skilled nursing facilities" (p. 68).

GROUPS FOR CARETAKERS OF OLDER ADULTS

Caregivers are crucial in the daily care and well-being of older adults who may not be able to take care of themselves completely (Thomas & Martin, 2006). The phenomenon of groups for caretakers of older adults is a relatively recent development (Santrock, 2006). It stems from the "advancements in medical science, technology, and health care" that enable human beings to live longer (Dobson & Dobson, 1991, p. 178). With this increased life span, middle-aged adults—the children of older adults—are often finding themselves as caretakers of this population, although they have limited information and few role models. As a group, they "experience problems with confinement, infringement on lifestyle, restricted social life, work and family conflicts, and emotional and physical stress" (Thomas & Martin, 1997, p. 44). The result is often frustration, resentment, and physical and emotional strain. To address these concerns, groups for caretakers have been formed.

A number of different kinds of caretaker groups are available, ranging from those for direct relatives to those for nursing home staff members. Their common denominator is that they primarily attempt to provide their members with information and support (Kennedy & Tanenbaum, 2000). Therefore, caretaker groups are mainly psychoeducational and psychotherapeutic in nature. Often they are short term, closed ended, and meet at nontraditional hours, such as early evening. Through the caretaker group, a bond is formed among participants that helps them to realize the universal nature of their situations (Dobson & Dobson, 1991; Hinkle, 1991). For nonrelative caretakers, especially those concerned with providing services to the dying, groups help them ventilate their feelings and revitalize themselves and their efforts (Smith & Maher, 1991).

Overall, groups for caretakers are preventive in nature. They affirm, support, and educate. They help link caretakers with others who can help them handle both unique and universal problems (Myers et al., 1991). They provide a means for participants to renew their own mental health and to concentrate on the interactional tasks ahead of them. As the older adult population increases, groups for caretakers of older adults will become more necessary and more prevalent.

◆ *Questions from Experience* ◆

Whom do you know who has looked after an older relative? What are some of the difficulties and concerns they have had? How do you think a group for caretakers could be or could have been of help to them?

STRENGTHS AND LIMITATIONS OF GROUPS FOR OLDER ADULTS

Strengths

Being a member of a group has numerous benefits for older people. The strengths are related to both the quantity and the quality of interpersonal relationships that older adults have (Horswill, 1993). Group members become more aware of their needs, commonalities, unique traits, and possibilities through sharing in a group. They are also able to find support for and resolution to their problems and concerns. Gaining a sense of the universality of their concerns may be especially key in such groups (Hawkins, 1983). Belonging to a group, especially with people who are around the same age, assists participants in realizing that they are not alone in their focus on "body image, physical ailments, and fear of mental deterioration" (Hawkins, 1983, p. 187). Through sharing, they come to develop a sense of community and a feeling of belonging (Thomas, 1991). This type of atmosphere contributes to their overall wellness.

Another strength of a group for older adults is that it gives its members an opportunity to try out different responses and initiate new behaviors. Older persons often engage in **growing times**, when fresh learning occurs on an individual and interpersonal level (Wrenn, 1989). This process may involve merely a better appreciation of what they encounter or where they have been, or it may entail a physical action, such as talking or taking on a different life role. Within a group, especially if it is psychoeducationally oriented, older individuals can experiment with behaviors they never had an opportunity to try when they were younger. Doing so can help them fulfill their sense of what is ideal and give them a more positive view of themselves.

A third positive aspect of group membership involves the process of formal and applied learning. A popular movement in the United States since the 1970s is the **elder hostel**, in which older individuals live and study together for a time, often on a college campus. This way of learning helps elders gain new knowledge and reinforce one another as achievers, and it promotes social cohesion. Often an older person's life experience allows him or her to become the teacher as well as the student. Learning groups are not just for the young (Johnson & Johnson, 2006).

Groups for older adults can also enhance self-concept (O'Brien, Johnson, & Miller, 1979). Through groups, older adults can be helped to focus on some of the advantages of growing old. For instance, many older individuals find comfort in integrating different aspects of their lives. Such reflection and ongoing involvement foster hope and ward off depression. Persons in such situations become contributors to society.

Finally, groups for older adults provide a series of checks and balances for those who participate in them. They shift responsibility for growth and development from caretakers or relatives to the persons in the group (Mardoyan & Weis, 1981). Participants in groups are empowered to take control of their present lives and to resolve past difficulties as best they can. This type of emphasis promotes growth in a way not usually possible in other one-to-one relationships because more ideas are shared and processed. For instance, through meeting with peers, elders may learn to focus more in their lives on what they select to do, how they optimize their opportunities, and how they compensate for factors related to aging, such as slowing down (Baltes & Baltes, 1990). The late Arthur Rubinstein, an admired concert pianist who performed well into his 80s, used many of these factors, such as selecting pieces that were difficult but not dependent on speed.

Limitations

One limitation of groups for older adults is they are labor intensive. Finding an environment that is suitable and setting it up in a way that is conducive to good communication takes time and effort.

Groups for older adults also require their leaders to have specialized skills that may be anxiety producing at best. A leader of a group of this nature must face his or her own mortality and also be sensitive to the life and death issues of those in the group. Such understanding is not easily achieved.

In groups for older adults, especially the old-old, group members and leaders have to face real loss. The death of a member may occur during the group or shortly thereafter. Dealing with loss and death is never easy, and group members and even leaders may be hesitant to invest as much in the group or its members because of this possibility.

A fourth limitation of groups for older adults is that they often have more limited goals than other groups, and members tend to be more limited in accomplishing them. Group workers who like to see dynamic progress and outcomes may be disappointed in conducting groups for older adults.

Finally, while working with a group for older adults, group workers and even members of the group itself will most likely have to deal with the caretakers of other members (Thomas & Martin, 2006). Although many of these encounters will be positive, they can also be a source of stress to the leader and members because of the energy they require.

SUMMARY AND CONCLUSION

Only since the late 1950s have aging and the aged been rigorously studied in the United States. With a growing number of individuals reaching age 65 and older, however, the importance of studying and working with this population has increased rapidly. Older adults have unique concerns and potentials that are often denied or overlooked. They bring to any situation a wealth of experience and talent as well as life circumstances unique to their time and informative to others.

Group work with older adults is still basically in its infancy. Before 1980, there was almost no professional literature on working with groups of older people (Myers, 1989). Now, research and approaches are more refined (Henderson & Gladding, 2004; Myers

et al., 1991; Thomas & Martin, 2006). However, questions still remain about what works best with which populations and when, even though Zimpfer (1987) has stated that, when older adults "client's needs are diagnosed correctly, the treatment often seems to work no matter what it is" (p. 91). Seven major types of groups are most frequently used therapeutically with older adults: reality orientation, remotivation therapy, reminiscing and life review, therapy and counseling, topic- and theme-focused, member specific, and eGroups. Psychoeducational and task groups that involve older adults, such as the Gray Panthers and the American Association of Retired Persons, are groups in which those over 65 may actively participate. Such groups offer social connections and support seldom found in other groups for older adults. Local religious and civic groups also offer support for some. Each of these types of groups has advantages and limitations.

In general, groups are quite appropriate and useful for older adults because groups may help them to integrate their lives more fully, find support, and develop a sense of universality. Furthermore, groups help older people combat loneliness and a sense of isolation. They may also give older adults a sense of orientation in time and place and an opportunity to continue to grow and develop.

Setting up a group for older adults depends on the leader's background and the participants' needs. Basically, many of the procedures for establishing groups are those required when working with other populations. However, group leaders need to be sensitive to time factors, foci, and themes that are especially appropriate for older adults. It is crucial, too, that the needs and interests of both men and women be considered in setting up groups (Horswill, 1993). For example, activities that center around both social and task-related opportunities should be included. This may mean setting up groups that focus on quilting bees, crafts, dances, and woodwork as well as seminars on travel, Social Security policies, and health insurance benefits.

When leaders direct their attention to these matters and come to terms with their own prejudices about age and their own sense of aging, they can promote positive interactions and development within groups of elderly. As the qualitative and quantitative aspects of groups for older adults grow, so will other activities connected with them. Among the most important of these related occurrences will be groups for caretakers of the aged. Such groups can help relatives and professionals of older adults maintain their own mental health and give optimal care through psychoeducational and psychotherapeutic means.

CLASSROOM EXERCISES

1. Divide into teams and investigate the most recent professional literature on any of the primary types of groups mentioned in this chapter. Report back to the class as a whole on your findings and which approaches seem to work best with which populations of older adults.

2. Draw a picture of yourself at age 80. Then work backward and make a drawing of yourself for each preceding decade until you reach your present age decade. After you have finished the drawings, role-play one of the ages you have drawn with a classmate and talk about how it feels to be that age and what concerns you have.

3. Collect data for a week from popular media, such as television, magazines, and newspapers, that demonstrate ageism or a lack of ageism. Share your findings with classmates in a group of four. Make recommendations to the class as a whole from your groups on three ways that ageism can be positively countered.

4. Think of your experiences with older people when you were a child. Talk with other classmates in a group of three about what your experiences taught you about the aged and what impressions they still make on your life. How would your past affect your present performance as a leader for an elderly group?

PART THREE

LEADING GROUPS FROM A
THEORETICAL PERSPECTIVE

CHAPTER 15

PSYCHOANALYTIC, TRANSACTIONAL ANALYSIS, AND REALITY THERAPY GROUPS

Scott Cunningham/Merrill

*We sit like strangers in hard-backed chairs
    at right angles from each other—
On the corners our sentences meet
    reflecting our thoughts and lives.
Slowly, messages in our minds
    make a move, a personal process
        whose destination is undetermined
But develops as we detect
    a crowd of quick-passing, open questions
That linger in our conversations
    after the sights of people
    have vanished with the fading light
And self-understanding has broken through
    as we travel from dusk into night.* *

*From "In the Midst of the Puzzles and Counseling Journey" by Samuel T. Gladding, 1978, *Personnel and Guidance Journal, 57,* p. 148. Copyright ACA. Reprinted with permission. No further reproduction authorized without written permission of the American Counseling Association.

The aftereffects of a group are often long lasting. Individuals usually enter groups as strangers but leave with a different understanding of themselves and others. These changes may be positive or negative but are rarely neutral. Conducting a group from a theoretical position is one factor that can influence a group for better or worse.

In this chapter, psychoanalytic, transactional analysis (TA), and reality therapy group work are examined. Although psychoanalytic approaches to groups are not as popular as they once were, they are still employed in a number of settings. In addition, psychoanalytic theory has influenced a number of other approaches either directly or indirectly, including TA and reality therapy.

The founder of TA, Eric Berne, initially trained to be a psychoanalytic therapist. However, Berne reacted to Freud's theory, believing it was too limited and focused in areas, such as psychosexual development, that he did not consider particularly useful or helpful. Thus, he developed a more pragmatic approach to working with groups in a variety of settings. Berne kept in his approach the concept of interactive ego states as it is found in psychoanalysis, but the internal and external dynamics of Berne's theory differ markedly from that of Freud.

Reality therapy was founded by William Glasser, who was initially trained to be a psychoanalyst but grew disenchanted with this approach. Since its development in the 1950s and 1960s, however, reality therapy has evolved. In the 1980s, **control theory**, a complete system for explaining how the brain works, was added to reality therapy (Glasser, 1985, 1986c; Wubbolding, 1988, 1991). Choice theory replaced control theory as the base of reality therapy in the 1990s (Glasser & Breggin, 2001; Wubbolding, 2001). The latest developments regarding reality therapy can be found on the William Glasser Institute Web site (www.wglasserinst.com). Like TA, reality therapy was initially employed more in groups than with individuals.

PSYCHOANALYTIC GROUPS

Psychoanalytic theory assumes that in-depth change takes years to produce. Therefore, it is usually oriented toward individuals with deep underlying psychological problems. However, this theory has changed from its original individual orientation to include groups. Psychoanalytic group work has several historical roots (Rutan, 1999).

Freud (1959), although never interested in conducting psychotherapy groups, did conduct psychoeducational groups on Wednesday nights meetings at his home at 19 Berggasse Street in Vienna, Austria (Barlow, Fuhrman, & Burlingame, 2004). He applied his psychoanalytic theory to groups in 1922 in his book *Group Psychology and the Analysis of the Ego*. In this work, Freud examined the nature of groups and how they influence individuals' lives. He concluded that a "group" is similar to a **primal horde** and that leaders of both function as substitute "parental figures" (Slavson, 1964). Freud also stressed the importance of ego development within a group context and the reconstruction of the family unit among group members.

Several physicians in the United States began using psychoanalytic theory as a basis for group psychotherapy before World War I. Among the most notable was E. W. Lazell (1921), who conducted group psychotherapy with schizophrenics. Trigant Burrow (1927) was the first to apply the term **group analysis** to the treatment of individuals in psychoanalytically oriented groups. He emphasized that social forces affect individuals' behaviors. Paul Schilder and Louis Wender were also pioneers in experimenting with group psychotherapy from a psychoanalytic perspective in New York in the 1930s (Shaskan & Roller, 1985). Both worked with psychotic, hospitalized adults, but Schilder also used group psychotherapy with prisoners, whereas Wender employed the approach with discharged patients (Gazda, 1968).

It was not until 1938, however, that a psychoanalytic model of group work was implemented on a sustained basis. Alexander Wolf, a psychiatrist and psychoanalyst, is generally credited with being the first to apply psychoanalytic principles and techniques systematically to groups (Corey, 2004; Ruitenbeek, 1970). He developed his analytical approach based more on economic reasons (i.e., the financial strain of clients to pay for individual services in the 1930s) than on an interest in groups. He quickly realized the utility of psychoanalytic groups, however, and became an enthusiastic supporter of them. Another early contributor to the psychoanalytic group work model was Samuel Slavson, who formed activity groups for children ages 8 to 15 based on psychoanalytic principles. He described his approach as **situational therapy** (Mullan & Rosenbaum, 1978).

One of the interesting outcomes of the psychoanalytic group movement is that at least two models for conducting groups have developed. Alexander Wolf created a model that stresses **psychoanalysis in groups**. In this model, the focus is on the individual, and the major tools of the psychoanalytic method are used: transference, dream interpretation, historical development analysis, interpretation of resistance, and free association. In contrast, George Bach (1954) and W. R. Bion (1959) developed models totally different from Wolf's, referred to as **group psychoanalysis**. These models emphasize that the whole group is the client and that group dynamics are an essential feature to analyze. Bion's point of view is similar to general systems theory (Bertalanffy, 1968), whereas Bach's view is based on field theory (Lewin, 1951). Both practitioners maintained that groups may manifest healthy or unhealthy influences on those within them. Generally, the most practiced form of psychoanalytically oriented group work emphasizes individual therapy in a group context (i.e., psychoanalysis in groups) (Seligman, 1982).

◆ *Questions from Experience* ◆

Think about the groups you have been in and how you have noticed change. What has been your experience? Have you seen more individuals change as a result of being in a group, or more groups change as a result of group dynamics? Relate your experience to the theories of psychoanalysis in a group and group psychoanalysis.

Premises of Psychoanalytically Oriented Groups

Regardless of the model, some basic premises underlie all psychoanalytically oriented groups. These common denominators deal with the major tenets of classic psychoanalytic theory as well as the belief that psychoanalysis is possible in a group setting. The importance of freeing unconscious thoughts, of making the unconscious more conscious, and of using specific techniques to do so (e.g., free association, transference, interpretation) is universally emphasized. Individuals who undergo psychoanalysis, regardless of the setting, should function better as a result of the experience because they have resolved intrapsychic conflicts.

The major assumptions of classic psychoanalytic theory are premised on the importance of the interaction among the id, ego, and superego. The **id**, the first system within the

Table 15.1

Psychosexual stages of development.

Stage	Age	Emphasis
Oral	Birth to 1 year	Gratification through sucking, biting; chief zone of pleasure is the mouth.
Anal	1st to 2nd year	Gratification through the withholding or eliminating of feces; chief zone of pleasure is the anus.
Phallic	3rd to 5th year	Gratification through stimulation of the genital area, sexual fantasy; resolution comes in giving up wish to possess opposite-sex parent and identifying with same-sex parent.
Latency	6th to 11th year	This is a period devoted to activity and achievement with peers; it is a quiet time sexually.
Genital	12th year on	This is the time of relating to persons of the opposite gender in an appropriate manner if previous stages have been resolved successfully.

personality to develop, is primarily where human instincts reside (Nye, 2000). The id is amoral, functions according to the pleasure principle, and contains a person's psychic energy (*libido*).

The **ego** is the "executive of the mind," works according to the reality principle, and tries to reduce the tension of the id. A strong ego is necessary for a healthy personality to develop.

The **superego** represents the values of parents and parental figures within the individual. It operates on the moral principle by punishing the person when he or she disobeys parental messages through the *conscience* and by rewarding the person through the ego *ideal* when parental teachings are followed. The superego strives for perfection and is seldom satisfied with less (Nye, 2000). In this regard, it is as unrealistic as the id.

Equally important as the interaction of these three ego states is the classic psychoanalytic theory hypothesis that individuals pass through **four stages of psychosexual development** during the first 20 years of life: oral, anal, phallic, and genital, with a period of latency between the phallic and genital stages. Each of these stages is named for a zone of pleasure at a particular age in a person's growth (see Table 15.1).

Failure to resolve the development tasks associated with these stages by being overindulged or excessively frustrated results in **fixation** (i.e., a tendency to cope with the outside world in a manner similar to that employed in the stage in which one is stuck). To overcome fixation requires that people regress to that time and come to terms with themselves and significant others who were involved in the fixation process. Ideal development can then go on and result in an ability to interrelate well with the self (with the ego in control of the id and the superego) and with others. A number of **defense mechanisms** (i.e., ways of protecting a person from being overwhelmed by anxiety), such as repression or denial, are overused when a person is not coping adequately (see Table 15.2). The main task of classic psychoanalysis is to undo fixation and to help people gain insight.

As implied previously, a major premise espoused by a number of psychoanalytic theorists (Foulkes & Anthony, 1965; Locke, 1961; Wolf & Schwartz, 1962) is that psychoanalysis is possible in a group setting. Any objections to its use in such a context, they imply, can easily

Table 15.2
Psychoanalytic defense mechanisms.

• Repression	The most basic of the defense mechanisms, repression is the unconscious exclusion of distressing or painful thoughts and memories. All other defense mechanisms make some use of repression.
• Denial	In this process, a person refuses to see or accept any problem or troublesome aspect of life. Denial operates at the preconscious or conscious level.
• Regression	When individuals are under stress, they often return to a less mature way of behaving.
• Projection	Instead of stating what one really thinks or feels, he or she attributes an unacceptable thought, feeling, or motive onto another.
• Rationalization	This defense mechanism involves giving an "intellectual reason" to justify a certain action. The reason and the action are connected only in the person's mind after the behavior has been completed.
• Reaction Formation	When an individual behaves in a manner that is just the opposite of how he or she feels, it is known as a "reaction formation." This type of behavior is usually quite exaggerated, such as acting especially nice to someone whom one dislikes intensely.
• Displacement	This defense is a redirection of an emotional response onto a "safe target." The substitute person or object receives the feeling instead of the person directly connected with it.

be overcome. Group psychoanalysis as well as psychoanalysis in a group is more a modification of individual analysis than a distinct school of thought (Slavson, 1964). However, group psychoanalysis and psychoanalysis in a group differ from Freud's original opinions about group members. In groups that are psychoanalytically oriented, (a) group members do not necessarily view the group leader as an ego ideal, (b) group members are not necessarily passive and dependent, (c) group standards are not always those of the leader, (d) group members' reactions to the group and to its leader are not the same, and (e) group members do not repress their aggression in deference to the group leader (Durkin, 1964).

Schleidlinger (1952) and Spotnitz (1961) stress two other points regarding the differences between conducting psychoanalysis in a group and doing so individually. They emphasize that certain processes, such as transference, are more intense in groups because of the interaction of members. Furthermore, factors highlighted in individual psychoanalysis, such as individual differences and genetic factors, are not emphasized as much in a group setting.

Basically, psychoanalytically oriented groups can be practiced on either a regressive-reconstructive or a repressive-constructive basis. The first approach (the **regressive-reconstructive model**) emphasizes that participants will become responsible for themselves and for society. It stresses the importance of being a creator of society as well as a transmitter of patterns. Therefore, it pushes participants to continue to change after the group has ended. The **repressive-constructive model** puts more focus on adaptation and adjustment of participants without stressing the creation of newness within culture (Mullan & Rosenbaum, 1978). Both approaches emphasize that a major change in personality is the goal of the group, which comes about only if there is sufficient regression followed by reconstruction.

Practice of Psychoanalytic Theory in a Group

The practice of psychoanalytic theory in a group is related to the premises of the theory in general. Because the theory emphasizes regression and resolution of previously unresolved stages of psychosexual development, membership in the group is usually restricted to either psychiatric patients or analytically oriented individuals. Therefore, the practice of psychoanalysis in groups is mainly applicable to counseling and psychotherapy groups. Although aspects of psychoanalytic theory may be included in a psychoeducational group, these same factors are not prevalent in a task/work group.

Most psychoanalytic groups are heterogeneous by design. The reason for this type composition is that such groups are more reflective of the world at large than homogeneous groups, and they promote transference and interaction while discouraging conformity (Wolf & Schwartz, 1962). Psychoanalytic groups should have about six to nine members and meet once or twice a week for at least 90 minutes (Mullan & Rosenbaum, 1978). There is no fixed number of sessions, but some groups of this type will meet more than 200 times (i.e., 300 hours).

The most important techniques used in the psychoanalytic approaches to groups parallel those employed in individual analysis. Each technique is examined separately here, although in practice they are used together and integrated.

Free Association

Free association in individual psychoanalysis is aimed at uncovering unconscious materials that have never been revealed or that have been repressed because they are too painful to keep in the conscious mind. In group psychoanalysis, the purpose of free association is similar, but the technique is also used to promote spontaneity, interaction, and feelings of unity in the group. In a group, free association works as a type of "free-floating discussion" (Foulkes & Anthony, 1965) in which group members report their feelings or impressions immediately.

One way to promote group free association is through the "go-round technique" (Wolf, 1963). This procedure encourages all members to share their feelings and impressions about others in the group at its beginning by saying whatever they think. In this way, members become more active within the group process and not only give personal impressions but receive interpersonal information as well. Interpersonal perceptions are very important in the development of the human personality (Mead, 1934).

Dream Analysis

Dream analysis is just as essential in group psychotherapy as it is in individual psychoanalysis. In both cases, individuals must be prepared to share. In an early session, the group leader asks members to describe a recent dream, a recurring dream, or even a daydream. Through sharing, group members get to know one another better and, at the same time, are able to be more concrete in handling their feelings associated with the dream and in managing themselves in general.

Dream content is manifest (i.e., conscious) and latent (i.e., hidden). *Manifest* content is the obvious and recallable features of the dream, such as who was in it. *Latent* content is the symbolic features of the dream that escape first analysis, such as water being a symbol for life. Psychoanalytic groups work on dreams at both levels. By giving their interpretations and free associations to others' dreams, group members gain insight into themselves and the group process as a whole. Dreams work on an interpersonal as well as an intrapersonal level in group psychotherapy (Kolb, 1983).

CASE EXAMPLE: Douglas Discloses a Dream

Douglas joined the psychoanalytic therapy group because he found the theory behind the practice of psychoanalysis intriguing. His group emphasized both the growth of the individual and the development of the group as a whole. Members were encouraged to share dreams or daydreams in the group.

Douglas had a dream where he was a peacemaker between two rival parties who were heavily armed. He told the group that he saw himself step between the two people—a teenage boy and girl who were both pointing guns at one another. He felt no fear until after he calmed the situation

down, but later he trembled when he realized he could have been killed in their conflict.

The group gave various feedback interpretations to Douglas ranging from keeping peace internally between his id and superego to stopping conflict in the group. Douglas's group leader, Fran, questioned him about how the dream was similar to other life experiences he had had. The emphasis was overall on the regressive-reconstruction model.

What do you think the interpretation of Douglas's dream would have been if the repressive-constructive model had been used?

Interpretation

Interpretation focuses on helping clients gain insights into their past or present behavior. Interpretations are generally made by group leaders in the earliest stages of the group because group members seldom possess the sophistication to do so adequately and appropriately (Stoller, 1968). Some group leaders who follow Melanie Klein's psychoanalytic method will make interpretations at the beginning of the group to try to make contact with an individual's unconscious (Mullan & Rosenbaum, 1978). Most will wait, however, until they are sure that a therapeutic alliance has been formed with group members and that members are able to work productively with interpreted material. In the later stages of the group, members interpret and give feedback to one another.

There are generally three levels of interpretation: thematical, constructional, and situational (Clark, 1993). *Thematical* interpretation is broad based and covers the whole pattern of a person's existence, such as self-defeating behavior. A leader might say, for instance, to a person who displays this behavior, "Pat, you seem to keep shooting yourself in the foot." *Constructional* interpretation focuses on thought patterns and the way group members express themselves, such as "I just can't win." *Situational* interpretation is context centered and emphasizes the immediate interactions within the group, such as members talking about trivia rather than meaningful or relevant issues. For example, the leader might observe, "This group is having a hard time getting down to work. Everyone seems to want to avoid real issues."

Using interpretation in group settings has several drawbacks and should be employed with caution. One of the biggest drawbacks is that the group leader will become overly involved with one member of the group and not give needed attention to others (Posthuma, 2002). Interpretation may also be rejected by group members and make them defensive, thereby halting the progress of the group. Finally, interpretation may divert the group's attention from the individual goals of members.

Resistance

Resistance works in overt and covert ways to keep the group from making progress. Overtly, it may take the form of rebellion by group members against the leader (Saravay, 1978). Covertly, it is demonstrated when group members get bogged down in details and become preoccupied with the unimportant (Corey, 2004). If the group is to make progress, then resistance must be confronted. Although the group leader may take the initiative in doing this, group members may also confront one another about the behaviors being displayed in the group. For example, Juanita may say to Skip, "I sense you are reluctant for us to talk about our past histories. Every time the subject comes up, you say 'Let's wait and discuss that later.'" Psychoanalytically oriented group work is an especially good approach to use with very resistant clients.

Transference

Transference can be displayed by individuals or by groups. In a group, transference is "a specific form of interpersonal perceptual distortion" in which persons project inappropriate emotions and unresolved conflicts onto a group leader or group members (Lev-Wiesel, 2003, p. 230). It usually occurs when members have come to know one another fairly well. A manifestation of transference might be when Jill says to Randy, "You really don't like me. I can just tell it from the way you look at me."

In psychoanalysis, transference is encouraged, and clients are helped to work through unresolved experiences of the past and gain insight into their present patterns of interaction. Group members can often assist one another in this process, which Wolf (1975) describes as the most important work in psychoanalytic groups.

Participants in psychoanalytically oriented groups are helped to see patterns of transference when the group leader directs their attention to present interactions and invites them to examine how much they are investing in relationships with one another and the leader. Transference in group psychoanalysis has broader dimensions than in individual psychoanalysis.

Projective Identification

Projective identification, sometimes just referred to as **identification,** is one of the most complex and potentially disruptive behaviors that can occur in a group. The manifestation of projective identification involves multiple members and occurs, for example, when an individual who "experiences marked self-contempt projects these feelings onto another person in the group. . . . The projector then vicariously identifies with the recipient's feelings of self-contempt," and other members of the group are drawn into either scapegoating or counterattacking (Clark, 1997, p. 85). The result is that group development is arrested, and in place of trust feelings of shame, hostility, and aggression surface.

To combat this destructive dynamic, which may even be directed at the group leader, a psychoanalytic group worker must use a combination of group skills, including moderating and clarifying projective identification, blocking, confronting, cognitively restructuring, reframing, and interpreting behavior patterns (Clark, 1997). The employment of these measures first involves recognizing what is happening in the group. If projective identification develops without measures being taken to counter it, then the group may reach a point at which the leader is limited in what he or she can do.

◆ *Questions from Experience* ◆

When have you seen any of the psychoanalytic techniques just described used whether professionally or not? What was your impression of the effectiveness of the techniques you saw displayed?

Role of the Psychoanalytically Oriented Group Leader

The role of the psychoanalytically oriented group leader varies with the characteristics and emphases of the groups he or she is leading. The stage of the group's development is an important variable as well. As a rule, psychoanalytic group leaders should be objective, warm, and relatively anonymous. They should strive to conceal, rather than reveal, information about themselves while at the same time attempting to foster transference. The group leader should promote a positive atmosphere within the group to help members feel free to explore and express themselves. They should also have directional and stimulational skills to keep the group moving and revitalize it if it gets bogged down in resistance (Slavson, 1964).

The psychoanalytic group leader is of necessity not a member of the group but, at the same time, he or she must avoid taking a dictatorial attitude toward group members. The leaders who function most effectively try to transfer some leadership responsibility to the group when appropriate (Wolf, 1963; Wolf & Schwartz, 1962). They should recognize each participant's potential to contribute to the good of the group as well as the potential power of the group as a whole.

Psychoanalytic group leaders should acknowledge their mistakes while making every effort to guide members toward their fullest development by encouraging transference and discouraging destructive alliances. Wolf (1963) believes that effective psychoanalytic group leaders promote members' interpersonal relationships above member and group leader relationships. Foulkes (1964) thinks that because psychoanalytically oriented group leaders do not wish to be the main attention of the groups they facilitate, they should be referred to as **conductors**.

CASE EXAMPLE: Ivan the Interpreter

After years of doing individual analysis, Ivan decided to conduct a group. He read the literature on what a psychoanalytic group leader should do and plunged right in. The group generally went well, except that Ivan tended to be authoritarian. He kept tight reins on the group and consistently spent so much time making interpretations of what was happening that group members started referring to him as "Ivan the Interpreter."

From what you know about leadership in psychoanalytic groups, what would you advise Ivan to do to make the group better?

Desired Outcome of Psychoanalytically Oriented Groups

Psychoanalytic group theory emphasizes stages of development of individual group members rather than of the group as a whole. Therefore, psychoanalytically oriented group work differs from other therapeutic systems that concentrate attention on the growth of the group. Wolf (1963) notes that not all clients pass through the same stage of treatment at the same time, but, for those who do, the desired **stages of psychoanalytically oriented groups** are as follows:

1. *Preliminary individual analysis*—In this stage, all individuals in the group are interviewed individually by the group leader. Their suitability for the group experience is assessed along with their diagnostic difficulty. Persons found to be too anxious or potentially unsettling for a group experience are referred for individual treatment. Ground rules for conducting group sessions are explored at this time.

2. *Establishment of rapport through dreams and fantasies*—Group members are asked to discuss a recent dream, recurring dream, or fantasy they have. The idea is to encourage group participation by having members report on themselves and help others interpret or free-associate on their experience. This stage usually begins around the second or third session of the group.

3. *Analysis of resistance*—This stage manifests itself when group members become reluctant to share themselves with others. At such times, individual defenses are examined and handled. Resistance may take many forms, but it is usually recognized when group participants are either too cooperative or too reluctant. For example, if Natasha says to the leader, "I'm ready to do anything you ask me to do," she may be essentially resisting initiatives to change and is passing control of the group to the leader instead of to herself. The task of the group leader is to uncover and correct these barriers to therapeutic growth.

4. *Analysis of transference*—Transference occurs when participants project feelings onto the group leader, other group members, or significant others. Transference basically gets in the way of reality testing. In this stage, then, the focus is on discovering and breaking up "irrelevant, repetitious, and irrational ways of viewing others" (Hansen, Warner, & Smith, 1980, p. 49). In this process, transference interactions are examined as close to the time of their occurrence as possible. Individual members are also asked to examine their feelings and involvement with other members of the group. For example, Paula may be asked to look at how she always blames others when she does not get her way. Her "your fault" way of dealing with failure is thereby challenged when group members respond to her accusations by making her examine what she might be doing that contributes to failures.

5. *Working through*—In this stage, individuals are required to accompany insight with action (Wolf, 1949). For example, if Paula realizes that she is her own worst obstacle to accomplishing goals, then she will be challenged by the group to start acting differently. The process of working through involves the participants' resolution of transference investments. The ability to deal with transference appropriately enables clients to terminate from the group.

6. *Reorientation and social integration*—The last stage of psychoanalytically oriented group treatment is reached when clients demonstrate that they are able to
   deal appropriately with the realities and pressures of life. This means they do
   not become overanxious or overcompliant when requests are made of them.

Hansen et al. (1980) note that the six-stage model of psychoanalytic group change is not as
distinct as presented here. Participants develop at different levels and may regress at different times in the group. Nevertheless, it is desirable that they pass through all six stages.
It is usually the group leader who decides when a person has made a good adjustment and
is ready to leave the group.

Evaluation of Psychoanalytically Oriented Groups

As with other methods, a psychoanalytical orientation in groups presents both strengths
and drawbacks. By realizing these factors before a group begins, leaders and members will
be able to benefit most from this model for group work.

Strengths and Contributions

A major advantage of psychoanalytically oriented groups compared with individual psychoanalysis is that group members can experience transference feelings with others in the
group as well as with the group leader (i.e., **multiple transferences**) (Esman, 1990). The
broad range of feelings that are generated and worked through in a group enables individuals to learn more about themselves than they might otherwise.

A second strength of the psychoanalytic group approach is that members have an
opportunity to work with others in the group to resolve current as well as past problems.
For example, Valbak (2001) reported good outcomes for most bulimic patients involved in
long-term group analysis. In their treatment, the individuals in this group were able not
only to work on their current dysfunctional behaviors but also to resolve some past difficulties. Because of the emphases on the past and the present, therapeutic progress can be
made more rapidly in some cases than would otherwise be possible if treatment were
focused on only one dimension of life.

A third plus for psychoanalytically oriented groups is that group members realize that
they each experience and express a wide range of feelings. In a successful group, members
develop "their capacities to contain, express, and integrate a full range of positive and negative affective components" even if some of these emotions have historically been over-
whelming (Nusbaum, 2000, pp. 300–301). Thus, members within the group demonstrate
different feelings, and everyone learns that uncomfortable emotions can be released without unduly upsetting oneself or group members.

A final strength of this type of group is its emphasis on long-term personality change
through the group process (Moreno, 1998). For individuals who need major changes in
the ways they interact with others at a basic level, psychoanalytically oriented groups may
be beneficial. They are usually conducted in psychiatric hospital settings and complement
other long-term change treatments used in such environments. They are often open
ended, so members can take maximum advantage of the help they can offer. For example,
Kleinberg (1995) suggests that adults in midlife can be significantly helped through group

treatment to work through stagnation, both in the group and in their own lives, and in the process become more generative.

Limitations

The limitations of psychoanalytically oriented groups are pointed out by those with and without an analytic background. One contention is that free association is not possible in a group setting. Group members tend to be interrupted in groups and may be unable to link their thoughts. Locke (1961) answers this criticism by stating that it is not absolutely necessary that free association come from one person. Comments from others may contribute significantly to the free association of the entire group or the individual.

A second limitation of the psychoanalytic approach to group work is that too often those within the "psychoanalytic establishment" read and absorb only their own papers and thoughts (Ruitenbeek, 1970). This type of inbreeding prevents more creative thinking and innovations. For instance, as noted previously, psychoanalytically oriented groups are mainly employed in counseling and psychotherapeutic settings. Do they also have potential for psychoeducational and task/work groups? At this point, because of the isolation of practitioners and theorists, that question has barely been addressed.

A third criticism of the psychoanalytically oriented groups is that the theory on which they are based is deterministic, biologically biased, and oriented toward a pathological view of human nature. Those who criticize psychoanalytic groups from this basis point out that the aim of such groups is geared toward "coping" rather than growth. They also state that women may experience bias in these experiences, especially if they are nontraditional women, and that group members in general may be perceived as "sick" rather than "stuck" in their development. In general, these critics point out that psychoanalysis as a theory seems to overanalyze everything, even in groups.

Finally, psychoanalytically oriented groups and the theory of psychoanalysis are criticized for a lack of openness to rigorous scientific investigation. Case reports, rather than empirically designed comparison studies, are most often used to document the effectiveness of the theory and its method. Critics of this approach point out the need for more rigor in determining for whom this theoretical group approach is best suited.

Learning More

Psychoanalytical theory and its application to group work are among the oldest approaches still practiced today. This way of working with groups is based on a number of concepts originated by Sigmund Freud and his disciples. Many psychoanalytically based practitioners of group work belong to the

American Group Psychotherapy Association, Inc.
25 East 21st Street, 6th Floor
New York, NY 10010
212-477-2677
www.groupsinc.org

This association sponsors seminars, institutes, and conferences, and it produces the *International Journal of Group Psychotherapy,* which is widely read and respected. Other publications relevant to psychoanalysis are the *Psychoanalytic Quarterly,* the *International*

Journal of Psychoanalysis, the *American Psychoanalytic Association Journal, the International Psychoanalytic Review,* the *Chicago Annual of Psychoanalysis,* and the *International Journal of Psychoanalytic Psychotherapy*. A wealth of contemporary literature is available on psychoanalysis and its various applications to modern life, including working with groups.

TRANSACTIONAL ANALYSIS GROUPS

Transactional analysis (TA) has been oriented toward groups since its inception. In TA groups, the emphasis is on understanding intrapersonal and interpersonal dynamics and participatory learning through interaction and homework assignments. TA theorists and practitioners have explored cultural frames of reference and intergroup encounters, too (James, 1994). Eric Berne believed that groups are more efficient in helping individuals understand their personal life scripts than individual counseling or psychotherapy (Barnes, 1977; Berne, 1966). However, to participate in a group, individuals must learn basic TA concepts, such as "ego state," "stroke," and "script" (Newell, 2002). They must also be willing to work on past experiences in a present context.

For the **redecision school of TA** (Goulding, 1987), in which the emphasis is on intrapsychic processes, groups are the main choice of treatment. Groups provide a living experience in which members are able to examine themselves and their histories in a precise way. Individuals can then change their life scripts. For the other two schools of TA— **classic**, which emphasizes present interactions (Berne, 1964), and **cathexis**, which emphasizes reparenting (James, 2002)—groups are also employed frequently. Thus, the emphasis of TA groups is on both interpersonal (i.e., the classic model) and intrapersonal (i.e., the cathexis and redecision models) (Barnes, 1977). In addition, TA is geared toward working on task/work group communication processes, such as those between employer and employee and among co-workers (Nykodym, Ruud, & Liverpool, 1986).

Premises of Transactional Analysis Groups

TA theory has multiple aspects (Hargaden & Sills, 2002). The basic concepts revolve around the development and interaction of what Berne (1964) called an **ego state**—"a system of feelings accompanied by a related set of behavior patterns" (p. 23). Three basic ego states—Parent, Adult, and Child—exist and operate within every individual and can be observed in the dynamic interactions of individuals with one another (Rath, 1993) (see Figure 15.1).

Each ego state functions in its own special way, as follows:

1. The **Parent ego state** is dualistic—both nurturing and critical (or controlling). "The function of the *Critical Parent* is to store and dispense the rules and protection for living. The function of the *Nurturing Parent* is to care for, to nurture" (Grimes, 1988, p. 53). Typical statements from the Critical Parent are "Be home by seven" and "Watch what you are doing." Typical statements from the Nurturing Parent are "Rest for a while" and "Here, let me take your coat."

Figure 15.1

TA ego states.

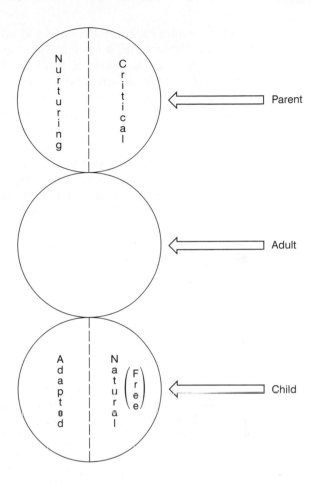

2. The **Adult ego state** functions like a computer in that it receives and processes information from the Parent, the Child, and the environment. It then makes the best decision possible. The Adult is the realistic, logical part of the person. A typical statement coming from the adult is "The appointment is this afternoon. I need to be on time."

3. The **Child ego state** is divided into two parts. The *Adapted Child* conforms to the rules and wishes of Parent ego states within the self and others. It is compliant and easy to get along with. A typical Adapted Child statement would be "I'm going to do what you ask because I am a good boy/girl." The *Free Child* (or *Natural Child*) reacts more spontaneously. It has fun and is curious and playful. It takes care of its needs without regard for others while using its intuition to read nonverbal cues. For instance, the Free Child might say, "Come on, let's have fun!"

There are four basic ways to identify which ego state individuals are in at a particular moment: behavioral, social, historical, and phenomenological (Woollams, Brown, & Huige, 1977). It is important to be aware of the ego states of people, for it affects the manner in which they interact with themselves and others. For example, a person who is operating from a Parent ego state is more likely to be critical or supportive than is a person who is operating from a Child ego state. Likewise, if an individual uses one ego state exclusively—for example, the Adult—then he or she is less likely to be flexible in thought and action than is a person who uses all three ego states.

Knowledge of their own ego states empowers individuals and those working with them to assess which types of transactions they are most likely to have and to take corrective measures, if needed (Hargaden & Sills, 2002). This type of information helps these persons avoid playing **"games,"** which Berne (1964) defined as "an ongoing series of complementary ulterior transactions progressing to a well-defined, predictable outcome" (p. 48). Games are played on three levels, and almost all of them are destructive and result in negative payoffs (i.e., *rackets*). *First-degree games* are the least harmful and may even be considered socially acceptable (e.g., "Blemish"). In these games, minor faults are highlighted, such as when Pat says to Suzanne, "You look great except for your hair." *Second-degree games* are more serious and usually result in some physical confrontation (e.g., "Uproar"). The interactive process in second-degree games leaves the people involved feeling negative, such as when Jim is called names by Mohammed. *Third-degree games* are deadly and often played for keeps (e.g., "Cops and Robbers"). There is nothing socially redeemable about third-degree games, for example, if Ed is caught stealing from the elderly and tries to fight his way free from the police.

People who play games operate from three distinct positions: (a) the *victim* (who appears to be innocent), (b) the *persecutor* (who appears to cause problems), and (c) the *rescuer* (who is seen as a problem solver or hero to the victim). Individuals who play games often switch between these roles as the *drama triangle* (Karpman, 1968) illustrates (see Figure 15.2). Games have a social as well as an individual dynamic, and they are often played on a group or organizational level on either an intra- or intergroup basis (Summerton, 1993).

TA also emphasizes several other beliefs about human nature. For instance, it holds that persons are born with positive tendencies to grow and develop, but this potential must be nurtured to become a reality (Dusay & Steiner, 1971). It likewise stresses that individuals structure their time to obtain **strokes** (i.e., physical or psychological recognition) in six major ways: (a) withdrawal, (b) ritual, (c) pastimes, (d) work, (e) games, and (f) intimacy (Berne, 1972). These ways of interacting can be represented through the use of an **egogram** (i.e., a bar graph) and will not change unless a person actively decides to change the amount of time spent engaging in certain behaviors (Dusay & Dusay, 1989) (see Figure 15.3).

Figure 15.2

Drama (Karpman) triangle.

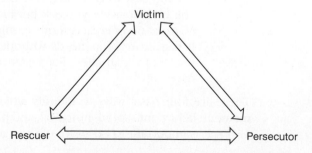

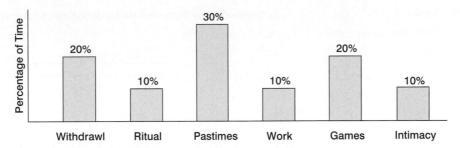

Figure 15.3

An egogram.

Over their life span, people gradually develop **scripts**, or habitual patterns of behavior, that influence how they spend their time—for example, as losers, nonwinners, or winners (Berne, 1972; Capers, 1975). Most people initially script their lives as a Child in the *I'm Not OK—You're OK* stance (i.e., powerless) but change to an Adult stance in later life as they affirm an *I'm OK—You're OK* position (characterized by trust and openness) (Harris, 1967). Other options open to them are *I'm OK—You're Not OK* (i.e., projection of blame onto others) and *I'm Not OK—You're Not OK* (i.e., hopeless and self-destructive).

Scripts include **transactions** (i.e., social action between two or more people). These transactions are manifested in social (overt) and psychological (covert) levels (Dusay & Dusay, 1989). Clear transactions with no hidden agenda are *complementary transactions*. For example,

Person 1:	What time is it?
Person 2:	It is 3 o'clock.

Crossed transactions are those in which a response is returned from an unexpected or inappropriate ego state. When this occurs, the person initiating the conversation often feels hurt and withdraws. Here is an example:

Person 1	(Adult ego state): What time is it?
Person 2	(Critical Parent): You are always in a hurry.

Ulterior transactions (which are often represented by dotted lines) (Dusay & Dusay, 1989) occur when a message appears to be sent on one level but is actually transmitted on another level. Often such transactions will seem to be from an Adult ego state but are actually coming from the Child. They are represented by the designation "Adult/Child."

Person 1	(Adult/Child message): Want some coffee at my place?
Person 2	(Adult/Child message): I'd really like that.

Figure 15.4 illustrates these three transactions.

Through transactions, individuals receive strokes (i.e., physical or psychological recognition). Strokes can be anything from a quick glance to a verbal comment. When positive strokes are not forthcoming, persons will work for negative strokes by using ulterior means. Games are the result and bad feelings the payoff in such cases.

Figure 15.4

Three types of interpersonal transactions.

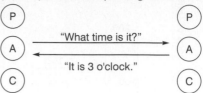

1. *Complementary* (both persons are operating from the same ego state)

"What time is it?"

"It is 3 o'clock."

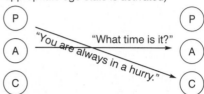

2. *Crossed* (an inappropriate ego state is activated)

"What time is it?"

"You are always in a hurry."

3. *Ulterior* (two ego states operate simultaneously, one disguises the other)

"Want some coffee at my place?"

"I'd really like that."

"Want to fool around?"

"Sure."

◆ *Questions from Experience* ◆

When have you seen people operating from what TA describes as parent, adult, child ego states? In examining your own life, from which ego states do you see yourself operating frequently? What do you think about the concepts of games? When have you seen them being played?

Practice of Transactional Analysis in a Group

TA is preferably used in groups. Groups serve as a setting in which people can become more aware of themselves, the structure of their individual personality, the transactions they have with others, the games they play, and the scripts they act out. Such awareness enables persons to see themselves more clearly so that they can change what they want to change and strengthen what they want to strengthen (James & Jongeward, 1971). TA is most appropriate in such settings as classrooms, especially when combined with behavioral approaches, to help children move into the OK position (Newell, 2002).

According to Berne (1966), the objective in group treatment settings is to "fight the past in the present in order to assure the future" (p. 250). The Child and Parent ego states represent the past, whereas the present is embodied in the Adult. There needs to be appropriate relations among these three ego states for people to function productively. The Adult ultimately needs to be most dominant in deciding which ego state will be displayed.

Therapeutic Contracts

All TA groups are based on the participants' ability and willingness to make and work on **therapeutic contracts** (Dusay & Dusay, 1989; Stewart, 2000). Contracts are specific, measurable, concrete statements of what participants intend to accomplish during the group. They place responsibility on members for clearly defining what, how, and when they want to change. Contracts can be made in all types of groups: task/work, psychoeducational, counseling, and psychotherapeutic. From the beginning of groups, members should learn that change is a shared responsibility and that they cannot passively wait for the group leader to assume the direction for working in a group. In short, the contract establishes the departure point for group activity. Well-written contracts make it clear that participants are getting what they want from the group (Dusay, 1983). They are based on decisions made by the Adult ego state (Dusay & Dusay, 1989).

Generally, "TA contracts have the four major components of a legal contract" (Dusay & Dusay, 1989, p. 428). These aspects include (a) *mutual assent*—clearly defining a goal from an adult perspective and joining with the therapist's Adult as an ally, (b) *competency*—agreeing on what can realistically be expected, (c) *legal object*—an objective, and (d) *consideration*—a fee or price for services. An example of a group contract is an agreement by members of an industrial group to remain together long enough to complete a mutually agreed-on activity, such as eliminating discriminatory language from company contracts. An individual contract includes personal goals, such as giving individuals in one's daily life more compliments than criticisms. Group members usually meet weekly to assess the progress made in pursuing their goals.

Classic Contracts

Classic school contracts are carried out with an emphasis on one or more of the following: (a) structural analysis, (b) transactional analysis, (c) game analysis, and (d) life script analysis (Berne, 1961). "To achieve the most complete treatment, all four need to be accomplished; each one is built upon the previous level and must be completed in order" (Donigian & Hulse-Killacky, 1999, p. 116). In *structural analysis,* all group members become aware of the structure of their ego states and how they function. Members are encouraged to "decontaminate" any ego state that is not operating properly. An example of a contaminated ego state occurs when a person who appears to speak from the Adult ego state is instead speaking from the Parent ego state, as in, "Children should be seen and not heard."

TA involves the diagnosing of interactions among group members to determine whether they are *complementary* (i.e., from appropriate and expected ego states), *crossed* (i.e., from inappropriate and unexpected ego states), or *ulterior* (i.e., from a disguised ego state, such as the Child speaking as if it were an Adult).

Game analysis includes an examination of destructive and repetitive behavioral patterns and an analysis of the ego states and types of transactions involved. Because games prevent intimacy (Berne, 1964), it is crucial that they be eliminated. The classical TA group devotes considerable time to helping members become aware of the games they initiate and participate in. With this knowledge, they can come to develop intimate and nonmanipulative relationships (Corey, 2004).

Finally, on the deepest level, classic TA school groups do **life script analyses**, which are people's basic plans involving transactions and games (Steiner, 1974). Typically, scripts are made on an unconscious level when individuals are children (before age 5). They determine life plans, such as living a tragic or happy existence (Berne, 1961). It is said that Berne lived a tragic life script, choosing to die of a "broken heart" at age 60 like his mother, without having known real intimacy (Steiner, 1974). As a general rule, script analysis is difficult to do in a group. Feelings resulting from such an experience, such as depression or discouragement, must be handled carefully and skillfully.

Redecision Contracts

Groups have within them curative factors because of their social nature (Berne, 1966). All properly conducted TA groups give their members knowledge and insight into their lives. A special form of TA, **redecision theory**, helps clients make redecisions while they are in their Child ego state (Goulding & Goulding, 1979; McCormick, 1995). This task is accomplished by having these individuals reexperience a past event as if it were now present. This process usually involves combining TA and Gestalt approaches and may be geared toward individuals or couples in a group (Tyler, 1995). Persons who engage in the redecision process first make a contract to address significant symptoms they wish to change. Then they take actions that focus on rackets and games they have experienced. They are taught that they are responsible for both their feelings and their actions (Goulding, 1975).

The next step of this process is for group members to explore the sources that led them to make a particular life decision. Accountability is stressed as is power for changing. Helpless or so-called cop-out words, such as *can't, perhaps,* and *try,* are not accepted. Once members redecide and make a change by actually reliving psychologically an early scene from their past, group members offer them reinforcement and encouragement to continue. Group leaders help such individuals focus on how they will conduct themselves in a new way outside the group and develop a needed support system to continue the changes they have made. Fantasizing what lies ahead and how they will cope is also a part of this process (Goulding, 1987).

Role of the Transactional Analysis Group Leader

TA group leaders are more than just members of the groups they lead. They stand apart as "primarily listeners, observers, diagnosticians, and analysts—and, secondarily, process facilitators" (Donigian & Hulse-Killacky, 1999, p. 115). These groups are leader centered and, although member–member transactions occur, they do not have the same effect as a leader–member interaction.

Overall, transactions in TA groups that are between the group leader and a member are considered major; those that occur among group members are minor. A group is functioning optimally when major and minor transactions involving all members take place and when attitudinal and behavioral changes occur in group members. By staying detached, the leader is able to see more clearly than group members the games that are occurring and is thereby able to analyze and intervene more dynamically than individual members can.

It is vital that TA group leaders understand themselves well from a TA perspective and that they adopt an "I'm OK" life position because they are teachers within the group. They must have a thorough understanding of how TA concepts operate in their own lives before they try to help others apply these concepts. Also, if TA leaders are going to be able to establish rapport with group members and help them change, then they must think well of themselves most of the time.

The leader has four specific roles within the TA group (Corey, 2004; Grimes, 1988). **Protection** involves keeping members safe from psychological or physical harm. **Permission** centers on giving group members directives to behave against the injunctions of their parents. (**Injunctions** are Parent commands recorded by the Child that call for the Child to adopt certain roles, such as "Do as you are told.") **Potency** is the use of appropriate counseling techniques in certain situations. For example, making a contract for change and active listening are two appropriate and potent counseling techniques. Finally, **operations** are very specific techniques employed by TA group leaders that include interrogation, specification, confrontation, explanation, illustration, confirmation, interpretation, and crystallization (Berne, 1966; Gladding, 2005). For instance, a group leader may confront a member about the inconsistencies shown between the member's speech and behavior.

Desired Outcome of Transactional Analysis Groups

If a TA group is successful, then group members will learn about themselves through their analysis of structures, transactions, games, and scripts. The knowledge they acquire from this process will enable them to think, feel, and behave differently if they so choose. They are freed from old Parent messages (injunctions) and early, self-defeating scripts made by their Child. They may adopt an "I'm OK—You're OK" position in life and "get on" with themselves in a positive way (Newell, 2002).

Woollams and Brown (1978) view the process that leads to this desired outcome as going through seven steps: (a) trust in the other, (b) trust in self, (c) moving into group, (d) work, (e) redecision, (f) integration, and (g) termination. These steps are usually intertwined, and rarely can they be distinguished from one another. At the point of termination, however, group members should have accomplished what they set out to do or have a contract for finishing their goal(s) (Tudor, 1995). TA promotes the integration of the person in multimodal ways; however, the outcome in TA is not likely to be accomplished unless its practitioners borrow behavioral and affective techniques and procedures from other theories.

CASE EXAMPLE: Thomas and the TA Group

Thomas was tired of always being put down by his peers. Therefore, when a chance came for him to join a TA counseling group, he jumped at it. He thought that through the use of TA in a group he could gain a greater perspective on both himself and those with whom he associated.

He was not disappointed. He signed a contract to work on the way he presented himself to others and got down to work immediately. Through the group he realized that he often spoke from his Child Ego State and that he invited criticism and putdowns in his life from the Parent Ego State of many of his acquaintances. Therefore, Thomas made modifications in his speech patterns. He learned to speak more often from the Adult Ego State and he stopped himself from getting hooked into playing games with others.

Thomas's success is truly inspirational. Why do you think he would be a typical or atypical member of a TA group? Besides modifying his ego states speech, what other tools do you think a TA group could help Thomas learn and how might they help him?

Evaluation of Transactional Analysis Groups

TA groups are potentially powerful ways of helping individuals work together for the good of themselves and others. However, they have limits as well as strengths.

Strengths and Contributions

There are a number of strengths associated with employing TA theory in group work. First is the cognitive clarity of the language used to explain TA concepts (Grimes, 1988; Yalom, 2005). TA works in groups by helping members to understand how they function intra- and interpersonally and how they came to make the decisions in life they did. The clarity of TA concepts is also useful in helping group members realize what they need to do to change. This approach stresses intellectual insight as the initial basis for doing things differently.

A second strength of TA is its simplicity (O'Hearne, 1977). TA concepts can be readily grasped, and the theory can be used in its most elementary form in just a few hours. The almost immediate applicability of TA makes it popular with group leaders who want their members to gain intellectual understanding quickly and make practical strides in resolving difficult relationships (Sigmund, 1995).

Another strength of using TA in groups is that individuals "move faster toward getting well" (Harris, 1967, p. 204). Group members who make progress toward achieving their goals reinforce others in the group to do the same. This dynamic, although not particularly emphasized, occurs in both subtle and overt ways and helps group members achieve results not possible in individual treatment formats.

A final strength of using TA in groups is that it can be used in task/work, psychoeducational, counseling, and psychotherapy settings, and it can be combined effectively with other more action-centered approaches, such as Gestalt or behavioral, to produce a dynamic method of change (Goulding & Goulding, 1979; James & Jongeward, 1971; Newell, 2002; Tyler, 1995). Such combinations help group members put their contracts and thoughts into achievable forms.

Limitations

A major drawback of TA is its restrictive interpretation of the complexities of human nature by categorizing them into a limited number of games, ego states, and scripts (Yalom, 2005). People are more complex than the concepts of TA, and group members may find themselves restricted in dealing with complicated situations because of a shortage of TA concepts to describe what is happening. It is also difficult to use TA language uniformly and correctly.

A second limitation of TA in groups is its strong emphasis on understanding. This cognitive focus is further complicated because some TA leaders use the structure and vocabulary of TA to "avoid genuine contact with their clients or to keep them from revealing their reactions" (Corey, 2004, p. 356). These types of behaviors set up barriers and constitute a misuse of TA theory while lessening the impact of the approach on participants. "If the group becomes immersed in analysis to the exclusion of spontaneous interaction and emotional expression, it has the potential to become merely an intellectual exercise" (Vander Kolk, 1985, p. 66).

Another limitation of TA in groups is its neglect of emphasizing group process (Yalom, 2005). TA centers largely on member–leader interaction and does not effectively use other group dynamics, such as interpersonal learning, cohesiveness, and universality. Future research in TA needs to focus on controlled research designs that will allow investigators to contrast and compare TA techniques in groups uniformly (Kapur & Miller, 1987).

A fourth limitation of the use of TA in groups is the lack of empirical evidence to support its effectiveness. Although Dusay and Dusay (1984) cite "hard data gain" as an outcome of TA treatment, little research has been done on TA groups per se. The *Transactional Analysis Journal* is interested in publishing such studies but so far has received relatively few.

Learning More

TA is akin to psychoanalysis in its emphasis on ego states. However, TA is much more cognitive in nature and is less concerned with the unconscious. There are hundreds of certified transactional analysts throughout the world. Most TA group practitioners belong to the

International Transactional Analysis Association (ITAA)
2186 Rheem Drive #B-1 Pleasanton, CA 94588
http://www.itaa-net.org/

The ITAA publishes material on TA theory and practice. Especially noteworthy is its professional periodical, the *Transactional Analysis Journal*. The ITAA also provides workshops and educational training in the practice of TA.

REALITY THERAPY GROUPS

Reality therapy has a dynamic history. Its growth and development have been phenomenal. Originally, reality therapy "had no systematic theory, only the empirical idea that individuals are responsible for what they do" (Glasser, 1984, p. 320). Glasser developed and employed his approach at the Ventura (California) School for Girls, his first employer. The approach is still quite popular in educational settings (Glasser, 1999; Stehno, 1995). In such settings, raising the self-esteem of low-achieving students and helping them alter their behaviors and attitudes are often emphasized (Comiskey, 1993; Williamson, 1992). Reality therapy has been used so successfully in educational settings that a Quality School Consortium of more than 200 schools using reality therapy principles has developed (www.wglasserinst.com/quality.htm/).

In addition, reality therapy has been applied to many populations of those seeking mental health services (Glasser, 1969, 1976, 1986b; Glasser & Breggin, 2001). Reality therapy has also gained a foothold in task/work environments, such as the **total quality movement (TQM)**, in which an emphasis is placed on working cooperatively and productively in small groups. It has also been examined in light of its sensitivity to cultural issues of clients and bias (Cunningham, 1995) and has been found to be effective in multiple cultures (e.g., In & Hwang, 1997; Peterson, Chang, & Collins, 1998).

Premises of Reality Therapy Groups

Reality therapy, as a theoretical approach, differs from other common-sense ways of working in groups. It emphasizes that "all behavior is generated within ourselves for the purpose of satisfying one or more basic need" (Glasser, 1984, p. 323). Unlike most other helping theories, Glasser claims that human behavior is a reaction not to outside events but rather to internal needs. **Reality therapy's four human psychological needs** are belonging, power, freedom, and fun, whose origin is the "new" human brain. There is also one physiological need, survival, which originated in the "old" human brain (Glasser, 1985). "No matter what the presenting problem, all clients seen in counseling are struggling unsuccessfully to satisfy one or more of these basic needs" (Glasser, 1986c, p. 3) (see Figure 15.5).

Glasser (1965, 1984, 1985, 1999, 2001, 2003) states that reality therapy also differs from other psychotherapeutic systems in the following ways:

1. It rejects the concept of mental illness. People choose to act psychotically or neurotically in an attempt to control the world to some extent and to satisfy their needs. The only behavior we can control is our own.
2. It emphasizes the present as the "cutting edge" of people's lives and focuses on how individuals can effectively control the world they live in and choose behaviors that are best for them. Such behavior is especially important in the four major personal relationships that cause problems: husband–wife, parent–child, teacher–student, and manager–worker.
3. It does not deal with transference but relates to clients' perceptions.
4. It does not consider the unconscious or dreams but rather present awareness in an attempt to make that awareness even greater.
5. It stresses that persons must judge their own behaviors in light of personal and societal values. Contrary to O. Hobart Mowrer's introduction to Glasser's first book, *Reality Therapy* (1965), reality therapists do not take a moral position.

Figure 15.5

Reality therapy as a theoretical therapy.

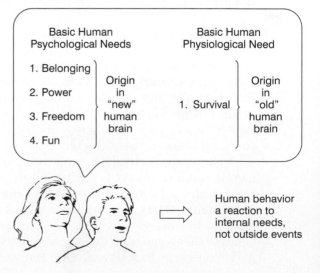

6. It attempts to teach people a better way of fulfilling their needs and taking responsibility for themselves. In essence, Glasser sees all psychotherapy as teaching and all psychoeducation as psychotherapeutic.

Glasser believes that third-force psychology with its humanistic emphasis, as represented by the writings of Abraham Maslow, is closely aligned with reality therapy. Mowrer's (1967) **integrity therapy**, which stresses helping people live up to their own moral convictions, also has much in common with reality therapy.

Yet, a main emphasis of reality therapy is also cognitive and behavioral in nature. Wubbolding (1991, 1992, 2001) has created an acronym, WDEP, as a pedagogical tool, that summarizes reality therapy and provides a memory peg for retaining, applying, and implementing the principles of reality therapy. In WDEP, W = wants, D = direction and doing, E = evaluation, and P = planning.

Practice of Reality Therapy in a Group

The practice of reality therapy in a group setting is basically a rational and pragmatic process. It emphasizes observable behavior in a here-and-now setting (Glasser, 1992, 2000). For example, what is someone in the group doing now in regard to personal and relationship difficulties? If the process goes smoothly, then group members will give up unproductive and self-defeating behaviors, such as trying to control others and making themselves miserable in the process. Instead, they will commit to new action patterns that they have mutually agreed on with the group leader (Bigelow & Thorne, 1969). One such choice might be to give up the belief that others are responsible for the ways they feel and to choose to accept the personal freedom they have to control their own thoughts, feelings, and behaviors.

Group leaders apply reality therapy concepts in many different ways. The main focus, however, is to help clients take responsibility for their actions, find better ways to meet their needs, and change inappropriate or destructive ways of behaving (Glasser & Breggin, 2001). Wubbolding (2001) is one of the masters of applying the theory to groups. He stressed that there are two main components involved in using reality therapy in groups: setting up the environment and applying proper procedures using the WDEP framework.

Setting up the environment involves establishing an atmosphere in which work within the group can take place. Wubbolding (1999, 2001) suggests a list of ABCDE do's and don't's: **A**lways **b**e **c**ourteous and **d**etermined as well as **e**nthusiastic (i.e., look for the positive). Don't **a**rgue, **b**elittle, **c**riticize, **d**emean, or get lost in **e**xcuses. In many ways, Wubbolding's suggestions for setting up the environment are similar to steps one, six, and seven of **Reality Therapy's original eight basic steps** (Glasser, 1984; Glasser & Zunin, 1973). All of the steps in the process are listed here, although reality therapy has evolved a great deal since its debut:

1. *Make friends/establish a meaningful relationship.* In this first step, the reality therapist attempts to establish rapport with each group member. People are usually involved in groups because of a need to connect with others. Therefore, the group leader can take the initial step in fulfilling this need. This process is achieved by having the group leader both screen applicants and then engage them in conversation or activity soon after they come to the group. In doing so, the leader

determines, with the help of the group member, what he or she pictures as a way of meeting his or her basic needs. This picture comes from within the internal world of the group member (Glasser, 1986c) and is drawn out by the leader through skillful questioning and interactions (Wubbolding, 1988).

2. *Emphasize present behaviors/Ask, "What are you doing now?"* This second step focuses in on the process of choice. Reality therapists stress the importance of using thinking and acting, rather than feeling or physiology, to bring about change (Glasser, 1986a). Therefore, group members are asked to concentrate on behaviors they can control in the present. For example, members have choices in the ways they think about and interact with other group members and the group leader. For instance, Willie can choose to avoid Florence and Jamie in the group, or he can face them and share with them his perception that they are always putting him down.

3. *Stress whether clients' actions are getting them what they want.* The emphasis here is on group members' judging their behaviors and learning that their behaviors are within their control. A part of this process focuses on personal values, whereas a second part underlines reasonable rules by which societal systems live. Persons with difficulties may be acting against their own best judgment or the collected wisdom of society (Glasser, 1986c). For example, if Tess becomes upset every time someone ignores her but her actions do not bring about changes, then she may be confronted with the fruitlessness of what she is doing.

4. *Make a positive plan to do better.* This is a critical stage in the group process. It involves "planning, advising, helping, and encouraging" (Glasser, 1984, p. 336). It is based on the accomplishment of the first three stages. The plan of action is the individual's, but group members and the leader can be effective in providing input and suggestions that will make the plan even more potent. Wubbolding (1988) suggests that an effective plan has the following components:
   a. Ties in closely with a member's needs
   b. Is simple and easy to understand
   c. Is realistic and attainable
   d. Includes positive actions
   e. Is independent of others' contributions
   f. Is practiced regularly
   g. Is immediately doable
   h. Is process oriented
   i. Is open to constructive input by group members by being written down and well formulated

5. *Get a commitment to follow the positive plan.* It is not enough to formulate a plan of action; group members must follow through. "A plan that does not have the client's firm commitment is likely to fail" (Barr, 1974, p. 67). In making a commitment, group members take responsibility for their lives and, in the process, gain more control. For example, if George commits himself to 15 minutes of exercise a day, then he achieves control of his body and time in a new way.

6. *No excuses.* At times, group members will not succeed in their plans of action. In such cases, the group leader and members simply acknowledge that the person failed. The past is not brought up, and excuses are not discussed. Accepting

excuses gives persons in the group the idea that they are weak, cannot change, and are, in effect, unable to control their lives (Wubbolding, 1988, 1991). Instead, individuals are helped to formulate another plan (usually a modification of the original one) and are encouraged to try again. Sometimes the plan is broken down into smaller steps than previously for, as Glasser and Zunin (1973) point out, "It is much better to have client success in small stages than to try to effect a large change and experience failure" (p. 301).

7. *No punishment.* "Punishment is the infliction of pain with no reasonable way to reduce or end the pain no matter what the wrongdoer does" (Glasser, 1984, p. 337). It is the opposite of choice and control and often leads to individuals acting in negative or self-defeating ways. Therefore, reality therapy (similar to Adlerian-based theory) stresses that persons who do not follow their plans of action must live with the natural consequences. This usually means they do not get what they want. This type of response, along with the group's encouragement, will often motivate them to try again.

8. *Never give up.* Change often takes time, especially if the client has a long history of failure. Group leaders persevere with group members who are slow to change. This consistency begins to become internalized by clients. They realize that the leader is like a good friend who does not give up easily. With this realization, they often become more willing to try new behaviors, and the process of change can begin. For example, Betsy may internally remind herself that her group leader still believes she can lose the weight she committed to dropping. Therefore, she renews her commitment and effort.

In addition to this eight-step procedure, Wubbolding (1988, 1991) suggests four special techniques that are applicable to setting up the environment of a reality therapy group: (a) skillful use of questioning, (b) self-help procedures, (c) use of humor, and (d) use of paradox.

Skillful *questioning* has already been covered. It is crucial that the group leader ask open-ended and inviting questions to help members become more explorative. For example, the leader might say, "Clarence, what do you hope to get out of this group?"

Self-help procedures are those in which there is a focus on the positive. Behaviors that members would like to change are targeted. A real effort is made by the member and the group to implement actions, such as learning new social skills, that will lead to success.

Glasser advocates the use of *humor* in many of his publications. Wubbolding's emphasis on this procedure is to stress its timing, focus, and the importance of trust in the process. Humor should never put people down. Rather, it should be used to help individuals gain an awareness of a situation not easily obtainable in another way. For example, in regard to self, the group leader might say, "Whenever I think I've learned all the answers about groups, the groups change the questions."

Finally, in regard to using **paradox**, Wubbolding (1999) stresses that with some group members, change is best brought about indirectly rather than directly, as Glasser recommends. In these situations, the power of humor (catching someone "off guard") is often effective, but there is a danger of being misunderstood. To be successful, group leaders may employ paradox (i.e., asking members to do the opposite of what they want) so that the message they give, such as "go slowly," is taken seriously and disobeyed for the good of the group member. Most reality therapy group leaders are not initially able to use paradox successfully.

Applying proper procedures in working with groups using the WDEP framework revolves around specific behaviors. In the "W" part of this process, group members are asked what they want. The question is geared toward cultural considerations and the commitment of the person in the group. The leader presses for both specifics of the answer and a level of commitment indicating that the person is fully dedicated to achieving the want and will do what it takes to reach a goal. The "D" part of the procedure is initially focused on what the person is doing but extends to where he or she is going. If a camera could take a picture of both the doing and the going aspects of the person's life, then the person, group members, and the group leader would have a clear idea of the person's present reality and direction.

"E" represents self-evaluation and is to reality therapy what interpretation is to psychoanalysis—the directive to strategic therapy and the disputation to REBT (Wubbolding, 1999). A self-evaluation can take a behavioral, emotional, or cognitive form. The important thing is that this evaluation must be realistic and honest. Finally, there is the "P" part of Wubbolding's way of working in groups. The P stands for a plan of action. It is direction based, outlining where the person should go. A good plan is **s**imple, **a**ttainable, **m**easurable, **i**mmediate, and **c**ontrolled by the planner. Wubbolding (1999) combines the first letters of the words describing good plan to form the acronym SAMIC. He, like Glasser, believes that a group leader must be persistent and never give up on a client, although the leader may work with the client to develop a new plan.

◆ *Questions from Experience* ◆

One of the major tenets of reality/choice therapy is to never give up on a person. When have you seen that idea work? What made it work? Are there circumstances where it would be best to give up on a person?

Role of the Reality Therapy Group Leader

As has been noted, reality therapy group leaders are active and involved with group members. They strive to be warm, confronting individuals who keep pointing out reality to group members in a direct, caring manner. For example, as the group leader, George may say to June, "Is what you are doing now working?"

Glasser (1965) lists four criteria for effective reality therapy leaders. First, they must be responsible persons who are able to fulfill their own needs. Next, they must be mentally strong and able to resist group members' pleas for sympathy and excuses for nonproductive behavior. A third quality is acceptance of group members for who they are, at least initially. Finally, reality therapy group leaders must be emotionally involved or supportive of each group member. Fulfilling these criteria is developmental. Leaders must be mentally and emotionally mature and comfortable with themselves before they can work with group members and help them bring about needed changes.

Corey (2004) states that reality therapy practitioners must strive to carry out other functions, too. Among the most prevalent is serving as a personal model of responsible behavior (i.e., being a success identity). Group members are likely to emulate leaders whether leaders wish them to or not. In addition to working in this way, reality therapy group leaders must also foster the process of self-evaluation in their members. They may do this through modeling the self-evaluation process in themselves. Furthermore, leaders establish a structure and limits for group sessions and assist group members in understanding the scope of the group process and the need to apply what they have learned in the group to their own daily lives. Hansen et al. (1980) state that in carrying out their responsibilities within the group, reality therapy leaders will generally be eclectic in the techniques they employ.

Desired Outcome of Reality Therapy Groups

If the reality therapy group process is successful, then members will realize several benefits. Among the most important is the change they will experience in moving past self-defeating patterns of behavior. These individuals will no longer be stuck in repetitive and nonproductive activity. Instead, they will engage in new behaviors designed to help them achieve responsible, present-oriented goals (Glasser, 1984, 1986c). They will realize that, just as the group leader did not give up or punish them when they were not successful with their positive plans of action, they do not have to become discouraged, defeated, or punitive when they do not initially achieve what they want.

Group members come away from the reality therapy experience with a greater awareness of their values. Through the group, they realize they have a choice in what they do (Glasser, 1986a). They are free to realize the role they play in taking control of their lives. Outside events and past histories lose much of their power if individuals learn one of the basic premises of the reality therapy approach—they are responsible and can choose to change.

CASE EXAMPLE: Raquel Becomes a Reality Therapy Leader

Raquel has been involved as a reality therapist for years. She holds the highest training credentials available, but she has never led a reality therapy group. So when she planned to launch her group from her regular client load she was a bit nervous. That anxiety was soon overcome as she got down to business.

Raquel chose a group of 10 adolescent, acting-out boys from her school and screened them. Nine expressed interest in her group for learning new behaviors and were chosen. Each week Raquel worked with the boys to make a plan and to stick with it. No excuses for failure were allowed, and she did not give up on even Burt, who had five straight weeks of not following through on what he proposed. When the 12-week group ended, the boys had bonded and were reluctant to end the experience. However, they all agreed that they were more successful than previously with their teachers, families, friends, and even themselves.

Do you think reality therapy is more successful on those whom others have given up on, or does the background of group members really make a difference? Why?

Evaluation of Reality Therapy Groups

Reality therapy has been used in a number of different kinds of groups and is among the most versatile of the theories used in groups. Nevertheless, it has limitations as well as strengths.

Strengths and Contributions

Several strengths of reality therapy make it an attractive and productive method to use in group settings. First, reality therapy emphasizes accountability (Wubbolding, 2001). Individuals are responsible for deciding what they value and wish to change in their lives. They learn that they must work on implementing these changes. Therefore, responsibility is placed squarely where it should be—on the shoulders of group members. They may act on the seven deadly habits that destroy relationships: "criticizing, blaming, complaining, nagging, threatening, punishing and bribing or rewarding to control," or they may improve their relationships through enacting the seven caring habits of relationships: "supporting, encouraging, listening, accepting, trusting, respecting, and negotiating differences" (Glasser, 2005, p. 21).

A second strength of this approach is its stress on action and thinking, as opposed to feeling and physiology (Glasser, 1986a, 2000). By emphasizing that group members make plans and carry them out, reality therapy breaks the inertia of the past and makes it more likely that clients will be able to change. Part of this action/thinking process involves refusing to accept excuses and not punishing (Glasser, 1984; Wubbolding, 1999). The action/thinking dimension of reality therapy is aimed in a positive direction—toward fostering needed and appropriate change.

A third valuable dimension of a reality therapy group is its viability with people in the society on which others have given up (Glasser & Breggin, 2001). For example, delinquents, prisoners, and addicts are groups that are often neglected or ineffectively served by mental health professionals (Dugan & Everett, 1998). Reality therapy groups make it possible to work productively with these populations and others that are viewed as incorrigible or difficult. This approach is also effective in crisis counseling and long-term group counseling, such as with victims of rape (McArthur, 1990).

A fourth strength of this approach is its emphasis on definable procedures for working with individuals in groups (Glasser, 1986b; Wubbolding, 1987, 1999). Reality therapy is straightforward in emphasizing what group leaders need to do and when. It has become more flexible through the years, with practitioners other than Glasser adding new techniques to its repertoire—for example, paradoxical methods and the employment of teaching metaphors and stories (Wubbolding, 1991).

A final strength of using reality therapy in groups is that the treatment continues only until participants are able to resolve difficulties. As a way of promoting positive change, reality therapy is a relatively brief approach (Wubbolding, 1988, 1999). Most individuals have only limited time to work on their difficulties, whether therapeutically or in an organizational context. Reality therapy is geared to that reality and helps group members become involved with others and reinforce each person's plans that were successful. In this way, reality therapy is similar to solution-focused brief therapy.

Limitations

One drawback of reality therapy is its emphasis on the exchange of communication, either verbal or written (Glasser, 1984). Many reality therapists use contracts in their groups to have members clarify exactly what their goals are. Individuals who cannot or will not communicate in this way do not benefit very much from this approach.

A second limitation is its simplicity. Glasser's eight-step method of conducting a group or Wubbolding's WDEP model may be misapplied by "mechanical" group leaders who do not understand or appreciate the complexity of human nature and change. These individuals are likely to be too controlling or rigid so that group members do not get the opportunity to struggle with their own issues.

A third drawback of reality therapy is its extreme position on some issues. Certainly, it can be argued that mental illness diagnoses are overused; however, to deny that there is genetically based mental illness and to insist that people choose to behave in mentally ill ways, as Glasser does, probably overstates the case (Glasser, 1984, 1986a; Glasser & Breggin, 2001). Likewise, it can be stated that some theories overemphasize the unconscious or the past, but that matter is different from the reality therapy perspective of refusing to deal with the unconscious and denying the importance of past events except as a way of understanding present behaviors.

A fourth limitation of this theory in group work is its lack of proven effectiveness. Glasser argues that reality therapy is one of the most popular theories in educational, correctional, and substance abuse programs (Evans, 1982), but the validity of this theory has not been researched thoroughly (Ford, 1982), although this weakness is being addressed through periodicals such as the *International Journal of Reality Therapy*. Until the theory is investigated more deeply, however, its use will continue to be questioned.

A final limitation of reality therapy is its emphasis on conformity and utility. Group members are expected to conform to the reality of those with the most power (Glasser, 1986a). Although this emphasis may be pragmatic, it may also discourage more creative and independent behaviors. It also takes the emphasis away from changing one's environment. Reality therapy is not the only theory that focuses more on individual change within the group than on environmental change. Like other approaches with this emphasis (i.e., most individual theories of counseling), the drawback is that attention to larger and important issues may be bypassed or ignored.

Learning More

Reality therapy is a dynamic approach to working with groups that now uses choice theory as its underlying base. The theory and its treatment were originally developed by William Glasser, but reality therapy has been popularized and explained in depth by both Glasser and Robert Wubbolding. Both run institutes where training and educational materials may be obtained. Their addresses are as follows:

> The William Glasser Institute
> 22024 Lassen Street, Suite #118
> Chatsworth, CA 91311-3600
> Telephone: 818-700-8000
> http://www.wglasser.com/whatisrt.htm/

> Center for Reality Therapy
> 7672 Montgomery Road #383
> Cincinnati, OH 45236-4204
> Telephone: 513-561-1911
> http://www.realitytherapywub.com/

SUMMARY AND CONCLUSION

Psychoanalytic, transactional analysis, and reality therapy groups have deep historical roots that both unite and divide them. Practitioners of these approaches continue today in a variety of group settings.

Psychoanalytic groups concentrate primarily on resolving individuals' unconscious thoughts and psychosexual stages. They are primarily employed in psychotherapeutic and long-term counseling groups. Techniques such as free association, transference, and interpretation of dreams are frequently used, as in individual analysis. However, the dynamics of groups make analysis quite different. The group leader is seen as the expert and directs group members in revealing repressed materials. Group members may or may not be encouraged to help one another or to look beyond their own needs, depending on the orientation of the leader.

If the group is successful, then group members will pass through a number of individual developmental stages, including working toward insight and a reorientation to their environments. They will be more aware of the past, the range of their feelings, and how they function in the present. The psychoanalytic group approach stresses long-term personality change through the group process. Psychoanalytic procedures are still in need of better documentation and refinement. The debate continues for those in this tradition about how to work best with the individual in a group setting and whether individual techniques can be employed effectively in groups of this type.

Transactional analysis has often been used in groups since its inception in the 1950s. It is frequently thought of as a group treatment approach, although it has been employed with individuals and families, too (Barnes, 1977; Corey, 2004; Dusay & Dusay, 1989). Transactional analysis is also used in task/work settings. The major thrust of the transactional analysis group is to concentrate on analyzing

ego states (Parent, Adult, Child) that individuals within the group are using. The group leader helps group members become aware of how they are functioning and how they might change their patterns of interaction. Cognitive understanding is emphasized initially in this process.

When the group is functioning properly, group members interact with one another (**minor transactions**). However, the major focus of the group is on leader–member interactions (**major transactions**). Thus, the transactional analysis group is leader centered and does not take advantage of group dynamics. Practitioners of this approach are still in the process of validating the effectiveness of transactional analysis groups. However, the theory is simple, clear, and can easily be used by members of groups in coming to better understand their structure, transactions, games, and life scripts.

Reality therapy is a unique theory in that it has some similarities to behaviorism and phenomenology. These similarities include its emphasis on perception and action and its de-emphasis on the past, the unconscious, and emotions. Yet reality therapy is distinct. It has incorporated choice theory into itself. At its core, it stresses the employment of action and thoughts.

Reality therapy groups used to follow a fairly well-formulated eight-stage approach, and some still do. This approach is specific but may become superficial in the hands of an inexperienced group leader. In the 1980s, some theorists encouraged developing new techniques and incorporating them into this format. Wubbolding led the way. An increased emphasis on reality therapy practice has led to the uniform training of leaders by Glasser in California and Wubbolding in Ohio.

As a result of being in a reality therapy group, members should become more aware of their values and more focused on changing their behaviors instead of trying to change others. It is hoped they will make choices in their lives and be responsible and accountable for all they do. Many group leaders, such as those working in education, mental health, and business, find reality therapy to be effective with the populations they serve. Although popular, reality therapy still needs a more solid research base.

CLASSROOM EXERCISES

1. Compare and contrast psychoanalytic and TA group work in regard to theory, method, group leader's role, and desired outcome. How do they overlap? How are they distinct? Share your impressions with three other classmates in a small-group setting.

2. A criticism of William Glasser is that he believes people choose to be mentally ill. What is your opinion about the origin and maintenance of mental illness? Do you think you have to agree with Glasser to be an effective practitioner of reality therapy?

3. What is your favorite part of each of the theories presented in this chapter? Which aspect did you like least? Discuss your thoughts and feelings concerning these theories with another class member.

4. Based on what you have learned about group work stages, which theory—psychoanalysis, TA, or reality therapy—do you think would work best with children, adolescents, adults, and older adults? Why?

CHAPTER 16

ADLERIAN, PERSON-CENTERED, AND EXISTENTIAL GROUPS

In eyes there is beauty
*   not found in words.*
Soft, clear expression
*   surrounded by light*
Slowly contracting in the warmth of our day
*   and growing in the depths of our nights,*
Opening up new worlds before us
*   as vividly as a good camera lens*
*   properly set and focused.*
Your eyes find mine
*   sometimes in our sessions*
Looking with you into the present
*   while catching glimpses of a darkened past*
*   that blurs sometimes in a flash.*
Silently, you expose hidden feelings
*   through unspoken language we share the moment.**

**From "Reflections," by Samuel T. Gladding, 1975, in *Personnel and Guidance Journal, 53,* p. 429. Copyright ACA. Reprinted with permission. No further reproduction authorized without written permission of the American Counseling Association.*

Adlerian, person-centered, and existential theories of group work are humanistically based ways of working with people. They are geared to picking up clients' messages that are conveyed verbally through spoken language as well as nonverbally, such as with eye movements or hand signals. These approaches stress the importance of congruence in human interactions. They also recognize the impact of subjective experiences in people's lives and in the life of a group. In these three models of group work, an emphasis is placed on here-and-now phenomena—that is, on being present in the moment. There is also a focus within these theories on the creation of personal and interpersonal awareness and finding meaning in life (Day & Matthes, 1992; Frankl, 2000).

Each theory has developed over the years and continues to evolve. Many of the techniques of these approaches have been incorporated into other group models. Thus, many of the once-unique features of these theories, such as confrontation and a focus on awareness and meaning in life, have become universally accepted as important dimensions in other ways of conducting groups.

ADLERIAN GROUPS

Adlerian theory has always had a group focus. It concentrates on the inherent social interest of persons and emphasizes social development, cooperation, and education. As mentioned in Chapter 1, Alfred Adler was an early user of groups for psychotherapeutic and psychoeducational purposes (Manaster & Corsini, 1982). He used groups to counsel parents as early as 1922. He often employed co-therapists in his work at the Vienna Child Guidance Clinics (Rosenbaum, 1978) and frequently had others observe his groups (Wilfried Datler & Johannes Gstach, personal communication, June 26, 2001). However, Adler never developed a theory of group work beyond the major principles he advocated in his approach to individual psychology (Donigian & Hulse-Killacky, 1999). It was left to Adler's followers to develop a group approach based on his principles.

Five such theorists who helped refine Adlerian concepts for group work were Rudolf Dreikurs, Manford Sonstegard, Oscar Christensen, Raymond Corsini, and Donald Dinkmeyer. Dreikurs became the major impetus behind the establishment of group procedures based on Adlerian theory. He introduced group therapy into private practice in 1929 in Vienna and then again in the United States in the late 1930s (Dreikurs, 1950; Terner & Pew, 1978). Christensen, Sonstegard, and Corsini applied Adlerian principles to family counseling groups (Christensen & Marchant, 1983; Dreikurs, Corsini, Lowe, & Sonstegard, 1959). Dinkmeyer and his colleagues (Dinkmeyer & Sperry, 2000) are most noted for packaging Adlerian group models, including the development of kits for specific populations, such as parents and children, with step-by-step instructions for leaders.

Premises of Adlerian Groups

Chief among the major tenets of Adlerian theory is that people are primarily motivated by social interest (Corsini, 1988; Donigian & Hulse-Killacky, 1999). **Social interest** has been defined as "not only an interest in others but an interest in the interests of others" (Ansbacher, 1977, p. 57). "From the Adlerian point of view the essence of normality is having a feeling of concern for others" (Corsini, 1988, p. 10). This concern is expressed as a positive attitude toward people (Sonstegard, 1998). Such a feeling can be and is developed in a group context.

Other major concerns that undergird Adlerian theory are as follows:

1. *The purposefulness of all behavior*—Adlerians believe that individuals do not act randomly. They act with a goal in mind, although they are sometimes not aware of their goal (Dreikurs, 1950). For instance, if Beverly lashes out at Carmen, her intent may be to protect her privacy, although she may say afterward, "I'm not sure why I just did that." The general direction of life is from minus (inferiority) to plus (perfection, i.e., completeness) (Ansbacher & Ansbacher, 1956).

2. *The subjective nature of perception*—Adlerians emphasize the phenomenological nature of human behavior. People perceive the world based on their experiences, not objectively. Therefore, if Eric has known only abuse in his life, then he may perceive the world as a hostile place.

3. *The holistic nature of people*—For Adlerians, people are a unified whole, not a collection of parts. People are more like trees, which grow from seeds and branch out, than they are like machines, such as automobiles, which are a collection of parts (Corsini, 1988). From this perspective, one answer is usually inadequate to explain even a simple act.

4. *The importance of developing a healthy style of life*—A **style of life** is the way one prefers to live and relate to others. Adlerians stress that a faulty lifestyle is based on competitiveness and on striving to be superior to others. Lifestyles are often not noticed when a person is in a favorable situation but manifest themselves when the person faces difficulties (Adler, 1956). Lifestyles are developed early in a person's development (around age 5), but they are open to change.

5. *The self-determinism of the individual to chart a future based on expected consequences of behavior* (Corsini, 1988; Hawes, 1985)—Adlerians stress that people are creative and can choose from among a wide range of possible behaviors (Manaster & Corsini, 1982; Sonstegard, 1998). All behavioral disorders are based on failures to choose wisely.

◆ *Questions from Experience* ◆

When, either in public or private life, have you ever seen someone fail to choose wisely? What do you think was going on in that person's mind? Do you think facts or emotions are predominant in an unwise decision?

Practice of Adlerian Theory in a Group

Adlerian groups are primarily psychoeducational in nature, although some of these groups are therapeutically oriented and they are often conducted in a counseling context. The groups are "heterodox with respect to procedures" (Corsini, 1988, p. 19) but nevertheless have many unifying aspects. The idea in all Adlerian groups is that people can learn from one another. As Dreikurs (1969) points out, "Since . . . problems and conflicts are recognized in their social nature, the group is ideally suited not only to highlight and reveal the nature of a person's conflicts and maladjustments but to offer corrective influences" (p. 43). Some groups are more didactic than others.

In **Adlerian parent education** groups, for example, developmental and preventive aspects of parenting are stressed. These groups focus on empowering parents to consider the dynamics and purposes of their children's behaviors, and they encourage group members' discussion and interaction. Change in parental behaviors is expected before a change will occur in their children. These groups also stress cooperation among family members as a goal, and they emphasize the use of logical and natural consequences to avoid power struggles. The Adlerian approach promotes parent discussion groups with a trained leader and a set curriculum. This orientation is democratic, and regular family council meetings are encouraged as a forum where all members in a family voice concerns and needs.

One variation of an Adlerian psychoeducational group is the **C group** (Dinkmeyer, 1973). The name is based on each component of the group: collaboration, consultation, clarification, confrontation, concern, confidentiality, and commitment. All aspects of the group begin with a *c*. Since the 1970s, the C group approach has been updated and is now packaged under the label **Systematic Training for Effective Parenting (S.T.E.P.)**. Another Adlerian parent education program is *Active Parenting Today in 3: Your Three Part Guide to a Great Family* (Popkin, 2006).

At least three unifying factors link Adlerian groups together regardless of their form. One is the emphasis on an **interpretation of a person's early history**. To promote change, it is helpful for group members to recognize and understand how they created their own lifestyles. Therefore, if Eleanor is miserable, she had an active part in becoming this way. A second similarity in Adlerian groups is the practice of stressing individual, interpersonal, and group process goals during the duration of the group. **Individual goals** may involve developing insight into the creation of a mistaken lifestyle and taking corrective measures. **Interpersonal goals** may entail becoming more socially oriented and involved with other individuals experiencing life difficulties. **Group process goals** may center around promoting and experiencing a cooperative climate in the group. In an Adlerian group, Shuford can come to realize he has isolated himself from others and simultaneously reach out to specific people in the group, as well as the group itself, in overcoming this isolation.

Another linkage that unifies Adlerian groups in practice is the phases they go through. For instance, Dreikurs (1969) has outlined four phases of Adlerian group counseling, and they have been elaborated on by Sonstegard and Bitter (1998b):

1. establishing and maintaining a proper therapeutic relationship by promoting cohesion
2. exploring the dynamics that are operating within the individual (i.e., where motivations and interactions are at work)
3. communicating to the individual an understanding of self, such as an understanding of the individual's goals
4. envisioning new alternatives and choices (i.e., a more useful pattern of living).

After an initial screening of members, an Adlerian counseling group begins with an emphasis on the leader's part to promote cooperation and an egalitarian spirit. Group members may contract formally or informally to work on areas that have personal meaning to them. After the proper participatory atmosphere has been created, participants are invited to explore their own lifestyles and understand more clearly how their present behavior promotes or deters their current functioning in all life tasks (Mosak, 2005). Some of the ways this second phase of the group is conducted include exploring family constellations, early recollections, and basic mistakes.

After this analysis, group members are ready to move into the **insight and reorientation phases of the group**. The insight phase involves helping individuals understand why they made the choices they did in the past. It often is accompanied by the group leader's use of interpretation. Interpretation is offered as a tentative hypothesis in these groups, such as "Could it be . . . ?" or "I wonder if . . . ?" For example, "Joan, I wonder if there is a connection between your sister's success and your pattern of abandoning projects just when you are doing well in them?"

In the final phase, **reorientation**, counseling group members are encouraged to act differently and take more control of their lives. Such a procedure means taking risks, acting "as if" they were the people they wished to be and "catching themselves" in old, ineffective patterns and correcting them. For example, Damany may resolve to act as if he does not need the backing of his parents to make a successful career choice. In this case, he sets up an appointment with a career counselor and begins exploring vocational possibilities he never considered before.

Role of the Adlerian Group Leader

Although co-leading groups is common in the Adlerian approach (Mosak, 2005), a number of qualities characterize effective individual Adlerian group leaders. The ideal leader is a well-balanced person who possesses certain characteristics: adaptability, courage, humor, sincerity, an acceptance of others, and an openness that promotes honest interchange with group members. Adlerian group leaders need a positive attitude that instils hope in others that change is possible (Sonstegard, 1998). In addition, group leaders must have good knowledge of their clients and be active in attacking in a timely manner the **faulty logic** (i.e., irrational ideas) their clients hold. They further need to help clients clarify lifestyles and encourage group members to act.

Corsini (1988) states that the personality of the Adlerian group leader is as important as the techniques he or she employs. Mosak (2005) agrees that the personhood of the leader is crucial. He also stresses that for the leader to be effective, he or she must feel free to share opinions and feelings. Therefore, the group leader is a participant in the group process in a collaborative manner. The leader models the behavior that group members should demonstrate (Dinkmeyer & Sperry, 2000) and creates the proper attitude in the group (Donigian & Hulse-Killacky, 1999).

Overall, Adlerian group leaders focus on understanding present behavioral patterns of group members and challenging them to change. Effective leaders use group dynamics to help groups help themselves. For example, the leader may encourage group members to confront one another about specific behaviors with the realization that, in so doing, members learn something about their own beliefs and goals in life.

In working with groups of children, Adlerian leaders may primarily use **encouragement** (wherein leaders imply faith in the child by stating their belief that behavior change is possible), **natural consequences** (i.e., living with the results of a particular behavior, such as getting lost because one did not follow directions), and **acting "as if"** (where in children act as if they are the ideal person they wish to be). With adult groups, more systematic plans may be employed. Leaders may use the three techniques just mentioned plus others, such as **task setting** (members set short-range, attainable goals and eventually work up to long-term, realistic objectives) and **push button** (members are helped to realize they have choices in their lives about which stimuli they pay attention to and remember). In either case, Adlerian leaders strive to stay true to the theory behind the process yet also be inventive.

CASE EXAMPLE: Alicia Acts "As If"

When Alicia joined the Adlerian parents' group, she was uncertain about herself and the roles she played in the lives of her family, especially her children. She married young and had had two children, now 5 and 7, almost immediately. They seemed to run wild and she did not get much help from her husband.

Through the group, though, she began to get ideas on what she could do to improve her life and those of her children and husband. One such idea was to act "as if." Utilizing this technique, Alicia acted as if she were confident in properly disciplining her children and instructing her husband on ways he could help with the children. Interestingly enough, not only did Alicia feel better about herself and what was happening in her family, but her children and husband did, too.

What other Adlerian-based techniques would you advise Alicia to use? What is the rationale for your choice?

Desired Outcome of Adlerian Groups

The outcomes of Adlerian group practice focus primarily on the growth and actions of the individual within the group rather than the group itself. In this respect, Adlerian groups are similar to psychoanalytic and transactional analysis (TA) groups. Because there is greater variety in the types of groups offered by Adlerians than in those offered by psychoanalysts and TA leaders, specific outcomes differ, as does the focus of these approaches.

On a global level, members of an Adlerian group should be more socially oriented, personally integrated, and goal directed when the group ends. They should have also corrected faulty beliefs, eliminated competitive behavioral stances, and become more in contact with family-of-origin issues. Children in Adlerian groups should recognize more clearly the logical consequences of their actions and who they can be; parents, teachers, and other adults who work with children should be more cognizant of children's faulty belief systems (i.e., that they must be superior, helpless, powerful, or deficient), and corrective measures to take in helping them eliminate misguided thoughts and behaviors (Dreikurs, 1968). Generally, children in Adlerian groups are worked with more directly than any other age group.

Adolescents in Adlerian groups are specifically helped to deal better with their own and others' perceptions of themselves and to realize they do not have to engage in competitive behaviors to be accepted. There are a number of ways to promote cooperative behaviors among adolescents (see Table 16.1).

Table 16.1
Typical faulty goals of adolescents.

Faulty Beliefs	Goals	Examples	Adult Reactions	Peer Group Reactions	Reactions to Corrective Feedback	Alternative Corrective Methods
I am worthwhile and belong only:						
When I am best at everything	Superiority	Super striving for best grades, most honors, first in the class, etc.	Approval	Admiration	Justifies striving	Avoid blanket approval Promote courage to be imperfect Encourage social cooperation
When I have widespread peer social acceptance	Popularity (social climbing)	Constantly attempting to obtain widespread peer social acceptance	Approval	Acceptance Subgroup envy or annoyance	Superficial compliance Friendly disagreement	Avoid blanket approval Encourage independent activity
When I live up completely to all standards of established adult society	Conformity	Constantly tries to please, particularly adults rather than peers, with good behavior, grades, etc.	Approval	Annoyance (with some envy)	Superficial compliance	Avoid blanket approval Encourage peer social activities Encourage individuality
When I am in complete control or free from outside control	Defiance: Independence struggle	Arguments over hair, dress, etc.	Annoyance Irritation Anger	Acceptance Approval	Continue to argue Defiant compliance	Avoid arguing Suggestions at other times
	Aggression	Vandalism Fighting Delinquency	Anger Hurt Revenge	Rejection by most Subgroup acceptance	Strike back	Avoid hurt and anger Don't strike back Reasonable limits and use of consequences
	Withdrawal	Runaway Truancy Suicide	Fear Alarm	Indifference Some sympathy	Passive response No improvement	Avoid hysterical reaction Encourage social participation
When I prove and enjoy myself sexually	Sexual promiscuity	High level of intimate sexual activity with others	Disgust Shock Disapproval	Rejection by most Subgroup acceptance	Defiant rejection	Avoid shock and disgust Encourage desire for self-respect and respect of others

374

"When I am..."	Goal	Behavior				Recommended response
When I am completely supported and consoled in my shortcomings	Inadequacy	Gives up easily; Displays dependence	Pity Hopelessness	Pity Indifference	Meager effort, then gives up again	Avoid discouraged reaction or pity; Provide opportunities for small successes and encouragement
When others find me completely charming and pleasing	Charm	Fascinating and pleasing with smooth talk and behavior	Charmed and flattered sometimes mixed with annoyance	Charmed Flattered Pleased Envious	Steps up charm Pouting Withdrawal	Be unimpressed but friendly; Remain courteous and insist on effort
If I am physically beautiful or strong	Beauty Strength	Excessive attention to and dependence on physical appearance	Admiration sometimes mixed with envy or irritation	Admiration sometimes mixed with envy	Ignoring	Avoid praise; Encourage nonphysical pursuits, e.g., reading, art, music
When I am "superman" or "superwoman"	Sexism	Boys: Macho behavior Girls: Clinging-vine behavior	General approval Some annoyance	General approval Some annoyance	Rejection	Avoid blanket approval; Encourage contrasting "feminine" or "masculine" attitudes and behaviors
When I am completely involved in learning or discussing ideas	Intellectualizing	Very bookish	Approval	Indifference Subgroup acceptance	Argument	Avoid blanket approval; Encourage social leisure activities
When I am fully involved in religious ideas and activities	Religiosity	Deep involvement in religious ideas and activities; Regular and frequent attendance at church	Approval sometimes mixed with concern or annoyance	Ignored by most Subgroup acceptance	Pity Defensiveness	Avoid blanket approval or arguments; Encourage exploratory thinking and talking

375

Source: From "Typical Faulty Goals of Adolescents" by E. W. Kelly and T. J. Sweeney, 1979, *The School Counselor, 26,* pp. 239–241. Copyright ACA. Reprinted with permission. No further reproduction authorized without written consent of the American Counseling Association.

With families and adults, Adlerian groups are directed toward social adjustment. Members of these groups are helped to understand that the basic problems in families and social relationships are people oriented and that relationships built on democratic principles, which foster healthy interactions, work best.

Although little literature is available on Adlerian task/work groups, the outcome from these groups should emphasize social cooperation and teamwork (Larson & LaFasto, 1989). Task/work group members may realize anew how much more they can accomplish when working together rather than separately.

Evaluation of Adlerian Groups

As with psychoanalytically oriented and TA groups, it is crucial to be aware of Adlerian theory and the nature of Adlerian groups before participating in them. The theory and practice of Adler's ideas have distinct strengths and limitations.

Strengths and Contributions

A strength associated with Adlerian groups is that they are usually nonthreatening. Adlerian groups are also generally helpful to participants because of their educational emphasis. Many Adlerian groups are based on a healthy, rather than a sick, operational model (Mosak, 2005). In these groups, members often enjoy the experience and feel they come out with concrete ways to handle specific everyday problems, such as children, spouse, or work situations.

A second strength of Adlerian group theory and practice is that methods associated with this approach are logical and based on "common sense" (Corsini, 1988; Sweeney, 1999). Most group participants do not feel put off by the terms or procedures used. In addition, most group leaders are able to learn and use Adlerian concepts in a relatively short time. The fact that this approach encourages democratic participation is useful for both the members and the leader in promoting openness and dialogue.

A third attractive feature of Adlerian groups is that they are holistic. Most Adlerians will typically employ a cognitive method to help participants understand the materials being presented, but they will also address behavioral and affective aspects of the person.

A fourth strength of Adlerian group work is its eclectic nature (Sweeney, 1999). Adlerians are not tied to rigid procedures and methods. For instance, Adlerian group leaders may make use of psychodrama and other active therapeutic techniques (Mosak, 2005). In addition, Adlerian groups stress common concepts of the Adlerian approach such as the value of social interests, goal-directed behavior, individual indivisibility, and the importance of family constellations.

Another strong point of the Adlerian approach is its flexibility in working with varied populations. Different forms of Adlerian groups are used with children (Sonstegard & Dreikurs, 1973; Sonstegard & Bitter, 1998b), adolescents (Kelly & Sweeney, 1979; Sonstegard & Bitter, 1998a), parents (Croake, 1983; Dreikurs & Soltz, 1964), and families (Lowe, 1982). In addition, Adlerian group work has been found to be successful with such diverse clients as those seeking relief from loneliness (Brough, 1994) and those enrolled in outpatient substance abuse programs (Prinz & Arkin, 1994).

Limitations

A drawback of Adlerian group work is the leader's style. Adlerians are unified in respect to their philosophy of equality and theory of personality development, but they follow their own style in regard to procedure. They "have no guidelines other than their experience" (Corsini, 1988, p. 14). The emphasis placed on different aspects of the approach is left entirely to the group leader. Therefore, if the group leader deviates somewhat from Adlerian principles, the group may have difficulty.

Another limitation of the groups derived from Adlerian theory is the narrowness of their scope. The Adlerian approach assumes that all problems are socially based. Although many difficulties may be so oriented, some problems have different causes that are not addressed in Adlerian groups. For example, in a work group, the processes set up to produce a product may be at fault rather than the people involved. Likewise, an impoverished environment or government regulations may contribute to friction between people whether they wish to be social or not.

A third limitation of Adlerian groups is their lack of uniformity of method. Most notable Adlerian theorists have achieved success because of their individual ability to translate Adlerian principles into practice. Although some followers of Adler (e.g., Dinkmeyer & Sperry, 2000; Kelly & Sweeney, 1979) have translated Adlerian principles into more unified practice techniques, the Adlerian approach still lacks concreteness of techniques in group work.

Finally, the research on which Adlerian group work is based is relatively weak (Manaster & Corsini, 1982). In response to this deficiency, Corsini (1988) contends that all group-based research lacks support. Yet, if Adlerian groups are to achieve prominence, more data must be generated to document their effectiveness.

Learning More

Adlerian theory is practiced worldwide. Its emphasis on social living makes it a popular approach to group work. For more information on Adlerian organizations and institutes, contact the

> North American Society of Adlerian Psychology (NASAP)
> 614 Old West Chocolate Ave.
> Hershey, PA 17033
> Phone: 717-579-8795
> Web page: http://www.alfredadler.org/
> E-mail: info@alfredadler.org

NASAP also publishes a newsletter and a quarterly periodical, the *Journal of Individual Psychology*. Both are filled with announcements and information on the practice of Adlerian theory. The latter is more scholarly and research based.

PERSON-CENTERED GROUPS

The growth and development of person-centered group work is linked to the theory and personal influence of Carl Rogers (Rogers, 1967, 1970, 1980). Initially, Rogers developed what he termed a *nondirective* counseling approach in reaction to the directive methods used by psychoanalytic therapists and other counselor-practitioners of the 1940s. E. G. Williamson, for example, emphasized the role of the counselor as the expert and director of the therapeutic process. Rogers had learned from his clients that when they were in charge of their own therapy and were truly accepted and understood by him as a therapist, they improved faster and better than when he directed their actions. During the 1940s and 1950s, Rogers focused on individual clients and worked to prove his theory of counseling. At the same time, he developed a *self theory of personality* (Rogers, 1951, 1957, 1959). The main exception to this emphasis was his use of groups to work with counselors-in-training.

In the 1960s, Rogers expanded his focus to the small group as well as to the individual. His emphasis away from a strictly individual approach (which he had emphasized in his 1951 book *Client-Centered Therapy*) was in keeping with the times. The T-group (i.e., training group) model was well established in the 1960s as a result of the work of the National Training Laboratories. Therapy groups in psychiatry settings were also used widely. For Rogers, the T-group approach was too impersonal because of its primary attention to theory, group dynamics, and strictly social material. Groups in psychiatric settings were not appropriate for the general population with whom Rogers preferred to work. So, Rogers adapted some of the T-group structure and combined it with his own clinical approach and positive humanistic views into what he called the **basic encounter group**, in which "individuals come into much closer and direct contact with one another than is customary in ordinary life" (Rogers, 1967, p. 270).

In the 1970s, variations of these types of groups went by many names, for example, *personal growth groups, sensory awareness groups, sensitivity groups,* and *human relations groups*. They were very popular and experienced "wild flower growth" (Hansen, Warner, & Smith, 1980, p. 158). California became the Mecca for those interested in a basic encounter-group type of experience, but the phenomenon rapidly spread across the country and gained wide acceptance, especially among college students and the middle class. "In its heyday, the decade between 1962 and 1972, a reasonable estimate would be that several million people participated in some form of encounter group" (Bebout, 1978, p. 323). The publicity around encounter groups during this time among the general public was rarely favorable (Lifton, 1972; Yalom, 2005). This reaction was due to the inappropriate and abusive use of such groups by a few publicity-seeking and untrained individuals. By the 1980s, the popularity of encounter groups had waned, but much of their basic format still survives.

Rogers became interested in large-group phenomena in the 1970s and initiated a new group format—the **community for learning**—in which about 100 people lived and worked together for 2 weeks at a time. Furthermore, Rogers applied person-centered theory to the more formal and established groups found in couples and families (Rogers, 1972, 1977, 1980). The flexibility of the person-centered approach is truly impressive (Raskin & Rogers, 2005). Here, the focus is on Rogers's work with small groups because his involvement and research with these groups is better documented than with other groups with which he worked.

Premises of Person-Centered Groups

Basic encounter groups, as defined by Rogers (1970), are built on several premises. The first is a trust in the inner resources of persons. As Rogers (1980) puts it, "Individuals have within themselves vast resources for self-understanding and for altering their self-concepts, basic attitudes, and self-directed behavior; these resources can be tapped if a definable climate of facilitative psychological attitudes can be provided" (p. 115).

A second underlying premise of this approach is a sense of trust in the group to help members develop their potential without being directed in a certain way by a leader. This is essentially a belief that encounter groups will promote the basic positive growth tendency that resides within individuals (Rosenbaum, 1974). Rogers (1970) emphasizes that movement in encounter groups will be positive, even when initially ill defined. "The group will move—of this I am confident—but it would be presumptuous to think that I can or should direct that movement toward a specific goal" (p. 45).

A third major tenet of Rogers's approach is the idea that certain conditions must be created within the group for the group and its members to maximize their full potential (Rogers, 1970). *Communication*—for example, the expression by the group leader and group members of empathy, genuineness (congruence), and acceptance (unconditional positive regard)—is necessary. In addition, group members must engage in **active listening** (i.e., hearing meanings behind words and behind nonverbal gestures); self-disclose and unmask pretensions and facades; deal with immediate issues of concern; and, when needed, **confront** (i.e., challenge incongruencies in thoughts and actions). "An underlying assumption of an encounter group is that somewhere along the way, people have lost the art of communication" (Hansen et al., 1980, p. 167).

Finally, encounter groups are based on the understanding that a qualified person with special training and experience will facilitate them. Group leaders must be skilled in allowing group members to struggle to express themselves. Furthermore, they must be integrated personally as well as educated professionally.

As opposed to a T group (the National Training Laboratory model developed by Kurt Lewin and colleagues in the 1940s), basic encounter groups are less structured, theoretical, here-and-now oriented, and task oriented. Members are free to talk about their past and present because encounter groups do not make a distinction between "growth and development goals and psychotherapy goals" (Shaffer & Galinsky, 1989, p. 211). Encounter groups also tend to be more process based and more confrontational in feedback than are T-groups.

As a rule, basic encounter groups are more open to allowing a wider range of expressible behaviors than are T-groups. Those who join them are usually more focused on broadening their own **personal growth** (i.e., a global emphasis that stresses development as a result of experiences, such as travel or encounter) as opposed to working on personal growth issues (i.e., an individual emphasis that springs from a perceived deficit or need). However, both deficit and enhancement issues may be dealt with in the group.

Overall, basic encounter groups are established on the premise that individuals who participate in them are relatively healthy. They were initially referred to as **group therapy for normals** (Yalom, 2005). In addition, it is assumed that these individuals (usually 8 to 18 in number and strangers to one another) will voluntarily commit to attend a select number of group sessions and work on developing a greater sense of awareness and acceptance of themselves and others. They will help themselves and others become more skilled in using personal and interpersonal assets as the group continues.

◆ *Questions from Experience* ◆

One of the factors that hurt the encounter group movement was the variations of it that were tried by untrained group leaders. Do you still see groups of any type, from teams to task forces, in your community that are led by individuals who appear not to know what they are doing? How does that affect the perception of groups where you live?

Practice of Person-Centered Theory in a Group

Certain procedures (i.e., techniques and processes) are common to all encounter groups. One of the most crucial is the creation of a psychological climate in which group members can risk being themselves. To achieve such a therapeutic climate, Rogers (1970) uses an **unstructured group** format in which members can freely express their thoughts and feelings. Trust must also be established. Group members who do not trust one another do not disclose much about themselves or relate very well to others. They fail to develop within the group (Gibb & Gibb, 1969). Group leaders can facilitate the development of trust by disclosing their own negative and positive feelings as they occur. For instance, if group members are simply describing past events in their lives instead of dealing with present experiences, then the group leader may say, "I do not think this group as a whole or you as individual members will make much progress unless or until you focus your attention and remarks on what is occurring now in your life."

Feedback and communication are also critical components in encounter group experiences. No real contact can occur between individuals without the expression of feedback and communication. *Feedback* involves one person giving another his or her perception of a behavior. For example, Claudia may say to Karl, "I really like the way you were honest in telling me how you felt about what I suggested to you." *Communication of thoughts and feelings* is best conveyed when clearly understood language and gestures are used. For instance, Matthew may say to Henrique in a serious manner, "It's frustrating when you close up when I ask you to say more about your opinions."

The process in which these basic techniques are employed and the **Rogerian-oriented encounter group 15-stage process** (Rogers, 1970) is well defined, although the stages do not always occur in a clear-cut sequence and may vary from group to group:

1. *Milling around*—In the initial stage of the group, members are often confused about who is responsible for conducting the group and what they are supposed to be doing. This confusion results in frustration, silence, and a tendency to keep conversations on a superficial level. Milling around is largely a warm-up activity that prevents members from getting down to business.
2. *Resistance*—Group members enter the group with both public and private selves. They tend to avoid exposing their private selves until they have built trust in other members. Therefore, members try to protect themselves and others from revealing too much too fast.
3. *Revealing past feelings*—As trust begins to develop, group members start to talk about their feelings, but only those that are safe to expose (e.g., the past).

The talk at this point is on there-and-then experiences (i.e., those that are historical) and those that are nonthreatening to expose. Members often act as if what they are saying is related to the present, but in reality it seldom is.

4. *Expression of negative feelings*—As the group develops, initial here-and-now feelings are expressed, but generally in a negative manner. Most of these feelings are directed toward the leader, and they are generally in the form of blame for not providing enough structure. For example, Ralph may say to Kevin, the group leader, "I wish you would either become more active in this group or find us a new leader." Negative feelings are safer to express than positive ones. Rogers hypothesizes that negative feelings occur first because members (a) want to test the trustworthiness of the group and (b) are less vulnerable to rejection if they are negative rather than positive.

5. *Expression of personally meaningful material*—At this stage, real trust in the group is established. Group members feel free to explore and talk about important meaningful events in their lives. They usually start off being more negative than positive but change as other group members accept them more. For instance, Peggy may say to the group, "I want to tell you more about myself than you have heard so far," and then begin to talk about some experiences in her life that she has made known to only very few people.

6. *Communication of immediate interpersonal feelings*—At this point in the life of the group, members begin to be affected by and respond to other group members. They indicate to others how their comments and actions are perceived. For instance, Charles may say to Steve, "Your comments about your life decisions strike me as those of a man with deep regret." Genuine encounter occurs at this point, and participants are ready to deal with one another.

7. *Development of a healing capacity in the group*—After members have expressed personal feelings about themselves and others, they begin to reach out to one another. This is accomplished after members offer warmth, compassion, understanding, and caring to others in the group who have shared their concerns. It is the caring attitude of group members more than the expertise of the group facilitator that Rogers believes is of the utmost importance. Therefore, when Tommy tells Jean that he cares about her as a person regardless of her past, Jean can begin to take risks.

8. *Self-acceptance and the beginning of change*—As members are accepted more, they become increasingly aware of their own behaviors and feelings and are consequently less rigid. In the process, they open themselves to changes that will lead to more changes. For instance, when Freddie realizes that other members like him even when he is not perfect, he begins to loosen up in what he says and to whom he directs his words.

9. *Cracking of facades*—Encounter group members tend to drop the masks they have been wearing and become more genuine. This process is known as the *cracking of facades*. Group members become less tolerant of facades as the group develops, and they often demand, rather than ask, that individuals stop relating in a polite or superficial way.

10. *Feedback*—Through feedback, group members become more self-aware. For instance, Mark may not realize that he is considered to be authoritarian unless

other members of the group tell him in the form of feedback. In this stage of the group, feedback is primarily constructive and greatly enhances the ability of a member to perceive how others see him or her.

11. *Confrontation*—At this stage in the process, confrontations of group members become more pronounced as members realize the group is reaching a climax. Confrontation is in the form of both positive and negative feedback.

12. *Helping relationships outside the group*—This stage is a parallel to stage 7, but group members experience healing and helping relationships with one another outside the formal group experience. This process helps them resolve any misunderstandings and develop new relationships.

13. *The basic encounter*—Genuine person-to-person contact is the overriding characteristic at this point in the group. Members come to realize how satisfactory and meaningful it is to relate to one another in such a way. Therefore, George seeks to become closer to Brenda, Betty, and Barry than previously because he realizes how much he learns from them about himself and human interaction patterns.

14. *Expressions of closeness*—As the group nears completion, group members express positive feelings about their experience and about one another. A sense of group spirit develops more strongly. Thus, Todd may say to the group as a whole, "I feel as if each of you is a member of my family."

15. *Behavior changes*—Behavior changes, the result of increased congruence, are more pronounced toward the end of a group. Members tend to act in a more open, honest, caring manner, and they carry these behaviors into everyday life experiences after the group terminates. For example, Mickey may be more open with strangers after the group than he ever thought about being before.

Role of the Person-Centered Group Leader

Group leaders of person-centered groups derive their direction from group members. Usually, such leaders view the groups with which they work as being capable and having the inner resources to direct and develop themselves as individuals and as a group (Raskin & Rogers, 2005). The leadership style of such persons is generally less active than in many other approaches to group work, although Rogers tends to be more confrontive in groups than in individual counseling sessions. Research (Bates & Goodman, 1986; Berenson, Mitchell, & Laney, 1968) indicates that effective facilitators confront their clients more frequently in a positive way, using empathy and positive regard, than do noneffective leaders.

Generally, leaders of Rogerian-based groups are paradigms "for interpersonal effectiveness, modeling the therapeutic norms of openness, congruence, warmth, genuineness, and acceptance" and for creating a climate within the group that promotes the development of relationships (Ohlsen, Horne, & Lawe, 1988, p. 68). Group leaders, who are known as **facilitators**, do not use gimmicks and planned procedures. Interpretation and other expert-oriented procedures are ignored, too. Instead, a person-centered group leader participates as a member of the group and shares struggles with the group. In doing so, the leader attempts to understand each person in the group on a more personal basis and accepts him- or herself and others genuinely (Bozarth, 1981).

Overall, person-centered group leaders carry out five distinct functions: (1) conveying warmth and empathy, (2) attending to others, (3) understanding meaning and content, (4) conveying acceptance, and (5) linking (Boy & Pine, 1999; Posthuma, 2002). These functions are expressed through such basic group skill techniques as listening, supporting, reflecting, sharing, affirming, clarifying, summarizing, engaging, and, of course, encountering. Overall, leaders use themselves as instruments of change (Raskin, 1986a, 1986b), and they convey the core conditions of empathy, congruence, and acceptance (Thorne, 1992). Their attitude toward the group helps create a climate that makes a difference in the growth of group members.

CASE EXAMPLE: Carey Experiences the Climate

When Carey entered the person-centered group, she was as tight as a clam. She did not make eye contact and she did not speak up. Other members wondered why she was there, and initially Carey did, too. She had come out of a desire to break her old habits of being withdrawn, but because she immediately retreated into a shell, she had second thoughts about whether she should have come to the group session or not.

Interestingly, no one pressed her to talk or do anything. They seemed comfortable with Carey the way she was. The same atmosphere prevailed during the second meeting of the group and continued to prevail thereafter.

As Carey became more comfortable, she opened up more at first with brief comments and later with well-thought-out statements. She seemed to be enjoying the group when it ended, and 3 months later when the group had a reunion, Carey actually arrived early.

What does Carey's experience in the group tell you about the power of acceptance and openness? Do you think Carey would have fared as well in other theory-oriented group? If so, which one(s) and why?

Desired Outcome of Person-Centered Groups

Person-centered encounter groups are intended for group members to develop self-awareness and awareness of others and to grow. The goal of personal growth is connected to what Rogers and others describe as **self-actualization** (i.e., becoming all that one can be) (Day & Matthes, 1992). Another goal is more openness to experience, especially as it relates to intimacy and meaningfulness with others. Behavior change is hoped for as group members alter their physical gestures and become more relaxed. Finally, there is the desired goal of becoming less alienated from oneself and others (Donigian & Hulse-Killacky, 1999).

Rogers (1970) reports that the desired outcomes of his approach and actual results have been very consistent. In a systematic follow-up study that he conducted, questionnaires were sent to 500 participants of small groups led by him and his associates. The study was conducted 3 to 6 months after the group had ended. Only two individuals felt the group experience had been damaging to them, whereas most surveyed reported the group had a positive and long-lasting impact on their behavior. Although there are some problems in doing survey research, it appears that person-centered encounter group members felt that they benefited from their experiences.

Other researchers, notably Lieberman, Yalom, and Miles (1973), found less positive results, stating that almost 10% of the participants they researched reported that marathon person-centered encounter groups were damaging to them. It should be noted that Rogerians do not prefer marathons, or group experiences that last more than 12 hours (Landreth, 1984). More and better research needs to be conducted on the overall impact of basic encounter groups. Some research of this nature is being conducted in Japan (Hirayama, 1993; Yamamoto, 1995) and has been conducted in the United States (Braaten, 1989, 1990). The outcome of Rogerian-oriented groups is meant to be positive and long lasting.

Evaluation of Person-Centered Groups

Person-centered groups have factors that are beneficial for some individuals in some situations. They also have limitations. The pros and cons of the approach are connected with who is included in the group as well as how the group is used.

Strengths and Contributions

The basic encounter group movement has helped traditional group leaders, especially those working from a psychotherapeutic perspective, to become aware of the importance of enhancing the development of the total individual. Until the 1960s, the focus of group psychotherapists was on reduction, rather than expansion, of group participants' experiences. After encounter groups gained popularity, group psychotherapists were inclined to stress patients' assets as well as try to alleviate their deficiencies (Yalom, 2005).

A second strength of the person-centered approach has been its emphasis on the group leader. The heart of the basic encounter group is the group facilitator (Donigian & Hulse-Killacky, 1999; Yalom, 2005). The facilitator's task is to have a genuine interest in others and to be able to set up conditions for personal growth. Few other group approaches concentrate as much on the leader as a person. However, most group models have been positively influenced by the person-centered emphasis on the importance of the leader, and a spillover effect has resulted. "The traditional 'blank screen' demeanor [of the group leader] is just not possible anymore with most clients" (Lieberman, 1977, p. 26).

A third positive contribution of the basic encounter group model is the emphasis on improving personal communication skills. Maliver (1973) notes that after an encounter group experience, participants are more aware of irritating mannerisms in their communication patterns and may change their behaviors as a result. The change is often long-lasting and productive, leading to both enhanced personal development and a significant contribution to the range of human relations skills participants acquire (Hall et al., 1999; Raskin & Rogers, 2005).

A fourth positive influence of basic encounter groups has been in the area of research technology. Yalom (2005) states that before the basic encounter group movement, research of group psychotherapy sessions was rather crude and unimaginative. Since then, empirical research has become more sophisticated and is rooted in the encounter group tradition of investigation (e.g., Bates & Goodman, 1986; Hayashi, 1990; Yamamoto, 1995).

Another strength and contribution of the Rogerian model of conducting groups is that it has led to several other educational models that use it as the basis for their work. For instance, some parent education programs are based on Rogerian group theory. Thomas

Gordon's (1970) **Parent Effectiveness Training (PET)** is an example of one such program that follows this model. In PET, an emphasis is on communication skills. Parents are encouraged to recognize their positive and negative feelings toward their children and come to terms with their own humanness. A major hypothesis of this approach is that *active listening* (i.e., hearing what is implied as well as what is actually said) and *acceptance* (i.e., acknowledging what is happening as opposed to evaluating it) will decrease family conflicts and promote individual growth (Resnick, 1981).

Finally, person-centered encounter groups have made group work acceptable for "normals." Because group participants are not seen as "sick," the group can work with individuals on personal development without the stigma of negative labeling. Such an atmosphere has a beneficial effect on a person's willingness to take risks and try out new behaviors.

Limitations

A limitation of encounter groups is that they may be dangerous to participants who need therapy or structure and who try to use these groups as they would more organized psychotherapy groups (Lieberman et al., 1973; Vander Kolk, 1985). Persons with mental retardation, severe brain damage, multiple disabilities, or severe emotional disturbances need greater structure and guidance than basic encounter groups provide. These individuals are not ready for the openness of encounter groups and may regress as a result of such an experience.

A second limitation of basic encounter groups is the way in which members and leaders are chosen. There are generally no rules for the selection of encounter group members (Meador, 1975; Wood, 1982). Some individuals may talk their way into such groups by convincing group leaders they can benefit from the experience. Group leader training is also not stressed in this tradition, so encounter group facilitators may end up being too passive or too caught up in a **crash-program mentality** in which group experiences are carried out to excess (Yalom, 2005). The ethical issue of not screening members and not requiring rigor in the training of group facilitators is critical. Too many problems can result from a lack of screening and training.

A third criticism of the person-centered approach is that it may not lead anywhere. Rogerians as a group have "had little interest in directing the group's conscious attention to its own processes" (Shaffer & Galinsky, 1989, p. 211). Although the qualities espoused by basic encounter group leaders are quite appropriate for beginning a group, the group's movement may come to a halt because there is no reliance on techniques to motivate members or stir members in a particular direction (Corey, 2004). The emphasis on the personhood of the facilitator and the lack of emphasis on technique may not be productive for some groups (Cain, 1993).

A fourth limitation of basic encounter groups is their history. In the 1960s and 1970s, basic encounter groups became so popular that they were nearly a fad. As a result, they may have lost some of their influence and power, at least in the United States. Participants in basic encounter groups emerged from their experiences in the 1960s and 1970s talking about "finding themselves" and "discovering others." Although the language and the experiences were valid for the time, they may not be as relevant for individuals now, and some skepticism about these groups still exists. Indeed, as Yalom (2005) points out, it is difficult to find a basic encounter group experience now,

386 PART THREE Leading Groups from a Theoretical Perspective

although much of the structure and technology of this type of group survive in large group awareness programs, such as est and Lifespring.

A final limitation of basic encounter groups centers on the research methods used to evaluate them and their success. The **self-report research format** used by Rogers (1970), in which participants write out or check off how they are different as a result of the group, has been attacked as inadequate by empirically oriented investigators. These researchers state that this type of research does not measure the complexity of personal change in a group of this type. Similarly, the claims of success for basic encounter groups are questionable. There were, and still are, variations of person-centered encounter groups throughout the world, so it is hard to determine exactly which variables have contributed to the success of which groups and how.

Learning More

Although person-centered theory began as an individually based way of helping, it evolved into a powerful way to work with groups. One of the primary person-centered group programs is the

Center for Studies of the Person
1150 Silverado, Suite #112
La Jolla, CA 92037
www.centerfortheperson.org

One of the best films on person-centered group work is a classic titled *Journey into Self* (McGaw, Farson, & Rogers, 1968). The film shows Rogers and Richard Farson leading a basic encounter group. Equally important, it shows these co-facilitators demonstrating the basic qualities Rogers conceptualized as important to a group leader: empathy, genuineness, caring, and spontaneity.

Articles or person-centered therapy can be found in a number of professional counseling and psychology periodicals. In addition, for individuals seeking a hands-on experience, biennial international forums on the person-centered approach are held throughout the world.

EXISTENTIAL GROUPS

Existentialism is a philosophy that addresses what it means to be human. This philosophy has been applied to the helping professions only since the mid-1940s (Tamm, 1993). The focus of existential therapy is human existence, particularly the thoughts and anxieties that come with being a human. Existentialists share some beliefs, such as the importance of values, freedom, and responsibility in living one's life. The nature of discovering meaning in the midst of everyday life, as well as in absurd and tragic events, is also an emphasis of this approach. "Existentialism focuses on understanding of the person's subjective view of the world" and, thus, is a phenomenological approach (Corey, 2004, p. 239).

However, existentialism is not united as a theory. Rather, what is described as existentialism is built on the work of such prominent writers as Martin Heidegger, Soren Kierkegaard, Miguel de Unamuno, Jean-Paul Sartre, Martin Buber, Paul Tillich, R. D. Laing,

Viktor Frankl, and Rollo May. These writers stress the importance of balance in human life, where the freedom to choose is counterweighed against the responsibility for choice. In existential thought, life is full of angst as well as joy. There is a paradox to human existence that the more one lives life fully, the greater one is aware of death. This paradox is not morbid but instead simply highlights the fine line in life between being and not being (Mullan, 1992).

Because many existential writers are literary figures, atheists, and theologians and therefore write from different traditions, a great deal of misunderstanding and misinterpretation arises regarding what existentialism is in traditional helping situations. "Many people perceive the existentialist philosophy as obscure and Godless, redundant and solipsistic, reactionary and anti-establishment" (Carroll, Bates, & Johnson, 2004, p. 15). Others have found existential ideas to be "lucid, spiritual, challenging, and comforting" (Carroll et al., 2004, p. 15). In actuality, existential theory is open to many interpretations, and few people find it neutral.

Existential groups in the United States have become popular since the 1960s owing to at least two factors. One has been the rapid change in lifestyles among Americans. The increase in technology, the breakdown of the family, and the accelerated pace of work have caused many people to seek a deeper understanding of who they are and what things mean. In addition, the writings and media presentations of Irvin Yalom (2005), Rollo May (1953, 1977), and Viktor Frankl (2000) have helped people focus on applying existential philosophy and therapy to everyday life as well as counseling situations. All three of the aforementioned professionals are excellent writers and presenters who have made existentialism relevant and have set up treatment formats, such as psychotherapy groups, in a form with popular appeal.

Premises of Existential Groups

Existential groups are based on several premises, among them the belief that people form their lives by the choices they make. Human beings, unlike other living things, are aware of their existence and of the fact that they will die. Thus, they have freedom to make choices and with it the freedom of responsibility for what they do and become (Frankl, 1997). Put another way, people are the authors of their lives for better or worse. They can make their lives meaningful, according to Frankl (2000), in one of three ways: (a) doing a deed, or achieving or accomplishing something; (b) experiencing a value, such as the intrinsic worth of a work of nature, culture, or love; and (c) suffering, by finding a proper attitude toward unalterable fate.

A person who does not actively seek meaning in life, from an existentialist's perspective, chooses despair or psychopathology. Therefore, humans are constantly challenged to relinquish actions and values that are meaningless to them and to embrace new behaviors and thoughts that give them a sense of meaning. The idea is to integrate the best of the old and the new together. Therefore, existentialism is a process of evaluating and simultaneously releasing and incorporating objects and events in life's quest for meaning.

This demand to discard and obtain so that life can be lived to the fullest creates tension and anxiety. The result can be that the person either refuses to take risks or becomes spurred on to seek and make positive choices for his or her life. For example, Grant may be inspired by an existential view to overcome his natural shyness and decide to speak up in his classroom environment. Taking this risk, an act of intention and courage, may result in Grant being recognized for his scholarship and developing new friendships and extracurricular activities. In contrast, Pearl may give into her shyness and not respond to teachers' questions. The result may be that she depreciates herself and becomes more estranged from her classmates.

Practice of Existential Theory in a Group

Existential groups are usually conducted with an emphasis on psychotherapy, counseling, and occasionally psychoeducation. Each member is seen as starting out on an equal footing with the others. "Each gradually scoops out and shapes a particular life space in the group" (May & Yalom, 2005, p. 293). In the group, it is important that members come to realize more fully their potential as human beings and their responsibilities for making healthy and self-directed choices (May, 1983). One of the first goals is to increase **self-awareness**. Corey (2004, p. 241) refers to this increase as helping group members "discover their unique 'being-in-the-world.'" Such a discovery comes through questions, such as "Who am I?" and "Where am I going?" Thus, Darlene may constantly compare and contrast her understanding of herself in reference to others in the group. As such, she may raise her consciousness about herself in the world and discover new possibilities.

It is hoped that hand in hand with awareness is an increase in **personal responsibility**, especially as it relates to interpersonal modes of behavior. Responsibility is "the keystone of the group therapeutic process" (May & Yalom, 2005, p. 292). People cannot live unto themselves without contracting what existential philosopher Soren Kierkegaard described as a "sickness unto death." Nothing in the world has meaning completely by itself. Rather, significance is found only by constantly being responsible for making meaning out of what we do or what occurs to us. In a group situation, it is not enough that Andy relates information about what has happened to him. Instead, he must take responsibility for assigning a meaning to events by thinking and experiencing them as thoroughly as possible in an interpersonal way. Thus, Jorge's descriptions of his childhood have relevance for Andy concerning his own childhood as he thinks about the meaning of events in this period of his life.

In combination with awareness and responsibility is productively handling **anxiety** (Deurzen-Smith, 1997). Being anxious is an unavoidable human emotion. It comes in the facing of new challenges and decision making. People can deny they are anxious in such situations, but to do so makes their lives less fulfilling. Therefore, in a group, members must face their anxiety by seeing their lives as a journey that will ultimately never stop changing or be secure and will end. Thus, when Gene can say to the group that he is nervous about his new relationships at work, he has made a positive step in handling himself and the anxiety that would otherwise paralyze him instead, as in this case, of inspiring him on to a fuller life.

Along with handling anxiety comes a struggle to **search for meaning** in life. Meaning is not something anyone else can give a person but rather something a person must find for him- or herself. Searching for meaning in even simple events, such as the sharing of food, constitutes a choice between being and nonbeing (i.e., death). Death and nonbeing can take many forms, from traumatic experiences, such as having a life-threatening illness, to more mundane times, such as boredom (Greenstein & Breitbart, 2000). Thus, when Gus recognizes that he is dying as a professional because he does not read the literature or take continuing education courses, he has made progress in reclaiming and renewing his life. He has avoided a psychological death.

◆ *Questions from Experience* ◆

When have you felt most alive in your life? What were you doing? How would you relate that feeling to existential theory?

Role of the Existential Group Leader

"Group leaders who work from within an existential framework find that leading a group is an intensive and personal experience" (Carroll et al., 2004, p. 15). This leadership carries with it a responsibility to be active and reflective. Existential group leaders are always thinking and taking risks. They are aware and sensitive to the concerns of others in the group. They do not take the role of an expert but rather the role of a fellow traveler in life (Tamm, 1993). As such, they use anxiety and other uncomfortable emotions in a productive way to help group members realize that these feelings will lead them toward deeper awareness.

Group leaders work hard to develop close relationships with all members of a group. In existential groups, meaningful change is believed to occur only when there is personal contact and interaction. These encounters are ones in which information can be carefully considered and discussed. Another primary job of existential group leaders is **confrontation**—that is, pointing out discrepancies between what people in the group say they want to do and what they are doing. For example, a group leader might say to a member that she keeps talking about inventing a new way to process foods but reports that she has stopped cooking. The leader would ask, "How do these two facts interrelate?"

In addition, group leaders use themselves in existential groups as a source of knowledge in regard to human experience and a model of how to be. Leaders are calm in the presence of the turmoil that may go on within a person or a group. They relate how they have faced difficulties and how they have made choices that enabled them. They talk about the meaning they have experienced in their own lives and how they have made risks or overcome obstacles. Through such self-disclosure, members become more aware not only of the leader but also of themselves.

Desired Outcome of Existential Groups

If the existential group process is successful, then members will realize several benefits. First, they will be more aware of themselves and the choices they have in regard to growth and development. Thus, Christopher will come to realize that even when he decides to postpone a decision he is really making a decision; that is, he is deciding to delay. Members of existential groups will also become more self-determining in what they do. They will refuse to be one of a crowd unless they consciously make that choice. In addition, they will realize that their feelings, even the emotions that seem most painful, can be a source of motivation for them (Greenstein & Breitbart, 2000).

Another outcome of an existential group experience may be that members find new meaning in all aspects of their lives. They no longer take even simple matters for granted but instead realize that, in nature and in their lives, much can be learned from their encounters in the world, even if some of their interactions are initially disconcerting. Related to this emphasis on meaningfulness is highlighting present, here-and-now experiences. The paradox of the human experience is that we are both alone and connected. We are alone in having to decide what we will do or how we will interpret our world. In addition, we are born and die alone. Yet, there is a connectedness to life that those in an existential group ideally come to know and appreciate (Greenstein, 2000). Relationships bring out our humanness, our humanity, and sometimes our humor.

A third outcome of an existential group is an emphasis on becoming authentic. **Authenticity** is the ability to affirm oneself and to make the most of discovering and using one's talents and creativity (Tillich, 1952). Like the other qualities people strive to develop in an existential group, the process of being true to oneself and of developing one's abilities is a lifelong challenge. Thus, DiAnna may claim her talent as a dancer, thereby dedicating herself to go to dance rehearsals regularly and participate in recitals to maximize her potential.

Finally, in an existential group, a desired outcome and possibility is increased interpersonal responsibility (May & Yalom, 2005). In the group, members learn how others view their behaviors, how their behaviors make others feel, how their behaviors create the opinions others have of them, and how their behaviors influence their opinions of themselves. Thus, Jack may come to realize that, when he interrupts and tries to focus the group on himself, other members see his behavior as rude and egotistical and shun him, which makes him feel worse than when his interrupting behavior began.

Overall, as the result of being in an existential group, members of such groups better understand themselves, interpersonal relationships, and their immediate worlds. The group becomes a microcosm of how members are seen and consequently function in their environments. From an existential group experience, members come to realize that life is a journey both shared and solitary.

CASE EXAMPLE: Mason and the Meaningfulness

Mason has been a drifter all his life. He has wondered in and out of educational institutions and work environments. He has been married and divorced twice. Therefore with a menial job and little hope, he attended the free lecture on existentialism at the public library. He was taken by the concepts and asked the lecturer if there was any follow-up he could take. Several books were recommended, which Mason devoured. He then found an open-ended existential discussion group.

He has been attending the group now for 3 months. He seems most content with the content that is being delivered and the discussions that follow. He thinks he is finding some direction in his life. He wonders if what he is experiencing is group therapy.

What do you think? Why?

Evaluation of Existential Groups

Just like other approaches, existentialist groups have certain strengths and limitations. Some of these qualities are inherent in the philosophy of existentialism; others are specific to concerns of individuals in groups.

Strengths and Contributions

One strength of existential groups is that they deal with ultimate issues in life and present their members with opportunities to explore their values and lifestyles in depth. It is difficult to be in an existential group and not question both how you are living and the meaning of events in life. The realities of death and loss, for instance, become more significant factors and concerns (May & Yalom, 2005; Viorst, 1986). After participating in an existential group, participants often let go of past patterns, customs, and beliefs and come to find a different focus for their lives.

Another strength of existential groups is that they provide a framework for other forms of group work. For instance, "the existential concepts of encounter and responsibility are . . . essential factors in psychodrama" (Avrahami, 1995). Likewise, the approach of Alcoholics Anonymous, for example, is consistent with existential philosophy and group work (Page & Berkow, 1998).

A third positive feature regarding existential groups is that they deal with group members in a holistic way in the present (Lowenstein, 1993). Concerns about specific behaviors or past events are not the focus. Therefore, existentialist group members cannot blame or shirk responsibility for who they are as total people and what they are doing here and now.

The versatility of existential theory in groups is another of its strengths. In working with cancer patients in groups, existential theory has been combined with cognitive theory (Kissane et al., 1997) as well as with experiential activities (van der Pompe, Duivenvoorden, Antoni, & Visser, 1997) to produce positive results.

Finally, existential groups are applicable to individuals from a wide range of cultures, especially, for example, African American women who have suffered because of open or subtle prejudice and discrimination (Pack-Brown, Whittington-Clark, & Parker, 1998). The philosophy and emphasis of this approach is open and intriguing. Overall, existential group work has a wide appeal because the theory behind it focuses on one's reason for being and the unavoidable exigencies of life in an unpredictable world.

Limitations

One limitation of existential groups, which is also a drawback to other humanistic approaches to working with groups, is that this approach is most useful and beneficial for members who are verbal, can communicate effectively, and are not afraid to confront issues that are painful (Lowenstein, 1993).

Another minus associated with existential groups is that the theory that supports these groups has limited applicability outside of counseling and psychotherapy settings. Psychoeducational and task/work groups are seldom based on this approach to working with groups.

A third limitation of existentialism in groups is that it takes maturity, life experience, and close supervision to practice this approach (Deurzen-Smith, 1997). There is no unifying way to be a practitioner of existentialism. Thus, the nature of existentialism as a theory and a practice presents problems in training future existential group leaders.

Finally, existentialism and existential groups are broadly based and do not generally deal with specific behaviors or concerns. Group members who need information or immediate answers are not good candidates for this way of working in groups.

Learning More

Existential theory is practiced in groups and with individuals in a number of countries. The most prominent professional organization devoted to existential issues in counseling is the

Society for Existential Analysis
BM Existential
London, England WC1N 3XX
Telephone: 07000 473337
E-mail: exist@cwcom.net

This society publishes the *Journal of the Society of Existential Analysis* and provides courses and advanced training in the field. Its membership is interdisciplinary and includes helping professionals from varied backgrounds as well as philosophers.

An excellent Web site for exploring existential psychotherapy is http://members.aol.com/timlebon/extherapy.htm#ExistentialLinks

For individuals interested in seeing an existential therapist conduct a group, Irvin Yalom's videotape series, *Understanding Group Psychotherapy* (1990), is recommended. This three-volume videotape features Yalom leading inpatient and outpatient groups. It includes an interview with Yalom.

SUMMARY AND CONCLUSION

In this chapter, the various nuances of Adlerian, person-centered, and existential groups have been discussed. Adlerian group work is a social, democratic, relationship-oriented approach to working with individuals. As such, it emphasizes the importance of change in the present while understanding the development of past faulty beliefs and behaviors based on the influence of the family and peer group. Many Adlerian concepts, such as inferiority complex, encouragement, and empathy, have been absorbed into other theories of helping (Corsini, 1988; Hansen et al., 1980). Nevertheless, Adlerian theory is still a viable way of assisting groups of individuals in a wide range of group settings to grow, change, and achieve. A real strength of the Adlerian approach to working with groups is its flexibility in relation to children, adolescents, adults, parents, and families. The application of Adlerian theory to different groups is psychoeducationally based and, therefore, nonthreatening and helpful to most.

Adlerian group work will need a stronger base of research support in the future if it is going to continue to prosper. More uniformity and concreteness of methodology will also have to be employed. For now, however, Adlerian group work offers a viable and positive alternative to other types of groups. By leading groups that are shorter in length, more health focused, and more socially oriented, Adlerians have carved out a unique niche in the group work field from which others have borrowed but which they have not superseded.

Person-centered groups, especially their most famous form, the basic encounter group, are both a historical footnote in the group work movement and a present reality. Many individuals participated in basic encounter groups in the 1960s and 1970s. The influence of these groups lives on in these people's memories as well as in some groups that are still conducted according to the encounter group model.

Carl Rogers (1970) introduced the concept and format of basic encounter groups in the 1960s. They caught on quickly and were widely imitated, partially because of the transitional nature of the period. As a scientist-practitioner,

Rogers investigated the impact of these groups and generally found them to make a positive contribution to the lives of individuals participating in them. True to his theory and belief about human nature, he set up the groups in a largely unstructured way, believing that the goodness and growth within people would emerge. He noted how the typical group session developed and wrote about his findings.

Today, encounter groups survive primarily in a less formal format but are the basis of several religious and self-help groups (Yalom, 2005). The bad publicity and negative findings associated with these groups in the past probably mean they will not emerge as a widespread popular movement again. Yet, their legacy in the group field is noteworthy. They contributed to new expectations of members and leaders in groups, and they fostered attention on how communication patterns change in a group setting and how group research should be conducted.

In comparison with person-centered groups, existential groups, like Adlerian groups, have increased in popularity over the years. Their growth can be attributed to the writings and influence of clinicians such as Irvin Yalom, Rollo May, and Viktor Frankl. The hectic, rapid, and uncertain nature of modern existence, including a new quest for spiritual matters, also has made these groups appealing to a number of individuals seeking greater self-understanding and meaning in their lives.

Existential groups, like Adlerian and person-centered groups, focus on relationships. A predominant belief underlying these groups is that techniques follow understanding within the groups between members and the leader. Therefore, the existential approach in group work can incorporate other major theoretical perspectives and even borrow techniques from these models (Vontress, 1996). The flexibility of existential group work is one of its strengths. In addition, its use in multicultural groups reflects the appropriateness of this theory of group work as one of the universal ways of working with people in groups.

Overall, Adlerian, person-centered, and existential theories are and have been important ways of conducting groups. Leaders in these approaches are challenged to renew and develop different means and methods whereby these theories may be used even more in groups in the future, especially in groups that are not primarily counseling and psychotherapy oriented.

CLASSROOM EXERCISES

1. Read a recent article (published in the last 5 years) on an Adlerian, person-centered, or existential group. Discuss the content of the article with three other classmates. What were the major findings?

2. Would you have to change your personal style of interaction to become a leader of an Adlerian, a person-centered, or an existential group (e.g., become more aware, become more/less active)? Discuss the changes you would have to make, if any, with a classmate and then with the class as a whole.

3. With another classmate, compare the Adlerian, person-centered or existential approaches to group work with psychoanalytic emphasis. Keep your remarks focused on the comparisons between the approaches you choose. Share your remarks with another pair.

4. With which groups of people do you think an Adlerian group would work best? With which group of people do you think a person-centered group would be a good fit? With which groups of people do you think an existential group would be most effective? Explain your answer as it relates to the philosophy and pragmatics of each approach, and if possible the research you have found that supports your view.

CHAPTER 17

GESTALT AND PSYCHODRAMA GROUPS

Laimute Druskis/PH College

I remember doing role plays in your group
  trying to look cool, while my palms sweated
    and my heart beat as fast as a hummingbird's wing.
You were supportive . . . giving me a part of the warmth
  you brought with you that summer
    while encouraging me to explore the universe
      that was myself.
Other classes, other seasons came as quickly as the sound
  of laughter and as silently as sorrow.
With you in mind I traveled the road to conventions
  and engaged in counseling conversations
Sharing all the light and darkness that came to be.*

*From "First Thoughts . . . A Reflection on Professional Friendship" by Samuel T. Gladding, 1989, *Journal of Humanistic Education and Development, 27,* p. 190. Copyright ACA. Reprinted with permission. No further reproduction authorized without the written permission of the American Counseling Association.

Gestalt and psychodrama groups are experiential in nature and generally stress interpersonal interactions and learning through awareness and enactment. Although they are powerful approaches in group settings, Gestalt therapy and psychodrama include both individual and group emphases (Moreno, 1946; Yontef & Jacobs, 2005).

Fritz Perls and his collaborators, Laura Perls and Paul Goodman, founded Gestalt therapy (Yontef & Jacobs, 2005). Fritz Perls was originally trained as a psychoanalyst and, while a practitioner in his native Germany, he incorporated Kurt Goldstein's holistic theory and Wilhelm Reich's idea of *"body armor"* (a notion that gave substance to Freud's concept of resistance) into his clinical work. Perls was forced to flee Nazism in the early 1930s because of his Jewish background. He settled in South Africa, where he encountered the holistic work of Jan Smuts. Then he immigrated to the United States, where his coauthored book *Gestalt Therapy* (Perls, Hefferline, & Goodman, 1951/1994) was published. The book outlined the major tenets of his theory and gained national prominence after his move in 1963 to the Esalen Institute in Big Sur, California.

Psychodrama is one of the oldest and most dynamic theories devised for working with groups. Its originator, Jacob L. Moreno, initially experimented with his theory in the streets of Vienna after World War I with an enactment procedure known as "The Living Newspaper." He spent the rest of his life developing and refining the concepts and practice of psychodrama both in Austria and in the United States (Moreno, 1984; Nolte, 1989). Although psychodrama gained notoriety in the United States as a therapeutic intervention at Moreno's psychodrama theater in Beacon, New York, and at St. Elizabeth's Hospital in Washington, DC, it is applicable in a number of settings and is practiced all over the world (Blajan-Marcus, 1974; Moreno, 1949). One of the most productive spin-offs of this approach is the common use of role-play within psychoeducational, psychotherapeutic, and management groups (Blatner, 1996, 2005; Corsini, 1966).

In this chapter, the essential natures of both Gestalt therapy and psychodrama are examined. Specifically, the emphases of these approaches, the premises behind them, their practice in a group setting, the role of leaders in such groups, desired outcomes, and strengths and limitations of these ways of working are explored. Resources are given for learning more about each theory, especially in group work.

GESTALT GROUPS

Gestalt therapy is an experiential and humanistic approach to change that focuses on working with client **awareness**. In the Gestalt environment, there is an emphasis on the teaching of awareness skills in a variety of ways. Although Gestalt therapy is practiced on many levels, Fritz Perls claimed that clients could be treated by Gestalt group therapy alone (Yontef & Jacobs, 2005). This assertion was never accepted by most Gestalt therapists and still is not today. Rather, Gestalt group therapy complements individual and couples work but does not replace them as treatment modalities.

In the original Gestalt workshops, "Perls and his immediate disciples preferred to focus on the group solely as a backdrop for individual work" (Shaffer & Galinsky, 1989, p. 121). Thus, they would concentrate on one individual at a time. The person who wanted to "work" would sit in the "**hot seat**" with his or her chair facing that of the therapist or leader. The rest of the group served as a kind of "**Greek chorus**" in the background of the encounter where they resonated and empathized with the one who was working and thereby gained insights into themselves and others through the process of identification. Work sessions would last from 10 to 30 minutes and end with a mutually decided closure.

Overall, Perls was a deep thinker and concerned about the problems of existence (Perls, 1974), but his unique, unconventional, complex, and eccentric lifestyle contributed to a basic misunderstanding of him and his theory (Perls, 1969b). It was the ideas and processes generated by Perls, however, combined with those of Kepner (1980) and Zinker (1977), that have evolved into what is now known as the *Gestalt group process.*

Premises of Gestalt Groups

Four basic assumptions underlie Gestalt groups, according to Latner (1973). First is the **principle of holism** (integration). Often individuals will carry around **emotional debris** (i.e., "unfinished business") from their past. These concerns are usually linked to resentment and incomplete separation from a lost love object. Through a series of prescribed exercises (e.g., an empty chair technique in which the distressed person is given an opportunity to role-play and speak to a missing person, say "good-bye," and feel all sides of a situation), integration occurs. The person becomes more complete—that is, more than the sum of his or her individual experiences.

A second assumption involves the **principle of awareness**. People are free to choose only when they are *self-aware:* in touch with their existence and what it means to be alive. The concept of awareness includes all sensations, thoughts, and behaviors that individuals experience. It is the "what" of existence and is always focused in the **here and now** (i.e., the present). Awareness often results in insight when a person "owns" his or her control and responsibility over a situation. Awareness and **dialogue** (i.e., talk between others and oneself or between different aspects of oneself) are two primary therapeutic tools in Gestalt therapy.

Third is the **principle of figure/ground**. The *figure* in one's personal life is composed of experiences that are most important, such as deciding how one will approach a hostile person. *Background* is composed of experiences that are less pressing, such as what one will do after dinner. Healthy persons take care of their figural (most important) needs first. As figural needs are met, these individuals become more aware of background needs, some of which become figural and require work.

The fourth principle of the Gestalt approach is the **principle of polarities**. If people are to meet their needs, then they must first differentiate their perceptual field into opposites/poles—for example, active/passive, good/bad. The idea is for clients to express both sides of a polarity or conflict and then integrate this experience holistically. Too often people fail to resolve conflicts within themselves and with others because they are not in contact with the opposite sides of the situation. For example, if Fran sees her father as only good, then she will not be able to deal with her relationship with him realistically, especially given the fact that when growing up she had a "love/hate" experience with him.

Overall, Gestalt group process is a complex phenomenon built on the previously cited premises. It is based on the assumption that groups are multidimensional systems that operate on several levels at once. Groups, and people, are holistic, with all of their functions interrelated. It is impossible to understand the person in the group outside of the context of the group. Another assumption is that people are *proactive* (i.e., they take the initiative) in making choices, especially if they are self-aware and living in the present (Passons, 1975). As an approach, Gestalt theory views individuals as neither positive nor negative but as **intrinsically neutral**—that is, without a predetermined set of responses.

In addition, Gestalt therapy is premised on the idea that individuals will experience a certain amount of "elasticity" between their more pressing needs (figure) and their less pressing needs (background). **Elasticity** is the ability to move from one set of needs to another and back. It is the elasticity of the figure-ground formation on which selfhood is rooted as individuals define themselves in regard to the needs of which they are most aware. Another way of explaining this phenomenon is to say that people perceive their selves changing in an expanding and contracting way depending on their needs.

A final major idea of the Gestalt approach is that **awareness** (i.e., a total organismic response) gives people self-cohesiveness and enables them. If individuals are healthily aware of themselves and their environments, then they choose an active way of dealing with the polarities of their lives. This usually means they integrate the opposite aspects of these polarities and make a choice based on all the information available. Therefore, Gestalt group process stresses increasing awareness, choice, meaningfulness, integrative wholeness, and closure (Mullan & Rosenbaum, 1978; Vander Kolk, 1985).

◆ *Questions from Experience* ◆

When have you been most aware of needs in your life? When have you noticed changes of needs from figure/ground to ground/figure in your development? How has this awareness and the changes that come with it contributed to your dialogue with others and yourself?

Practice of Gestalt Theory in a Group

Gestalt group process is often misperceived as individual "hot seat" psychotherapy in a group setting (Shaffer & Galinsky, 1989; Yalom, 2005), even though Perls (1967) distinguished his workshop style, in which he would often interact with someone in this manner, from other forms of Gestalt groups. Actually, Gestalt groups function in several ways.

One typical way is for the Gestalt leader to focus on one person in the presence of other group members and work with him or her. This is more of a traditional West Coast practice, according to Latner (1973), in which Gestalt practitioners who have been heavily influenced by Perls pay attention to the issues of self-awareness, centering, and responsibility (Corey, 2004).

The traditional East Coast style of Gestalt group work is more interactive, involving direct, here-and-now communication among group members. "This model is similar to Yalom's model for existential group therapy" (Yontef & Jacobs, 2005, pp. 328–329). It is interpersonal in nature (Earley, 2000).

A third model is a mixture of the two models just described with a balance between interaction and one-on-one focus (Yontef, 1990). This style, which has no geographic identification, is sometimes referred to as **dual-focused Gestalt group work** (Harman, 1988). One older variation of this model is the so-called **floating hot seat** (Polster & Polster, 1973; Yontef & Jacobs, 2005) in which interaction is promoted by encouraging group members to work on exploring their own personal issues when someone else in the group touches on an issue that has personal relevance for them. A newer form of this approach is Kepner's (1980) Gestalt group process in which attention is systematically focused on (a) the individual at the intrapersonal level, (b) two or more people at the interpersonal level, and (c) the group as a systematic unit. Kepner's **trilevel model of Gestalt group work** illustrates how dynamic Gestalt group work can be. Overall, there is no one style of Gestalt group practice.

Despite diversity in operating procedures, Gestalt group practitioners share many common beliefs and practices. First, they stay centered on the here and now (i.e., present experiences). They do this by asking how and what questions, instead of why. This focus allows the most pressing needs of clients to surface and to be addressed (Westwood, Keats, & Wilensky, 2003). Second, Gestalt group practitioners ask their group members to work on a specific problem to help foster greater awareness. Sometimes, group members may be actively involved in helping a member process what is happening in his or her work. At other times, the interaction is between the group leader and the group member, with the rest of the group functioning as a background. Regardless, the focus is on individual responsibility and integration (Perls, 1969a).

A third quality that Gestalt practitioners share is their emphasis on behavioral, rather than cognitive, processes (Zinker, 1977). Inviting group members to participate in a therapeutic or growth experience, rather than to talk about their problem, is helpful for most. Finally, Gestalt practitioners use a series of experiments and exercises to help their members achieve greater awareness and growth (Resnikoff, 1988). **Experiments** are nonplanned experiences that occur spontaneously in the session. For example, if a group member starts waving her arms when talking about how she wishes to be free of her present life circumstances, then the group leader might say to her, "Melody, develop that more," at which time the member might begin to exaggerate the arm movement into a winglike flapping motion. In response to this motion, the leader might encourage the member to "fly," at which point the member might take off and pretend to fly around the room. The experience would then be processed. **Exercises**, in contrast, are planned activities that have been used previously to help group members become more aware. For example, having Tom, a group member, role-play a situation is a type of exercise.

Both experiments and exercises revolve around five main themes: (a) enactment, (b) directed behavior, (c) fantasy, (d) dreams, and (e) homework (Polster & Polster, 1973). They all occur in the present and are chosen for the specific purpose of promoting growth. Some of the better known exercises are explored here.

Making the rounds is a warm-up game in Gestalt groups in which confrontation is heightened. In this exercise, group members are asked to say something they usually do not verbalize. For example, Anita might say to all group members, "I am afraid to tell you about myself . . . because . . ." or "When I try to ask for help from you, I feel . . . ." In such cases, Anita makes the rounds with all other members and may become aware and feel like working through some unfinished materials of the past, in which case rounds would be suspended. Then Anita would work with the group leader and other group members on a particular concern.

Two other types of enactment are **rehearsal** and role reversal. In a rehearsal, group members are invited to say out loud what they are thinking internally. For example, they may note how much they struggle to please others and perform properly. They are then free to decide whether they wish to spend their time and energy in this manner. In a **role reversal**, people act the opposite of what they feel. For instance, Craig, who is feeling inadequate, will act adequate, even bold. By doing so, he gets a feel for an area he previously denied.

Body language is another exercise in which group members are invited to participate. Here the emphasis is placed on what a person's body is doing, such as a hand tapping a chair or a leg kicking. The leader asks, "What is your hand saying?" or "What is your leg doing?" Participants are then free to emphasize what their behaviors mean. They may do this through exaggerating the behavior or simply noting its present movement. The result is an integration of mind and body awareness.

Another technique often used in Gestalt groups is **changing questions to statements**. This procedure requires a group member who has raised a question to make it into a statement. For instance, the question "Do you really think that is why you did not succeed?" would be changed to "I do not think that is why you were unsuccessful." Changing questions to statements helps all group members become more aware of their true feelings. It also helps eliminate **condemning questions** that put people down and prevent them from seeing situations more honestly and openly. "Don't you think you should feel differently?" is an example of a condemning question.

The **empty chair technique** is designed to help group members deal with different aspects of their personalities (Fagan & Shepherd, 1970). This technique is often used in individual Gestalt sessions but is also effective in group settings. Two variations of the technique are discussed here. In both, an empty chair is placed in front of the group member who wishes to work. In the first variation, the participant is asked to put into the chair all of the feelings that are opposite of the way he or she usually feels, such as anger, aggression, and impulsiveness. The individual then switches seats and becomes the feelings put into the chair. A dialogue is promoted between the polar parts of the individual, with the person changing chairs every time he or she switches feelings. The idea is to promote an integration of feelings and thoughts.

In the second variation, **unfinished business** (i.e., the tendency of a person to relive past thoughts and feelings in the present) is the focus. Unfinished business usually centers on unacknowledged grief, anger, or loss of objects, and it remains in the background of people's lives, inhibiting their ability to function realistically in the present. Participants who have unfinished business are often asked to put the object, feeling, or person in the empty chair and say good-bye. Sometimes another group member can play the part of whatever was placed in the chair and say good-bye in return.

A variation of the integrative empty chair technique is the **top dog/underdog dialogue**. In this method, group members are asked to examine the *top-dog introjections* they have taken in from parents (usually represented by "should" and "you") and their own real feelings about situations (usually represented by "I" statements). For example, "You should always be polite, but sometimes I do not feel that way." They then are asked to carry on a dialogue between these two aspects of themselves before the group or with another group member and try to become more aware of their true self-identity and ways to act that would be appropriate.

Fantasy exercises are another popular method used in Gestalt group work. Corey (2004) notes that fantasy can be employed to help group members (a) be more concrete in assessing their feelings, (b) deal with catastrophic experiences, (c) explore and express feelings of guilt and shame, and (d) become more involved in the group. It is not necessary that group members live out their fantasies, for example, conveying their repressed feelings of resentment to an elderly relative. Just the fact that they are acting as if they were doing what they have hoped for is helpful to most in becoming more integrative and holistic.

Dream work is seen by Perls (1969a) as "the royal road to integration." It is used in both individual and group work by having those who dream recreate and relive the dream in the present. By doing so, these individuals become all parts of the dream. They may do this through working alone in the group setting or having others in the group act out different parts of the dream. This latter idea is known as *dream work as theater* (Zinker, 1977). It assumes that basic archetypal themes exist that all group members share and can benefit from experiencing.

Dreams are expressions of the polarities within individuals in Gestalt theory. Therefore, it is important to act out the different parts and become conscious of the forces within. Rainwater (1979) suggests that people explore their dreams by asking themselves certain questions, such as "What am I feeling?" "What do I want?" "What am I doing?" and "What is my dream telling me?" By questioning and enacting with others, individuals become more aware, integrated, and empowered to act.

Provost (1999) describes a 6-week growth group based on Gestalt, Jungian, and humanistic theories that helps participants process and understand their dreams. The group, including the leader, uses the **energy field** (i.e., the sum total of individual members' energies and attention in the group) to help a group member expand the dialogue and action within the original dream but beyond itself. By so doing, dream work becomes a means for understanding oneself and the group in which one is working.

Coven (2004) found that Gestalt Group Dreamwork could be effective with an Asian population, specifically Taiwanese. Contrary to cultural stereotypes, "participants readily enacted roles, were personally open, and expressed intense feelings" (p. 175). However, Coven cautions that his experience may be atypical because of the preparation he did beforehand and the demonstration nature of his workshop. Nevertheless, it seems clear that "dream work facilitates group cohesion and is fun, stimulating, and powerful in assisting with the development of personal insight" (Berube, 1999, p. 98).

Homework is a technique that primarily involves group members practicing outside the group what they have learned inside the group. For example, Carole may learn through homework assignments to make statements to her colleagues, such as "This room feels cold to me," instead of asking them condemning questions such as "Aren't you aware that you have the thermostat set too low and that people are freezing in this room because of your actions?" Homework helps group members achieve closure on unresolved issues as well. For instance, Ishu may speak to his parents about how he felt neglected as a child and then bring the results of this discussion back to the group to process.

CASE EXAMPLE: Gerard Has a Gestalt Experience

Gerard has lived a lonely life drifting in and out of jobs and relationships. He is depressed and has been having a hard time lately defining himself as anything other than a "loser." He lives near a university, however, and recently he heard of a professor who was offering a group experience for depressives. Gerard applied, was screened, and joined the group.

His first day he was surprised to find that instead of introducing each other verbally, the college professor, who was the group leader, had members cut out pictures and words from magazines and newspapers and either place them in a bag (if they were not ready to share) or paste them on a bag if the pictures and words represented aspects of the person that the individual was willing

to share. Gerard found he put more of his material in the bag than on it. However, as the weeks went by, he occasionally pulled something out of his bag and shared it with other group members.

The group was active throughout its 14 sessions. Gerard did not hold back, and he was able to voice his concerns by relating his dreams, reversing roles, and rehearsing new ways of relating to others. He felt energized at the end of each session.

How do you think Gerard's experience would have differed had he enrolled in a person-centered group? The fact that Gerard was energized seemed helpful to him. What might he have done with the energy or even with the group to maximize his experience?

Role of the Gestalt Group Leader

The group leader is central to the functioning of the Gestalt group. The leader is usually the person who "determines much of what will take place, and with whom and when such interaction will occur" (Hansen, Warner, & Smith, 1980, p. 217). One of the leader's jobs is to help group members locate their **impasses** (i.e., the places in which they get stuck) and work ways through them so awareness and growth will take place (Corey, 2004). To achieve this goal and promote a therapeutic breakthrough, the leader may intentionally frustrate group members by refusing to play their manipulative games, such as being helpless or stupid. Perls (1969a) puts it this way: "My function as a therapist is to help you to the awareness of the here and now, and to frustrate you in any attempt to break out of this" (p. 74). The leader balances challenging group members with supporting them.

Zinker (1977) sees the leader's role in this process as an artist. It is up to the leader to create an atmosphere that promotes growth within the group and the group's own creativity. To do so, the group leader must self-disclose and allow things to happen. He or she must be "agenda free" and block off any attempts by group members or the group as a whole to desert the "now." This may mean that the leader asks group members or the group, "What is happening to you (us) now?" It also means that the group leader makes sure everyone speaks for him- or herself by using "I" messages instead of "you" messages (Donigian & Hulse-Killacky, 1999), for example, "I feel happy when dancing" rather than "You feel happy when dancing." Whenever possible and appropriate, "should" messages are changed to "want to" messages.

Overall, as Levin and Shepherd (1974) have pointed out, Gestalt group leaders play several roles during the group's life span: (a) expert-helper; (b) seer, communications expert; (c) frustrator; (d) creator; and (e) teacher. Leaders must balance these roles with personal integrity and have the strength to withstand pressures from the group not to stay in the present. They must not rely on gimmicks to try to promote the growth of group members, yet they cannot be passive (Resnikoff, 1988). They must trust their intuition and play their hunches. In many ways, competent Gestalt group leaders are "catalysts" (Shaffer & Galinsky, 1989). They keep group members focused on "now" issues and help them increase awareness and find personal/interpersonal resolutions for issues that emerge.

Desired Outcome of Gestalt Groups

As a result of a Gestalt group, members should be more aware of themselves in the here and now. They should also change (Flores, 1988). It is hoped they will have shed **layers of neurosis** (i.e., the *phony*—being unauthentic; the *phobic*—being afraid to really see themselves as they are; and the *impasse*—where their maturity is stuck). Then they can come to realize self-growth through *implosiveness*—feeling their deadness—and *explosiveness*—releasing pent-up energy to be authentic and alive to all feelings (Perls, 1970). The bottom line is that members will be more congruent in themselves (mind and body) and with others. They will not be mired down in worrying about the past and will become more self-regulating. The experiential quality of Gestalt groups is especially beneficial for persons who are predominantly cognitive, for it forces them to use other ways of relating.

Thousands of people have experienced favorable results through participating in Gestalt groups (Yontef & Simkin, 2005). In a well-designed study, Lieberman, Yalom, and Miles (1973) actually found Gestalt group members rated their experience first among 17 different groups in regard to pleasantness and constructiveness. They felt they had learned a great deal and were enthusiastic. They rated their group leader highly. The key to whether a Gestalt group is beneficial is whether the leader is well trained.

Evaluation of Gestalt Groups

Strengths and limitations of Gestalt groups must be recognized before individuals decide to enroll in or conduct such groups. Whether a Gestalt group is right for a person or a situation depends on that particular individual or situation.

Strengths and Contributions

One strength of Gestalt groups is their particular suitability to group leaders "who have a humanistic, existential approach to helping others" (Vander Kolk, 1985, p. 82). Gestalt group work lends itself well to leaders who are creative and who strive to bring out the creativity in others. It emphasizes the affective dimension of human existence, which is often neglected in groups. When people's emotional arousal is raised, they are often more persuadable (Young, 2001).

A second strength of Gestalt groups is that the focus within the groups is on working through impasses and becoming more integrated. Members may help one another feel more connected and less alone than if Gestalt work were conducted individually. As Frew

(1983) points out, there is power in the group that comes from member and group inter-action as well as from leader and member interaction.

A third strong point of Gestalt groups is the variety of exercises and experiences they foster. Gestalt group work is usually intense and active (Day & Matthes, 1992). By partici-pating in planned and spontaneous activities, group members come to realize different aspects about themselves than they might through just talking. The group is also influen-tial in forcing members out of previously unproductive patterns of interacting.

Gestalt groups are also quite powerful in working with a variety of difficulties, from addiction (Browne-Miller, 1993) to issues faced by couples (Curman & Curman, 1994). The versatility of Gestalt groups make them popular with a number of clinicians, especially those who work in settings where talking and the exchange of words are not as effective as movement.

Another strength of the Gestalt groups is the abundance of training institutes available to professionals who wish to learn this approach. Several publications are devoted to this approach, too, including *The Gestalt Journal*. Group leaders have a reservoir of rich resources available to them, if they are careful in screening the backgrounds of those with whom they work and study (Yontef & Simkin, 2005).

Limitations

The limitations of Gestalt theory and practice in groups mirror its strengths. First, the Gestalt approach tends to eschew the cognitive side of human nature. Perls and the Gestalt theory are often accused of being anti-intellectual and concerned only with affec-tive and bodily experiences. Perls's famous statement "Lose your mind and come to your senses" is often quoted in support of this criticism.

A second limitation of Gestalt groups is that group leaders are sometimes not able to help the group help itself, that is, to work through impasses. When this occurs, there is individual leader–member interaction, or there is uncontrolled group pressure on individ-uals to do things they are not ready to do. Either case is nonproductive at best and can be destructive.

A third limitation of the Gestalt approach is the potential danger of abusing tech-niques and people. Unless the group leader is particularly sensitive to the needs of group members, he or she may become mechanical in showing off techniques and not really be helpful. Ethical questions are of major concern if the group leader opens up members' feelings and then does not help them resolve these emotions in an integra-tive fashion. Although there are a number of state, national, and international associa-tions for Gestalt therapy, there is still much to be done in standardizing the practice of this theory.

Finally, Gestalt groups are extremely difficult to research (Fagan & Shepherd, 1970). Very little empirical research has been conducted on them. Although Simkin (1975) may be correct in saying, "Most Gestalt therapists are busy practicing their art rather than eval-uating it" (p. 283), more research must be conducted if this approach is to continue within the mainstream of group work (Rudestam, 1982). Yalom (1985), for instance, has already dismissed some aspects of Gestalt group work by saying, "I feel that Perls's group therapy technique is ill-founded and makes inefficient use of a group's therapeutic poten-tial" (p. 453).

Learning More

A number of centers support and encourage the practice of Gestalt theory in group work and in counseling and therapy. One of the most productive of these centers is

> Association for the Advancement of Gestalt Therapy
> AAGT—Administrator
> Silvie Falschlunger
> 60 Waller Ave.
> White Plains, NY 10605
> http://www.aagt.org/

The Gestalt Therapy Network (http://www.gestalttherapy.net/) is another informative link and provides a forum where Gestalt Therapist as all levels can "talk to each other, learn from each other and create a network of shared interests and resources."

The Gestalt Therapy Page (http://www.gestalt.org/) a project sponsored by The Gestalt Journal Press (i.e., Center for Gestalt Development), also provides good information. This Center for Gestalt annually publishes *The Gestalt Directory,* which includes information about Gestalt practitioners and training programs throughout the world. It also produces *The Gestalt Journal,* a semiannual periodical that is devoted to publishing articles on the theory and practice of Gestalt theory.

PSYCHODRAMA GROUPS

Psychodrama, a way of exploring the human psyche through dramatic action, was created and developed by Moreno in the 1920s and 1930s (D'Amato & Dean, 1988; Goldman & Morrison, 1984). The idea evolved out of Moreno's creativity, which was fostered by his encounters with children and his love for spontaneity and the theater. In essence, psychodrama became an extension of Moreno's personality. He advocated a group approach in an era of intrapersonal emphasis. Therefore, many of his contributions to the field of group work (e.g., his emphasis on action and his focus on the here and now) have never been properly acknowledged.

The main forerunner of psychodrama was the "**Theater of Spontaneity**," which Moreno originated in 1921 in Vienna. Participants in the theater were "radical young artists" who entertained the Viennese "with dramatic productions that were improvised on the stage. This kind of action took many forms; one was the '**Living Newspaper**,' in which recent happenings—sometimes local incidents, sometimes developments in world politics—were spontaneously dramatized" (Anderson, 1974, p. 209). Moreno found that those who played nonscripted and unrehearsed parts, as well as members of the audience, experienced an emotional **catharsis** (a release of pent-up feelings) as a result of participating in or observing the dramatic enactment. Shortly thereafter, psychodrama as a formal system was conceptualized, with Moreno (1923, 1984) stressing the uniqueness of the approach by having clients relive, instead of retell or analyze, their conflicts.

Premises of Group Psychodrama

Psychodrama is sometimes viewed as "nothing more than a grand extension of the clinical interview" (Greenberg, 1974b, p. 13), but it is actually much more. Psychodrama is similar to psychoanalysis in that it emphasizes a freeing of individuals from the irrational forces that bind them into dysfunctional patterns of behaving. The goals of these two approaches are the same; however, psychodrama differs radically from psychoanalysis in its emphasis on action. The client is removed from the usual one-to-one relationship with the psychotherapist or counselor and is given an opportunity to act out and experience various aspects of his or her problem(s) within a group setting. In contrast to psychoanalysis, psychodrama emphasizes personal interaction and encounter, focus on here and now, spontaneity and creativity, full expression of feelings, and reality testing (Brown-Shaw, Westwood, & DeVries, 1999).

A focused emphasis of psychodrama is on the holistic interaction of the protagonist in his or her drama. The group leader is the producer of the drama. In the process, the protagonist reworks his or her life as both a player and a playwright (Blatner, 2000). In action, "habitual verbal defenses are circumvented" (Blatner, 2005) and new realizations occur. For instance, a psychodrama leader might say to Bob, a group member, "Show the group how your interactions with your father affected your view of work." Bob would then enact by himself, or with others, scenes that came to mind between his father and him. Such enactments would be based on memories and shown in dramatic form rather than discussed. The result would be new awareness on Bob's part that he could then discuss, and observations from group members of what they noticed in Bob's enactment(s) could be shared. Basically, psychodrama is predicated on the assumption that humans in society are continually evolving and can become aware of matters pertaining to their lives at any developmental stage. Persons who are open to themselves begin to realize their strengths as well as their liabilities. Such realizations make them more capable of meeting external demands in creative ways.

At the heart of psychodrama is the **encounter**, an existentialist concept that involves total physical and psychological contact among persons on an intense, concrete, and complete basis in the here and now. The encounter can relate to past events, anticipated ones, or present circumstances, but it always involves taking a moment or a particular situation in one's life and expanding it in various dimensions (Leveton, 2001). One particular dimension that the encounter deals with is **surplus reality**—"psychological experience that transcends the boundaries of physical reality" (Blatner, 2005, p. 429). These experiences, which include relationships with those who have died or were never born or with God, are often as important to people as their actual experiences with physical entities. For example, Jodie may still grieve for the child she lost in childbirth. In the encounter, she can express her feelings through dramatically reliving the scene of loss and the ways she might have handled or dealt with the tragedy at that time. Overall, the encounter is the experience of identity and total reciprocity, summed up by Moreno (1914) in the following poetic way:

> A meeting of two: eye to eye, face to face. And when you are near I will tear your eyes out and place them instead of mine, and you will tear my eyes out and will place them instead of yours, and I will look at you with your eyes and you will look at me with mine. (p. 3)

The main concepts that emphasize Moreno's premise on experiencing one's situation fully in the here and now are spontaneity and creativity, situation, tele, catharsis, and insight (Greenberg, 1974b). **Spontaneity** is the response people make that contains "some degree of adequacy to a new situation or a degree of novelty to an old situation"

(Moreno, 1945a, p. xii). The purpose of spontaneity is to liberate one's self from scripts and stereotypes and gain new perspectives on life. Responding in new creative ways is part of this process. For example, Mildred, instead of panicking when she is given a math test, now begins to sit calmly and study the whole exam before making a response.

Situation is the emphasis on the present, where "natural barriers of time, space, and states of existence are obliterated" (Greenberg, 1974b, pp. 16–17). Under these circumstances, clients are able to work on past problems, future fears, and current difficulties in a here-and-now atmosphere. For instance, Lucas plans for his graduation from high school, college, and an entry-level job by confronting his fear of success and his present lack of self-confidence.

Tele is the total communication of feelings between people, "the cement which holds groups together" (Moreno, 1945a, p. xi). It is experienced most when it occurs between two people. At its best, it involves complete interpersonal and reciprocal empathy. In a tele, Mitch and Sandy tell each other which qualities they most admire in the other and how it makes them feel when they think they have expressed one or more of these qualities, such as empathy and poise.

Catharsis and insight are the "end products" of spontaneity and tele (Greenberg, 1974b). Catharsis involves an emotional purging, such as when Delilah screams out in regard to her mother, "All I ever wanted you to do was love me!" While one of the end products of spontaneity and tele, catharsis is "the beginning of reparation and healing" because what was disowned, such as suffering and grief, is now personally accepted, expressed, and integrated (Westwood et al., 2003, p. 123). **Insight** is a related concept, consisting of immediate new perceptions and understandings about one's problems that occur during or after the experience of catharsis. For instance, in the preceding example, Delilah might say after her cathartic experience, "I never realized I was so angry." Psychodrama participants and the audience may experience both catharsis and insight.

◆ *Questions from Experience* ◆

When have you ever felt relief by either reenacting an event or reliving an experience with another person where you both told and showed them what had happened to upset or disturb you?

Practice of Psychodrama in a Group

The practice of psychodrama is multidimensional. First, physical and personal factors must be considered, such as a stage, a protagonist, actors, a director, and an audience (Blatner, 1996, 2005; Haskell, 1973) (see Figure 17.1). Second, techniques must be employed in a methodological manner (Holmes & Karp, 1991; Moreno, 1959).

The **stage** is the area where the action takes place. It may be a formal platform, or it may simply be a part of a room. In essence, the stage is wherever the participants want it to be. For instance, Jason says to his psychodrama group, "The corner of the room will be my stage this time." Most groups find it beneficial to have the stage in a separate place

Figure 17.1

The psychodrama stage.

Source: Adapted from *Acting In: Practical Applications of Psychodramatic Methods* (2nd ed.), by A. Blatner, 1988, Springer Publishing Company, Inc., New York 10012. Copyright © 1988 by Springer Publishing Company, Inc. Used by permission.

from where the group meets to remind members that the enactments are clearly different from verbal interchanges (Blatner, 1996).

The **protagonist** is the person who is the subject of the psychodrama enactment (Blatner, 1996, 2005). He or she may play many parts. For example, in a psychodrama, Laura as the protagonist played different parts of herself, from being sweet and innocent to being mean and spiteful. At times, the protagonist may step out of a scene and observe. Regardless, the goal of the protagonist is to express freely the thoughts, feelings, concerns, and issues relevant to the role he or she plays in the psychodrama. A key element to being a protagonist is spontaneity.

Actors are those who play the parts of other important people or objects in the play. They are called "auxiliaries" and, with prompting from the protagonist, they can play the protagonist's double, an antagonist, or even a piece of furniture. In the same psychodrama, an auxiliary could play more than one part, such as being the protagonist's best friend and worst enemy.

The **director** is the person who guides the protagonist in the use of the psychodramatic method to help that person explore his or her problem (Blatner, 1996). The director is roughly equivalent to the group leader in other theoretical approaches.

Finally, the **audience** is a term used to describe others who may be present during the psychodrama. These individuals may become auxiliaries, but many may not actively participate. "The purpose of the audience is to give feedback regarding what they saw, heard, and felt during the psychodrama" (Ohlsen, Horne, & Lawe, 1988, p. 100). Sometimes the audience will become involved while the psychodrama is being conducted and make sound effects or comments at the request of the director. For example, the audience might be directed to repeat to Rhonda when she gets angry and makes a mistake, "Keep cool. Use your head. Keep cool. Use your head." In such cases, the audience becomes a *chorus*.

The techniques employed in psychodrama are dependent on many variables. Among the most important factors that influence which techniques will be used are the situation of the protagonist, the skill of the director, the availability of actors, the size of the audience, the goals of the session, and the phase in which the psychodrama is operating. Special situations will require different skills. For example, Blatner (1996) states that some psychodrama techniques are best employed when the objective is to clarify the protagonist's feelings (e.g., monodrama, soliloquy, the double). Others are used to facilitate the expression of emotion (e.g., amplification, asides, exaggeration of nonverbal actions). Yet other techniques (e.g., role reversal, audience feedback, nonverbal interaction exercises) are completed in self-awareness situations. The psychodrama process generally goes through three phases: warm-up (preaction), action, and integration.

1. **Warm-up phase**—The warm-up phase is characterized by the director making sure he or she is ready to lead the group and that group members are ready to be led. This process may involve both verbal and nonverbal activity designed to put everyone in the right frame of mind to conduct the psychodrama and at the same time establish trust and an atmosphere of spontaneity (Blatner, 2005; Moreno, 1940). For instance, the director may walk around arranging furniture while speaking to all participants. Then he or she may lead the group in some get-acquainted exercises, in which participants are placed in dyads. After these activities, the group as a whole may engage in action exercises (e.g., sensory awareness methods, guided imagery), which help members discover common themes within the group as well as focus more on individual concerns. Overall, the warm-up is experiential in nature and allows members to process some of the technical procedures they will experience in the actual psychodrama (Holmes & Karp; 1991; Leveton, 2001). The end of the warm-up dovetails into the action phase of psychodrama.

2. **Action phase**—This part of the psychodrama process involves the enactment of protagonists' concerns (Blatner, 1996; Haskell, 1973). The director helps each protagonist who chooses to work "set the stage" for a specific scene in the here and now. Group participants are assigned auxiliary ego roles of significant others or things in the protagonist's life. Then the opening scene is portrayed, and the protagonist and auxiliary egos are given an opportunity to refine their roles and gear their interaction from the surface to the most significant events. The director may encourage the protagonist at this point to do a role reversal so that he or she can feel more empathy or projection of feelings. Other techniques that are often employed are the use of soliloquy, the double technique, and asides. All are targeted toward helping the protagonist elaborate on feelings.

Finally, the protagonist is helped to work through the situation by developing other adaptive attitudes and behavioral responses. Working through may mean repeating a scene using new behavioral strategies every time. It may also involve role reversals or even the use of modeling. The crucial thing in the action stage is that protagonists express repressed emotions and find a new, effective way to act.

3.   **Integration phase**—This last phase of psychodrama involves discussion and closure. After the action phase, a protagonist is off balance, vulnerable, and in need of support. The director encourages the group to give the protagonist as much personal, supportive, and constructive feedback as possible during this time. Feedback focuses initially on the affective, rather than the intellectual, aspects of the enactment. Toward the end of the group, some cognitive aspects of what has been experienced are appropriate to express (Blatner, 1996; Corey, 2004). At the completion of this phase, an emphasis is placed on understanding and integration so the protagonist can act differently if any similar situations arise. Figure 17.2 illustrates how the intensity of emotions in these three phases of psychodrama changes over time.

There are literally hundreds of psychodrama techniques with many variations, so only a few major techniques (creative imagery, magic shop, sculpting, soliloquy, monodrama, double and multiple double, role reversal, and mirror) are considered here. Their use varies and is dictated by the circumstances within a particular psychodrama (Holmes, Karp, & Watson, 1995; Karp, Holmes, & Tauvon, 1998).

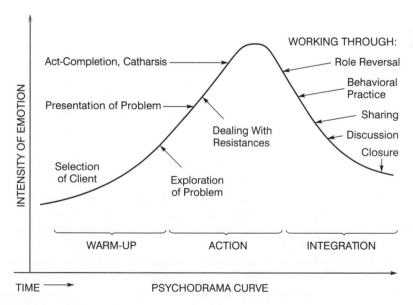

Figure 17.2
Psychodrama curve.
Source: Adapted from *Acting In: Practical Applications of Psychodramatic Methods* (2nd ed., p. 86), by A. Blatner, 1988, Springer Publishing Company, Inc., New York 10012. Copyright © 1988 by Springer Publishing Company, Inc. Used by permission.

1. **Creative imagery**—This warm-up technique consists of inviting psychodrama participants to imagine neutral or pleasant objects and scenes. The idea is to help participants become more spontaneous. For instance, Del realizes he can create a picture of a sunrise from a mountaintop although he lives on a coastal plain.

2. **The magic shop**—This warm-up technique is especially useful for protagonists who are undecided or ambivalent about their values and goals. It involves a storekeeper (the director or an auxiliary ego) who runs a magic shop filled with special qualities. The qualities are not for sale but may be bartered (Verhofstadt & Leni, 2000). Thus, if Leroy as the protagonist wants better relationship skills with others, then he may have to give up irrational anger in exchange.

3. **Sculpting**—In this exercise, group members use nonverbal methods to arrange other group members into a configuration like that of significant persons with whom they regularly deal, such as family members, office personnel, or social peers. The positioning involves body posturing and assists group members in seeing and experiencing their perceptions of significant others in a more dynamic way. For example, by arranging her family members with their backs toward her, Regina realizes how shut out of her family of origin she felt when she was growing up.

4. **Soliloquy**—This technique involves the protagonist (i.e., the client) giving a monologue about his or her situation, as he or she is acting it out. For instance, the person who is driving home from work alone may give words to the thoughts that are uppermost on his or her mind, such as "I feel life is unfair." A variation on this activity is the *therapeutic soliloquy* technique, in which private reactions to events in the protagonist's life are verbalized and acted out, usually by other actors (i.e., auxiliary egos). For example, other group members may push and tug at each other, showing Helena her ambivalence about going on to graduate school.

5. **Monodrama** (autodrama)—In this technique, the protagonist plays all the parts of the enactment; no auxiliary egos are used. The person may switch chairs or talk to different parts of the self. The monodrama is a core feature of Gestalt therapy. For instance, Walt becomes the significant thoughts he has about his upcoming marriage and has a dialogue between these expressions in different chairs arranged in a circle.

6. **Double and multiple double**—The double is an extremely important technique in psychodrama. The group facilitator or a group member designated by the director takes on the role of the protagonist's alter ego and helps the protagonist express true inner feelings more clearly (Leveton, 2001). The double follows the lead of the director but can also make feeling statements to guide the director in case he or she misses a cue (Monterio-Leitner, 2001).

In cases in which the protagonist has ambivalent feelings, the multiple double technique is used. In these situations, two or more actors represent different aspects of the protagonist's personality. The doubles may speak at once or take turns but, through their input, the protagonist should gain a better idea of what his or her thoughts and feelings are.

Doubles can emphasize or **amplify** statements made by the protagonist in a number of ways. Speaking to the protagonist in the first person, the double or doubles may verbalize nonverbal communications, question one's self, interpret what is being said and not said, contradict feelings, make a self-observation, or engage in denial (Blatner, 1996, 2000). For instance, referring to Irene's changing jobs, her double says, "I wonder for whom I am doing this, myself or my children?"

An effective double then will reach the very core of the protagonist's experience, and the protagonist will feel confirmed and understood.

7.   **Role reversal**—In this technique, the protagonist literally switches roles with another person on stage and plays that person's part. For instance, Zelda becomes Claudia and acts like her. Zerka Moreno (1983) states that role reversal encourages the maximum expression of conflict; however, Blatner (2005) maintains that role reversal is another core part of psychodrama and one of the most important action techniques in it, especially in the action phase.

8.   **Mirror**—In this activity, the protagonist watches from offstage while an auxiliary ego mirrors the protagonist's posture, gesture, and words. This technique is often used in the action phase of psychodrama to help the protagonist see him- or herself more accurately. For instance, Rufus learns through watching Buster mirror him that he is not the clearheaded, decisive person he imagined himself to be.

Role of the Psychodrama Group Leader

The director is the leader of a psychodrama and as such wears many hats. Moreno (1953, 1964) suggests that the **director** serves as a producer, a facilitator, an observer, and an analyzer. The director sets norms and models skills that ensure safety and personal control (Brown-Shaw et al., 1999). Furthermore, the director builds his or her skills in three interdependent areas:

1.   knowledge of methods, principles, and techniques,
2.   understanding of personality theory and its relationship to developing an evolving philosophy of life, and
3.   his or her own personality development and maturity. (Blatner, 1996)

In addition to a broad general knowledge of life and human nature, a director is expected to have completed specific course work in subject areas such as general psychology, group process, humanistic psychology, communication theory, and nonverbal communications.

The director's function is to conduct such tasks as leading the warm-up experience, encouraging the development of trust and spontaneity, establishing a structure so that protagonists can identify and work on significant issues in their lives, protecting members from abuse by others, and bringing some type of closure to group sessions (Haskell, 1973; Ohlsen et al., 1988). To conduct these tasks properly, potential directors should have experienced many psychodramas and received direct supervision from more experienced directors. Overall, Corsini (1966) concludes that effective group directors possess three qualities: creativity, courage, and charisma. These individuals work very hard for the good of the group and often must take risks to help group members begin achieving goals.

CASE EXAMPLE: Monique Delivers a Monologue

Monique has wrestled with the impulsive side of herself for years. She idealizes calmness and can see herself being poised. Sometimes she achieves this demeanor, but often she becomes flustered in her dealing with others or her work on the job and impulsively fires off an email or blurts out a sentence that she later regrets. Her inability to control herself in frustrating situations has cost her promotions and raises. Therefore, when someone suggested that Monique try psychodrama, she was ready. She thought almost anything would help and doing psychodrama would allow her to learn something more about her actions and how she might control them better.

During the warm-up phrase of her first psychodrama session, Monique was led through a guided imagery exercise by her director, Sharon. She found herself emotionally charged from the experience as she could see herself in various ways. During the action phase of the session, Monique volunteered to be the protagonist and while in that role, she delivered a monologue (i.e., a soliloquy) while acting out her problem with impulsivity. She both was surprised by her words and actions and found comfort in the help from other actors to her wish for control. During the integrative phase of the psychodrama, Sharon and other members of the group gave Monique constructive feedback, such as the comment: "When you seemed to think about your behaviors, you were able to talk yourself into acting calmer." Monique left the session feeling supported and stronger.

Although you may not have been in a psychodrama session, when have you found yourself supported by others as you told or showed them a situation with which you were dealing? How do you connect that experience to psychodrama?

Desired Outcome of Psychodrama Groups

The desired outcome of psychodrama can be described as the creation of catharsis, insight, and emotional resolution (Moreno, 1964). Yablonsky (1976) states that Moreno's goal in psychodrama is "to develop a 'theatrical cathedral' for the release of the natural human spontaneity and creativity that he believed existed naturally in everyone" (p. 274). Through psychodrama, individuals should be able to experience and work through past, present, or anticipated events that have caused them distress. When they have gained emotional and cognitive insight by acting out their difficulties, they will reach a stage of renewed self-awareness, readjustment, integration, acceptance, control, and prevention.

It is essential, not just desirable, that participants in psychodramas be willing to take risks and be open to constructive feedback from the audience and director. One of the desirable spinoffs from psychodrama is the learning that takes place when one is not the main protagonist. A definite **spillover effect** from this approach results for others who are helping or watching a main character reach resolution on important issues. This effect is often that they see themselves as interacting in a new and better way.

Evaluation of Psychodrama Groups

Psychodrama groups can be quite powerful and have much to commend them as ways of working with others. However, they are not without limitations.

Strengths and Contributions

A major strength of psychodrama is its diversity (Greenberg, 1974a). Psychodrama is appropriately used in psychotherapeutic environments as well as in psychoeducational and business settings. For example, the Harvard Law School uses certain aspects of psychodrama to help students practice interpersonal skills they have difficulty performing (Bordone, 2000). Furthermore, psychodrama can be employed with individuals of all age, educational, and socioeconomic levels. For instance, Amatruda (2006) helped 10-to 13-year-old elementary school children in a special education program communicate more positively with one another and improve their status with peers by using action techniques and psychodrama methods. Students' negative behaviors in the classroom decreased, interactions with one another were more positive, and attitudes toward their own potential increased as a result of the psychodrama-based conflict resolution and skill-building training. Other forms of psychodrama have been used in family therapy, addiction treatment, the training of theologians, the sensitizing of leaders, and the supervision of counselors (Gendron, 1980; Wilkins, 1995). A unique use of psychodrama is in the middle-school grades to help teachers and counselors demonstrate the concept of roles (Shaffer, 1997) and to describe and prevent bullying behavior (Beale & Scott, 2001). A novel form of psychodrama is a structured "guided autobiography," which is used with older people as an educational exercise with natural therapeutic potential (Brown-Shaw et al., 1999).

Another positive aspect of psychodrama is its teaching potential. Group members learn a great deal about themselves through their active participation (Kranz & Lund, 1993). Similarly, as Zerka Moreno (1983) points out, professionals in various mental health specialties can also use psychodrama to learn how they interact and resolve matters with difficult clients. Psychodrama gives these professionals a feeling for situations, instead of just thoughts about them.

A third strength of a psychodrama group is its fostering of creativity and spontaneity within leaders and members (Coven, Ellington, & Van Hull, 1997). A major problem that people have is their inability to find resolutions to stressful or harmful situations. Psychodrama promotes creative and spontaneous ways to help people find solutions to transitional or permanent problems. By acting on a difficulty in the confines of a safe environment, the protagonist gets a feel for how things can be different and may practice acting accordingly (Moreno, 1987). For example, Peter realizes in the calm atmosphere of the group that he can respond to a negative statement by ignoring it, using humor, becoming negative himself, or using confrontation. Before the psychodrama group, he only ignored such statements.

A fourth positive aspect of psychodrama is its integrative and vicarious effect. Psychodrama emphasizes action coupled with emotional release. A by-product of this process is the change in thoughts that accompanies changes in behavior and emotion (Coven et al., 1997). This change is not limited to just the protagonist but can extend to members of the audience as well. As the psychodrama concludes, a good psychodrama director "shifts the focus to the audience and discusses the impact of their experiences, parts of the psychodrama with which they identified, issues they got in touch with, and what they learned from the psychodrama in general" (Ohlsen et al., 1988, p. 105).

A final strength of psychodrama is the input and feedback the audience and actors give the protagonist and each other (Moreno, 1964). Psychodrama promotes interaction and experiential learning among group members. It makes good use of the group format. Many of the dynamics that occur in psychodrama are described regularly in the *Journal of Group Psychotherapy, Psychodrama, and Sociometry* and other periodicals in group work.

Limitations

A major limitation of psychodrama is the danger of overexposing the protagonist to him- or herself as well as to the audience (Greenberg, 1974a). A sense of timing and knowledge of what hidden factors need to be exposed are crucial. The ability of a psychodrama director to know when and what to emphasize is one that takes years to develop and requires both courage and creativity (Corsini, 1966). First attempts at helping are not as polished as later efforts, and sometimes everyone involved struggles in the process.

Another area of considerable concern to many professional group workers is the quantity and quality of the research underlying psychodrama (D'Amato & Dean, 1988; Kellermann, 1987). Role playing, one aspect of psychodrama, has the potential to change individual attitudes and behaviors (Janis & Mann, 1954; Mann, 1967). However, psychodrama is more than just role playing. As D'Amato and Dean (1988) point out, there is a need for more controlled research of the factors that make up the approach. Even the "taproot of the theory"—that is, when problems are acted out, the client's mind-set becomes more spontaneous—has never been empirically verified (D'Amato & Dean, 1988, p. 312).

A third limitation of psychodrama is connected with the availability of training (Greenberg, 1974a). As pointed out previously, it is recommended that directors be involved in a large number of psychodramas and take specific courses in human development and group work (Blatner, 1996). At present, there are few training centers for directors. In addition, experience and course work alone are not enough. Needed qualities of directors go beyond experience with observing/participating and studying to also include intuition and charisma, which vary considerably in human personality. There is the danger that some psychodrama groups may differ radically from others because of self-awareness and knowledge of the director. Since 1975, the American Board of Examiners in Psychodrama, Sociometry and Group Psychotherapy has tried to ensure more uniformity in professional standards for directors.

A final criticism of psychodrama is that it may focus too much on expression of feelings rather than change in behavior. A lot of emphasis in psychodrama is placed on affect and present experiences, as opposed to cognitive awareness and exploration of the past. If the group is not carefully constructed, then the emotional part of the theory and the here-and-now emphasis will override the integrative aspect of the approach.

Learning More

Psychodrama is one of the most interesting and active forms of group work. Professionals who wish to practice it must undergo extensive training. One of the most prominent organizations devoted to the study and furtherance of psychodrama is the

> American Society for Group Psychotherapy and Psychodrama (ASGPP)
> 301 North Harrison Street, Suite 508
> Princeton, NJ 08540
> Telephone: 609-452-1339
> Web site: http://www.asgpp.org/

The ASGPP publishes an excellent professional periodical, the *Journal of Group Psychotherapy, Psychodrama, and Sociometry*. It also holds conferences and provides training opportunities for its members.

SUMMARY AND CONCLUSION

Two active group therapy approaches have been examined in this chapter—Gestalt and psychodrama. These theories stress interpersonal interactions and behaving before processing.

The influence of Gestalt groups was most prominent in the late 1960s and early 1970s, when they were perceived as exciting and active places to work. The processes within these groups, when properly conducted, helped group members become self-aware and integrated. The approach worked on an individual, interpersonal, and group level. Most often, it was associated with Fritz Perls and a dynamic one-on-one encounter, but the approach eventually became diversified. More than just gimmicks are now employed in Gestalt groups to help members in their growth (Reshnikoff, 1988).

Gestalt group processes have received favorable reviews from their participants (Lieberman et al., 1973), but controversy still surrounds the use of these groups. Part of the controversy is based on a lack of empirical evidence to support the effectiveness of Gestalt groups. A second part is connected with the perception that the groups are all action and no thought. Gestalt group leaders will have to take more productive steps in the future to set aside these criticisms and form uniform standards for training and conducting groups (Yontef & Simkin, 2005).

Psychodrama continues to be one of the most exciting forms of group work. Although it has largely been used in psychotherapy and counseling settings, aspects of it are quite appropriate in psychoeducational and task/work environments. This approach to groups requires a great deal of action or participation on the part of all involved. Within the psychodrama, protagonists work out their problems and are free to release feelings and try new behaviors with the help of others and themselves. Psychodrama goes through stages and needs an expert and experienced director to work properly. The process is exciting and one of the most powerful group approaches available.

CLASSROOM EXERCISES

1. Which of the Gestalt exercises listed in this chapter do you think would be effective if you were leading a counseling group? Would they be the same if you were leading a psychoeducational group or a task group? Discuss your answer with the group as a whole.

2. What do you find most appealing about Gestalt groups? What is the least appealing aspect of these groups? In what way is the action-oriented philosophy of this approach a strength or a weakness compared to the other group approaches with which you are now familiar?

3. Discuss in groups of three how psychodrama has influenced other forms of group work. Which techniques have other group approaches borrowed from psychodrama? How do they use these techniques differently? Show, as well as tell, others of your impressions and findings.

4. In groups of four or five, do literature searches on the writings of either Jacob or Zerka Moreno. As a class, discuss how psychodrama has evolved.

CHAPTER 18

RATIONAL-EMOTIVE BEHAVIOR THERAPY AND BEHAVIORAL THERAPY GROUPS

In the long-shadowed days of winter
when the cold seeps through to the depths of your thoughts
*   and engraves crystal frost on morning windows,*
You awaken inner dreams—
*   images that have laid dormant since summer*
*   when you, warmed by the August sun,*
*   built sandcastles and called your expectations by name.*
Slowly, with chilled fingers,
*   you handle slow-moving memories,*
*   examining them like slightly blurred pictures,*
Under the light from a nearby lamp
*   that flickers off and on*
*   like the sound of your voice*
*   which flows in broken waves.**

*From "Awakening" by Samuel T. Gladding, 1977, *The School Counselor, 24,* p. 184. Reprinted with permission. No further reproduction authorized without permission of the American Counseling Association.

416

T houghts and behaviors play a positive role in people's lives. They are expressed through memories, awareness, projection, and actions. Thoughts and behaviors may also have a negative impact on people, especially when they occur involuntarily and are negative (e.g., with the traumatic recalling of events in posttraumatic stress syndrome) or when actions are irrational and skewed (e.g., losing one's temper quickly, becoming hysterical).

Cognitive and behavioral theories of group work focus primarily on how thought processes and actions affect the overall functioning of group members. These theories include a wide variety of approaches, such as an emphasis on cognitive restructuring, a focus on modifying observable behaviors, and a combined cognitive-behavioral emphasis that stresses the importance of integrating thoughts and behavior in a social learning format (Kennedy & Tanenbaum, 2000). Overall, **cognitive and behavioral approaches to human relations** are based on a theory of personality that maintains that how one thinks or behaves largely determines how one feels and functions (Beck & Weishaar, 2005; Wilson, 2005) and what one does indicates who one is. Rational-emotive behavior therapy (REBT) and behavioral therapy are the two theories examined here. They have followed the trend of other helping approaches by expanding their strategies and techniques through the years.

Cognitive and behavioral theories, as a rule, are frequently combined when they are employed. In this chapter, similarities and differences between these approaches are highlighted in regard to group work. Like other theories examined in this section, these models are used with individuals, groups, and families. They came into prominence at about the same time (the late 1950s and early 1960s), influencing how practitioners have conceptualized and conducted groups ever since. These approaches have a history of being used extensively in psychoeducational, counseling, and psychotherapeutic groups and occasionally in task/work groups.

RATIONAL-EMOTIVE BEHAVIOR THERAPY GROUPS

Rational-emotive behavior therapy (REBT) was originally known as rational-emotive therapy (RET) but changed its name when its founder, Albert Ellis (2005), decided his approach needed to be more reflective of what the theory actually did: focus on behavior as well as cognitions. Although the name change came in 1993, the employment of various forms of REBT has been evolving for decades (Dryden, 1994; O'Connor, 2001). In fact, Ellis (1996) emphasizes that REBT is one of the most humanistic and creative psychotherapies ever formulated, and Weinrach (1995, 1996), among others, has documented its effectiveness.

Rational-emotive behavior therapy groups originated in 1958 when Ellis noticed that working in groups was beneficial and economical for his clients (Vander Kolk, 1985; Weinrach, 1980). From the beginning, REBT groups have been quite varied (Ellis, 1997). Sometimes the groups are as large as 100 and meet for the purpose of demonstrating REBT principles, a skills-learning approach. In such cases, the emphasis is on a combination of psychoeducational and psychotherapeutic principles regarding a specific topic, such as dealing with anxiety, depression, or interpersonal relationships (Wessler, 1986).

Other types of groups conducted by REBT practitioners are open-ended and closed-ended psychotherapy and counseling sessions that may include group marathons (Ellis & Dryden, 1997). Most REBT groups of this nature usually meet weekly, with open-ended ones being conducted on an indefinite basis over a number of months and closed-ended ones seldom meeting for more than 10 to 12 sessions. Marathons are conducted on a 12- to 36-hour basis depending on the leader and setting.

Regardless of form, the number of members in REBT groups is usually limited to a dozen. This arrangement allows group members the chance to interact with other people, to take verbal and nonverbal risks, to receive maximum feedback, to learn from others' experiences, and to make contributions to the group as a whole (Ellis, 2005). The dynamic interaction among members in such settings is not possible on a one-to-one level.

Premises of Rational-Emotive Behavior Therapy Groups

The underlying premises of REBT are both stoic and humanistic. Rational-emotive behavior therapy is based on the idea that one's thinking about events, not external circumstances, produces feelings and behaviors. "Ellis believes that emotional troubles are rooted in personal perceptions of unchangeable facts, such as another person's unkindness" (O'Connor, 2001, p. 32). Individuals who have negative, faulty, or irrational thoughts about matters become emotionally disturbed or upset. Their **self-talk** (i.e., the messages people give themselves internally) influences their mental health and actions in nonproductive ways. This phenomenon is just as true for leaders of groups as for people in general (Browne, 2005). Therefore, to behave rationally, individuals need first to control their thoughts and behaviors (Ellis, 1962, 1995, 2005). If persons can change their irrational beliefs and behaviors to rational ones, then they will suffer less and actually enjoy life (Wessler, 1986).

The process of change is built on an **A-B-C model of human interaction** (see Figure 18.1), in which "A" is the event, "B" is the thought process, and "C" is the feeling state resulting from one's thoughts. To change negative or nonproductive feelings, individuals need to think differently. According to Ellis, there are **four types of thoughts: negative, positive, neutral, and mixed**. Negative thoughts concentrate on painful or disappointing aspects of an event; positive thoughts focus on just the opposite. Neutral cognitions are those that are neither positive nor negative, whereas those that are mixed contain elements of the other three thought processes.

Although people are entitled to feel as much emotion as they want about events, Ellis's approach allows individuals to control their affect by switching the focus of their

Figure 18.1
The ABC model of human interaction.

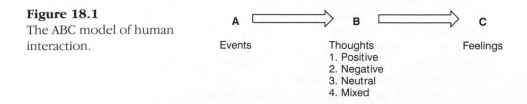

A   Events

B   Thoughts
1. Positive
2. Negative
3. Neutral
4. Mixed

C   Feelings

thoughts from, say, negative to neutral (Ellis, 1988; Harper & Ellis, 1975). For example, if Paige does not speak to Carmen at a meeting, then Carmen may think that she was slighted or that Paige was preoccupied with another task and simply missed an opportunity to speak. If Carmen chooses the second way to think, then she will not get upset, whereas the first way of thinking will result in anger. In switching their thoughts from negative to neutral or even positive, people can make better-informed decisions and relate productively with themselves and others.

Rational-emotive behavior therapy stresses the **dual nature of human beings**. Individuals have both rational and irrational beliefs that can be modified through disputation (Ellis, 1976). Self-rating is discouraged in this approach because no one can live up to a label, such as "good," and individuals tend to become discouraged when they act differently from what they believe is perfect behavior for themselves. Therefore, Ellis advocates that individuals see themselves as "fallible human beings" who act in certain ways in specific circumstances. By avoiding labels and forms of the verb *to be* (e.g., *am, are, was*), people are able to live more rational lives (Harper & Ellis, 1975).

Overall, REBT can be thought of as a philosophy of life as well as a treatment for changing behaviors (Weinrach, 1996; Wessler & Hankin, 1988). If individuals can learn to think more rationally, then they are more likely to stop inappropriately evaluating themselves, others, and events in the world over which they have no control (Ellis, 2005; Wessler, 1986). By doing so, they can also quit **making wishes into demands**, for example, using *should, ought,* and *must* in regard to an action. They are then released to deal with themselves and their environments realistically.

Practice of Rational-Emotive Behavior Therapy in a Group

Rational-emotive behavior therapy groups vary according to the type of group being led. Some groups are open ended, with a constant influx of new members; others are closed ended and limited to the same people who began the group (Wessler & Hankin, 1988). Regardless of the format, REBT groups tend to be didactic, philosophical, and skills oriented (Corey, 2004; Hansen, Warner, & Smith, 1980). The leader introduces REBT theory to the group, and then group members are asked to share troublesome problems or concerns that are usually of a personal nature. These situations are analyzed using the ABCs of therapeutic intervention (Dryden, 1999). Group members, as well as the leader, give feedback and suggestions to the person who initially presented (Ellis, 2005). The feedback is in the form of disputation, which takes three main forms: cognitive, imaginal, and behavioral (Gladding, 2005). The process is most effective if all three forms are used (Walen, DiGiuseppe, & Wessler, 1980).

Cognitive disputation involves direct questioning, reasoning, and persuasion. It may involve asking the question "Why?"—an inquiry seldom employed in helping relationships such as counseling and psychotherapy. For example, group members might ask one another, "Why must that occur?" Cognitive disputation also involves monitoring one's self-talk in regard to giving oneself irrational or absolute messages. Sichel and Ellis (1984) have developed a self-help form to assist clients in identifying irrational beliefs (see Figure 18.2).

A (ACTIVATING EVENTS OR ADVERSITIES)

```

```

- Briefly summarize the situation you are disturbed about (what would a camera see?)
- An *A* can be *internal* or *external, real* or *imagined.*
- An *A* can be an event in the *past, present,* or *future.*

IBs (IRRATIONAL BELIEFS)   **D (DISPUTING IBs)**

```

```

To identify IBs, look for:

- Dogmatic Demands
  (musts, absolutes, shoulds)

- Awfulizing
  (It's awful, terrible, horrible)

- Low Frustration Tolerance
  (I can't stand it)

- Self/Other Rating
  (I'm/he/she is bad, worthless)

To dispute ask yourself:

- Where is holding this belief getting me?
  Is it *helpful* or *self-defeating?*

- Where is the evidence to support the
  existence of my irrational belief? Is it
  consistent with social reality?

- Is my belief *logical?* Does it follow from
  my preferences?

- Is it really *awful* (as bad as it could be)?

- Can I really not *stand* it?

Figure 18.2
Rational-emotive behavior therapy (REBT) self-help form.
Source: Reprinted with permission of Windy Dryden & Jane Walker.

C (CONSEQUENCES)

Major unhealthy negative **emotions:**

Major self-defeating **behaviors:**

Unhealthy negative emotions include:

- Anxiety
- Depression
- Rage
- Low Frustration Tolerance
- Shame/Embarassment
- Hurt
- Jealousy
- Guilt

E (EFFECTIVE NEW PHILOSOPHIES)   E (EFFECTIVE EMOTIONS & BEHAVIORS)

New healthy
negative emotions:

New constructive
behaviors:

To think more rationally, strive for:

- Non-Dogmatic Preferences
  (wishes, wants, desires)

- Evaluating Badness
  (It's bad, unfortunate)

- High Frustration Tolerance
  (I don't like it, but I can stand it)

- Not Globally Rating Self or Others
  (I—and others—are falliable human
  beings)

Healthy negative emotions include:

- Disappointment

- Concern

- Annoyance

- Sadness

- Regret

- Frustration

Figure 18.2, *continued*

Imaginal disputation, a technique devised by Maxie Maultsby (1984), has participants seeing themselves in stressful situations and examining their self-talk. Then they go through the sequence again, but in the process modify their self-talk so it is more rational. For example, individuals might imagine themselves taking a major test while initially telling themselves they did not have a chance to pass. The same scene would then be envisioned in which group members would tell themselves more positive or neutral statements, such as "I have studied hard and I am ready" or "I will think each question through before putting down an answer." The REBT self-help form can be of value to these individuals, too.

Behavioral disputation involves many forms, from reading (bibliotherapy) to role playing in the group. Often enactment of the problem in the group setting and possible ways of handling it are used. Homework may then be assigned in the form of emotive-dramatic exercises, such as a **shame attack** (in which the person actually does what he or she dreaded and finds the world does not fall apart regardless of the outcome). For example, a shame attack for Shirley might involve speaking to Ned and confirming in her mind that her self-worth is not based on whether he responds. Ellis actually used such a behavioral exercise in his early adulthood (Dryden, 1989). Being shy around women, he actually forced himself to speak to literally 100 women one day, all of whom he did not know. Ellis even went a step farther by asking these women he did not know out for a date. Many of the women did not speak back to him and none of them went out with him. Through this experiment, he found that his world did not come unraveled when he was ignored or rejected. His rational thinking served him well.

◆ *Questions from Experience* ◆

When have you ever had a disappointment and realized that your world did not end? How did your thinking help you put the situation into perspective?

Very little attention is paid to past events in an REBT group. It is not that past events are unimportant. However, the focus of the group is on the here and now (Wessler & Hankin, 1988). In general, REBT groups, which are primarily focused on counseling and psychotherapy, use a "no holds barred approach" (Hansen et al., 1980, p. 243). Virtually no restrictions are placed on the types of subjects that can be discussed. The important point is that members of the group learn to handle themselves better in a variety of difficult situations by thinking rationally and behaving accordingly. In many ways, REBT groups can be conceptualized as psychoeducational in both theory and practice. Members learn a new way of life and, through sharing with one another, reinforce appropriate ideas and behaviors.

The REBT approach to group work is not limited to just intellectually bright individuals. Rather, it is appropriate for persons functioning at all levels. It is used with children, adolescents, adults, and the elderly (Ellis, 1997). Most often, the approach stresses remediation.

Figure 18.3

Jeff's mad thermometer.

Source: From "Childhood Anxieties, Fears, and Phobias: A Cognitive-Behavioral Psycho-situational Approach" by R. M. Grieger and J. D. Boyd, 1983, in *Rational-Emotive Approaches to Problems of Childhood* (p. 234) by A. Ellis and M. E. Bernard (Eds.). New York: Plenum. Reprinted with permission.

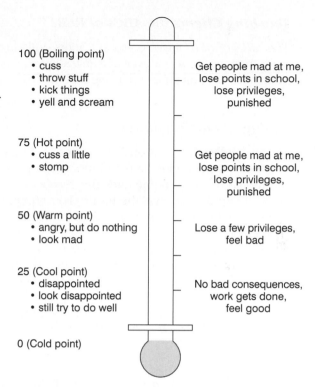

100 (Boiling point)
• cuss
• throw stuff
• kick things
• yell and scream

Get people mad at me, lose points in school, lose privileges, punished

75 (Hot point)
• cuss a little
• stomp

Get people mad at me, lose points in school, lose privileges, punished

50 (Warm point)
• angry, but do nothing
• look mad

Lose a few privileges, feel bad

25 (Cool point)
• disappointed
• look disappointed
• still try to do well

No bad consequences, work gets done, feel good

0 (Cold point)

However, at the Living School (a private school for children in New York City) or other similar institutes, the emphasis is on prevention (Ellis & Bernard, 1983). For example, the teacher of the ABCs of REBT may illustrate through drawings and other graphic means how emotions develop and what children can do to stay in control of themselves at potentially emotional times (see Figure 18.3).

Regardless of where they participate in an REBT group, members are exposed to a wide variety of cognitive and behavioral methods. Among the best known of these techniques are actively disputing clients' thoughts, persuading them to work from an REBT viewpoint, teaching clients the ABCs of REBT, and giving clients feedback on the rational outcomes of their thoughts. Disputing clients' thoughts has already been covered, so the other three techniques are briefly discussed.

The REBT Viewpoint

Persuading clients to work from an **REBT viewpoint** simply involves getting them to believe that the premises on which REBT is based are valid and applicable to their situations. Many REBT group specialists spend at least half of their time in initial individual or group sessions highlighting studies that show that the ideas on which REBT was founded are valid. For instance, as a group leader, Laurie may talk to group members at length about ancient wisdom as well as modern research on the power of thought to affect a person's way of living.

Teaching Clients the ABCs of REBT

The *ABCs of REBT* involve group leaders outlining to members how feelings are derived from thoughts. It is one way of persuading clients to work from a rational-emotive viewpoint and teaching them a valuable tool they can use at the same time.

Giving Clients Feedback

Giving **feedback** on rational outcomes of thoughts requires that the group leader and members suspend judgment and function cognitively. Feedback refers to the final results of rational thinking. Sometimes this feedback is worded in the present; on other occasions, it is projected into the future. For example, Bart may say to Lindsey, "If you keep thinking rationally about your studies, I expect you'll be a logical candidate for medical school in the future."

In addition to the techniques already mentioned, group members are encouraged to role-play their situations (often in the group) and to find appropriate models to emulate (or copy). The main focus is not just to teach skills but to promote and foster a way of life. Ellis (1979) states this view as follows: "Just as skill training enables clients to change their perceptions of their abilities, so does helping them to perceive themselves differently enable them to acquire better skills" (p. 133).

Role of the Rational-Emotive Behavior Therapy Group Leader

"The Rational-Emotive group is leader-centered. It is the leader's task to make sure that the group is philosophically and cognitively based" (Hansen et al., 1980, p. 246). In REBT groups, the leader encourages rational thinking in a number of ways (Ellis, 1974a, 1974b), including the following:

1. Teaching group members about the origins of emotions
2. Being active in the group process by challenging and probing
3. Encouraging group members to help one another to think rationally
4. Using activity-oriented experiences in the group and homework assignments outside the group
5. Allowing the expression of feelings previously hidden by group members. These emotions are then dealt with in a practical, rational way.

In psychotherapeutic and counseling groups, the group leader encourages members to work as **auxiliary counselors** once someone has presented a problem. When they do, participants benefit from multiple inputs (Ellis, 2005; Ellis & Dryden, 1997). The group leader also serves as a model for the group and reveals how he or she practices REBT in daily life. "The leader's objective is to help participants give up their demands for perfection" (Vander Kolk, 1985, p. 108). Techniques used by the group leader do not vary that much from other group approaches and are usually a combination of cognitive, behavioral, and affective-based interventions, such as confrontation, challenging, persuasion, role playing, and imagining.

CASE EXAMPLE: Carlos Learns to Calm Down

Carlos has always been emotional. Traditionally, he has not thought through problems but has reacted to situations with feelings ranging from anger to delight. While he loves the highs, he loathes the lows. Therefore, his goal in the REBT group he joined was to be more level in his emotional responses, that is, to calm down.

Initially, becoming calmer was harder for Carlos than he thought. It took him awhile to master the ABCs of REBT and to learn how to really apply them. He was used to going to either positive or negative ways of reacting to events instead of to neutral or mixed ways of responding. Therefore, he asked members of the group to role play with him. They put him in situations that were prone to have a lot of emotion attached to them, such as winning the lottery or being in an accident. Eventually, through practice and feedback, Carlos learned to respond in a neutral or mixed way to events with the option that he could choose to feel as much or as little emotion as he wanted.

Desired Outcome of Rational-Emotive Behavior Therapy Groups

A primary desired outcome of a REBT group is for group members to learn how to think rationally. If they can learn how to control their thought processes, as Carlos did in the case example, they will be able to deal more effectively with a wide variety of problems. For example, insurance representatives who reduce their type A behavior (e.g., aggressive, hostile, impatient) do a better job in relating to their customers, their product, and themselves (Moller & Botha, 1996).

A second objective is for group members to achieve a particular goal in their own lives connected with overcoming an irrational belief using REBT, such as anxiety (Cowan & Brunero, 1997). Knowing how to implement the theory is not enough; it must be practiced, too, both inside and outside of the group context. For instance, if Dottie knows REBT theory but does not apply the process to her own life, then she is limiting herself.

A third expected result of an REBT group is that members should have a better knowledge of how REBT can be employed in situations with which they have no firsthand experience. Knowing this will allow them to be helpful in addressing novel, nondevelopmental problems.

A final payoff from participating in an REBT group is that members gain the experience of personally understanding the process of change. For example, victims of childhood sexual abuse who overcome their depression through group rational-emotive behavior therapy (Rieckert & Moller, 2000) understand the difficulties of changing their thoughts, emotions, and behaviors. Therefore, they can be more empathetic with others who are in the process of trying to modify their cognitions, feelings, and actions (Wessler & Hankin, 1988).

Evaluation of Rational-Emotive Behavior Therapy Groups

As with other types of groups, REBT groups have inherent strengths and limitations. These groups are primarily psychoeducationally, psychotherapeutic, and counseling focused, but REBT theory can be employed in task/work groups as well.

Strengths and Contributions

A strength of employing REBT theory in group work is the focus of the approach on the importance of cognition in influencing people's emotions and actions (Weinrach, 1996). The role of thoughts in helping relationships is the emphasis in many other forms of group work. However, rational-emotive behavior therapy is one of the few integrative theories used in a group that places primary importance on cognitions as they are related to behaviors and affect. In this regard, REBT is broad based and similar to multimodal theories of clinicians such as Arnold Lazarus (1985) in stressing a multitude of specific treatments.

A second strength of the REBT group approach is how Ellis has demystified the process of using REBT in a group setting. The essentials of REBT can be taught quickly to counselors and clients alike. It is relatively easy for everyone involved in the group process to learn how to take charge of themselves and help others in the group (Ellis, 1997).

Another positive associated with REBT groups is that they may be the perfect environments for clients who are phasing out of individual therapeutic counseling (Wessler & Hankin, 1988). The group helps persons in transition see themselves more clearly by giving them feedback. These groups also equip their members further by assisting them in refining their skills in rational thinking.

A fourth strength of using REBT theory in groups is versatility. REBT theory is geared toward working with large segments of the population. Wolfe (1995), for instance, reports that REBT women's groups, including those focused on sexuality, aging, authority, dependency, power, and risk taking, all have had positive results. These groups emphasize prevention as well as remediation. The basic tenets of this theory are easy to understand and implement with persons from a wide variety of settings and backgrounds.

A final strength of REBT groups is the opportunities they provide for members to do homework assignments, take verbal and nonverbal risks, and learn from the experiences of others, both inside and outside the formal group context (Ellis, 2005). Such groups emphasize action as well as talk (Rieckert & Moller, 2000). Books, such as *A New Guide to Rational Living* (Harper & Ellis, 1975) and *How to Stubbornly Refuse to Make Yourself Miserable About Anything—Yes, Anything!* (Ellis, 1988), are often assigned reading between sessions.

Limitations

One limitation of REBT is its traditional focus on the individual, not the group (Wessler & Hankin, 1988). Although group members learn a lot about their ability to control thoughts, emotions, and behaviors, they do not usually learn a lot about group dynamics.

Another limitation of the REBT approach is its confrontive and directive stance. Group leaders and members may push a member to get rid of faulty beliefs and adopt new thought patterns before he or she is ready. This trade-off may not be in the best interest of the participant because it has not been personalized. Hence, faulty beliefs may not really be discarded, and rational ones may not really be adopted.

A third limitation of REBT groups is that borderline-disturbed members may actually get worse (Wessler & Hankin, 1988). Some individuals, especially those who require a great deal of individual attention or those who have a low intellectual capacity, may do better in individual sessions. Because the emphasis in REBT is not on a close client–counselor/leader relationship, these individuals may receive more of the personal and professional attention they need in non-REBT settings.

A final limitation of REBT groups is the lack of rigorous research specifically on them. Ellis (1982) claims that REBT groups are effective, but his research is based more on cognitive groups in general than on REBT groups in particular. A review of outcome studies of REBT by McGovern and Silverman (1986) is more convincing, and Solomon and Haaga (1995) suggest that methodological limitations of REBT research have caused researchers to underestimate REBT's effectiveness. Nevertheless, greater uniformity in regard to methodology is needed in REBT group research. Studies such as those by Rieckert and Moller (2000), where control and treatment groups were used in measuring the effectiveness of REBT groups for adult victims of childhood sexual abuse, hold promise. There must be more such studies.

Learning More

REBT, a cognitive-behavioral counseling, psychotherapy, and psychoeducational theory that deals with changing emotions, has been found to be an effective treatment in group work for a number of problems. Its founder, Albert Ellis, has been especially prolific and influential in counseling and psychology circles. The best known training facility for learning more about REBT is the

> Albert Ellis Institute
> 45 East 65th Street
> New York, NY 10021 6593
> Telephone: 212-535-0822
> E-mail: Info@rebt.org

The institute offers a variety of material on REBT, including official programs of study. The *Journal of Rational Emotive and Cognitive Behavior Therapy* is a primary source of articles on REBT.

BEHAVIORAL THERAPY GROUPS

Behavioral theories have a long and diversified history stretching back to the beginning of the 20th century (Wilson, 2005). John B. Watson (1913) is often credited as being the primary advocate of **respondent conditioning** at the beginning of the 1900s. His views were similar to those of Ivan Pavlov in that he believed all human responses were learned through association. B. F. Skinner (1953) attacked the passivity of respondent conditioning, stressing the need for organisms to be active in the environment to learn. His **operant conditioning** model, which led to the development of applied behavioral analysis, emphasizes that behavior is a function of its consequences. Albert Bandura (1969) went even further, stating that much learning is obtained through **social modeling** (i.e., imitation of observation).

Thus, the behaviorist point of view is really a combination of opinions and procedures that since the 1950s has been collectively called **behavior therapy**. Those who consider themselves to be behaviorists emphasize learning and modification of behaviors as opposed to the treatment of underlying symptoms. They are aware that many behaviors are linked to one another. To break the chain of maladaptive responses, practitioners must determine associations and make appropriate interventions (Hollander & Kazaoka, 1988; Wilson, 2005).

Behaviorism includes so-called **radical behaviorists,** such as Skinner (1974), who avoid any mentalistic concepts and concentrate exclusively on observable actions, as well as the so-called **cognitive behaviorists**, such as David Meichenbaum (1977, 1986) and Aaron Beck (1976), who believe that thoughts play a major part in determining action and that thoughts are behaviors. Behaviorism became popular in counseling and human relations training in the 1960s (Krumboltz, 1966; Krumboltz & Thoresen, 1969) at about the same time groups did. The sophistication of each, alone and in combination, has grown since.

Premises of Behavioral Therapy Groups

In general, **behaviorists** inside and outside group settings emphasize overt processes, here-and-now experiences, learning, changing maladaptive actions, defining specific goals, and scientific support for techniques (Spiegler & Guevremont, 1993). As a group, these practitioners offer a wide variety of concrete and pragmatic procedures that are tailored to the needs of particular individuals and empirically verified. A few of the more prevalent techniques are positive reinforcement, extinction, desensitization, and modeling (Hollander & Kazaoka, 1988; Rimm & Cunningham, 1985). These techniques are applied systematically, and a great deal of planning goes into delineating which procedures will be most effective for which clients. Overall, behaviorism can simply be defined as a "learning process" in which helpers "employ a systematic procedure to help clients accomplish a particular change in behavior" (Hosford & deVisser, 1974, p. 15).

In groups, "practically all of the theoretical and conceptual materials drawn from behavior theory and integrated into the area of behavior therapy are germane" (Hollander & Kazaoka, 1988, p. 279). **Behavioral groups** are either interpersonal or transactional, depending on the purposes of the leader and members. *Interpersonal groups* are highly didactic and involve specified goals that usually center on self-improvement, such as daily living or study skills. They are essentially psychoeducational. *Transactional groups* are more heterogeneous and focus on broader, yet specific, goals. For example, transactional groups might concentrate on the proper display of a wide variety of social skills in cross-cultural interactions, such as making introductions, accepting compliments, or saying good-bye. They focus on each person in the group as well as on the group itself. They are most similar to group counseling.

Practice of Behavioral Therapy in a Group

Behavioral groups may form for a variety of purposes that range from learning life skills (Gazda, Ginter, & Horne, 2001) to treating a disorder, such as insomnia (Backhaus, Hohagen, Voderholzer, & Riemann, 2001). Regardless, there are specific stages and principles that universally apply to behavioral groups (Rose, 1977, 1983; Hollander & Kazaoka, 1988).

The first stage can be labeled *forming the group.* It consists of the organizational details that must be addressed before a group can begin. These details involve the purpose of the group, its membership, and the frequency and length of its meetings. Of these factors, Hollander and Kazaoka (1988) consider the homogeneity or heterogeneity of the problem to be most crucial. Clients with different target behaviors require completely different approaches (Lobitz & Baker, 1979).

Stage 2 involves *establishing the initial group attraction and identity.* The leader plays a major role in this process by conducting pregroup individual interviews in which members are able to explore their goals more deeply. These interviews also stress the connection of group members with one another (Rose, 1980).

The third stage can best be described as the *establishment of openness and sharing in the group.* The leader promotes this type of behavior by letting group members know what is expected, introducing subgroups to one another, and modeling what he or she is asking group members to do. For example, if the purpose of the group is to focus on increasing one's comfort in speaking in public, then the leader may speak out in the group before asking other members to do likewise.

Stage 4, *establishing a behavioral framework for all participants,* is really the beginning of the working stage in the group. At this juncture, group leaders introduce their members to the behavioral frame of reference that will directly control the conduct of group members. The **antecedent–response–consequence model of behaviorism** formulated by Bijou, Peterson, and Ault (1968) is an excellent way to present such a concept. This model states that behavior is functionally related to its antecedents and consequent events. Therefore, behavior is purposeful, although some behaviors may not be productive. Once group members learn this **A-B-C model**, they are better able to assess their own actions and monitor them, especially in regard to prebehavior cues and postbehavior rewards. They can then report more accurately the changes they make inside and outside the group. In essence, this way of thinking gives the group and its members a tool that can be used to evaluate specific behaviors being tried.

Related to this stage is the creation of **positive expectations** within group members. Individuals who expect to be successful are much more likely to achieve their goals. Hollander and Kazaoka (1988) include the establishment of positive expectations as a separate stage, but here it is considered a substage of stage 4.

Establishing and implementing a model for change is the fifth stage. At this point, group members become more specific in what they are attempting to do. They identify and pinpoint the behaviors they have targeted to change, keep a baseline on how often they occur, implement appropriate change techniques, and assess their degree of success (Madsen & Madsen, 1970). As highlighted previously, intervention techniques can take many forms. "There is no 'approved list' of techniques the use of which enables one to call himself [or herself] a behavioral counselor" (Krumboltz & Thoresen, 1969, p. 3).

Some of the most frequently used techniques are reinforcement, extinction, contingency contracts, shaping, modeling, behavioral rehearsal, coaching, cognitive restructuring, and the buddy system (Posthuma, 2002). They are briefly described here.

Reinforcement is the key to behavioral groups. Within a group, members reinforce one another for changing specified behaviors. Usually, the reinforcement is positive and takes the form of verbal and nonverbal approval or praise. In some cases, reinforcement will be negative; that is, it will involve the removal of something from the group, such as criticism. In either case, the probability of a response is increased through reinforcement (Nye, 2000). One objective in behavioral groups is to teach individual group members to positively reinforce one another and to learn how to reinforce themselves. For example, Carter may say to Larry, "I like the way you spoke up for yourself in group today. I wonder, how can you reward yourself for such behavior?" At that point, Larry would be asked to suggest ways Carter and other group members could reinforce him.

Extinction is the process of lowering the rate at which a behavior occurs through withdrawing the reinforcers that have been maintaining it. Eventually, the targeted behavior will stop altogether. This technique is usually used in combination with other behavioral methods so group members have a behavior to replace the one being eliminated. Extinction might be used when a group member is talking about irrelevant material. In such a case, the group leader would ignore the behavior and get other group members to ignore it, too. Only when the group member focused on relevant material would he or she receive the attention of the group and its leader.

Contingency contracts spell out the behaviors to be performed, changed, or discontinued; the rewards associated with the achievement of these goals; and the conditions under which rewards are to be received. Most often contingency contracts will be used in groups of children, rather than with adults, because many adults find them offensive. Usually contingency contracts are written out as quasi-formal documents (e.g., see Figure 18.4).

Shaping involves teaching behaviors through successive approximation and chaining. This gradual step process allows members to learn a new behavior over time and practice parts of it to perfection. Before undertaking shaping in a group, group leaders need to be aware of the specific response sequence they wish to establish—what follows what and how, a process known as **chaining**. For example, in teaching his beginning swim class the arm movement of the side stroke, Landon had them learn in gradual steps. First, they extended one arm and reached out with their hand as in "picking an apple." Then they lowered that arm pretending in the process to give the apple they picked to the hand of the other arm at their waist. That hand was lowered to an imaginary basket where the invisible apple was dropped and the motion was repeated again. Implementing such a procedure, when carefully planned, will usually lead to new and improved behaviors.

Modeling is learning through observing someone else (Bandura, 1965, 1977). Behavioral group leaders often model appropriate behaviors for their members (Trotzer, 2007). Likewise, group members sometimes serve as good models for others in the group. Modeling is an especially powerful tool in group settings when those who are modeling resemble group members (Bandura, 1969, 1977). For example, in a group for shy children, a participant may imitate an assertive behavior if he or she views another child in the group acting in such a manner (Meichenbaum, 1977). Videotape feedback can often be used in the modeling process so group participants are able to see others like themselves or even themselves engaging in desired behaviors (Rose & Edleson, 1987; Smokowski, 2003). Two strategies exist for using video modeling in groups. "The group leader can bring in existing tapes or videodiscs of actors demonstrating desired skills. Passively watching these tapes can spur active discussion that is useful to the group. Alternatively, the group can produce its own modeling videotapes, writing and acting out scenarios that are unique to the group" (Smokowski, 2003, p. 14).

Chocolate Chip Cookie Contract

I, _____*Joe Smith*_____ , do hereby on this 10th day of June, 1998, commit myself to contract with _____*Jane Jones*_____ .
_____*Joe Smith*_____ agrees to forfeit specified monies as outlined below to _____*Jane Jones*_____ upon failing to comply with the criterion for limited chocolate chip cookie eating as set forth below. Joe Smith will report to Jane Jones each day the number of chocolate chip cookies he has consumed outside her presence. Jane Jones will collect $1.50 for every chocolate chip cookie consumed by Joe Smith above the listed number for the day. Joe Smith will reward himself with a $1.00 in his "tennis ball box" for every day he meets or breaks his target behavior. Joe Smith promises to be honest and accurate in his counting of chocolate chip cookies consumed and report to Jane Jones immediately before Jane's bedtime (11 P.M.) every night. Jane Jones is free to do with the collected money anything she wishes. Joe Smith will hold no animosity toward her for performing her duties and spending the money in whatever way she wishes. This contract will be in effect for a period of ____*8*____ days (until June 18th) after which Joe Smith will be free to eat as many chocolate chip cookies a day as he desires.

Date _____*June 10, 1998*_____

Signed _____*Joe Smith*_____

_____*Jane Jones*_____

Specified number of cookies
allowed to be eaten by
Joe Smith

Date	Maximum number of chocolate chip cookies that can be eaten in a day by Joe Smith
June 11	11
June 12	9
June 13	7
June 14	5
June 15	3
June 16	1
June 17	0
June 18	0

Figure 18.4
Cookie contract.

◆ *Questions from Experience* ◆

What skills have you learned by modeling others? When did you learn them? How have they served you?

Behavioral rehearsal consists of practicing a desired behavior until it is performed the way one wishes. The process consists of gradually shaping a behavior and getting corrective feedback. It is frequently used after a person has viewed a model enacting the desired behavior (Smokowski, 2003). In such cases, especially with complex behavior, the person who wishes to acquire the behavior will practice what he or she has observed in the presence of other group members and the leader. The person will then receive feedback and suggestions on what was done and make modifications accordingly. For example, Hernando may have watched a videotape on assertiveness skills. Coming back into the group, the following scenario might happen.

Leader:	"Hernando, you have had a chance to practice assertiveness skills at home imitating the models you have seen on the videotape. Are you ready to practice them in the group?"
Hernando:	"I will need a partner to work with. Anyone want to volunteer?"
Betsy:	"I'll be the salesperson who is trying to sell you two suits when you only want to buy one."
Hernando:	"Sounds good. Let's begin."
Betsy:	"We have a special on suits, sir. If you buy two you save $100."
Hernando:	"That's nice, but I just need one suit."
Betsy:	"But think of the money you will save!"
Hernando:	"Think of the extra money I'll spend."
Betsy:	"Sir, it's only money. You can afford it and you will be getting a bargain."
Hernando:	"No, thank you. Now I would like to look for a suit."

At this point the role play might end and Hernando would receive feedback from the group and discuss with them what he did, how he did it, and whether there were other things he could have done.

The group setting is ideal for such a procedure because it offers safety to the practitioner and a chance to experiment. The more similar the rehearsal is to the actual conditions under which it will take place outside the group, the more likely it is to be performed successfully and generalized (i.e., be effective over a wide variety of conditions) in a particular environment (Cormier & Cormier, 1998).

Coaching is a process of providing group members with general principles for performing desired behaviors. It works best when the coach sits behind the group member who is rehearsing (see Figure 18.5). If the member forgets what to do next or questions why he or she is doing it, then the coach can intervene. Over time, coaching should be diminished, a process known as *fading*.

Cognitive restructuring is a process in which group members are taught to identify, evaluate, and change self-defeating or irrational thoughts that negatively influence their

Figure 18.5

Coaching.

Source: From an original idea by
Mark Miller, professor of counseling,
Louisiana Technical University,
Ruston. Used with permission.

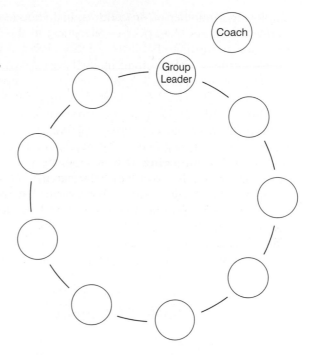

behavior. This process is accomplished by getting group members to vocalize their self talk
before others and change it when necessary from negative to either neutral or positive
(Posthuma, 2002). It is similar to what Ellis (1962) and Beck (1976) propose in regard to modifying the way one thinks. One of the best methods for implementing this process is Meichenbaum's (1977) **self-instructional training**. In this procedure, the group member is trained
to become aware of his or her maladaptive thoughts (self-statements). Next, the group leader
models appropriate behaviors while verbalizing the reasons behind these strategies. Finally,
the group member performs the designated behaviors while verbally repeating the reasons
behind the actions and then conducts these behaviors giving him- or herself covert messages.

Rose (1986) has identified a number of cognitive restructuring procedures, including
corrective information, thought stopping, relabeling, disputing irrational beliefs, imagery,
stress inoculation, relaxation exercises, and systematic problem solving. Rose (1983) has
also outlined a method of using cognitive restructuring within a group setting that
involves the use of teaching, practice, and performance similar to that of Meichenbaum.

In the **buddy system**, members are paired up in dyadic teams to mutually reinforce
and support each other (Hollander & Kazaoka, 1988). This type of learning appears to
enhance the change process for each dyad and the entire group.

Stage 6, *generalization and transference of treatment to the natural environment,*
marks the beginning of group termination. **Generalization** involves the display of behaviors in environments outside where they were originally learned, such as at home or work.
It indicates that transference into another setting has occurred. Generalizing behaviors
and transferring them to another setting does not happen by chance. Skilled group leaders must ensure that these processes are implemented (Wilson, 2005). They do so by

employing a number of procedures, including assigning behavioral homework, training significant others (e.g., peers, colleagues) in the individuals' environments to reinforce them for appropriate behaviors, and consulting with group members about particular problems they may have in making behavioral switches (Corey, 2004; Rose, 1983).

The seventh and final stage of behavior groups is *maintaining behavior change and fading out of the need for the group's support.* **Maintenance** is defined as being more consistent in doing the actions desired without depending on the group or its leader for support. In this stage, emphasis is placed on increasing group members' self-control and self-management (Mahoney & Thoresen, 1974; Thoresen & Mahoney, 1974). This may be done by **self-monitoring**, in which members are asked "to keep detailed, daily records of particular events or psychological reactions" (Wilson, 2005, p. 216). For example, in a group for the management of weight control, individuals monitor their calorie intake and reactions to eating certain foods. They then transfer this behavioral technique outside the group setting. If they find this strategy does not help, then they would rejoin another weight management group and try another technique. The results of the chocolate chip cookie contract (which your author once participated in to become healthier) (Figure 18.6) illustrate the basic components of a detailed self-monitoring program.

Role of the Behavioral Therapy Group Leader

Behavioral group leaders have a number of leadership responsibilities. Corey (2004) lists some of their primary functions as screening group members, teaching them about group process, assessing their progress in the group, determining the effectiveness of techniques employed in the group, and reinforcing members' achievements of specific goals. Vander Kolk (1985), although not disagreeing, conceptualizes the behavioral group leader as a systematic planner who identifies problems in behavioral terms and works with group members to achieve their objectives through the employment of appropriate strategies. "The most common strategies are instruction, feedback, modeling, behavioral rehearsal, social reinforcement, and homework assignments" (p. 127).

Overall, the behavioral group leader is a participant-observer (Hansen et al., 1980; Rose, 1983). The leader is much more active and direct at the beginning of the group but delegates more responsibility to group members as sessions go on (Axelrod, 1977). Leaders use as many techniques and instruments as possible, including videos, in helping their group members bring about desired changes. Belkin (1988) describes this leadership style as that of a "manager of contingencies" (p. 391). If the leader performs adequately, then group members will help reinforce one another in a positive manner.

Behavioral group leaders may come from any of the major mental health professions (e.g., counseling, social work, psychology, nursing, psychiatry) or the business and management domains. Many will need specialized training beyond that which they received in graduate school. Hollander and Kazaoka (1988) recommend 2 years of postgraduate training as a prerequisite to becoming a behavioral group leader. They also advocate that behavioral groups be co-led by a male and a female to model a coequal relationship and show group members that persons of different genders and backgrounds can work together harmoniously. For those wishing to become behavioral therapists, the **Association for Advancement of Behavioral Therapy (AABT)** is the major organization with which to affiliate.

Baseline Chocolate Chip Cookie–Eating Behavior

Date	# of cookies per day	Contract for Treatment
June 1	10	Chocolate chip cookie eating will be
June 2	14	decreased by two cookies a day during
June 3	8	the treatment period. The subject will
June 4	10	either earn or lose money as specified
June 5	11	in the chocolate chip cookie contract
June 6	13	for his behavior.
June 7	9	
June 8	11	
June 9	12	
June 10	10	

Baseline average—11 cookies per day

Treatment Chocolate Chip Cookie–Eating Behavior

Date	Target Behavior # of cookies per day	Actual Behavior # of cookies per day	Difference	Money earned (+) or lost (–)
June 11	11	8	–3	+$1.00
June 12	9	5	–4	+$1.00
June 13	7	4	–3	+$1.00
June 14	5	5	0	+$1.00
June 15	3	3	0	+$1.00
June 16	1	2	+1	– $1.50
June 17	0	0	0	+$1.00
June 18	0	0	0	+$1.00

Total money earned (+) or lost (–) +$5.50

Figure 18.6
Chocolate chip cookie–eating behavior.

Desired Outcome of Behavioral Therapy Groups

As a result of a behavioral group experience, participants should achieve a number of objectives. Many behavioral groups tend to be individually focused, yet goals for the group as a whole may be achieved. The magnitude of change and its impact depends on how well the group functions and how dedicated group members are. If all goes well, some or all of the following should occur.

First, members will be more aware of which specific behaviors they and others have that need changing and how to accomplish that. It is highly likely that they will become more sensitive about areas of their lives that they would like to modify. For example, in a behavioral group experience, Blair realized that if she was going to be effective in communicating with others, then she had to shorten her sentences and focus her ideas in a clearer way.

Second, it is hoped that participants will be able to assess how well they have altered their behaviors as well as what they still need to do to generalize them to their daily living environments. For example, in checking her chart on speaking up in the group, Margo realizes she has improved. However, in monitoring her behavior outside the group, she sees she has not changed. Therefore, in working with the behavioral group, Margo asks members for suggestions on how to generalize what she is doing in the group to situations outside it.

A third outcome of the group is that members will be more cognizant of new models for achieving their desired goals. This outcome objective dovetails with the second outcome focus. Behavioral groups are centered around learning, and one of the primary lessons learned in these settings is that there are many ways to modify behaviors, such as behavioral rehearsals and real-life experiences. Take, for example, an art group in which young novices are beginning to experiment with form and textures. By watching the group leaders and other group members, an individual in such a setting should begin to realize that many ways to achieve the desired end results are possible.

In addition to individual achievements, behavioral group members may realize more fully the power of group reinforcement. As a result of this psychological and social support, they may structure their life within groups differently. For example, Ed may now say to his friends when he is in doubt, "How am I doing?"

Finally, group members may become more behaviorally oriented in resolving their own difficulties outside a group setting. In other words, they may make behaviorism more a way of life. As such, they may concentrate on shaping, reinforcing, extinguishing, or modifying behaviors in their immediate environments. For instance, some behaviorally based parent training courses become internalized and integrated into the lives of their participants because of the overall positive effect that takes place in their lives.

CASE EXAMPLE: Alberto and AA

Alberto joined Alcoholics Anonymous (AA) after being discharged from a detoxification center. He did not know what to expect, but he thought the group might be able to help. Initially, he tried to be quiet, but he noticed that members who spoke up and were honest were reinforced by the group. He also was quick to observe that the group reinforced his abstinence from drinking and even paired him up with a buddy he could call at any time when he felt like he might be giving into the temptation to take a drink.

Alberto did not classify AA as a strict behavioral group because it had other components, but he did notice how much of what went on in the group was behavioral.

When have you been in groups that used a lot of behavioral principles? How did the structure of the group and the behavioral techniques help you?

Evaluation of Behavioral Therapy Groups

Because behaviorism has a long history and strong research methods, groups based on this theory are probably among the easiest to evaluate.

Strengths and Contributions

A major strength of behavioral groups is their focus on helping their members to learn new ways of functioning (Spiegler & Guevremont, 1993). Consider, for example, people with obsessive-compulsive disorders. Using group behavioral approaches, such individuals can learn to modify or rid themselves of recurrent, unwanted, and ritualized thoughts and behaviors they feel compelled to carry out (Fisher & Himle, 1998; Kobak, Rock, & Greist, 1995). Likewise, many individuals who have difficulty with interpersonal relationships of a less severe nature may benefit from behavioral groups. Usually these persons display excessive or limited behavioral skills; for example, they talk too much or not enough. Behavioral groups directly instruct their members on ways to improve interpersonal and personal skills so problems are alleviated.

A second strength of the behavioral approach is the impressive research it has generated (Rose, 1983). A number of journals are devoted exclusively to behavior therapy (Wilson, 2005). In addition, researchers of this approach are investigating its impact in groups under controlled conditions (Zimpfer, 1984). Annual reviews on behavioral and cognitive-behavioral groups and their methods are constantly being compiled (e.g., Upper & Ross, 1980). Major texts on behavioral treatment approaches continue to be published regularly, and the number of self-help books based on the application of cognitive behavioral therapy is growing (Baker & Brownell, 1999).

Yet a third strength of behavioral groups is that they are relatively short term and here and now focused (Gazda et al., 2001; Hollander & Kazaoka, 1988). Behavioral psychotherapy and counseling groups, for instance, are seldom conducted more than once a week over an 8- to 12-month period and last 90 to 120 minutes a session. This period is relatively brief, especially when compared with psychoanalytic groups. Members have specific goals to work on that are measurable. Psychoeducational and task/work behavioral groups are equally of a short-term duration.

A fourth strength of behavioral groups is their versatility. For example, behaviorally oriented groups can be used to

- teach specific skills, such as assertion (Alberti & Emmons, 2002) or parent education (Lewis, 1986; White & Mullis, 1997);
- work on certain problem areas, such as phobic behavior (Wolpe, 1958);
- address holistic issues (Lazarus, 1981); and
- improve functioning in four typical depression areas of the elderly—grief and bereavement, role transitions, role disputes, such as marital conflict, and interpersonal deficits, such as difficulties making new friends or accepting care (Kennedy & Tanenbaum, 2000).

There are very few problems that behaviorists do not address. Each group is tailored to the needs of its members (Rose, 1983).

A fifth strength of the behavioral approach is its emphasis on promoting self-control among its members once the group ends. In some ways, the behavioral group is like an incubator that fosters specific growth in its participants and that keeps developing after the group experience terminates.

A final positive about the behavioral group focus is that behavioral theories can be combined with other approaches (e.g., cognitive theories) to create a multimodal way of working with groups and their members. Cognitive-behavioral group psychotherapy, for instance, is a very popular way of working with individuals in groups to help them integrate their thoughts and behaviors (Sedgwick, 1989). It is also an effective way to help cultural minority groups, such as African American women, to alter their thinking and influence their sense of well-being and mental health (Pack-Brown, Whittington-Clark, & Parker, 1998).

Limitations

Behavioral groups have disadvantages, too. One is that group members may become overdependent on the group for support and encouragement. In such cases, these individuals become "group junkies/addicts" and use the group for inappropriate reinforcement. Although this type of behavior is rare, it may occur if the leader and participants do not work hard on generalization and termination issues.

A second limitation of behavioral group work is that some of its methods can be too rigidly applied. In such situations, too much emphasis is placed on techniques and not enough on individuals. Groups in which this occurs have leaders who are underinvolved with members and overinvolved in changing behaviors. They work like mechanics instead of like human development specialists.

A third limitation of the behavioral approach is its tendency to ignore the past and the unconscious (Rose, 1977). Early history has only so much influence on people, but behaviorally based groups do not consider any influence of early history or repressed thoughts. This theory is not appropriate for those trying to resolve early childhood experiences that are still problematic.

A fourth limiting aspect of behavioral groups is their lack of focus on broad life issues (T. M. Elmore, personal communication, 1997). Behavioral groups are much more likely to concentrate on particular events or skills in their members' lives than on members' lives as a whole. As a result, some changes brought about in the group may not last because of members' inabilities to see a connection between what they have learned and the rest of their lives.

The behavioral approach is also limited in its concentration on just behavior, whether overt or covert. Behavioral groups are not particularly concerned about feelings but rather the dynamics behind them (T. M. Elmore, personal communication, 1997). Persons who wish to become more aware of their emotions are better served in another setting.

Finally, behavioral groups are not unified theoretically and work best with well-motivated members (Hollander & Kazaoka, 1988). More work is needed in bringing the different theories that underlie this group procedure together and in making it more applicable for individuals whose motivation is low. To their credit, many behaviorists are actively engaged in trying to rectify these deficits.

Learning More

Behavioral therapy focuses on behavioral and cognitive-behavioral therapy, assessment, and analysis. The organization to which most behaviorally based group workers belong to is the

Association for Advancement of Behavior Therapy
305 Seventh Avenue
New York, NY 10001-6008
Telephone: 212-647-1890 or 1-800-685-AABT
Web site: www.aabt.org/aabt

The AABT sponsors continuing education programs and symposia. It produces professional publications, too (e.g., *Behavior Therapy, Cognitive and Behavioral Practice, Behavior Therapist*).

SUMMARY AND CONCLUSION

Rational-emotive behavior therapy and behavioral approaches are popular ways of working with groups. Each may be used effectively with groups, provided group workers have prepared the group and themselves to operate according to the principles of these approaches.

REBT is frequently used in group settings, particularly group counseling and psychotherapy. It makes use of a number of affective, behavioral, and cognitive methods to help its group members bring about change. A primary aspect of this approach is the initial teaching needed to educate group members that feelings are derived from thoughts, not events. After this information is clearly understood, the group proceeds with the leader being in charge but with other participants acting as "auxiliary counselors."

REBT groups stress role playing and homework assignments as well as recognition of thoughts. Disputations are usually employed to get rid of faulty, irrational thinking and help participants take better control of their lives. Overall, REBT groups enable their members to learn from one another and recognize their shortcomings more quickly than is often the case in individual sessions. These groups are highly structured and didactic and do not stress group dynamics as much as some other approaches. In many ways, REBT groups function in a psychoeducational format even when they are emphasizing psychotherapeutic changes.

The behavioral position, although diverse, focuses on empowering its group members by concentrating on self-improvement skills. Individuals in these groups learn how to manage excessive amounts of behavior or learn new behaviors. The three primary behavior methods for teaching in these groups are respondent learning, operant conditioning, and social learning. Contracts are often used in behaviorally oriented groups to help members focus on the behaviors they wish to change. As a group, behaviorists employ many techniques to promote and foster change with their group members, including reinforcement, extinction, shaping, cognitive restructuring, coaching, the buddy system, and problem-solving rehearsals.

Within groups, members offer support to one another, although this approach is often more leader-to-member than member-to-member focused. A real strength of the behavioral approach to group work is the solid learning theory base behind it. Excellent research also exists to back behavioral approaches to group work. Table 18.1 provides a comparative summary of the 10 theories covered in Part III.

Table 18.1

A comparison of theoretical approaches to group work.

Approach	Psychoanalytic	Transactional Analysis	Reality Therapy	Adlerian
Premise	Emphasis on freeing unconscious thoughts and making the unconscious more conscious; focus on interaction of id, ego, and superego; four stages of psychosexual development; defense mechanisms.	Three basic ego states: Child, Parent, and Adult; potential for growth must be nurtured in a person; can determine ego states through behavioral, social, historical, and phenomenological; avoid playing "games" through knowledge of ego states.	Behavior is generated from within to meet one or more basic needs; basic psychological needs: belonging, power, freedom, and fun; physiological need is survival; rejects concept of mental illness; present is emphasized; focus on clients' perceptions and present awareness; focus on taking responsibility for oneself.	Concern for social interest; emphasis on the purposefulness of all behavior; focus on the subjective nature of perception and holistic nature of people; emphasis on developing a healthy lifestyle and the self-determinism of the individual to chart a future based on expected consequences of behavior.
Practice	Membership generally restricted to psychiatric patients or analytically oriented individuals; groups are heterogeneous by design; use techniques such as dream analysis, interpretation, resistance, and transference.	TA most often used in groups; therapeutic contracts are what client intends to accomplish during group process; game analysis; life script analysis; redecision theory: helps clients make redecisions while in the Child ego state.	Basically a rational process; emphasizes observable behavior in the here and now; eight basic steps to reality therapy; techniques include use of humor, paradox, questioning, and self-help procedures.	Primarily psychoeducational; emphasis on individuals learning from one another; focus on interpretation of person's early history; stress on individual, interpersonal, and group process goals; four phases of group process.
Role of leader	Should be objective and relatively anonymous; should foster transference while keeping self-disclosure to a minimum; promotes positive atmosphere; should have directional and stimulation skills; serve as conductors rather than dictators.	Serve primarily as listener, observer, diagnostician, and analyst; secondarily serve as facilitator; groups are leader centered; leaders stay detached; serve as teachers; basic roles: protector, permission, potency, and operations.	Active and involved with group members; strive to be warm and confronting; always pointing out reality in a direct and caring manner; serve as a model of responsible behavior; must foster self-evaluation process in group members; establish structure and limits for group sessions.	Must have good knowledge of clients to attack "faulty logic"; challenges group members to change present behavior; uses encouragement and natural consequences; leader shares opinions and feelings; serves as a model for the group; creates proper attitude in group.

Desired outcomes	For members to grow as individuals; to pass through various stages of development such as preliminary individual analysis; establishment of rapport through dreams and fantasies; analysis of resistance; analysis of transference; working through; reorientation and social integration.	Group members will learn about themselves through their analysis of structures, transactions, games, and scripts; to be freed from old parental messages and early self-defeating messages from their Child state; to be enabled to think, feel, and behave differently; to adopt the "I'm OK—You're OK" life position.	Members will move past self-defeating patterns of behavior; engage in new behaviors to help achieve responsible, present-oriented goals; greater awareness of values; the realization that there is a choice; outside events and history lose their power.	Focus on the growth and actions of individual within the group rather than the group itself; members should be more socially oriented, personally integrated, and goal directed; correct faulty beliefs; eliminate competitive behavioral stances; be more in touch with family-of-origin issues.
Strengths	Opportunity to experience transference feelings with other group members as well as group leader; opportunity to resolve current problems as well as issues from the past; members learn that they experience and express a wide range of emotions; emphasis on long-term personality change.	The clarity of the language used to explain TA concepts—stresses intellectual insight as initial basis for change; strength in its simplicity and easily grasped concepts; fast-paced—group members moving forward reinforce one another to change; can be used in a variety of settings and combined with various other approaches, such as Gestalt.	Emphasizes accountability; stress on action and thinking—the refusal to accept excuses; viability with members of society on which others have given up; definable procedures for working in groups; treatment continues only until clients can solve their difficulties.	Usually nonthreatening in nature; generally helpful because of educational emphasis; methods associated with Adlerian are logical and based on common sense; concepts easily grasped; theory is holistic—emphasis on cognitive, behavioral, and affective sides of human nature; eclectic nature of the theory; flexible in working with different populations.
Limitations	Free association may not be possible in group setting; those in psychoanalytic field tend to read and use only their own works—hinders creativity in counseling experience; theory is deterministic, biologically biased, and oriented toward a pathological view of human nature; lack of scientific investigations.	Restrictive interpretation of human nature—people are more complex than TA concepts suggest; strong emphasis on cognitive understanding—TA may become more of an intellectual exercise than expression and interaction; lack of empirical evidence to support its effectiveness.	Emphasis on either verbal or written communication; may be too simple—steps in the change process may be misapplied by the clients or counselor; extreme positions on certain issues such as mental illness; lack of proven effectiveness; emphasis on conformity and utility.	Style of leader—Adlerians follow their own style in regard to procedure; narrowness of Adlerian scope—assumes all problems are socially based; lack of uniformity of method; research on Adlerian is relatively weak.

Approach	Person Centered	Existential	Gestalt	Psychodrama
Premise	Emphasis on trusting the inner resources of persons; trust in group to develop their potential without direction from leader; certain conditions must be met within group for group to reach full potential; qualified person serves as facilitator; focus on personal growth groups composed of generally healthy individuals.	People are the authors of their lives for better or worse; they have the freedom to choose and are responsible for their choices; constant search for meaning through discarding meaningless actions and values and embracing new and meaningful thoughts and behaviors; search for meaning may cause tension and anxiety.	"Principle of holism" (integration of unfinished business); person must be self-aware to be free to make choices; healthy persons meet figural needs first; express both sides of a polarity and then integrate; groups operate on several levels at once; people are proactive in making choices; individuals are viewed as intrinsically neutral; awareness gives people self-cohesiveness and enables them.	Emphasizes freeing persons from dysfunctional patterns of behavior; strong focus on action; opportunity to act out and experience various aspects of problems in group setting; emphasis on personal here and now; full expression of feelings.
Practice	Establish climate in which group members can risk being themselves; unstructured format; must establish sense of trust in group; feedback and communication of thoughts and feelings necessary for contact to occur among members; 15 stages in group process.	Emphasis on psychotherapy, counseling, and occasionally psychoeducation; work toward increasing self-awareness and personal responsibility; productively handling anxiety; struggle to search for meaning in life; emphasis on becoming authentic.	Focus on individual within the group; dual-focused Gestalt work; floating hot seat; trilevel model of Gestalt group work centered on the here and now; ask what and how; work on specific problem to increase self-awareness; emphasis on behavioral rather than cognitive; participation in growth experience; use experiments and exercises.	Multidimensional in nature; consider personal and physical factors; techniques must be employed in a methodological manner; three phases are warm-up, action, and integration; hundreds of psychodrama techniques—a few major ones are creative imagery, sculpting, magic shop, soliloquy, role reversal, and mirror.
Role of leader	Confronts in a positive manner; conveys warmth and empathy, attending, understanding meaning and content; conveys acceptance, linking; derives direction from group; facilitator who participates as a group member; more passive form of leadership.	Must be active and reflective; consistently thinking and taking risks; work to build close relationships with all members; confrontative; to be used as a source of knowledge in regard to the human experience; serves as a model of how to be appropriately self-disclosing.	Leader is central to function of the group; helps members locate impasses and work through them to awareness; balances challenging and supporting members; an "artist" who creates an atmosphere that promotes growth; serves as expert-helper, frustrater, communications expert, creator and teacher; serves as a catalyst for change.	Director serves as producer, facilitator, observer, and analyzer; leads warm-up, encourages development of trust and spontaneity, establishes a structure, protects members from abuse by other members; brings closure to group sessions.

Desired outcomes	Development of self-awareness and awareness of others; personal growth; self-actualization; more openness to experience intimacy and meaningfulness with others.	Members will be more aware of themselves and the choices they have in regard to growth and development; to become more self-determining; to find new meaning in all aspects of life; better understanding of self and the world—life is a journey.	More awareness in the here and now; to shed layers of neuroses; members will be more congruent in themselves and with others.	Creation of catharsis—insight and emotional resolution; to experience and work through past, present, or anticipated events that have caused distress; to reach a stage of renewed self-awareness, readjustment, integration, acceptance, control, and prevention; spillover effect—one learns even when one is not the "main character."
Strengths	Focus on enhancing the development of the total individual; focus on improving communication skills; makes group work acceptable for the "normal" population.	Deals with ultimate issues in life and presents opportunities to explore values and lifestyles in depth; provide a framework for other forms of group work; deal with members holistically in the present; applicable for a wide range of cultures	Suitability to group leaders who have a humanistic existential approach to helping others; lends itself well to creative individuals; emphasizes the affective dimension of human experiences; focus on working through impasses and becoming integrated; variety of exercises and experiments; abundance of training institutes.	Diversity—can be used in a variety of settings with all levels of age, education, and socioeconomic status; teaching potential; fostering of creativity and spontaneity within leaders and members; integrative and vicarious effect; input and feedback of audience.
Limitations	Less than ideal for individuals who need therapy or structure; method by which leaders and group members are chosen; lack of structure may mean that group process goes nowhere; the history of person-centered groups; research not necessarily reliable.	Most useful for individuals who have no trouble communicating, even when dealing with painful issues; limited applicability outside of counseling and therapy environments; maturity, life experience, and close supervision are necessary to practice this approach; broad based and does not generally deal with specific behaviors or concerns; not appropriate for those who need information or immediate answers.	Eschews cognitive side of human nature; group leaders may not be able to help members work through impasses; there is a potential danger for abusing techniques and people; difficulty in researching Gestalt groups.	Danger of overexposing the protagonist to him- or herself as well as to the audience; lack of quality research underlying psychodrama; few training centers for directors; too much focus on expression of feelings without change in behavior.

Approach	REBT	Behavioral
Premise	One's thinking about events produces feelings rather than situations themselves; ABC model of human interaction; four types of thought: negative, positive, neutral, and mixed; stress on the dual nature of humans; philosophy of life as well as treatment.	Emphasis on learning and modification of behaviors; no focus on treatment of underlying problems; two major groups—radical and cognitive behaviorists; learning process in which helpers use specific, planned techniques to accomplish behavioral change; groups are either interpersonal or transactional.
Practice	Groups vary between open and closed ended; tend to be didactic, philosophical, and skills oriented; REBT theory introduced by leader; members share problems or concerns; members and leader give feedback and suggestions; little attention to past—focus on here and now; role play and modeling.	Seven specific stages apply to all types of behavioral groups; frequently used techniques include reinforcement, extinction, shaping, contingency contracts, modeling, behavior rehearsal, coaching, and cognitive restructuring.
Role of leader	Leader-centered groups; leader encourages rational thinking; encourages members to act as auxiliary counselors for other members; serves as model for group; helps members give up their demands for perfection.	Screening group members; teaching about group process; assessing members' progress; evaluating techniques; reinforcing member achievements; systematic planner who identifies problems in behavioral terms; overall a participant-observer; more active and directive at beginning of group and later delegates responsibility.

Desired outcomes	To learn to think rationally; to achieve a particular goal connected with overcoming an irrational belief; increased knowledge of how REBT can be employed in new experiences; to gain the experience of personally understanding the process of change.	Awareness of specific behaviors that need changing and how to accomplish that; ability to assess behavioral changes; increases cognizance of new models for achieving desired goals; to realize the power of group reinforcement; may become more behaviorally oriented in resolving other difficulties.
Strengths	Focus on the importance of cognition and behavior in influencing emotions and actions; can be quickly taught to everyone involved; may be perfect for persons phasing out of individual therapy; versatility; emphasizes remediation and prevention; emphasis on action as well as discussion.	Focus on helping members learn new ways of functioning; impressive research in the field; short term and very focused; versatility—can be used to teach specific skills, work on problem areas, and address holistic issues; emphasis on promoting self-control after termination; can be combined with other approaches.
Limitations	Traditional focus on individual rather than entire group; may be too confrontive and directive at times; borderline-disturbed individuals may become worse in REBT; lack of reliable group research.	Members may become overdependent on group for support; too much emphasis on techniques; tendency to ignore the past and unconscious; lack of focus on broad life issues; emphasis only on behavior—lack of concern about feelings; not theoretically unified; works best with well motivated.

445

CLASSROOM EXERCISES

1. Write down your thoughts about working in groups as opposed to working with individuals. After you have spent about 5 minutes writing down as many thoughts as you can, pair up with another class member and discuss which of your thoughts are primarily positive, negative, neutral, and mixed. Notice how the tone of the thought affects you as a person, and talk to your classmate about what you observe happening to you in discussing your thoughts. How do you think what you experience is similar to that of group members in a REBT-based group?

2. In a group of four, have each person demonstrate to the others a minor change in his or her behavior, such as walking differently or using more mannerisms when talking. Get feedback from the group about what the behavior looked like and its impact. Discuss how each person might or might not benefit from modifying some aspect of his or her behavior.

3. In groups of three, check major periodicals or citation indexes in your library for articles on the use of REBT and behavioral groups. Report back what you have found to the class and what patterns you have noticed in articles related to these theories.

4. Have a class debate, between two teams of five class members each, on the pros and cons of using the two theories covered in this chapter. Poll the class after the debate on which points they remember each side making and why they remember those emphases.

APPENDIX A

ASSOCIATION FOR SPECIALISTS IN GROUP WORK: BEST PRACTICE GUIDELINES

The Association for Specialists in Group Work (ASGW) is a division of the American Counseling Association whose members are interested in and specialize in group work. We value the creation of community, as well as service to our members, clients, and the profession; we value leadership as a process to facilitate the growth and development of individuals and groups.

The Association for Specialists in Group Work recognizes the commitment of its members to the Code of Ethics and Standards of Practice (as revised in 1995) of its parent organization, the American Counseling Association, and nothing in this document shall be construed to supplant that code. These Best Practice Guidelines are intended to clarify the application of the ACA Code of Ethics and Standards of Practice to the field of group work by defining Group Workers' responsibility and scope of practice involving those activities, strategies, and interventions that are consistent and current with effective and appropriate professional ethical and community standards. ASGW views ethical process as being integral to group work and views Group Workers as ethical agents. Group Workers, by their very nature in being responsible and responsive to their group members, necessarily embrace a certain potential for ethical vulnerability. It is incumbent on Group Workers to give considerable attention to the intent and context of their actions because the attempts of Group Workers to influence human behavior through group work always have ethical implications. These Best Practice Guidelines address Group Workers' responsibilities in planning, performing, and processing groups.

JOURNAL FOR SPECIALISTS IN GROUP WORK, Vol. 23 No. 3, September 1998, 237–244 © 1998 Sage Publications, Inc.

SECTION A: BEST PRACTICE IN PLANNING
A.1. Professional Context and Regulatory Requirements

Group Workers actively know, understand, and apply the ACA Code of Ethics and Standards of Best Practice, the ASGW Professional Standards for the Training of Group Workers, these ASGW Best Practice Guidelines, the ASGW diversity competencies, the ACA Multicultural Guidelines, relevant state laws, accreditation requirements, relevant National Board for Certified Counselors Codes and Standards, their organization's standards, and insurance requirements affecting the practice of group work.

A.2. Scope of Practice and Conceptual Framework

Group Workers define the scope of practice related to the core and specialization competencies defined in the ASGW Training Standards. Group Workers are aware of personal strengths and weaknesses in leading groups. Group Workers develop and are able to articulate a general conceptual framework to guide practice and a rationale for use of techniques that are to be used. Group Workers limit their practice to those areas for which they meet the training criteria established by the ASGW Training Standards.

A.3. Assessment

a. *Assessment of self.* Group Workers actively assess their knowledge and skills related to the specific group(s) offered. Group Workers assess their values, beliefs, and theoretical orientation and how these affect the group, particularly when working with a diverse and multicultural population.

b. *Ecological assessment.* Group Workers assess community needs, agency or organization resources, sponsoring organization mission,

447

staff competency, attitudes regarding group work, professional training levels of potential group leaders regarding group work, client attitudes regarding group work, and multicultural and diversity considerations. Group Workers use this information as the basis for making decisions related to their group practice or for implementing groups for which they have supervisory, evaluation, or oversight responsibilities.

A.4. Program Development and Evaluation

a. *Group Workers identify the type(s) of group(s) to be offered and how they relate to community needs.*

b. *Group Workers concisely state in writing the purpose and goals of the group.* Group Workers also identify the role of the group members in influencing or determining the group goals.

c. *Group Workers set fees consistent with the organization's fee schedule, taking into consideration the financial status and locality of prospective group members.*

d. *Group Workers choose techniques and a leadership style appropriate to the type(s) of group(s) being offered.*

e. *Group Workers have an evaluation plan consistent with regulatory, organization, and insurance requirements, where appropriate.*

f. *Group Workers take into consideration current professional guidelines when using technology, including but not limited to Internet communication.*

A.5. Resources

Group Workers coordinate resources related to the kind of group(s) and group activities to be provided, such as: adequate funding, the appropriateness and availability of a trained coleader, space and privacy requirements for the type(s) of group(s) being offered, marketing and recruiting, and appropriate collaboration with other community agencies and organizations.

A.6. Professional Disclosure Statement

Group Workers have a professional disclosure statement that includes information on confidentiality and exceptions to confidentiality; theoretical orientation;

information on the nature, purpose(s), and goals of the group; the group services that can be provided; the role and responsibility of group members and leaders; Group Workers' qualifications to conduct the specific group(s); specific licenses, certifications, and professional affiliations; and address of licensing/credentialing body.

A.7. Group and Member Preparation

a. *Group Workers screen prospective group members if appropriate to the type of group being offered.* When selection of group members is appropriate, Group Workers identify group members whose needs and goals are compatible with the goals of the group.

b. *Group Workers facilitate informed consent.* Group Workers provide in oral and written form to prospective members (when appropriate to group type): the professional disclosure statement, group purpose and goals, group participation expectations including voluntary and involuntary membership, role expectations of members and leader(s), policies related to entering and exiting the group, policies governing substance use, policies and procedures governing mandated groups (where relevant), documentation requirements, disclosure of information to others, implications of out-of-group contact or involvement among members, procedures for consultation between group leader(s) and group member(s), fees and time parameters, and potential impacts of group participation.

c. *Group Workers obtain the appropriate consent forms for work with minors and other dependent group members.*

d. *Group Workers define confidentiality and its limits (for example, legal and ethical exceptions and expectations; waivers implicit with treatment plans, documentation, and insurance usage).* Group Workers have the responsibility to inform all group participants of the need for confidentiality and potential consequences of breaching confidentiality; they must explain that legal privilege does not apply to group discussions (unless provided by state statute).

A.8. Professional Development

Group Workers recognize that professional growth is a continuous, ongoing, developmental process throughout their career.

a. *Group Workers remain current and increase knowledge and skill competencies through activities such as continuing education, professional supervision, and participation in personal and professional development activities.*

b. *Group Workers seek consultation and/or supervision regarding ethical concerns that interfere with effective functioning as a group leader.* Supervisors have the responsibility to keep abreast of consultation, group theory, and process and to adhere to related ethical guidelines.

c. *Group Workers seek appropriate professional assistance for their own personal problems or conflicts that are likely to impair their professional judgment or work performance.*

d. *Group Workers seek consultation and supervision to ensure appropriate practice whenever working with a group for which all knowledge and skill competencies have not been achieved.*

e. *Group Workers keep abreast of group research and development.*

A.9. Trends and Technological Changes

Group Workers are aware of and responsive to technological changes as they affect society and the profession. These include but are not limited to changes in mental health delivery systems, legislative and insurance industry reforms, shifting population demographics and client needs, and technological advances in Internet and other communication and delivery systems. Group Workers adhere to ethical guidelines related to the use of developing technologies.

SECTION B: BEST PRACTICE IN PERFORMING
B.1. Self-Knowledge

Group Workers are aware of and monitor their strengths and weaknesses and the effects these have on group members.

B.2. Group Competencies

Group Workers have a basic knowledge of groups and the principles of group dynamics and are able to perform the core group competencies, as described in the ASGW Professional Standards for the Training of Group Workers. In addition, Group Workers have

adequate understanding and skill in any group specialty area chosen for practice (psychotherapy, counseling, task, psychoeducation, as described in the ASGW Training Standards).

B.3. Group Plan Adaptation

a. *Group Workers apply and modify knowledge, skills, and techniques appropriate to group type and stage and to the unique needs of various cultural and ethnic groups.*

b. *Group Workers monitor the group's progress toward the group goals and plan.*

c. *Group Workers clearly define and maintain ethical, professional, and social relationship boundaries with group members as appropriate to their role in the organization and the type of group being offered.*

B.4. Therapeutic Conditions and Dynamics

Group Workers understand and are able to implement appropriate models of group development, process observation, and therapeutic conditions.

B.5. Meaning

Group Workers assist members in generating meaning from the group experience.

B.6. Collaboration

Group Workers assist members in developing individual goals and respect group members as coequal partners in the group experience.

B.7. Evaluation

Group Workers include evaluation (both formal and informal) between sessions and at the conclusion of the group.

B.8. Diversity

Group Workers practice with broad sensitivity to client differences including but not limited to ethnic, gender, religious, sexual, psychological maturity, economic class, family history, physical characteristics or limitations, and geographic location. Group Workers continuously seek information regarding the cultural issues of the diverse population with whom they are working, both by interaction with participants and by using outside resources.

B.9.   Ethical Surveillance

Group Workers employ an appropriate ethical decision-making model in responding to ethical challenges and issues and in determining courses of action and behavior for self and group members. In addition, Group Workers employ applicable standards as promulgated by ACA, ASGW, or other appropriate professional organizations.

SECTION C: BEST PRACTICE IN GROUP PROCESSING
C.1.   Processing Schedule

Group Workers process the workings of the group with themselves, group members, supervisors, or other colleagues, as appropriate. This may include assessing progress on group and member goals, leader behaviors and techniques, group dynamics and interventions, as well as developing understanding and acceptance of meaning. Processing may occur both within sessions and before and after each session, at time of termination, and later follow-up, as appropriate.

C.2.   Reflective Practice

Group Workers attend to opportunities to synthesize theory and practice and to incorporate learning outcomes into ongoing groups. Group Workers attend to session dynamics of members and their interactions and also attend to the relationship between session dynamics and leader values, cognition, and affect.

C.3.   Evaluation and Follow-Up

a. *Group Workers evaluate process and outcomes.* Results are used for ongoing program planning, improvement and revisions of current group, and/or for professional research literature. Group Workers follow all applicable policies and standards in using group material for research and reports.
b. *Group Workers conduct follow-up contact with group members, as appropriate, to assess outcomes or when requested by a group member(s).*

C.4.   Consultation and Training With Other Organizations

Group Workers provide consultation and training to organizations in and out of their setting, when appropriate. Group Workers seek out consultation as needed with competent professional persons knowledgeable about group work.

ASSOCIATION FOR SPECIALISTS IN GROUP WORK: PRINCIPLES FOR DIVERSITY-COMPETENT GROUP WORKERS

PREAMBLE

The Association for Specialists in Group Work (ASGW) is committed to understanding how issues of diversity affect all aspects of group work. This includes but is not limited to: training diversity-competent group workers; conducting research that will add to the literature on group work with diverse populations; understanding how diversity affects group process and dynamics; and assisting group facilitators in various settings to increase their awareness, knowledge, and skills as they relate to facilitating groups with diverse memberships.

As an organization, ASGW has endorsed this document with the recognition that issues of diversity affect group process and dynamics, group facilitation, training, and research. As an organization, we recognize that racism, classism, sexism, heterosexism, ableism, and so forth, affect everyone. As individual members of this organization, it is our personal responsibility to address these issues through awareness, knowledge, and skills. As members of ASGW, we need to increase our awareness of our own biases, values, and beliefs and how they impact the groups we run. We need to increase our awareness of our group members' biases, values, and beliefs and how they also impact and influence group process and dynamics. Finally, we need to increase our knowledge in facilitating, with confidence, competence, and integrity, groups that are diverse on many dimensions.

DEFINITIONS

For the purposes of this document, it is important that the language used is understood. Terms such as "dominant," "nondominant," and "target" persons

JOURNAL FOR SPECIALISTS IN GROUP WORK, Vol. 24 No. 1, March 1999, 7–14 © 1999 Sage Publications, Inc.

and/or populations are used to define a person or groups of persons who historically, in the United States, do not have equal access to power, money, certain privileges (such as access to mental health services because of financial constraints, or the legal right to marry, in the case of a gay or lesbian couple), and/or the ability to influence or initiate social policy because of unequal representation in government and politics. These terms are not used to denote a lack of numbers in terms of representation in the overall U.S. population. Nor are these terms used to continue to perpetuate the very biases and forms of oppression, both overt and covert, that this document attempts to address.

For the purposes of this document, the term "disabilities" refers to differences in physical, mental, emotional, and learning abilities and styles among people. It is not meant as a term to define a person, such as a learning disabled person, but rather in the context of a person with a learning disability.

Given the history and current cultural, social, and political context in which this document is written, the authors of this document are limited to the language of this era. With this in mind, we have attempted to construct a "living document" that can and will change as the sociopolitical and cultural context changes.

THE PRINCIPLES
I. Awareness of Self

A. Attitudes and Beliefs

1. Diversity-competent group workers demonstrate movement from being unaware to being increasingly aware and sensitive to their own race, ethnic and cultural heritage, gender, socioeconomic status (SES), sexual orientation, abilities, and religion and spiritual beliefs, and to valuing and respecting differences.

2. Diversity-competent group workers demonstrate increased awareness of how their own race, ethnicity, culture, gender, SES, sexual orientation, abilities, and religion and spiritual beliefs are impacted by their own experiences and histories, which in turn influence group process and dynamics.

3. Diversity-competent group workers can recognize the limits of their competencies and expertise with regard to working with group members who are different from them in terms of race, ethnicity, culture (including language), SES, gender, sexual orientation, abilities, religion, and spirituality and their beliefs, values, and biases. (For further clarification on limitations, expertise, and type of group work, refer to the training standards and best practice guidelines, Association for Specialists in Group Work, 1998; and the ethical guidelines, American Counseling Association, 1995.)

4. Diversity-competent group workers demonstrate comfort, tolerance, and sensitivity with differences that exist between themselves and group members in terms of race, ethnicity, culture, SES, gender, sexual orientation, abilities, religion, and spirituality and their beliefs, values, and biases.

B.   Knowledge

1. Diversity-competent group workers can identify specific knowledge about their own race, ethnicity, SES, gender, sexual orientation, abilities, religion, and spirituality, and how they personally and professionally affect their definitions of "normality" and the group process.

2. Diversity-skilled group workers demonstrate knowledge and understanding regarding how oppression in any form—such as, racism, classism, sexism, heterosexism, ableism, discrimination, and stereotyping—affects them personally and professionally.

3. Diversity-skilled group workers demonstrate knowledge about their social impact on others. They are knowledgeable about communication style differences, how their style may inhibit or foster the group process with members who are different from themselves along the different dimensions of diversity, and how to anticipate the impact they may have on others.

C.   Skills

1. Diversity-competent group workers seek out educational, consultative, and training experiences to improve their understanding and effectiveness in working with group members who self-identify as Indigenous Peoples, African Americans, Asian Americans, Hispanics, Latinos/ Latinas, gays, lesbians, bisexuals, or transgendered persons and persons with physical, mental/ emotional, and/or learning disabilities, particularly with regard to race and ethnicity. Within this context, group workers are able to recognize the limits of their competencies and: (a) seek consultation, (b) seek further training or education, (c) refer members to more qualified group workers, or (d) engage in a combination of these.

2. Group workers who exhibit diversity competence are constantly seeking to understand themselves within their multiple identities (apparent and unapparent differences), for example, gay, Latina, Christian, working class, and female, and are constantly and actively striving to unlearn the various behaviors and processes they covertly and overtly communicate that perpetuate oppression, particularly racism.

II.   Group Worker's Awareness of Group Member's Worldview

A.   Attitudes and Beliefs

1. Diversity-skilled group workers exhibit awareness of any possible negative emotional reactions toward Indigenous Peoples, African Americans, Asian Americans, Hispanics, Latinos/Latinas, gays, lesbians, bisexuals, or transgendered persons and persons with physical, mental/emotional and/or learning disabilities that they may hold. They are willing to contrast in a nonjudgmental manner their own beliefs and attitudes with those of Indigenous Peoples, African Americans, Asian Americans, Hispanics, Latinos/Latinas, gays, lesbians, bisexuals, or transgendered persons and persons with physical, mental/ emotional, and/or learning disabilities who are group members.

2. Diversity-competent group workers demonstrate awareness of their stereotypes and preconceived notions that they may hold

toward Indigenous Peoples, African Americans, Asian Americans, Hispanics, Latinos/Latinas, gays, lesbians, bisexuals, or transgendered persons and persons with physical, mental/emotional, and/or learning disabilities.

B.   Knowledge

1. Diversity-skilled group workers possess specific knowledge and information about Indigenous Peoples, African Americans, Asian Americans, Hispanics, Latinos/Latinas, gays, lesbians, bisexuals, and transgendered people and group members who have mental/emotional, physical, and/or learning disabilities with whom they are working. They are aware of the life experiences, cultural heritage, and sociopolitical background of Indigenous Peoples, African Americans, Asian Americans, Hispanics, Latinos/Latinas, gays, lesbians, bisexuals, or transgendered persons and group members with physical, mental/emotional, and/or learning disabilities. This particular knowledge-based competency is strongly linked to the various racial/minority and sexual identity development models available in the literature (Atkinson, Morten, & Sue, 1993; Cass, 1979; Cross, 1995; D'Augelli & Patterson, 1995; Helms, 1992).

2. Diversity-competent group workers exhibit an understanding of how race, ethnicity, culture, gender, sexual identity, different abilities, SES, and other immutable personal characteristics may affect personality formation, vocational choices, manifestation of psychological disorders, physical "disease" or somatic symptoms, help-seeking behavior(s), and the appropriateness or inappropriateness of the various types of and theoretical approaches to group work.

3. Group workers who demonstrate competency in diversity in groups understand and have the knowledge about sociopolitical influences that impinge upon the lives of Indigenous Peoples, African Americans, Asian Americans, Hispanics, Latinos/Latinas, gays, lesbians, bisexuals, or transgendered persons and persons with physical, mental/emotional, and/or learning disabilities. Immigration issues, poverty, racism, oppression, stereotyping, and/or powerlessness adversely impacts many of these individuals and therefore impacts groups process or dynamics.

C.   Skills

1. Diversity-skilled group workers familiarize themselves with relevant research and the latest findings regarding mental health issues of Indigenous Peoples, African Americans, Asian Americans, Hispanics, Latinos/Latinas, gays, lesbians, bisexuals, or transgendered persons and persons with physical, mental/emotional, and/or learning disabilities. They actively seek out educational experiences that foster their knowledge and understanding of skills for facilitating groups across differences.

2. Diversity-competent group workers become actively involved with Indigenous Peoples, African Americans, Asian Americans, Hispanics, Latinos/Latinas, gays, lesbians, bisexuals, or transgendered persons and persons with physical, mental/emotional, and/or learning disabilities outside of their group work/counseling setting (community events, social and political functions, celebrations, friendships, neighborhood groups, etc.) so that their perspective of minorities is more than academic or experienced through a third party.

III.   Diversity-Appropriate Intervention Strategies

A.   Attitudes and Beliefs

1. Diversity-competent group workers respect clients' religious and/or spiritual beliefs and values, because they affect worldview, psychosocial functioning, and expressions of distress.

2. Diversity-competent group workers respect indigenous helping practices and respect Indigenous Peoples, African Americans, Asian Americans, Hispanics, Latinos/Latinas, gays, lesbians, bisexuals, or transgendered persons and persons with physical, mental/emotional, and/or learning disabilities and can identify and utilize community intrinsic help-giving networks.

3. Diversity-competent group workers value bilingualism and sign language and do not view another language as an impediment to group work.

B.   Knowledge

1. Diversity-competent group workers demonstrate a clear and explicit knowledge and understanding of generic characteristics of group

work and theory and how they may clash with the beliefs, values, and traditions of Indigenous Peoples, African Americans, Asian Americans, Hispanics, Latinos/Latinas, gays, lesbians, bisexuals, or transgendered persons and persons with physical, mental/emotional, and/or learning disabilities.

2. Diversity-competent group workers exhibit an awareness of institutional barriers that prevent Indigenous Peoples, African Americans, Asian Americans, Hispanics, Latinos/Latinas, gays, lesbians, bisexuals, or transgendered members and members with physical, mental/emotional, and/or learning disabilities from actively participating in or using various types of groups, that is, task groups, psychoeducational groups, counseling groups, and psychotherapy groups or the settings in which the services are offered.

3. Diversity-competent group workers demonstrate knowledge of the potential bias in assessment instruments and use procedures and interpret findings, or actively participate in various types of evaluations of group outcome or success, keeping in mind the linguistic, cultural, and other self-identified characteristics of the group member.

4. Diversity-competent group workers exhibit knowledge of the family structures, hierarchies, values, and beliefs of Indigenous Peoples, African Americans, Asian Americans, Hispanics, Latinos/Latinas, gays, lesbians, bisexuals, or transgendered persons and persons with physical, mental/emotional, and/or learning disabilities. They are knowledgeable about the community characteristics and the resources in the community as well as about the family.

5. Diversity-competent group workers demonstrate an awareness of relevant discriminatory practices at the social and community level that may be affecting the psychological welfare of persons and access to services of the population being served.

C. Skills

1. Diversity-competent group workers are able to engage in a variety of verbal and nonverbal group-facilitating functions, dependent upon the type of group (task, counseling, psychoeducational, psychotherapy), and the multiple, self-identified status of various group members

(such as Indigenous Peoples, African Americans, Asian Americans, Hispanics, Latinos/Latinas, gays, lesbians, bisexuals, or transgendered persons and persons with physical, mental/emotional, and/or learning disabilities). They demonstrate the ability to send and receive both verbal and nonverbal messages accurately, appropriately, and across/between the differences represented in the group. They are not tied down to one method or approach to group facilitation and recognize that helping styles and approaches may be culture-bound. When they sense that their group facilitation style is limited and potentially inappropriate, they can anticipate and ameliorate its negative impact by drawing upon other culturally relevant skill sets.

2. Diversity-competent group workers have the ability to exercise institutional intervention skills on behalf of their group members. They can help a member determine whether a "problem" with the institution stems from the oppression of Indigenous Peoples, African Americans, Asian Americans, Hispanics, Latinos/Latinas, gays, lesbians, bisexuals, or transgendered persons and persons with physical, mental/emotional, and/or learning disabilities, such as in the case of developing or having a "healthy" paranoia, so that group members do not inappropriately personalize problems.

3. Diversity-competent group workers do not exhibit a reluctance to seek consultation with traditional healers and religious and spiritual healers and practitioners in the treatment of members who are self-identified Indigenous Peoples, African Americans, Asian Americans, Hispanics, Latinos/Latinas, gays, lesbians, bisexuals, and transgendered persons and/or group members with mental/emotional, physical, and/or learning disabilities when appropriate.

4. Diversity-competent group workers take responsibility for interacting in the language requested by the group member(s) and, if not feasible, make an appropriate referral. A serious problem arises when the linguistic skills of a group worker and a group member or members, including sign language, do not match. The same problem occurs when the linguistic skills of one member or several members do not match. This being the case, the group worker, should (a) seek a translator with cultural knowledge and appropriate

professional background, and (b) refer to a knowledgeable, competent bilingual group worker or a group worker competent or certified in sign language. In some cases, it may be necessary to have a group for group members of similar languages or to refer the group member for individual counseling.

5. Diversity-competent group workers are trained and have expertise in the use of traditional assessment and testing instruments related to group work, such as in screening potential members, and they also are aware of the cultural bias/limitations of these tools and processes. This allows them to use the tools for the welfare of diverse group members following culturally appropriate procedures.

6. Diversity-competent group workers attend to as well as work to eliminate biases, prejudices, oppression, and discriminatory practices. They are cognizant of how sociopolitical contexts may affect evaluation and provision of group work and should develop sensitivity to issues of oppression, racism, sexism, heterosexism, classism, and so forth.

7. Diversity-competent group workers take responsibility in educating their group members to the processes of group work, such as goals, expectations legal rights, sound ethical practice, and the group worker's theoretical orientation with regard to facilitating groups with diverse membership.

CONCLUSION

This document is the "starting point" for group workers as we become increasingly aware, knowledgeable, and skillful in facilitating groups whose memberships represent the diversity of our society. It is not intended to be a "how to" document. It is written as a call to action and/or a guideline and represents ASGW's commitment to moving forward with an agenda for addressing and understanding the needs of the populations we serve. As a "living document," the Association for Specialists in Group Work acknowledges the changing world in which we live and work and therefore recognizes that this is the first step in working with diverse group members with competence, compassion, respect, and integrity. As our awareness, knowledge, and skills develop, so too will this document evolve. As our knowledge as a profession grows in this area and as the sociopolitical context in which this document was written changes, new editions of these *Principles for Diversity-Competent Group Workers* will arise. The operationalization of this document (article in process) will begin to define appropriate group leadership skills and interventions as well as make recommendations for research in understanding how diversity in group membership affects group process and dynamics.

REFERENCES

American Conseling Association. (1995). *Code of ethics and standards.* Alexandria, VA: Author.

Association for Multicultural Counseling and Development. (1996). *Multicultural competencies.* Alexandria, VA: American Counseling Association.

Association for Specialists in Group Work. (1991). Professional standards for training of group workers. *Together, 20,* 9–14.

Association for Specialists in Group Work. (1998). Guidelines for best practice. *Journal for Specialists in Group Work, 23,* 237–244.

Atkinson, D. R., Morten, G., & Sue, D. W. (Eds.). (1993). *Counseling American minorities* (4th ed.). Madison, WI: Brown & Benchmark.

Cass, V. C. (1979). Homosexual identity formation: A theoretical model. *Journal of Homosexuality, 4,* 219–236.

Cross, W. E. (1995). The psychology of Nigrescence: Revising the cross model. In J. G. Ponterotto, J. M. Casas, L. A. Suzuki, & C. M. Alexander (Eds.), *Handbook of multicultural counseling* (pp. 93–122). Thousand Oaks, CA: Sage.

D'Augelli, A. R. & Patterson, C. J. (Eds.). (1995). *Lesbian, gay and bisexual identities over the lifespan.* New York: Oxford University Press.

Helms, J. E. (1992). *A race is a nice thing to have.* Topeka, KS: Context Communications.

ASSOCIATION FOR SPECIALISTS IN GROUP WORK: PROFESSIONAL STANDARDS FOR THE TRAINING OF GROUP WORKERS

PREAMBLE

For nearly two decades, the Association for Specialists in Group Work (herein referred to as ASGW or as the Association) has promulgated professional standards for the training of group workers. In the early 1980s, the Association published the ASGW Training Standards for Group Counselors (1983), which established 9 knowledge competencies, 17 skill competencies, and clock-hour baselines for various aspects of supervised clinical experience in group counseling. The focus on group counseling embodied in these standards mirrored the general conception of the time that whatever counselors did with groups of individuals should properly be referred to as group counseling.

New ground was broken in the 1990 revision of the ASGW Professional Standards for the Training of Group Workers with (a) the articulation of the term *group work* to capture the variety of ways in which counselors work with groups; (b) differentiation of core training, deemed essential for all counselors, from specialization training required of those intending to engage in group work as part of their professional practice; and (c) the differentiation among four distinct group work specializations: task and work group facilitation, group psychoeducation, group counseling, and group psychotherapy. Over the 10 years in which these standards have been in force, commentary and criticism has been elicited through discussion groups at various regional and national conferences and through published analyses in the ASGW's journal, the *Journal for Specialists in Group Work*.

From Donald E. Ward, Journal for Specialists in Group Work, 25 *(4), p. 327, Copyright 2000 by Sage Publications, Inc. Reprinted by permission of Sage Publications, Inc.*

In this Year-2000 revision of the ASGW Professional Standards for the Training of Group Workers, the foundation established by the 1990 training standards has been preserved and refined by application of feedback received through public discussion and scholarly debate. The Year 2000 revision maintains and strengthens the distinction between core and specialization training, with requirements for core training and aspirational guidelines for specialization training. Furthermore, the definitions of group work specializations have been expanded and clarified. Evenness of application of training standards across the specializations has been assured by creating a single set of guidelines for all four specializations, with specialization-specific detail being supplied when necessary. Consistent with both the pattern for training standards established by the Council for Accreditation of Counseling and Related Educational Programs accreditation standards and past editions of the ASGW training standards, the Year 2000 revision addresses both content and clinical instruction. Content instruction is described in terms of both coursework requirements and knowledge objectives, whereas clinical instruction is articulated in terms of experiential requirements and skill objectives. This revision of the training standards was informed by and profits from the seminal ASGW Best Practice Guidelines (1998) and the ASGW Principles for Diversity-Competent Group Workers (1999). Although each of these documents have their own form of organization, all address the group work elements of planning, performing, and processing and the ethical and diversity-competent treatment of participants in group activities.

PURPOSE

The purpose of the Professional Standards for the Training of Group Workers is to provide guidance to counselor training programs in the construction of their curricula for graduate programs in counseling (e.g., master's, specialist, and doctoral degrees and other forms of advanced graduate study). Specifically, core standards express the ASGW's view on the minimum training in group work all programs in counseling should provide for all graduates of their entry-level, master's degree programs in counseling, and specialization standards provide a framework for documenting the training philosophy, objectives, curriculum, and outcomes for each declared specialization program.

Core Training in Group Work

All counselors should possess a set of core competencies in general group work. The ASGW advocates for the incorporation of core group work competencies as part of required entry-level training in all counselor preparation programs. The ASGW's standards for core training are consistent with and provide further elaboration of the standards for accreditation of entry-level counseling programs identified by the Council for Accreditation of Counseling and Related Educational Programs (CACREP, 1994). Mastery of the core competencies detailed in the ASGW training standards will prepare the counselor to understand group process phenomena and to function more effectively in groups in which the counselor is a member. Mastery of basic knowledge and skill in group work provides a foundation that specialty training can extend but does not qualify one to independently practice any group work specialty.

Specialist Training in Group Work

The independent practice of group work requires training beyond core competencies. ASGW advocates that independent practitioners of group work must possess advanced competencies relevant to the particular kind of group work practice in which the group work student wants to specialize (e.g., facilitation of task groups, group psychoeducation, group counseling, or group psychotherapy). To encourage program creativity in development of specialization training, the specialization guidelines do not prescribe minimum trainee competencies. Rather, the guidelines establish a framework within which programs can develop unique training experiences using scientific foundations and best practices to achieve their training objectives. In providing these guidelines for specialized training, ASGW makes no presumption that a graduate program in counseling must provide training in a group work specialization or that adequate training in a specialization can be accomplished solely within a well-rounded master's degree program in counseling. To provide adequate specialization training, completion of post-master's options, such as certificates of post-master's study or doctoral degrees, may be required. Furthermore, there is no presumption that an individual who may have received adequate training in a given declared specialization will be prepared to function effectively with all group situations in which the graduate may want or be required to work. It is recognized that the characteristics of specific client populations and employment settings vary widely. Additional training beyond that which was acquired in a specific graduate program may be necessary for optimal, diversity-competent, group work practice with a given population in a given setting.

DEFINITIONS

Group Work: A broad professional practice involving the application of knowledge and skill in group facilitation to assist an interdependent collection of people to reach their mutual goals, which may be intrapersonal, interpersonal, or work related. The goals of the group may include the accomplishment of tasks related to work, education, personal development, personal and interpersonal problem solving, or remediation of mental and emotional disorders.

Core Training in Group Work: Includes knowledge, skills, and experiences deemed necessary for general competency for all master's degree–prepared counselors. ASGW advocates for all counselor preparation programs to provide core training in group work regardless of whether the program intends to prepare trainees for independent practice in a group work specialization. Core training in group work is considered a necessary prerequisite for advanced practice in group work.

Specialization Training in Group Work: Includes knowledge, skills, and experiences deemed necessary for counselors to engage in independent practice of group work. Four areas of advanced practice, referred to as *specializations,* are identified: task group facilitation, group psychoeducation, group counseling, and group psychotherapy. This list is not presumed to be exhaustive and although there may be no sharp boundaries between the specializations, each has recognizable characteristics that have professional utility. The definitions for these group work specializations have been built upon the American Counseling Association's (ACA) model definition of counseling (adopted by the ACA Governing Council in 1997), describing the methods typical of the working stage of the group being defined, the typical purposes to which those methods are put, and the typical populations served by those methods. Specialized training presumes mastery of prerequisite core knowledge, skills, and experiences.

Specialization in Task and Work Group Facilitation:

- The application of principles of normal human development and functioning
- through group-based educational, developmental, and systemic strategies
- applied in the context of here-and-now interaction
- that promote efficient and effective accomplishment of group tasks
- among people who are gathered to accomplish group task goals.

Specialization in Psychoeducation Group Leadership:

- The application of principles of normal human development and functioning
- through group-based educational and developmental strategies
- applied in the context of here-and-now interaction
- that promote personal and interpersonal growth and development and the prevention of future difficulties
- among people who may be at risk for the development of personal or interpersonal problems or who seek enhancement of personal qualities and abilities.

Specialization in Group Counseling:

- The application of principles of normal human development and functioning
- through group-based cognitive, affective, behavioral, or systemic intervention strategies
- applied in the context of here-and-now interaction

- that address personal and interpersonal problems of living and promote personal and interpersonal growth and development
- among people who may be experiencing transitory maladjustment, who are at risk for the development of personal or interpersonal problems, or who seek enhancement of personal qualities and abilities.

Specialization in Group Psychotherapy:

- The application of principles of normal and abnormal human development and functioning
- through group-based cognitive, affective, behavioral, or systemic intervention strategies
- applied in the context of negative emotional arousal
- that address personal and interpersonal problems of living, remediate perceptual and cognitive distortions or repetitive patterns of dysfunctional behavior, and promote personal and interpersonal growth and development
- among people who may be experiencing severe and/or chronic maladjustment.

CORE TRAINING STANDARDS
I.   Coursework and Experiential Requirements

A.   Coursework requirements
Core training shall include at least one graduate course in group work that addresses but is not limited to scope of practice, types of group work, group development, group process and dynamics, group leadership, and standards of training and practice for group workers.

B.   Experiential requirements
Core training shall include a minimum of 10 clock hours (20 clock hours recommended) observation of and participation in a group experience as a group member and/or group leader.

II.   Knowledge and Skill Objectives

A.   Nature and Scope of Practice
1. *Knowledge objectives.* Identify and describe:
   a.   the nature of group work and the various specializations within group work,

b. theories of group work including commonalities and distinguishing characteristics among the various specializations within group work,

c. and research literature pertinent to group work and its specializations.

2. *Skill objectives*. Demonstrate skill in:

a. preparing a professional disclosure statement for practice in a chosen area of specialization

b. and applying theoretical concepts and scientific findings to the design of a group and the interpretation of personal experiences in a group.

B. Assessment of Group Members and the Social Systems in Which They Live and Work

1. *Knowledge objectives*. Identify and describe:

a. principles of assessment of group functioning in group work

b. and use of personal contextual factors (e.g., family of origin, neighborhood of residence, organizational membership, cultural membership) in interpreting behavior of members in a group.

2. *Skill objectives*. Demonstrate skill in:

a. observing and identifying group process,

b. observing the personal characteristics of individual members in a group,

c. developing hypotheses about the behavior of group members,

d. and employing contextual factors (e.g., family of origin, neighborhood of residence, organizational membership, cultural membership) in interpretation of individual and group data.

C. Planning Group Interventions

1. *Knowledge objectives*. Identify and describe:

a. environmental contexts that affect planning for group interventions,

b. the impact of group member diversity (e.g., gender, culture, learning style, group climate preference) on group member behavior and group process and dynamics in group work,

c. and principles of planning for group work.

2. *Skill objectives*. Demonstrate skill in:

a. collaborative consultation with targeted populations to enhance ecological validity of planned group interventions

b. and planning for a group work activity including such aspects as developing overarching purpose, establishing goals and objectives, detailing methods to be used in achieving goals and objectives, determining methods for outcome assessment, and verifying ecological validity of plan.

D. Implementation of Group Interventions

1. *Knowledge objectives*. Identify and describe:

a. principles of group formation including recruiting, screening, and selecting group members;

b. principles for effective performance of group leadership functions;

c. therapeutic factors within group work and when group work approaches are indicated and contraindicated;

d. and principles of group dynamics including group process components, developmental stage theories, group member roles, and group member behaviors.

2. *Skill objectives*. Demonstrate skill in:

a. encouraging participation of group members;

b. attending to, describing, acknowledging, confronting, understanding, and responding empathically to group member behavior;

c. attending to, acknowledging, clarifying, summarizing, confronting, and responding empathically to group member statements;

d. attending to, acknowledging, clarifying, summarizing, confronting, and responding empathically to group themes;

e. eliciting information from and imparting information to group members;

f. providing appropriate self-disclosure;

g. maintaining group focus and keeping a group on task;

h. and giving and receiving feedback in a group setting.

E. Leadership and Coleadership

1. *Knowledge objectives*. Identify and describe:

a. group leadership styles and approaches,

b. group work methods including group worker orientations and specialized group leadership behaviors,

c. and principles of collaborative group processing.

2. *Skill objectives.* To the extent opportunities for leadership or coleadership are provided, demonstrate skill in:
   a. engaging in reflective evaluation of one's personal leadership style and approach,
   b. working cooperatively with a coleader and/or group members,
   c. and engaging in collaborative group processing.

F.   Evaluation

1. *Knowledge objectives.* Identify and describe:
   a. methods for evaluating group process in group work
   b. and methods for evaluating outcomes in group work.
2. *Skill objectives.* Demonstrate skill in:
   a. contributing to evaluation activities during group participation
   b. and engaging in self-evaluation of personally selected performance goals.

G.   Ethical Practice, Best Practice, Diversity-Competent Practice

1. *Knowledge objectives.* Identify and describe:
   a. ethical considerations unique to group work,
   b. best practices in group work,
   c. and diversity competent group work.
2. *Skill objectives.* Demonstrate skill in:
   a. evidencing ethical practice in planning, observing, and participating in group activities;
   b. evidencing best practice in planning, observing, and participating in group activities;
   c. and evidencing diversity-competent practice in planning, observing, and participating in group activities.

SPECIALIZATION GUIDELINES
I.   Overarching Program Characteristics

A. The program has a clearly specified philosophy of training for the preparation of specialists for independent practice of group work in one of the forms of group work recognized by the ASGW (i.e., task and work group facilitation, group psychoeducation, group counseling, or group psychotherapy).

1. The program states an explicit intent to train group workers in one or more of the group work specializations.
2. The program states an explicit philosophy of training, based on the science of group work, by which it intends to prepare students for independent practice in the declared specialization(s).

B. For each declared specialization, the program specifies education and training objectives in terms of the competencies expected of students completing the specialization training. These competencies are consistent with:
   1. the program's philosophy and training model,
   2. the substantive area(s) relevant for best practice of the declared specialization area, and
   3. standards for competent, ethical, and diversity-sensitive practice of group work.

C. For each declared specialization, the program specifies a sequential, cumulative curriculum, expanding in breadth and depth and designed to prepare students for independent practice of the specialization and relevant credentialing.

D. For each declared specialization, the program documents achievement of training objectives in terms of student competencies.

II.   Recommended Coursework and Experience

A. *Coursework.* Specialization training may include coursework that provides the student with a broad foundation in the group work domain in which the student seeks specialized training.
   1. *Task/Work Group Facilitation.* Coursework includes but is not limited to organizational development, management, and consultation, theory and practice of task and/or work group facilitation.
   2. *Group Psychoeducation.* Coursework includes but is not limited to organizational development, school and community counseling and/or psychology, health promotion, marketing, program development and evaluation, organizational consultation, theory and practice of group psychoeducation.

3. *Group Counseling.* Coursework includes but is not limited to normal human development, health promotion, and theory and practice of group counseling.
4. *Group Psychotherapy.* Coursework includes but is not be limited to normal and abnormal human development, assessment and diagnosis of mental and emotional disorders, treatment of psychopathology, and theory and practice of group psychotherapy.

B. *Experience.* Specialization training includes:
1. *Task/Work Group Facilitation.* Experience includes a minimum of 30 clock hours (45 clock hours recommended) supervised practice facilitating or conducting an intervention with a task or work group appropriate to the age and clientele of the group leader's specialty area (e.g., school counseling, student development counseling, community counseling, mental health counseling).
2. *Group Psychoeducation.* Experience includes a minimum of 30 clock hours (45 clock hours recommended) supervised practice conducting a psychoeducation group appropriate to the age and clientele of the group leader's specialty area (e.g., school counseling, student development counseling, community counseling, mental health counseling).
3. *Group Counseling.* Experience includes a minimum of 45 clock hours (60 clock hours recommended) supervised practice conducting a counseling group appropriate to the age and clientele of the group leader's specialty area (e.g., school counseling, student development counseling, community counseling, mental health counseling).
4. *Group Psychotherapy.* Experience includes a minimum of 45 clock hours (60 clock hours recommended) supervised practice conducting a psychotherapy group appropriate to the age and clientele of the group leader's specialty area (e.g., mental health counseling).

III.   Knowledge and Skill Elements

In achieving its objectives, the program has and implements a clear and coherent curriculum plan that provides the means whereby all students can acquire and demonstrate substantial understanding of and competence in the following areas:

A. *Nature and Scope of Practice.* The program states a clear expectation that its students will limit their independent practice of group work to those specialization areas for which they have been appropriately trained and supervised.
B. *Assessment of Group Members and the Social Systems in Which They Live and Work.* All graduates of specialization training will understand and demonstrate competence in the use of assessment instruments and methodologies for assessing individual group member characteristics and group development, group dynamics, and process phenomena relevant for the program's declared specialization area(s). Studies should include but are not limited to:
1. methods of screening and assessment of populations, groups, and individual members who are or may be targeted for intervention;
2. methods for observation of group member behavior during group interventions;
3. and methods of assessment of group development, process, and outcomes.
C. *Planning Group Interventions.* All graduates of specialization training will understand and demonstrate competence in planning group interventions consistent with the program's declared specialization area(s). Studies should include but are not limited to:
1. establishing the overarching purpose for the intervention;
2. indentifying goals and objectives for the intervention;
3. detailing methods to be employed in achieving goals and objectives during the intervention;
4. selecting methods for examining group process during group meetings, between group sessions, and at the completion of the group intervention;
5. preparing methods for helping members derive meaning from their within-group experiences and transfer within-group learning to real-world circumstances;
6. determining methods for measuring outcomes during and following the intervention;

7. and verifying ecological validity of plans for the intervention.

D. *Implementation of Group Interventions.* All graduates of specialization training will understand and demonstrate competence in implementing group interventions consistent with the program's declared specialization area(s). Studies should include but are not limited to:

1. principles of group formation including recruiting, screening, selection, and orientation of group members;
2. standard methods and procedures for group facilitation;
3. selection and use of referral sources appropriate to the declared specialization;
4. identifying and responding constructively to extra-group factors which may influence the success of interventions;
5. applying the major strategies, techniques, and procedures;
6. adjusting group pacing relative to the stage of group development;
7. identifying and responding constructively to critical incidents;
8. identifying and responding constructively to disruptive members;
9. helping group members attribute meaning to and integrate and apply learning;
10. responding constructively to psychological emergencies;
11. and involving group members in within-group session processing and on-going planning.

E. *Leadership and Coleadership.* All graduates of specialization training will understand and demonstrate competence in pursuing personal competence as a leader and in selecting and managing the interpersonal relationship with a coleader for group interventions consistent with the program's declared specialization area(s). Studies should include but are not limited to:

1. characteristics and skills of effective leaders,
2. relationship skills required of effective coleaders,
3. and processing skills required of effective coleaders.

F. *Evaluation.* All graduates of specialization training will understand and demonstrate competence in evaluating group interventions con-

sistent with the program's declared specialization area(s). Studies should include, but are not limited to, methods for evaluating participant outcomes and participant satisfaction.

G. *Ethical Practice, Best Practice, and Diversity-Competent Practice.* All graduates of specialization training will understand and demonstrate consistent effort to comply with principles of ethical, best practice, and diversity-competent practice of group work consistent with the program's declared specialization area(s). Studies should include but are not limited to:

1. ethical considerations unique to the program's declared specialization area,
2. best practices for group work within the program's declared specialization area,
3. and diversity issues unique to the program's declared specialization area.

IMPLEMENTATION GUIDELINES

Implementation of the Professional Standards for the Training of Group Workers requires a commitment by a program's faculty and a dedication of program resources to achieve excellence in preparing all counselors at core competency level and in preparing counselors for independent practice of group work. To facilitate implementation of the training standards, the ASGW offers the following guidelines.

Core Training in Group Work

Core training in group work can be provided through a single, basic course in group theory and process. This course should include the elements of content instruction detailed below and may also include the required clinical instruction component.

Content Instruction

Consistent with accreditation standards (CACREP, 1994, Standard II.J.4), study in the area of group work should provide an understanding of the types of group work (e.g., facilitation of task groups, psychoeducation groups, counseling groups, psychotherapy groups); group development, group dynamics, and group leadership styles; and group leadership methods and skills. More explicitly, studies should include but not be limited to the following:

- principles of group dynamics including group process components, developmental stage theories, and group members' roles and behaviors;

- group leadership styles and approaches including characteristics of various types of group leaders and leadership styles;
- theories of group counseling including commonalities, distinguishing characteristics, and pertinent research and literature;
- group work methods including group leader orientations and behaviors ethical standards, appropriate selection criteria and methods, and methods of evaluating effectiveness;
- approaches used for other types of group work, including task groups, prevention groups, support groups, and therapy groups;
- and skills in observing member behavior and group process, empathic responding, confronting, self-disclosing, focusing, protecting, recruiting and selecting members, opening and closing sessions, managing, explicit and implicit teaching, modeling, and giving and receiving feedback.

Clinical Instruction

Core group work training requires a minimum of 10 clock hours of supervised practice (20 clock hours of supervised practice is recommended). Consistent with CACREP (1994) standards for accreditation, the supervised experience provides the student with direct experiences as a participant in a small group and may be met either in the basic course in group theory and practice or in a specially conducted small group designed for the purpose of meeting this standard (CACREP, 1994, Standard II.D). In arranging for and conducting this group experience, care must be taken by program faculty to assure that the ACA ethical standard for dual relationships and ASGW standards for best practice are observed.

Specialist Training in Group Work

Though ASGW advocates that all counselor training programs provide all counseling students with core group work training, specialization training is elective. If a counselor training program chooses to offer specialization training (e.g., task group facilitation, group psychoeducation, group counseling, group psychotherapy), ASGW urges institutions to develop their curricula consistent with the ASGW standards for that specialization.

Content Instruction

Each area of specialization has its literature. In addition to basic coursework in group theory and process, each specialization requires additional coursework providing specialized knowledge necessary for professional application of the specialization.

- *Task Group Facilitation:* Coursework in such areas as organization development, consultation, management, or sociology so students gain a basic understanding of organizations and how task groups function within them.
- *Group Psychoeducation:* Coursework in community psychology, consultation, health promotion, marketing, and curriculum design to prepare students to conduct structured consciousness-raising and skill-training groups in such areas as stress management, wellness, anger control and assertiveness training, and problem solving.
- *Group Counseling:* Coursework in normal human development, family development and family counseling, assessment and problem identification of problems in living, individual counseling, and group counseling, including training experiences in personal growth or counseling group.
- *Group Psychotherapy:* Coursework in abnormal human development, family pathology and family therapy, assessment and diagnosis of mental and emotional disorders, individual therapy, and group therapy, including training experiences in a therapy group.

Clinical Instruction

For task group facilitation and group psychoeducation, group specialization training recommends a minimum of 30 clock hours of supervised practice (45 clock hours of supervised practice is strongly suggested). Because of the additional difficulties presented by group counseling and group psychotherapy, a minimum of 45 clock hours of supervised practice is recommended (60 clock hours of supervised practice is strongly suggested). Consistent with CACREP (1994) standards for accreditation, supervised experience should provide an opportunity for the student to perform under supervision a variety of activities that a professional counselor would perform in conducting group work consistent with a given specialization (i.e., assessment of group members and the social systems in which they live and work, planning group interventions, implementing group interventions, leadership and coleadership, and within-group, between-group, and end-of-group processing and evaluation).

In addition to courses offering content and experience related to a given specialization, supervised clinical experience should be obtained in practica and internship experiences. Following the model provided by CACREP (1994) for master's practica, we recommend that one quarter of all required supervised clinical experience be devoted to group work.

- *Master's practicum:* At least 10 clock hours of the required 40 clock hours of direct service should be spent in supervised leadership or coleadership experience in group work, typically in task group facilitation,

group psychoeducation, or group counseling (at the master's practicum level, experience in group psychotherapy would be unusual) (CACREP, 1994, Standard III.H.1).

- *Master's internship:* At least 60 clock hours of the required 240 clock hours of direct services should be spent in supervised leadership or coleadership in group work consistent with the program's specialization offering(s) (i.e., in task group facilitation, group psychoeducation, group counseling, or group psychotherapy).
- *Doctoral internship:* At least 150 clock hours of the required 600 clock hours of direct service should be spent in supervised leadership or coleadership in group work consistent with the program's specialization offering(s) (i.e., in task group facilitation, group psychoeducation, group counseling, or group psychotherapy).

REFERENCES

Association for Specialists in Group Work (ASGW) (1983). *ASGW professional standards for group counseling.* Alexandria, VA: Author.

Association for Specialists in Group Work (ASGW). (1990). *Professional standards for the training of group workers.* Alexandria VA: Author.

Association for Specialists in Group Work (ASGW). (1998). ASGW best practice guidelines. *Journal for Specialists in Group Work, 23,* 237–244.

Association for Specialists in Group Work (ASGW). (1999). ASGW principles for diversity-competent group workers. *Journal for Specialists in Group Work, 24,* 7–14.

Council for Accreditation of Counseling and Related Educational Programs (CACREP). (1994). *CACREP accreditation standards and procedures manual.* Alexandria, VA: Author.

GLOSSARY

AARP a leading group for those age 55 and above to learn which social and political events affect them most

A-B-C model of human interaction "A" is the event, "B" is the thought process, and "C" is the feeling state resulting from one's thoughts. To change negative or nonproductive feelings, individuals need to think differently (i.e., positive or neutral).

A-B-C-D-E worksheet an approach to ethical decision making that uses a mnemonic device to remind group leaders and members of what they should do. The letters of this worksheet stand for Assessment, Benefit, Consequences and Consultation, Duty, and Education.

accommodating a behavior in which individuals neglect their own concerns to satisfy the concerns of others

acting "as if" an Adlerian therapeatic technique wherein someone acts "as if" he or she were the person he or she wishes to be

action-centered view of groups the view that groups for children under 12 years of age should involve play and action

action exercises sensory awareness methods or guided imagery used in the psychodrama warm-up phase to help members discover common themes within the group as well as focus more on individual concerns

action-oriented group techniques techniques that require group members to behave in an active manner (e.g., role playing, using "I" statements)

action phase the second part of the psychodrama process, which involves the enactment of protagonists' concerns

active listening to hear the tone and meanings behind verbal communication and to pick up on messages in nonverbal behaviors

activity group guidance (AGG) group guidance involving activities that are developmental in nature; typically includes coordinated guidance topics

actors those who play the parts of other important people or objects in a psychodrama play. They are called *auxiliaries*. With prompting from the protagonist, they can play the protagonist's double, an antagonist, or even a piece of furniture. In the same psychodrama, an auxiliary could play more than one part, such as being the protagonist's best friend and worst enemy.

Adlerian parent education stresses cooperation among family members as a goal and emphasizes the use of logical and natural consequences to avoid power struggles. There is

a democratic emphasis to this orientation, and regular family council meetings are held for all members to voice concerns and needs. The Adlerian approach stresses parent discussion groups with a trained leader and a set curriculum.

adolescence the age span from 13 to 19, although it can be extended to include some individuals up to age 25; a time of unevenness and paradoxes marked by extensive personal changes

adult children of alcoholics (ACoAs) adults who grew up in families in which one or both parents abused alcohol. These individuals developed coping mechanisms for dealing with their alcoholic family system, such as denial or overcompensation, that are usually not functional for a mature lifestyle. Dealing with feelings about the past as well as learning behaviors for coping and life skills are therapeutic foci for these persons.

Adult ego state (TA) the realistic, logical part of a person, which functions like a computer in that it receives and processes information from the Parent, the Child, and the environment

adulthood a somewhat nebulous term implying that a person has reached physical, mental, social, and emotional maturity

advice/evaluation telling people how to behave or judging them

advice giving instructing someone what to do in a particular situation. It is seldom appropriate or needed in most groups. It prevents members from struggling with their own feelings and keeps advice givers from having to recognize shortcomings in their own lives.

ageism discrimination against older people based on their age

aging process a biological phenomenon composed of physiological changes as well as a mental process of considering oneself older

airtime the amount of time available for participation in the group

Alcoholics Anonymous (AA) an organization that helps alcoholics gain and maintain control of their lives by remaining sober; established in the late 1930s

alternated a form of group co-leadership; one leader takes responsibility for a specific time or session, and the other leader provides support

altruism sharing experiences and thoughts with others; helping them by giving of one's self; working for the common good

American Group Psychotherapy Association (AGPA) a psychoanalytically oriented organization established by Samuel R. Slavson in 1943

American Society of Group Psychotherapy and Psychodrama (ASGPP) a professional group association established by Jacob L. Moreno between 1941 and 1942

amplify to emphasize statements made by the protagonist in psychodrama. Examples include verbalizing nonverbal communications, questioning one's self, interpreting statements based on what is being said and not said, contradicting feelings, self-observing, and engaging in denial.

analyzing/interpreting explaining the reasons behind behavior without giving the person an opportunity for self-discovery

antecedent–response–consequence model of behaviorism a model that basically states that behavior is functionally related to its antecedents and consequent events

anxiety tension; an uneasy feeling that accompanies decision making or performance

apprehension anxiety; a moderate amount helps group members key in on what they are experiencing and what they want to do

apprenticed a form of group co-leadership in which the more experienced leader takes charge of the group to demonstrate for a novice leader how to work with a group

A-R-C model (see *antecedent–response–consequence model of behaviorism*)

assessing members' growth and change a technique similar to personal reviews but, in assessment, the emphasis is on individuals' memories of themselves at the beginning of the group and now. The idea of such an exercise is to have members see and share significant gains with themselves and others.

Association for Advancement of Behavioral Therapy (AABT) the major professional organization for behavioral therapists

Association for Specialists in Group Work (ASGW) formed in 1973; a division within the American Counseling Association

asynchronous a type of online group, such as an e-mail listserv; messages can be formatted as typed and sent at any time, whether or not the receiver is online, too

attack on the group leader when members of the group become hostile or rebellious in regard to a leader's authority or conduct of the group. Underlying reasons for such attacks are subgrouping, fear of intimacy, and extragroup socializing.

attractiveness a multidimensional concept that basically refers to members positively identifying with others in the group

audience a term used to describe others who may be present during the psychodrama. Some may become auxiliaries.

authenticity the ability to affirm oneself and to make the most of discovering and using one's talents and creativity

authoritarian group leaders leaders who envision themselves as experts. They interpret, give advice, and generally direct the movement of the group much as a parent controls the actions of a child. They are often charismatic and manipulative. They feed off of obedience, expect conformity, and operate out of the wheel model.

autodrama see *monodrama*

authoritative power power predicated on social position or responsibility in an organization

autonomy the promotion of self-determination or the power to choose one's own direction in life. In groups, it is important that group members feel they have a right to make their own decisions.

auxiliary counselors group members who act as cocounselors once someone has presented a problem; occurs when a rational-emotive behavioral therapy group leader encourages it to help participants benefit from multiple input

avoiding when individuals do not immediately pursue their concerns or those of other persons

avoiding conflict when the group ignores areas of tension or silences or discounts members who expose the group's disagreements

awareness Gestalt term for a total organismic response to the environment so that a person gains insight and control over situations and becomes responsible in achieving a healthy response to life events

"BA" (basic assumption) activity a classification devised by Wilfred Bion for the emotional pattern of an antiwork group (as opposed to a "W" [work group]). BA groups can be broken down further into three subpatterns: *BA Dependency* (where members are overdependent on the group leader), *BA Pairing* (where members are more interested in being with one another than in working on a goal), and *BA Fight–Flight* (where members become preoccupied with either engaging in or avoiding hostile conflict).

band-aiding the misuse of support; process of preventing others from fully expressing their emotional pain

basic encounter group also known as *encounter group;* first established by Carl Rogers to describe his approach to group work; focuses on individuals' awareness of their own emotional experiences and the behaviors of others; emphasis is placed on the awareness and exploration of intrapsychic and interpersonal issues. Encounter groups are often known as *personal growth groups* because the emphasis in these groups is on personal development.

BASIC ID A. Lazarus's multimodal model for helping; includes the components of behavior, affect, sensation, imagery, cognition, interpersonal relations, and drugs

basic skills training (BST) approach to groups developed at the National Training Laboratories in the 1940s; predecessor of the *T-group* movement

behavior therapy the collective behaviorist point of view, a combination of opinions and procedures about behavior and how to influence it

behavioral disputation rational-emotive behavioral therapy treatment that involves many forms, from reading (bibliotherapy) to role playing in the group. Often enactment of the problem within the group setting and possible ways of handling it are used. Homework may then be assigned in the form of *shame attacks* (in which the person actually does what he or she dreaded and finds the world does not fall apart regardless of the outcome).

behavioral groups either interpersonal or transactional groups depending on the purposes of the leader and members. (a) *Interpersonal groups* are highly didactic and involve specified goals that usually center on self-improvement. (b) *Transactional groups* are more heterogeneous and focus on broader, yet specific, goals.

behavioral rehearsal practicing a desired behavior until it is performed the way one wishes. The process consists of gradually shaping a behavior and getting corrective feedback.

behaviorists inside and outside group settings, leaders who emphasize overt processes, here-and-now experiences, learning, changing maladaptive actions, defining specific goals, and scientific support for techniques

beneficence promoting the good of others. It is assumed in groups that leaders and members will work hard for the betterment of the group as a whole.

blind quadrant information originally unknown to oneself but known to others when the group began

blocking related to protecting, in which the leader intervenes in the group activity to stop counterproductive behavior. This intervention can be done on a verbal or a nonverbal level.

blocking role an anti-group member role. Individuals who take this role act as aggressors, blockers, dominators, recognition seekers, and self-righteous moralists.

body language a Gestalt concept in which emphasis is placed on what a person's body is doing, such as a hand tapping

boundaries physical and psychological parameters under which a group operates, such as starting and ending on time

brainstorming a way to stimulate divergent thinking; requires an initial generating of ideas in a nonjudgmental manner. The premise of this approach is that creativity and member participation are often held back because of the critical evaluation of ideas and actions by other group members.

buddy system where members in a behavioral group are paired up in dyadic teams to mutually reinforce and support each other

burnout a state of physical and emotional exhaustion

C group a type of Adlerian parent education group; each component of the group—collaboration, consultation, clarification, confrontation, concern, confidentiality, and commitment—begins with a *c*. The group is primarily

psychoeducational. It emphasizes developmental and preventive aspects of parenting.

capping the process of easing out of emotional interaction and into cognitive reflection; especially useful during termination

career awareness and self-exploration groups groups that combine brief lectures on particular subjects, such as types of careers, self-disclosure, trust, self-esteem, and communications, with small-group interaction

career change groups groups for adults in midlife that are both psychoeducational and psychotherapeutic in nature

career support groups groups geared to life-span issues of work

caring genuine concern for others

catharsis a release of pent-up feelings, such as anger or joy; a psychoanalytic concept

cathexis school (of TA) a branch of transactional analysis that emphasizes reparenting

chain in this group arrangement, people are positioned or seated along a line, often according to their rank. Communication is passed from a person at one end of the configuration to a person at the other end through others. The chain is a popular way to run some group organizations, such as the military. Disadvantages of the chain include indirectness of communication, lack of direct contact with others, and frustration in relaying messages through others.

chaining specific behavioral response sequences linked or chained to one another and used in shaping behavior

changing questions to statements Gestalt procedure that requires a group member who has raised a question to rephrase it as a statement

Chicanas women of Mexican descent

Child ego state (TA) divided into two parts (a) *Adapted Child* conforms to the rules and wishes of Parent ego states within the self and others; (b) *Free Child* (or natural child) reacts more spontaneously, has fun, and is curious and playful. It takes care of its needs without regard for others while using its intuition to read nonverbal cues.

circle in this group configuration, all members have direct access to one another, and there is implied equality in status and power. The disadvantage of this arrangement is the lack of a perceived leader in the structure unless the identified leader is active and direct. Overall, the circle is probably the best structured way to ensure group members have an opportunity for equal airtime.

clarify the purpose when group leaders remind members and the group as a whole what the appropriate behavioral interactions or foci in the group are and why

clarity of purpose the first step in the preplanning process; determining what the group is set up to accomplish

classic school (of TA) a branch of transactional analysis that emphasizes present interactions

closed-ended groups that do not admit new members after the first session

coaching a process of providing a group member with general principles for performing desired behaviors. It works best when the coach sits behind the group member who is rehearsing.

code of ethics a set of standards and principles that organizations create to provide guidelines for their members to follow in working with the public and one another

cognitive and behavioral approaches to human relations based on a theory of personality that maintains that how one thinks largely determines how one feels and behaves

cognitive behaviorists behaviorists who believe thoughts play a major part in determining action and that thoughts are behaviors

cognitive disputation a process in REBT that involves direct questioning, reasoning, and persuasion

cognitive restructuring a process in which group members are taught to identify, evaluate, and change self-defeating or irrational thoughts that negatively influence their behavior

cognitively restructure to think of and perceive oneself differently

cohesion the togetherness of a group; "we-ness"

cohesiveness (see *cohesion*)

co-leader a professional or a professional-in-training who undertakes the responsibility of sharing the leadership of a group with another leader in a mutually determined manner. The use of co-leaders in groups occurs often when membership is 12 or more.

collaborating the process in which individuals work with others to find some solution that fully satisfies everyone's concerns

collaboration sharing facts and feelings with other members in a group; helping a member obtain a personal goal when there is no observable reward for the other members of a group

collective counseling Alfred Adler's form of group counseling

commitment when participants begin to evaluate their performances and the performances of others in terms of accomplishment of the group's goals

communication facilitator a group leader who reflects the content and feeling of members and teaches them how to do likewise. This process focuses on both the expression of words and the emotion behind these communications. In addition, the leader stresses the importance of speaking congruently—that is, using "I" messages to state what one wants or thinks.

community for learning a large-group phenomenon in the 1970s initiated by Carl Rogers in which about 100 people live and work together for 2 weeks at a time

competing pursuing personal concerns at other people's expense

compromising attempting to find some expedient, mutually acceptable solution that partially satisfies both parties

conceptual skills thinking skills that enable group leaders to delineate dominant themes and concerns of clients while simultaneously choosing a particular helpful response

condemning questions questions that put people down and prevent them from seeing situations more honestly and openly (e.g., "Don't you think you should feel differently?")

conductors the term used to refer to psychoanalytically oriented group leaders who do not wish to be the main attention of the groups they facilitate

confidentiality the explicit agreement that what is said within a group will stay in the group; the right of group members to reveal personal thoughts, feelings, and information to the leader and other members of the group and expect that in no way will nonmembers of the group learn of it. Not keeping confidences is like gossiping and is destructive to the group process.

conflict involves matters in which people struggle in resolving significant issues in their lives, such as authority, intimacy, growth, change, autonomy, power, and loss

conflict management an approach premised on the belief that conflict can be positive. Thus, the focus in conflict management is on directing conflict toward a constructive dialogue.

conflict management orientations ways of handling conflict in a group (e.g., competing, accommodating, collaborating, sharing, avoiding)

conflict resolution based on the underlying notion that conflict is essentially negative and destructive, with the primary focus on ending a specific conflict

confront to challenge incongruencies in thoughts and actions

confrontation challenging group members to look at the discrepancies and incongruencies between their words and their actions

consciousness-raising (C-R) group a group set up to help its participants become more aware of the issues they face and choices they have within their environment

consensual validation involves checking out one's behaviors with a group of other people

contact-focused group theory a conceptualization of groups in which the purpose of groups is highlighted; three primary contact groups described in this model are group guidance, group counseling, and group psychotherapy

contagion the process in which member behavior elicits group interaction on either an emotional or a behavioral level

content functions the actual words and ideas exchanged between leaders and members

contingency contracts contracts that spell out the behaviors to be performed, changed, or discontinued; the rewards associated with the achievement of these goals; and the conditions under which rewards are to be received

continuing education units (CEUs) credits for participating in professional educational programs

contract an agreement, verbal or written, of what group members or the group as a whole will do and when

control theory a complete system for explaining how the brain works; added to base of reality therapy in the 1980s to make it more complete

cooperation group members working together for a common purpose or good

cooperative learning groups study groups established so that assigned tasks can be divided and accomplished; members are responsible for meeting regularly and teaching one another what they have learned

core mechanisms of group leadership core skills of group leadership (i.e., emotional stimulation, caring, meaning attribution, and executive function)

corrective emotional experience a hallmark of the working stage of a group; a group member is helped by others to interact interpersonally in an appropriate way through reality testing responses

corrective recapitulation of the primary family group reliving early familial conflicts correctly and resolving them

counseling groups see *counseling/interpersonal problem-solving groups*

counseling/interpersonal problem-solving groups groups that focus on each person's behavior and growth or change within the group in regard to a particular problem or concern

countertransference a leader's emotional responses to members that are a result of the leader's own needs or unresolved issues with significant others

couples group therapy proponents of couples group therapy list many advantages for it, including (a) identification by group members of appropriate and inappropriate behaviors and expectations by others, (b) development of insight and skills through observing other couples, (c) group feedback and support for the ventilation of feelings and changed behavior, and (d) lower cost

crash-program mentality when group experiences are carried out to excess

creative imagery a warm-up technique consisting of inviting psychodrama participants to imagine neutral or pleasant objects and scenes. The idea is to help participants become more spontaneous.

creativity the act of taking elements from the environment and arranging or rearranging them in such a way that something new and useful is formed

crisis-centered groups groups formed because of some emergency, such as conflict between rival groups

critical incident in the life of the group an event that has the power to shape or influence the group positively or negatively

critical-incident model a model focusing on a number of critical incidents in the life of a group of any type. The

trainee, after studying group dynamics, watches a videotape of his or her instructor handling a number of different situations in a group. Then the trainee co-leads a group under the instructor's supervision and makes strategic interventions geared to the incidents in the particular group. Trainees are taught self-management skills as well as ways to deal with specific group situations.

critical incident stress debriefing (CISD) groups groups that help victims of violence deal with its repercussions, such as feelings of helplessness, anxiety, depression, and disorganization, lasting one 1- to 3-hour session

culturally encapsulated holding stereotyped views of others who differ from oneself and acting accordingly

curative (therapeutic) factors within groups eleven group factors (instillation of hope, universality, imparting of information, altruism, corrective recapitulation of the primary family group, development of socialization techniques, imitative behavior, interpersonal learning, group cohesiveness, catharsis, and existential factors) that contribute to the betterment of individuals in the group; first researched by Irvin Yalom

cutting off another term for blocking; defined two ways: (a) making sure that new material is not introduced into the group too late in the session for the group to adequately deal with it; (b) preventing group members from rambling

cyclotherapy process the idea that after the group meets, it continues to evolve and can be conceptualized as forever forming, with certain issues returning from time to time to be explored in greater depth

defense mechanisms ways of protecting a person from being overwhelmed by anxiety, such as repression or denial; overused when a person is not coping adequately

delegating the group leader's assignment of a task to the group or one or more of its members

democratic group leaders group-centered leaders who trust group participants to develop their own potential and that of other group members. They serve as facilitators of the group process and not as directors of it. They cooperate and collaborate with the group and share responsibilities with group members.

denial acting as if an experience does not exist or will never end

density of time the fullness of time and eventfulness; both seem to lessen with age

dependency group members who present themselves as helpless and incapable but refuse to listen to feedback. They are help-rejecting complainers and encourage the behavior of advice givers and band-aiders in a group.

Developing Understanding of Self and Others–Revised (DUSO–R) a commercial classroom guidance program based on Adlerian theory

development of socializing techniques learning basic social skills

developmental factors variables such as the age, gender, and maturity level of those involved in a group

developmental group counseling psychoeducational groups often used for teaching basic life skills

developmental psychoeducational groups groups that focus on common concerns of adolescents, such as identity, sexuality, parents, peer relationships, career goals, and educational/institutional problems. Individuals who join these groups do so out of a sense of need.

devil's advocate procedure procedure in which one or more members in the group are asked to question group decisions with a firm skepticism before the group reaches a conclusion

diagnosing an activity in which the leader identifies certain behaviors and categories into which a person or group fits. Diagnosing in groups does not usually include psychological instruments but is based more on leader observations.

dialogue talk between others and oneself or between different aspects of oneself; one of the two primary therapeutic tools in Gestalt therapy (along with *awareness*)

director the person who guides the protagonist in the use of the psychodramatic method to help that person explore his or her problem. The director is roughly equivalent to the group leader in other theoretical approaches but serves as a producer, a facilitator, an observer, and an analyzer.

discussion teams small groups used to promote involvement in guidance activities. In this arrangement, a large group is divided into four or five teams that are then seated in semicircles around the room. This formation has the advantage of getting members involved with one another and raising the level of excitement among them. The disadvantages are that interaction is mainly limited to a small number of individuals and that other group members do not get the advantage of participating in all the groups.

double and multiple double important techniques in psychodrama. The *double* consists of an actor taking on the role of the protagonist's alter ego and helping the protagonist express true inner feelings more clearly. In cases in which the protagonist has ambivalent feelings, the *multiple double* technique is used. In these situations, two or more actors represent different aspects of the protagonist's personality. The doubles may speak at once or take turns but, through their input, the protagonist should gain a better idea of what his or her thoughts and feelings are.

drawing out the opposite of cutting off or blocking; a process in which group leaders purposefully ask more silent members to speak to anyone in the group, or to the group as a whole, about anything on their minds or a specific subject

dream analysis a psychotherapeutic technique. In group psychotherapy, individuals must first be prepared to share. This preparation can occur through the group leader asking members in an early session to describe a recent dream, a recurring dream, or even a daydream. Through sharing, group members get to know one another better and at the same time are able to be more concrete in handling their feelings associated with the dream and in

managing themselves in general. *Dream content* is either *manifest* (conscious) or *latent* (hidden). Manifest content consists of the obvious and recallable features of the dream, such as who was in it. Latent content is the symbolic features of the dream that escape first analysis.

dream work seen by Fritz Perls as "the royal road to integration." It is used by having those who dream recreate and relive the dream in the present. By doing so, these individuals become all parts of the dream. They may do this through working alone in the group setting or having others in the group act out different parts of the dream (i.e., *dream work as theater*).

dual-focused Gestalt group work a Gestalt approach in which attention is concentrated on group process, with the power of individual work within the group

dual nature of human beings an REBT concept that individuals are both rational and irrational

dual relationships when group leaders find themselves in two potentially conflicting roles with their group members

dyads groups of two

eating disorders groups professionally led psychotherapeutic and support groups for individuals who have obsessive and distorted ideas in regard to thinness and body image

eclectic a composite of theoretical approaches

educational and developmental procedure a group training model consisting of four components: (a) content, (b) decision making, (c) eventual leadership style, and (d) dual process

educational groups see *psychoeducational groups;* another name for such groups

ego (psychoanalysis) the "executive of the mind"; works according to the reality principle and tries to reduce the tension of the id

ego state (TA) a system of feelings accompanied by a related set of behavior patterns; the three basic TA ego states are Parent, Adult, and Child

egogram (TA) a bar graph showing how people structure their time in six major ways: (a) withdrawal, (b) ritual, (c) pastimes, (d) work, (e) games, and (f) intimacy

eight basic steps of reality therapy (see *reality therapy's original eight basic steps*)

elasticity a Gestalt term describing the ability to move from one set of needs to another and back

elder hostel a place where older individuals live and study together for a select period

emotional ambivalence feelings of loss, sadness, and separation mixed with those of hope, joy, and accomplishment

emotional debris unfinished business

emotional impact of separation includes dealing with loss, putting the separation in perspective, becoming aware of the limited value of searching for causes of separation, becoming more cognizant of systems interactions (family, work, social network), using the past as a guide to the future, and moving from a dyadic to a monadic identity

emotional response of separation focuses on continuing relationships with an ex-spouse; recognizing the influence of the separation on family, friends, and children; working and dating; and making sexual adjustments

emotional stimulation sharing on an affective level as well as intellectual level

empathizing putting oneself in another's place in regard to subjective perception and emotion and yet keeping one's objectivity. It demands a suspension of judgment and a response to another person that conveys sensitivity and understanding.

empty chair technique a Gestalt technique designed to help group members deal with different aspects of their personalities (e.g., a person is given an opportunity to role-play and speak to a missing person with whom he or she has unfinished business)

encounter an existentialist concept that involves total physical and psychological contact between persons on an intense, concrete, and complete basis in the here and now; a psychodrama concept

encounter group (see *basic encounter group*)

encouragement an Adlerian technique of having group members examine their lifestyles in regard to mistaken perceptions and take note of their assets, strengths, and talents. Encouragement is one of the most distinctive Adlerian procedures.

energy field the sum total of individual members' energies and attention in a group

ethics suggested standards of conduct based on a set of professional values

evaluation questionnaire serves the purpose of helping group members be concrete in assessing the group in which they have participated. This questionnaire can take many forms but is best if kept brief. An evaluation questionnaire should cover at least three aspects of the group: the leadership of the group, the facilities in which the group was held, and the group's effectiveness in achieving its objectives.

excursions a part of synectics in which members actually take a break—a vacation—from problem solving and engage in exercises involving fantasy, metaphor, and analogy. The idea is that the material generated in these processes can later be reintegrated back into the group.

executive function the role of the leader to manage the group as a social system that allows the group and its members to achieve specific goals

exercises planned activities that have been used previously to help group members become more aware; structured activities that the group does for a specific purpose

existential factors accepting responsibility for one's life in basic isolation from others; recognizing one's own mortality and the capriciousness of existence

existential variables immediate feelings and interactions, such as conflict, withdrawal, support, dominance, and change

experiments nonplanned experiences that occur spontaneously in the group session

extinction the process of lowering the rate at which a behavior occurs by withdrawing the reinforcers that have been maintaining it so the targeted behavior will cease

facilitating as done by group leaders, helping open up communication among group members

facilitative feedback telling another person the effect he or she has on you as a compliment or confrontation

facilitative/building role a role that adds to the functioning of a group in a positive and constructive way. Members who take on such a role may serve as initiators of actions and ideas, information seekers, opinion seekers, coordinators, orienters, evaluators, or recorders.

facilitators term for Rogerian group leaders

families in high-risk environments families living in neighborhoods prone to violence

family councils a form of family group meetings originated by Alfred Adler

family reenactment a situation in which family-of-origin issues continue to be an influence on people throughout their lives, such as in groups that resemble families in many ways

fantasy exercises a method used in Gestalt group work to help group members (a) be more concrete in assessing their feelings, (b) deal with catastrophic experiences, (c) explore and express feelings of guilt and shame, and (d) become more involved in the group. It is not necessary for group members to live out their fantasies.

farewell-party syndrome a dynamic in which group members emphasize only the positive aspects of what has occurred in the group, instead of what they have learned. This type of focus tends to avoid the pain of closure.

faulty logic irrational ideas that clients hold

feedback involves one person giving another his or her perception of a behavior, sharing relevant information with other people, such as how they appear to others, so they can make decisions about whether they would like to change. Feedback information should be given in a clear, concrete, succinct, and appropriate manner.

fidelity loyalty and duty; keeping one's promise and honoring one's commitment. In group work, fidelity involves stating up front what the group will focus on and then keeping that pledge.

field theory Kurt Lewin's approach to groups, which emphasizes the interaction between individuals and their environments. It is based on the ideas of Gestalt psychology, in which there is an interdependence of part–whole relationships.

fishbowl the use of in and out circles in conducting a group

fishbowl procedure (see *group observing group*)

fixation a tendency to cope with the outside world in a manner similar to that employed in an earlier stage of development in which one is stuck. To overcome fixation requires that people regress to that time and come to terms with themselves and significant others who were involved in the fixation process.

floating hot seat Gestalt technique in which interaction is promoted by encouraging group members to work on exploring their own personal issues when someone else in the group touches on an issue that has personal relevance for them

focus groups temporary groups composed of representative samples of individuals concerned with issues, products, and/or outcomes; increasingly used by businesses and politicians

focusers on others those who become self-appointed group "assistant leaders" by questioning others, offering advice, and acting as if they do not have any problems

follow-up reconnecting with group members after they have had time to process what they experienced in the group and work on their goals/objectives

formal feedback structured; may be set up through use of a *time-limited round*

forming, or orientation, stage of the group a stage characterized by initial caution associated with any new experience. During this time, group members try to avoid being rejected by others, the leader, or even themselves.

four stages of psychosexual development oral, anal, phallic, and genital

four types of thoughts: negative, positive, neutral, and mixed an REBT concept; (a) negative thoughts concentrate on painful or disappointing aspects of an event, (b) positive thoughts focus on just the opposite, (c) neutral cognitions are those that are neither positive nor negative, and (d) mixed thoughts contain elements of the other three thought processes

free association in group psychoanalysis, used to promote spontaneity, interaction, and feelings of unity in the group. In a group, free association works as a type of "free-floating discussion" in which group members report their feelings or impressions immediately.

game analysis (TA) an examination of destructive and repetitive behavioral patterns and an analysis of the ego states and types of transactions involved

games (TA) an ongoing series of complementary ulterior transactions progressing to a well-defined, predictable outcome. Games are played on three levels, and almost all of them are destructive and result in negative payoffs (i.e., *rackets*). *First-degree* games are the least harmful; minor faults are highlighted. *Second-degree* games are more serious; interactive process in second-degree games leaves the people involved feeling negative. *Third-degree* games are deadly and often played for keeps; there is nothing socially redeemable about third-degree games. People who play games operate from three distinct positions: (a) the *victim* (who appears to be innocent), (b) the *persecutor* (who appears to cause problems), and (c) the *rescuer* (who is seen as a problem-solver or hero to the victim). Individuals who play games often switch among these roles.

GAP matrix for groups the "goals and process" model of group types; originated by Waldo and Bauman

general systems theory a theory that emphasizes circular causality as opposed to linear causality

generalization the display of behaviors in environments other than where they were originally learned

generativity a goal of midlife, according to Erik Erikson, in which people seek to be creative in their lives and work for the benefit of others and the next generation

genogram a type of family tree

goals specific objectives that individuals in the group or the group as a whole wishes to accomplish

go-rounds also known as *rounds;* a procedure in which every group member comments briefly (usually a sentence or two) as his or her turn comes up around the circle

Gray Panthers a psychoeducational and advocacy task group for the elderly

Greek chorus (see *hot seat*)

group a collection of two or more individuals who meet in face-to-face interaction, interdependently, with the awareness that each belongs to the group and for the purpose of achieving mutually agreed-on goals

group analysis a term first applied to the treatment of individuals in psychoanalytically oriented groups by Trigant Burrow. He emphasized that social forces affect individuals' behaviors.

group-based training In this model, specific skills used in groups are first identified and defined by trainers. Examples are given in which this skill might be used. The flexibility of using various skills is stressed in this presentation. Next, both videotapes and role-plays are used to show trainees how a particular skill is employed. The third step in this procedure is structured practice in which each trainee demonstrates how he or she would use the skill that has been demonstrated. This enactment is then critiqued. Finally, group leader trainees, after learning all the group skills, are asked to demonstrate their group facilitation skills in 20-minute unstructured practice sessions. They are observed leading a group and given feedback on the use of skills they implemented during this time as well as those that they did not use.

group-centered perspective focuses on members and interpersonal processes

group cohesion a sense of "we-ness"

group cohesiveness the proper therapeutic relationship among group members, group members and the group leader, and the group as a whole so that a sense of we-ness is fostered

group collusion involves cooperating with others unconsciously or consciously to reinforce prevailing attitudes, values, behaviors, or norms. The purpose of such behavior is self-protection, and its effect is to maintain the status quo in the group.

group-conducted pregroup screening process a way of screening potential group members by placing them in a group and observing how they interact

group content information discussed within a group

group dynamics a term originally used by Kurt Lewin to describe the interrelations of individuals in groups

group exercises (see *exercises*)

group generalist model a model entailing five steps: (a) the trainer models leader behavior for the total group; (b) the group is broken into subgroups of five or six, and each subgroup member practices leading a small-group discussion; (c) after each discussion, some aspect of the subgroup's behavior is processed (e.g., anxiety); (d) the subgroup critiques the leader's behavior; and (e) following practice by each trainee, the total group shares observations and conclusions about the activity

group interaction the way members relate to one another with nonverbal and verbal behaviors and the attitudes that go with them. Group interaction exists on a continuum, from extremely nondirective to highly directive.

Group Leader Self-Efficacy Instrument (GLSI) a 36-item scale for measuring group leader self-efficacy

group norming (see *norming*)

group observing group when a group breaks into two smaller groups and each observes the other function (as outsiders) for a set amount of time; sometimes called a *fishbowl procedure*

group process the interactions of group members as the group develops

group process goals in Adlerian groups, goals center around promoting and experiencing a cooperative climate within the group

group processing when a neutral third party observes and offers feedback to the group about what is occurring among members and in the group itself

group psychoanalysis a model that emphasizes that the whole group is the client and that group dynamics are an essential feature to analyze

group psychotherapy a group that addresses personal and interpersonal problems of living among people who may be experiencing severe and/or chronic maladjustment; specializes in personality reconstruction. It is meant to help people who have serious, long-term psychological problems. As such, this type of group is found most often in mental health facilities, such as clinics or hospitals.

group setting the group's physical environment

group structure the way a group is set up physically as well as how the group members interact or structure themselves in relationship to others

group for survivors of suicide group for adults that helps them break out of isolation and resolve grief issues specific to suicide; can also be conducted on a self-help and support group basis

group techniques exercises that are structured so that group members interact with one another

group therapy for normals premise of basic encounter groups: individuals who participate are relatively healthy

group work According to the Association for Specialists in Group Work, "a broad professional practice involving the application of knowledge and skill in group facilitation to assist an interdependent collection of people to reach their mutual goals, which may be intrapersonal, interpersonal, or work related. The goals of the group may include the accomplishment of tasks related to work, education, personal development, personal and interpersonal problem solving, or remediation of mental and emotional disorders."

groups for victims of abuse groups set up to help victims of abuse break the cycle of isolation so common to this population and to interrelate in a healthy, dynamic way

groupthink a group situation in which there is a deterioration of mental efficiency, reality testing, and moral judgment that results from in-group pressures

groupware the collective name of computer support for something a group does

growing times when fresh learning occurs on an individual and interpersonal level

growth-centered groups groups that focus on the personal and social development of people and are set up to explore feelings, concerns, and behaviors about a number of everyday subjects

guidance groups see *psychoeducational groups;* another name for such groups

"guidance hour" also called *"guidance room";* the term used for a homeroom at school in the 1930s; responsibilities of the teacher were to establish friendly relationships with students, discover their abilities and needs, and develop right attitudes with them toward school, home, and the community

Hawthorne effect changes in behavior as a result of observation/manipulation conditions under which a person or group works

HELPING D. B. Keat's multimodal framework for helping: Health, Emotions, Learning, Personal Interactions, Imagery, Need to Know, and Guidance

here and now the present

heterogeneous groups groups composed of dissimilar persons. Such groups can broaden members' horizons and enliven interpersonal interactions.

heuristic discovering, usually through research and investigation

hidden quadrant in the Johari window, contains undisclosed information known only to oneself initially

highly structured groups groups with a predetermined goal and a plan designed to enable each group member to reach an identified goal with minimum frustration. Such groups are usually used in teaching skills that may be transferred to a wide range of life events.

high-risk families families prone to violence

holding the focus helping members concentrate on a specific topic or person for a set length of time

homework working outside the group itself, members implement behaviors they have addressed or practiced within the group. These real-life situations help them realize more fully what they need to work on in the group.

homogeneous groups groups composed of similar persons

hope both a cognitive and an emotional experience in groups. Cognitively, the belief that what is desired is also possible and that events will turn out for the best; emotionally, the feeling that what one wishes for will occur. The importance of hope is that it energizes group members and the group as a whole.

hot seat the place in Gestalt group therapy where the person who wants to work sits with his or her chair facing that of the therapist or leader; the rest of the group serves as a kind of "Greek chorus" in the background of the encounter, where they resonate and empathize with the one who is working and gain insights into themselves and others through the process of identification.

humor the ability to laugh at oneself and the group in a therapeutic and nondefensive manner; an especially important quality during the working stage of the group

hypokinesis physical inactivity

I/We/It a conceptualization of the group process in which attention is given to personal, interpersonal, and product outcomes

icebreaker an activity designed to promote communication between two or more people in a group

ice-breaking exercises introductory activities that link people together. Such exercises increase the group members' awareness of one another and/or remind members of what they did in previous sessions.

id (psychoanalysis) the first system within the personality to develop; primarily where human instincts reside. It is amoral, functions according to the pleasure principle, and contains the psychic energy *(libido)* of the person.

identification a "normal" developmental process in which individuals see themselves as being similar to one another

imaginal disputation a technique that has participants see themselves in stressful situations and examine their self-talk

imago (i.e., image) relationship therapy image therapy; an eclectic approach to working with couples that includes elements of psychoanalysis, transactional analysis, Gestalt psychology, cognitive therapy, and systems theory

imitative behavior modeling actions of other group members

imparting of information instruction on how to deal with life problems, usually through group discussion

impasses in Gestalt theory, the places where group members get stuck

in and out circles often referred to as the *fishbowl*. The inner circle promotes a sense of closeness, but those in the outer circle may feel left out and become bored. To help promote participation by everyone, group leaders can assign tasks for the outside group members to do while they observe the inside group.

incorporation personal awareness and appreciation of what the group has accomplished both on an individual and a collective level

individual goals in Adlerian groups, involves developing insight into the creation of a mistaken lifestyle and taking corrective measures

individually conducted pregroup screening procedure intake interview used to determine who will join a particular group

influential power based on the idea of persuasion and manipulation of others through convincing them that a certain course of action is correct

informal feedback reactions solicited of members by the group leader; provided in an unstructured way at any time. Such an invitation is likely to increase spontaneity and sensitivity.

information statement a written description of what a group is about and what is expected of its members

informational power premised on the idea that those who know more are able to exert control over situations, including those involving people

informed consent statement a document a group member signs acknowledging that the individual is aware of the group activity in which he or she is about to participate and is doing so voluntarily

injunctions (TA) parent commands recorded internally by a child that call for the individual to adopt certain roles

inner circle/outer circle approach a Native American group approach in which members are organized into two concentric circles. Inner circle members release their pain and frustrations, expressed as clenched fists, into the open palms of the outer circle members.

insight consists of immediate new perceptions and understandings about one's problems; often occurs during or after the experience of catharsis

insight and reorientation phases of the group in Adlerian groups, involves helping individuals understand why they made the choices they did in the past, often accompanied by the use of interpretation on the group leader's part that is offered as a tentative hypothesis

instillation of hope a process in which group members come to realize that their issues are resolvable

integrating conflicting ideas to form new solutions the idea behind integration is consensus. In using this strategy, group leaders try to get all parties to reexamine a situation and identify points of agreement.

integration phase last phase of psychodrama; involves discussion and closure

integrity one of Erikson's virtues; the total integration of life experiences into a meaningful whole

integrity therapy stresses helping people live up to their own moral convictions; has some commonality with reality therapy

intellectualization behavior characterized by an emphasis on abstraction with a minimal amount of affect; the use of thoughts and a sophisticated vocabulary to avoid dealing with personal feelings

intentional civil liability cases include situations such as (a) *battery* (the unconsented touching of a person); (b) *defamation* (injury to a person's character or reputation either through verbal *[slander]* or written *[libel]* means); (c) *invasion of privacy* (violation of the right to be left alone); and (d) *infliction of mental distress* (outrageous behavior on the part of the therapist or the group leader)

interactional catalyst occurs when group leaders promote interaction among group members without calling attention to themselves. It is a functional process that continues throughout the group and can take various forms, such as questioning whether two or more group members have something to say to each other and then being silent to see what happens.

interactive journal writing the process wherein group members keep logs of their thoughts, feelings, impressions, and behaviors within a group and exchange them in all directions—member–leader, member–member, and leader–member

interpersonal goals in Adlerian groups, involves becoming more socially oriented and involved with other individuals experiencing life difficulties

interpersonal style of group leadership leadership that focuses on transactions between individuals in the group

interpretation a psychoanalytic technique that focuses on helping group members gain insights into their past or present behavior; generally made by group leaders in the earliest stages of the group because group members seldom possess the sophistication to do so adequately and appropriately at this time. There are three levels of interpretation: *thematical*—broad based, covering the whole pattern of a person's existence, such as self-defeating behavior; *constructional*—focusing on thought patterns and the way group members express themselves; and *situational*—context centered, emphasizing the immediate interactions within the group.

interpretation of a person's early history in Adlerian groups, group members' recognition and understanding of the ways they created their own lifestyles

intervention cube concept model for training group leaders (see *critical-incident model*)

intrapersonal style of group leadership leadership that concentrates on the inward reactions of individual members of the group

intrinsically neutral as an approach, Gestalt theory views individuals as neither positive nor negative (i.e., without a predetermined set of responses)

involvement group members' active participation with one another and investment of themselves in the group

job support groups groups for people who have lost their jobs and need emotional support; who want to learn how to achieve career goals and are willing to spend a good deal of time in doing so; and who are unemployed

and are emotionally struggling with the stigma, shame, and isolation of their situations

jogging group approach built on the premise that physical exercise is an important element that contributes to people's abilities to perform better in all areas of life. The jogging group itself combines an hour of exercise, in the form of walking, jogging, or running, with another hour of group process.

Johari Awareness Model also known as *Johari Window;* a representative square with four quadrants that is often used to show what happens in group interactions when the group and its members are working or not working

joining the process by which leaders and group members connect with one another psychologically and/or physically

journal letters a way of ending a group; members and the leader write about their experiences in the group and give their letters to one another

journals also known as *logs;* in this experience, group members are required to write their reactions to the events of each session. This process enables them to spot inconsistencies in their reactions more quickly than if they simply talked about them.

justice fairness; refers to the equal treatment of all people. This virtue implies that everyone's welfare is promoted and that visible differences in people, such as gender or race, do not interfere with the way they are treated.

laissez-faire leaders leaders in name only. They do not provide any structure or direction for their groups. Members are left with the responsibility of leading and directing.

law a body of rules recognized by a state or a community as binding on its members

Law of Triviality the time a group spends discussing any issue is in inverse proportion to the consequences of the issue

layers of neurosis in Gestalt theory, those aspects of people that keep them from being healthy: the *phony*—being unauthentic; the *phobic*—being afraid to really see themselves as they are; and the *impasse*—where their maturity is stuck

leader-centered group autocratic; the leader instructs the followers in the "right" way. The leader-centered group is based on obedience from followers.

leaderless groups groups that rotate the leadership role among members (e.g., self-help groups)

leveling a process in which group members are encouraged to interact freely and evenly with one another. In leveling, group members who are underparticipatory are drawn out and those who are excessively active are helped to modify their behavior.

life script analyses (TA) an examination of people's basic life plans involving transactions and games

life-skills group a type of guidance/psychoeducational group, especially designed for those who have a deficit of behavior. Emphasis is on a "how-to" approach to learning new behaviors; may include the use of films, plays, demonstrations, role-plays, and guest speakers (see *developmental group counseling*).

life-skills training focuses on helping persons identify and correct deficits in their life-coping skills and learn new appropriate behaviors

limits the outer boundaries of a group in regard to behaviors that will be accepted within the group

linear a cause-and-effect explanation

linking the process of connecting persons with one another by pointing out to them what they share in common. Linking strengthens the bonds between individuals and the group as a whole.

Living Newspaper a dramatic technique devised by Jacob Moreno in psychodrama in which recent happenings—sometimes local incidents, sometimes developments in world politics—were spontaneously dramatized

logs (see *journals*)

low facilitative responses (a) *advice/evaluation* (telling people how to behave or judging them); (b) *analyzing/interpreting* (explaining the reasons behind behavior without giving the person an opportunity for self-discovery); (c) *reassuring/supportive* (trying to encourage someone yet dismissing the person's real feelings)

magic shop a warm-up technique in psychodrama that is especially useful for protagonists who are undecided or ambivalent about their values and goals. It involves a storekeeper (the director or an auxiliary ego) who runs a magic shop filled with special qualities. The qualities are not for sale but may be bartered.

maintenance in this stage, an emphasis is placed on increasing group members' self-control and self-management (e.g., when a behavioral group member is consistent in doing the actions desired without depending on the group or its leader for support)

maintenance role a person who contributes to the social-emotional bonding of members and the group's overall well-being. When interpersonal communication in the group is strained, there is a need to focus on relationships. Persons who take on such roles are socially and emotionally oriented. They express themselves by being encouragers, harmonizers, compromisers, commentators, and followers.

major transactions a transactional analysis term that describes when the major focus of the group is on group leader–member interactions

making the rounds a warm-up technique in which each member is given a chance to speak about a particular topic. In Gestalt groups, confrontation is heightened as group members are asked to say something they usually do not verbalize.

making wishes into demands using *should, ought,* and *must* in regard to a desired action

malpractice bad practice; implies the group leader has failed to render proper service because of either negligence or ignorance

malpractice suit a claim against a professional made by a "plaintiff" who seeks a monetary award based on a specific amount of damages—physical, financial, and/or emotional

manipulators group members who use feelings and behaviors to get their way regardless of what others want or need. Often they are angry.

marathon groups originated by George Bach and Fred Stoller in 1964 as a way of helping people become more authentic with themselves; usually held for extended periods, such as 24 or 48 hours; group members are required to stay together. As time passes, members become tired and experience a breakdown in their defenses and an increase in their truthfulness.

marriage enrichment a psychoeducational and growth group for marrieds aimed at helping them have healthier relationships

meaning attribution refers to the leader's ability to explain to group members in a cognitive way what is occurring in the group

mediation having a third party hear arguments about a situation and then render a decision

member-specific groups related to topic-specific groups; focus on particular transitional concerns of individual members, such as grief, hospitalization, or institutionalized day care. Basically, member-specific groups may be conducted for older adults or for members of their families.

memory decay where more frequent life events of group members overshadow previous group experiences

midlife ages 40 to 65 years

minor transactions a transactional analysis term to describe when the group is functioning properly, when group members interact with one another

mirror in this psychodrama activity, the protagonist watches from offstage while an auxiliary ego mirrors the protagonist's posture, gestures, and words. This technique is often used in the action phase of psychodrama to help the protagonist see him- or herself more accurately.

mixed-gender groups groups composed of both males and females

mixed groups groups that defy fitting any category. They encompass multiple ways of working with their members and may change their emphasis frequently. For example, some groups that are instructive are also simultaneously or consequentially therapeutic. The prototype for a mixed group is a *self-help group*.

modeler of appropriate behavior when group leaders consciously pick and choose actions they think group members need to learn through passive and active demonstrations; can include deliberate use of self-disclosure, role-plays, speech patterns, and acts of creativity

modeling a social behavioral method used to teach group members complex behaviors in a relatively short period by copying/imitating

modification a technique in which the group leader must use a logical sequence by first "acknowledging the emotional reaction of a member" receiving negative feedback and then affirming the "potentially constructive intent" of the sender

monodrama also known as *autodrama;* in this technique, the protagonist plays all the parts of the enactment; no auxiliary egos are used. The person may switch chairs or talk to different parts of the self.

monopolizers group members who, because of their own anxiety, dominate conversation by not giving other persons a chance to participate verbally

monopolizing when a person or persons within the group dominate the group's time through talking

multimodal method using verbal and nonverbal means for conveying information

multiple-family group therapy (MFGT) involves treating several families together at the same time. It requires the use of co-leaders and has many of the same advantages that couples group therapy has, including the fact that families can often serve as cotherapists for one another.

multiple transferences in psychoanalytic groups, when group members can experience transference feelings with others in the group as well as with the group leader

mutual help group see *self-help group*

mythopoetic refers to a process of ceremony, drumming, storytelling/poetry reading, physical movement, and imagery exercises designed to create a "ritual process"; a process often used in men's groups

narcissistic groups groups that develop cohesiveness by encouraging hatred of an out-group or by creating an enemy. As a result, regressive group members are able to overlook their own deficiencies by focusing on the deficiencies of the out-group.

National Training Laboratories (NTL) a group training facility in Bethel, Maine, established by Kurt Lewin and associates in the late 1940s

natural consequences living with the results of a particular behavior, such as not following instructions (an Adlerian concept)

negative group variables group action that includes, but is not limited to, avoiding conflict, abdicating group responsibilities, anesthetizing to contradictions within the group, and becoming narcissistic

nominal-group technique (NGT) a six-step process involving the generation both verbally and in writing of a number of ideas/solutions connected with a problem statement. This exercise does not require the open exposure of members as much as brainstorming and ends with a vote, discussion, and revote on priorities for resolving a situation. The time period for the group is 45 to 90 minutes, after which the group, composed of people from diverse settings, is disbanded and the members thanked for their participation.

nondevelopmental counseling and psychotherapy groups adolescent groups that tend to focus mainly on concerns of adults and society, such as drug use, school problems (e.g., poor grades, truancy), or deviant behavior.

Usually, these groups are set up by a school, agency, or court, and troubled adolescents are forced to attend.

nondevelopmental factors unpredictable qualities such as the nature of a problem, the suddenness of its appearance, the intensity of its severity, and the present coping skills

nonmaleficence avoiding doing harm. To act ethically, leaders and members of groups must be sure the changes they make in themselves and help others to make are not going to be damaging.

nonverbal behaviors behaviors that make up more than 50% of the messages communicated in social relationships, such as in groups, and are usually perceived as more honest and less subject to manipulation than verbal behaviors. Four categories of nonverbal behavior are body behaviors, interaction with the environment, speech, and physical appearance.

nonverbal cues such behaviors as body posture and facial expression

norming process in which members form an identity as a group and a sense of "we-ness" prevails; there is enthusiasm, cooperation, and cohesiveness at this time. In many ways, the norming stage parallels the forming stage in regard to its emphasis on positive feelings. Norming, like storming, lasts for only a few sessions; it sets the pattern for the next stage: performing (i.e., working).

norms rules and standards of behavior. Groups typically accept both *prescriptive* norms, which describe the kinds of behaviors that should be performed, and *proscriptive* norms, which describe the kinds of behaviors that are to be avoided.

old individuals over the age of 75

old-old individuals over the age of 85; they are likely to experience declines in health and overall functioning

open quadrant in the Johari window, one that contains information that is generally known to self and others

open ended groups that admit new members at any time

open-ended questions questions that invite more than a one- or two-word response

operant conditioning emphasizes that behavior is a function of its consequences

operations specific techniques employed by transactional analysis group leaders, such as interrogation, specification, confrontation, explanation, illustration, confirmation, interpretation, and crystallization

paradox asking members to do the opposite of what you want in the hope they will disobey

parent education groups primarily psychoeducational groups focusing on the raising of children. Rudolph Dreikurs began setting up these groups in the 1950s using Alfred Adler's theory and ideas.

Parent Effectiveness Training (PET) a Rogerian-based parent education program. In PET, there is an emphasis on communication skills, and parents are encouraged to recognize their positive and negative feelings toward their children and come to terms with their own humanness. A major hypothesis of this approach is that *active listening* (i.e., hearing what is implied as well as what is actually said) and *acceptance* (acknowledging what is happening as opposed to evaluating it) will decrease family conflicts and promote individual growth.

Parent ego state (TA) dualistic in being both nurturing and critical (or controlling). The function of the *Critical Parent* is to store and dispense the rules and protection for living. The function of the *Nurturing Parent* is to care for (i.e., to nurture).

Parents Without Partners (PWP) a popular national organization whose groups for the divorced and widowed tend to be psychoeducational or self-help

PARS model (Processing: Activity, Relationship, Self) a model for examining processing in an individual, group, or family situation

pat on the back a closing exercise in which members draw the outline of their hand on a piece of white paper that is then taped on their back. Other group members then write closing comments that are positive and constructive about the person on the hand outline or on the paper itself.

peer group supervision see *peer supervision*

peer supervision practitioners meeting on a regular basis to consult with one another about particularly difficult group situations

permission (TA) centers on giving group members directives to behave against the injunctions of their parents

personal growth Rogerian term; a global emphasis that stresses development as a result of experiences, such as travel or encounter; the opposite of *personal growth* issues—an individual emphasis that springs from a perceived deficit or need

personal power a strategy often used in mature relationships. Personal power's source is from the individual and his or her ability to persuade others to follow a select course of action.

personal responsibility an existentialist concept, being responsible for making meaning out of what one does or what occurs

personalization skills using one's own personal attributes, such as openness or humor, to full advantage in a group setting

phyloanalysis the biological principles of group behavior

physical structure the arrangement of group members in relationship to one another

planning for continued problem resolution an activity that may be completed in a group before or after individual good-byes are said. It involves making a specific plan of what group members will do to continue their progress after the group ends. It should include when and how certain activities will be carried out, but others' expectations should not be part of the plan.

polarities two interrelated, interdependent, opposite poles, such as career and family

polarization when a group becomes divided into different and opposing subgroups or camps

position power a strategy often used when there are immature relationships between individuals. Position power is derived from the status of people's titles, such as "group leader" or "group facilitator."

positive expectations behavioral theory that individuals who expect to be successful are much more likely to achieve their goals

positive group variables a collection of favorable group factors, such as member commitment; readiness of members for the group experience; the attractiveness of the group for its members; a feeling of belonging, acceptance, and security; and clear communication

potency the use of appropriate counseling techniques in certain situations to bring about change

power the capacity to bring about certain intended consequences in others' behavior

preadolescents children in the latency period with an age range from 9 to 13 years

premature termination when individuals quit a group abruptly or when the group experience ends suddenly because of actions by the leader. There are three types of premature termination: the termination of the group as a whole, the termination of a successful group member, and the termination of an unsuccessful group member.

preschool and early school-aged children ages 5 through 9

pretraining orienting members of a group on what to expect of the group before it meets

primal horde Freud's conceptualization of a group; he thought leaders within the group function as *parental figures*

primary affiliation groups groups to which people most identify as belonging, such as a family or peers

primary tension awkwardness about being in a strange situation

principle ethics ethics based on obligations. They focus on finding socially and historically acceptable answers to the question "What shall I do?" Codes of ethics are based on principle ethics (i.e., actions stemming from obligations).

principle of awareness Gestalt assumption that people are free to choose only when they are *self-aware*—that is, in touch with their existence and what it means to be alive; awareness includes all sensations, thoughts, and behaviors of the individual

principle of figure/ground Gestalt principle. The *figure* in one's personal life is composed of experiences that are most important; the *background* is composed of experiences that are less pressing.

principle of holism Gestalt term for *integration*

principle of polarities Gestalt belief that if people are to meet their needs, then they must first differentiate their perceptual field into opposites/poles—for example, active/passive, good/bad. People fail to resolve conflicts because they are not in contact with the opposite sides of the situation.

problem-centered groups small groups set up to focus on one particular concern (e.g., coping with stress)

process observer a professional human services person who is neutral in regard to the group agenda and personalities; as part of the procedure of group processing, observes and gives feedback to the group on what and how they are doing

process-play a simulation model for group work training wherein students respond to superficial characteristics, such as whether a member is tall or is wearing green

process skills observable behaviors used to run groups, such as summarization, immediacy, and confrontation. By improving these skills, group leaders become more versatile in their interactions with group members and the group as a whole.

processing helping group members to identify and examine what occurred in a group in order to understand themselves and the group better

professional liability insurance insurance designed specifically to protect a group worker from financial loss in case of a civil suit

professional skills actions such as behaving appropriately in a crisis, safeguarding confidentiality, and turning in reports connected with the group in a timely manner

projecting the future asking group members to imagine what changes they would like to make in the short term and long term

projective identification, sometimes referred to as just *identification*, one of the most complex and potentially disruptive behaviors that can occur in a group. The manifestation of projective identification involves multiple members and occurs, for example, when an individual who experiences marked self-contempt projects these feelings onto another person in the group.

promoting hope one of the basic "therapeutic" factors described by Irving Yalom. If members believe that their situations can be different and better, then they are likely to work harder in the group.

promoting a positive interchange a condition that, when created, can help members become more honest with themselves and others and promote cohesion in the group

protagonist the person who is the subject of the psychodrama enactment; may play many parts

protecting involves the leader safeguarding members from unnecessary attacks by others in the group

protection involves a group leader keeping members safe from psychological or physical harm

pseudo-acceptance false acceptance; harmony is stressed over everything; prevents anxiety but also progress in a group

psychic numbing members anesthetizing themselves to contradictions in the group

psychoanalysis in groups focus is on the individual; the major tools of the psychoanalytic method are transference, dreams interpretation, historical development analysis, interpretation of resistance, and free association

psychodrama an interpersonal group approach in which participants act out their emotions and attempt to clarify conflicts; a way of exploring the human psyche through dramatic action; created and developed by Jacob Moreno; psychodrama process generally goes through three phases: (a) warm-up (preaction), (b) action, and (c) integration

psychoeducational groups groups originally developed for use in educational settings. They are premised on the idea that education is about changing perceptions as well as acquiring knowledge.

psychotherapy and counseling groups for the elderly geared toward the remediation of specific problems faced by the aging, such as role changes, social isolation, physical decline, and fear of the future

publicizing a group the way a group is announced; an appropriate activity in the planning substage of forming

push button an Adlerian technique wherein individuals are helped to realize that they have choices in their lives regarding which stimuli they pay attention to and remember

questioning a query that is sometimes a disguise for a statement. If group members are constantly questioning one another, then they are safe from exposing their true selves. Questions keep the group focused on why something occurred and prevent members from concentrating on what is happening now.

radical behaviorists behaviorists who avoid any mentalistic concepts and concentrate exclusively on observable actions

rape survivors' group a group for victims of rape aimed at helping them decrease their sense of isolation and stigma while learning to model effective coping strategies

rating sheet an evaluation form members fill out and return before they terminate a group or a group session. Members can rate themselves, other members, and the leader on a number of dimensions, including involvement, risk taking, goals, emotional involvement, feedback, and productivity

rational-emotive behavior therapy (REBT) based on the idea that it is one's thinking about events that produces feelings, not situations themselves. Individuals who have negative, faulty, or irrational thoughts become emotionally disturbed or upset and act in nonproductive ways, whereas those with more neutral or positive thoughts feel calmer and behave constructively.

reality-oriented groups set up for older individuals who have become disoriented to their surroundings. These groups, although educationally focused, are therapeutically based in that their emphasis is on helping group members become more attuned to where they are with respect to time, place, and people.

reality testing a skill used when a group member makes an important decision (e.g., changing jobs, taking a risk). At such moments, the leader will have other group members give feedback to the one who is contemplating a change on how realistic they see the decision being. Through this process, the person is able to evaluate more thoroughly his or her decision.

reality therapy founded by William Glasser, this theory emphasizes that all behavior is generated within ourselves for the purpose of satisfying one or more basic needs

reality therapy's original eight basic steps (a) Make friends; establish a meaningful relationship. (b) Emphasize present behaviors; ask, "What are you doing now?" (c) Stress whether clients' actions are getting them what they want. (d) Make a positive plan to do better. (e) Get a commitment to follow the positive plan. (f) No excuses. (g) No punishment. (h) Never give up.

reality therapy's four human psychological needs belonging, power, freedom, and fun; one physiological need: survival

reassuring/supportive trying to encourage someone, yet dismissing the person's real feelings

REBT viewpoint involves convincing group that the premises on which REBT is based are valid and applicable to their situations

recycling when individuals who have not benefited from a group experience go through a similar group to learn lessons missed the first time

redecision school of TA emphasis is on intrapsychic processes; groups provide a living experience in which members are able to examine themselves and their histories in a precise way. Individuals can then change their life scripts.

redecision theory a special form of transactional analysis; helps clients make redecisions while they are in their Child ego state. This task is accomplished by having these individuals reexperience a past event as if it were now present.

referrals transfers of members to another group; made when group leaders realize they cannot help certain members achieve designated goals or when there is an unresolvable conflict between leaders and members. The group leader should make appropriate referrals since he or she cannot be all things to all people. The referral process itself involves four steps: (a) identifying the need to refer, (b) evaluating potential referral sources, (c) preparing the client for the referral, and (d) coordinating the transfer.

reframing conceptualizing potentially negative actions in a positive way

regressive-reconstructive model (group psychoanalysis) emphasizes that participants will become responsible for themselves and for society. It stresses the importance of being a creator of society as well as a transmitter of patterns. It pushes participants to continue to change after the group has ended.

rehearsal (a) when members show others in the group how they plan to act in particular situations; (b) in Gestalt groups, when members are invited to say out loud what they are thinking

reinforcemen any behavior, positive or negative, that increases the probability of a response

relationship groups groups that focus on helping women break out of the dependency and caretaking roles they often find themselves in and connecting with themselves and others in a healthy, growth-producing way. In such groups, the emphasis is on being-in-relation, where one's needs as well as others' needs are met. The groups are short term (6 weeks) and goal oriented.

reminiscing groups originated in the 1960s; based on the importance of "life review." They help individuals who are not yet at the older life stage to comprehend and appreciate more fully who they are and where they have been. Persons in these groups share memories, increase personal integration, and become more aware of their lives and the lives of those their age. Insight gained from this process helps these persons realize more deeply their finiteness and thus prepare for death.

remotivation therapy groups groups aimed at helping older clients become more invested in the present and future. Their membership is composed of individuals who have "lost interest" in any time frame of life except the past.

reorientation in Adlerian groups, when members are encouraged to act differently and take more control of their lives. Such a procedure means taking risks, acting "as if" they were the person they wished to be, and "catching themselves" in old, ineffective patterns and correcting them.

repressive-constructive model (group psychoanalysis) focuses on adaptation and adjustment of participants without stressing the creation of newness within culture

resistance any behavior that moves the group away from areas of discomfort or conflict and prevents it from developing; works in overt and covert ways (e.g., rebellion by group members against the leader; getting bogged down in details; becoming preoccupied with the unimportant)

resisters group members who do not actively participate in the group and/or act as barriers to helping the group develop

respondent conditioning also known as *classical conditioning;* behavioral view that human responses are learned through association

reviewing and summarizing the group experience a procedure during termination in which group members recall and share special moments they remember from the group

Rogerian-oriented encounter group 15-stage process

1. *Milling around*—In the initial stage of the group, members are often confused about who is responsible for conducting the group and what they are supposed to be doing. This confusion results in frustration, silence, and a tendency to keep conversations on a superficial level.

2. *Resistance*—Group members tend to avoid exposing their private selves until they have built trust in other members. Members try to protect themselves and others from revealing too much too fast.

3. *Revealing past feelings*—As trust begins to develop, group members start to talk about their feelings but only those that are safe to expose (e.g., the past). The talk at this point is on there-and-then experiences (i.e., those that are historical) that are nonthreatening to expose.

4. *Expression of negative feelings*—As the group develops, initial here-and-now feelings are expressed, but generally in a negative manner. Most of these feelings are directed toward the leader, and they are in the form of blame for not providing enough structure.

5. *Expression of personally meaningful material*—Real trust in the group is established at this stage. Group members feel free to explore and talk about important meaningful events in their lives.

6. *Communication of immediate interpersonal feelings*—At this point in the life of the group, members begin to be affected by and respond to other group members. They indicate to others how their comments and actions are perceived.

7. *Development of a healing capacity in the group*—After members have expressed personal feelings about themselves and others, they begin reaching out to one another. This is accomplished by offering warmth, compassion, understanding, and caring to group members who have shared their concerns.

8. *Self-acceptance and the beginning of change*—As members are accepted more, they become increasingly aware of their own behaviors and feelings and are consequently less rigid. In the process, they open themselves to changes.

9. *Cracking of facades*—The tendency in encounter groups for members to drop the masks they have been wearing and become more genuine.

10. *Feedback*

11. *Confrontation*

12. *Helping relationships outside the group*—This stage is a parallel to stage 7, but group members experience healing and helping relationships with one another outside the formal group experience.

13. *The basic encounter*—Genuine person-to-person contact is the overriding characteristic at this point in the group.

14. *Expressions of closeness*—As the group nears completion, group members express positive feelings about their experience and about one another. A sense of group spirit develops.

15. *Behavior changes*—Behavior changes, the result of increased congruence, are more pronounced; members tend to act in a more open, honest, caring manner; and their behaviors are carried with them into everyday life experiences after the group terminates.

role a dynamic structure within an individual (based on needs, cognitions, and values) that usually comes to life under the influence of social stimuli or defined positions. The manifestation of a role is based on the individual's expectation of self and others and the interactions one has in particular groups and situations.

role collision when there is a conflict between the role an individual plays in the outside world (e.g., being a passive observer) and the role expected within the group (e.g., being an active participant)

role confusion occurs when a group member (or members) simply does not know what role to perform. This often happens in leaderless groups where members do not know if they are to be assertive in helping establish an agenda or to be passive and just let the leadership emerge.

role incompatibility when a person is given a role within the group (e.g., being the leader) that he or she neither wants nor is comfortable exercising

role playing assuming an identity that differs from one's present behavior. Role playing is a tool for bringing a specific skill and its consequences into focus. It is vital for experiential learning in the group.

role reversal a psychodrama technique in which the protagonist literally switches roles with another person on stage and plays that person's part; group members act the opposite of what they feel

role transition when a person is expected to assume a different role as the group progresses but does not feel comfortable doing so

rounds also known as *go-rounds;* the process of giving members of a group an equal chance to participate in the group by going around the circle in which they are sitting and asking each person to make a comment on a subject that is presently before the group

row formation a group in which attention is focused toward the front. This arrangement is good for making a presentation, but it limits, and even inhibits, group interaction

rules the guidelines by which groups are run

sarcasm masked feelings disguised through the use of clever language, such as biting humor

saying good-bye the final words members exchange with others at the end of a group that wraps it up, at least on an affective/cognitive level. Members are encouraged to own their feelings and express their thoughts at this time, especially in regard to what others in the group have meant to them.

scapegoat to blame others for one's own problems

screened when potential group members are interviewed before the group in regard to their suitability for the group

screening a three-part process that begins when group leaders formulate the type of group they would like to lead. Next is the process of *recruitment,* in which the leader must make sure not to misrepresent the type of group that is to be conducted and to publicize it properly. Finally, there is the task of interviewing applicants by the leader to determine whether they will benefit from and contribute to the group.

scripts (TA) patterns of behavior that influence how people spend their time. Most people initially script their lives as a Child in the *I'm Not OK—You're OK* stance (powerless) but change to an Adult stance in later life as they affirm an *I'm OK—You're OK* position (characterized by trust and openness). Other options open to them are *I'm OK— You're Not OK* (projection of blame onto others) and *I'm Not OK—You're Not OK* (hopeless and self-destructive).

sculpting an exercise in which group members use nonverbal methods to arrange others in the group into a configuration like that of significant persons with whom they regularly deal, such as family members, office personnel, or social peers. The positioning involves body posturing and assists group members in seeing and experiencing their perceptions of significant others in a more dynamic way.

search for meaning the search to find significance in one's life, even in the mundane events

secondary affiliation groups groups with which people least identify

secondary tension intragroup conflict

self-actualization realistically living up to one's potential; being the best one can be

self-awareness a state of being in touch with one's existence and what it means to be alive; includes all sensations, thoughts, and behaviors of an individual

self-disclosure revealing to the group personal information of which the group was previously unaware. It involves listening and receiving feedback as well as speaking. One of the strongest signs of trust in a group is self-disclosure.

self-efficacy a person's judgment of his or her capacity to organize and execute a course of action required to attain a designated type of performance

self-help groups groups that usually do not include professional leaders but are led by paraprofessionals or group members. Examples of such groups are Alcoholics Anonymous (AA) and Compassionate Friends.

self-instructional training in this procedure, the group member is trained to become aware of his or her maladaptive thoughts (self-statements). Next, the group leader models appropriate behaviors while verbalizing the reasons behind these strategies. Finally, the group member performs the designated behaviors while verbally repeating the reasons behind the actions and then conducts these behaviors, giving himself or herself covert messages.

self-monitoring behavioral group members keeping detailed, daily records of particular events or psychological reactions

self-report format research method used by Rogers and nonbehaviorists in which participants write out or check off how they have changed as a result of the group experience

self-talk the messages people give themselves internally

semicircle arrangement a half-circle group structure in which members can see one another; discussion is likely to involve almost everyone. However, if the group is too large (e.g., more than 20), persons may not feel that they are a group.

sensitivity groups (see *basic encounter group*)

setting up the environment establishing an atmosphere in which work within the group can take place

settling-down period a time when members test one another and the group collectively before the group unifies

shame attack an REBT technique in which a person actually does what he or she dreaded and finds the world does not fall apart regardless of the outcome

shaping teaching behaviors through successive approximation and chaining. This gradual step process allows group members to learn a new behavior over time.

shared a form of group co-leadership in which each leader takes charge of the group momentarily as he or she sees fit

shifting the focus moving group members to a different topic area or person

silent members group members who are reticent to speak in the group owing to anger, nonassertiveness, reflection, shyness, or slowness in the assessment of their thoughts and feelings

simulated group counseling model a model for introducing graduate students to the dynamics within a group; the students role-play group members for a number of weeks

single-subject research design a procedure in which leaders follow one of two methods in evaluating their groups. In the first method, they follow an ABAB design to evaluate the relationship of an intervention on changes that may occur in the group. In the other method, leaders employ a multiple-baseline design that more randomly measures change across subject, variables, or situations.

SIPA (structure, involvement, process, and awareness) a model for achieving group goals in group guidance

situation a psychodrama technique in which an emphasis is placed on the present; natural barriers of time, space, and states of existence are obliterated

situational therapy activity groups for children ages 8 to 15 based on psychoanalytic principles first created by Samuel Slavson

Skilled Group Counseling Scale 18 skills organized into three stages: (a) counseling and exploration, (b) understanding, and (c) action

Skilled Group Counseling Training Model a model for helping beginning group workers learn and transfer group counseling skills to actual group counseling sessions

social ecology context of a group

social group work organizing individuals into purposeful and enriching groups; first begun by Jane Addams at Hull House in Chicago for immigrants and the poor

social influence how interaction in groups exerts an influence on actions, attitudes, and feelings of people

social interest an Adlerian term defined as not only an interest in others but also an interest in the interests of others

social modeling learning as a result of imitation of others' behaviors

sociogram a tool of sociometry that plots out group interactions

sociometry a phenomenological methodology for investigating interpersonal relationships

soliloquy a psychodrama technique that involves the protagonist (i.e., the client) giving a monologue about his or her situation as he or she is acting it out. A variation on this activity is the therapeutic soliloquy technique, in which private reactions to events in the protagonist's life are verbalized and acted out, usually by other actors (i.e., auxiliary egos).

solution-focused debriefing (SFD) groups groups that help victims of violence deal with its repercussions, such as feelings of helplessness, anxiety, depression, and disorganization, spanning seven stages in 3 weeks for enhanced recovery. These groups emphasize a specific distressing incident, focus on the here and now, and include only persons who have witnessed the same violent episode.

sophistry a cognitive, psychotherapeutic group technique for assessing offenders' (and involuntary clients') "private logic" (i.e., way of thinking) and helping them change. This method helps counselors get beyond offenders' resistance. It employs paradox (i.e., telling resistant clients not to change), use of hidden reasons in a group debate, and a reorientation phase to get offenders to examine their thinking.

specialty/standards model an approach to conceptualizing groups in which they are defined according to their purpose, focus, and needed competencies. The ASGW has defined standards for four types of groups: psychoeducational, counseling, psychotherapy, and task/work.

spillover effect the impact for others who are helping or watching a main character in a psychodrama reach resolution on important issues; they see themselves as interacting in a new and better way.

spontaneity in psychodrama, the response people make that contains some degree of adequacy to a new situation or a degree of novelty to an old situation. The purpose of spontaneity is to liberate one's self from scripts and stereotypes and gain new perspectives on life.

stage in psychodrama, the area in which the action takes place

stages of psychoanalytically oriented groups

1. *Preliminary individual analysis*—Individuals in the psychoanalytically oriented group are interviewed individually by the group leader for their suitability for the group experience.

2. *Establishment of rapport through dreams and fantasies*—Group members are asked to discuss a recent dream, recurring dream, or a fantasy they have. The idea is to encourage group participation by having all members report on themselves and help others interpret or free associate on their experience.

3. *Analysis of resistance*—When group members become reluctant to share themselves with others and individual defenses are examined and dealt with.

4. *Analysis of transference*—When transference interactions are examined as close to the time of their occurrence as possible. Individual members are also asked to examine their feelings and involvement with other members of the group.

5. *Working through*—When individuals are required to accompany insight with action.

6. *Reorientation and social integration*—When clients demonstrate they are able to deal with the realities and pressures of life in an appropriate fashion without becoming overanxious or overcompliant when requests are made of them.

storming a time of conflict and anxiety in a group when it moves from primary tension (awkwardness about being in a strange situation) to secondary tension (intragroup conflict). It is a period when group members and leaders struggle with issues related to structure, direction, control, catharsis, and interpersonal relationships.

strokes (TA) verbal, psychological, or nonverbal recognition

structured activities (see *exercises*)

structuring the group running the group according to a preset prescribed plan or agenda

study groups types of task groups, typically involving three to four students who meet at least weekly to share information, knowledge, and expertise about a course in which they all are enrolled. The idea is that each group member will support and encourage the others and will obtain insight and knowledge through the group effort.

style of life Adlerian term; the way one prefers to live and relate to others. Adlerians stress that a faulty lifestyle is based on competitiveness and striving to be superior to others.

subgrouping occurs when a large group breaks down into several smaller groups, each with its own identity and each existing as part of the larger group. Groups do not function well as a whole when subgrouping develops.

subgroups cliques of group members who band together, often to the detriment of the group as a whole

Succeeding in School lessons a series of 10 lessons created by Gerler and Anderson (in 1986) that deal with modeling after successful people in school while learning to feel comfortable and responsible. Succeeding focuses on promoting cooperative efforts; enhancing student self-concept; and learning appropriate school skills, such as listening and asking for help.

summarizing reflections by group members that recall significant events or learning experiences in the group

superego a psychoanalytic term that represents the values of parents and parental figures within the individual. It operates on the moral principle by punishing the person when he or she disobeys parental messages through the *conscience* and by rewarding the person through the *ego ideal* when parental teachings are followed. The *superego* strives for perfection.

support groups types of self-help groups in which members share a common concern and have a professional group leader

supporting the act of encouraging and reinforcing others. Its aim is to convey to persons that they are perceived as adequate, capable, and trustworthy. Through the act of supporting, group members feel affirmed and are able to risk new behaviors because they sense a backing from the group.

suppressing conflict a strategy that consists of playing down conflict. It is often used when issues are minor. It keeps emotions under control and helps group leaders build a supportive climate.

surplus reality psychological experience that transcends the boundaries of physical reality. These experiences, which include relationships with those who have died or were never born, or with God, are often as important to people as their actual experiences with physical entities; a psychodrama concept.

sweat lodge ceremony a type of Native American group ceremony and ritual that leads to explanation, transition, purification, and emergence

SYMLOG System for the Multiple Level Observation of Groups

synchronous a type of online group; members must be online and logged in to the site of a group at a designated time to receive messages

synectics from the Greek, means the joining together of different and apparently irrelevant elements. Synectics theory applies to the integration of diverse individuals into a problem-stating, problem-solving group.

system a set of elements standing in interaction

systematic group leadership training involves the teaching of basic skills to beginning group leaders. It is a six-step method that includes the videotaping of trainees leading a group before being introduced to the skill they are to learn (steps 1 and 2). Then the trainees read about and see a new skill demonstrated (steps 3 and 4). Finally, trainees critique their original videos and then make new videotapes demonstrating the skill they have just been taught (steps 5 and 6).

Systematic Training for Effective Parenting (S.T.E.P.) an Adlerian-based parent education program

systemically in a circular manner

systems theory a theory that focuses on the interconnectedness of elements. From this perspective, a group as an organism is composed of other organisms, commonly called members and a leader, who over time relate to each other face to face, processing matter, energy, and information (see *general systems theory*).

talking circle a sweat lodge ceremony tradition in which participants express their thoughts and feelings in both prayer and conversation with themselves and others

task processing ways of accomplishing specific goals in a group

task setting an Adlerian therapeutic technique wherein individuals set short-range, attainable goals and eventually work up to long-term, realistic objectives

task/work groups groups whose emphasis is on accomplishment and efficiency in completing identified work goals. They are united in their emphasis on achieving a successful performance or a finished product through collaborative efforts. Task/work groups take the form of task forces, committees, planning groups, community organizations, discussion groups, and learning groups.

Tavistock Institute of Human Relations a group research facility in Great Britain

teachable moment a time when people are ready and able to learn

team a number of persons associated together in work or activity, such as in athletic or artistic competition, in which members of a group act and perform in a coordinated way to achieve a goal. Teams differ from basic groups in four main ways: (a) They have shared goals, as opposed to individual goals in most groups. (b) They stress an interdependency in working more than do groups. (c) They require more of a commitment by members to a team effort. (d) They are by design accountable to a higher level within the organization than are groups.

team building effective development of a team through managing conflict, promoting interpersonal relationships, and achieving consensus

Team Player Inventory (TPI) a 10-item assessment instrument that denotes the degree to which individuals are predisposed toward organizational team-working environments

teamwork all members of a group working together cooperatively

tele the total communication of feelings among people; involves complete interpersonal and reciprocal empathy; a psychodrama concept

termination a transition event that ends one set of conditions so that other experiences can begin. Termination provides group members an opportunity to clarify the meaning of their experiences, to consolidate the gains they have made, and to make decisions about the new behaviors they want to carry away from the group and apply to their everyday lives.

Theater of Spontaneity a forerunner of psychodrama formulated by Jacob L. Moreno in 1921

theater style a type of group structure in which members are seated in lines and rows

theme group a group that focuses on a particular problem or theme

themes specific topics or subjects related to the genuine interests of the participants, thereby holding their interest and inviting their participation. Many adolescent groups work best when they are structured around themes.

theory a way of organizing what is known about some phenomenon to generate a set of interrelated, plausible, and, above all, refutable propositions about what is unknown. A theory guides empirical inquiry and is useful in testing hypotheses.

Theory X leader an autocratic and coercive leader who basically believes people are unambitious and somewhat lazy

Theory Y leader a nondirective and democratic leader who thinks that people are self-starters and will work hard if given freedom

Theory Z leader a facilitative leader who helps encourage group members to participate in the group and trust that individual and collective goals will be accomplished through the process of interaction

therapeutic contracts in transactional analysis groups, specific, measurable, concrete statements of what participants intend to accomplish during the group. They place responsibility on members for clearly defining what, how, and when they want to change. TA contracts have the four major components of a legal contract: (a) *mutual assent*—clearly defining a goal from an adult perspective and joining with the therapist's Adult as an ally; (b) *competency*—agreeing to what can realistically be expected; (c) *legal object*—an objective; and (d) *consideration*—a fee or price for services.

therapeutic factors (see *curative factors within groups)*

therapeutic fairy tale a projective group activity meant to help persons focus on the future and renew their effort in the group. In this process, individuals are asked to write a fairy tale in a 6- to 10-minute time frame. They are to begin their story with "Once upon a time," and in it they are to include (a) a problem or predicament; (b) a solution, even if it appears outlandish; and (c) a positive, pleasing ending. The tale is then discussed in regard to personal and group goals.

time limit for the group the number of meeting times that the group will meet, usually announced in advance

time-limited round a technique in which each individual has the same amount of time, usually 1 or 2 minutes each, to say whatever he or she wishes

timely teaching when a particular event stimulates thinking and discussion among students

top dog/underdog dialogue Gestalt method in which group members are asked to examine the *top-dog introjections* they have taken in from parents (usually represented by *shoulds* and *you)* and their own real feelings about situations (usually represented by "I" statements). They then are asked to carry on a dialogue between these two aspects of themselves before the group or with another group member and try to become more aware of their true self-identity and ways to act that would be appropriate.

topic-specific groups centered around a particular topic, such as widowhood, bibliotherapy, sexuality, health, or the arts. They are designed ultimately to improve the quality of daily living for older people. They also assist the aged to find more meaning in their lives and to establish a support group of like-minded people.

total quality group implemented by the Japanese under the direction of task/work group master W. Edwards Deming; focus on problem solving related to consumer satisfaction and quality issues in business

total quality movement (TQM) in task/work environments, an emphasis on working cooperatively and productively in small groups

TRAC model of groups a model of groups known by the acronym TRAC (tasking, relating, acquiring, and contacting). Each letter represents an area in the total picture of group work. *Tasking* groups are focused on task achievement. *Relating* groups achieve objectives to increase the options for movement within the life of each person. *Acquiring* groups are directed toward learning outcomes that members can apply to others. In contrast, *contacting* groups are focused on the individual growth of members.

traditional leader a person who is controlling and exercises power from the top down as an expert; may be appropriate in running a hierarchical group that is diverse and whose members are physically separated

traffic director when the group leader helps members become aware of behaviors that open communication channels and those that inhibit communication

training group a group for beginning leaders designed to help them recognize and work out major personal and professional issues that affect their ability to conduct groups (e.g., criticism, anxiety, jealousy, need for control)

training group (T-group) approach to groups developed at the National Training Laboratories in the 1940s; primary attention to theory, group dynamics, and social material involving groups

trait approach the idea that some persons emerge as leaders because of their personal qualities

transactional analysis (TA) involves the diagnosing of interactions among group members to determine if they are *complementary* (from appropriate and expected ego states), *crossed* (from inappropriate and unexpected ego states), or *ulterior* (from a disguised ego state)

transactional skills qualities that help group members interact

transactions (TA) social actions between two or more people, manifested in social (overt) and psychological (covert) levels

transference the displacement of affect from one person to another; the projection of inappropriate emotions onto the leader or group members

transformational leader a person who empowers group members and shares power with them in working toward the renewal of a group; may be needed when a group is floundering

transformational skills helping members and the group achieve new behaviors

transient children children who have moved to a new community and a new school

transition period the time after the forming process and the working stage; it includes the storming and before norming stages

trilevel model of Gestalt group work attention is systematically focused on (a) the individual at the intrapersonal level, (b) two or more people at the interpersonal level, and (c) the group as a systematic unit

tying things together linking; connecting members with one another in regard to their similarities

unfinished business emotional debris from a person's past

unintentional civil liability a lack of intent to cause injury

universality a sense of commonness that group members feel in regard to their experiences when compared with others

universalization one's realization that others may have the same concerns

unknown quadrant in the Johari window, contains material hidden from self and others because of lack of opportunity

unstructured group used in experientially based situations and employed where process rather than product is emphasized

users of sarcasm persons who mask their feelings through the use of clever language that has a biting humor

using eyes to scan the group and notice nonverbal reactions

using power to resolve the conflict a strategy involving the imposition of someone's will on someone else. The source of power may be derived either from one's status (position) or from one's personality. *Position* power is most often used when there are immature relationships between individuals. Position power is derived from the status of people's titles, such as "group leader" or "group facilitator." *Personal* power is employed more frequently in mature relationship situations. The source of power in such a situation is from the individual and his or her ability to persuade others to follow a select course of action. By using power, a leader is able to quickly resolve a crisis, but the use of power often creates *win–lose atmospheres.*

veracity truthfulness. In group work, veracity is important in almost all phases of the group's development. Group members and leaders who are not truthful with themselves or others set up situations in which a good working relationship is impossible to achieve.

verbal behavior when group members speak to one another. The content of speech between people along with its tone and emphases.

virtue ethics focus on the character traits of the counselor (or group worker) and nonobligatory ideals to which professionals aspire rather than on solving specific ethical dilemmas

"W" (work group) (see *task/work groups*)

warm-up phase in psychodrama, characterized by the director making sure he or she is ready to lead the group and that group members are ready to be led

we/they mentality when practitioners of other points of view are seen as "uninformed," "naive," or "heretical"

we/they tendency when there is an overemphasis on identifying with a particular group, group members may tend to develop an antagonism toward other groups

wheel in this group arrangement, there is a center spoke, a leader, through which all messages go. Members have the advantage of face-to-face interaction with the leader, but they may become frustrated by the inability to communicate with another group member directly.

wisdom one of Erikson's virtues; the ability to make effective choices among alternatives

withdrawal from the conflict a strategy that involves group leaders distancing themselves from conflict and postponing interventions

working out a compromise when each party involved gives up a little to obtain a part of what they wanted and to avoid conflict. The result is a win–win situation in which cooperative behavior and collaborative efforts are encouraged. This approach is effective in groups when resources are limited.

working stage most unified and productive group stage that focuses on the achievement of individual and group goals and the movement of the group itself as a system

wounded healers fellow sufferers who have overcome their hurt; it is assumed in self-help groups that these individuals are able to deal most effectively with one another by coming together and sharing through disclosing, listening, and learning

written projections a process whereby members are asked to see themselves or their groups in the future as having been successful and to describe what the experience is like. They are able to play with their fantasies at times as well as be realistic.

Y this group arrangement combines the structural elements of the wheel and the chain—there is a perceived leader. The efficiency of the unit is second only to that of the wheel in performance. Like a chain, the Y may frustrate group members who wish to have direct contact and communication with one another. Information is not equally shared or distributed.

yearbook feedback saying nice but insignificant things about a person, as high school students do when they write in annuals

young adulthood ages 20 to 40 years, in which identity and intimacy are two intense primary issues

young-old individuals between ages 65 and 75

REFERENCES

Abudabeth, N., & Aseel, H. A. (1999). Transcultural counseling and Arab Americans. In J. McFadden (Ed.), *Transcultural counseling* (2nd ed., pp. 283–296). Alexandria, VA: American Counseling Association.

Ackerman, N. (1958). *The psychodynamics of family life.* New York: Basic Books.

Adams, K. (1993). *The way of the journal.* Lutherville, MD: Sidran.

Addington, J. (1992). Separation group. *Journal for Specialists in Group Work, 17,* 20–28.

Adler, A. (1956). *The individual psychology of Alfred Adler.* New York: Basic Books.

Agazarian, Y. M. (1997). *Systems-centered therapy for groups.* New York: Guilford.

Akos, P. (2000). Building empathic skills in elementary school children through group work. *Journal for Specialists in Group Work, 25,* 214–223.

Akos, P. (2004). Investing in experiential training appropriate for preservice school counselors. *Journal for Specialists in Group Work, 29,* 327–342.

Akos, P., & Martin, M. (2003). Transition groups for preparing students for middle school. *Journal for Specialists in Group Work, 28,* 139–154.

Alberti, R. E., & Emmons, M. L. (2002). *Your perfect right: A guide to assertive behavior* (8th ed). San Luis Obispo, CA: Impact.

Alexander, V. (1999). Ethics-based decision-making: A psychoeducational workshop for adult diversion programs. *Journal for Specialists in Group Work, 24,* 208–219.

Alfred, A. R. (1992). Members' perceptions of coleaders' influence and effectiveness in group psychotherapy. *Journal for Specialists in Group Work, 17,* 42–53.

Allan, J., & Bardsley, P. (1983). Transient children in the elementary school: A group counseling approach. *Elementary School Guidance & Counseling, 17,* 162–169.

Allen, R. D. (1931). A group guidance curriculum in the senior high school. *Education, 52,* 189–194.

Allport, F. (1924). *Social psychology.* Boston: Houghton Mifflin.

Allport, G. W. (1954). *The nature of prejudice.* Garden City, NY: Anchor.

Allport, G. W. (1955). *Becoming: Basic considerations for a psychology of personality.* New Haven, CT: Yale University Press.

Altarriba, J., & Bauer, L. M. (1998). Counseling the Hispanic client: Cuban Americans, Mexican Americans, and Puerto Ricans. *Journal of Counseling & Development, 76,* 389–396.

Altholz, J. A. S. (1978). Group psychotherapy with the elderly. In I. M. Burnside (Ed.), *Working with the elderly: Group process and techniques* (pp. 354–370). North Scituate, MA: Duxbury.

Amatruda, M-J. (2006). Conflict resolution and social skill development with children. *Journal of Group Psychotherapy, Psychodrama & Sociometry, 58,* 168–181.

American Association of Retired Persons. (2006). *A profile of older Americans.* Washington, DC: Author.

American Counseling Association. (2005). *Code of ethics and standards of practice.* Alexandria, VA: Author.

American Group Psychotherapy Association. (2002). *Guidelines for the training of group psychotherapists.* New York: Author.

Anderson, B. S., & Hopkins, B. R. (1996). *The counselor and the law* (4th ed.). Alexandria, VA: American Counseling Association.

Anderson, K. J. (1995). The use of a structured career development group to increase career identity: An exploratory study. *Journal of Career Development, 21,* 279–291.

Anderson, W. (1974). J. L. Moreno and the origins of psychodrama: A biographical sketch. In I. A. Greenberg (Ed.), *Psychodrama: Theory and therapy* (pp. 205–211). New York: Behavioral Publications.

Anderson, W. (1982). A training module for preparing group facilitators. *Journal for Specialists in Group Work, 7,* 119–124.

Andrews, H. B. (1995). *Group design and leadership: Strategies for creating successful common-theme groups.* Needham Heights, MA: Allyn & Bacon.

Andronico, M. P., & Horne, A. M. (2004). Counseling men in groups: The role of myths, therapeutic factors, leadership, and rituals. In J. L. DeLucia-Waack, D. A. Gerity, C. R. Kalodner, & M. T. Riva (Eds.), *Handbook of group counseling and psychotherapy* (pp. 456–468). Thousand Oaks, CA: Sage.

Ansbacher, H. L. (1977). Individual psychology. In R. J. Corsini (Ed.), *Current personality theories.* Itasca, IL: Peacock.

Ansbacher, H. L., & Ansbacher, R. R. (Eds.). (1956). *The individual psychology of Alfred Adler.* New York: Basic Books.

Aponte, H. J. (1994). How personal can training get? *Journal of Marital and Family Therapy, 20,* 3–15.

Appleton, V. E., & Dykeman, C. (1996). Using art in group counseling with Native American youth. *Journal for Specialists in Group Work, 21,* 224–231.

Appley, D. G., & Winder, A. E. (1973). *T-groups and therapy groups in a changing society.* San Francisco: Jossey-Bass.

Armstrong, S. A., & Berg, R. C. (2005). Demonstrating group process using *12 Angry Men. Journal for Specialists in Group Work, 30,* 135–140.

Arp, R. S., Holmberg, K. S., & Littrell, J. M. (1986). Launching adult students into the job market: A support group approach. *Journal of Counseling and Development, 65,* 166–167.

Asch, S. E. (1951). Effects of group pressure upon the modification and distortion of judgment. In H. Guetzkow (Ed.), *Groups, leadership, and men* (pp. 177–190). Pittsburgh: Carnegie.

Association for Specialists in Group Work. (1989). *Ethical guidelines for group counselors.* Alexandria, VA: Author.

Association for Specialists in Group Work. (1991). *Ethical guidelines for group counselors and professional standards for the training of group workers.* Alexandria, VA: Author.

Association for Specialists in Group Work. (1998). Best practice guidelines. *Journal for Specialists in Group Work, 23,* 237–244.

Association for Specialists in Group Work. (1999). Principles for diversity-competent group workers. *Journal for Specialists in Group Work, 24,* 7–14.

Association for Specialists in Group Work. (2000). Professional standards for the training of group workers. *Journal for Specialists in Group Work, 25,* 327–342.

Atkinson, D. R., Morten, G., & Sue, D. W. (Eds.). (1993). *Counseling American minorities: A cross cultural perspective* (4th ed.). Madison, WI: Brown & Benchmark.

Avrahami, E. (1995). Elements of relinquishment in psychodrama: Choice-relinquishing junctions in the psychodramatic process of the protagonist. *Journal of Group Psychotherapy, Psychodrama and Sociometry, 48,* 96–112.

Axelrod, S. (1977). *Behavior modification for the classroom teacher.* New York: McGraw-Hill.

Aylmer, R. C. (1988). The launching of the single young adult. In B. Carter & M. McGoldrick (Eds.), *The changing family life cycle* (2nd ed., pp. 191–208). New York: Gardner.

Azar, B. (1997, July). Teambuilding isn't enough: Workers need training, too. *APA Monitor, 28*(7), 14–15.

Baca, L. M., & Koss-Chioino, J. D. (1997). Development of a culturally responsive group counseling model for Mexican American adolescents. *Journal of Multicultural Counseling and Development, 25,* 130–141.

Bach, G. (1954). *Intensive group psychotherapy.* New York: Ronald.

Bach, G. R. (1967). Marathon group dynamics: Some functions of the professional group facilitator. *Psychological Reports, 20,* 995–999.

Backhaus, J., Hohagen, F., Voderholzer, U., & Riemann, D. (2001). Long-term effectiveness of a short-term cognitive-behavioral group treatment for primary insomnia. *European Archives of Psychiatry and Clinical Neuroscience, 251,* 35–41.

Baker, C. W., & Brownell, K. D. (1999). Binge eating disorder: Identification and management. *Nutrition in Clinical Care, 2,* 344–353.

Baker, S. (1996). Take care not to define developmental guidance too narrowly. *School Counselor, 43,* 243–244.

Baker, S. B., Thomas, R. N., & Munson, W. W. (1983). Effects of cognitive restructuring and structural group discussion as primary prevention strategies. *School Counselor, 31,* 26–33.

Bales, R. F. (1951). *Interaction process analysis.* Reading, MA: Addison-Wesley.

Bales, R. F. (1980). *SYMLOG: A case study kit.* New York: Free Press.

Bales, R. F., Cohen, S. P., & Williamson, S. A. (1979). *SYMLOG: A system for the multiple level observation of groups.* New York: Free Press.

Baltes, P. B., & Baltes, M. M. (Eds.). (1990). *Successful aging: Perspectives from the behavioral sciences.* New York: Cambridge University Press.

Baltimore, M. L. (1997). Multifamily group psychotherapy: Implementation and process. In S. T. Gladding (Ed.), *New developments in group counseling* (pp. 55–57). Greensboro, NC: ERIC.

Bandura, A. (1965). Behavioral modifications through modeling procedures. In L. Krasner & L. P. Ullman (Eds.), *Research in behavior modification.* New York: Holt, Rinehart & Winston.

Bandura, A. (1969). *Principles of behavior modification.* New York: Holt, Rinehart & Winston.

Bandura, A. (1977). *Social learning theory.* Upper Saddle River, NJ: Prentice Hall.

Bandura, A. (1986). *Social foundations of thought and action: A social cognitive theory.* Upper Saddle River, NJ: Prentice Hall.

Barker, R. A. (1997). How can we train leaders if we do not know what leadership is? *Human Relations, 50,* 343–362.

Barkhaus, R. S., Adair, M. K., Hoover, A. B., & Bolyard, C. W. (1985). *Threads* (3rd ed.). Dubuque, IA: Kendall/Hunt.

Barlow, S. H., Fuhrman, A. J., & Burlingame, G. M. (2004). The history of group counseling and psychotherapy. In J. L. DeLucia-Waack, D. A. Gerity, C. R. Kalodner, & M. T. Riva (Eds.), *Handbook of group counseling and psychotherapy* (pp. 3–22). Thousand Oaks, CA: Sage.

Barnes, G. (1977). Introduction. In G. Barnes (Ed.), *Transactional analysis after Eric Berne* (pp. 1–31). New York: Harper & Row.

BarNir, A. (1998). Can group- and issue-related factors predict choice shift? A meta-analysis of group decisions on life dilemmas. *Small Group Research, 29,* 308–338.

Baron, R. A. (1974). The aggression-inhibiting influence of nonhostile humor. *Journal of Experimental Social Psychology, 10,* 23–33.

Barr, N. I. (1974). The responsible world of reality therapy. *Psychology Today, 7,* 64–68.

Baruth, L. G., & Manning, M. L. (2007). *Multicultural counseling and psychotherapy: A lifetime perspective* (4th ed.). Upper Saddle River, NJ: Prentice Hall.

Bass, B. M. (1995). The meaning of leadership. In J. T. Wren (Ed.), *The leader's companion* (pp. 37–38). New York: Free Press.

Bata, E. J. (2006). Men, aging, and environmental trends. *The Advocate, 29*(1), 1, 10–11.

Bates, B., & Goodman, A. (1986). The effectiveness of encounter groups: Implications of research for counseling practice. *British Journal of Guidance and Counseling, 14,* 240–251.

Bates, M., Johnson, C. D., & Blaker, K. E. (1982). *Group leadership: A manual for group counseling leaders* (2nd ed.). Denver, CO: Love.

Bateson, G., & Ruesch, J. (1951). *Communication: The social matrix of psychiatry.* New York: Norton.

Bauman, S., & Waldo, M. (1998). Improving the goals and process (GAP) matrix for groups: Incorporating feedback from the field. *Journal for Specialists in Group Work, 23,* 215–224.

Beale, A. V., & Scott, P. C. (2001). "Bullybuster": Using drama to empower students to take a stand against bullying behavior. *Professional School Counseling, 4,* 300–305.

Beaver, M. L. (1983). *Human service practice with the elderly.* Upper Saddle River, NJ: Prentice Hall.

Bebout, J. (1978). Basic encounter groups: Their nature, method, and brief history. In H. Mullan & M. Rosenbaum (Eds.), *Group psychotherapy: Theory and practice* (2nd ed., pp. 305–329). New York: Free Press.

Beck, A. T. (1976). *Cognitive therapy and the emotional disorders.* New York: International Universities Press.

Beck, A. T., & Weishaar, M. E. (2005). Cognitive therapy. In R. J. Corsini & D. Wedding (Eds.), *Current psychotherapies* (7th ed., pp. 238–268). Itasca, IL: Peacock.

Becvar, D. S. (1982). The family is not a group—Or is it? *Journal for Specialists in Group Work, 7,* 88–95.

Bednar, R. L., & Kaul, T. J. (1985). Experiential group research: Results, questions, and suggestions. In S. L. Garfield & A. Bergin (Eds.), *Handbook for psychotherapy and behavior change* (3rd ed.). New York: Wiley.

Bednar, R. L., & Lawlis, G. F. (1971). Empirical research in group psychotherapy. In S. L. Garfield & A. Bergin (Eds.), *Handbook of psychotherapy and behavior change* (pp. 812–838). New York: Wiley.

Beitin, B. K., & Allen, K. R. (2005). Resilience in Arab American couples after September 11, 2001: A systems perspective. *Journal of Marital and Family Therapy, 31,* 251–267.

Belkin, G. S. (1988). *Introduction to counseling.* Dubuque, IA: Brown.

Bell, J. E. (1961). *Family group therapy.* Public Health Monograph No. 64. Washington, DC: U.S. Government Printing Office.

Bemak, F., & Chung, R. C-Y. (2004). Teaching multicultural group counseling: Perspectives for a new era. *Journal for Specialists in Group Work, 29,* 31–41.

Bemak, F., & Epp, L. R. (1996). The 12th curative factor: Love as an agent of healing in group psychotherapy. *Journal for Specialists in Group Work, 21,* 118–127.

Benjamin, A. (1981). *The helping interview* (3rd ed.). Boston: Houghton Mifflin.

Benne, K. D., & Sheats, P. (1948). Functional roles of group members. *Journal of Social Issues, 4,* 2.

Bennis, W. G., & Shepard, H. A. (1956). A theory of group development. *Human Relations, 9,* 415–437.

Berenson, B. G., Mitchell, K. M., & Laney, R. C. (1968). Therapeutic conditions after therapist-initiated confrontation. *Journal of Clinical Psychology, 24,* 363–364.

Berne, E. (1961). *Transactional analysis in psychotherapy.* New York: Grove.

Berne, E. (1964). *Games people play: The psychology of human relationships.* New York: Grove.

Berne, E. (1966). *Principles of group treatment.* New York: Grove.

Berne, E. (1972). *What do you say after you say hello?* New York: Grove.

Bernstein, B. E., & Hartsell, T. L., Jr. (2005). *The portable lawyer for mental health professionals: An A-Z guide to protecting your clients, your practice, and yourself* (2nd ed.). New York: Wiley.

Bersoff, D. N. (1996). The virtue of principle ethics. *The Counseling Psychologist, 24,* 86–91.

Bertalanffy, L. von (1968). *General systems theory: Foundations, development, application.* New York: Braziller.

Berube, E., & Berube, L. (1997). Creating small groups using school and community resources to meet student needs. *School Counselor, 44,* 294–302.

Berube, L. (1999). Dream work: Demystifying dreams using a small group for personal growth. *Journal for Specialists in Group Work, 24,* 88–101.

Bieschke, K. J., Gehlert, K. M., Wilson, D., Matthews, C. R., & Wade, J. (2003). Qualitative analysis of multicultural awareness in training groups. *Journal for Specialists in Group Work, 28,* 325–338.

Bigelow, G. S., & Thorne, J. W. (1969). Reality versus client-centered models in group counseling. *School Counselor, 16*(1), 91–94.

Bijou, S. W., Peterson, R. P., & Ault, M. H. (1968). A method to integrate descriptive and experimental field studies at the level of data and empirical concepts. *Journal of Applied Behavior Analysis, 1,* 175–191.

Bion, W. R. (1948). Experience in groups. *Human Relations, 1,* 314–329.

Bion, W. R. (1959). *Experiences in groups.* New York: Basic Books.

Bisio, T. A., & Crisan, P. (1984). Stress management and nuclear anxiety: A structured group experience. *Journal of Counseling and Development, 63,* 108–109.

Black, C. (1981). *It will never happen to me.* Denver, CO: M.A.C.

Blajan-Marcus, S. (1974). Psychodrama and its diverse uses. In I. A. Greenberg (Ed.), *Psychodrama: Theory and therapy* (pp. 47–55). New York: Behavioral Publications.

Blatner, A. (1988). *Acting in: Practical applications of psychodramatic methods* (2nd ed.). New York: Springer.

Blatner, A. (1996). *Acting in: Practical applications of psychodramatic methods* (3rd ed.). New York: Springer.

Blatner, A. (2000). *Foundations of psychodrama: History, theory, and practice* (4th ed.). New York: Springer.

Blatner, A. (2005). Psychodrama. In R. J. Corsini & D. Wedding (Eds.), *Current psychotherapies* (7th ed., pp. 405–438). Belmont, CA: Thompson.

Bleck, R. T., & Bleck, B. L. (1982). The disruptive child's play group. *Elementary School Guidance & Counseling, 17,* 137–141.

Blocher, D. H. (1987). On the uses and misuses of the term theory. *Journal of Counseling and Development, 66,* 67–68.

Blum, D. J., & Jones, L. A. (1993). Academic growth group and mentoring program for potential dropouts. *School Counselor, 40,* 207–217.

Bly, R. (1990). *Iron John: A book about men.* Reading, MA: Addison-Wesley.

Bond, K. (1993). Classroom guidance: The get along gang. *Elementary School Guidance & Counseling, 27,* 303–304.

Bonner, H. (1959). *Group dynamics.* New York: Ronald.

Bordone, R. C. (2000). Teaching interpersonal skills for negotiating and for life. *Negotiation Journal, 16,* 377–385.

Borgers, S. B., & Koenig, R. W. (1983). Uses and effects of modeling by the therapist in group therapy. *Journal for Specialists in Group Work, 8,* 133–138.

Bormann, E. G. (1975). *Discussion and group methods: Theory and practice* (2nd ed.). Glenview, IL: Addison Wesley Longman.

Boutwell, D. A., & Myrick, R. D. (1992). The go for it club. *Elementary School Guidance & Counseling, 27,* 65–72.

Bowman, R. L., & Bowman, V. E. (1998). Life on the electronic frontier: The application of technology to group work. *Journal for Specialists in Group Work, 23,* 428–445.

Bowman, R. P. (1987). Small-group guidance and counseling in schools: A national survey of school counselors. *School Counselor, 34,* 256–262.

Bowman, V. E., & Boone, R. K. (1998). Enhancing the experience of community: Creativity in group work. *Journal for Specialists in Group Work, 23,* 388–410.

Boy, A. V., & Pine, G. J. (1982). *Client-centered counseling: A renewal.* Boston: Allyn & Bacon.

Boy, A. V., & Pine, G. J. (1999). *A person-centered foundation for counseling and psychotherapy* (2nd ed.). Springfield, IL: Thomas.

Bozarth, J. D. (1981). The person-centered approach in the large community group. In G. Gazda (Ed.), *Innovations to group psychotherapy* (2nd ed.). Springfield, IL: Thomas.

Braaten, L. J. (1989). The effects of person-centered group therapy. *Person-Centered Review, 4,* 183–209.

Braaten, L. J. (1990). The different patterns of group critical incidents in high and low cohesion sessions of group psychotherapy. *International Journal of Group Psychotherapy, 40,* 477–493.

Brabender, V. (1985). Time-limited inpatient group therapy: A developmental model. *International Journal of Group Psychotherapy, 3,* 373–390.

Brammer, L. M., Abrego, P. J., & Shostrom, E. L. (1993). *Therapeutic psychology.* Upper Saddle River, NJ: Prentice Hall.

Brammer, L. M., & MacDonald, G. (2003). *The helping relationship* (8th ed.). Boston: Allyn & Bacon.

Brandler, S. M. (1985). The senior center: Informality in the social work function. In G. S. Getzel & M. J. Mellor (Eds.), *Gerontological social work practice in the community* (pp. 195–210). New York: Haworth.

Brandstatter, H., & Farthofer, A. (1997). Personality in social influence across tasks and groups. *Small Group Research, 28,* 146–163.

Brantley, L. S., Brantley, P. S., & Baer-Barkley, K. (1996). Transforming acting-out behavior: A group counseling program for inner-city elementary school pupils. *Elementary School Guidance & Counseling, 31,* 96–105.

Brenner, V. (1999). Process-play: A simulation procedure for group work training. *Journal for Specialists in Group Work, 24,* 145–151.

Brewer, J. M. (1942). *History of vocational guidance.* New York: Harper.

Bridbord, K., DeLucia-Waack, J. L., Jones, E., & Gerrity, D. A. (2004). The nonsignificant impact on an agenda setting treatment for groups: Implications for future research and practice. *Journal for Specialists in Group Work, 29,* 301–315.

Brinson, J. A., & Lee, C. C. (1997). Culturally responsive group leadership: An integrative model for experienced practitioners. In H. Forester-Miller & J. A. Kottler (Eds.), *Issues and challenges for group practitioners* (pp. 43–56). Denver, CO: Love.

Brough, M. F. (1994). Alleviation of loneliness: Evaluation of an Adlerian-based group therapy program. *Individual Psychology, 50,* 40–51.

Brown, B. M. (1996, Fall). A time for unity. *Together, 25*(1), 1, 6.

Brown, B. M. (1997, March). Psychoeducation group work. *Counseling and Human Development, 29,* 1–16.

Brown, S., & Beletsis, S. (1986). The development of family transference in groups for adult children of alcoholics. *International Journal of Group Psychotherapy, 36,* 97–114.

Brown, S. P., Lipford-Sanders, J., & Shaw, M. (1995). *Kujchagulia—Uncovering the secrets of the heart: Group work with African American women on predominantly white campuses. Journal for Specialists in Group Work, 20,* 151–158.

Brown, S. P., Parham, T. A., & Yonker, R. (1996). Influence of a cross-cultural training course on racial identity attitudes of white women and men: Preliminary perspective. *Journal of Counseling & Development, 74,* 510–516.

Browne, F. R. (2005). Self-talk of group counselors: The research of Rex Stockton. *Journal for Specialists in Group Work, 30,* 289–297.

Browne-Miller, A. (1993). *Gestalting addiction: The addiction-focused group therapy of Dr. Richard Louis Miller.* Stanford, CT: Ablex.

Brown-Shaw, M., Westwood, M., & DeVries, B. (1999). Integrating personal reflection and group-based enactments. *Journal of Aging Studies, 13,* 109–119.

Buban, M. E., McConnell, S. C., & Duncan, B. L. (1988). Children's fears of nuclear war: Group intervention strategies. *Journal for Specialists in Group Work, 13,* 124–129.

Burlew, L. D., Jones, J., & Emerson, P. (1991). Exercise and the elderly: A group counseling approach. *Journal for Specialists in Group Work, 16,* 152–158.

Burlingame, G. M., Fuhriman, A., & Johnson, J. (2004). Process and outcome in group counseling and psychotherapy. In J. L. DeLucia-Waack, D. A. Gerity, C. R. Kalodner, & M. T. Riva (Eds.), *Handbook of group counseling and psychotherapy* (pp. 49–61). Thousand Oaks, CA: Sage.

Burlingame, G. M., Fuhriman, A., & Mosier, J. (2003). The differential effectiveness of group psychotherapy: A meta-analytic perspective. *Group Dynamics: Theory, Research, and Practice, 7,* 3–12.

Burns, J. M. (1978). *Leadership.* New York: Harper.

Burnside, I. M. (1978). Responsibilities of the preceptor. In I. M. Burnside (Ed.), *Working with the elderly: Group processes and techniques* (pp. 88–100). North Scituate, MA: Duxbury.

Burnside, I. M. (1986). *Working with the elderly: Group processes and techniques* (2nd ed.). Monterey, CA: Wadsworth.

Burnside, I. M. (1993). Themes in reminiscence groups with older women. *International Journal of Aging and Human Development, 37,* 177–189.

Burrow, T. (1927). *The social basis of consciousness.* New York: Harcourt, Brace & World.

Burrow, T. (1928). The basis of group-analysis or the analysis of the reactions of normal and neurotic individuals. *British Journal of Medical Psychology, 8,* 196–206.

Butler, L. (1987). Anatomy of collusive behavior. *NTL Connections, 4,* 1–2.

Butler, R. N. (1975). *Why survive? Being old in America.* New York: Harper & Row.

Cain, D. J. (1993). The uncertain future of client-centered counseling. *Journal of Humanistic Education and Development, 31,* 133–138.

Campbell, C. A. (1991). Group guidance for academically undermotivated children. *Elementary School Guidance & Counseling, 25,* 302–307.

Campbell, C. A. (1993). Play, the fabric of elementary school counseling programs. *Elementary School Guidance & Counseling, 28,* 10–16.

Campbell, C., & Bowman, R. P. (1993). The "fresh start" support club: Small group counseling for academically retained children. *Elementary School Guidance & Counseling, 27,* 172–185.

Campbell, C. A., & Brigman, G (2005). Closing the achievement gap: A structured approach to group counseling. *Journal for Specialists in Group Work, 30,* 67–82.

Campbell, R. E., & Cellini, J. V. (1980). Adult career development. *Counseling and Human Development, 12,* 1–8.

Capers, H. (1975). Winning and losing. *Transactional Analysis Journal, 5,* 257–258.

Cappetta, L. K. (1996). The effectiveness of small group counseling for children of divorce. *School Counselor, 43,* 317–310.

Capuzzi, D., & Gross, D. (1980). Group work with the elderly: An overview for counselors. *Personnel and Guidance Journal, 59,* 206–211.

Capuzzi, D., & Gross, D. R. (2006). Group counseling: Elements of effective leadership. In D. Capuzzi, D. R. Gross, & M. D. Stauffer (Eds.), *Introduction to group counseling* (pp. 57–88). Denver, CO: Love.

Carkhuff, R. (1971). *Helping and human relations* (Vols. 1 & 2). New York: Holt, Rinehart & Winston.

Carroll, M., Bates, M., & Johnson, C. (2004). *Group leadership* (4th ed.). Denver, CO: Love.

Carroll, M. R. (1981). End the plague on the house of guidance—Make counseling part of the curriculum. *NASSP Bulletin, 65,* 17–22.

Carroll, M. R. (1986). *Group work: Leading in the here and now* [Film]. Alexandria, VA: American Counseling Association.

Carroll, M. R., & Levo, L. (1985). The association for specialists in group work. *Journal of Counseling and Development, 63,* 453–454.

Carroll, M. R., & Wiggins, J. D. (1997). *Elements of group counseling* (2nd ed.). Denver, CO: Love.

Carter, E. F., Mitchell, S. L., & Krautheim, M. D. (2001). Understanding and addressing clients' resistance to group counseling. *Journal for Specialists in Group Work, 26,* 66–80.

Carter, R. T. (1991). Cultural values: A review of empirical research and implications for counseling. *Journal of Counseling & Development, 70,* 164–173.

Carter, R. T., & Akinsulure-Smith, A. M. (1996). White racial identity and expectations about counseling. *Journal of Multicultural Counseling and Development, 24,* 218–228.

Carty, L. (1983). Shalom: A developmental group model for young adults. *Journal for Specialists in Group Work, 8,* 205–210.

Castore, G. (1962). Number of verbal interrelationships as a determinant of group size. *Journal of Abnormal and Social Psychology, 64,* 456–457.

Chau, K. L. (1992). Needs assessment for group work with people of color: A conceptual formulation. *Social Work with Groups, 15,* 53–66.

Chauvin, J. C., & Remley, T. P., Jr. (1996). Responding to allegations of unethical conduct. *Journal of Counseling and Development, 74,* 563–568.

Chen, M., & Han, Y. S. (2001). Cross-cultural group counseling with Asians: A stage-specific interactive approach. *Journal for Specialists in Group Work, 26,* 111–128.

Chen, M., Noosbond, J. P., & Bruce, M. A. (1998). Therapeutic document in group counseling: An active change agent. *Journal of Counseling and Development, 76,* 404–411.

Chen, Z., Lawson, R. B., Gordon, L. R., & McIntosh, B. (1996). Group-think: Deciding with the leader and the devil. *Psychological Record, 46,* 581–590.

Cheng, W. D. (1995, Fall). Pacific perspective. *Together, 24*(1), 8.

Cheng, W. D. (1996, Winter). Pacific perspective. *Together, 24*(2), 10.

Cheng, W. D., Chae, M., & Gunn, R. W. (1998). Splitting and projection identification in multicultural group counseling. *Journal for Specialists in Group Work, 23,* 372–387.

Childers, J. H., Jr. (1986). Group leadership training and supervision: A graduate course. *Journal for Specialists in Group Work, 11,* 48–52.

Childers, J. H., Jr., & Burcky, W. D. (1984). The jogging group: A positive-wellness strategy. *AMHCA Journal, 6,* 118–125.

Childers, J. H., Jr., & Couch, R. D. (1989). Myths about group counseling: Identifying and challenging misconceptions. *Journal for Specialists in Group Work, 14,* 105–111.

Chiu, T. L. (1997). Problems caused for mental health professionals worldwide by increasing multicultural populations and proposed solutions. *Journal of Multicultural Counseling and Development, 24,* 129–140.

Choate, L. H., & Henson, A. (2003). Group work with adult survivors of childhood abuse and neglect: A psychoeducational approach. *Journal for Specialists in Group Work, 28,* 106–121.

Chong, W. H. (2005). The role of self-regulation and personal agency beliefs: A psychoeducational approach with Asian high school students in Singapore. *Journal for Specialists in Group Work, 30,* 343–361.

Christensen, O. C., & Marchant, W. C. (1983). The family counseling process. In O. C. Christensen & T. G. Schramski (Eds.), *Adlerian family counseling* (pp. 29–55). Minneapolis, MN: Educational Media.

Christensen, T. M., & Kline, W. B. (2000). A qualitative investigation of the process of group supervision with group counselors. *Journal for Specialists in Group Work, 25,* 376–393.

Christensen, T. M., & Kline, W. B. (2001). The qualitative exploration of process-sensitive peer group supervision. *Journal for Specialists in Group Work, 26,* 81–99.

Christensen, T. M., Hulse-Killacky, D., Sagado, Jr., R. A., Thornton, M. D., & Miller, J. L. (2006). Facilitating reminiscence groups: Perceptions of group leaders. *Journal for Specialists in Group Work, 31,* 73–88.

Chung, R. C.-Y. (2004). Group counseling with Asian. In J. L. DeLucia-Waack, D. A. Gerity, C. R. Kalodner, & M. T. Riva (Eds.), *Handbook of group counseling and psychotherapy* (pp. 200–212). Thousand Oaks, CA: Sage.

Chung, R. C.-Y., Bemak, F., & Okazaki, S. (1997). Counseling Americans of Southeast Asian descent. In C. C. Lee (Ed.), *Multicultural issues in counseling* (2nd ed., pp. 207–231). Alexandria, VA: American Counseling Association.

Claiborn, C. D. (1987). Science and practice: Reconsidering the Pepinskys. *Journal of Counseling and Development, 65,* 286–288.

Claiborn, C. D., Goodyear, R. K., & Horner, P. A. (2001). Feedback. *Psychotherapy, 38,* 401–405.

Clark, A. J. (1992). Defense mechanisms in group counseling. *Journal for Specialists in Group Work, 17,* 151–160.

Clark, A. J. (1993). Interpretation in group counseling: Theoretical and operational issues. *Journal for Specialists in Group Work, 18,* 174–181.

Clark, A. J. (1995). Modification: A leader skill in group work. *Journal for Specialists in Group Work, 20,* 14–17.

Clark, A. J. (1997). Projective identification as a defense mechanism in group counseling and therapy. *Journal for Specialists in Group Work, 22,* 85–96.

Clark, A. J., & Seals, J. M. (1984). Groups counseling for ridiculed children. *Journal for Specialists in Group Work, 9,* 157–162.

Clark, J., Blanchard, M., & Hawes, C. W. (1992). Group counseling for people with addictions. In D. Capuzzi & D. R. Gross (Eds.), *Introduction to group counseling* (pp. 103–119). Denver, CO: Love.

Claypoole, S. D., Moody, E. E., Jr., & Peace, S. D. (2000). Moral dilemma discussions: An effective group intervention for juvenile offenders. *Journal for Specialists in Group Work, 25,* 394–411.

Cobia, D. C., & Henderson, D. A. (2007). *Developing an effective and accountable school counseling program* (2nd ed.). Upper Saddle River, NJ: Prentice Hall.

Coche, E. (1984). Group psychotherapy for group therapists. In F. Kaslow (Ed.), *Psychotherapy with psychotherapists.* New York: Haworth.

Coe, D. M., & Zimpfer, D. G. (1996). Infusing solution-oriented theory and techniques into group work. *Journal for Specialists in Group Work, 21,* 49–57.

Coffman, S. G., & Roark, A. E. (1988). Likely candidates for group counseling: Adolescents with divorced parents. *School Counselor, 35,* 246–252.

Cohen, A. M., & Smith, R. D. (1976). *Critical incidents in growth groups: Theory and techniques.* La Jolla, CA: University Associates.

Cohen, R. J., & Mariano, W. E. (1982). *Legal guidebook in mental health.* New York: Free Press.

Colmani, S. A., & Merta, R. J. (1999). Using the sweat lodge ceremony as group therapy for Navajo youth. *Journal for Specialists in Group Work, 24,* 55–73.

Comiskey, P. E. (1993). Using reality therapy group training with at-risk high school freshmen. *Journal of Reality Therapy, 12,* 59–64.

Comstock, D. L., Duffey, T., & St. George, H. (2002). The relational-cultural model: A framework for group process. *Journal for Specialists in Group Work, 27,* 254–272.

Connors, J. V., & Caple, R. B. (2005). A review of group systems theory. *Journal for Specialists in Group Work, 30,* 93–110.

Conyne, R. K. (1983). The social ecology of group work. *Journal for Specialists in Group Work, 8,* 2.

Conyne, R. K. (1996). The Association for Specialists in Group Work Training Standards: Some considerations and suggestions for training. *Journal for Specialists in Group Work, 21,* 155–162.

Conyne, R. K. (1998). Personal experience and meaning in group work leadership: The views of the experts. *Journal for Specialists in Group Work, 23,* 245–256.

Conyne, R. K. (2003). Group work issues: Past, present, future. *Journal for Specialists in Group Work, 28,* 291–298.

Conyne, R. K., & Bemak, F. (2004). Teaching group work from ecological perspective. *Journal for Specialists in Group Work, 29,* 7–18.

Conyne, R. K., & Silver, R. (1980). Direct, vicarious, and vicarious process experiences. *Small Group Behavior, 11,* 419–429.

Conyne, R. K., & Wilson, F. R. (1998). Toward a standards based classification of group work offerings. *Journal for Specialists in Group Work, 23,* 177–184.

Conyne, R. K., Wilson, F. R., & Tang, M. (2000). Evolving lessons from group work involvement in China. *Journal for Specialists in Group Work, 25,* 252–268.

Conyne, R. K., Wilson, F. R., & Ward, D. E. (1997). *Comprehensive group work.* Alexandria, VA: American Counseling Association.

Coppock, M. W. (1993). Small group plan for improving friendships and self-esteem. *Elementary School Guidance & Counseling, 28,* 152–154.

Corazzini, J. G., Williams, K., & Harris, S. (1987). Group therapy for adult children of alcoholics: Case studies. *Journal for Specialists in Group Work, 12,* 156–161.

Corey, G. (2004). *The theory and practice of group counseling* (6th ed.). Pacific Grove, CA: Brooks/Cole.

Corey, M. S., & Corey, G. (2006). *Groups: Process and practice* (7th ed.). Pacific Grove, CA: Brooks/Cole.

Corey, G., Corey, M. S., & Callanan, P. (2007). *Issues and ethics in the helping professions* (7th ed.). Pacific Grove, CA: Brooks/Cole.

Corey, G., Corey, M. S., Callanan, P. J., & Russell, J. M. (2003). *Group techniques* (3rd ed.). Pacific Grove, CA: Brooks/Cole.

Corey, G., Corey, M. S., & Haynes, R. (1999). *Ethics in action: Student video and workbook.* Pacific Grove, CA: Brooks/Cole.

Corey, G., & Herlihy, B. (Eds.). (2006). *ACA ethical standards casebook* (5th ed.). Alexandria, VA: American Counseling Association.

Cormier, L. S., & Cormier, W. H. (1998). *Interviewing strategies for helpers* (4th ed.). Pacific Grove, CA: Brooks/Cole.

Cormier, L. S., & Hackney, H. (2005). *The professional counselor: A process guide to helping* (5th ed.). Boston: Allyn & Bacon.

Cornish, P. A., & Benton, D. (2001). Getting started in healthier relationships: Brief integrated dynamic group counseling in a university counseling setting. *Journal for Specialists in Group Work, 26,* 129–143.

Corsini, R. J. (1957). *Methods of group psychotherapy.* Chicago: James.

Corsini, R. J. (1966). *Roleplaying in psychotherapy.* New York: Free Press.

Corsini, R. J. (1988). Adlerian groups. In S. Long (Ed.), *Six group therapies* (pp. 1–43). New York: Plenum.

Cottone, R. R., & Tarvydas, V. M. (2007). *Ethical and professional issues in counseling* (3rd ed.). Upper Saddle River, NJ: Prentice Hall.

Couch, R. D. (1995). Four steps for conducting a pregroup screening interview. *Journal for Specialists in Group Work, 20,* 18–26.

Couch, R. D., & Childers, J. H., Jr. (1987). Leadership strategies for instilling and maintaining hope in group counseling. *Journal for Specialists in Group Work, 12,* 138–143.

Coulson, W. R. (1972). *Groups, gimmicks and instant gurus.* New York: Harper & Row.

Coulson, W. R. (1974). *A sense of community.* Columbus, OH: Merrill/Prentice Hall.

Courtois, C. A. (1988). *Healing the incest wound.* New York: Norton.

Courtois, C. A., & Leehan, J. (1982). Group treatment for grown-up abused children. *Personnel and Guidance Journal, 60,* 564–566.

Coven, A. B. (2004). Gestalt group dreamwork demonstrations in Taiwan. *Journal for Specialists in Group Work, 29,* 175–184.

Coven, A. B., Ellington, D. B., & Van Hull, K. G. (1997). The use of Gestalt psychodrama in group counseling. In S. T. Gladding (Ed.), *New developments in group counseling* (pp. 17–18). Greensboro, NC: ERIC.

Cowan, D., & Brunero, S. (1997). Group therapy for anxiety disorders using rational emotive behaviour therapy. *Australian and New Zealand Journal of Mental Health Nursing, 6,* 164–168.

Cowie, H., & Rivers, I. (2000). Going against the grain: Supporting lesbian, gay and bisexual clients as they "come out." *British Journal of Guidance & Counseling, 28,* 503–513.

Cowley, G. (1997, June 30). How to live to 100. *Newsweek,* 56–67.

Cox, H. G. (2006). *Later life: The realities of aging* (6th ed.). Upper Saddle River, NJ: Prentice Hall.

Cox, J. R. (1999). *A guide to peer counseling.* New York: Jason Aronson.

Crawford, R. L. (1994). *Avoiding counselor malpractice.* Alexandria, VA: American Counseling Association.

Croake, J. W. (1983). Adlerian parent education. *Counseling Psychologist, 11,* 65–71.

Cross, W. (2005). On research considerations. *International Journal of Group Psychotherapy, 55,* 455–463.

Cummings, A. L. (2001). Teaching group process to counseling students through the exchange of journal letters. *Journal for Specialists in Group Work, 26,* 7–16.

Cummings, A. L. Hoffman, S., & Leschied, A. W. (2004). A pscyhoeducational group for aggressive adolescent girls. *Journal for Specialists in Group Work, 29,* 285–299.

Cummins, P. N. (1996). Preparing clients with eating disorders for group counseling: A multimedia approach. *Journal for Specialists in Group Work, 21,* 4–10.

Cunningham, L. M. (1995). Control theory, reality therapy, and cultural bias. *Journal of Reality Therapy, 15,* 15–22.

Curman, M., & Curman, B. (1994). The Gestalt couples group. In G. Wheeler & S. Backman (Eds.), *On intimate ground: A Gestalt approach to working with couples* (pp. 229–242). San Francisco: Jossey-Bass.

D'Amato, R. C., & Dean, R. S. (1988). Psychodrama research—therapy and theory: A critical analysis of an arrested modality. *Psychology in the Schools, 25,* 305–314.

Daniels, J., D'Andrea, M., Omizo, M., & Pier, P. (1999). Group work with homeless youngsters and their mothers. *Journal for Specialists in Group Work, 24,* 164–185.

Dannison, L., & Nieuwenhuis, A. (Eds.). (1996). *Second time around—Grandparents raising grandchildren.* Kalamazoo: Western Michigan University.

Dansby, V. S. (1996). Group work within the school system: Survey of implementation and leadership role issues. *Journal for Specialists in Group Work, 21,* 232–242.

Davenport, D. S. (2004). Ethical issues in the teaching of group counseling. *Journal for Specialists in Group Work, 29,* 43–49.

Davies, D., & Kuypers, B. (1985). Group development and interpersonal feedback. *Group and Organizational Studies, 10,* 184–208.

Day, B., & Matthes, W. (1992). A comparison of Jungian, person-centered, and Gestalt approaches to personal growth groups. *Journal for Specialists in Group Work, 17,* 105–115.

DeAngelis, T. (1992, November). Best psychological treatment for many men: Group therapy. *APA Monitor, 23,* 31.

DeAngelis, T. (1997, March). Do online support groups help for eating disorders? *APA Monitor, 28*(3), 43.

Deck, M. D., & Saddler, D. L. (1983). Freshmen awareness groups: A viable option for high school counselors. *School Counselor, 30,* 392–397.

Delbecq, A. L., & Van de Ven, A. H. (1971). A group process model for problem identification and program planning. *Journal of Applied Behavioral Science, 7,* 466–492.

Delbecq, A. L., Van de Ven, A. H., & Gustafson, D. H. (1975). *Group techniques for program planning.* Glenview, IL: Scott, Foresman.

DeLucia-Waack, J. L. (1996a). Multicultural group counseling: Addressing diversity to facilitate universality and self-understanding. In J. L. DeLucia-Waack (Ed.), *Multicultural counseling competencies: Implications for training and practice* (pp. 157–195). Alexandria, VA: American Counseling Association.

DeLucia-Waack, J. L. (1996b). Multiculturalism is inherent in all group work. *Journal for Specialists in Group Work, 21,* 218–223.

DeLucia-Waack, J. L. (1997a). Measuring the effectiveness of group work: A review and analysis of process and outcome measures. *Journal for Specialists in Group Work, 22,* 277–293.

DeLucia-Waack, J. L. (1997b). The importance of processing activities, exercises, and events to group work practitioners. *Journal for Specialists in Group Work, 22,* 82–84.

DeLucia-Waack, J. L. (1998). What is the relationship between therapeutic factors and group work effectiveness really? *Journal for Specialists in Group Work, 23,* 235–236.

DeLucia-Waack, J. L. (1999a, August). *Group psychotherapy and outcome measures.* Paper presented at the annual convention of the American Psychological Association, Boston.

DeLucia-Waack, J. L. (1999b). Supervision for counselors working with eating disorders groups: Countertransference issues related to body image, food, and weight. *Journal of Counseling & Development, 17,* 379–388.

DeLucia-Waack, J. L. (1999c). What makes an effective group leader? *Journal for Specialists in Group Work, 24,* 131–132.

DeLucia-Waack, J. (2000a). Effective group work in the schools. *Journal for Specialists in Group Work, 25,* 131–132.

DeLucia-Waack, J. L. (2000b). International group work. *Journal for Specialists in Group Work, 25,* 227–228.

DeLucia-Waack, J. L. (2000c). The field of group work: Past, present, and future. *Journal for Specialists in Group Work, 25,* 323–326.

DeLucia-Waack, J. L. (2001a). Mentoring future group workers. *Journal for Specialists in Group Work, 26,* 107–110.

DeLucia-Waack, J. L. (2001b). *Using music in children of divorce groups: A session-by-session manual for counselors.* Alexandria, VA: American Counseling Association.

DeLucia-Waack, J. L. (2002). A written guide for planning and processing group sessions in anticipation of supervision. *Journal for Specialists in Group Work, 27,* 341–357.

DeLucia-Waack, J. L. (2004). Multicultural groups. In J. L. DeLucia-Waack, D. A. Gerity, C. R. Kalodner, & M. T. Riva (Eds.), *Handbook of group counseling and psychotherapy* (pp. 167–168). Thousand Oaks, CA: Sage.

DeLucia-Waack, J. L., & Birdbord, K. H. (2004). Measures of group process, dynamics, climate, leadership behaviors, and therapeutic factors. In J. L. DeLucia-Waack, D. A. Gerity, C. R. Kalodner, & M. T. Riva (Eds.), *Handbook of group counseling and psychotherapy* (pp. 120–135). Thousand Oaks, CA: Sage.

DeLucia-Waack, J. L., & Donigian, J. (2004). *The practice of multicultural group work.* Belmont, CA: Thompson.

DeLucia-Waack, J. L., & Fauth, J. (2004). Effective supervision of group leaders. In J. L. DeLucia-Waack, D. A. Gerity, C. R. Kalodner, & M. T. Riva (Eds.), *Handbook of group counseling and psychotherapy* (pp. 136–150). Thousand Oaks, CA: Sage.

DeLucia-Waack, J. L., & Gerrity, D. (2001). Effective group work for elementary school-age children whose parents are divorcing. *The Family Journal: Counseling and Therapy for Couples and Families, 9,* 273–284.

DeLucia, J. L., Coleman, V. D., & Jensen-Scott, R. L. (1992). Cultural diversity in group counseling. *Journal for Specialists in Group Work, 17,* 194–195.

Denholm, C. J., & Uhlemann, M. R. (1986). Organizing the child, preadolescent, and adolescent group literature: A pragmatic teaching tool. *Journal for Specialists in Group Work, 11,* 163–173.

Dennis, H. (1978). Remotivation therapy groups. In I. M. Burnside (Ed.), *Working with the elderly: Group processes and techniques* (pp. 219–235). North Scituate, MA: Duxbury.

Dennis-Small, L. (1986). *Life skills for adolescents.* Ann Arbor, MI: ERIC/CAPS (ED 278883).

DeRoma, V. M., Root, L. P., & Battle, J. V. (2003). Pretraining in group process skills: Impact on anger and anxiety in combat veterans. *Journal for Specialists in Group Work, 28,* 339–354.

deShazer, S. (1985). *Keys to solution in brief therapy.* New York: Norton.

deShazer, S. (1988). *Clues: Investigating solutions in brief therapy.* New York: Norton.

Deurzen-Smith, E. van. (1997). *Everyday mysteries: Existential dimensions of psychotherapy.* London: Routledge.

DeVries, B., Birren, J. E., & Deutchman, D. E. (1995). Methods and uses of the guided autobiography. In B. K. Haight & J. D. Webster (Eds.), *The art and science of reminiscing* (pp. 165–177). Philadelphia: Taylor & Francis.

Dies, R. R. (1983). Clinical implications of research on leadership in short-term group psychotherapy. In R. R. Dies & K. R. MacKenzie (Eds.), *Advances in group psychotherapy: Integrating research and practice* (pp. 27–78). New York: International Universities Press.

DiGiulio, J. F. (1992). Early widowhood: An atypical transition. *Journal of Mental Health Counseling, 14,* 97–109.

Diller, J. V. (2007). *Cultural diversity: A primer for the human services* (3rd ed.). Belmont, CA: Thompson.

Dinkmeyer, D. C. (1973). The parent "C" group. *Personnel and Guidance Journal, 52,* 252–256.

Dinkmeyer, D., & Dinkmeyer, D., Jr. (1982). *Developing understanding of self and others, D-2* (rev. ed.). Circle Pines, MN: American Guidance Service.

Dinkmeyer, D., & Muro, J. J. (1979). *Group counseling: Theory and practice* (2nd ed.). Itasca, IL: Peacock.

Dinkmeyer, D., Jr., & Sperry, L. (2000). *Adlerian counseling and psychotherapy* (3rd ed.). Upper Saddle River, NJ: Merrill/Prentice Hall.

Dobson, J. E., & Dobson, R. L. (1991). Changing roles: An aging parents support group. *Journal for Specialists in Group Work, 16,* 178–184.

Donigian, J. (1993). Duality: The issue that won't go away. *Journal for Specialists in Group Work, 18,* 137–140.

Donigian, J., & Hulse-Killacky, D. (1999). *Critical incidents in group therapy* (2nd ed.). Pacific Grove, CA: Brooks/Cole.

Donigian, J., & Malnati, R. (1997). *Systemic group therapy.* Pacific Grove, CA: Brooks/Cole.

Dorland, J. M., & Fischer, A. R. (2001). Gay, lesbian, and bisexual individuals' perceptions: An analogue study. *Counseling Psychologist, 29,* 532–547.

Dossick, J., & Shea, E. (1988). *Creative therapy: 52 exercises for groups.* Sarasota, FL: Professional Resource Exchange.

Dossick, J., & Shea, E. (1990). *Creative therapy II: 52 more exercises for groups.* Sarasota, FL: Professional Resource Exchange.

Downing, T. K. E., Smaby, M. H., & Maddux, C. D. (2001). A study of the transfer of group counseling skills from training to practice. *Journal for Specialists in Group Work, 26,* 158–167.

Draper, K., Ritter, K. B., & Willingham, E. U. (2003). Sand tray group counseling with adolescents. *Journal for Specialists in Group Work, 28,* 244–260.

Dreikurs, R. (1950). *Fundamentals of Adlerian psychology.* New York: Greenberg.

Dreikurs, R. (1968). *Psychology in the classroom* (2nd ed.). New York: Harper & Row.

Dreikurs, R. (1969). Group psychotherapy from the point of view of Adlerian psychology. In H. M. Ruitenbeek (Ed.), *Group therapy today: Styles, methods, and techniques.* New York: Adline-Atherton.

Dreikurs, R., & Corsini, R. J. (1954). Twenty years of group psychotherapy. *American Journal of Psychiatry, 110,* 567–575.

Dreikurs, R., Corsini, R., Lowe, R., & Sonstegard, M. (Eds.). (1959). *Adlerian family counseling.* Eugene: University of Oregon Press.

Dreikurs, R., & Soltz, V. (1964). *Children: The challenge.* New York: Duell, Sloan, & Pearce.

Driver, H. I. (1958). *Counseling and learning through small-group discussion.* Madison, WI: Monona.

Drum, D. J., & Knott, J. E. (1977). *Structured groups for facilitating development: Acquiring life skills, resolving life themes, and making life transitions.* New York: Human Science Press.

Dryden, W. (1989). Albert Ellis: An efficient and passionate life. *Journal of Counseling and Development, 67,* 539–546.

Dryden, W. (1994). Reason and emotion in psychotherapy: Thirty years on. *Journal of Rational Emotive and Cognitive Behavior Therapy, 12,* 83–99.

Dryden, W. (1999). *Rational emotive behavior therapy: A training model.* New York: Springer.

Dryfoos, J. G. (1990). *Adolescents at risk: Prevalence and prevention.* New York: Oxford University Press.

Dryfoos, J. G. (1993). Schools as places for health, mental health, and special services. In R. Takanshi (Ed.), *Adolescence in the 1990s.* New York: Teachers College Press.

Dufrene, P. M., & Coleman, V. D. (1992). Counseling Native Americans: Guidelines for group process. *Journal for Specialists in Group Work, 17,* 229–234.

Dugan, J. R., & Everett, R. S. (1998). An experimental test of chemical dependency for jail inmates. *International Journal of Offender Therapy and Comparative Criminology, 42,* 360–368.

Duncan, D. M., & Brown, B. M. (1996). Anxiety and development of conceptual complexity in group counselors-in-training. *Journal for Specialists in Group Work, 21,* 252–262.

Dunphy, D. (1968). Phases, roles, and myths in self-analytic groups. *Journal of Applied Behavioral Science, 4,* 195–225.

Durbin, D. M. (1982). Multimodal group sessions to enhance self-concept. *Elementary School Guidance & Counseling, 16,* 288–295.

Durkin, H. E. (1964). *The group in depth.* New York: International Universities Press.

Durkin, H. E. (1975). The development of systems theory and its implications for the theory and practice of group therapy. In L. R. Wolberg & M. L. Aronson (Eds.), *Group therapy: 1975—An overview* (pp. 8–20). New York: Stratton.

Durkin, J. E. (1981). *Living groups: Group psychotherapy and general systems theory.* New York: Brunner/Mazel.

Dusay, J. M. (1983). Transactional analysis in groups. In H. I. Kaplan & B. J. Sadock (Eds.), *Comprehensive group psychotherapy* (2nd ed.). Baltimore: Williams & Wilkins.

Dusay, J. M., & Dusay, K. M. (1989). Transactional analysis. In R. Corsini & D. Wedding (Eds.), *Current psychotherapies* (4th ed., pp. 404–453). Itasca, IL: Peacock.

Dusay, J., & Steiner, C. (1971). Transactional analysis in groups. In H. I. Kaplan & B. J. Sadock (Eds.), *Comprehensive group psychotherapy* (pp. 198–240). Baltimore: Williams & Wilkins.

Dye, A. (1997). The multiple T: A procedure for teaching group counseling skills. In S. T. Gladding (Ed.), *New developments in group counseling* (pp. 125–127). Greensboro, NC: ERIC.

Earley, J. (2000). A practical guide to fostering interpersonal norms in a Gestalt group. *Gestalt Review, 4,* 138–151.

Eddy, W. B., & Lubin, B. (1971). Laboratory training and encounter groups. *Personnel and Guidance Journal, 49,* 625–635.

Edelwich, J., & Brodsky, A. (1992). *Group counseling for the resistant client.* New York: Lexington.

Egge, D. L., Marks, L. G., & McEvers, D. M. (1987). Puppets and adolescents: A group guidance workshop approach. *Elementary School Guidance & Counseling, 21,* 183–192.

Ekloff, M. (1984). The termination phase in group therapy: Implications for geriatric groups. *Small Group Behavior, 15,* 565–571.

Elliott, G. (1989). An interview with George M. Gazda. *Journal for Specialists in Group Work, 14,* 131–140.

Ellis, A. (1962). *Reason and emotion in psychotherapy.* New York: Stuart.

Ellis, A. (1974a). Rational-emotive therapy in groups. *Rational Living, 9,* 15–22.

Ellis, A. (1974b). Rationality and irrationality in the group therapy process. In D. S. Milman & G. D. Goldman (Eds.), *Group process today* (pp. 78–96). Springfield, IL: Thomas.

Ellis, A. (1976). The biological basis of irrational thinking. *Journal of Individual Psychology, 32,* 145–168.

Ellis, A. (1977). Fun as psychotherapy. In A. Ellis & R. Grieger (Eds.), *Handbook of rational-emotive therapy* (Vol. 1, pp. 262–270). New York: Springer.

Ellis, A. (1979). Rational-emotive therapy. In A. Ellis & J. M. Whitely (Eds.), *Theoretical and empirical foundations of rational-emotive therapy.* Pacific Grove, CA: Brooks/Cole.

Ellis, A. (1982). Rational-emotive group therapy. In G. M. Gazda (Ed.), *Basic approaches to group therapy and group counseling* (3rd ed.). Springfield, IL: Thomas.

Ellis, A. (1986). Rational-emotive therapy approaches to overcoming resistance. In A. Ellis & R. Grieger (Eds.), *Handbook of rational-emotive therapy* (Vol. 2, pp. 246–274). New York: Springer.

Ellis, A. (1988). *How to stubbornly refuse to make yourself miserable about anything—Yes, anything!* Secaucus, NJ: Lyle Stuart.

Ellis, A. (1995). Changing rational-emotive therapy (RET) to rational emotive behavioral therapy (REBT). *Journal of Rational Emotive and Cognitive Behavioral Therapy, 13,* 85–89.

Ellis, A. (1996). The humanism of rational emotive behavior therapy and other cognitive behavior therapies. *Journal of Humanistic Education and Development, 35,* 69–88.

Ellis, A. (1997). REBT and its application to group therapy. In J. Yankura & W. Dryden (Eds.), *Special applications of REBT: A therapist's casebook* (pp. 131–161). New York: Springer.

Ellis, A. (2005). Rational-emotive behavior therapy. In R. J. Corsini & D. Wedding (Ed.), *Counseling psychotherapies* (7th ed., pp. 166–201). Belmont, CA: Wadsworth.

Ellis, A., & Bernard, M. E. (Eds.). (1983). *Rational-emotive approaches to the problems of childhood.* New York: Plenum.

Ellis, A., & Dryden, W. (1997). *The practice of rational-emotive therapy.* New York: Springer.

Emerson, S. (1988). Female student counselors and child sexual abuse: Theirs and their clients'. *Counselor Education and Supervision, 28,* 15–21.

Emerson, S. (1995). A counseling group for counselors. *Journal for Specialists in Group Work, 20,* 222–231.

Ender, S. C. (1985). Study groups and college success. *Journal of College Student Personnel, 26,* 469–471.

Enright, A. B., Butterfield, P., & Berkowitz, B. (1985). Self-help and support groups in the management of eating disorders. In D. M. Garner & P. Garfinkel (Eds.), *Handbook of psychotherapy for anorexia nervosa and bulimia* (pp. 419–512). New York: Guilford.

Epstein, N. B., & Bishop, D. S. (1981). Problem centered systems therapy of the family. *Journal of Marital and Family Therapy, 7,* 23–31.

Erikson, E. H. (1963). *Childhood and society* (2nd ed.). New York: Norton.

Erikson, E. H. (1968). *Identity: Youth and crisis.* New York: Norton.

Erwin, K. T. (1997). *Group techniques for aging adults: Putting geriatric skills enhancement into practice.* Philadelphia: Routledge.

Esman, A. H. (Ed.). (1990). *Essential papers on transference.* New York: New York University Press.

Espin, O. M. (1987). Psychological impact of migration on Latinas. *Psychology of Women Quarterly, 11,* 489–503.

Evans, D. B. (1982). What are you doing? An interview with William Glasser. *Personnel and Guidance Journal, 60,* 460–465.

Evans, T. D., & Kane, D. P. (1996). Sophistry: A promising group technique for the involuntary client. *Journal for Specialists in Group Work, 21,* 110–117.

Fagan, J., & Shepherd, I. (1970). *Gestalt therapy now.* Palo Alto, CA: Science and Behavior Books.

Falco, L. D., & Bauman, S. (2004). The use of process: Notes in the experiential component of training group workers. *Journal for Specialists in Group Work, 29,* 185–192.

Fall, K. A., & Wejnert, T. J. (2005). Coleader stages of development: An application of Tuckman and Jensen (1977). *Journal for Specialists in Group Work, 30,* 309–327.

Farrell, W. (1974). *The liberated man.* New York: Random House.

Faust, V. (1968). *The counselor-consultant in the elementary school.* Boston: Houghton Mifflin.

Festinger, L. (1954). A theory of social comparison processes. *Human Relations, 7,* 117–140.

Fine, G. A. (1977). Humour in situ: The role of humour in small group culture. In A. J. Chapman & R. Grieger (Eds.), *Handbook of rational-emotive therapy* (Vol. 2, pp. 246–274). New York: Springer.

Fine, L. (1979). Psychodrama. In R. J. Corsini (Ed.), *Current psychotherapies* (2nd ed.). Itasca, IL: Peacock.

Finn, C. A. (2003). Helping students cope with loss: Incorporating art into group counseling. *Journal for Specialists in Group Work, 28,* 155–165.

Firestein, B. A. (1999). New perspectives on group treatment with women of diverse sexual identities. *Journal for Specialists in Group Work, 24,* 306–315.

Fischer, D. J., & Himle, J. A. (1998). Group behavioral therapy for adolescents with obsessive-compulsive disorder: Preliminary outcomes. *Research on Social Work Practice, 8,* 629–636.

Fletcher, T., & Hinkle, J. S. (2002). Adventure based counseling: An innovation in counseling. *Journal of Counseling and Development, 80,* 277–285.

Flores, P. J. (1988). *Group psychotherapy with addicted populations.* New York: Haworth.

Folken, M. H. (1991). The importance of group support for widowed persons. *Journal for Specialists in Group Work, 16,* 172–177.

Foltz, M.-L., Kirby, P. C., & Paradise, L. V. (1989). The influence of empathy and negative consequences on ethical decisions in counseling situations. *Counselor Education and Supervision, 28,* 219–228.

Ford, D. (1997). Counseling middle-class African Americans. In C. C. Lee (Ed.), *Multicultural issues in counseling* (pp. 81–108). Alexandria, VA: American Counseling Association.

Ford, E. E. (1982). Reality therapy in family therapy. In A. M. Horne & M. M. Ohlsen (Eds.), *Family counseling and therapy.* Itasca, IL: Peacock.

Forester-Miller, H., & Duncan, J. A. (1990). The ethics of dual relationships in the training of group counselors. *Journal for Specialists in Group Work, 15,* 88–93.

Forsyth, D. (2005). *Group dynamics* (4th ed.). Belmont, CA: Wadsworth.

Foulkes, S. H. (1964). *Therapeutic group analysis.* London: Allen & Unwin.

Foulkes, S. H., & Anthony, E. J. (1965). *Group psychotherapy: The psychoanalytic approach* (2nd ed.). Baltimore: Penguin.

Framo, J. L. (1981). The integration of marital therapy with family of origin sessions. In S. Gurman & D. P. Kniskern (Eds.), *Handbook of family therapy* pp. 133–158. New York: Brunner/Mazel.

France, M. H. (1984). Responding to loneliness: Counselling the elderly. *Canadian Counsellor, 18,* 123–129.

Frankl, V. (1962). *Man's search for meaning: An introduction to logotherapy.* New York: Washington Square Press.

Frankl, V. E. (1997). *Viktor Frankl— Recollections: An autobiography.* New York: Plenum.

Frankl, V. E. (2000). *Man's search for meaning: An introduction to logotherapy,* New York: Beacon.

Franks, J. C. (1983). Children. In J. A. Brown & R. H. Pate, Jr. (Eds.), *Being a counselor: Directions and challenges* (pp. 195–206). Pacific Grove, CA: Brooks/Cole.

Freeman, B., & McHenry, S. (1996). Clinical supervision of counselors-in-training: A nationwide survey of ideal delivery, goals, and theoretical influences. *Counselor Education and Supervision, 36,* 144–158.

French, J. R. P., Jr., & Raven, B. (1960). The bases of social power. In D. Cartwright & A. Zander (Eds.), *Group dynamics* (2nd ed., pp. 607–623). Evanston, IL: Row, Peterson.

Freud, S. (1949). *Group psychology and the analysis of the ego.* New York: Hogarth.

Freud, S. (1959). *Group psychology and the analysis of the ego.* New York: Liveright.

Frew, J. E. (1983). Encouraging what is not figural in the Gestalt group. *Journal for Specialists in Group Work, 8,* 175–181.

Friedman, W. H. (1989). *Practical group therapy.* San Francisco: Jossey-Bass.

Fry, W. F., & Salameh, W. A. (Eds.). (1993). *Advances in humor and psychotherapy.* Sarasota, FL: Pro Resources.

Fuhrmann, B. S., & Washington, C. S. (1984). Substance abuse and group work: Tentative conclusions. *Journal for Specialists in Group Work, 9,* 62–63.

Fukuyama, M. A., & Coleman, N. C. (1992). A model for bicultural assertion training with Asian-Pacific

American college students: A pilot study. *Journal for Specialists in Group Work, 17,* 210–217.

Furr, S. R. (2000). Structuring the group experience: A format for designing psychoeducational groups. *Journal for Specialists in Group Work, 25,* 29–49.

Furst, W. (1953). Homogeneous versus heterogeneous groups. *International Journal of Psychotherapy, 3,* 59–66.

Gainor, K. A. (1992). Internalized oppression as a barrier to effective group work with black women. *Journal for Specialists in Group Work, 17,* 235–242.

Gardner, J. W. (1990). *On leadership.* New York: Free Press.

Garrett, M. T. (2004). Sound of the drum: Group counseling with Native Americans. In J. L. DeLucia-Waack, D. A. Gerity, C. R. Kalodner, & M. T. Riva (Eds.), *Handbook of group counseling and psychotherapy* (pp. 169–182). Thousand Oaks, CA: Sage.

Garrett, M. T., & Osborne, W. L. (1995). The Native American sweat lodge as metaphor for group work. *Journal for Specialists in Group Work, 20,* 33–39.

Garrett, M. T., Garrett, J. T., & Brotherton, D. (2001). Inner circle/outer circle: A group technique based on Native American healing circles. *Journal for Specialists in Group Work, 26,* 17–30.

Gazda, G. M. (1968). Group psychotherapy: Its definition and history. In G. M. Gazda (Ed.), *Innovations to group psychotherapy* (pp. 3–14). Springfield, IL: Thomas.

Gazda, G. M. (1985). Group counseling and therapy: A perspective on the future. *Journal for Specialists in Group Work, 10,* 74–76.

Gazda, G. M. (1989). *Group counseling: A developmental approach* (4th ed.). Boston: Allyn & Bacon.

Gazda, G. M., Ginter, E. J., & Horne, A. M. (2001). *Group counseling and group psychotherapy: Theory and practice.* Boston: Allyn & Bacon.

Gendron, J. M. (1980). *Moreno: The roots and the branches and bibliography of psychodrama, 1972–1980; and sociometry, 1970–1980*. Beacon, NY: Beacon House.

George, R. L., & Dustin, D. (1988). *Group counseling: Theory and practice*. Upper Saddle River, NJ: Prentice Hall.

Gerler, E. R., Jr. (1982). *Counseling the young learner*. Upper Saddle River, NJ: Prentice Hall.

Gerler, E. R., Jr. & Anderson, R. F. (1986). The effects of classroom guidance on success in school. *Journal of Counseling and Development, 65,* 78–81.

Gerrity, D. A. (1998). A classification matrix using goals and process dimensions: Issues for therapy groups. *Journal for Specialists in Group Work, 23,* 202–207.

Gerrity, D. A., & Peterson, T. L. (2004). Groups for survivors of childhood sexual abuse. In J. L. DeLucia-Waack, D. A. Gerity, C. R. Kalodner, & M. T. Riva (Eds.), *Handbook of group counseling and psychotherapy* (pp. 497–517). Thousand Oaks, CA: Sage.

Gerstein, L. H., & Hotelling, K. (1987). Length of group treatment and changes in women with bulimia. *Journal of Mental Health Counseling, 9,* 162–173.

Gibb, J. R. (1961). Defensive communication. *Journal of Communication, 11,* 141–148.

Gibb, J. R., & Gibb, L. M. (1969). Role freedom in a TORI group. In A. Burton (Ed.), *Encounter: The theory and practice of encounter groups* (pp. 42–57). San Francisco: Jossey-Bass.

Gibbs, J. (1965). Norms: The problems of definition and classification. *American Journal of Sociology, 70,* 586–594.

Gigliotti, R. J. (1988). Sex differences in children's task group performance. *Small Group Behavior, 19,* 273–293.

Gillam, S. L., Hayes, R. L., & Paisley, P. O. (1997). Group work as a method of supervision. In S. T.

Gladding (Ed.), *New developments in group counseling* (pp. 133–135). Greensboro, NC: ERIC.

Gillen, M. C., & Balkin, R. S. (2006). Adventure counseling as an adjunct to group counseling in hospital and clinical settings. *Journal for Specialists in Group Work, 31,* 153–164.

Gillis, H. L., & Gass, M. A. (2004). Adventure therapy with groups. In J. L. DeLucia-Waack, D. A. Gerity, C. R. Kalodner, & M. T. Riva (Eds.), *Handbook of group counseling and psychotherapy* (pp. 593–605). Thousand Oaks, CA: Sage.

Ginott, H. (1968). Group therapy with children. In G. Gazda (Ed.), *Basic approaches to group psychotherapy and group counseling*. Springfield, IL: Thomas.

Giordano, F. G. (1995). The whole person at work: An integrative vocational intervention model for women's workplace issues. *Journal for Specialists in Group Work, 20,* 4–13.

Gladding, S. T. (1968/1989). *A poem in parting.* Unpublished manuscript, Wake Forest University, Winston-Salem, NC.

Gladding, S. T. (1975). Reflections. *Personnel and Guidance Journal, 53,* 429.

Gladding, S. T. (1975). Still life. *North Carolina Personnel & Guidance Journal, 4,* 28.

Gladding, S. T. (1977). Awakening. *The School Counselor, 24,* 184–185.

Gladding, S. T. (1978). In the midst of the puzzles and counseling journey. *Personnel and Guidance Journal, 57,* 148.

Gladding, S. T. (1979). A restless presence: Group process as a pilgrimage. *School Counselor, 27,* 126–127.

Gladding, S. T. (1986). Circles. *ASGW Newsletter, 14,* 3.

Gladding, S. T. (1988). *Ancestral thoughts.* Unpublished manuscript.

Gladding, S. T. (1989). First thoughts ... A reflection on professional friendship. *Journal of Humanistic Education and Development, 27,* 190–191.

Gladding, S. T. (1989). *Group dynamics.* Unpublished manuscript, University of Alabama, Birmingham.

Gladding, S. T. (1989). *In anticipation.* Unpublished poem, University of Alabama, Birmingham.

Gladding, S. T. (1990). Journey. *Journal of Humanistic Education and Development, 28,* 142.

Gladding, S. T. (1990). Secrets—Revised. *Journal of Humanistic Education and Development, 28,* 141.

Gladding, S. T. (1993). *Beginnings.* Unpublished manuscript, Wake Forest University, Winston-Salem, NC.

Gladding, S. T. (1993). *In reflection.* Unpublished manuscript, Wake Forest University, Winston-Salem, NC.

Gladding, S. T. (1994a). *Effective group counseling.* Greensboro, NC: ERIC/CASS.

Gladding, S. T. (1994b). *Transitions.* Unpublished manuscript, Wake Forest University, Winston-Salem, NC.

Gladding, S. T. (1994b, January). *The place of hope in the group.* Presentation at the Second National Conference of the Association for Specialists in group work, St. Petersburg, FL.

Gladding, S. T. (1997). *Earth traveler.* Unpublished manuscript, Wake Forest University, Winston-Salem, NC.

Gladding, S. T. (1997). *Rainbow.* Unpublished manuscript, Wake Forest University, Winston-Salem, NC.

Gladding, S. T. (2001). *In his element.* Unpublished manuscript, Winston-Salem, NC.

Gladding, S. T. (2002). *Becoming a counselor: The light, the bright, and the serious.* Alexandria, VA: American Counseling Association.

Gladding, S. T. (2004). *Counseling as an art: The creative arts in counseling* (3rd ed.). Alexandria, VA: American Counseling Association.

Gladding, S. T. (2005). *Counseling: A comprehensive profession* (5th ed.). Upper Saddle River, NJ: Merrill/Prentice Hall.

Gladding, S. T. (2006). *The counseling dictionary* (2nd ed.). Upper Saddle River, NJ: Pearson.

Gladding, S. T. (2007). *Family therapy: History, theory, and practice* (4th ed.). Upper Saddle River, NJ: Prentice Hall.

Glaize, D. L., & Myrick, R. D. (1984). Interpersonal groups or computers? A study of career maturity and career decidedness. *Vocational Guidance Quarterly, 32,* 168–176.

Glanz, E. C., & Hayes, R. W. (1967). *Groups in guidance* (2nd ed.). Boston: Allyn & Bacon.

Glaser, B. A., Webster, C. B., & Horne, A. M. (1992). Planning a group: An instructional project for graduate students. *Journal for Specialists in Group Work, 17,* 84–88.

Glass, J. S., & Benshoff, J. M. (1999). PARS: A processing model for beginning group leaders. *Journal for Specialists in Group Work, 24,* 15–26.

Glasser, W. (1965). *Reality therapy: A new approach to psychiatry.* New York: Harper & Row.

Glasser, W. (1969). *Schools without failure.* New York: Harper & Row.

Glasser, W. (1976). *Positive addiction.* New York: Harper & Row.

Glasser, W. (1984). Reality therapy. In R. J. Corsini (Ed.), *Current psychotherapies* (3rd ed., pp. 320–353). Itasca, IL: Peacock.

Glasser, W. (1985). *Control theory: A new explanation of how we control our lives.* New York: Harper & Row.

Glasser, W. (1986a). *The basic concepts of reality therapy* (chart). Canoga Park, CA: Institute for Reality Therapy.

Glasser, W. (1986b). *Control theory in the classroom.* New York: Harper & Row.

Glasser, W. (1986c). *The control theory–reality therapy workbook.* Canoga Park, CA: Institute for Reality Therapy.

Glasser, W. (1992). Reality therapy. *New York State Journal for Counseling and Development, 7,* 5–13.

Glasser, W. (1999). *Choice theory: A new psychology of personal freedom.* New York: HarperCollins.

Glasser, W. (2000). *Reality therapy in action.* New York: HarperCollins.

Glasser, W. (2001). *Counseling with choice theory.* New York: HarperCollins.

Glasser, W. (2003). *Warning: Psychiatry can be hazardous to your mental health.* New York: HarperCollins.

Glasser, W. (2005). *Treating mental health as a public health problem: A new leadership role for the helping professions.* Chatsworth, CA: William Glasser Inc.

Glasser, W., & Breggin, P. R. (2001). *Counseling with choice theory.* New York: HarperCollins.

Glasser, W., & Zunin, L. M. (1973). Reality therapy. In R. Corsini (Ed.), *Current psychotherapies.* Itasca, IL: Peacock.

Glassman, S. M., & Wright, T. L. (1983). In, with, and of the group: A perspective on group psychotherapy. *Small Group Behavior, 14,* 96–106.

Gloria, A. M. (1999). Apoyando estudiantes Chicanas: Therapeutic factors in Chicana college student support groups. *Journal for Specialists in Group Work, 24,* 246–259.

Glosser, G., & Wexler, D. (1985). Participants' evaluation of educational/support groups for families of patients with Alzheimer's disease and other dementias. *The Gerontologist, 25,* 232–236.

Golden, L. B. (1987). Prosocial learning groups with young children. *Elementary School Guidance & Counseling, 22,* 31–36.

Goldman, E. E., & Morrison, D. S. (1984). *Psychodrama: Experience and process.* Dubuque, IA: Kendall/Hunt.

Goldstein, A. P., Heller, K., & Sechrest, L. B. (1966). *Psychotherapy and the psychology of behavior.* New York: Wiley.

Goldstein, A., Sprafkin, R., Gershaw, N. J., & Klein, P. (1980). *Skill-streaming the adolescent: A structured learning approach to teaching prosocial skills.* Champaign, IL: Research Press.

Gonzalez-Lopez, G., & Taylor, B. A. (1997, April). Contributing to the empowerment of inner city immigrant families: Group therapy in a Latino barrio school. *Family Therapy News, 28,* 20–21.

Goodnough, G. E., & Ripley, V. (1996). Structured groups for high school seniors making the transition to college and to military service. *School Counselor, 44,* 230–234.

Goodyear, R. K. (1981). Termination as a loss experience for the counselor. *Personnel and Guidance Journal, 59,* 347–350.

Gordon, K. (1924). Group judgments in the field of lifted weights. *Journal of Experimental Psychology, 7,* 398–400.

Gordon, P. A., Winter, R., Feldman, D., & Dimick, K. (1996). Group work for persons with multiple sclerosis. *Journal for Specialists in Group Work, 21,* 243–251.

Gordon, T. (1970). *Parent effectiveness training.* New York: Wyden.

Gordon, W. (1961). *Synectics: The development of creative capacity.* New York: Harper & Row.

Gore-Felton, C., & Spiegel, D. (1999). Enhancing women's lives: The role of support groups among breast cancer patients. *Journal for Specialists in Group Work, 24,* 274–287.

Gossett, T. F. (1998). *Race: The history of an idea in America* (2nd ed.). New York: Oxford University Press.

Gough, P. B. (1987). The key to improving schools: An interview with William Glasser. *Phi Delta Kappa, 68,* 656–662.

Goulding, M., & Goulding, R. (1979). *Changing lives through redecision therapy.* New York: Brunner/Mazel.

Goulding, R. (1975). The formation and beginning process of transactional analysis groups. In G. Gazda (Ed.), *Basic approaches to group psychotherapy and group counseling* (2nd ed.). Springfield, IL: Thomas.

Goulding, R. (1987). Group therapy: Mainline or sideline? In J. K. Zeig (Ed.), *The evolution of psychotherapy* (pp. 300–311). New York: Brunner/Mazel.

Graber, J. A., & Brooks-Gunn, J. (1996). *Transitions through adolescence*. Hillsdale, NJ: Erlbaum.

Greeley, A. T., Garcia, V. L., Kessler, B. L., & Gilchrest, G. (1992). Training effective multicultural group counselors: Issues for a group training course. *Journal for Specialists in Group Work, 17*, 196–209.

Greenberg, I. A. (1974a). Audience in action through simulated psychodrama. In I. A. Greenberg (Ed.), *Psychodrama: Theory and therapy* (pp. 457–486). New York: Behavioral Publications.

Greenberg, I. A. (1974b). Moreno: Psychodrama and the group process. In I. A. Greenberg (Ed.), *Psychodrama: Theory and therapy* (pp. 11–28). New York: Behavioral Publications.

Greenburg, S. L., Lewis, G. J., & Johnson, J. (1985). Peer consultation groups for private practitioners. *Professional Psychology: Research and Practice, 16*, 437–447.

Greene, R. R. (1986). *Social work with the aged and their families*. New York: Aldine de Gruyter.

Greenstein, M. (2000). The house that's on fire: Meaning-centered psychotherapy pilot group for cancer patients. *American Journal of Psychotherapy, 54*, 501–511.

Greenstein, M., & Breitbart, W. (2000). Cancer and the experience of meaning: A group psychotherapy for people with cancer. *American Journal of Psychotherapy, 54*, 486–500.

Grieger, R. M., & Boyd, J. D. (1983). Childhood anxieties, fears, and phobias: A cognitive-behavioral psycho-situational approach. In A. Ellis & M. E. Bernard (Eds.), *Rational-emotive approaches to problems of childhood* (pp. 211–239). New York: Plenum.

Grimes, J. (1988). Transactional analysis in group work. In S. Long (Ed.), *Six group therapies* (pp. 49–113). New York: Plenum.

Guarnaschelli, J. S. (1994). Men's support groups and the men's movement: Their role for men and for women. *Group, 18*, 197–211.

Guerney, B. G., Jr. (1977). *Relationship enhancement: Skill-training programs for therapy problem prevention and enrichment*. San Francisco: Jossey-Bass.

Gumaer, J. (1984). *Counseling and therapy for children*. New York: Free Press.

Gumaer, J. (1986). Working in groups with middle graders. *School Counselor, 33*, 230–238.

Gumaer, J., & Martin, D. (1990). Group Ethics: A multimodal model for training knowledge and skill competencies. *Journal for Specialists in Group Work, 15*, 94–103.

Gumaer, J., & Scott, L. (1985). Training group leaders in ethical decision making. *Journal for Specialists in Group Work, 10*, 198–204.

Gumaer, J., & Scott, L. (1986). Group workers' perceptions of ethical and unethical behavior of group leaders. *Journal for Specialists in Group Work, 11*, 139–150.

Guy, J. (1987). *The personal life of the psychotherapist*. New York: Wiley.

Hage, S. M., & Nosanow, M. (2000). Becoming stronger at broken places: A model for group work with young adults from divorced families. *Journal for Specialists in Group Work, 25*, 50–66.

Halas, C. (1973). All women's groups: A view from inside. *Personnel and Guidance Journal, 52*, 91–95.

Hall, E., Hall, C., Harris, B., Hay, D., Biddulph, M., & Duffy, T. (1999). An evaluation of the long-term outcomes of small-group work for counsellor development. *British Journal of Guidance and Counselling, 27*, 99–112.

Hall, G. S. (1904). *Adolescence*. New York: Appleton.

Hall, J., & Hawley, L. (2004). Interactive process notes: An innovative tool in counseling groups. *Journal for Specialists in Group Work, 29*, 193–205.

Hamburg, D. A., & Takanishi, R. (1989). Preparing for life: The critical transition of adolescence. *American Psychologist, 44*, 825–827.

Haney, H., & Leibsohn, J. (2001). *Basic counseling responses in groups*. Belmont, CA: Wadsworth.

Hansen, J. C., Warner, R. W., & Smith, E. J. (1980). *Group counseling: Theory and process* (2nd ed.). Chicago: Rand McNally.

Hare, A. P. (1962). *Handbook of small group research*. Glencoe, IL: Free Press.

Hargaden, H., & Sills, C. (2002). *Transactional analysis: A relational perspective*. East Sussex: Brunner-Routledge.

Harman, M. J. (1991). The use of group psychotherapy with cancer patients: A review of recent literature. *Journal for Specialists in Group Work, 16*, 56–61.

Harman, M. J., & Withers, I. (1992). University students from homes with alcoholic parents: Considerations for therapy groups. *Journal for Specialists in Group Work, 17*, 37–41.

Harman, R. L. (1988). Gestalt group therapy. In S. Long (Ed.), *Six group therapies* (pp. 217–255). New York: Plenum.

Harper, B. L. (1985). Say it, review it, enhance it with a song. *Elementary School Guidance & Counseling, 19*, 218–221.

Harper, F. D. (1984). Group strategies with black alcoholics. *Journal for Specialists in Group Work, 9*, 38–43.

Harper, R. L., & Ellis, A. (1975). *A new guide to rational living*. Upper Saddle River, NJ: Prentice Hall.

Harris, H. L., Altekruse, M. K., & Engels, D. W. (2003). Helping Freshmen student athletes adjust to college life using psychoeducational groups. *Journal for Specialists in Group Work, 28*, 64–81.

Harris, S. A. (1996). Childhood roles and the interpersonal circle: A model for ACOA groups. *Journal for Specialists in Group Work, 21*, 39–48.

Harris, S. A., & MacQuiddy, S. (1991). Childhood roles in group therapy: The lost child and the mascot. *Journal for Specialists in Group Work, 16*, 223–229.

Harris, T. A. (1967). *I'm OK—You're OK*. New York: Harper & Row.

Harvill, R., Masson, R. L., & Jacobs, E. (1983). Systematic group leader training: A skills development approach. *Journal for Specialists in Group Work, 8,* 226–232.

Harvill, R., West, J., Jacobs, E. E., & Masson, R. L. (1985). Systematic group leader training: Evaluating the effectiveness of the approach. *Journal for Specialists in Group Work, 10,* 2–13.

Haskell, M. R. (1973). *The psychodramatic method* (4th ed.). Long Beach: California Institute of Socioanalysis.

Hatch, K. D., & McCarthy, C. J. (2003). Challenge course participation as a component of experiential groups for counselors in training. *Journal for Specialists in Group Work, 28,* 199–214.

Hawes, E. C. (1985). Personal growth groups for women: An Adlerian approach. *Journal for Specialists in Group Work, 10,* 19–27.

Hawkins, B. L. (1983). Group counseling as a treatment modality for the elderly: A group snapshot. *Journal for Specialists in Group Work, 8,* 186–193.

Hayashi, M. (1990, On the significance of co-facilitator relationship in their encounter group. *Japanese Journal of Psychology, 61,* 184–187.

Hayes, R. L. (1990). Developmental group supervision. *Journal for Specialists in Group Work, 15,* 225–238.

Hayes, R. L. (1991). Group work and the teaching of ethics. *Journal for Specialists in Group Work, 16,* 24–31.

Henderson, D. A., & Gladding, S. T. (2004). Group counseling with older adults. In J. L. DeLucia-Waack, D. A. Gerity, C. R. Kalodner, & M. T. Riva (Eds.), *Handbook of group counseling and psychotherapy* (pp. 469–478). Thousand Oaks, CA: Sage.

Hendrix, F. G., & Sedgwick, C. (1989). Group counseling with the elderly. In G. M. Gazda (Ed.), *Group counseling: A developmental approach* (pp. 195–211). Boston: Allyn & Bacon.

Hendrix, H. (1988). *Getting the love you want*. New York: Holt, Rinehart & Winston.

Heppner, P. P. (1981). Counseling men in groups. *Personnel and Guidance Journal, 60,* 249–252.

Herlihy, B., & Remley, T. P., Jr. (1995). Unified ethical standards: A challenge for professionalism. *Journal of Counseling and Development, 74,* 130–133.

Herlihy, B., & Remley, T. (2001). Legal and ethical challenges in counseling. In D. C. Locke, J. E. Myers, & E. L. Herr (Eds.), *The handbook of counseling* (pp. 69–90). Thousand Oaks, CA: Sage.

Hern, B. G., & Weis, D. M. (1991). A group counseling experience with the very old. *Journal for Specialists in Group Work, 16,* 143–151.

Hersey, P., & Blanchard, K. H. (1969). Life-cycle theory of leadership. *Training and Development Journal, 23,* 26–34.

Hershenson, D. B., & Power, P. W. (1987). *Mental health counseling*. New York: Pergamon.

Higgins, E., & Warner, R. (1975). Counseling blacks. *Personnel and Guidance Journal, 53,* 383–386.

Higgs, J. A. (1992). Dealing with resistance: Strategies for effective group. *Journal for Specialists in Group Work, 17,* 67–73.

Hill, M., Glaser, K., & Harden, J. (1995). A feminist model for ethical decision making. In E. J. Rave & C. C. Larsen (Eds.), *Ethical decision making in therapy: Feminist perspectives* (pp. 18–37). New York: Guilford.

Hillkirk, J. (1993, December 21). World famous quality expert dead at 93. *USA Today,* B1–B2.

Hillman, B. W., & Reunion, K. B. (1978). Activity group guidance: Process and results. *Elementary School Guidance & Counseling, 13,* 104–111.

Himes, C. L., Hogan, D. P., & Eggebeen, D. J. (1996). Living arrangements of minority elders. *Journal of Gerontology, 51A,* 542–548.

Hines, M. (1988). Similarities and differences in group and family therapy. *Journal for Specialists in Group Work, 13,* 173–179.

Hines, P. L., & Fields, T. H. (2002). Preschool screening issues for school counselors. *Journal for Specialists in Group Work, 27,* 358–376.

Hinkle, J. S. (1991). Support group counseling for caregivers of Alzheimer's disease patients. *Journal for Specialists in Group Work, 16,* 185–190.

Hinkle, J. S. (1993). Training school counselors to do family counseling. *Elementary School Guidance & Counseling, 27,* 252–257.

Hirayama, E. (1993). A scale measuring individual processes in encounter groups. *Japanese Journal of Psychology, 63,* 419–424.

Hitchings, P. (1994). Psychotherapy and sexual orientation. In P. Clarkston & M. Pokorny (Eds.), *The handbook of psychotherapy* (pp. 119–132). London: Routledge.

Hollander, M., & Kazaoka, K. (1988). Behavior therapy groups. In S. Long (Ed.), *Six group therapies* (pp. 257–326). New York: Plenum.

Holmes, P., & Karp, M. (Eds.). (1991). *Psychodrama: Inspiration and technique*. New York: Routledge.

Holmes, P., Karp, M., & Watson, M. (1995). *Psychodrama since Moreno*. New York: Routledge.

Homrich, A. M., & Horne, A. M. (1997). Multiple family group therapy (MFGT). In S. T. Gladding (Ed.), *New developments in group counseling* (pp. 51–53). Greensboro, NC: ERIC.

Hopson, B., & Hough, P. (1976). The need for personal and social education in secondary schools and further education. *British Journal of Guidance and Counseling, 4,* 16–27.

Horne, A. M. (1996). The changing world of group work. *Journal for Specialists in Group Work, 21,* 2–3.

Horne, A. M. (1999, January). *Working with men in groups*. Paper presented at the Association for Specialists in Group Work Group-A-Rama, Albuquerque, NM.

Horne, A. M.. (2001). *Family counseling and therapy* (3rd ed.). Itasca, IL: F. E. Peacock.

Horne, S. (1999). From coping to creating change: The evolution of women's groups. *Journal for Specialists in Group Work, 24,* 231–245.

Horswill, R. K. (1993). Are typical senior center group activities better suited for women than for men? *Journal for Specialists in Group Work, 18,* 45–48.

Hosford, R. E., & deVisser, L. A. J. M. (1974). *Behavioral approaches to counseling: An introduction.* Washington, DC: AGPA Press.

Hoskins, M. (1984, April). *Guidelines for writing therapeutic fairy tales.* Paper presented at the Fourth Annual Conference of the National Association for Poetry Therapy, Hempstead, NY.

Howard, J. (1970). *Please touch.* New York: McGraw-Hill.

Howlin, P., & Yates, P. (1999). The potential effectiveness of social skills groups for adults with autism. *Autism, 3,* 299–307.

Hsiung, R. C. (2000). The best of both worlds: An online self-help group hosted by a mental health professional. *CyberPsychology & Behavior, 3,* 935–950.

Hudson, P. E., Doyle, R. E., & Venezia, J. F. (1991). A comparison of two group methods of teaching communication skills to high school students. *Journal for Specialists in Group Work, 16,* 255–263.

Huey, W. C. (1983). Reducing adolescent aggression through group assertive training. *School Counselor, 30,* 193–203.

Hulse-Killacky, D. (1993). Personal and professional endings. *Journal of Humanistic Education and Development, 32,* 92–94.

Hulse-Killacky, D., Killacky, J., & Donigian, J. (2001). *Making task groups work in your world.* Upper Saddle River, NJ: Prentice Hall.

Hulse-Killacky, D., Schumacher, B., & Kraus, K. (1994, April). *Effective group leadership.* Presentation at the annual convention of the American Counseling Association, Minneapolis.

Hulse-Killacky, D., Schumacher, B., & Kraus, K. (1999). Visual conceptualizations of meetings: A group work design. *Journal for Specialists in Group Work, 24,* 113–124.

Hummel, D. L., Talbutt, L. C., & Alexander, M. D. (1985). *Law and ethics in counseling.* New York: Van Nostrand Reinhold.

Hurst, J. B., & Vanderveen, N. (1994). Effective management of polarities: Educating men to manage unsolvable problems. *Journal for Specialists in Group Work, 19,* 211–216.

Huss, S. N., & Ritchie, M. (1999). Effectiveness of a group for parentally bereaved children. *Journal for Specialists in Group Work, 24,* 186–196.

In, J. K., & Hwang, M. G. (1997). The effect on internal control and achievement motivation based on R. T. group activity—Making the world I want. *Korean Journal of Counseling and Psychotherapy, 9,* 81–99

Ivey, A. E. (1971). *Microcounseling: Innovations in interviewing training.* Springfield, IL: Thomas.

Ivey, A. (1973). Microcounseling: The counselor as trainer. *Personnel and Guidance Journal, 51,* 311–316.

Ivey, A. E., & Ivey, M. B. (2007). *Intentional interviewing and counseling: Facilitating client development in a multicultural society* (6th ed.). Pacific Grove, CA: Brooks/Cole.

Ivey, A. E., Pedersen, P. B., & Ivey, M. B. (2001). *Intentional group counseling: A microskills approach.* Pacific Grove, CA: Brooks/Cole.

Jacobs, E. (1992). *Creative counseling techniques: An illustrated guide.* Odessa, FL: Psychological Assessment Resources.

Jacobs, E. E., Masson, R. L., & Harvill, R. L. (2006). *Group counseling: Strategies and skills* (5th ed.). Pacific Grove, CA: Brooks/Cole.

James, L., & Martin, D. (2002). Sand tray and group therapy: Helping parents cope. *Journal for Specialists in Group Work, 27,* 390–405.

James, M. (2002). *It's never too late to be happy: Reparenting yourself for happiness.* Sanger, CA: Quill Driver Books.

James, M., & Jongeward, D. (1971). *Born to win: Transactional analysis with Gestalt experiments.* Reading, MA: Addison-Wesley.

James, N. (1994). Cultural frame of reference and intergroup encounters: A TA approach. *Transactional Analysis Journal, 24,* 206–210.

Janis, I. L. (1971). Group think. *Psychology Today, 5,* 36–43, 74–76.

Janis, I. L. (1972). *Victims of groupthink.* Boston: Houghton Mifflin.

Janis, I. L. (1982). *Groupthink: Psychological studies of policy decisions and fiascos* (2nd ed.). Boston: Houghton Mifflin.

Janis, I. L., & Mann, L. (1954). Effectiveness of emotional role playing in modifying smoking habits and attitudes. *Journal of Experimental Research in Personality, 1,* 84–90.

Johnson, D. W. (2000). *Reaching out: Interpersonal effectiveness and self-actualization* (7th ed.). Boston: Allyn & Bacon.

Johnson, D. W., & Johnson, F. P. (2006). *Joining together* (9th ed.). Boston: Allyn & Bacon.

Johnson, I. H., Torres, J. S., Coleman, V. D., & Smith, M. C. (1995). Issues and strategies in leading culturally diverse counseling group. *Journal for Specialists in Group Work, 20,* 143–150.

Johnson, W. Y., & Wilborn, B. (1991). Group counseling as an intervention in anger expression and depression in older adults. *Journal for Specialists in Group Work, 16,* 133–142.

Johnson, W., & Kottman, T. (1992). Developmental needs of middle school students: Implications for counselors. *Elementary School Guidance & Counseling, 27,* 3–14.

Jones, K. D. (2002). Group play therapy with sexually abused preschool children: Group behaviors and interventions. *Journal for Specialists in Group Work, 27,* 377–389.

Jones, K. D., & Robinson, E. H. (2000). Psychoeducational groups: A model for choosing topics and exercises appropriate to group stages. *Journal for Specialists in Group Work, 25,* 356–365.

Jourard, S. M. (1971). *The transparent self* (2nd ed.). New York: Van Nostrand.

Juhnke, G. A., & Osborne, W. L. (1997). The solution-focused debriefing group: An integrated postviolence group intervention for adults. *Journal for Specialists in Group Work, 22,* 66–76.

Juntunen, C. L., Cohen, B. B., & Wolszon, L. R. (1997). Women and anger: A structured group. *Journal for Specialists in Group Work, 22,* 97–110.

Kaczkowski, H. (1979). Group work with children. *Elementary School Guidance & Counseling, 14,* 44–51.

Kalodner, C. R., & Coughlin, J. W. (2004). Psychoeducational and counseling groups to prevent and treat eating disorders and disturbances. In J. L. DeLucia-Waack, D. A. Gentry, C. R. Kalodner, & M. T. Riva (Eds.), *Handbook of group counseling and psychotherapy.* Thousand Oaks: Sage.

Kane, C. M. (1995). Fishbowl training in group process. *Journal for Specialists in Group Work, 20,* 183–188.

Kapur, R., & Miller, K. (1987). A comparison between therapeutic factors in TA and psychodynamic therapy groups. *Transactional Analysis Journal, 17,* 294–300.

Karp, M., Holmes, P., & Tauvon, K. B. (Eds.). (1998). *The handbook of psychodrama.* Philadelphia: Routledge.

Karpman, S. (1968). Fairy tales and script drama analysis. *Transactional Analysis Bulletin, 7,* 39–43.

Katz, J. H. (1985). The sociopolitical nature of counseling. *The Counseling Psychologist, 13,* 615–624.

Katzenbach, J., & Smith, D. (1993). *The wisdom of teams.* Cambridge, MA: Harvard Business School Press.

Kauff, P. F. (1977). The termination process: Its relationship to separation–individuation phase of development. *International Journal of Group Psychotherapy, 27,* 3–18.

Kauffman, E., Dore, M. M., & Nelson-Zlupko, L. (1995). The role of women's therapy groups in the treatment of chemical dependence. *American Journal of Orthopsychiatry, 65,* 355–363.

Keat, D. B. (1974). *Fundamentals of child counseling.* Boston: Houghton Mifflin.

Keat, D. B. (1979). *Multimodal therapy with children.* New York: Pergamon.

Keat, D. B., Metzgar, K. L., Raykovitz, D., & McDonald, J. (1985). Multimodal counseling: Motivating children to attend school through friendship groups. *Journal of Humanistic Education and Development, 23,* 166–175.

Keel, L. P. (1998). A task group practitioner's response to Waldo and Bauman's article on regrouping the categorization of group work. *Journal for Specialists in Group Work, 23,* 192–195.

Keene, M., & Erford, B. T. (2007). *Group activities: Firing up for performance.* Upper Saddle River, NJ: Prentice Hall.

Kees, N. L. (1999). Women together again: A phenomenological study of leaderless women's groups. *Journal for Specialists in Group Work, 24,* 288–305.

Kees, N. L., & Jacobs, E. (1990). Conducting more effective groups: How to select and process group exercises. *Journal for Specialists in Group Work, 15,* 21–29.

Kees, N. L., & Leech, N. (2004). Practice trends in women's groups: An inclusive view. In J. L. DeLucia-Waack, D. A. Gerrity, C. R. Kalonder, & M. T. Riva (Eds.), *Handbook of group counseling and psychotherapy* (pp. 445–455). Thousand Oaks, CA: Sage.

Kellerman, H. (1979). *Group psychotherapy and personality: Intersecting structures.* New York: Grune & Stratton.

Kellermann, P. F. (1987). Outcome research in classical psychodrama. *Small Group Behavior, 18,* 459–469.

Kelly, E. W., & Sweeney, T. J. (1979). Typical faulty goals of adolescents. *School Counselor, 26,* 236–246.

Kelly, V. A. (2006). Women of courage: A personal account of a wilderness-based experiential group for survivors of abuse. *Journal for Specialists in Group Work, 31,* 99–111.

Kelman, H. C. (1963). The role of the group in the induction of therapeutic change. *International Journal of Group Psychotherapy, 13,* 399–442.

Kennedy, G. J., & Tanenbaum, S. (2000). Psychotherapy with older adults. *American Journal of Psychotherapy, 54,* 386–407.

Kepner, E. (1980). Gestalt group process. In B. Feder & R. Ronall (Eds.), *Beyond the hot seat: Gestalt approaches to group* (pp. 5–24). New York: Brunner/Mazel.

Kerr, M. E., & Bowen, M. (1988). *Family evaluation: An approach based on Bowen theory.* New York: Norton.

Keyton, J. (1993). Group termination: Completing the study of group development. *Small Group Research, 24,* 84–100.

Khng, R. H. H. (2001). Tiptoe out of the closet: The before and after of the increasingly visible gay community. *Journal of Homosexuality, 40,* 81–97.

Kim, B. S. K., Atkinson, D. R., & Umemoto, D. (2001). Asian cultural value and the counseling process: Current knowledge and directions for future research. *Counseling Psychologist, 29,* 570–603.

Kim, B. S. K., Omizo, M. M., & D'Andrea, M. J. (1998). The effects of culturally consonant group counseling on the self-esteem and internal locus of control orientation among Native American adolescents. *Journal for Specialists in Group Work, 23,* 145–163.

Kincade, E. A., & Kalodner, C. R. (2004). The use of groups in college and university counseling centers. In J. L. DeLucia-Waack, D. A. Gerrity,

C. R. Kalonder, & M. T. Riva (Eds.), *Handbook of group counseling and psychotherapy* (pp. 366–377). Thousand Oaks, CA: Sage.

Kissane, D. W., Bloch, S., Miach, P., Smith, G. C., Seddon, A., & Keks, N. (1997). Cognitive-existential group therapy for patients with primary breast cancer—Techniques and themes. *Psycho-Oncology, 6,* 25–33.

Kitchener, K. S. (1984a). Ethics and counseling psychology: Distinctions and directions. *The Counseling Psychologist, 12,* 15–18.

Kitchener, K. S. (1984b). Intuition, critical evaluation, and ethical principles: The foundation for ethical decisions in counseling psychology. *The Counseling Psychologist, 12,* 43–55.

Kitchener, K. S. (1986). Teaching applied ethics in counselor education: An integration of psychological processes and philosophical analysis. *Journal of Counseling and Development, 64,* 306–310.

Kivlighan, D. M., Jr., Coleman, M. N., & Anderson, D. C. (2000). Process, outcome, and methodology in group counseling research. In S. D. Brown & R. W. Lent (Eds.), *Handbook of counseling psychology* (3rd ed., pp. 767–796). New York: Wiley.

Kivlighan, D. M., Jr., & Luiza, J. W. (2005). Examining the credibility gap and the mum effect: Rex Stockton's contributions to research on feedback in groups. *Journal for Specialists in Group Work, 30,* 253–269.

Kizner, L. R. (1999). Small group counseling with adopted children. *Professional School Counseling, 2*(3), 226–231.

Klaw, E., & Humphreys, K. (2004). The role of peer-led mutual help groups in promoting health and well-being. In J. L. DeLucia-Waack, D. A. Gerrity, C. R. Kalodner, & M. T. Riva (Eds.), *Handbook of group counseling and psychotherapy* (pp. 630–640). Thousand Oaks, CA: Sage.

Kleinberg, J. L. (1995). Group treatment of adults in midlife. *International Journal of Group Psychotherapy, 45,* 207–222.

Kline, T. J. B. (1999). The Team Player Inventory: Reliability and validity of a measure of predisposition toward organizational team-working environments. *Journal for Specialists in Group Work, 24,* 102–112.

Kline, T. J. B. (2001). Predicting team performance: Testing a model in a field setting. *Journal for Specialists in Group Work, 26,* 185–197.

Kline, W. B. (1990). Responding to "problem" members. *Journal for Specialists in Group Work, 15,* 195–200.

Kline, W. B. (1997). Groups as a whole dynamics and the "problem" member: Conceptualization and intervention. In S. T. Gladding (Ed.), *New developments in group counseling* (pp. 93–95). Greensboro, NC: ERIC.

Kline, W. B. (2003). *Interactive group counseling and therapy.* Upper Saddle River, NJ: Merrill/Prentice Hall.

Knight, B. G. (1996). *Psychotherapy with older adults* (2nd ed.). Newbury Park, CA: Sage.

Kobak, K. A., Rock, A. L., & Greist, J. H. (1995). Group behavior therapy for obsessive-compulsive disorders. *Journal for Specialists in Group Work, 20,* 26–32.

Kochendofer, S. A., & Culp, D. (1979). Relaxation group—Intake procedure. *Elementary School Guidance & Counseling, 14,* 124.

Kolb, G. E. (1983). The dream in psychoanalytic group therapy. *International Journal of Group Psychotherapy, 33,* 41–52.

Kominars, K. & Dorheim, L. (2004). Group approaches to substance abuse treatment. In J. L. DeLucia-Waack, D. A. Gerity, C. R. Kalodner, & M. T. Riva (Eds.), *Handbook of group counseling and psychotherapy* (pp. 563–575). Thousand Oaks, CA: Sage.

Konstam, V. (1995). Anger: A neglected group treatment issue with cardiac transplantation recipients and their families. *Journal for Specialists in Group Work, 20,* 189–194.

Korchin, S. J. (1976). *Clinical psychology.* New York: Basic Books.

Korda, L. J., & Pancrazio, J. J. (1989). Limiting negative outcome in group practice. *Journal for Specialists in Group Work, 14,* 112–120.

Kormanski, C. (1982). Leadership strategies for managing conflict. *Journal for Specialists in Group Work, 7,* 112–118.

Kormanski, C. (1990). Team building patterns of academic groups. *Journal for Specialists in Group Work, 15,* 206–214.

Kormanski, C. (1999). *The team: Explorations in group process.* Denver, CO: Love.

Kormanski, C., & Eschbach, L. (1997). From group leader to process consultant. In H. Forester-Miller & J. A. Kottler (Eds.), *Issues and challenges for group practitioners* (pp. 133–164). Denver, CO: Love.

Kormanski, C. L., & Mozenter, A. (1987). A new model of team building: A technology for today and tomorrow. In J. W. Pfeiffer (Ed.), *The 1987 annual: Developing human resources* (pp. 255–268). San Diego, CA: University Associates.

Kottler, J. A. (1983). *Pragmatic group leadership.* Pacific Grove, CA: Brooks/Cole.

Kottler, J. A. (1986). *On being a therapist.* San Francisco: Jossey-Bass.

Kottler, J. A. (1994). *Advanced group leadership.* Pacific Grove, CA: Brooks/Cole.

Kottler, J.A. (2001). *Learning group leadership: An experiential approach.* Boston: Allyn & Bacon.

Kottler, J. A., & Forester-Miller, H. (1998). Personal and social change in the lives of group leaders. *Journal for Specialists in Group Work, 23,* 338–349.

Kranz, P. L., & Lund, N. (1993). A reflective analysis through the vision and voices of an undergraduate psychodrama class. *Journal of Group Psychotherapy, Psychodrama, and Sociometry, 46,* 32–39.

Kraus, K. L., & Hulse-Killacky, D. (1996). Balancing process and content in groups: A metaphor. *Journal for Specialists in Group Work, 21,* 90–93.

Kraus, K. L., DeEsch, J. B., & Geroski, A. M. (2001). Stop avoiding challenging situations in group counseling. *Journal for Specialists in Group Work, 26,* 31–47.

Krieg, F. J. (1988). *Group leadership training and supervision manual for adolescent group counseling in schools* (3rd ed.). Muncie, IN: Accelerated Development.

Krieger, K. M., & Stockton, R. (2004). Technology and group leadership training: Teaching group counseling in an online environment. *Journal for Specialists in Group Work, 29,* 343–359.

Krivatsy-O'Hara, S., Reed, P., & Davenport, J. (1978) Group counseling with potential high school dropouts. *Personnel and Guidance Journal, 56,* 510–512.

Krumboltz, J. D. (Ed.). (1966). *Revolution in counseling: Implications of behavioral science.* Boston: Houghton Mifflin.

Krumboltz, J., & Thoresen, C. E. (1969). *Behavioral counseling: Cases and techniques.* New York: Holt, Rinehart & Winston.

Kübler-Ross, E. (1973). *On death and dying.* London: Tavistock.

Kulic, K. L., Horne, A. M., & Dagley, J. C. (2004). A comprehensive review of prevention groups for children and adolescents. *Group Dynamics: Theory, Research, and Practice, 8,* 139–151.

Kymissis, P. (1993). Group psychotherapy with adolescents. In H. Kaplan & B. J. Sadock (Eds.), *Comprehensive group psychotherapy* (3rd ed.). Baltimore: Williams & Wilkins.

Lacoursiere, R. (1974). A group method to facilitate learning during the stages of a psychiatric affiliation. *International Journal of Group Psychotherapy, 24,* 114–119.

Lacoursiere, R. B. (1980). *The life cycle of groups: Group development stage theory.* New York: Human Sciences Press.

LaFountain, R. M., & Garner, N. E. (1996). Solution-focused counseling groups: The results are in. *Journal for Specialists in Group Work, 21,* 128–143.

LaGaipa, J. (1977). The effects of humour on the flow of social conversation. In A. J. Chapman & H. C. Foot (Eds.), *It's a funny thing, humour* (pp. 421–427). New York:

Lake, R. G. (1987). *The sweat lodge: An ancient medicine for modern sickness.* Mesa, AZ: Self Discovery Magazine.

Lakin, M. (1985). *The helping group: Therapeutic principles and issues.* Reading, MA: Addison-Wesley.

Landreth, G. L. (1984). Encountering Carl Rogers: His views on facilitating groups. *Personnel and Guidance Journal, 62,* 323–326.

Lanier, E., & Robertiello, R. C. (1977). A small group of patients discuss their experiences and feelings about working with therapists of different races. *Journal of Contemporary Psychotherapy, 9,* 42–44.

Lanning, W. (1986). Development of the supervisor emphasis rating form. *Counselor Education and Supervision, 27,* 331–342.

Larrabee, M. (1982). Working with reluctant clients through affirmation techniques. *Personnel and Guidance Journal, 60,* 105–109.

Larson, C. E., & LaFasto, F. M. J. (1989). *TeamWork.* Newbury Park, CA: Sage.

Latham, V. M. (1987). Task type and group motivation. *Small Group Behavior, 18,* 56–71.

Latner, J. (1973). *The Gestalt therapy book.* New York: Julian.

Laughlin, P. R. (1988). Collective induction: Group performance, social combination processes, and mutual majority and minority influence. *Journal of Personality and Social Psychology, 54,* 254–267.

Lazarus, A. A. (1976). *Multimodal behavior therapy.* New York: Springer.

Lazarus, A. A. (1981). *The practice of multimodal therapy.* New York: McGraw-Hill.

Lazarus, A. A. (Ed.). (1985). *Casebook of multimodal therapy.* New York: Guilford.

Lazarus, A. A. (1989). *The practice of multimodal therapy: Systematic, comprehensive, and effective psychotherapy.* Baltimore: Johns Hopkins University Press.

Lazell, E. W. (1921). The group treatment of dementia praecox. *Psychoanalytic Review, 8,* 168–179.

Leaman, D. R. (1983). Group counseling to improve communication skills of adolescents. *Journal for Specialists in Group Work, 8,* 144–150.

Leavitt, H. J. (1951). Some effects of certain communication problems on group performance. *Journal of Abnormal and Social Psychology, 46,* 38–50.

LeCroy, C. W. (1986). An analysis of the effects of gender on outcome in group treatment with young adolescents. *Journal of Youth and Adolescence, 15,* 497–508.

Lee, C. C. (1995, Fall). Group work for a new millennium. *Together, 24*(1), 4.

Lee, C. C. (1997). Cultural dynamics: Their importance in culturally responsive counseling. In C. C. Lee (Ed.), *Multicultural issues in counseling* (2nd ed., pp. 15–30). Alexandria, VA: American Counseling Association.

Lee, C. C., Armstrong, K. L., & Brydges, J. L. (1996, January). *The challenges of a diverse society: Counseling for mutual respect and understanding.* Denver, CO: Love.

Lee, R. S. (1993). Effects of classroom guidance on student achievement. *Elementary School Guidance & Counseling, 27,* 163–171.

Leech, N. L., & Kees, N. L. (2005). Researching women's groups: Findings, limitations, and recommendations. *Journal of Counseling & Development, 83,* 367–373.

LeMasters, E. E., & DeFrain, J. (1989). *Parents in contemporary America* (5th ed.). Belmont, CA: Wadsworth.

Leong, F. T. L. (1992). Guidelines for minimizing premature termination among Asian American clients in group counseling. *Journal for Specialists in Group Work, 17,* 218–228.

LeShan, E. (1990). *It's better to be over the hill than under it: Thoughts on life over 60.* New York: Newmarket.

Lessner, J. W. (1974). The poem as a catalyst in group work. *Personnel and Guidance Journal, 53,* 33–38.

Leveton, E. (2001). *A clinician's guide to psychodrama* (3rd ed.). New York: Springer.

Levin, J. S., Taylor, R. J., & Chatters, L. M. (1994). Race and gender differences in religiosity among older adults: Findings from four national surveys. *Journal of Gerontology, 49,* S137–S145.

Levin, L. S., & Shepherd, I. L. (1974). The role of the therapist in Gestalt therapy. *The Counseling Psychologist, 4,* 27–30.

Lev-Wiesel, R. (2003). The group stories fabric technique (GSFT): A clinical tool for understanding transference issues in group psychotherapy. *Journal for Specialists in Group Work, 28,* 227–243.

Lewin, K. (1940). Formulation and progress in psychology: University of Iowa studies. *Child Welfare, 16,* 9–42.

Lewin, K. (1944). The dynamics of group action. *Educational Leadership, 1,* 195–200.

Lewin, K. (1948). *Resolving social conflicts: Selected papers on group dynamics.* New York: Harper.

Lewin, K. (1951). *Field theory in social science.* New York: Harper.

Lewis, M. I., & Butler, R. N. (1984). Life-review therapy: Putting memories to work. In I. M. Burnside (Ed.), *Working with the elderly: Group processes and techniques* (2nd ed., pp. 50–59). Monterey, CA: Wadsworth.

Lewis, W. M. (1986). Group training for parents of children with behavior problems. *Journal for Specialists in Group Work, 11,* 194–199.

Lieberman, M. A. (1977). Problems in integrating traditional group therapies with new forms. *Journal of International Group Psychotherapy, 27,* 19–33.

Lieberman, M. A., Yalom, I. D., & Miles, M. (1973). *Encounter groups: First facts.* New York: Basic Books.

Lifton, W. M. (1972). *Groups: Facilitating individual and societal change.* New York: Wiley.

Light, R. (1994, March). *Effective teaching.* Presentation at Faculty Development Seminar, Wake Forest University, Winston-Salem, NC.

Linehan, M. M. (1993). *Skills training manual for treating borderline personality disorder.* New York: Guilford.

Linton, J. M. (2003). A preliminary qualitative investigation of group processes in group supervision. *Journal for Specialists in Group Work, 28,* 215–226.

Lobitz, W. C., & Baker, E. L. (1979). Group treatment of sexual dysfunction. In D. Upper & S. M. Ross (Eds.), *Behavior group therapy.* Champaign, IL: Research Press.

Locke, N. (1961). *Group psychoanalysis: Theory and technique.* New York: New York University Press.

Long, S. (1988). The six group therapies compared. In S. Long (Ed.), *Six group therapies* (pp. 327–338). New York: Plenum.

Lowe, R. N. (1982). Adlerian/Dreikursian family counseling. In A. M. Horne & M. M. Ohlsen (Eds.), *Family counseling and therapy* (pp. 329–359). Itasca, IL: Peacock.

Lowenstein, L. F. (1993). Humanism-existentialism as a basis of psychotherapy. *International Journal of Mental Health, 22,* 93–102.

Luft, J. (1963). *Group processes: An introduction to group dynamics.* Palo Alto, CA: National Press.

Luft, J. (1984). *Group processes: An introduction to group dynamics* (3rd ed.). Palo Alto, CA: Mayfield.

MacDevitt, J. W. (1987). Conceptualizing therapeutic components of group counseling. *Journal for Specialists in Group Work, 12,* 76–84.

MacKenzie, K., & Livesley, W. (1983). Developmental model for brief groups. In R. E. Dies & K. R. MacKenzie (Eds.), *Advances in group psychotherapy: Integrating research and practice* (pp. 101–116). New York: International Universities Press.

MacKenzie, K., & Livesley, W. (1984). Developmental stages: An integrating theory of group psychotherapy. *Canadian Journal of Psychiatry, 29,* 247–251.

Mackler, L., & Strauss, C. (1981). Bion's bibliography. In L.R. Wolberg & M. L. Aronson (Eds.), *Group and family therapy.* New York: Brunner/Mazel.

MacNair-Semands, R. R. (1997, August). Using new instruments to enhance group therapy. In J. Corazzini (Chair), *Integral features of group psychotherapy.* Symposium conducted at the annual meeting of the American Psychological Association, Chicago.

MacNair-Semands, R. R. (1998). Encompassing the complexity of group work. *Journal for Specialists in Group Work, 23,* 208–214.

MacNair-Semands, R. R. (2004). Theory, practice, and research of grief groups. In J. L. DeLucia-Waack, D. A. Gerity, C. R. Kalodner, & M. T. Riva (Eds.), *Handbook of group counseling and psychotherapy* (pp. 318–331). Thousand Oaks, CA: Sage.

Madsen, C. H., Jr., & Madsen, C. K. (1970). *Teaching/discipline.* Boston: Allyn & Bacon.

Mahler, C. A. (1969). *Group counseling in the schools.* Boston: Houghton Mifflin.

Mahler, C. A. (1971). Group counseling. *Personnel and Guidance Journal, 49,* 601–610.

Mahoney, M. J., & Thoresen, C. E. (1974). *Self-control: Power to the person.* Pacific Grove, CA: Brooks/Cole.

Malekoff, A. (1997). *Group work with adolescents.* New York: Guilford.

Maliver, B. L. (1973). *The encounter game.* New York: Stein & Day.

Manaster, G. G., & Corsini, R. J. (1982). *Individual psychology: Theory and practice.* Itasca, IL: Peacock.

Mann, L. (1967). The effects of emotional role playing on smoking attitudes and behavior. *Journal of Experimental Social Psychology, 3,* 334–348.

Maples, M. F. (1988). Group development: Extending Tuckman's theory. *Journal for Specialists in Group Work, 13,* 17–23.

Maples, M. F. (1992). Steamwork: An effective approach to team building. *Journal for Specialists in Group Work, 17,* 144–150.

Marbley, A. F. (2004). His eye is on the sparrow: A counselor of color's perception of facilitating groups with predominantly White members. *Journal for Specialists in Group Work, 29,* 247–258.

March, L. C. (1935). Group therapy and the psychiatric clinic. *Journal of Nervous and Mental Disorders, 32,* 381–392.

Mardoyan, J. L., & Weis, D. M. (1981). The efficacy of group counseling with older adults. *Personnel and Guidance Journal, 60,* 161–163.

Marrotta, S. A., Peters, B. J., & Paliokas, K. L. (2000). Teaching group dynamics: An interdisciplinary model. *Journal for Specialists in Group Work, 25,* 16–28.

Marrow, A. J. (1969). *The practical theorist.* New York: Basic Books.

Martin, V., & Thomas, M. C. (2000). A model psychoeducation group for shy college students. *Journal for Specialists in Group Work, 25,* 79–88.

Maslow, A. H. (1962). *Toward a psychology of being.* Princeton, NJ: Van Nostrand.

Masters, W. H., & Johnson, V. E. (1970). *Human sexual inadequacy.* Boston: Little, Brown.

Mathis, R. D., & Tanner, Z. (2000). Structured group activities with family-of-origin themes. *Journal for Specialists in Group Work, 25,* 89–103.

Matthews, C. O. (1992). An application of general system theory (GST) to group therapy. *Journal for Specialists in Group Work, 17,* 161–169.

Maultsby, M. C., Jr. (1984). *Rational behavior therapy.* Upper Saddle River, NJ: Prentice Hall.

May, R. (1953). *Man's search for himself.* New York: Norton.

May, R. (1977). *The meaning of anxiety* (rev. ed.). New York: Norton.

May, R. (1983). *The discovery of being: Writings in existential psychology.* New York: Norton.

May, R., & Yalom, I. (2005). Existential psychotherapy. In R. J. Corsini & D. Wedding (Eds.), *Current psychotherapies* (7th ed., pp. 269–298). Belmont, CA: Thompson.

Maynard, P. E. (1980). Group counseling with the elderly. *Counseling and Values, 24,* 227–235.

Mayo, E. (1945). *The social problems of an industrial civilization.* Cambridge, MA: Harvard University Press.

Mazza, N., & Vinton, L. (1999). A nationwide study of group work in nursing homes. *Activities, Adaptation & Aging, 24,* 61–73.

McArthur, M. J. (1990). Reality therapy with rape victims. *Archives of Psychiatric Nursing, 4,* 360–365.

McBride, M. C., & Emerson, S. (1989). Group work with women who were molested as children. *Journal for Specialists in Group Work, 14,* 25–33.

McCarthy, C., Mejia, O. L., & Liu, H. T. (2000). Cognitive appraisal theory: A psychoeducational approach for understanding connections between cognition and emotion in group work. *Journal for Specialists in Group Work, 25,* 104–121.

McClure, B. A. (1990). The group mind: Generative and regressive groups. *Journal for Specialists in Group Work, 15,* 159–170.

McClure, B. A. (1994). The shadow side of regressive groups. *Counseling and Values, 38,* 77–89.

McCormick, P. (1995). Redecisions required for mental health. *Transactional Analysis Journal, 25,* 321–326.

McCullough, P. G., & Rutenberg, S. K. (1988). Launching children and moving on. In B. Carter & M. McGoldrick (Eds.), *The changing family life cycle* (2nd ed., pp. 285–309). New York: Gardner.

McGaw, W. H., Farson, R. E., & Rogers, C. R. (Producers). (1968). *Journey into self* [Film]. Berkeley: University of California Extension Media Center.

McGovern, T. E., & Silverman, M. (1986). A review of outcome studies of rational-emotive therapy from 1977 to 1982. In A. Ellis & R. Grieger (Eds.), *Handbook of rational-emotive therapy* (Vol. 2). New York: Springer.

McGregor, D. (1960). *The human side of enterprise.* New York: McGraw-Hill.

McKown, H. C. (1934). *Home room guidance.* New York: McGraw-Hill.

McManus, P. W., Redford, J. L., & Hughes, R. B. (1997). Connecting to self and others: A structured group for women. *Journal for Specialists in Group Work, 22,* 22–30.

McMurray, D. (1992). When it doesn't work: Small-group work in adolescent sexuality education. *School Counselor, 39,* 385–389.

McRoberts, C., Burlingame, G. M., & Hoag, M. J. (1998). Comparative efficacy of individual and group psychotherapy: A meta-analytic perspective. *Group Dynamics, 2,* 101–117.

McRoy, C. R., & Brown, B. M. (1996). Effect of conceptual level on group conflict interaction. *Journal for Specialists in Group Work, 21,* 11–17.

McWhirter, B. T., McWhirter, E. H., & McWhirter, J. J. (1988). Groups in Latin America: Comunidades eclesial de base as mutual support groups. *Journal for Specialists in Group Work, 13,* 70–76.

McWhirter, J. J. (1995). Emotional education for university students. *Journal of College Student Psychotherapy, 10,* 27–38.

McWhirter, J. J., Nichols, E., & Banks, N. M. (1984). Career awareness and self-exploration (CASE) groups: A self-assessment model for career decision making. *Personnel and Guidance Journal, 62,* 580–582.

McWhirter, P. T., & McWhirter, J. J. (1996). Transition-to-work group: University students with learning disabilities. *Journal for Specialists in Group Work, 21,* 144–148.

Mead, G. H. (1934). *Mind, self, and society*. Chicago: University of Chicago Press.

Mead, M. (1972). *Blackberry winter*. New York: Morrow.

Meador, B. D. (1975). Client-centered group therapy. In G. Gazda (Ed.), *Basic approaches to group psychotherapy and group counseling* (2nd ed.). Springfield, IL: Thomas.

Meara, N. M., Schmidt, L. D., & Day, J. D. (1996). Principles and virtues: A foundation for ethical decision, policies, and character. *The Counseling Psychologist, 24*, 4–77.

Meichenbaum, D. H. (1977). *Cognitive-behavior modification: An integrative approach*. New York: Plenum.

Meichenbaum, D. H. (1986). Cognitive-behavior modification. In F. H. Kanfer & A. P. Goldstein (Eds.), *Helping people change*. New York: Pergamon.

Melnick, J., & Wood, M. (1976). Analysis of group composition research and theory for psychotherapeutic and growth oriented groups. *Journal of Applied Behavioral Science, 12*, 493–512.

Merriam-Webster's Collegiate Dictionary (11th ed.). (2003). Springfield, MA: Merriam-Webster.

Merta, R. J. (1995). Group work: Multicultural perspectives. In J. G. Ponterotto, J. M. Casas, L. A. Suzuki, & C. M. Alexander (Eds.), *Handbook of multicultural counseling* (pp. 567–585). Thousand Oaks, CA: Sage.

Michaels, M. L. (2006). Stepfamily enrichment program: A preventive intervention for remarried couples. *Journal for Specialists in Group Work, 31*, 135–152.

Miles, M. B. (1957). Human relations training: How a group grows. *Teachers College Record, 55*, 90–96.

Miles, R. (1993). I've got a song to sing. *Elementary School Guidance & Counseling, 28*, 71–75.

Miller, M. J. (1986). On the perfectionistic thoughts of beginning group leaders. *Journal for Specialists in Group Work, 11*, 53–56.

Miller, S. P., & Hudson, P. (1994). Using structured parent groups to provide parental support. *Intervention in School and Clinic, 29*, 151–155.

Milman, D. S., & Goldman, G. D. (1974). Introduction. In D. S. Milman & G. D. Goldman (Eds.), *Group process today*. Springfield, IL: Thomas.

Milsom, A., Akos, P., & Thompson, M. (2004). A psychoeducational group approach to postsecondary transition planning for students with learning disabilities. *Journal for Specialists in Group Work, 29*, 395–411.

Mitchell, C. L. (1993). The relationship of clinicians' values to therapy outcome ratings. *Counseling and Values, 37*, 156–164.

Mitchell, J. T., & Everly, G. S. (1993). *Critical incident stress debriefing: An operations manual for the prevention of traumatic stress among emergency services and disaster workers*. Ellicott City, MD: Chevron.

Moleski, S. M., & Kiselica, M. S. (2005). Dual relationships: A continuum ranging from destructive to the therapeutic. *Journal of Counseling & Development, 83*, 3–11.

Molina, B., Brigman, G., & Rhone, A. (2003). Fostering success through group work with children who celebrate diversity. *Journal for Specialists in Group Work, 28*, 166–184.

Moller, A. T., & Botha, H. C. (1996). Effects of a group rational-emotive behavior therapy program on the type A behavior pattern. *Psychological Reports, 78*, 947–961.

Monterio-Leitner, J. (2001, March). *Psychodrama: When and why to use doubling*. Presentation at the annual convention of the American Counseling Association, San Antonio, TX.

Moore, J., & Herlihy, B. (1993). Grief groups for students who have had a parent die. *School Counselor, 41*, 54–59.

Moore, M. M., & Freeman, S. J. (1995). Counseling survivors of suicide: Implications for group postvention. *Journal for Specialists in Group Work, 20*, 40–47.

Moreno, J. K. (1998). Long-term psychodynamic group psychotherapy for eating disorders: A descriptive case report. *Journal for Specialists in Group Work, 23*, 269–284.

Moreno, J. L. (1914). *Einladung zu einer Begegnung*. Vienna: Anzuengruber.

Moreno, J. L. (1923). *Das Stegif Theatre*. Berlin: Kiepenheur.

Moreno, J. L. (1940). The mental catharsis and the psychodrama. *Sociometry, 3*, 209–244.

Moreno, J. L. (1945a). *Psychodrama*. New York: Beacon House.

Moreno, J. L. (Ed.). (1945b). *Group psychotherapy: A symposium*. New York: Beacon House.

Moreno, J. L. (1946). *Psychodrama: Volume 1*. New York: Beacon House.

Moreno, J. L. (1953). *Who shall survive?* New York: Beacon House.

Moreno, J. L. (1964). *Psychodrama: Volume 1* (rev. ed.). New York: Beacon House.

Moreno, J. L. (1984). Reflections on my method of group psychotherapy and psychodrama. In H. Greenwald (Ed.), *Active psychotherapy* (pp. 130–143). New York: Aronson.

Moreno, Z. T. (1949). History of the sociometric movement in headlines. *Sociometry, 12*, 255–259.

Moreno, Z. T. (1959). A survey of psychodramatic techniques. *Group Psychotherapy, 12*, 5–14.

Moreno, Z. T. (1966). Evolution and dynamics of the group psychotherapy movement. In J. L. Moreno (Ed.), *The international handbook of group psychotherapy*. New York: Philosophical Library.

Moreno, Z. T. (1983). Psychodrama. In H. I. Kaplan & B. J. Sadock (Eds.), *Comprehensive group* (2nd ed.). Baltimore: Williams & Wilkins.

Moreno, Z. T. (1987). Psychodrama, role theory, and the concept of the social atom. In J. K. Zeig (Ed.), *The evolution of psychotherapy* (pp. 341–366). New York: Brunner/Mazel.

Morgan, B., & Hensley, L. (1998). Supporting working mothers through group work: A multimodal psychoeducational approach. *Journal for Specialists in Group Work, 23,* 298–311.

Morgan, R. (2004). Groups with offenders and mandated clients. In J. L. DeLucia-Waack, D. A. Gerrity, C. R. Kalodner, & M. T. Riva (Eds.), *Handbook of group counseling and psychotherapy* (pp. 388–400). Thousand Oaks, CA: Sage.

Morgan, R. D., Garland, J. T., Rozycki, A. T., Reich, & Wilson, S. (2005). Group therapy goals: A comparison of group therapy providers and male inmates. *Journal for Specialists in Group Work, 30,* 159–172.

Morran, D. K. (1982). Leader and member self-disclosing behavior in counseling groups. *Journal for Specialists in Group Work, 7,* 218–223.

Morran, D. K., Robison, F. F., & Stockton, R. (1985). Feedback exchange in counseling groups: An analysis of message content and receiver acceptance as a function of leader versus member delivery, session, and valence. *Journal of Counseling Psychology, 32*(5), 7–67.

Morran, D. K., Stockton, R. Cline, R. J., & Teed, C. (1998). Facilitating feedback exchange in groups: Leader interventions. *Journal for Specialists in Group Work, 23,* 257–268.

Morran, D. K., Stockton, R., & Whittingham, M. H. (2004). Effective leader interventions for counseling and psychotherapy groups. In J. L. DeLucia-Waack, D. A. Gerity, C. R. Kalodner, & M. T. Riva (Eds.), *Handbook of group counseling and psychotherapy* (pp. 91–103). Thousand Oaks, CA: Sage.

Mosak, H. H. (2005). Adlerian psychotherapy. In R. J. Corsini & D. Wedding (Eds.), *Current psychotherapies* (7th ed., pp. 52–95). Belmont, CA: Thompson.

Mowrer, O. H. (Ed). (1967). *Morality and mental health.* Chicago: Rand McNally.

Mullan, H. (1992). Existential therapists and their group therapy practices. *International Journal of Group Psychotherapy, 42,* 453–468.

Mullan, H., & Rosenbaum, M. (1978). *Group psychotherapy* (2nd ed.). New York: Free Press.

Muller, L. E. (2002). Group counseling for African American males: When all you have are European American counselors. *Journal for Specialists in Group Work, 27,* 299–313.

Muller, L. E., & Hartman, J. (1998). Group counseling for sexual minority youth. *Professional School Counseling, 1,* 38–42.

Munich, R. L., & Astrachan, B. (1983). Group dynamics. In H. I. Kaplan & B. J. Sadock (Eds.), *Comprehensive group psychotherapy* (2nd ed., pp. 15–23). Baltimore: Williams & Wilkins.

Murphy, J. J. (1997). *Solution-focused counseling in middle and high schools.* Alexandria, VA: American Counseling Association.

Murstein, B. I., & Brust, R. G. (1985). Humor and interpersonal attraction. *Journal of Personality Assessment, 49,* 637–640.

Myers, I. (1962). *Myers-Briggs Type Indicator.* Princeton, NJ: Educational Testing Service.

Myers, J. E. (1989). *Infusing gerontological counseling into counselor preparation.* Alexandria, VA: American Counseling Association.

Myers, J. E. (1990). Aging: An overview for mental health counselors. *Journal of Mental Health Counseling, 12,* 245–259.

Myers, J. E., Poidevant, J. M., & Dean, L. A. (1991). Groups for older persons and their caregivers: A review of the literature. *Journal for Specialists in Group Work, 16,* 197–205.

Myrick, R. D. (2003). *Developmental guidance and counseling: A practical approach* (4th ed.). Minneapolis: Educational Media Corporation.

Napier, R. W., & Gershenfeld, M. K. (2004). *Groups: Theory and experience* (7th ed.). Boston: Houghton Mifflin.

Nasser-McMillan, S. C., & Hakim-Larson, J. (2003). Counseling considerations among Arab Americans. *Journal of Counseling and Development, 81,* 150–159.

Negy, C. (2004). *Cross-cultural psychotherapy: Toward a critical understanding of diverse clients.* Reno, NV,: Bent Tree Press.

Nelson, J. R., Dykeman, C., Powell, S., & Petty, D. (1996). The effects of a group counseling intervention on students with behavioral adjustment problems. *Elementary School Guidance & Counseling, 31,* 21–33.

Neugarten, B. (1970). Dynamics of transition of middle age to old age: Adaptation and the life cycle. *Journal of Geriatric Psychiatry, 4,* 71–87.

Neugarten, B. L. (1979). Time, age and the life cycle. *American Journal of Psychiatry, 136,* 887–894.

Neukrug, E., Milliken, T., & Walden, S. (2001). Ethical complaints made against credential counselors: An updated survey of state licensing boards. *Counselor Education and Supervision, 41,* 57–70.

Newcomb, T. (1943). *Personality and social change.* New York: Dryden.

Newell, S. (2002). *Behavioural management in the classroom: A transactional analysis approach.* London: David Fulton.

Nichols, M. (1986). *Turning forty in the '80s.* New York: Norton.

Nims, D. R. (1998). Search for self: A theoretical model for applying family systems to adolescent group work. *Journal for Specialists in Group Work, 23,* 133–144.

Nims, D. R. (2002). A collaborative psychoeducational group work training program for residential workers in the juvenile justice system. *Journal for Specialists in Group Work, 27,* 287–298.

Nitza, A. G. (2005). Mechanisms of change: The contributions of Rex Stockton to group development and outcome in research and practice. *Journal for Specialists in Group Work, 30,* 271–281.

Nolan, E. J. (1978). Leadership interventions for promoting personal mastery. *Journal for Specialists in Group Work, 3,* 132–138.

Nolte, J. (1989). Remembering J. L. Moreno. *Journal of Group Psychotherapy, Psychodrama, & Sociometry, 42,* 129–137.

Nusbaum, G. A. (2000). A case illustration of combined treatment using a psychodynamic group for women sexual abuse survivors to address and modify self-punitive superego trends. *Group, 24,* 289–302.

Nye, R. D. (2000). *Three psychologies: Perspectives from Freud, Skinner, and Rogers* (6th ed.). Pacific Grove, CA: Brooks/Cole.

Nykodym, N., Ruud, W., & Liverpool, P. (1986). Quality circles: Will transaction analysis improve their effectiveness? *Transactional Analysis Journal, 16,* 182–187.

O'Brien, C. R., Johnson, J. L., & Miller, B. (1979). Counseling the aging: Some practical considerations. *Personnel and Guidance Journal, 57,* 288–291.

O'Connor, E. (2001, May). Psychology's original "survivor." *Monitor on Psychology, 32*(5), 32.

O'Connor, G. G. (1980). Small groups: A general systems model. *Small Group Behavior, 11,* 145–173.

O'Halloran, T. M., & McCartney, T. J. (2004). An evaluation of the use of technology as a tool to meet group training standards. *Journal for Specialists in Group Work, 29,* 65–74.

O'Hanlon, B., & Weiner-Davis, M. (1989). *In search of solutions: A new direction in psychotherapy.* New York: Norton.

O'Hearne, J. J. (1977). Pilgrim's progress. In G. Barnes (Ed.), *Transactional analysis after Eric Berne* (pp. 458–484). New York: Harper & Row.

O'Malley, F., & Allen, J. G. (1993). Adolescent group therapy. *Bulletin of the Menninger Clinic, 57,* 265–267.

O'Neil, J. M., & Egan, J. (1992). Men's gender role transitions over the life span: Transformations and fears of femininity. *Journal of Mental Health Counseling, 14,* 305–324.

Ohlsen, M. M. (1977). *Group counseling* (2nd ed.). New York: Holt, Rinehart & Winston.

Ohlsen, M. M. (1979). *Marriage counseling in groups.* Champaign, IL: Research Press.

Ohlsen, M. M., Horne, A. M., & Lawe, C. F. (1988). *Group counseling* (3rd ed.). New York: Holt, Rinehart & Winston.

Okech, J. E. A., & Kline, W. B. (2005). A qualitative exploration of group co-leader relationships. *Journal for Specialists in Group Work, 30,* 173–190.

Okech, J. E. A., & Kline, W. B. (2006). Competency concerns in group co-lead relationships. *Journal for Specialists in Group Work, 31,* 165–180.

Okun, B. F. (1984). *Working with adults.* Pacific Grove, CA: Brooks/Cole.

Olson, M. J., & McEwen, M. A. (2004). Grief counseling groups in a medium-security prison. *Journal for Specialists in Group Work, 29,* 225–236.

Olson, S. K., & Brown, S. L. (1986). A relocation support group for women in transition. *Journal of Counseling and Development, 64,* 454–455.

Omizo, M. M., & Omizo, S. A. (1988a). Group counseling's effects on self-concept and social behavior among children with learning disabilities. *Journal of Humanistic Education and Development, 26,* 109–117.

Omizo, M. M., Cubberly, W. E., & Longano, D. M. (1984). The effects of group counseling on self-concept and locus of control among learning disabled children. *Humanistic Education and Development, 23,* 69–79.

Ormont, L. R. (1984). The leader's role in dealing with aggression in groups. *International Journal of Group Psychotherapy, 34,* 553–572.

Ormont, L. R. (1988). The leader's role in resolving resistances to intimacy in the group setting. *International Journal of Group Psychotherapy, 38,* 29–45.

Osborn, A. F. (1957). *Applied imagination.* New York: Scribner.

Ouchi, W. (1981). *Theory Z.* Reading, MA: Addison-Wesley.

Pack-Brown, S. P., & Fleming, A. (2004). An Afrocentric approach to counseling groups with African Americans. In J. L. DeLucia-Waack, D. A. Gerity, C. R. Kalodner, & M. T. Riva (Eds.), *Handbook of group counseling and psychotherapy* (pp. 183–197). Thousand Oaks, CA: Sage.

Pack-Brown, S. P., & Whittington-Clark, L. E. (2002). I am because we are! Afrocentric approaches to group work. Farmingham, MA: Microtraining Associates (www.emicrotraining.com).

Pack-Brown, S. P., Whittington-Clark, L. E., & Parker, W. M. (1998). *Images of me: A guide to group work with African American women.* Boston: Allyn & Bacon.

Page, B. J. (2004). Online group counseling. In J. L. DeLucia-Waack, D. A. Gerity, C. R. Kalodner, & M. T. Riva (Eds.), *Handbook of group counseling and psychotherapy* (pp. 609–620). Thousand Oaks, CA: Sage.

Page, B. J., Delmonico, D. L., Walsh, J., L'Amoreaux, N. A., Danninhirsh, C., Thompson, R. S., et al. (2000). Setting up on-line support groups using The Palace software. *Journal for Specialists in Group Work, 25,* 133–145.

Page, B. J., & Hulse-Killacky, D. (1999). Development and validation of the Corrective Feedback Self-Efficacy Instrument. *Journal for Specialists in Group Work, 24,* 37–54.

Page, B.J., Jencius, M. J., Rehfuss, M. C., Foss, L. L., Dean, E. P., Petruzzi, M. L., et al. (2003). PalTalk online groups: Process and reflections on students' experience. *Journal for Specialists in Group Work, 28,* 35–41.

Page, B. J., Mitchell, C., Olson, S., & Vernon, D. (2000, October). *Ethical issues in group work: What decisions will you make?* Paper presented at the Southern Association for Counselor Education and Supervision, Greensboro, NC.

Page, B. J., Pietrzak, D. R., & Lewis, T. F. (2001). Development of the Group Leader Self-Efficacy Instrument. *Journal for Specialists in Group Work, 26,* 168–194.

Page, R. C., & Berkow, D. N. (1998). Group work as facilitation of spiritual development for drug and alcohol abusers. *Journal for Specialists in Group Work, 23,* 285–297.

Paisley, P., Swanson, L., Borders, S., Cassidy, N., & Danforth, C. (1994, March). *Counseling children using play media and the expressive arts.* Presentation at the North Carolina Counseling Association Conference, Charlotte.

Pan, P. J. D. (2000). The effectiveness of structured and semistructured Satir model groups in family relationships with college students in Taiwan. *Journal for Specialists in Group Work, 25,* 305–318.

Pan, P. J. D., Chang, S.-H., & Yu, Y.-Y. (2005). A support group for home-quarantined college students exposed to SARS: Learning from practice. *Journal for Specialists in Group Work, 30,* 363–374.

Paradise, L. V., & Kirby, P. C. (1990). Some perspectives on the legal liability of group counseling in private practice. *Journal for Specialists in Group Work, 15,* 114–118.

Paradise, L. V., & Siegelwaks, B. J. (1982). Ethical training for group leaders. *Journal for Specialists in Group Work, 7,* 162–166.

Parcover, J. A., Dunton, E. C., Gehlert, K. M., & Mitchell, S. L. (2006). Getting the most from group counseling in college counseling centers. *Journal for Specialists in Group Work, 31,* 37–49.

Parker, C. L. (1975). A desensitization group for adult community leaders. *Personnel and Guidance Journal, 54,* 48–49.

Parker, W. M., Freytes, M., Kaufman, C. J., Woodruff, R., & Hord, R. (2004). The mentoring lab: A small group approach for managing emotions from multicultural counseling training. *Journal for Specialists in Group Work, 29,* 361–375.

Parkinson, C. N. (1957). *Parkinson's law and other studies in administration.* Boston: Houghton Mifflin.

Parr, G., Haberstroh, S., & Kottler, J. (2000). Interactive journal writing as an adjunct in group work. *Journal for Specialists in Group Work, 25,* 229–241.

Parsons, T., & Shils, E. A. (1951). *Toward a general theory of action.* Cambridge, MA: Harvard University Press.

Passons, W. R. (1975). *Gestalt approaches in counseling.* New York: Holt, Rinehart & Winston.

Patterson, C. H. (1958). The place of values in counseling and psychotherapy. *Journal of Counseling Psychology, 5,* 216–223.

Patterson, C. H. (1985). New light for counseling theory. *Journal of Counseling and Development, 63,* 349–350.

Patterson, C. H. (1986). *Gimmicks in groups.* Paper presented at the annual convention of the American Association for Counseling and Development, Los Angeles.

Patterson, L. E., & Eisenberg, S. (2000). *The counseling process* (5th ed.). Pacific Grove, CA: Brooks/Cole.

Pearson, J. E. (1988). A support group for women with relationship dependency. *Journal of Counseling and Development, 66,* 394–396.

Pearson, R. E. (1985). A group-based training format for basic skills of small-group leadership. *Journal for Specialists in Group Work, 10,* 150–156.

Peck, M. S. (1983). *People of the lie.* New York: Simon & Schuster.

Pedersen, P. (1997a). *Culture-centered counseling interventions.* Thousand Oaks, CA: Sage.

Pedersen, P. (1997b, July). The positive consequences of a culture-centered perspective. *Counseling Today, 40,* 20.

Pedersen, P. (2000). *A handbook for developing multicultural awareness* (3rd ed.). Alexandria, VA: American Counseling Association.

Perls, F. (1967). Group vs. individual therapy. *A Review of General Semantics, 24,* 306–312.

Perls, F. (1969a). *Gestalt therapy verbatim.* New York: Bantam.

Perls, F. (1969b). *In and out of the garbage pail.* New York: Bantam.

Perls, F. (1970). Four lectures. In J. Fagan & I. L. Shepherd (Eds.), *Gestalt therapy now.* New York: Harper & Row.

Perls, F. (1974). *The Gestalt approach and eye witness to therapy.* Ben Lomond, CA: Science and Behavior Books.

Perls, F., Hefferline, R. F., & Goodman, P. (1951/1994). *Gestalt therapy: Excitement & growth in the human personality.* New York: The Gestalt Journal Press.

Perrone, K. M., & Sedlacek, W. E. (2000). A comparison of group cohesiveness and client satisfaction in homogeneous and heterogeneous groups. *Journal for Specialists in Group Work, 25,* 243–251.

Peterson, A. V., Chang, C., & Collins, P. L. (1998). The effects of reality therapy and choice theory training on self concept among Taiwanese university students. *International Journal for the Advancement of Counseling, 20,* 79–83.

Peterson, J. V., & Nisenholz, B. (1987). *Orientation to counseling.* Boston: Allyn & Bacon.

Pfeiffer, J. W., & Jones, J. E. (Eds.). (1972–1980). *A handbook of structured exercises for human relations training* (Vols. 1–8). San Diego, CA: University Associates.

Pfeiffer, J. W., & Jones, J. E. (Eds.). (1969–1975). *A handbook of structured experiences for human relations training* (Vols. 1–5). La Jolla, CA: University Associates.

Phelps, R. E., & Luke, E. (1995). A structured group for dealing with self-criticism. *Journal for Specialists in Group Work, 20,* 48–58.

Phillips, T. H., & Phillips, P. (1992). Structured groups for high school students: A case study of one district's program. *School Counselor, 39,* 390–393.

Piercy, F., Sprenkle, D., & Wetchler, J. L. (1996). *Family therapy sourcebook* (2nd ed.). New York: Guilford.

Piper, W. E., & Ogrodniczuk, J. S. (2004). Brief group therapy. In J. L.

DeLucia-Waack, D. A. Gerrity, C. R. Kalodner, & M. T. Riva (Eds.), *Handbook of group counseling and psychotherapy* (pp. 641–650). Thousand Oaks, CA: Sage.

Pistole, M. C. (1991). Termination: Analytic reflections on client contact after counselor relocation. *Journal of Counseling and Development, 69,* 337–340.

Pistole, M. C. (1997). Attachment theory: Contributions to group work. *Journal for Specialists in Group Work, 22,* 7–21.

Plotkin, R. (1978, March). Confidentiality in group counseling. *APA Monitor,* p. 14.

Polcin, D. L. (1991). Prescriptive group leadership. *Journal for Specialists in Group Work, 16,* 8–15.

Polster, I., & Polster, M. (1973). *Gestalt therapy integrated: Contours of theory and practice.* New York: Brunner/Mazel.

Ponzo, Z. (1991). Critical factors in group work: Clients' perceptions. *Journal for Specialists in Group Work, 16,* 16–23.

Popkin, M. (2006). *Active parenting Now in 3: Your Three Part Guide to a Great Family.* Atlanta, GA: Active Parenting.

Posthuma, B. W. (2002). *Small groups in therapy settings* (4th ed.). Boston: Allyn & Bacon.

Pottick, K. J. (1988). Jane Addams revisited: Practice theory and social economics. *Social Work with Groups, 11,* 11–26.

Price, G. E., Dinas, P., Dunn, C., & Winterowd, C. (1995). Group work with clients experiencing grieving: Moving from theory to practice. *Journal for Specialists in Group Work, 20,* 159–167.

Prinz, J., & Arkin, S. (1994). Adlerian group therapy with substance abusers. *Journal of Individual Psychology, 50,* 349–358.

Provost, J. A. (1999). A dream focus for short/term growth groups. *Journal for Specialists in Group Work, 24,* 74–87.

Rainwater, J. (1979). *You're in charge! A guide to becoming your own therapist.* Los Angeles: Guild of Tutors Press.

Rambo, T. (1997). The use of creative arts in adolescent group therapy. In S. T. Gladding (Ed.), *New developments in group counseling* (pp. 31–33). Greensboro, NC: ERIC.

Randall, D. A., Jr. (1995). Curative factor rankings for female incest survivor groups: A summary of three studies. *Journal for Specialists in Group Work, 20,* 232–239.

Rapin, L. S. (2004). Guidelines for ethical and legal practice in counseling and psychotherapy groups. In J. L. DeLucia-Waack, D. A. Gerity, C. R. Kalodner, & M. T. Riva (Eds.), *Handbook of group counseling and psychotherapy* (pp. 151–165). Thousand Oaks, CA: Sage.

Raskin, N. J. (1986a). Client-centered group psychotherapy. Part I: Development of client-centered groups. *Person-Centered Review, 1,* 272–290.

Raskin, N. J. (1986b). Client-centered group psychotherapy. Part II: Research on client centered groups. *Person-Centered Review, 1,* 389–408.

Raskin, N. J., & Rogers, C. R. (2005). Person-centered therapy. In R. J. Corsini & D. Wedding (Eds.), *Current psychotherapies* (7th ed., pp. 130–165). Belmont, CA: Thompson.

Rath, I. (1993). Developing a coherent map of transactional analysis theories. *Transactional Analysis Journal, 23,* 201–215.

Rayle, A. D., Sand, J. K., Brucato, T., & Ortega, J. (2006). The "Comadre" group approach: A wellness-based group model for monolingual Mexican women. *Journal for Specialists in Group Work, 31,* 5–24.

Reilly, A. J., & Jones, J. E. (1974). Teambuilding. In J. W. Pfeiffer & J. E. Jones (Eds.), *The annual handbook of group facilitators* (pp. 227–237). San Diego, CA: University Associates.

Remley, T. P., Jr. (1996). The relationship between law and ethics. In B.

Herlihy & G. Corey (Eds.), *ACA ethical standards casebook* (5th ed., pp. 285–292). Alexandria, VA: American Counseling Association.

Remley, T. P., Jr., & Herlihy, B. (2005). *Ethical, legal, and professional issues in counseling* (2nd ed.). Upper Saddle River, NJ: Prentice Hall.

Remley, T. P., Jr., & Reeves, T. G. (1989, March). *Beyond the formal classroom: Faculty/graduate student relationships.* Paper presented at the annual meeting of the American Association for Counseling and Development, Boston.

Resnick, J. L. (1981). Parent education and the female parent. *The Counseling Psychologist, 9,* 55–62.

Resnikoff, R. (1988, October). *Gestalt couples therapy.* Paper presented at the 46th Annual Conference of the American Association for Marriage and Family Therapy, New Orleans, LA.

Rice, A. H. (2004). Group treatment of depression. In J. L. DeLucia-Waack, D. A. Gerity, C. R. Kalodner, & M. T. Riva (Eds.), *Handbook of group counseling and psychotherapy* (pp. 532–546). Thousand Oaks, CA: Sage.

Riddle, J., Bergin, J. J., & Douzenis, C. (1997). Effects of group counseling on the self-concept of children of alcoholics. *Elementary School Guidance & Counseling, 31,* 192–203.

Rieckert, J., & Moller, A. T. (2000). Rational-emotive behavior therapy in the treatment of adult victims of childhood sexual abuse. *Journal of Rational Emotive and Cognitive Behavior Therapy, 18,* 87–101.

Rimm, D. C., & Cunningham, H. M. (1985). Behavior therapies. In S. J. Lynn & J. P. Garske (Eds.), *Contemporary psychotherapies: Models and methods* (pp. 221–260). Columbus, OH: Merrill.

Riordan, R. J., & Beggs, M. S. (1988). Some critical differences between self-help and therapy groups. *Journal for Specialists in Group Work, 13,* 24–29.

Riordan, R. J., & Kahnweiler, W. (1996). Job support groups: Three configurations. *Journal of Counseling and Development, 74,* 517–520.

Riordan, R. J., & Matheny, K. B. (1972). Dear diary: Logs in group counseling. *Personnel and Guidance Journal, 50,* 379–382.

Riordan, R. J., & White, J. (1996). Logs as therapeutic adjuncts in group. *Journal for Specialists in Group Work, 21,* 94–100.

Ritchie, M. H., & Huss, S. N. (2000). Recruiting and screening of minors for group counseling. *Journal for Specialists in Group Work, 25,* 146–156.

Rittenhouse, J. (1997). Feminist principles in survivor's groups: Out-of-group contact. *Journal for Specialists in Group Work, 22,* 111–119.

Riva, M. T. (2004). Best practices in groups. In J. L. DeLucia-Waack, D. A. Gerity, C. R. Kalodner, & M. T. Riva (Eds.), *Handbook of group counseling and psychotherapy* (pp. 63–64). Thousand Oaks, CA: Sage.

Riva, M. T., & Korinek, L. (2004). Teaching group work: Modeling group leader and member behaviors in the classroom to demonstrate group theory. *Journal for Specialists in Group Work, 29,* 55–63.

Riva, M. T., Lippert, L., & Tackett, M. J. (2000). Selection practices of group leaders: A national survey. *Journal for Specialists in Group Work, 25,* 157–169.

Riva, M. T., Wachtel, M., & Lasky, G. B. (2004). Effective leadership in counseling and psychotherapy. In J. L. DeLucia-Waack, D. A. Gerity, C. R. Kalodner, & M. T. Riva (Eds.), *Handbook of group counseling and psychotherapy* (pp. 37–48). Thousand Oaks, CA: Sage.

Rivera, E. T. (2004). Psychoeducational and counseling groups with Latinos. In J. L. DeLucia-Waack, D. A. Gerity, C. R. Kalodner, & M. T. Riva (Eds.) *Handbook of group counseling and psychotherapy* (pp. 213–223). Thousand Oaks, CA: Sage.

Rogers, C. R. (1951). *Client-centered therapy.* Boston: Houghton Mifflin.

Rogers, C. R. (1957). The necessary and sufficient conditions of therapeutic personality change. *Journal of Consulting Psychology, 21,* 95–103.

Rogers, C. R. (1959). A theory of therapy, personality, and interpersonal relationships, as developed in the client-centered framework. In S. Koch (Ed.), *Psychology: A study of science.* New York: McGraw-Hill.

Rogers, C. R. (1967). The process of the basic encounter group. In J. F. T. Bugenthal (Ed.), *Challenges of humanistic psychology.* New York: McGraw-Hill.

Rogers, C. R. (1970). *Carl Rogers on encounter groups.* New York: Harper & Row.

Rogers, C. R. (1972). *Becoming partners: Marriage and its alternatives.* New York: Delacorte.

Rogers, C. R. (1977). *Carl Rogers on personal power: Inner strength and its revolutionary impact.* New York: Delacorte.

Rogers, C. R. (1980). *A way of being.* Boston: Houghton Mifflin.

Rokeach, M. (2001). *Understanding human values.* New York: Free Press.

Rokeach, M., Smith, P. W., & Evans, R. I. (1960). Two kinds of prejudice or one? In M. Rokeach (Ed.), *The open and closed mind* (pp. 132–168). New York: Basic Books.

Rolland, C. B., & Neitzschman, L. (1996). Groups in schools: A model for training middle school teachers. *Journal for Specialists in Group Work, 21,* 18–25.

Rollock, D. A., Westman, J. S., & Johnson, C. (1992). A black student support group on a predominantly white university campus: Issues for counselors and therapists. *Journal for Specialists in Group Work, 17,* 243–252.

Romano, J. L. (1998). Simulated group counseling: An experiental training model for group work. *Journal for Specialists in Group Work, 23,* 119–132.

Romano, J. L., & Cikanek, K.L. (2003). Group work and computer applications: Instructional components for graduate students. *Journal for Specialists in Group Work, 28,* 23–34.

Romano, J. L., & Sullivan, B. A. (2000). Simulated group counseling for group work training: A four-year research study of group development. *Journal for Specialists in Group Work, 25,* 366–375.

Rose, S. D. (1977). *Group therapy: A behavioral approach.* Upper Saddle River, NJ: Prentice Hall.

Rose, S. D. (1980). *A casebook in group therapy: A behavioral-cognitive approach.* Upper Saddle River, NJ: Prentice Hall.

Rose, S. D. (1982). Group counseling with children: A behavioral and cognitive approach. In G. M. Gazda (Ed.), *Basic approaches to group psychotherapy and group counseling* (3rd ed.). Springfield, IL: Thomas.

Rose, S. D. (1983). Behavior therapy in groups. In H. I. Kaplan & B. J. Sadock (Eds.), *Comprehensive group psychotherapy* (2nd ed.). Baltimore: Williams & Wilkins.

Rose, S. D. (1986). Group methods. In F. H. Kanfer & A. P. Goldstein (Eds.), *Helping people change: A textbook of methods* (3rd ed., pp. 437–469). New York: Pergamon.

Rose, S. R. (1987). Social skill training in middle childhood: A structured group research. *Journal for Specialists in Group Work, 12,* 144–149.

Rose, S. R. (2001). Group work to promote the occupational functioning of Ethiopian minority men with disabilities who have immigrated to Israel. *Journal for Specialists in Group Work, 26,* 144–155.

Rose, S. D., & Edleson, J. L. (1987). *Working with children and adolescents in groups.* San Francisco: Jossey-Bass.

Roseman, I., Antonion, A. A., & Jose, P. (1996). Appraisal determinants of emotions: Constructing a more accurate and comprehensive theory. *Cognition and Emotion, 10,* 241–277.

Rosen, K. H., & Bezold, A. (1996). Dating violence prevention: A didactic support group for young women. *Journal of Counseling and Development, 74,* 521–525.

Rosenbaum, M. (1974). An overview of group psychotherapy and the present trend. In D. S. Milman & G. D. Goldman (Eds.), *Group process today: Evaluation and perspective* (pp. 15–36). Springfield, IL: Thomas.

Rosenbaum, M. (1978). The cotherapeutic method in the psychoanalytic group. In H. Mullan & M. Rosenbaum (Eds.), *Group psychotherapy: Theory and practice* (2nd ed., pp. 153–173). New York: Free Press.

Rothke, S. (1986). The role of interpersonal feedback in group psychotherapy. *International Journal of Group Psychotheraphy, 36,* 225–240.

Rudestam, K. E. (1982). *Experiential groups in theory and practice.* Pacific Grove, CA: Brooks/Cole.

Rugel, R. P. (1991). Closed and open systems: The Tavistock group from a general system perspective. *Journal for Specialists in Group Work, 16,* 74–84.

Ruitenbeek, H. M. (1970). *The new group therapies.* New York: Avon.

Rutan, J. S. (1999). Psychoanalytic group psychotherapy. In J. R. Price & D. R. Hescheles (Eds.), *A guide to starting psychotherapy groups* (pp. 151–166). San Diego, CA: Academic Press.

Rybak, C. J., & Brown, B. M. (1997). Group conflict: Communication patterns and group development. *Journal for Specialists in Group Work, 22,* 31–42.

Sack, R. T. (1985). On giving advice. *AMHCA Journal, 7,* 127–132.

Safran, J. S., & Safran, S. P. (1985). Teaching behavioral awareness in groups. *Elementary School Guidance & Counseling, 20*(9), 1–96.

Saidla, D. D. (1990). Cognitive development and group stages. *Journal for Specialists in Group Work, 15,* 15–20.

Salgado de Synder, V. N. (1987). Factors associated with acculturative stress and depressive symptomatology among married Mexican immigrant women. *Psychology of Women Quarterly, 11,* 475–488.

Saltmarsh, R. E., Jenkins, S. J., & Fisher, G. L. (1986). The TRAC model: A practical map for group process and management. *Journal for Specialists in Group Work, 11,* 30–36.

Sampson, E. E., & Marthas, M. (1981). *Group process for the health profession* (2nd ed.). New York: Wiley.

Sandhu, D. S. (1997). Psychocultural profiles of Asian and Pacific Islander Americans: Implications for counseling and psychotherapy. *Journal of Multicultural Counseling and Development, 25,* 7–22.

Santrock, J. W. (2006). *Life-span development* (10th ed.). Columbus, OH: McGraw-Hill.

Saravay, S. M. (1978). A psychoanalytic theory of group development. *International Journal of Group Psychotherapy, 28,* 481–507.

Saroyan, J. S. (1990). The use of music therapy in an adolescent psychiatric unit. *Journal of Group Psychotherapy, 43,* 139–142.

Satir, V. (1964). *Conjoint family therapy: A guide to theory and technique.* Palo Alto, CA: Science & Behavior Books.

Sayger, T. V. (1996). Creating resilient children and empowering families using a multifamily group process. *Journal for Specialists in Group Work, 21,* 81–89.

Schafer, M., & Crichlow, S. (1996). Antecedents of groupthink. *Journal of Conflict Resolution, 40,* 415–435.

Schilder, P. (1939). Results and problems of group psychotherapy in severe neurosis. *Mental Hygiene, 23,* 87–98.

Schleidlinger, S. (1952). *Psychoanalysis and group behavior.* New York: Norton.

Schlossberg, N. K. (1981). A model for analyzing human adaptation to transition. *The Counseling Psychologist, 9,* 2–18.

Schlossberg, N.K., Waters, E., & Goodman, J. (1995). *Counseling adults in transition* (2nd ed.). New York: Springer.

Schultz, B. (1982). *Legal liabilities in psychotherapy.* San Francisco: Jossey-Bass.

Schuster, E. (1998). A community bound by words: Reflections on a nursing home writing group. *Journal of Aging Studies, 12,* 137–147.

Schutz, W. (1958). *FIRO: A three dimensional theory of interpersonal behavior.* New York: Holt, Rinehart & Winston.

Schutz, W. (1966). *FIRO-B: Interpersonal underworld.* Palo Alto, CA: Science & Behavior Books.

Schutz, W. (1967). *Joy: Expanding human awareness.* New York: Grove.

Schutz, W. (1973). Encounter. In R. Corsini (Ed.), *Current psychotherapies.* Itasca, IL: Peacock.

Schutz, W. C. (1971). *Here comes everybody.* New York: Harper & Row.

Schwartz, J. P., & Waldo, M. (1999). Therapeutic factors in spouse-abuse group treatment. *Journal for Specialists in Group Work, 24,* 197–207.

Schwartz, J. P., & Waldo, M. (2003). Reducing gender role conflict among men attending partner abuse prevention groups. *Journal for Specialists in Group Work, 28,* 355–369.

Scogin, F., & Pollio, H. (1980). Targeting and the humorous episode in group process. *Human Relations, 33,* 831–852.

Sedgwick, C. (1989). Cognitive-behavioral group therapy. In G. M. Gazda (Ed.), *Group counseling* (4th ed., pp. 427–437). Boston: Allyn & Bacon.

Seligman, M. (1982). Introduction. In M. Seligman (Ed.), *Group psychotherapy and counseling with special populations* (pp. 1–3). Baltimore: University Park Press.

Seligman, M. (1993). Group work with parents of children with disabilities. *Journal for Specialists in Group Work, 18,* 115–126.

Shaffer, J., & Galinsky, M. D. (1989). *Models of group therapy* (2nd ed.). Upper Saddle River, NJ: Prentice Hall.

Shaffer, W. (1997). Psychodrama technique in the middle school, or meanwhile back at Elsinore Castle. In S. T. Gladding (Ed.), *New developments in group counseling* (pp. 33–36). Greensboro, NC: ERIC/CASS.

Shapiro, J. L. (1978). *Methods of group psychotherapy and encounter: A tradition of innovation.* Itasca, IL: Peacock.

Sharma, A., & Cheatham, H. E. (1986). A women's center support group for sexual assault victims. *Journal of Counseling and Development, 64,* 525–527.

Shaskan, D., & Roller, B. (1985). *Paul Schilder: Mind explorer.* New York: Human Sciences Press.

Shaw, B. R., McTavish, F., Hawkins, R., Gustafson, D. H., & Pingree, S. (2000). Experiences of women with breast cancer: Exchanging social support over the CHESS computer network. *Journal of Health Communication, 5,* 135–159.

Shechtman, Z. (2004). Group counseling and psychotherapy with children and adolescents: Current practice and reseach. In J. L. DeLucia-Waack, D. A. Gerity, C. R. Kalodner, & M. T. Riva (Eds.), *Handbook of group counseling and psychotherapy* (pp. 429–444). Thousand Oaks, CA: Sage.

Shechtman, Z., & Perl-Dekel, O. (2000). A comparison of therapeutic factors in two group treatment modalities: Verbal and art therapy. *Journal for Specialists in Group Work, 25,* 288–304.

Shechtman, Z., Vurembrand, N., Hertz-Lazarowitz, R. (1994). A dyadic and gender-specific analysis of close friendships of preadolescents receiving group psychotherapy.

Journal of Social and Personal Relationships, 11, 443–448.

Shepherd, C. R. (1964). *Small groups.* Scranton, PA: Chandler.

Sherif, M. (1936). *The psychology of group norms.* New York: Harper.

Sherif, M. (1937). An experimental approach to the study of attitudes. *Sociometry, 1,* 90–98.

Shulman, L. (1999). *The skills of helping individuals, families, groups and communities* (4th ed.). Itasca, IL: Peacock.

Sichel, J., & Ellis, A. (1984). *RET self-help form.* New York: Institute for Rational-Emotive Behavior Therapy.

Sidley, N. T. (Ed.). (1985). *Law and ethics: A guide for the health professional.* New York: Human Sciences Press.

Sigmund, E. (1995). A five-step model for problem resolution in difficult relationships. *Transactional Analysis Journal, 25,* 211–214.

Sileo, F. J., & Kopala, M. (1993). An A-B-C-D-E worksheet for promoting beneficence when considering ethical issues. *Counseling and Values, 37,* 89–95.

Silverman, M. (1976). The achievement motivation group: A counselor-directed approach. *Elementary School Guidance & Counseling, 11,* 100–106.

Silverman, P. R. (1986). The perils of borrowing: Role of the professional in mutual help groups. *Journal for Specialists in Group Work, 11,* 68–73.

Simkin, J. S. (1975). Gestalt therapy in groups. In G. M. Gazda (Ed.), *Basic approaches to group psychotherapy and group counseling* (2nd ed., pp. 265–286). Springfield, IL: Thomas.

Simpson, D. (1977). Handling group and organizational conflict. In J. Jones & J. W. Pfeiffer (Eds.), *1977 annual handbook for group facilitators* (pp. 120–122). La Jolla, CA: University Associates.

Singer, V. I., Tracz, S. M., & Dworkin, S. H. (1991). Reminiscence group therapy: A treatment modality for

older adults. *Journal for Specialists in Group Work, 16,* 167–171.

Skibbe, A. (1986). Assessing campus needs with nominal groups. *Journal of Counseling and Development, 64,* 532–533.

Skinner, B. F. (1953). *Science and human behavior.* New York: Macmillan.

Skinner, B. F. (1974). *About behaviorism.* New York: Knopf.

Sklare, G., Keener, R., & Mas, C. (1990). Preparing members for "here-and-now" group counseling. *Journal for Specialists in Group Work, 15,* 141–148.

Sklare, G. B., Sabella, R. A., & Petrosko, J. M. (2003). A preliminary study of the effects of group solution-focused guided imagery on recurring individual problems. *Journal for Specialists in Group Work, 28,* 370–381.

Sklare, G., Thomas, D. V., Williams, E. C., & Powers, K. A. (1996). Ethics and an experiential "here and now" group: A blend that works. *Journal for Specialists in Group Work, 21,* 263–273.

Slavson, S. R. (1945). Different methods of group therapy in relation to age levels. *Nervous Child, 4,* 196–210.

Slavson, S. R. (1948). Group therapy in child care and child guidance. *Jewish Social Service Quarterly, 25,* 203–213.

Slavson, S. R. (1962). Personality qualifications of a group psychotherapist. *International Journal of Group Psychotherapy, 12,* 411–420.

Slavson, S. R. (1964). *A textbook in analytic group psychotherapy.* New York: International Universities Press.

Smaby, M. H., Maddux, C. D., Torres-Rivera, E., & Zimmick, R. (1999). A study of the effects of a skills-based versus a conventional group counseling training program. *Journal for Specialists in Group Work, 24,* 152–163.

Smaby, M. H., Peterson, T. L., & Hovland, J. (1994). Total quality groups in business: Opportunities and challenges for specialists in group work. *Journal for Specialists in Group Work, 19,* 217–226.

Smead, R. S. (1994). *Skills for living: Group activities for elementary school students*. Champaign, IL: Research Press.

Smead, R. (1995). *Skills and techniques for group work with children*. Champaign, IL: Research Press.

Smead, R. S. (1996). *Skills and techniques for group work with youth*. Champaign, IL: Research Press.

Smiley, K. A. (2004). Structured groups for gay men newly diagnosed with HIV/AIDS. *Journal for Specialists in Group Work, 29,* 207–224.

Smith, D. C., & Maher, M. F. (1991). Group interventions with caregivers of the dying: The "Phoenix" alternative. *Journal for Specialists in Group Work, 16,* 191–196.

Smokowski, P. R. (2003). Beyond role-playing: Using technology to enhance modeling and behavioral rehearsal in group work practice. *Journal for Specialists in Group Work, 28,* 9–22.

Solomon, A., & Haaga, D. A. F. (1995). Rational emotive behavior therapy research: What we know and what we need to know. *Journal of Rational Emotive and Cognitive Behavior Therapy, 13,* 179–191.

Solotaroff, P. (1999). *Group*. New York: Berkley.

Sommers-Flanagan, R., Barrett-Hakanson, T., Clarke, C., & Sommers-Flanagan, J. (2000). A psychoeducational school-based coping and social skills group for depressed students. *Journal for Specialists in Group Work, 25,* 170–190.

Sonnenblick, M. D. (1997). The GALSS club: Promoting belonging among at-risk adolescent girls. *School Counselor, 44,* 243–245.

Sonstegard, M. A. (1998). The theory and practice of group counseling and group psychotherapy. *Journal of Individual Psychology, 54,* 217–250.

Sonstegard, M. A., & Bitter, J. A. (1998a). Adlerian group counsel-ing: Step by step. *Journal of Individual Psychology, 54,* 176–216.

Sonstegard, M. A., & Bitter, J. A. (1998b). Counseling children in groups. *Journal of Individual Psychology, 54,* 251–267.

Sonstegard, M., & Dreikurs, R. (1973). The Adlerian approach to group counseling of children. In M. M. Ohlsen (Ed.), *Counseling children in groups* (pp. 47–78). New York: Holt, Rinehart & Winston.

Spiegler, M. D., & Guevremont, D. C. (1993). *Contemporary behavior therapy* (2nd ed.). Pacific Grove, CA: Brooks/Cole.

Spira, J. L. (1997). Existential group therapy for advanced breast cancer and other life-threatening illnesses. In J. L. Spira (Ed.), *Group therapy for medically ill patients* (pp. 165–222). New York: Guilford.

Spotnitz, H. (1961). *The couch and the circle*. New York: Knopf.

Sprei, J., & Goodwin, R. A. (1983). Group treatment of sexual assault survivors. *Journal for Specialists in Group Work, 8,* 39–46.

Stanger, T., & Harris, Jr., R. S. (2005). Marathon group therapy: Potential for university counseling centers and beyond. *Journal for Specialists in Group Work, 30,* 145–157.

Stanley, P. H. (2006). Using the 5 P relay in task groups. *Journal for Specialists in Group Work, 31,* 25–35.

Starak, Y. (1988). Confessions of a group leader. *Small Group Behavior, 19,* 103–108.

Stehno, J. J. (1995). Classroom consulting with reality therapy. *Journal of Reality Therapy, 15,* 81–86.

Stein, H. (1993). Organizational psychohistory. *Journal of Psychohistory, 21,* 97–114.

Steiner, C. (1974). *Scripts people live: Transactional analysis of life scripts*. New York: Grove.

Steinglass, P. (1982). The roles of alcohol in family systems. In J. Oxford & J. Harwin (Eds.), *Alcohol and the family* (pp. 127–150). New York: St. Martin's.

Steinglass, P., Bennett, L. A., Wolin, S. J., & Reiss, D. (1993). *Alcoholic family*. New York: Basic Books.

Sternberg, R. J. (2004). Culture and intelligence. *American Psychologist, 59,* 325–338.

Stevens, M. J., Pfost, K. S., & Bruyere, D. (1983). Managing test anxiety: A group approach. *Journal of College Student Personnel, 24,* 88–89.

Stewart, I. (2000). *Transactional analysis counseling in action* (2nd ed.). London: Sage.

Stockton, R., & Morran, D. K. (1980). The use of verbal feedback in counseling groups: Toward an effective system. *Journal for Specialists in Group Work, 5,* 10–14.

Stockton, R., McDonnell, K. A., & Aldarondo, F. (1997). Application of a model for group leader instruction. In S. T. Gladding (Ed.), *New developments in group counseling* (pp. 129–131). Greensboro, NC: ERIC.

Stockton, R., & Moran, D. K. (1980). The use of verbal feedback in counseling groups: Toward an effective system. *Journal for Specialists in Group Work, 5,* 10–14.

Stockton, R., & Morran, D. K. (1982). Review and perspective of critical dimensions in therapeutic small group research. In G. M. Gazda (Ed.), *Basic approaches to group psychotherapy and group counseling* (3rd ed., pp. 37–83). Springfield, IL: Thomas.

Stockton, R., Morran, D. K., & Harris, M. (1991). Factors influencing group member acceptance of corrective feedback. *Journal for Specialists in Group Work, 16,* 245–254.

Stockton, R., Morran, D. K, & Krieger, K. K. (2004). An overview of current research and best practices for training beginning. In J. L. DeLucia-Waack, D. A. Gerity, C. R. Kalodner, & M. T. Riva (Eds.), *Handbook of group counseling and psychotherapy* (pp. 65–75). Thousand Oaks, CA: Sage.In

Stockton, R., Morran, D. K., & Nitza, A. G. (2000). Processing group events:

A conceptual map for leaders. *Journal for Specialists in Group Work, 25,* 343–355.

Stockton, R., Morran, D., & Velkoff, P. (1987). Leadership of therapeutic small groups. *Journal of Group Psychotherapy, Psychodrama & Sociometry, 39,* 157–165.

Stockton, R., & Toth, P. L. (1996). Teaching group counselors: Recommendations for maximizing preservice instruction. *Journal for Specialists in Group Work, 21,* 274–282.

Stogdill, R. M. (1969). Personal factors associated with leadership: A survey of the literature. In C. A. Gibb (Ed.), *Leadership* (pp. 91–133). Harmondsworth, England: Penguin.

Stogdill, R. M. (1974). *Handbook of leadership.* New York: Free Press.

Stoller, F. H. (1968). Focused feedback with video tape. Extending the group's focus. In G. M. Gazda (Ed.), *Innovations to group psychotherapy.* Springfield, IL: Thomas.

Stoltz, S. G. (1984). Recovering from foodaholism. *Journal for Specialists in Group Work, 9,* 51–61.

Stone, M. L., & Waters, E. (1991). Accentuate the positive: A peer group counseling program for older adults. *Journal for Specialists in Group Work, 16,* 159–166.

Storandt, M. (1983). *Counseling and therapy with older adults.* Boston: Little, Brown.

Strange, R. (1935). *The role of the teacher in personnel work.* New York: Bureau of Publications, Teachers College, Columbia University.

Streib, G., & Beck, R. (1981). Older families: A decade review. *Journal of Marriage and the Family, 42,* 937–956.

Strother, J., & Harvill, R. (1986). Support groups for relocated adolescent students: A model for school counselors. *Journal for Specialists in Group Work, 11,* 114–120.

Strupp, H. H., Hadley, S. W., & Gomes-Schwartz, B. (1977). *Psychotherapy for better or worse: The problem of negative effects.* New York: Aronson.

Sue, D. W. (1992). The challenge of multiculturalism: The road less traveled. *American Counselor, 1,* 6–14.

Sue, D. W., Arredondo, P., & McDavis, R. J. (1992). Multicultural counseling competencies and standards: A call to the profession. *Journal of Counseling and Development, 70,* 477–486.

Sullivan, E. M., Coffey, J. F., & Greenstein, R. A. (1987). Treatment outcome in a group geropsychiatry program for veterans. *The Gerontologist, 27,* 434–435.

Sullivan, M. (1983a). Introduction to women emerging: Group approaches. *Journal for Specialists in Group Work, 8,* 3–8.

Sullivan, M. (1983b). Women and career development: Group activities to overcome internal barriers. *Journal for Specialists in Group Work, 8,* 47–55.

Summerton, O. (1993). Games in organizations. *Transactional Analysis Journal, 23,* 87–103.

Sweeney, T. J. (1999). *Adlerian counseling: A practical approach for a new decade.* Philadelphia: Accelerated Development.

Swenson, L. C. (1997). *Psychology and law* (2nd ed.). Pacific Grove, CA: Brooks/Cole.

Tamm, M. E. (1993). Models of health and disease. *British Journal of Medical Psychology, 66,* 213–238.

Taub, D. J. (1998a). Building community on campus: Student affairs professionals as group workers. *Journal for Specialists in Group Work, 23,* 411–427.

Taub, D. J. (1998b). Promoting student development through psychoeducational groups: A perspective on the goals and process matrix. *Journal for Specialists in Group Work, 23,* 196–201.

Taulbee, L. R. (1978). Reality orientation: A therapeutic group activity for elderly persons. In I. M. Burnside (Ed.), *Working with the elderly: Group processes and techniques* (pp. 206–218). North Scituate, MA: Duxbury.

Taylor, L., Adelman, H. S., & Kaser-Boyd, N. (1986). Exploring minors' reluctance and dissatisfaction with psychotherapy. *Professional Psychology: Research and Practice, 16,* 418–425.

Tedder, S. L., Scherman, A., & Sheridan, K. M. (1984). Impact of group support on adjustment to divorce by single, custodial fathers. *AMHCA Journal, 6,* 180–189.

Tedder, S. L., Scherman, A., & Wantz, R. A. (1987). Effectiveness of a support group for children of divorce. *Elementary School Guidance & Counseling, 22,* 102–109.

Terner, J., & Pew, W. L. (1978). *The courage to be imperfect: The life and work of Rudolf Dreikurs.* New York: Hawthorn.

Thomas, K. W., & Kilmann, R. H. (1974). *Thomas-Kilmann Conflict Mode Instrument.* Tuxedo, NY: XICOM.

Thomas, M. B. (1992). *An introduction to marital and family therapy.* New York: Macmillan.

Thomas, M. C. (1991). Their past gives our present meaning—Their dreams are our future. *Journal for Specialists in Group Work, 16,* 132.

Thomas, M. C., & Martin, V. (1997). Helping older adults age with integrity, empowerment, and meaning through group counseling. In S. T. Gladding (Ed.), *New developments in group counseling* (pp. 43–45). Greensboro, NC: ERIC.

Thomas, M. C., & Martin, V. (2006). Group work: Elderly people and their caregivers. In D. Capuzzi, D. R. Gross, & M. D. Shauffer (Eds.), *Introduction to group work* (4th ed.) (pp. 484–514). Denver: Love.

Thomas, M. C., Martin, V., Alexander, J. J., Cooley, F. R., & Loague, A. M. (2003).Using new attitudes and technology to change the developmental counseling focus for older populations. *Counseling and Human Development, 35*(8), 1–8.

Thomason, T. C. (1991). Counseling Native Americans: An introduction for non–Native American counselors. *Journal of Counseling & Development, 69,* 321–326.

Thompson, C. L., & Henderson, D. A. (2007). *Counseling children* (7th ed.). Pacific Grove, CA: Brooks/Cole.

Thompson, E. C., III. (1987). The "Yagottawanna" group: Improving student self-perceptions through motivational teaching of study skills. *School Counselor, 35,* 134–142.

Thoresen, C. E., & Mahoney, M. J. (1974). *Behavioral self-control.* New York: Holt, Rinehart & Winston.

Thorne, B. (1992). *Carl Rogers.* Newbury Park, CA: Sage.

Tillich, P. (1952). *The courage to be.* New Haven, CT: Yale University Press.

Tjosvold, D. (1986). Constructive controversy: A key strategy for groups. *Personnel, 63,* 39–44.

Tollerud, T. R., Holling, D. W., & Dustin, D. (1992). A model for teaching in group leadership: The pre-group interview application. *Journal for Specialists in Group Work, 17,* 96–104.

Torres Rivera, E., Wibur, M., Roberts-Wilbur, J., Phan, L. T., Garrett, M. T., & Betz, R. L. (2004). Supervising and training psychoeducational group leaders. *Journal for Specialists in Group Work, 29,* 377–394.

Toseland, R., & Siporin, M. (1986). When to recommend group treatment: A review of the clinical and group literature. *International Journal of Group Psychotherapy, 36,* 172–201.

Toth, P. L. (2005). The contributions of Rex Stockton to the field of group work: Implications and applications. *Journal for Specialists in Group Work, 30,* 199–202.

Toth, P. L., & Erwin, W. J. (1998). Applying skilled-based curriculum to teach feedback groups: An evaluation study. *Journal of Counseling & Development, 76,* 294–301.

Toth, P. L., & Stockton, R. (1996). A skill-based approach to teaching group counseling interventions.

Journal for Specialists in Group Work, 21, 101–109.

Treadwell, T. W., Kumar, V. K., Stein, S. A., & Prosnick, K. (1997). Sociometry: Tools for research and practice. *Journal for Specialists in Group Work, 22,* 52–65.

Trotzer, J. P. (1980). Develop your own guidance group: A structural framework for planning and practice. *School Counselor, 27,* 341–349.

Trotzer, J. P. (1988). Family theory as a group resource. *Journal for Specialists in Group Work, 13,* 180–185.

Trotzer, J. P. (1997, Spring). Gleanings of a process observer. *Together, 25*(3), 6.

Trotzer, J. P. (2004). Conducting a group: Guidelines for choosing and using activities. In J. L. DeLucia-Waack, D. A. Gerity, C. R. Kalodner, & M. T. Riva (Eds.), *Handbook of group counseling and psychotherapy* (pp. 76–90). Thousand Oaks, CA: Sage.

Trotzer, J. P. (2007). *The counselor and the group: Integrating theory, training, and practice* (4th ed.). Philadelphia: Brunner-Routledge.

Tsui, A. M., & Sammons, M. T. (1988). Group intervention with adolescent Vietnamese refugees. *Journal for Specialists in Group Work, 13,* 90–95.

Tuckman, B. (1965). Developmental sequence in small groups. *Psychological Bulletin, 63,* 384–399.

Tuckman, B. W., & Jensen, M. A. C. (1977). Stages of small-group development revisited. *Group and Organizational Studies, 2,* 419–427.

Tudor, K. (1995). What do you say about saying good-bye? Ending psychotherapy. *Transactional Analysis Journal, 25,* 228–233.

Tyler, N. (1995). PAIRS and redecision therapy. *Transactional Analysis Journal, 25,* 347–349.

U.S. Bureau of the Census. Census 2000 shows America's diversity. (March 12, 2001). Retrieved December 10, 2006, from http://www.census.gov/Press Release/www/releases.

Upper, D., & Ross, S. M. (Eds.). (1980). *Behavioral group therapy, 1980: An annual review.* Champaign, IL: Research Press.

Vacc, N. A., & Wittmer, J. P. (Eds.). (1980). *Let me be me: Special populations and the helping professions.* Muncie, IN: Accelerated Development.

Vacha-Haase, T., Ness, C. M., Dannison, L., & Smith, A. (2000). Grandparents raising grandchildren: A psychoeducational group approach. *Journal for Specialists in Group Work, 25,* 67–78.

Valbak, K. (2001). Good outcome for bulimic patients in long-term group analysis: A single-group study. *European Eating Disorders Review, 9,* 19–32.

Valdes, T. M., & McPherson, R. H. (1987). "Leaving home": A family of origin group for college students. *Journal of College Student Personnel, 28,* 466–467.

Van der Pompe, G., Duivenvoorden, H. J., Antoni, M. H., & Visser, A. (1997). Effectiveness of a short-term group psychotherapy program on endocrine and immune function in breast cancer patients: An exploratory study. *Journal of Psychosomatic Research, 42,* 453–466.

Van Hoose, W. H., & Paradise, L. V. (1979). *Ethics in counseling and psychotherapy: Perspectives in issues and decision-making.* Cranston, RI: Carroll.

Van Hoose, W., & Kottler, J. (1977). *Ethical and legal issues in counseling and psychotherapy.* San Francisco: Jossey-Bass.

Van Hoose, W., & Kottler, J. (1985). *Ethical and legal issues in counseling and psychotherapy* (2nd ed.). San Francisco: Jossey-Bass.

Vander Kolk, C. J. (1985). *Introduction to group counseling and psychotherapy.* Upper Saddle River, NJ: Prentice Hall.

Verhofstadt, D., & Leni, M. F. (2000). The "magic shop" technique in psychodrama: An existential-dialectical view. *International Journal of Action Methods: Psychodrama,*

Skill Training, and Role Playing, 53, 3–15.

Vernon, A. (1990). *Thinking, feeling, behaving: An emotional educational curriculum for children grades 1–6.* Champaign, IL: Research Press.

Villalba, J. A. (2003). A psychoeducational group for limited-English proficient Latino/Latina children. *Journal for Specialists in Group Work, 28,* 261–276.

Vinson, A. (1992). Group counseling with victims of abuse/incest. In D. Capuzzi & D. R. Gross (Eds.), *Introduction to group counseling* (pp. 165–181). Denver, CO: Love.

Vinson, M. L. (1995). Employing family therapy in group counseling with college students: Similarities and a technique employed by both. *Journal for Specialists in Group Work, 20,* 240–252.

Viorst, J. (1971). *The tenth good thing about Barney.* New York: Aladdin.

Viorst, J. (1986). *Necessary losses.* New York: Simon & Schuster.

Vontress, C. E. (1996). A personal retrospective on cross-cultural counseling. *Journal of Multicultural Counseling and Development, 24,* 156–166.

Vriend, J. (1985). We've come a long way, group. *Journal for Specialists in Group Work, 10,* 63–67.

Vriend, J., & Dyer, W. W. (1973). Counseling the reluctant client. *Journal of Counseling Psychology, 20,* 240–246.

Wagenheim, G., & Gemmill, G. (1994). Feedback exchange: Managing group closure. *Journal of Management Education, 18,* 265–269.

Walden, S. L. (1997). The counselor/client partnership in ethical practice. In B. Herlihy & G. Corey (Eds.), *Boundary issues in counseling: Multiple roles and responsibilities* (pp. 40–47). Alexandria, VA: American Counseling Association.

Waldo, M. (1985). A curative factor framework for conceptualizing group counseling. *Journal of Counseling and Development, 64,* 52–58.

Waldo, M., & Bauman, S. (1998). Regrouping the categorization of group work: A goals and process (GAP) matrix for groups. *Journal for Specialists in Group Work, 23,* 164–176.

Walen, S. R., DiGiuseppe, R., & Wessler, R. L. (1980). *A practitioner's guide to RET.* New York: Oxford University Press.

Walsh, F. (1988). The family in later life. In B. Carter & M. McGoldrick (Eds.), *The changing family life cycle* (2nd ed., pp. 311–332). New York: Gardner.

Walsh, R. (1989). Asian psychotherapies. In R. J. Corsini & D. Wedding (Eds.), *Current psychotherapies* (4th ed., pp. 546–559). Itasca, IL: Peacock.

Walter, C. A. (2005). Support groups for widows and widowers. In G. L. Greif & P. H. Ephross (Eds), *Group work with populations at risk* (2nd ed., pp. 109–125). New York: Oxford.

Walters, R. (1989). Nonverbal communication in group counseling. In G. M. Gazda (Ed.), *Group counseling: A developmental approach* (4th ed.). Boston: Allyn & Bacon.

Walton, M. (1991). *Deming management at work.* New York: Putnam.

Wanlass, J., Moreno, J. K., & Thomson, H. M. (2005). Group therapy for eating disorders: A retrospective case study. *Journal for Specialists in Group Work, 30,* 47–66.

Ward, D. E. (1982). A model for the more effective use of theory in group work. *Journal for Specialists in Group Work, 7,* 224–230.

Ward, D. E. (1985). Levels of group activity: A model for improving the effectiveness of group work. *Journal of Counseling and Development, 64,* 59–64.

Ward, D. E. (1997). Factors influencing the development and quality of cooperative teamwork in groups. In S. T. Gladding (Ed.), *New developments in group counseling* (pp. 115–117). Greensboro, NC: ERIC/CASS.

Ward, D. E. (2004a). Introducing a special issue on teaching group work. *Journal for Specialists in Group Work, 29,* 1–2.

Ward, D. E. (2004b). The evidence mounts: Group work is effective. *Journal for Specialists in Group Work, 29,* 155–157.

Ward, D. E. (2006). Classification of groups. *Journal for Specialists in Group Work, 31,* 93–97.

Ward, D. E., & Litchy, M. (2004). The effective use of processing in groups. In J. L. DeLucia-Waack, D. A. Gerity, C. R. Kalodner, & M. T. Riva (Eds.), *Handbook of group counseling and psychotherapy* (pp. 104–119). Thousand Oaks, CA: Sage.

Waring, E. (1988). *Enhancing marital intimacy through cognitive self-disclosure.* New York: Brunner/Mazel.

Wasielewski, R. A., Scruggs, M. Y., & Scott, C. W. (1997). Student groups conducted by teachers: The teachers As Counselors (TAC) program. *Journal for Specialists in Group Work, 22,* 43–51.

Waters, E., McCarroll, J., & Penman, N. (1987). *Training mental health workers for the elderly: An instructor's guide.* Rochester, MI: Continuum Center.

Watkins, C. E. (1985). Countertransference: Its impact on the counseling situation. *Journal of Counseling and Development, 63,* 356–359.

Watson, D. L., & Tharp, R. G. (1981). *Self-directed behavior: Self-modification for personal adjustment* (3rd ed.). Pacific Grove, CA: Brooks/Cole.

Watson, G. (1928). Do groups think more effectively than individuals? *Journal of Abnormal and Social Psychology, 23,* 328–336.

Watson, J. B. (1913). Psychology as a behaviorist views it. *Psychological Review, 20,* 158–177.

Watzlawick, P. (1983). *The situation is hopeless, but not serious.* New York: Norton.

Wegscheider, S. (1981). *Another chance: Hope and health for the alcoholic family.* Palo Alto, CA: Science & Behavior Books.

Weiner, M. F. (1984). *Techniques of group psychotherapy*. Washington, DC: American Psychiatric Press.

Weinrach, S. G. (1980). Unconventional therapist: Albert Ellis. *Personnel and Guidance Journal, 59,* 152–160.

Weinrach, S. G. (1995). Rational emotive behavior therapy: A tough-minded therapy for a tender-minded profession. *Journal of Counseling & Development, 73,* 296–300.

Weinrach, S. G. (1996). Nine experts describe the essence of rational-emotive therapy while standing on one foot. *Journal of Counseling & Development, 74,* 326–331.

Weisman, C., & Schwartz, P. (1989). Worker expectations in group work with the frail elderly: Modifying the model for a better fit. *Social Work with Groups, 12,* 47–55.

Welfel, E. R. (2006). *Ethics in counseling and psychotherapy* (3rd ed.). Pacific Grove, CA: Brooks/Cole.

Wender, L. (1936). The dynamics of group psychotherapy and its application. *Journal of Nervous and Mental Diseases, 84,* 54–60.

Wenz, K., & McWhirter, J. J. (1990). Enhancing the group experience: Creative writing exercises. *Journal for Specialists in Group Work, 15,* 37–42.

Werstlein, P. O., & Borders, L. D. (1997). Group process variables in group supervision. *Journal for Specialists in Group Work, 22,* 120–136.

Wessler, R. L. (1986). Rational-emotive therapy in groups. In A. Ellis & R. Grieger (Eds.), *Handbook of rational-emotive therapy* (Vol. 2, pp. 295–315). New York: Springer.

Wessler, R. L., & Hankin, S. (1988). Rational-emotive therapy and related cognitively oriented psychotherapies. In S. Long (Ed.), *Six group therapies* (pp. 159–215). New York: Plenum.

Westwood, M. J., Keats, P. A., & Wilensky, P. (2003). Therapeutic enactment: Integrating individual and group counseling models for

change. *Journal for Specialists in Group Work, 28,* 122–138.

Wheeler, I., O'Malley, K., Waldo, M., Murphey, J., & Blank, C. (1992). Participants' perception of therapeutic factors in groups for incest survivors. *Journal for Specialists in Group Work, 17,* 89–95.

Whitaker, D. S., & Lieberman, M. (1964). *Psychotherapy through the group process*. New York: Atherton.

White, J., & Mullis, F. (1997). Parent education groups. In S. T. Gladding (Ed.), *New developments in group counseling* (pp. 47–49). Greensboro, NC: ERIC.

White, J., & Riordan, R. (1990). Some key concerns in leading parent education groups. *Journal for Specialists in Group Work, 15,* 201–205.

Whiteside, R. G. (1993). Making a referral for family therapy: The school counselor's role. *Elementary School Guidance & Counseling, 27,* 273–279.

Whitfield, C. L. (1987). *Healing the child within: Discovery and recovery for adult children of dysfunctional families*. Pompano Beach, FL: Health Communications.

Whyte, W. (1943). *Street corner society*. Chicago: University of Chicago Press.

Wilcox, D. W., & Forrest, L. (1992). The problems of men and counseling: Gender bias or gender truth? *Journal of Mental Health Counseling, 14,* 291–304.

Wilcoxon, A., Remley, T. R., Gladding, S. T., & Huber, C. H. (2007). *Ethical, legal and professional issues in the practice of marriage and family therapy* (4th ed.). Upper Saddle River, NJ: Prentice Hall.

Wilkins, P. (1995). A creative therapies model for the group supervision of counselors. *British Journal of Guidance and Counselling, 23,* 245–257.

Williams, C. B., Frame, M. W., & Green, E. (1999). Counseling groups for African American women: A focus on spirituality. *Journal for Specialists in Group Work, 24,* 260–273.

Williams, R. C., & Myer, R. A. (1992). The men's movement: An adjunct to traditional counseling approaches. *Journal of Mental Health Counseling, 14,* 393–404.

Williams, W. C., & Lair, G. S. (1988). Geroconsultation: A proposed decision-making model. *Journal of Counseling and Development, 67,* 198–203.

Williamson, E. (1958). Value orientation in counseling. *Personnel and Guidance Journal, 36,* 520–528.

Williamson, R. S. (1992). Using group reality therapy to raise self-esteem in adolescent girls. *Journal of Reality Therapy, 11,* 3–11.

Wilson, F. R., Rapin, L. S., & Haley-Banez, L. (2004). How teaching group work can be guided by foundational documents: Best practice guidelines, diversity principles, training standards. *Journal for Specialists in Group Work, 29,* 19–29.

Wilson, G. L., & Hanna, M. S. (1986). *Groups in context*. New York: Random House.

Wilson, G. T. (2005). Behavior therapy. In R. J. Corsini & D. Wedding (Eds.), *Current psychotherapies* (7th ed., pp. 202–237). Itasca, IL: Peacock.

Wolf, A. (1949). The psychoanalysis of groups. *American Journal of Psychotherapy, 3,* 529–557.

Wolf, A. (1963). The psychoanalysis of groups. In M. Rosenbaum and M. Berger (Eds.), *Group psychotherapy and group function* (pp. 273–327). New York: Basic Books.

Wolf, A. (1975). Psychoanalysis of groups. In M. Berger & M. Rosenbaum (Eds.), *Group psychotherapy and group function* (2nd ed., pp. 273–327). New York: Basic Books.

Wolf, A., & Schwartz, E. K. (1962). *Psychoanalysis in groups*. New York: Grune & Stratton.

Wolf, T. J. (1987). Group counseling for bisexual men. *Journal for Specialists in Group Work, 12,* 162–165.

Wolfe, J. L. (1995). Rational emotive behavior therapy women's groups: A twenty year retrospective. *Journal of Rational Emotive and*

Cognitive Behavior Therapy, 13, 153–170.

Wolpe, J. (1958). *Psychotherapy by reciprocal inhibition.* Stanford, CA: Stanford University Press.

Wood, J. K. (1982). Person-centered group therapy. In G. Gazda (Ed.), *Basic approaches to group psychotherapy and group counseling* (3rd ed.). Springfield, IL: Thomas.

Woody, R. H. (1988). *Protecting your mental health practice.* San Francisco: Jossey-Bass.

Woody, R. H., & Associates (Eds.). (1984). *The law and the practice of human services.* San Francisco: Jossey-Bass.

Woody, R. H., Hansen, J. C., & Rossberg, R. H. (1989). *Counseling psychology: Strategies and services.* Pacific Grove, CA: Brooks/Cole.

Woody, R. H., & Mitchell, R. E. (1984). Understanding the legal system and legal research. In R. H. Woody & Associates (Eds.), *The law and the practice of human services.* San Francisco: Jossey-Bass.

Woollams, S., & Brown, M. (1978). *Transactional analysis.* Dexter, MI: Huron Valley Institute.

Woollams, S., Brown, M., & Huige, K. (1977). What transactional analysts want their clients to know. In G. Barnes (Ed.), *Transactional analysis after Eric Berne* (pp. 487–525). New York: Harper & Row.

Worden, J. (1991). *Grief counseling and grief therapy* (2nd ed.). New York: Springer.

Wrenn, C. G. (1962). The culturally encapsulated counselor. *Harvard Educational Review, 32,* 444–449.

Wrenn, C. G. (1979). Proposed changes in counselor attitudes: Toward your job. *School Counselor, 27,* 81–90.

Wrenn, C. G. (1985). Afterward: The encapsulated counselor revisited. In P. Pedersen (Ed.), *Handbook of cross-cultural counseling and therapy* (pp. 323–329). Westport, CT: Greenwood.

Wrenn, C. G. (1989). Preface. In J. E. Myers (Ed.), *Infusing gerontological counseling into counselor preparation* (pp. 9–15). Alexandria, VA: American Counseling Association.

Wubbolding, R. E. (1987). A model for group activities related to teaching reality therapy. *Journal of Reality Therapy, 6,* 23–28.

Wubbolding, R. E. (1988). *Using reality therapy.* New York: Harper & Row.

Wubbolding, R. E. (1991). *Understanding reality therapy.* New York: Harper.

Wubbolding, R. E. (1992). *Cycle of counseling and supervision and coaching using reality therapy* (chart). Cincinnati, OH: Center for Reality Therapy.

Wubbolding, R. E. (1999, April). *Reality therapy in groups.* Presentation at the World Conference of the American Counseling Association. San Diego, CA.

Wubbolding, R. E. (2001). *Reality therapy for the 21st century.* New York: Brunner/Mazel.

Yablonsky, L. (1976). *Psychodrama: Resolving emotional problems through role playing.* New York: Basic Books.

Yalom, I. D. (1970). *The theory and practice of group psychotherapy.* New York: Basic Books.

Yalom, I. D. (1985). *The theory and practice of group psychotherapy* (2nd ed.). New York: Basic Books.

Yalom, I. D. (1990). *Understanding group psychotherapy* [Videotape]. Pacific Grove, CA: Books/Cole.

Yalom, I. (1995). *The theory and practice of group psychotherapy* (4th ed.). New York: Basic Books.

Yalom, I. D. (2005). *The theory and practice of group psychotherapy* (5th ed.). New York: Basic Books.

Yalom, I. D., & Lieberman, M. (1971). A study of encounter group casualties. *Archives of General Psychology, 25,* 16–30.

Yamamoto, G. (1995). The problems and effects of structured encounter groups as assessed by a follow-up survey. *Japanese Journal of Counseling Science, 28,* 1–20.

Yauman, B. E. (1991). School-based group counseling for children of divorce: A review of the literature. *Elementary School Guidance & Counseling, 26,* 130–138.

Yeaworth, R. C., McNamee, M. J., & Pozehl, B. (1992). The adolescent life change event scale: Its development and use. *Adolescence, 27,* 783–802.

Yontef, G. (1990). Gestalt therapy in groups. In I. Kutash & A. Wolf (Eds.), *Group psychotherapist's hand book.* New York: Columbia University Press.

Yontef, G., & Jacobs, L. (2005). Gestalt therapy. In R. J. Corsini & D. Wedding (Eds.), *Current psychotherapies* (7th ed., pp. 299–336). Belmont, CA: Thompson.

Yontef, G., & Simkin, J. S. (2005). Gestalt therapy. In R. J. Corsini & D. Wedding (Eds.). *Current psychotherapies* (4th ed., pp. 323–361). Itasca, IL: Peacock.

Young, M. E. (1992). *Counseling methods and techniques.* Upper Saddle River, NJ: Prentice Hall.

Young, M. E. (1998, November). *Megaskills.* Wake Forest University Counselor Education Program Seminar on Leadership and Ethics in Counseling, Winston-Salem, NC.

Young, M. E. (2001), *Learning the art & helping: Building blocks and techniques* (2nd ed.). Upper Saddle River, NJ: Prentice Hall.

Zajonc, R. B. (1965). Social facilitation. *Science, 149,* 269–274.

Zimpfer, D. G. (1984). Patterns and trends in group work. *Journal for Specialists in Group Work, 9,* 204–208.

Zimpfer, D. G. (1986). Planning for groups based on their developmental phases. *Journal for Specialists in Group Work, 11,* 180–187.

Zimpfer, D. G. (1987). Groups for the aging: Do they work? *Journal for Specialists in Group Work, 12,* 85–92.

Zimpfer, D. G. (1990). Group work for bulimia: A review of outcomes. *Journal for Specialists in Group Work, 15,* 239–251.

Zimpfer, D. G. (1991). Pretraining for group work: A review. *Journal for*

Specialists in Group Work, 16, 264–269.

Zimpfer, D. G. (1992). Group work with juvenile delinquents. *Journal for Specialists in Group Work, 17,* 116–126.

Zimpfer, D. G. (1992). Group work with adult offenders: An overview.

Journal for Specialists in Group Work, 17, 54–61.

Zimpfer, D. G., & Carr, J. J. (1989). Groups for midlife career change: A review. *Journal for Specialists in Group Work, 14*(2), 243–250.

Zinck, K., & Littrell, J. M. (2000). Action research shows group coun-

seling effective with at-risk adolescent girls. *Professional School Counseling, 4*(1), 50–60.

Zinker, J. (1977). *Creative process in group therapy.* New York: Vintage Books.

Name Index

SUBJECT INDEX